HANDBOOK OF MAJOR SOVIET NATIONALITIES

HANDBOOK OF MAJOR SOVIET NATIONALITIES

ZEV KATZ, Editor

ROSEMARIE ROGERS, Associate Editor

FREDERIC HARNED, Assistant Editor

 THE FREE PRESS
A Division of Macmillan Publishing Co., Inc.
NEW YORK

Collier Macmillan Publishers
LONDON

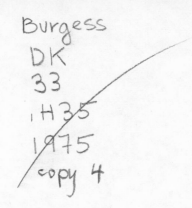

The Free Press
A Division of Macmillan Publishing Co., Inc.
866 Third Avenue, New York, N.Y. 10022

Collier Macmillan Canada, Ltd.

Library of Congress Catalog Card Number: 74–10458

Printed in the United States of America

printing number
3 4 5 6 7 8 9 10

Library of Congress Cataloging in Publication Data
Main entry under title:

Handbook of major Soviet nationalities.

    Includes bibliographies and index.
    1. Ethnology--Russia. 2. Russia. I. Katz, Zev,
ed. II. Rogers, Rosemarie, ed.   III. Harned,
Frederic T., ed. IV. Massachusetts Institute of Tech-
nology. Center for International Studies. V. Title.
VI. Title: Major Soviet nationalities.
DK33.H35 1975   914.7'06   74-10458
ISBN 0-02-917090-7

CONTENTS

EDITORS AND

CONTRIBUTORS

Zev Katz is with the Department of Russian Studies and Soviet and East European Research Center at Hebrew University of Jerusalem. As Research Associate of M.I.T. Center for International Studies, Dr. Katz was Project Director of studies of Soviet sociology. After undergraduate work at Teachers' College in Kazakhstan, USSR, Dr. Katz received an M.A. degree from Hebrew University of Jerusalem and a Ph.D. from London University. He taught at School for Political Studies at the Office of the Prime Minister in Israel and was Foreign Editor of the newspaper *Ha'aretz*. Dr. Katz has been Lecturer at Glasgow University, Essex University, and Harvard University, and was Research associate of the Russian Research Center at Harvard.

Rosemarie Rogers is Associate Professor at Fletcher School of Law and Diplomacy at Tufts University and Research Associate at M.I.T. Center for International Studies. She holds an M.A. from University of Texas and a Ph.D. in Political Science from M.I.T. Dr. Rogers is author of articles and research reports on the use of mass media and leisure time in the Soviet Union.

Frederic T. Harned is with the First National Bank of Louisville, Kentucky. During the period of this study, Mr. Harned was member of the research staff of M.I.T. Center for International Studies. He holds an undergraduate degree in Russian from Vanderbilt University and an M.A. from Harvard University, where he has done additional work toward a doctorate.

CONTRIBUTORS

Aman Berdi Murat is employed by Radio Liberty as U.S. Correspondent in the Turkestani Department. In 1941 he graduated from the Law School in Ashkhabad. He holds an LL.D. from University of Munich. Mr. Berdi Murat also holds an M.A. from Columbia University. He is a candidate for Ph.D.

Gustav Burbiel is Manager of Belorussian, Ukrainian, and Turco-Caucasian Department of Radio Liberty. He received a Ph.D. in Turkology and Slavistics from University of Hamburg. He taught Tatar and Azerbaidjani at Columbia University. Dr. Burbiel has written articles on Tatar literature and a major work entitled *Modern Tatar*, scheduled for publication.

Donald S. Carlisle is Associate Professor of Political Science at Boston College. He did his undergraduate work at Brown University and received a Ph.D. from Harvard University.

Richard B. Dobson is Ph.D. candidate in sociology at Harvard University, where he is associated with Russian Research Center and Center for International Affairs. Mr. Dobson received a B.A. in history from Stanford University and an A.M. in Soviet regional studies from Harvard University.

Stephen Fischer-Galati is Professor of History at University of Colorado and editor of *East European Quarterly*. His published books include *Ottoman Imperialism and German Protestantism; The New Rumania: From People's Democracy to Socialist Republic; Twentieth Century Europe: A Documentary History; Man, State, and Society in East European History*; and *Twentieth Century Rumania*. His articles have appeared in many periodicals.

Allen Hetmanek is author and lecturer on the USSR. He studied at University of Nebraska, Carleton College, University of Denver, and Georgetown University School of Foreign Service. He received a Ph.D. from Georgetown University.

Frank Huddle, Jr., is Ph.D. candidate in history and Middle Eastern languages at Harvard University, from which he received an M.A. in Middle Eastern studies. Mr. Huddle holds an undergraduate degree from Brown University and has done advanced work at Columbia University.

Mary K. Matossian is Associate Professor of History at University of Maryland. She received a B.A. and Ph.D. at Stanford University and an M.A. from American University of Beirut, Lebanon. She is author of *The Impact of Soviet Policies in Armenia*.

Richard Pipes, one-time Director of Russian Research Center, is Professor of History at Harvard University. He did his undergraduate work at Cornell University and received a Ph.D. from Harvard University. Dr. Pipes is author of many books and articles on Russian history, including *Formation of the Soviet Union, Karamzin's Memoir on Ancient and Modern Russia*, and *Social Democracy and the St. Petersburg Labor Movement*. Among books edited and co-edited are: *Russian Intelligentsia, Of the Russe Commonwealth*, and *Revolutionary Russia*.

Teresa Rakowska-Harmstone is Associate Professor of Political Science at Carleton University in Ottawa and Director of the university's Institute of Soviet and East European Studies. She taught at Douglass College, Rutgers University, and Carleton and was part-time visiting professor at McGill University and George Washington University's Institute for Sino-Soviet Studies. Dr. Rakowska-Harmstone holds a B.A. from McGill University, an M.A. from Radcliffe College, and a Ph.D. from Harvard University. She is the author of, among others, *Russia and Nationalism in Central Asia: The Case of Tadzhikistan* and co-editor with Adam Bromke of *Communist States in Disarray.*

Dina Rome Spechler is Lecturer in Government at Harvard University. She did her undergraduate studies at Radcliffe College and holds a Ph.D. from Harvard University. Dr. Spechler is author of articles and chapters on dissent in the Soviet Union.

Roman Szporluk is Associate Professor of History at University of Michigan and has been Research Associate in Ukrainian Studies at Harvard University and Associate of Russian Research Center at Harvard. Dr. Szporluk holds a law degree from Lublin State University, B. Litt. from Nuffield College at Oxford, and Ph.D. from Stanford University. He has published articles in American and British professional journals and is editor and co-translator of *Russia in World History: Selected Essays.*

Rein Taagepera is Assistant Professor of Political Science at University of California, Irvine. He is co-editor of *Problems of Mininations: Baltic Perspectives* and co-editor of *Baltic Events,* a bimonthly newsletter. He was research physicist with E. I. duPont de Nemours. Dr. Taagepera received a doctoral degree in physics from the University of Delaware. He has published work in radioactivity and luminescence.

Jan Zaprudnik is Assistant Manager of Belorussian, Ukrainian, and Turco-Caucasian Department of Radio Liberty and Adjunct Assistant Professor at Queens College, CUNY. He holds advance degrees in history from the Université Catholique de Louvain and a Ph.D. from New York University. Dr. Zaprudnik is editor and publisher of *Facts on Byelorussia.* He has published numerous articles in professional journals and delivered papers at international professional meetings.

ACKNOWLEDGMENTS

In addition to the editors and the authors of each chapter, many people contributed to the conception and completion of this volume.

Dr. Ithiel de Sola Pool and Dr. William E. Griffith, both Professors of Political Science at the Massachusetts Institute of Technology and senior members of the M.I.T. Center for International Studies, originated the idea for the study, helped to assemble the staff and enlist the contributors, and acted as Faculty Advisors throughout.

The three editors are fully identified in the preceding section on editors and contributors. It should be mentioned, however, that Dr. Rosemarie Rogers, in addition to her editorial contributions, collected, organized, and analyzed most of the data in the media section of the several chapters.

Special acknowledgment is owed to Ms. Patricia Perrier on whom fell the heavy day-to-day responsibility of ensuring that the work progressed on schedule. Ms. Perrier also provided the editorial guidance needed to produce consistent style, referencing, and format among the chapters. Mrs. Irirangi Coates Bloomfield prepared the index for this volume.

This volume was initially prepared under contract with the United States Information Agency. Distribution of this book does not indicate endorsement by the United States Information Agency, nor should the contents be construed as reflecting the official opinion of the Agency.

NOTES TO THE READER

This study was produced at the Center for International Studies, Massachusetts Institute of Technology. The study deals with seventeen Soviet nationalities —fifteen of which have their own Union republics, plus the Tatars and Jews. Each nationality is the subject of one chapter. The nationalities are grouped by geographical and/or cultural affinity in four of the parts: *The Slavs, The Baltics, The Transcaucasus,* and *Central Asia.* The fifth part, *Other Nationalities,* includes chapters on the Moldavians, the Tatars, and the Jews. The Appendix contains a set of comparative tables for all nationalities.

Except for the Russian chapter, the chapters are written to a uniform outline. *General Information* deals with territory, economy, history, demography, culture, and external relations. *Media* treats questions of language and media, as well as educational, cultural, and scientific institutions. *National Attitudes* analyzes national attitude formation, views of scholars, and current evidences of nationalism.

The reader will notice some variations in spellings of individuals' names and book and periodical titles among chapters and within chapters. There are two sources of this apparent inconsistency. First, there are no internationally agreed upon rules for transliterating Russian from the Cyrillic to the Latin alphabet. We have allowed each author to apply the rules most acceptable to him or her, except where we have attempted to standardize references cited in several chapters. Second, there is even less consensus on transliteration of the minority languages into the Latin alphabet. In the case of names and titles originally in one of the minority languages, we have allowed each author to make his or her own transliteration direct from the original language, rather than transliterating the equivalent Russian word.

Sources used more than once in a chapter are cited in abbreviated form in the footnotes, with full citations given in the list of references at the end of each chapter. Where several quotations are taken from a single source, reference is provided at the end of the last quotation. Similarly, where information in a paragraph is from one source, the source is cited at the end of the paragraph. Sources containing only one page are cited without page numbers. Except where noted, emphasis in quotations has been added.

INTRODUCTION: THE NATIONALITY PROBLEM

Richard Pipes

The nationality problem occupies a unique place in internal Soviet politics. The Soviet Union is the only major power where the dominant nationality barely has a majority. The 1970 census revealed that of 241.7 million inhabitants of the USSR only 129.0 million are of Russian nationality. This fact is so awkward that the compilers of the summary volume[1] failed anywhere in its 648 pages to provide the percentage of the whole which this figure represents—namely, 53.4. Given the much more rapid rate of growth of the non-Russian, and especially Asiatic, populations, the time may not be too distant when the "minorities" shall outnumber that nationality which has given the Soviet state its leadership and language.

A basic difficulty in studying the ethnic problems of the Soviet Union derives from the peculiar circumstances under which the Soviet Union and its predecessor, tsarist Russia, became multinational states. The

classic empires of the West came into being after the construction of national states had been completed. As a rule, the building of empires was a spilling over of surplus energies and resources of a national state that could no longer be accommodated within its own borders. Because of the peculiar geographic location of Europe as an appendage of the Eurasian continent, European imperial expansion directed itself across the seas and into other continents; hence, there was never doubt about the spatial separation between colony and metropolis. In sum, Western empire-building—that is, the acquisition of masses of other ethnic groups —was always chronologically and territorially distinct from the process involved in building the national state. The West European model, of course, is not of universal validity: the first great empire in world history, the Persian, was put together not by conquest of overseas territories but by expansion along land frontiers. The importance of the West European model, however, is that until recently it has served as raw material for the construction of theories

---

[1] *Itogi vsesoiuznoi perepisi naseleniya 1970 goda*, vol. IV (Moscow: Statistika 1973).

of nationalism and of ethnic conflict, and that this model still dominates the thinking of Russian leaders.

The expansion of Russia had a very different character from that known to Western experience. Being a continental power without natural frontiers and ready access to the seas, Russia has traditionally expanded along its territorial frontiers. Historically, the process of nation-building, which began in the fifteenth and sixteenth centuries, led to the conquest and absorption of other ethnic groups, starting with various Finnic and Turkic nationalities, and eventually including groups representing many Asian and some European populations. The chronological and geographic contiguity of the processes leading to the building of both the nation-state and empire has had the effect of blurring the two phenomena, tending to make Russians remarkably insensitive to ethnic problems. Characteristically, even liberal and social democratic groups in pre-revolutionary Russia were inclined to ignore ethnic problems and to treat demands of nationalities for a greater role in self-government as reactionary and enemy-inspired.

The basic tendency of Russian leaders, past and present, in dealing with ethnic problems has been to follow (unconsciously, of course) what may be called the French type of colonialism. In contrast to the British, the French have striven to extend to the ethnic (i.e., colonial) minorities the full rights and privileges of Frenchmen, hoping by this device, over the long run, to assimilate them. Muscovite and Imperial Russia did the same by opening the ranks of the privileged elite (the *dvorianstvo*) to the land-owning and educated elements of conquered nationalities.[2] The Soviet regime followed suit by allowing minority elites access to the Communist party apparatus and all the benefits and privileges which membership in it entails. This time-tested policy, however, which had enabled tsarist Russia in large measure to siphon off potential national resistance, no longer works

quite as well. The problem is that, whereas until the twentieth century primary allegiance in Eastern Europe tended to be directed toward one's social class, more recently, as a result of the breakdown of the estate structure and the spread of egalitarianism, society's primary allegiance has shifted toward the nation. Thus, the Tatar prince or Georgian landowner who in tsarist Russia may have felt greater affinity for his Russian equivalent than for the peasant of his own culture no longer exists; his democratized descendant has no choice but to identify with the Tatar or Georgian nation. Here we have a clear example of how democratization leads to an increase of national sensitivities and brings with it a rise in ethnic tensions—a fact quite unforseen by nineteenth-century liberal theorists.

It is customary to think of the Soviet Union as a veritable ethnic museum inhabited by over one hundred exotic national groups. Now, while it is true that the USSR has a large number of ethnic groups within its borders, most of them are so small as to be of interest primarily to the anthropologist, linguist, and demographer. Furthermore, it must be borne in mind that the Soviet government, in pursuing the traditional *divide et impera* policy, deliberately exaggerates ethnic differences among its minorities. From the political point of view the student of ethnic problems in the USSR confronts only a dozen or so groups, namely: (1) the Ukrainians and Belorussians who, as Slavs professing the Orthodox faith, are closely related to the Great Russians; (2) Moslems, nearly all Sunni by religion and Turkic by racial and linguistic background; (3) the two major Caucasian groups—Georgians and Armenians—close to the Moslems in culture and economy but separated from them by their Christian religion; (4) the Jews; (5) the three Baltic nationalities; and (6) a number of West European and East Asian groups, among whom the Germans are perhaps most important. According to the 1970 census, the groups enumerated above under rubrics 1–5 represent about 85 percent of the non-Russians inhabiting the Soviet Union. The problem, thus, is less complicated than Soviet policy makers would like to make it appear.

---

2 The tsarist policy was most successful in regard to nations whose nobility did not enjoy the same privileges as did the Russian equivalent. It was a complete failure when applied to the extremely privileged, proud nobility of Western provinces of the empire—e.g., Poland and the Baltic areas.

Clearly, the sense of national cohesion and common destiny differs from nationality to nationality. There are many ways of testing the intensity of nationalism, but the most reliable are probably criteria based on statistical evidence provided by censuses. These are: level of education, especially higher and specialized education; linguistic attachment, as measured by the proportion of people who regard their national language as the mother tongue; territorial concentration, the percentage of a given nationality residing in that nationality's republic; and intermarriage (for which, unfortunately, statistical data are exceedingly scarce). Of itself, none of these factors can tell us how viable is a given nationality.[3] The chapters which follow provide very good clues helping the attentive observer to gauge, as it were, the temperature of the national sentiment of various national groups. The material makes it quite clear, for example, that the nationalism of Georgians is much stronger than that of the Belorussians—a fact which can be demonstrated by non-statistical evidence as well.

If we follow demographic statistics from 1897 to 1970, we discover an interesting phenomenon bearing on number of ethnic groups and intensity of their nationalisms. Census statistics indicate that over the seven decades separating the first Russian census from the most recent one, the number of nationalities has tended to diminish as the smaller ethnic groups lose out to those major ones closest to them culturally and territorially. Thus, the Bashkirs have been steadily dissolving among the Tatars, the Abkhazians among the Georgians, the Kara-kalpaks among the Kazakhs, and so on. As a result, the nationalities structure of the Soviet Union is becoming streamlined, the minor Soviet nationalities growing leaner and the major ones fatter. In political terms, this means that the Great Russian majority confronts an increasingly difficult situation; it has to deal with fewer but stronger ethnic groups. These facts should

be borne in mind by anyone who assumes that all denationalization of ethnic minorities means Russification. In some respects, the contrary proposition is closer to the truth: denationalization of the minor ethnic groups reduces the likelihood of Russification.[4]

Why does national sentiment survive among the Soviet nationalities? Why do Soviet authorities have to stress continuously the desirability of the ethnic minorities "drawing together" (*sblizheniye*)? To this question there are many answers, the most obvious of which is that under conditions prevailing in the USSR—where one nationality comprises more than half of the population and controls, to boot, the state and its economy—"drawing together" means nothing else but Russification. The language of a single "Soviet nationality" would have to be Russian; so would its historic traditions and in time its customs. But this negative consideration, which obviously must dissuade any but the most career-minded or obtuse non-Russian from following his government's directives, is only part of the answer. National sentiment is more than a "thing in itself" which either exists or is exterminated. Historical experiences indicate that it represents a sum total of diverse social and cultural forces, many having nothing whatever to do with ethnicity. One reason nationalism possesses such extraordinary tenacity, why it has refused to dissolve in the acid bath of modernity, as nineteenth-century liberals and socialists had expected it to do, is that it constitutes more a result than a cause. One way to illustrate what we have in mind is to cite the complaint voiced recently by a West German official about unforeseen difficulties this country is experiencing with hordes of foreign *Gastarbeiter*: "We asked for workers and got human beings."

Perhaps the most important single element which keeps ethnic feelings alive in multinational states is competition for resources and services. This is true in every

---

3 The Jews, for example, score very low on all the above criteria except the first which, in their case, is of decisive importance. See Table A.19 in the Appendix, which indicates that there are almost twice as many Jews attending higher educational institutions as there are of the next group, the Georgians.

4 Ukrainians, Belorussians, Jews, and the West European groups, when they break off from their own ethnic groups, tend to Russify. It is probably true to say that the majority of Russified minorities come from these groups.

multinational society, but is a particularly potent factor in the USSR where the government enjoys a monopoly of national wealth and doles out products and services to society no more than it must. If we consider the nationality problem in the Soviet Union from this point of view, we can perceive why phenomena which in themselves appear neutral can nevertheless produce ethnic tension and conflict.

A basic fact of Russian history over the past thousand years has been colonization. V. O. Kliuchevsky once said that "the history of Russia is the history of a country which colonizes itself," [5] and the statement is as correct today as when he made it nearly a century ago. Russians are a people forever on the move. They move because the land on which they live is on the whole ill adapted to agriculture, yielding them little beyond bare subsistence and sometimes not even that. They migrate in search of virgin soil and easier conditions of life. The movement outward from the central forest zone, homeland of the Great Russian people, began to assume intensive forms in the mid-sixteenth century and shows no signs of abating. The 1970 census indicates the continued outflow of Great Russians to the borderlands, especially the western republics (Ukraine, Belorussia, and the three Baltic republics). It is a centrifugal movement of an elemental force.

In their migrations the Russians encroach upon territories inhibited by non-Russians, inevitably entering into competition with them over jobs, housing, schooling, and goods. It is a curious fact that, while the proportion of Great Russians in the USSR population as a whole tends steadily to diminish, the proportion of Russians residing in many border republics tends to rise. Between 1959 and 1970 the proportion of Great Russians living in the RFSFR has declined by 2.3 percentage points, the highest decline of the major nationalities—indicative of the unique intensity of Russian migration. The friction resulting from a migration of such persistence would be serious under any circumstances. What aggravates it is that in the past several decades the borderland popula-

tions (especially on the eastern periphery) have been growing more rapidly than the Russian. This means that pressure on resources and services created by the influx of Russians is intensified by a very high rate of local population growth. The recent decision to create large economic planning regions, in some cases encompassing more than one republic, was probably motivated by a desire to attenuate these conflicts. It marks an important step toward administrative amalgamation of the national republics into a unified state structure.

There was a time when, basing their expectations on what turned out to be an unrealistic view of the American "melting pot," most scholars believed the nationality problem in the Soviet Union was well on its way to "solution." Formal policy pronouncements in the USSR fed these expectations. There was, on paper, full equality of all ethnic groups, a federal system which seemed to balance neatly centrifugal and centripetal tendencies, and numerous outlets for cultural strivings. In the early years of the Soviet regime, indeed, a certain amount of liberalism in the treatment of the nationalities was in effect. In order to compensate the minorities for failure to honor its pledges of "national self-determination," the Soviet government in the 1920's offered many concessions short of self-government. But with Stalin's rise to power the course was rapidly reversed. From the beginning, Stalin based himself on support of lower-echelon *apparatchiki* who looked on the Soviet Union as a vast field of exploitation and would hear of no concessions to "aliens." To win them over, Stalin adopted a blatantly pro-Russian course which neither Khrushchev nor Brezhnev has altered in any substantial manner. The Soviet Union today is in effect an empire run like a nationally homogeneous state, suffering all the consequences of this contradiction. Western scholars in their majority have come to recognize this fact. The persistence of strong national sentiments is generally recognized, and disputes among specialists no longer concern the fact of minority nationalism, but its character and orientation. Our own view can be stated succinctly in a series of propositions:

---

5 *Kurs russkoi istorii* (Moscow, 1937): I: 20.

1. The nationality question in the Soviet Union has attained a decisive state of development. The Great Russian population can no longer expand outward into the borderland areas without running into stiff resistance. Where in the past Russians have run into isolated and scattered ethnic groups, they now confront solid national entities with all the trappings of national self-government. Demographically speaking, the Russians are declining vis-à-vis the ethnic minorities. It is probable that in the future the Russian population will not be able to penetrate in any significant numbers outside the confines of the RSFSR and Kazakhstan. Elsewhere Russian colonists will be increasingly regarded as outsiders. In short, we may be witnessing a solidification of ethnic frontiers separating Russians from the minorities.

2. The coming conflicts involving the nationalities and the Great Russians are likely to center on access to jobs, housing, schooling, and commodities. In order to overcome minority resistance, the Soviet government is likely to have recourse to basic administrative measures aiming at lowering the barriers separating the republics. In other words, we may see a slow and cautious dismantling of the pseudofederal structure created in 1922–1924. The recently announced regional economic plans may represent a step in this direction.

3. On the Great Russians, the situation is likely to produce an increased sense of frustration, intensifying chauvinism and xenophobia. The identification of the Soviet regime with the Russian people and Russian history, initiated by Stalin, has lately recurred with increasing frequency. One of the most important by-products of the nationality problem, therefore, is likely to be the growth of national sentiment, not only among minorities but also, and above all, among the Great Russians themselves.

Part I

THE SLAVS

Part I includes chapters on the Russians, Ukrainians, and Belorussians. Each chapter deals both with the nationality as an ethnic group and with the republic as a political-territorial unit.

The Ukrainian and Belorussian chapters are full-length presentations covering all topics listed in the chapter outline (see Notes to the Reader). The Russian chapter departs from this format, concentrating on the relationship of the Russians, as the dominant Soviet nationality, with the many minority nationalities in the USSR. The three nationalities covered in this part belong to the East Slav group; there is much affinity among them in language, religion, history, and way of life, and outsiders often regard them as one. Yet there are major differences and cleavages, especially between the Ukrainians and the Russians. Recently, this has been manifested by such phenomena as the struggle of the Ukrainians for their national language and the harsh suppression of the national movement in the Ukraine.

1 RUSSIA and THE RUSSIANS

Dina Rome Spechler

The focus of this handbook is primarily on the non-Russian or "minority" nationalities of the USSR. The history and culture of the dominant Russian nationality and the economic and historical development of the RSFSR are covered in many competent and easily available studies, and a comprehensive treatment of these subjects is beyond the scope of this survey.

Therefore, the following discussion is limited to factors particularly relevant to position of the Russians and of the RSFSR in relation to other Soviet nationalities. The Comparative Tables in the Appendix provide data on all nationalities studied, and further comments on position of the Russians appear in chapters on other individual nationalities. A reader interested in more detailed treatment of topics related to the Russians may want to consult studies listed in the references and supplementary bibliography at the end of this chapter.

Demographic Patterns and Trends

The Russians are the largest national group in the USSR. According to the latest census, taken in 1970, they comprise slightly more than half (53.37%) of the total population. Their weight in the population has been declining in recent years, however, since their rate of natural increase is one of the lowest of all the national groups. Among the major nationalities, only Latvians, Estonians, and Jews increased by a smaller percentage than the Russians in the period between the last two censuses

(1959–1970). (See Table A.2 in Appendix).

The republic in which most Russians live, the Russian Soviet Federated Socialist Republic (RSFSR), is the largest union republic. It extends from the Baltic to the Pacific and covers 6.5 million square miles, or 76% of the total area of the USSR, including 53.8% of the USSR's population.[1] Although the vast majority (83.5%) of Russians live in the RSFSR, this concentra-

---

[1] *Soviet Union*, 1969: 24.

tion is declining. The percentage point decline in share of the Russian population living in its own republic was 2.3 between 1959 and 1970, largest decline experienced by any Soviet nationality except the Tatars. The preponderance of Russians in population of the RSFSR is also declining; Russians made up 83.3% of that population in 1959 and 82.8% in 1970.[2]

The main component of Russian outmigration is movement away from rural areas. At first, this process was internal to Russia. It began in the nineteenth century, but accelerated noticeably after the late 1920s, when job opportunities in the cities became more plentiful. The Russian regions of the USSR possessed poor land resources and a surplus agricultural population and until recently sustained a high birth rate. Also, after collectivization conditions in the village became very difficult, people moved to town in search of better living conditions.[3]

Reasons for Russian expansion into non-Russian areas in the last decade differ, depending on area. In some regions, such as the Baltic republics of Latvia and Estonia, the influx has probably been due to attractiveness of these highly developed areas to the Russians and inability of the indigenous population, with even lower rates of natural increase than the Russians, to supply sufficient manpower for growing industry. Movement of Russians to Central Asia and Kazakhstan has been a consequence of intensive industrial development in these regions, combined with reluctance or inability of the native population to move to the cities. The modern mechanized agriculture developed in new areas such as the virgin lands was also manned by non-local labor, mainly Slavs.

Apart from these ethnic and economic reasons for Russian expansion, there are others stemming from the Soviet system itself. Introduction of the Soviet system into many non-Russian areas has meant bureaucratization of many spheres of social life and infusion of political and security ap-

---

[2] See Table A.7 in Appendix and *Census Data*: 17.
[3] Lewis, 1971: 159–160.

Table 1.1

Dispersion of Russians in Republics of USSR

	No. Russians	Rank by % of Total Russians in USSR	% of Total Russians in USSR	Rank by % of Republic Populations	Russians as % of Republic Population
USSR total	129,015,140	—	100	—	53.37
RSFSR	107,747,630	1	83.5	1	82.8
Ukrainian SSR	9,126,331	2	7.1	6	19.4
Kazakh SSR	5,521,917	3	4.3	2	42.4
Uzbek SSR	1,473,465	4	1.1	8	12.5
Belorussian SSR	938,161	5	0.7	12	10.4
Kirgiz SSR	855,935	6	0.7	4	29.2
Latvian SSR	704,599	7	0.5	3	29.8
Azerbaidzhan SSR	510,059	8	0.4	11	10.1
Moldavian SSR	414,444	9	0.3	10	11.6
Georgian SSR	396,694	10	0.3	14	8.5
Tadzhik SSR	344,109	11	0.3	9	11.9
Estonian SSR	334,620	12	0.3	5	24.7
Turkmen SSR	313,079	13	0.2	7	14.5
Lithuanian SSR	267,989	14	0.2	13	8.6
Armenian SSR	66,108	15	0.1	15	2.7

Sources: *Itogi 1970*: IV: 321; *Nar. khoz. 1972*: 516–681.

paratuses of Soviet power into non-Russian areas. Specialist personnel consists mainly of Slavs, and the language of business is Russian. The central Soviet authorities regard "intermingling" of nationalities as a positive development and promote it, utilizing many available levers of control and influence (see following sections).

One result of these migrations is that Russians have settled in significant numbers everywhere in the Soviet Union. (See Table 1.1.) Only in Lithuania and the Caucasus do they make up less than 10% of the population. In Latvia and Kirgizistan they are almost 30% and in Kazakhstan 42.4%, outnumbering the Kazakhs themselves. The Russian component of the population is also large in rural areas outside the RSFSR, recently opened up to argicultural and industrial development, and cities, where a significant minority (if not a majority) of the inhabitants are Russians. Kiev, Vilnius, and Tallinn, where Russians comprise 23%, 25%, and 40% of the population, respectively, are not unusual examples.[4] In Alma Ata, capital of Kazakhstan, 70.3% of the population is Russian, while only 12.1% is Kazakh.[5]

This urbanization is characteristic of Russians at home as well as "abroad"; 68% of all Russians in the RSFSR are urban dwellers. Russians rank second only to Jews in degree of urbanization and comprise nearly two thirds of the entire urban population of the USSR. (See Table A.9 in Appendix.)

Position in Soviet Society

Officially, the USSR is presented as composed of 15 equal union republics and many equal nationalities. Actually, the RSFSR alone accounts for three quarters of the territory, more than half of the population, and almost two thirds of the Communist party membership of the USSR as a whole. Moscow, capital of the RSFSR, is also capital of the USSR. On any of a series of vital indicators, the RSFSR and the Russians predominate over all other republics and nationalities of the USSR taken together, as shown in Tables 1.2 and 1.3.

With respect to political position, Russians make up 62.5% of the USSR party leadership (Politburo members) and 61% of all party members (1972 figures). While Georgians, Armenians, and possibly Jews also enjoy a more than proportional representation in the party, all other national groups are underrepresented. (See Table A.11 in Appendix.) Moreover, Russian presence in party organizations of the non-Russian republics is considerable, while non-Slavs do not generally participate in party work in republics other than their own. First secretaryship of the republic parties is usually held by a native, but the second secretary is almost always a Slav and usually a Russian. Chairman of the republic councils of ministers and their deputies are generally indigenous, but the critical position of republican KGB chief is most often held by a Russian.[6]

Russians also hold a disproportionate number of important posts in non-Russian republics outside the political hierarchies: in higher education, large-scale agriculture (the virgin lands of Kazakhstan), new industries in traditionally rural areas (Moldavia), and key industries such as Azerbaidzhani oil, Kazakh iron and steel, and Yakut oil fields. Heads of enterprises and construction projects in non-Russian areas tend to be Russian. Many Russians have escaped rural poverty by taking advantage of numerous employment opportunities which opened up in the cities of Central Asia in the last decade. Most jobs requiring education or skills have been given to Russians, and many nonskilled positions as well.[7]

---

4 *Nar. khoz. 1972:* 516–581, Lewis, 1971: 155; Szporluk, 1971: 83, 90; *New York Times* (July 31), 1972.
5 *Itogi 1970:* 233.
6 Forwood, 1970: 203–204.
7 *Ibid.;* Lewis, 1971: 161–163; Szporluk, 1971: 91.

Table 1.2

Indicators of Position of RSFSR within USSR

	RSFSR AS % OF USSR TOTAL
Population (1970)[a]	53.81
Territory[b]	76
Delegates to 22nd Party Congress (1961)[c]	63.1
RSFSR party members as % total CPSU membership (1971)[d]	64.0
RSFSR residents with secondary and higher education as % of total population with secondary and higher education (1970)[e]	55.8
Students in higher educational institutions (RSFSR as % of total, 1971)[f]	58
Number of scientific workers in RSFSR as % of total scientific workers (1971)[g]	69
Number of books published in RSFSR as % of total books published (1971)[h]	80
RSFSR production of oil as % of USSR total[i]	80.6
RSFSR production of electricity as % of USSR total[j]	63.5

[a] Table A.4 in Appendix.
[b] *Soviet Union*, 1969: 24.
[c] Rigby, 1968: 375.
[d] Computed from Table A.13.
[e] Computed from *Nar. khoz. 1972*: 36; *Nar. khoz. RSFSR, 1970*: 24.
[f, g, h] *Nar. khoz. RSFSR, 1971*: 29.
[i, j] *Nar. khoz. 1970*: 70.

The relative ease with which Russians gain access to the more responsible and desirable jobs in government and industry, even in non-Russian areas, reflects two other respects in which they occupy a favored or dominant position in Soviet society. One is the special status of their language; the other is the greater facility with which they can obtain a higher education. Unlike other Soviet languages, used in the official institutions of only one republic or region, Russian is the language of business everywhere in governmental and economic organizations. Most Russians speak Russian and only Russian, whether they live in the RSFSR or outside it. When they occupy administrative or supervisory posts, they assume their colleagues and subordinates will speak Russian and tend to hire only those who do; throughout the USSR natives are often refused employment if they do not know Russian well enough. Thus a knowledge of Russian is a necessity for political and economic advancement. As a result of this pressure,

49% or nearly half of all non-Russians are fluent in Russian (while only 3% of all Russians have found it important to learn another Soviet language well enough to claim fluency).[8]

Because of greater facility in the majority tongue, Russians enter higher educational institutions in larger percentages than do most other national groups. Also, Soviet establishments in science and higher education are heavily concentrated in big cities of the Russian republic (Moscow, Leningrad, Novosibirsk, Sverdlovsk). Russians rank fourth in the USSR—behind Jews, Georgians, and Armenians—in terms of the number of students for every 1,000 people of their nationality, and they comprise 60% of the total enrollment in higher education. (See Table A.19.) In fields requiring higher education, such as scientific work, Russian

---

[8] Forwood, 1970: 203–204; Lewis, 1971: 161–163; Szporluk, 1971: 91; *New York Times* (February 27), 1972. Computations based on *Census Data:* 14, 16–17.

Table 1.3

Indicators of Position of Russian People and Language in USSR

	RUSSIAN(S) AS % OF TOTAL	INDEX
Russians as % of total population of USSR (1970)[a]	53.4	1.00
Russians as % of total urban dwellers (1970)[b]	64.5	1.21
Russians as % of total rural population (1970)[c]	39.1	0.73
Russians as % of total CPSU members (1972)[d]	61.0	1.14
Russians as % of total secretaries of CC/CPSU (1973)[e]	100.0	1.87
Russians as % of total Politburo members (1973)[f]	62.5	1.17
Russians as % of total students in higher educational institutions (1970–1971)[g]	59.6	1.12
Russians as % of total scientific workers (1971)[h]	66.4	1.24
Fluent Russian speakers in total population (as native and second language—1970)[i]	75.9	1.42
Teachers of Russian language and literature as % of teachers of all Soviet languages and literatures in elementary and secondary schools of USSR (1971–1972)[j]	71.6	1.34
Copies of works of Russian literature as % of copies of works of literature of all Soviet languages (1971)[k]	78	1.46
Titles published in Russian as % of all titles in Soviet languages (1971)[l]	80	1.50
Copies of books published in Russian as % of all books published in Soviet languages (1971)[m]	84	1.57
Magazines in Russian language as % of magazines in all Soviet languages (1971)[n]	74	1.39
Newspapers in Russian as % of all newspapers in Soviet languages (1971)[o]	82.7	1.55

$$\text{Index} = \frac{\text{indicator}}{\text{Russians as \% of USSR population}}$$

NOTE: Because of high percentage of Russians in the USSR population (53.4%), even when the Russians reach 100% of the indicator, the index can show only 1.87 (as in case of secretaries of CC/CPSU in this table).

[a] Table A.2.
[b] Computed from *Itogi 1970*: 27.
[c] Computed from *Itogi 1970*: 35.
[d] Table A.11.
[e] Computed from data in Edward L. Crowley et al., eds., *Prominent Personalities in the USSR* (New Jersey: Scarecrow Press, 1968).
[f] Computed from data in *ibid.*; also *New York Times* (April 27), 1973.
[g] Table A.19.
[h] Table A.20.
[i] Computed from *Census Data*: 14, 16–17.
[j] Computed from *Nar. khoz. 1972:* 429.
[k] Computed from *Pechat' 1971*: 52.
[l, m] Computed from *Pechat' 1971*: 10.
[n] Computed from *Pechat' 1971*: 59.
[o] Computed from *Pechat' 1971*: 68.

predominance is even stronger (66% of all scientific workers), and overrepresentation of Russians in this educational elite (in comparison with their weight in the population) has been increasing in the last decade. (See Table A.20.)

Russian Influence and Official Policy

The influence of Russians in Soviet society is even greater than that revealed by their political, economic, linguistic, and educational position. This is the result of many years of official support for Russification and encouragement of Russian nationalism.

As an official policy, Russification has a long history. During the reign of Nicholas I (1825–1855), a deliberate process of inculcating Russian culture was initiated in the educational systems of parts of Poland, Belorussia, and Lithuania. At the same time the Russian Orthodox Church increased its proselytizing activities. Manifestations of local nationalism by subject peoples were crushed, and individuals thought to have led or inspired them, like the Ukrainian poet Taras Shevchenko, were arrested and exiled. The policy of Russification was given new impetus under Alexander III (1881–1894), when even peoples who had shown complete loyalty to the Russian throne were harassed. The Jews were subjected to violent pogroms, often instigated by the Black Hundreds, protofascist groups given official encouragement. The last tsar, Nicholas II, was an honorary member of one such group.[9]

Initially, for reasons of both policy and principle, Soviet leaders repudiated this approach to minority peoples of the Empire. On seizing power, the Bolsheviks sought to distinguish themselves in this respect from the nationalistic Whites. They issued a declaration guaranteeing the right of the "peoples of Russia" to self-determination—including secession, if they wished it—and promising abolition of all national privileges and restrictions. At the same time (November 1917), they addressed an appeal to Moslem inhabitants of the Empire.

Moslems of Russia [it read], Tatars of the Volga and the Crimea, Kirghiz and Sarts of Siberia and Turkestan, Turks and Tatars of Transcaucasia, Chechens and mountaineers of the Caucasus and

all you whose mosques and oratories have been destroyed, whose beliefs and customs have been trampled underfoot by the Tsars. . . . Your beliefs and usages, your national and cultural institutions are henceforth free and inviolable. Organize your national life freely and without hindrance. You have a right to this.[10]

These declarations were followed by a series of gestures calculated to win the sympathy of nationalist rebels in the border regions. Historic and sacred relics were returned to the Ukrainians and to several Moslem peoples. The Bolsheviks even banned further Russian settlement in areas inhabited by certain minorities (Kazakhs, Kalmyks, Chechen, and Ingush).[11]

During the first years after the Bolshevik revolution, the leaders looked with favor on national autonomy—political, cultural, or economic—as long as it did not conflict with "democratic centralism." All opposed Great Russian chauvinism in principle, and some actually fought it in practice. As believers in the imminence of a world proletarian revolution, prominent figures in the party favored a unitary supranational state in which all national distinctions would cease to exist. They were contemptuous, and perhaps even ashamed, of the history of Great Russian domination and oppression in the Empire. Lenin, for example, detested Russian chauvinism and declared that he would fight a "war to the death against it." He opposed enforced use of Russian in Soviet schools and supported education in local languages. His instructions on relations with the minorities demonstrated a concern that non-Russian traditions and pride should be respected and that Russians or Russified bureaucrats should administer minority peoples tactfully.[12]

For a while during the twenties, Lenin's

---

9 Schopflin, 1970: 191–198.

10 Quoted in Conquest, 1967: 22.
11 *Ibid.*
12 Schopflin, 1970: 191–198; Conquest, 1967: 144–147.

attitude continued to prevail in official policy. The Twelfth Party Congress, meeting in April 1923, condemned "survivals of great power chauvinism" in the outlook of Russian officials and the "contemptuous and soulless" attitudes of the latter toward the national republics. A resolution at the end of the congress declared that the party's most urgent task was the struggle against Great Russian chauvinism in its own ranks. Minority loyalty to Soviet rule would be won, party leaders hoped, by allowing native leaders to administer the governments and economies of their areas. Native languages were encouraged and alphabets for peoples without written languages were devised: these were media for communication of socialist ideas. Even some national military formations were created to assist in the defense of Soviet territory.[13]

All this changed, however, under Stalin, who apparently believed that to mobilize the population, the majority of which was Russian, for industrialization and defense, it was necessary publicly to identify the regime with the Russian people and Russian history. Beginning in the 1930's, he gradually made promotion of Russian nationalism and national symbols official policy. The Russian people and culture were glorified, their language extolled. Heroes of Russian history were celebrated—even those previously denounced by the Communists as tyrants and reactionaries. Russians were elevated to a position of primacy among the nationalities of the country. Official publications declared that they stood "at the head of the peoples of the USSR" and were "lead[ing] the struggle of all the peoples of the Soviet land for the happiness of mankind."[14]

Stalin feared development of distinct national identities and rise of nationalist sentiment among non-Russian peoples, for these could become the basis of secessionist or collaborationist movements in wartime. The republics, potential foci of minority loyalty, were therefore deprived of all ves-

tiges of political autonomy in the late 1930s. Most national cadres which had risen during 1917–1920 and in the twenties were destroyed in the purges of 1937–1939. The practice of placing Russians as secretaries in non-Russian party organizations was intensified. The foremost representatives of minority cultures were arrested, and Russification became the order of the day. Cyrillic script was imposed on the Moslem minorities, and Russian was made a compulsory subject in all non-Russian schools.[15]

Stalin's suspicion of the minority nationalities and his encouragement of Great Russian nationalism reached a peak during the war—the Great Fatherland War, in the Stalinist lexicon. Whole national groups were deported on the allegation they had aided the enemy or could potentially do so. In a famous speech, Stalin invoked symbols not of the "Soviet Union" but of "the Great Russian nation, the nation of Plekhanov and Lenin, of Belinsky and Chernyshevsky, of Pushkin and Tolstoi, of Glinka and Chaikovsky, of Gorky and Chekhov, of Sechenov and Pavlov, of Repin and Surikov, of Suvorov and Kutuzov." This passage, with long enumeration of exclusively Great Russian personages, was the essence of the new Stalinist system.[16]

When Stalin died, strident promotion of the Russian people abated and draconic measures against minority nationalities were repudiated, but essential attitudes of the leadership regarding the proper role of Russians and Russian culture did not change. Officially, Russians were still regarded as the most important ethnic group, although now instead of the "leading people" they were presented as the "elder brother" of the technologically less advanced and culturally inferior non-Russians. Political and cultural autonomy of minority nationalities was still seen as a threat to the power of the regime, and manifestations of national tradition—particularly in its religious form—were severely persecuted. Khrushchev declared that the Russian language would become the basis

13 Schopflin, 1970: 191–198; Conquest, 1956: 29–30.
14 Goldhagen, 1968: x; B. Volin, "Velikii russkii narod," *Bol'shevik*, (1938): IX: 36; *Malaya sovetskaya entsiklopediya* (Moscow, 1949), IX, cols. 319–326, quoted in Conquest, 1956: 38–39.

15 Schopflin, 1970: 191–198.
16 J. Stalin, *O velikoi otechestvennoi voine Sovetskogo Soyuza* (Moscow, 1944): 11, 28, quoted in Conquest, 1956: 40.

for a "fusion of the nations" of the USSR, a vision suggesting elimination of both separate identities of the national minorities and their corresponding political entities.[17]

Brezhnev and Kosygin have avoided Khrushchev's rhetorical flights and utopian projections, but they are quietly taking steps which seem intended to make his vision a reality. Russian language and culture are being brought to non-Russian areas in numerous ways while expression of minority identity is carefully contained and kept to modest proportions. The Khrushchev policy of promoting an "inter-republic exchange of cadres" continues to be implemented on a very large scale. Many thousands of new graduates and workers are sent each year to work in republics other than their own. Minority nationals are thereby cut off from nearly all contact with their native culture and for practical reasons absorb elements of available Russian culture. By contrast, Russians outside the RSFSR are amply supplied with schools, books, and periodicals to assist in retaining and spreading their culture. Mixed marriages between Russians and other nationals are encouraged in many areas, with the expectation that the non-Russian partner will assimilate.[18]

Russian is energetically promoted in every republic as a "second native tongue," although reciprocal efforts to induce Russians to learn other Soviet languages are usually ineffective. Journals devoted to improvement of Russian teaching in non-Russian areas have proliferated in recent years, and numerous regional and interrepublic conferences have been devoted to this object. There are more than twice as many teachers of Russian language and literature in elementary and secondary schools as teachers of all other Soviet languages and literatures together (336,000 as compared to 133,000). Schools in which instruction is conducted in minority languages (mostly through the first eight grades) tend to be small, ill equipped, and poorly staffed, while the Russian language schools are large, well equipped, and competently staffed. Lavish praise is heaped on parents who send their children to Russian language schools despite the censure of friends and neighbors. Moreover, this is frequently most convenient, especially in the cities. Once the Russians begin moving into an area, it is only a matter of time before the Russian language schools far outnumber the schools providing instruction in the indigenous language. Even in the latter institutions Russian is a required subject, whereas the local language is optional in Russian language schools.[19]

Soviet media policy is also designed to promote Russification. Traditional native themes are discouraged. Russian literature is published in much greater volume than the literature of all other nationalities together. In 1971, 78% of all copies of literary works published in the USSR were of Russian literature. The Russian language is similarly favored: of all titles published in Soviet languages in 1971, 80% were in Russian, as were 84% of all copies of all books published. Even within the non-Russian republics, it is not uncommon for more books to be published in Russian than in the indigenous language, and native writers find it more difficult to publish their work than Russian authors. The emphasis in magazine and newspaper publishing is the same: almost three times as many magazines and more than four times as many newspapers are published in Russian as in all other Soviet languages. Throughout the country the great bulk of radio and television broadcasting is also in Russian.[20] At the same time, publication and broadcasting in the national languages is continued, at considerable cost to the state.[21] This represents a tacit recognition by the central authorities that years of Russification have had only a limited effect.

No less important an instrument of Russification are the Russified natives appointed to high party and state posts in the republics. Some, like the party leaders in Estonia, are Russian in everything but birth: their education was Russian, as was their place of residence and work for many

17 Conquest, 1956: 28; Forwood, 1970: 204; Pipes, 1968: 3–4; Goldhagen, 1968: xi.
18 Bilinsky, 1968: 153–156; Szporluk, 1971: 91–92; *New York Times* (February 27, July 20), 1972.

19 Forwood, 1970: 204; Ornstein, 1968: 135; *Nar. khoz.* 1972: 429; Bilinsky, 1968: 160; *New York Times* (May 4, July 20), 1972.
20 *New York Times* (February 27, May 4, July 20), 1972; *Pechat'* 1971: 10, 52, 59, 68, 95–97.
21 See discussions of media in the remaining chapters, as well as Tables A.22 and A.23 in Appendix.

years. Others, like the recently appointed head of the Ukrainian party, while not Russian in background, are nonetheless willing to work for the creation of a single Soviet culture based primarily on Russian language, art, and traditions. They see it as their function to quash local resistance to this long-range goal. By installing men like this and dismissing them if they waver, the central authorities continue to encourage Russian political, cultural, and economic dominance over Soviet society.[22]

Revived Russian Nationalism and the Soviet Leadership

The pride in Russia and things Russian which underlies official policy is not confined to the leadership alone. Nor is it to be found solely among the peasant and worker masses, so often assumed a nation's chief repository of patriotism. Recent years have witnessed a great upsurge of interest in the Russian past and a striking outburst of nationalism among Russian intelligentsia. In part this nationalist revival may be a consequence of de-Stalinization. The denunciation of Stalin created an intellectual and emotional void in Soviet life. Ideology, regarded with acute suspicion by an over-propagandized generation, cannot fill this void. Nationalism is one of the few alternative faiths available. At the same time, manifestations of nationalism by the Russian intelligentsia may be an expression of both resentment and admiration of national ferment among the minorities.

This new trend has moderate-liberal, Slavophile-conservative, and extremist-chauvinist adherents. The aim of the first is primarily to rehabilitate elements of Russian tradition neglected or denigrated by successive Soviet rulers. The moderates engage in studies of Russian folk culture and language, icon painting, and church architecture; they write letters to the press decrying the destruction of churches and other historical monuments; and they give lectures on these topics in rural areas and workers' clubs. Many are members of one of the few spontaneously formed (though subsequently officially approved organizations in the USSR today, the Rodina (Motherland) Club. Some in this liberal category are established writers and officials.

The other two groups are sometimes referred to colloquially as *russity* [Russites]. The Russite extremist wing consists of Great Russian nationalists, who believe in the messianic role of a Russia preserved from further "disorderly hybridization" of nations, in which "the traditional Russian religion [occupies] an honorable position." Racist, chauvinist, anti-intellectual, and reactionary, the extremist Russites have published a manifesto in *samizdat* (*Slovo natsii*). Less extreme are Slavophile conservatives, contributors to the underground journal *Veche*. These people are similarly convinced of the importance of preserving the religion, culture, traditions, and distinct identity of the Russian nation. But they are not chauvinists and, unlike the authors of *Slovo natsii*, do not seek to make Russians the "dominating nation" in the USSR. Calling on all "Russian patriots" to join and support them, they urge cultivation of the unique qualities of the Russians and every other nation.[23] Writings of Russite authors appear not only in *samizdat*, but sometimes in the official press and books.[24]

The regime is divided in its opinion of the Russian nationalists. Evidently, some party leaders fear the extremist Russites might exacerbate national tensions and genuinely dislike their Russian supremacism and religiosity. But other powerful persons in the KGB, the party, and the military are

22 For examples of reliance on Russified republic leaders and dismissals for inadequate Russifying, see *New York Times* (March 13, October 1), 1972 and (April 23, July 14), 1973. See also chapters on the Ukraine, Latvia, and Georgia in this study.

23 "Word to the Nation," 1971: 191–199; Pospielovsky, 1973: 51–74; Scammel, 1971: 100; Palmer, 1970: 164; Amalrik, 1969: 64–65. See also Zev Katz, "Soviet Dissenters and Social Structure in the USSR" (Cambridge: Center for International Studies, MIT, April 1972, C/72–3).

24 See, for example, V. Kochetov, *What Do You Want?* (1969); Yury Ivanov, *Caution, Zionism!* (1969); Ivan Shevtsov, *In the Name of the Father and the Son* (1970).

believed highly sympathetic to the Russites and determined to promote and protect them. For some time an intense struggle seems to have been underway between these two groups. For awhile it seemed that the faction which disliked the Russites would be victorious. The party journal *Kommunist* condemned the line taken by both *samizdat* publications, and the editor of *Veche* was warned of his impending arrest.[25] A recent incident, however, suggests that supporters of the Russites are gaining the upper hand. In November 1972 the acting chief of the Central Committee's Ideological Section, Alexander P. Yakovlev,

published a lengthy attack on excessive Russian nationalism and overglorification of the Russian past.[26] Despite the endorsement this article received from the party's highest ranking ideologist, Mikhail Suslov, its author was removed from his post in April 1973 amid charges that he had been too critical of works on Russian nationalism.[27] Yakovlev was one of the most outspoken of the Russites, opponents, and his removal may mean that henceforth they can write and publish more freely. Official Russian nationalism seems to have joined forces with its unofficial variant in a rare alliance of state and society in the USSR.

Minority Attitudes Toward the Russians

The assessment of attitudes of the "minority" nationals toward the Russians is a very difficult—if not impossible—task. Nevertheless, certain currents are discernible.

Russifying policies of the regime and its tolerance of Great Russian chauvinism are keenly resented in minority areas. They are not made more palatable by the behavior of Russians, as perceived by other nationalities when Russians emigrate or are sent to these areas. As individuals they are sometimes portrayed as arrogant, as groups exclusive; they are reputed to treat indigenous peoples as less than equal and to segregate assiduously their places of residence and recreation. The feelings aroused by these practices find many outlets—in *samizdat*, in public protests, and most frequently in humor. Anti-Russian jokes are circulated in abundance among intelligentsia of some national minorities, stressing the alleged slowness, stupidity, lack of irony or sense of humor, lack of initiative, and general passivity of the *russak*.[28]

Anti-Russian sentiment of the minority nationalities is expressed in anti-Russian

activities, which find multiple forms and are sometimes supported by the local elite. The Tbilisi riots of 1956 in Georgia were a case in point, as were the violent clashes between Russians and Uzbeks during the Tashkent football matches in 1969 and the 1972–1973 protests in Lithuania.[29] Roi Medvedev, a Russian dissident, writes that in the Ukraine, Georgia, and Latvia local cultural institutions appoint only persons of local nationalities to important positions. This policy is designed to discriminate against Russians as well as other nationalities. Medvedev also proposes a change in the USSR constitution providing for a periodical referendum in each republic on its desire to remain part of the USSR.[30] The *samizdat Program of the Democratic Movement of the Soviet Union* stipulated that the national republics should have the right to fix quotas for settlement of nonlocal nationals within their borders; such a measure would be directed primarily against the Russians.[31] Evidence from recent émigrés suggests that local elites in the national areas make efforts to settle

25 Pospielovsky, 1973: 51–74; *Kommunist*, 1971: XV: 105–107, quoted in Pospielovsky, 1973; *New York Times* (July 19), 1971.
26 *Lit. gaz.* (November 15), 1972.
27 *New York Times* (May 7), 1973.
28 See, for example, the chapter on Latvia.

29 See the chapters on these nationalities.
30 Roi Medvedev, *Kniga o sotsialisticheskoi demokratii* (Amsterdam/Paris: Herzen Foundation, 1972): 75–111, 319–328.
31 *Programma Demokraticheskogo dvizheniya Sovetskogo Soyuza* (Amsterdam: Herzen Foundation, 1970), *passim*.

their nationals in Russianized cities and to stem further infusion of Russians into their territory.[32]

It must be stressed that the relationship between the non-Russian nationalities and the Russians is complex; it is not uniformly hostile. Some segments of the minority populations and their elite groups accept

---

[32] Zev Katz, "The New Nationalism in the USSR," *Midstream* (February, 1973): 3–13. See also chapter on the Tatars.

the Soviet-Russian culture willingly, feel at home with the Russian language, and have a very high regard for Russians as individuals and group. Still, anti-Russian sentiment is obviously strong among some non-Russian nationals. This, in turn, evokes resentment by Russians, intensifying their own national feelings. A vicious circle is created: Russian ascendancy breeds nationalism among minority nationalities, which intensifies Russian nationalism and drive for predominance.

REFERENCES

Allworth, 1971
    Edward Allworth, ed., *Soviet Nationality Problems* (New York: Columbia University Press, 1971).
Amalrik, 1969
    Andrei Amalrik, "Will the USSR Survive Until 1984?" *Survey* (Autumn 1969): LXXIII: 47–79.
Bilinsky, 1968
    Yaroslav Bilinsky, "Assimilation and Ethnic Assertiveness Among Ukrainians of the Soviet Union," in Goldhagen, 1968: 147–184.
Census Data
    "Census Data: Age, Education, Nationality," *Current Digest of the Soviet Press* (1971), XXIII: 16: 14–18.
Conquest, 1956
    Robert Conquest, *Soviet Russian Nationalism* (New York: Oxford University Press, 1956).
Conquest, 1967
    Robert Conquest, *Soviet Nationalities Policy in Practice* (New York: Praeger, 1967).
Forwood, 1970
    William Forwood, "Nationalities in the Soviet Union," in Schopflin, 1970: 199–208.
Goldhagen, 1968
    Erich Goldhagen, ed., *Ethnic Minorities in the Soviet Union* (New York: Praeger, 1968).
Harris, 1971
    Jonathan Harris, "The Dilemma of Dissidence," *Survey* (Winter 1971): XVI: 1: 107–122.
Itogi 1970
    Itogi vsesoyuznoi perepisi naseleniya

1970 goda, vol. IV (Moscow: Statistika, 1973).
Lewis, 1971
    Robert A. Lewis, "The Mixing of Russian and Soviet Nationalities and Its Demographic Impact," in Allworth, 1971: 117–167.
Lit. gaz.
    Literaturnaya gazeta (Moscow, weekly).
Nar. khoz. RSFSR 1970
    Narodnoye khozyaistvo RSFSR v 1970 godu (Moscow: Statistika, 1971).
Nar. khoz. RSFSR 1971
    Narodnoye khozyaistvo RSFSR v 1971 godu (Moscow: Statistika, 1972).
Nar. khoz. 1972
    Narodnoye whozyaistvo SSR 1922–1972: Yubileinyi statishchesii yezhegodnik (Moscow: Statistika, 1972).
Ornstein, 1968
    Jacob Ornstein, "Soviet Language Policy: Continuity and Change," in Goldhagen, 1968: 121–146.
Palmer, 1970
    S. T. Palmer, "The Restoration of Ancient Monuments," *Survey* (Winter/Spring 1970): LXXIV/LXXV: 163–174.
Pechat' 1971
    Pechat' v SSSR v 1971 godu (Moscow: Kniga, 1972).
Pipes, 1964
    Richard Pipes, "The Forces of Nationalism," *Problems of Communism* (January–February 1964): 1–6.
Pipes, 1967
    Richard Pipes, " 'Solving' the Nationality Problem," *Problems of Communism* (September–October 1967): 125–131.

Pospielovsky, 1973
  Dimitry Pospielovsky, "Russian National-
  ism in Samizdat," *Survey* (Winter 1973):
  XIX: 1: 51–74.
Rigby, 1968
  T. H. Rigby, *Communist Party Member-
  ship in the USSR, 1917–1967* (Princeton:
  Princeton University Press, 1968).
Scammel, 1971
  Michael Scammel, "Soviet Intellectuals
  Soldier On," *Survey* (Winter 1971): XVI:
  1: 99–106.
Schopflin, 1970
  George Schopflin, ed., *The Soviet Union*

and Eastern Europe: A Handbook* (New
  York: Praeger, 1970).
Soviet Union, 1969
  *Soviet Union—50 Years: Statistical Re-
  turns* (Moscow: Progress Publishers,
  1969).
Szporluk, 1971
  Roman Szporluk, "The Nations of the
  USSR in 1970," *Survey* (Autumn 1971):
  XVII: 4: 67–100.
"Word to the Nation," 1971
  "Word to the Nation," *Survey* (Summer
  1971): XVII: 3: 191–199.

Some Supplementary Readings on the Russians

and the RSFSR

RUSSIAN NATIONAL CHARACTER AND
ATTITUDES

Raymond A. Bauer and Alex Inkeles, *How
the Soviet System Works: Cultural, Psy-
chological, and Social Themes* (Cam-
bridge: Harvard University Press, 1956).
Geoffrey Gorer and John Rickman, *The
People of Great Russia: A Psychological
Study* (New York: Norton, 1962).
Margaret Mead, *Soviet Attitudes Toward
Authority* (New York: Schocken, 1966).
Klaus Mehnert, *Soviet Man and his World*
(New York: Praeger, 1958).
Colette Shulman, ed., *We the Russians* (New
York: Praeger, 1971).

RUSSIFICATION

Elizabeth E. Bacon, *Central Asians Under
Russian Rule: A Study in Culture Change*
(Ithaca: Cornell University Press, 1966).
Frederick C. Barghoorn, *Soviet Russian
Nationalism* (New York: Oxford Uni-
versity Press, 1956).
Maurice Hindus, *The Kremlin's Human
Dilemma: Russia after Half a Century of
Revolution* (New York: Doubleday, 1967).

RUSSIAN CULTURE

James H. Billington, *The Icon and the Axe:
An Interpretive History of Russian Cul-
ture* (New York: Vintage Books, 1966).
Paul Miliukov, *Outline of Russian Culture*
(New York: Barnes, 1942), 3 vols.

POSITION OF NATIONAL MINORITIES
VIS-À-VIS RUSSIANS

David J. Dallin, *The New Soviet Empire*
(London: World Affairs Book Club,
1951), chs. 6, 7.
Susan Jacoby, *Moscow Conversations* (New
York: Coward, McCann, & Geoghegan,
1972).
Jaan Pennar et al., *Modernization and
Diversity in Soviet Education, With
Special Reference to Nationality Groups*
(New York: Praeger, 1971).

RUSSIAN HISTORY AND ECONOMIC HISTORY.

Jerome Blum, *Lord and Peasant in Russia*
(New York: Atheneum, 1964).
Michael T. Florinsky, *Russia* (New York:
Macmillan, 1953), 2 vols.

RUSSIAN GEOGRAPHY

W. H. Parker, *An Historical Geography of
Russia* (Chicago: Aldine, 1969).

2 | THE UKRAINE and THE UKRAINIANS

Roman Szporluk

General Information

TERRITORY

The Ukrainian Soviet Socialist Republic occupies an area of 233,089 square miles, larger than France or any European country (excluding the RSFSR). It is divided into 25 provinces [*oblasty*], varying in size from 12,857 square miles (Odessa region) to 3,127 square miles (Chernovtsy).[1] The Ukraine's borders are 4,018 miles long— 2,574 miles are with the Soviet republics of Russia, Belorussia, and Moldavia, and 789.5 with Poland, Czechoslovakia, Hungary, and Rumania. Seashore comprises 654 miles. The Ukraine extends 818 miles from west to east and 555 miles from north to south.[2] Most of the Ukraine is plains, with mountains in the west and extreme south (Crimea).

The Ukraine is rich in minerals, including iron, manganese, chromite, titanium, lead-zinc, aluminum, mercury, and nickel. It has large reserves of hard coal, brown coal, petroleum, and natural gas.

Potassium, rock salt, solar salt, and sulfur also abound, as well as kaolin and other clays, cement raw materials, flux limestones, graphites, and building stone.[3]

The climate of most of the Ukraine is moderately continental. On the south coast of the Crimea, however, it approaches subtropical. Rainfall varies from 59 inches per year in mountainous areas of the Carpathians to 11–13 inches on the Black and Azov sea coasts. Largest river is the Dnieper, flowing for 749 miles through the republic. Almost all rivers feed into the Black and Azov seas. Other major rivers are the Dniester, Desna, Siversky Donets, Southern Bug, Pripyat, and Seym. The Ukraine has more than 3,000 natural lakes, 30 with an area of 4 square miles or more, and 13 more than 20 square miles. There are also artificial reservoirs, the largest on the Dnieper: the Kakhovka (832 square miles), the Kremenchug (985), and the Kiev (356 square miles).[4]

The Ukraine lies within three physico-

---

1 *Narodne hospodarstvo 1970:* 9.
2 *Soviet Ukraine,* 1970: 9.

3 *Ibid.:* 29–32.
4 *Ibid.:* 32–40.

geographic zones: the Mixed Forest, Forest-Steppe, and the Steppe. The Mixed-Forest belt is covered by soddy *podzolic* soils, the Forest–Steppe belt has a variety of subtypes of black earth [*chernozem*], and the Steppe belt is subdivided into three zones with different types of soils.[5] The growing season in the Mixed Forest belt (which embraces the northern part of the Ukraine) lasts 190–205 days; in the Forest-Steppe belt, 200–210 days; and, in the Steppe belt, 210–245 days.[6]

The Ukraine territory has been divided, within the all-Union regional scheme, into three economic regions. The Donetsk-Dnieper Region occupies an area of 85,290 square miles, or 36.7% of the Ukrainian territory, and includes the provinces [*oblasty*] of Voroshilovgrad, Dnepropetrovsk, Donetsk, Zaporozhe, Kirovograd, Poltava, Sumy, and Kharkov. The South-western Region, encompassing almost half of the Ukraine, includes the Vinnitsa, Volyn, Zhitomir, Transcarpathia, Ivano-Frankovsk, Kiev, Lvov, Rovno, Ternopol, Khmelnytsky, Cherkassy, Chernovtsy, and Chernigov *oblasty*. The Southern Region, of 43,745 square miles, includes the *oblasty* of the Crimea, Nikolaev, Kherson, and Odessa.[7]

ECONOMY

The Ukraine has been one of the most important economic areas of prerevolutionary Russia and the USSR. In 1912 it provided 18.3% of total Russian output of manufactures by value and employed 16.8% of the labor force.[8] According to another estimate, the Ukraine produced 24% of the entire industrial output of Russia before World War I.[9] In 1913 it produced over 20% of the output of large-scale industry, 78.2% of the coal, 57.7% of the steel, and over two thirds of the iron ore.[10]

Ukrainian agriculture was more advanced than that of Russia proper, although backward in comparison with the West. Wooden ploughs were still used in some localities in 1917, and about one half of the peasant farmers had no draft animals or implements of their own.[11]

In 1970, with 3% of the area and 19% of the population of the USSR, the Ukraine produced one third of the total USSR coal output, 48% of the pig iron, 40% of the steel, and 57% of the iron ore. The Ukraine was advanced in extractive industries and heavy machine industry, but markedly weaker in other respects, such as light industry and production of consumer durables.[12] Agriculture remains very important. In 1970 it produced 19% of all Soviet grain, 59% of the sugar beets, and 28% of the vegetables. The rail and road network of the Ukraine is relatively dense: with 3% of the area of the Soviet Union, it has 16% of the railway mileage and 18% of the automobile roads.

There is considerable variation in the level of economic development among different parts of the Ukraine. At the end of the 1960s industrial output per capita in the Donetsk-Dnieper Region was one third higher than in the South and over twice as high as in the Southwestern Region, the least developed area.[13] There is surplus rural population in the Ukraine, especially in the Southwestern Region. In 1959 an average able-bodied collective farm peasant worked (and was paid for) 198 days in a year (as compared to 255 in the Leningrad area and 249 in Siberia). By 1965 this had declined to 188.[14] Productivity of labor in agriculture is low, and much working time is wasted owing to shortcomings in management and organization.[15]

In 1970, 35.5% of the Ukrainian labor force was employed in industry and construction (28.9% in 1960), 31.7% in agriculture and forestry (46.5%), 7.5% in transport and communication (5.9%), 6.8% in trade, supplies, and public catering (4.9%), and 13.4% in education,

5 *Ibid.*: 41–43.
6 *Ibid.*: 55–58.
7 Voloboi and Popovkin, 1972: 52.
8 Seton-Watson, 1967: 658. The area considered here does not coincide exactly with the present Ukraine, which includes parts not in Russia in 1912.
9 *Soviet Ukraine*, 1970: 244.
10 *Ibid.*: 252.

11 *Ukraine, A Concise Encyclopaedia*, 1971: I: 845.
12 *Narodne hospodarstvo 1970*: 56–57.
13 *Ukraina, Teraźniejszosć i przeszłosć*, 1970: 128–129; *Naseleniye, trudovye resursy*, 1971: 171.
14 *Ibid.*: 148, 150.
15 *Ibid.*: 204.

medicine, and public health (9.7%).[16] In comparison, in Poland in 1969, 35% of the labor force was employed in industry and construction and 37% in agriculture and forestry. In Czechoslovakia the former constituted 46%, the latter 19%.[17]

Average monthly wage for Ukrainian workers and officials (excluding *kolkhoz* members but including employees of state farms) in 1970 was 115.2 rubles. Wages in construction averaged 135.0 rubles per month, in industry 130.1, in science 121.9, in transport 120.9, and in government service 111.8. The average wage in education was 102.2 rubles, in communication 92.3, in commerce and public catering 88.0, and in health 85.0. On state farms and auxiliary agricultural enterprises the average was 95.7 rubles per month.[18] No data are available on income of collective farmers, but it is known to be lower than that of state farm workers.

HISTORY

First historical state on the present territory of the Ukraine was Kievan Rus (ninth to eleventh centuries).[19] Eventually, it disintegrated into a number of principalities, of which Galicia and Volynia survived as independent states until the fourteenth century. The former became Polish in 1387, while the latter was subdued by Lithuania, which also conquered Kiev itself. In 1569 all the Ukrainian lands were united under Poland, which thereafter exerted a strong influence on the language, culture, politics, and society in the Ukraine. In 1648 the Ukrainians rose against Poland in a national insurrection, which reflected peasant opposition to serfdom, Orthodox religious protest against Polish Catholic expansionism, and Cossack resentment of their treatment as a military force under Polish control. The Ukrainians defeated the

Poles at first, but Polish counter-attacks led them to turn to Moscow for help.

In 1654 the Ukraine entered into relationship with Moscow, the precise nature of which has been disputed ever since. In 1667 the Ukraine was partitioned between Poland and the Tsardom of Muscovy. A truncated Ukraine (on the left bank of the Dnieper River) survived as an autonomous structure under Russia until 1764 when the elective office of *hetman* was abolished. The second and third partitions of Poland in 1793 and 1795 brought the rest of the Ukraine under Russian rule, with the exception of Galicia, which had come under Austrian control in 1772 and remained under Vienna until 1918. Russian expansion to the south, which led to the conquest of the northern Black Sea coast and the Crimea from the Tatars, opened these areas to Ukrainian settlers in the late eighteenth century.

Although the Ukrainian landed nobility generally accepted Russian rule, nationalist sentiments were never totally extinguished. They revived in strength during the Ukrainian literary and cultural awakening of the nineteenth century. The tsarist regime responded with a prohibition on printing in Ukrainian (1876–1905). Ukrainians were able to develop their culture more freely in Austrian Galicia, where their language was recognized in schools, civil administration, and courts of justice. By 1914 Lvov, the Galician capital, had three Ukrainian language dailies and a number of weekly and monthly periodicals. Ukrainian political parties, first formed in the 1890s, were represented in the Galician provincial assembly and the Austrian parliament in Vienna.

The outbreak of World War I in 1914 came when the Ukrainian national movement in Russia was still in its initial stages. The Ukrainian press, although no longer totally banned, suffered from systematic persecution by the tsarist administration. Cultural and educational organizations were usually allowed to exist for very brief periods. The vast majority of the peasantry was illiterate. Ukrainian was not allowed to be used or taught in public schools, political and national consciousness of the masses was low, and Russians were predominant in the cities. The weakness of

---

16 *Narodne hospodarstvo 1970:* 375. Figures in parentheses are all for 1960.
17 Pivovarov, 1972: 24.
18 *Narodne hospodarstvo 1970:* 381.
19 Material in this section is based, among others, on *Ukraine: A Concise Encyclopaedia*, 1963; Pipes, 1968; Rudnytsky, 1963; Seton-Watson, 1967; *Soviet Ukraine*, 1970; *Ukraina, Terazniejszosc i przeszłosc*, 1970.

Ukrainian nationalists became apparent in 1917, when they managed to get the Russian Provisional Government to recognize the Ukraine's autonomy but failed to establish an effective administration or army. On January 22, 1918, shortly after the Bolshevik takeover and the beginning of fighting between Ukrainian forces and those of the Russian Soviet government, the Ukrainian Central Council [*Rada*] proclaimed independence.

In February 1918 the Ukraine signed a peace treaty with Germany, Austria-Hungary, Turkey, and Bulgaria. German and Austrian troops entered the Ukraine, expelling the Red Army. The *Rada* soon clashed with the German occupation authorities—it was moderately socialist and favored land reforms while the Germans wanted to requisition grain. Subsequently, it was overthrown in a military coup led by General Skoropadsky ("the Ukrainian Mannerheim"). The Skoropadsky regime, conservative in outlook and employing many former tsarist officials, was opposed by peasantry and Ukrainian nationalist intelligentsia. When Imperial Germany surrendered and German troops began to leave the Ukraine, a popular uprising forced Skoropadsky to resign. His successor was the Directory, composed of former leaders of the *Rada*. The new government tried to compete with the Bolsheviks for support of the masses and promised radical reforms, labor legislation, and land reform. It did not establish an effective administration, and its armies melted away as soon as the Skoropadsky forces had been defeated. The Soviet armies, coming from north and east, expelled the Directory from Kiev. Then the Ukraine was plunged into a bloody civil war. Peasant anarchist bands roamed the countryside, while regular troops of the Directory faced enemies on all sides: Bolsheviks, anticommunist Russians, Poles, and Allied troops in the south. In 1920 the nationalist government, by then in exile in Poland, agreed to cede the western Ukraine to Poland in exchange for Polish help in expelling the Bolsheviks from Kiev. But this attempt failed disastrously, and in 1921 Poland concluded peace with Russia and the Soviet Ukraine at Riga.

Ukrainians in Austria did not participate in the events of 1917–1918 in the Russian Ukraine, but after the defeat of Austria they proclaimed a West Ukrainian Republic in November 1918. They were unable to join the war against the Russians because the area of this republic was claimed by Poland, and Polish-Ukrainian hostilities began on November 1, 1918. The war lasted until June 1919, and ended with Poland in occupation of all the western Ukraine. In 1923 the Allies provisionally granted Poland sovereignty over this area. Unlike the eastern part of the Ukraine, the West Ukrainian Republic had succeeded in establishing an efficient, disciplined administration and army. Its fall was due to lack of international support and superior military power of the Allied-equipped Polish forces.

Ukrainian lands under Soviet rule were constituted as the Ukrainian Soviet Socialist Republic· (The first Soviet Ukrainian government had been set up in Kharkov as early as December 1917, but a Soviet regime throughout the Ukraine was established only in 1919.) Formally, the Soviet Ukraine was tied to Russia by an alliance, but this was a fiction, since the Communist party of the Ukraine was in fact a regional subdivision of the Russian party. In December 1922 the Ukraine concluded a "treaty" forming the USSR, together with Russia, Transcaucasia, and Belorussia.

During the 1920s Soviet policies toward language and culture in the Ukraine were generally quite liberal; the Ukrainian Communist party enjoyed a measure of control over its affairs, and the peasantry remained in possession of its land. The 1930s, however, brought collectivization of agriculture, mass famine (in 1933 several million peasants died because of the imposition of excessive delivery quotas on the Ukraine, despite the protests of the Soviet Ukrainian government), and mass extermination of party and government cadres, as well as both party and nonparty intelligentsia. By 1938 a new party elite dominated the Ukraine, headed by N. S. Khrushchev, previously secretary of the Moscow party organization, as first secretary of the Communist party of the Ukraine. Also during the 1930s industries were built and towns grew in population. Many Ukrainians moved from the country to such cities as Kiev, Kharkov, Donetsk, Dnepropetrovsk, Voroshilovgrad, and Zaporozhe.

Poland never granted autonomy to its west Ukrainian provinces; essentially, its policies aimed at assimilation. Ukrainian liberal and democratic parties made an effort to function within the Polish system; the Ukrainian National Democratic Union became the most influential and representative political force. There were also two clandestine political organizations. The Communist party of the West Ukraine, on the extreme left wing, was *de facto* a territorial subdivision of the Polish Communist party, sharing the fate of the latter when it was purged, and most of its members in exile in the USSR were killed or imprisoned by Stalin. On the right, the Organization of Ukrainian Nationalists (OUN), founded in 1929, carried on sabotage against the Poles and assassinated many Polish officials and Ukrainian "collaborators." It stressed the primacy of "will" over "reason" and advocated a one-party regime for the future Ukraine, with a single ideology and a single leader. It hoped for an independent, OUN-ruled Ukraine in Hitler's promised territorial reorganization of Europe.

The August 1939 Stalin-Hitler pact was a blow to the OUN. After the Soviet army occupied eastern Poland in September, formally incorporating its Ukrainian area into the Ukrainian SSR, the organization continued its underground activities. During 1939–1940 it split into two wings, the radical Bandera faction and the more moderate Melnyk faction. The Nazi invasion of June 1941 brought further disillusionment when the Nazis refused to cooperate in any manner with the Ukrainian nationalists, even to the extent that they did with the Slovak and Croat satellite states. When the Bandera faction of the OUN proclaimed an independent Ukrainian state in Lvov on June 30, 1941, its members were arrested and sent to concentration camps. The Nazis planned to transform the Ukraine into a colony for Germans, not into a satellite, and least of all into a truly independent state.

Thus, during the war, organized Ukrainian nationalism was in conflict with both Nazis and Soviet partisans. Its zone of operation was limited to the former Polish territories, although attempts were made to broaden the base of the nationalist underground. The nationalist movement underwent an ideological and political evolution toward moderation in the underground, and in 1943–1944 officially renounced its totalitarian program in favor of a multiparty state, social reforms, and ideological pluralism. The OUN was instrumental in organizing a partisan army, the UPA, which engaged in armed struggle against the Germans and then against Soviet troops until the early 1950s.

The war extended the territory of the Ukrainian SSR considerably. In addition to the former Polish territory (western Ukraine), the following areas were added as a result of the war: Northern Bukovina and the Izmail district of Bessarabia (formerly part of Rumania), Transcarpathian Ruthenia (formerly part of Czechoslovakia). The Crimea (formerly part of the RSFSR) was transferred to the Ukraine in February 1954.[20]

Ukrainian human losses in the war were enormous, among the highest in Europe, compounded by the effects of the 1930s terror and the post–1945 arrests and deportations. In 1959, the first postwar census, the ratio of imbalance between men and women (4.7 million more women than men; 44.4% men, 55.6% women) indicated the magnitude of these losses.

In 1944, while his police and army were battling the UPA in the west Ukraine, Stalin granted all Soviet republics, including the Ukraine, the right to establish direct relations with foreign countries and to maintain their own military formations. These turned out to be essentially paper concessions, however. In 1945 the Ukraine joined the UN, but it never established diplomatic relations with foreign countries (British attempts to exchange ambassadors with Kiev in 1947 and 1950 were rebuffed) or a separate military force. In fact, after 1945, Stalin tightened Moscow's control over the Ukraine still further. In 1946 the Uniate Church was dissolved,[21] removing a strongly nationalist religious organization and a link with the West. Writers and historians were accused of nationalist deviations (1946–1947, 1950–1951), but no executions of artists or scholars took place.

---

20 See section on external relations.
21 See section on culture later in this chapter.

In the 1950s Khrushchev claimed that he had restrained Stalin in his struggle against the Ukrainian intelligentsia during the 1940s. He also attributed to Stalin hostility toward all Ukrainians and a desire to deport them all from the Ukraine.

In 1946 there was another famine in the Ukraine; however, it was less severe than that of 1933.

The death of Stalin in 1953 was followed immediately by a change in the top party post in the Ukraine; A. P. Kirichenko became the first Ukrainian first secretary of the Ukrainian Communist party. Promoted to the CPSU secretariat in Moscow in 1957, he was soon dismissed, succeeded by N. V. Podgorny, another Ukrainian, who in his turn was promoted to Moscow in 1963. Podgorny's successor in Kiev, P. Shelest, was demoted in 1972. He was succeeded by Shcherbitsky. Although Soviet policy in relation to the Ukrainians has generally been more moderate since 1953, there are various indications that the Moscow center has failed to this date to find a stable and mutually acceptable *modus vivendi* with the Ukraine, including the Ukrainian CP. The dismissal of Shelest, accused of being tolerant of, if not sympathetic to, Ukrainian nationalism, was followed by a personnel shakeup in the party, state, and cultural apparatus of the Ukraine, while periodic waves of arrests among the intelligentsia attest to a discontent in these circles as well.

DEMOGRAPHY

Population of the Ukraine on January 1, 1973, was 48,200,000,[22] an increase of more than 13% over 1959. In 1970 the Donetsk-Dnieper Region had 20,057,000 people, an increase of 13% over 1959; the Southwestern Region had 20,689,000, an increase of 9%, and the Southern Region had 6,380,000, a rise of 26%.[23] Ethnic Ukrainians made up 76.8% of the Ukraine's population in 1959 and 74.9% in 1970. Russian population increased from 16.9% to 19.4% in the same period. Ethnic Ukrainians con-

stituted 87.8% of the population in the Southwestern Region, 66.6% in the Donetsk-Dnieper Region, and 55% in the Southern Region. From 1959 to 1970, the percentage of Russians in the South moved from 30.9% to 34.0%, in the Donetsk-Dnieper Region from 24.8% to 27.9%, and in the Southwestern Region from 5.8% to 6.6%.[24]

The seven administrative *oblasty* of the so-called West Ukraine (administratively, they do not form a separate unit but belong to the Southwestern Region), not part of the USSR until World War II, displayed a different demographic and ethnic evolution in the intercensus period. While their population grew by about 12.2% between 1959 and 1970, from 7,800,000 to 8,755,000, their Ukrainian ethnic population advanced by 13.6%, as compared with 9.7% for the Ukraine as a whole and 8.7% for the entire Southwestern Region. Ukrainians made up 87.2% of the west Ukraine's population in 1959 and 88.7% in 1970. Russian population in the west Ukraine increased by 10.7%, less than the all-Union average, and a third of their Ukrainian increase, and the Russian share of the area's population dropped from 5.2% to 5.1%.[25] Thus, the western part of the republic became less Russified and the eastern part more so.[26]

In 1970 about 5.5 million Soviet Ukrainians lived in republics other than the Ukraine. The Russian republic had a Ukrainian population of 3,344,000 in 1970 (a decline from 3,359,000 in 1959), and the Ukrainian population of Moscow was 185,000. There were also 930,000 Ukrainians in Kazakhstan (an increase of 22%), 507,000 in Moldavia (an increase of 20%), and 191,000 in Belorussia (an increase of 44%). In the Baltic republics of Estonia, Latvia, and Lithuania, the Ukrainians increased 68% from 63,000 in 1959 to 106,000 in 1970.[27] Thus Ukrainians are ap-

---

22 *Rabochaya gazeta* (February 1), 1973.
23 *Narodne hospodarstvo 1970:* 18.

24 Calculated from *Radianska Ukrayina* (April 25), 1971.
25 *Ibid.*
26 The 446,000 Russians in the west Ukraine still represent a marked increase over prewar times, when the few Russians in the area were primarily refugees from the Soviet Union.
27 Calculated from *Izvestia* (April 17), 1971. The figures for Ukrainians in Moscow are in *Itogi 1970:* IV: 103.

parently emigrating to a majority of the republics except for the RSFSR. In the period between the censuses of 1959 and 1970, approximately 2.5 to 3 million Russians migrated from the Russian republic to other parts of the USSR; about 1 million moved to the Ukraine,[28] where immigration is higher than emigration.

In 1970, 55% of the population of the Ukraine lived in urban areas, up from 46% in 1959. The Donetsk-Dnieper Region had the highest percentage of urban population with 70%, followed by the Southern Region with 57%, while in the Southwestern Region, predominantly Ukrainian and including areas that had been non-Soviet before World War II, the urban share of the population was only 38%.[29]

Kiev, capital of the republic, is its largest city and the third largest in the USSR. In 1970 its population was 1,632,000, an increase of 47% over 11 years. Between 1959 and 1970 the proportion of Ukrainians in the capital rose from 60.2% to 64.8%.[30] Kharkov is second largest with 1,223,000 inhabitants in 1970 (a 28% increase over 1959), followed by Odessa, 892,000; Donetsk, 879,000; and Dnepropetrovsk, 862,000.[31]

In 1970 the Ukraine's birth rate was 15.2 per thousand; the death rate, 8.9; the natural growth rate, 6.3.[32] On January 15, 1970, the Ukraine's population under 20 years of age was 15,588,900, while that of age 60 and above was 6,563,800.[33]

The ethnic composition of the Communist party in the Ukraine in 1968 and of the total population in 1970 was as follows:

	NO., % IN COMMUNIST PARTY, 1968[34]		NO., % IN TOTAL POPULATION, 1970[35]	
Total Membership	2,138,800			
Ukrainians	1,391,682	65.1	35,283,857	74.9
Russian	569,131	26.6	9,126,331	19.4
Jewish	99,940	4.7	777,126	1.6
Belorussian	27,382	1.3	385,847	0.8
Polish	8,969	0.4	295,107	0.6

CULTURE

The Ukrainians possess a distinct folk culture, including songs, music, oral literary tradition, architecture, and dress.[36] Over the ages the churches, both Orthodox and Catholic, assimilated a variety of pre-Christian popular customs and this blend of Christian beliefs and local usages has given to Ukrainian religious practices an individual style and flavor.

The first formative influence on Ukrainian culture came from Byzantium, with the adoption of Christianity in the tenth century in the Greek Orthodox rather than the Roman Catholic version. The Eastern Slavs, including the future Ukrainians, received their Cyrillic script and written language, Church Slavonic, from the Orthodox peoples of the Balkans, who had developed them under the influence of Constantinople. Church Slavonic remained the Ukraine's literary language until the end of the eighteenth century and was used in some parts well into the nineteenth. It was also used in scholarly, especially theological, writings of the sixteenth and seventeenth centuries, and was language of instruction in the Kievan Academy (est. 1632), first institution of higher learning among the East

28 Bruk, 1972: 49.
29 *Narodne hospodarstvo 1970:* 18.

30 *Radianska Ukrayina* (April 25), 1971.
31 *Narodne hospodarstvo 1970:* 19–24.
32 *Ibid.:* 10.
33 *Narodne hospodarstvo 1970:* 30.
34 *Soviet Ukraine,* 1970: 190.
35 *Itogi 1970:* IV: 7: 152.
36 See *Ukraine: A Concise Encyclopaedia,* 1971: 524–668, for a detailed survey of architecture, sculpture, painting, music, theater, and cinema in the Ukraine.

Slavs. Not only language and literature, but also architecture, music, theatre, and painting were influenced over the centuries by Byzantium, the West (especially Poland), Russia, and the East (Turkey, Tatars). Samples of Renaissance architecture survive in Galicia to this day, as do palaces and churches built in various parts of the Ukraine in "Ukrainian Baroque," a blend of foreign and native styles.

Modern Ukrainian literature in the vernacular developed in the nineteenth century. Its leading representatives included Ivan Kotliarevsky, Taras Shevchenko, Marko Vovchok (Maria Vilinska), P. Kulish, Ivan Franko, M. Kotsiubynsky, and Lesia Ukrainka (Larisa Kosach). During 1876–1905, when Ukrainian publications were banned in the Russian Empire, writers from the Russian Ukraine published their works in Austria. Lvov became the center of Ukrainian culture. Lvov University had several Ukrainian chairs. Lvov was home to several major libraries in Ukrainian studies, as well as the Shevchenko Scientific Society. An important role in the formation of modern Ukrainian culture, especially historiography, belonged to the universities of Kharkov and Kiev; Ukrainian scholars from these universities produced fundamental editions of historical documents and many monographs.

While in the nineteenth century Ukrainian themes and motifs found their way into Russian culture (Gogol in literature, Glinka in music, Repin in painting), the tsarist regime tried to forestall the transformation of Ukrainian folklore into a separate, modern, urban-based culture. Ukrainian professional theater developed in the nineteenth century but performances in Ukrainian were banned in 1876; in the 1880s the ban was somewhat modified, but Ukrainian traveling companies were as a rule forbidden to perform in major Ukrainian cities (they were highly successful in St. Petersburg and Moscow), and they were also forbidden to stage translated plays and original plays depicting the life of the educated classes.

A lasting achievement of the briefly independent Ukraine (1918–1919) was establishment of the Ukrainian Academy of Sciences (since 1936 Academy of Sciences of the Ukrainian SSR) by Hetman Skoro-padsky. Its first president (V. Vernadsky) and members had been Ukrainian members of the Imperial Academy of Sciences in St. Petersburg. Also at that time, new Ukrainian universities were established in Kiev and Kamenets and the Ukrainian Academy of Fine Arts in Kiev. Kiev acquired its first regular repertory theater in Ukrainian. The beginnings made in 1918–1919 were continued on a much larger scale under the Soviet regime despite periodic efforts to quell them.

The 1920s are considered by Ukrainians in the West as a golden age of Ukrainian literature, theater, and painting. In the 1920s and early 1930s, Ukrainian films won international renown for the art of Dovzhenko, but Dovzhenko was forbidden to work in the Ukraine from the middle 1930s until his death in 1956. In 1933–1937 a number of writers, painters, theater producers, and other artists were arrested and executed; socialist realism replaced modern experimentation. In the late 1950s and early 1960s, a new wave, the generation born in the thirties, made its mark in Ukrainian letters. Many of its representatives were arrested either in 1965–1966 or in 1971–1972. A number of works which could not be published at home found publishers in the West, reestablishing direct cultural relations between Ukrainians in the USSR and those outside that had not existed since the 1920s. Soviet cultural policies have been more severe in the Ukraine than in Moscow or Leningrad; various Ukrainian composers of the younger generation have had works performed in Russia, but not in the Ukraine.

Similarly, young theater producers and actors, rebelling against the rigid cultural standards in Kiev, have been forced to seek work outside the republic. One was Les' Tanyuk, a producer and actor who, failing to get work in the Ukraine, became chief director of a Moscow theater. In an article entitled "Lethargy of Ukrainian Theater," published in Ukrainian in Czechoslovakia in 1968, Tanyuk complained that the Ukraine had proportionately fewer theaters than many other Soviet republics, while Kiev ranked far behind Moscow and Leningrad in this respect. (According to Tanyuk, Kiev had one Ukrainian theater of drama, in which modern plays can be performed, per more than one million inhabitants, while in Moscow there was one theater for every 315,000 and in Leningrad one for every 165,000 inhabitants.) Tanyuk objected to the absence of experimental theaters, contrasting this situation with conditions in Russia, Georgia, and Estonia.[37] Ukrainian intellectuals have been demanding the establishment of a new Ukrainian theater in Kiev for well over 15 years, unsuccessfully so far. Tanyuk was among those to propose a new theater; several speakers at an earlier congress of Ukrainian writers had done the same, including playwright V. Sobko and the then chairman of the Ukrainian Writers Union, Oles Honchar.[38]

Some Ukrainian dissenters have interpreted these restrictions as an indication that the regime wishes to maintain Ukrainian culture on a definitely provincial level so it will be unattractive to more talented artists and will not appeal to the intelligent public. Certainly it is true that as soon as a Ukrainian literary or cultural journal becomes independent-minded and wins a wide readership, a purge of its editorial board swiftly follows. (This point was made by the Ukrainian literary critic, Ivan Dzyuba, in his *Internationalism or Russification?*, published in the West in 1968. Dzyuba is currently serving a 5-year prison term.)[39] On the other hand, the Soviet government appears more tolerant of Ukrainian music and ballet, and such groups as the Virsky Dance Company or the Veryovka National Choir have performed successfully all over the USSR and abroad.

Until the end of the sixteenth century, Ukrainians were Orthodox in religion. Since that time the Orthodox and Uniate (i.e., united with Rome) have become the two principal churches. In 1946 the Uniate Church was dissolved after all its bishops and numerous lower clergy had been arrested. As with Jehovah's Witnesses, Uniate religious activities are forbidden in the USSR. The Orthodox Church, headed by the metropolitan of Kiev and Galicia, "Exarch of All Ukraine," is under the Moscow Patriarchate. The Metropolitanate publishes a Ukrainian language periodical, *Pravoslavnyi visnyk,* and has recently issued calendars and a prayer book. Most of its bishops are reported to be Ukrainian.[40]

EXTERNAL RELATIONS

The Ukraine has common borders with Rumania, Hungary, Czechoslovakia, and Poland. Of all the USSR's European republics, it has the most direct contacts with Eastern Europe. Until World War II the Ukraine's western provinces belonged to these countries at various times. Particularly important are historical and cultural links between the Ukraine and Poland: the Polish provinces of Kraków and Rzeszów and the Ukrainian provinces of Lvov, Ivano-Frankovsk, and Ternopol share six centuries of history, first within Poland, then in Austria, then again in Poland. Polish is generally understood in the west Ukraine, and the Polish press is available at newsstands in Lvov. Radio broadcasts from Warsaw and Kraków can be received in the west Ukraine. The province of Transcarpathia belonged to Hungary until 1918 and from 1939 to 1944, and to Czechoslovakia from 1919 to 1939. A Hungarian minority there has its own schools and periodical press. The province of Chernovtsy has a Rumanian minority; it belonged to Rumania from 1918 to 1940 and from 1941 to 1944.

Despite postwar population exchanges, Czechoslovakia, Poland, Rumania, and Yugoslavia have Ukrainian minorities. In each of these countries a Ukrainian language press and Ukrainian language elementary and secondary school systems exist. The University of Warsaw and the University of Prague boast chairs in Ukrainian philosophy and literature.

37 *Narodnyi kalendar na 1969 rik,* Presov, 1968, reprinted as "Letarhiya ukrayinskoho teatru," *Sucasnist',* 1969: VIII: 86–92; *Shliakh peremohy* (March 23, 30), 1969. Tanyuk was named as one of the young men for whom no work was available in the Ukraine in *Literaturna Ukrayina* (March 26), 1968: 2.

38 *Z'yizd psy'mennykiv,* 1967: 57, 168.

39 Dzyuba, 1968. In November 1973 Dzyuba was reported to have recanted and been released from prison. See *New York Times* (November 14), 1973: 8. See Dzyuba's statement in *Literaturna Ukrayina* (November 9), 1973: 4.

40 Bociurkiw, 1972: 209.

The Soviet authorities do not encourage cultural contacts between the Ukraine and Ukrainians in the East European Communist countries. Although the press from Poland or Czechoslovakia is available to Soviet citizens by subscription, the Ukrainian language periodicals published in those countries are not included in the official subscription catalog. They are delivered by mail, however, when a subscription is paid for by an individual in an East European country.

Official institutions of the Ukrainian SSR display much interest in activities of Ukrainians in the West. The society Ukrayina, also known as Society for Cultural Relations with Ukrainians Abroad, maintains contacts with West European, Canadian, and American Ukrainians. It publishes two weekly newspapers (News from Ukraine and Visti z Ukrayiny) and acts as host to delegations and excursions of "progressive" Ukrainian groups from Canada and the United States. The Ukrainian Society for Friendship and Cultural Relations with Foreign Countries maintains contacts with foreign organizations and individuals of non-Ukrainian background.

Judging by their press, the Soviets pay much attention to the activities of Ukrainian émigrés in the West. The daily press and various periodicals abound with articles criticizing such institutions as the Free University at Munich, the Shevchenko Society (Paris, New York, Winnipeg), the Ukrainian Congress Committee of America, and the Ukrainian Committee of Canada, and publications and leaders of these organizations. In more recent times alleged contacts between Ukrainian émigrés and "Maoists" in Peking have been the subject of comment in Kiev newspapers.[41]

The Ukrainian SSR is a member of the UN, maintaining a permanent delegation in New York. It is also a member of UNESCO, ILO, and other international organizations. Seven states have consulates-general in Kiev: Poland, Czechoslovakia, East Germany, Hungary, Rumania, Bulgaria, and Yugoslavia. Cuba, India, and Egypt have consulates in Odessa. The Ukraine has not taken advantage of its constitutional prerogative to establish diplomatic relations with foreign countries, and foreign consuls in Kiev are there through arrangement with the USSR government. Reportedly, the Ministry of Foreign Affairs of the Ukraine has officers on the staffs of Soviet embassies in countries such as Canada where considerable numbers of Ukrainians live.[42]

In recent years the Ukrainian Ministry of Trade has concluded agreements with the ministries of trade of Poland, Rumania, and Hungary on the exchange of articles of mass consumption and food products.[43] These exchanges appear to be of rather limited importance, and regular foreign trade relations are conducted by the USSR Ministry of Foreign Trade.

In the West little scholarly attention has been given to the relations of the Ukraine with foreign countries or to Kiev's role in formulation of Soviet foreign policy although two works exist, dealing, respectively, with the role of the Ukrainian and Belorussian republics in Soviet foreign policy immediately after World War II[44] and with the Ukrainian aspect of the Czechoslovak crisis of 1968.[45] In 1967 the Communist party of Canada sent an official delegation to the Ukraine, with the specific task of exploring Soviet handling of the nationality question. It published a report upon its return to Canada, containing a number of criticisms[46] along with words of praise. At first this report was accepted by the Central Committee of the Canadian Communist Party; then, after protests from Kiev, it was withdrawn.

There were unconfirmed reports that the then first secretary of the Ukrainian Communist party took a stand urging the invasion of Czechoslovakia in 1968 and later opposing President Nixon's visit to Moscow

41 Radio Liberty Research (March 10), 1972. "Kiev Attacks Ukrainian 'Pro-Chinese' Group," and "Peking Orientation of Ukrainian Nationalists Exposed," DSUP (August), 1972: 21–25.

42 Personal communication received by Roman Szporluk.
43 Visti z Ukrayiny (June 10), 1971: 4; Radianska Ukrayina (August 21), 1971: 3.
44 Aspaturian, 1960.
45 Hodnett and Potichnyj, 1970.
46 "Report of Delegation to Ukraine," Viewpoint, Discussion Bulletin issued by Central Committee, Communist party of Canada (January), 1968: V: 1: 1–13.

after the U.S. mining of Haiphong. In any case, Shelest was subsequently removed as first secretary. Whatever the truth of these reports, Ukrainian leaders have probably exerted little influence on the external relations of the USSR.

Media

LANGUAGE DATA

Together with Russian and Belorussian, Ukrainian belongs to the eastern group of Slavic languages. "The distinctive phonetic, grammatical and lexical features of the Ukrainian language have been discerned in written documents of the 12th century." [47] The Ukrainian script is based on Cyrillic, also used in Russian, Bulgarian, Serbian, Belorussian, and most languages of the USSR. Modern Ukrainian script has incorporated the orthographic reforms introduced by M. Kulish in the nineteenth century.[48] Literary Ukrainian grew out of Church Slavonic and linguistic forms specific to the region. Polish and Latin influences dating from the sixteenth to eighteenth centuries also affected its development. Modern Ukrainian is based on popular peasant speech, introduced to literature in the nineteenth century. Taras Shevchenko (1814–1861), who originated standard literary Ukrainian (as Pushkin did for Russian), employed a variety of Ukrainian dialects as well as old Church Slavonic elements.[49]

Ukrainian (see Table 2.1) is the second most widespread language in the USSR. Its native speakers include 35.9 million Ukrainians (of whom 2.6 million live outside the borders of the Ukraine) and 400,000 non-Ukrainian inhabitants of the Ukraine (Russians, Poles, Jews). In 1959, 73% of the population of the Ukrainian SSR, including 490,000 non-Ukrainians, said Ukrainian was their native language. In 1970 the proportion was down to 69%; Ukrainian was declared as a second language by 4.4

million people in 1970. One and a half million of this group were Ukrainians who considered Russian their first language.

Other speakers of Ukrainian as a second language included more than a quarter of the Russians and more than a third of the Jews in the Ukraine; altogether, 37.1 million people regarded Ukrainian as either first or second language.[50]

According to the 1970 census, over 41 million Soviet citizens in the Ukraine and outside its borders are familiar with the Ukrainian language. According to Soviet estimates, Ukrainian speakers abroad number 300,000 in Poland, over 70,000 in Czechoslovakia, 62,000 in Rumania, 40,000 in Yugoslavia, over 700,000 in Canada, over 1 million in the United States, and smaller numbers in Australia, Brazil, and other countries.[51]

LOCAL MEDIA

Soviet Print Media

Kiev is the principal center of Ukrainian newspaper and journal publishing, and the second largest publishing center in the USSR. Of a total of 103 journals published in the Ukraine in 1971, 99 appeared in Kiev, and one in each of the following: Lvov, Kharkov, Donetsk, and Dnepropetrovsk. All the newspapers of republican rank (i.e., those distributed throughout the Ukraine and offering subscriptions to the other republics and abroad) are published in Kiev.

Kiev has more diversified republican newspapers than any other union republic capital. They include the party government daily *Radianska Ukrayina* [*Soviet Ukraine*]

47 *Soviet Ukraine,* 1970: 474.
48 *Ukraine: A Concise Encyclopaedia,* 1963: 511–515.
49 *Ibid.,* 485–504. See also section on culture earlier in this chapter.

50 *Radianska Ukrayina* (April 25), 1971.
51 *Soviet Ukraine,* 1970: 474; *Itogi 1970:* IV: 331.

Table 2.1

Native and Second Languages Spoken by Ukrainians

(in thousands)

	Number of Ukrainians Residing		SPEAKING AS NATIVE LANGUAGE					SPEAKING AS SECOND LANGUAGE[a]		
			Ukrainian		Percentage Point Change 1959–1970	Russian		Percentage Point Change 1959–1970	Russian	Other Languages of Peoples of USSR
	1959	1970	1959	1970		1959	1970		1970	1970[b]
in Ukrainian SSR	32,158.5 (100%)	35,283.9 (100%)	30,072.3 (93.5%)	32,257.4 (91.4%)	−2.1	2,075.5 (6.5%)	3,018 (8.6%)	+2.1	10,091 (28.6%)	1,575 (4.5%)
in other Soviet republics	5,094.4 (100%)	5,469.4 (100%)	2,602.2 (51%)	2,668.1 (48%)	−3.0	2,465.6 (48.4%)	2,769 (50.6%)	+2.2	4,702 (86.0%)	878 (16.1%)
Total	37,252.9 (100%)	40,753.2 (100%)	32,680.6 (87.7%)	34,925.5 (85.7%)	−2.0	4,541.1 (12.3%)	5,787 (14.2%)	+1.9	14,793 (36.3%)	2,453 (6.0%)

Sources: *Itogi 1970: IV: 7*: 152–153. *Itogi SSSR 1959* and *Itogi Ukrainskoi SSR 1959*, tables 53, 54.

[a] No data are available for 1959, since no questions regarding command of a second language were asked in the 1959 census.

[b] Including Ukrainian, if not native language.

(which had a circulation of 520,000 in 1971) and two dailies for specialized audiences, *Robitnycha hazeta* [*Workers' Gazette*] and *Silski visti* [*Village News*]. *Workers' Gazette* also appears in Russian with identical text; the combined circulation is 320,000 (1971). *Village News* appears only in Ukrainian (circulation 390,000 in 1968). *Pravda Ukrainy* (circulation over 500,000 in 1971), the Russian counterpart to *Radianska Ukrayina*, devotes more attention to urban, economic, industrial, and managerial problems, while *Radianska Ukrayina* has much more material on ideological topics, as well as attacks on Ukrainian émigrés and their foreign friends. It also serves as watchdog over the rest of the Ukrainian press, reacting promptly to ideological errors.

Molod' Ukrayiny [*Youth of the Ukraine*] is the Young Communist League newspaper and appears five times per week. It had a circulation of 875,000 in 1971. It devotes a great deal of space to sports and feature articles on modern science and family problems. A Russian counterpart, *Komsomolskoye znamya*, had a much smaller circulation (131,500 in 1970), perhaps due to competition from the Moscow *Komsomolskaya pravda*, printed from matrices in a number of cities in the Ukraine (as are *Pravda* and other Moscow dailies).

The Ukrainian branch of DOSAAF, a paramilitary organization, publishes a weekly newspaper in Ukrainian, *Patriot batkivshchyny* [*Patriot of the Fatherland*] (128,000 in 1966), which may be the only non-Russian language publication in the USSR even remotely related to military affairs. *Literaturna Ukrayina*, semiweekly organ of the Ukrainian Writers Union, was the most liberal paper in the Ukraine in the early 1960s but in recent years has been closely controlled. *Sportyvna hazeta* [*The Sports Gazette*] appears three times a week (310,000 per issue in 1973).

Other Ukrainian newspapers include the organ of the Ministry of Culture, *Kultura i zhyttia* [*Culture and Life*], the teachers' newspaper *Radianska osvita* [*Soviet Education*], and *Druh chytacha* [*Reader's Friend*], not available outside the USSR. There are two children's weeklies, the Ukrainian *Zirka* [*Star*] (2.5 million per

issue) and the Russian *Iunyi Leninets* [*Young Leninist*] (1.6 million per issue). Two weeklies are for foreign readers: *Visti z Ukrayiny* and *News from Ukraine*. The latter had a circulation of 18,000 in 1971.

In addition to the republican papers, Kiev has three city and *oblast* newspapers in Ukrainian only. The evening paper, *Vechirniy Kyiv*, had a circulation of 307,500 in 1972. The other regional Kiev papers are the party *Kyivska pravda* (134,000 in 1972) and the Komsomol *Moloda hvardiya* (132,000 in 1966). As of 1972, the Ukraine had two other evening city papers: they belong to a special "lighter" category of Soviet dailies, printing more about problems of everyday city life and publishing a relatively large amount of advertisement; politics, on the other hand, takes up much less space. These papers were *Vechirniy Kharkiv* in Kharkov (130,000 in 1972) and *Dnipro vechirniy* in Dnepropetrovsk (est. 1972, 80,000 copies). In an apparent reversal of the press policy pursued by Shelest, two Russian language evening papers were established in July 1973: *Vecherniy Donetsk* in Donetsk and *Vecherniaya Odessa* in Odessa.

Since a majority of the population in both Kharkov and Dnepropetrovsk speaks Russian and probably is Russian,[52] and since Russian is the most influential language in Kiev despite its clear Ukrainian majority, the fact that the evening papers are published only in Ukrainian in those cities demonstrates that they can be distributed in predominantly Russian environments. This seems to confirm Soviet statements claiming that while Ukrainians in the Ukraine are generally bilingual, so are Russians, and that the latter use Ukrainian language media.[53]

There are significant variations in the language pattern of the provincial press. All *oblasty* carry Ukrainian party–Soviet papers, but some also carry Russian provincial papers. This is true in Donetsk and the Crimea, where in addition the Komsomol

52 The 1970 census data give figures for these provinces but not separately for the cities. *Itogi 1970:* IV: 172, 187.

53 Kurman and Lebedinskiy, 1968: 125; Yizhakevych, 1966: 170; Chizhikova, 1968: 24–25. Cf. *Itogi, 1970:* IV: 152–153.

papers come out exclusively in Russian. Local, district, and city newspapers in the Crimea are also exclusively Russian, while in Donetsk they are predominantly Russian. Voroshilovgrad, the easternmost *oblast* of the Ukraine, has a Komsomol paper in Ukrainian (its party papers are in both Russian and Ukrainian), and Ukrainian is used in the local press. In general, these three *oblasty* constitute the most Russified area in terms of press. Zaporozhe, Kharkov, and Odessa also have *oblast* papers in Russian, and some districts have local newspapers in the Russian language. Russian language *oblast* papers exist in only two of a total of 13 provinces of the Southwestern Region—in Lvov and Transcarpathia. They have lower circulations than Ukrainian counterparts. Transcarpathia also has Hungarian newspapers and Chernovtsy-Moldavian. Elsewhere in the republic the *oblast* newspapers are in Ukrainian only.

Two Ukrainian journals print over a million copies per issue. *Perets* [*Pepper*], a journal of humor and satire (the Ukrainian counterpart of Moscow's *Krokodil*), printed 2,620,000 copies per issue in 1973. The monthly *Radianska zhinka* [*Soviet Woman*] had a circulation of 1,755,000 during the same period. *Novyny kinoekranu* [*Screen News*], with a circulation of 500,000, was third most popular journal for adults in Ukrainian; the weekly illustrated magazine *Ukrayina*, fourth (355,000 per week).

Strictly political periodicals are *Komunist Ukrayiny*, theoretical and political monthly journal of the CP of the Ukraine appearing in both Russian (1973 circulation 59,000) and Ukrainian (112,500) and *Pid praporom leninizmu* (Russian version: *Pod znamenem leninizma* [*Under the Banner of Leninism*]), a more popular biweekly publication addressed to party activists and agitators. In 1972 the Ukrainian edition of the latter had a circulation of 262,000; the Russian, about 280,000.

Publications addressed to professional groups include *Radianske pravo* [*Soviet Law*] (over 55,000) and *Ekonomika Radians'koyi Ukrayiny* (in Ukrainian and Russian versions, each with a circulation of 10,000). The popular antireligious magazine *Liudyna i svit* [*Man and the World*] has a circulation over 150,000 and the much more sophisticated popular science (including social science) review, *Nauka i suspil'stvo* [*Science and Society*], over 60,000.

The Union of Writers of the Ukraine published three monthly journals in Ukrainian: *Vitchyzna* [*Fatherland*] (published in Kiev with a circulation of 25,000), *Zhovten'* [*October*] (published in Lvov; circulation, 20,000), which specializes in attacking Ukrainian nationalists past and present, and *Prapor* [*Banner*] (Kharkov; circulation, 14,000). The journal *Vsesvit* publishes foreign literature in Ukrainian translation and is jointly sponsored by the Writers Union and the Ukrainian Society for Friendship and Cultural Relations with Foreign Countries; in 1973 its circulation was 44,000. Art journals include *Muzyka* (20,000 per issue), *Ukrayinskyi teatr* (ca. 8,000), and *Obrazotvorche mystetstvo* (fine arts; ca. 15,000).

The Russian Orthodox Church in the Ukraine publishes a Ukrainian language journal, *Provoslavnyi visnyk* [*Orthodox Herald*]; its circulation is not known but several thousand copies per issue have reportedly been distributed among Ukrainian religious communities in Canada and the United States. Originally, it appeared in Lvov, but has been published in Kiev since 1971.)

Soviet Electronic Media

Kiev broadcasts three radio programs, two heard throughout the republic, the third local. The republic-wide programs are on the air from 6:00 A.M. to 1:00 A.M. The total volume of Ukrainian-language broadcasting amounts to 130 hours a day (including the republic, regional, and district broadcasts). There are no figures on the ratio of Ukrainian language broadcasts to those in Russian, but a major portion of the republic's scheduled listings consists of programs relayed from Moscow, and Ukrainian television also broadcasts partly in Russian. All Ukrainian radio stations carry Moscow news several times a day, and the popular program "Mayak" ["Beacon"] is also relayed into the Ukraine. A Ukrainian counterpart to "Mayak," the radio program "Promin" ["Ray"] has existed since 1965. It includes music, short news bulletins and commentaries, and special broadcasts for young people.

Until 1972 Kiev and other Ukrainian TV stations had only a single program each, in which they alternated Moscow telecasts with those produced locally. The Kiev TV Center was reorganized early in 1972 and two parallel channels, Central (from Moscow) and Ukrainian, may now be viewed in the Ukraine. Moscow TV, however, reaches a larger audience in the republic than does Ukrainian TV, with broadcast time, 12 hours daily, longer than that of the UTV (7 hour per day, part made up of local broadcasts originating outside Kiev, part including the Moscow broadcast, "Vremya").

The quality of Ukrainian TV is much poorer than that of the Central station, and its technical equipment is not as modern. Among provincial TV stations contributing to the channel, the Lvov station most frequently includes programs with a distinctly Ukrainian flavor; the station promotes not only traditional Ukrainian folk music and singing, but also works by more modern artists.

Foreign Media

Newspapers and journals published in East European Communist countries are generally available in major cities of the Ukraine, especially Kiev and Lvov—only exceptions are Ukrainian language publications from abroad.

Regularly, Soviet Ukrainian media mention foreign radio broadcasts in Ukrainian from the West, especially Radio Liberty and Voice of America. Radio Canada, Madrid, Rome, and Vatican are also mentioned. Recently doubling of VOA broadcast time in Ukrainian has been noted in the press.

Foreign radio programs in Ukrainian are jammed, but jamming is less effective in the countryside. The Soviet press and radio have been replying to criticism expressed in these programs, and it may be due to these foreign broadcasts that such names as

Karavansky, Chornovil, or Moroz[54] have appeared in the newspapers; originally, their arrests and trials had not been reported in the Soviet media. The press also responds to criticism in foreign publications printed in Ukrainian. Polemics at Ukrainian émigré journals such as *Suchasnist'*, *Ukrayinskyi samostiynyk*, or *Ukrayinske slovo* are a regular feature of *Zhovten'*, *Radianska Ukrayina*, *Literaturna Ukrayina*, and the Lvov *Vilna Ukrayina*.

EDUCATIONAL INSTITUTIONS

In the school year 1971–1972 there were over 27,500 general education schools in the Ukraine: in 4,700, Russian was the language of instruction; in 122, Rumanian or Moldavian; in 68, Hungarian; in a few others, Polish. In 427 schools, classes were taught in more than one language.[55] This leaves a balance of about 22,200 Ukrainian language schools. Twenty years earlier, in 1950–1951, there were 2,836 Russian language schools and close to 28,000 Ukrainian.[56] V. Swoboda, a British scholar of Ukrainian descent, has written that in 1958 73% of pupils in the Ukraine attended Ukrainian language schools, but only 66% in 1965.[57] An official Soviet publication stated that in 1966–1967 Ukrainian was language of instruction in about 82% of schools under the Ministry of Education of the Ukrainian SSR.[58] This percentage does not conflict with that given by Swoboda because schools differ vastly in size; a village four-year school may have less than a hundred students while an urban ten-year school may have a thousand.

Relatively complete data exist for schools in the three *oblasty* of the former Austrian

54 See later section of this chapter on recent manifestations of nationalism.
55 Malanchuk, 1972: 115, 117. Clearly Malanchuk was not including in the total evening schools for young adults and correspondence school for adults, of which the Ukraine had 2,300 in 1970. *Narodne hospodarstvo, 1970* lists 27,558 regular schools (p. 476) and, separately, 2,344 schools for adults for 1970 (p. 481).
56 Zuban', 1967: 87, 90.
57 Swoboda, 1971: 214.
58 *Soviet Ukraine*, 1970: 364.

Table 2.2

Publications in Ukrainian SSR

Language of Publication	Year	NEWSPAPERS			MAGAZINES			BOOKS AND BROCHURES		
		No.	Per Issue Circulation (1,000)	Copies/100 in Language Group[a]	No.	Per Issue Circulation (1,000)	Copies/100 in Language Group[a]	No. Titles	Total Volume (1,000)	Books & Brochures/100 in Language Group[a]
Russian	1959	381	2,430	23.9	N.A.	N.A.	N.A.	2,628	21,998	216.3
	1970	400	6,083	45.7	39	1,318	9.9	4,682	25,564	192.2
	1971	357	6,417	N.A.	39	1,334	N.A.	4,613	28,541	N.A.
Ukrainian	1959	919	5,458	17.8	N.A.	N.A.	N.A.	4,048	75,272	246
	1970	936	13,455	41.1	63	7,162	21.9	3,105	91,994	281
	1971	863	13,973	N.A.	63	7,884	N.A.	3,106	93,379	N.A.
Minority Languages	1959	15	39	N.A.	N.A.	N.A.	N.A.	N.A.	N.A.	N.A.
	1970	5	48	N.A.	0	0	0	17	301	N.A.
	1971	5	44	N.A.	0	0	0	15	194	N.A.
Foreign Languages	1959	0	0	0	N.A.	N.A.	N.A.	N.A.	N.A.	N.A.
	1970	6*	67*	N.A.	1	15	N.A.	329*	3,647*	N.A.
	1971	6*	N.A.	N.A.	1	15	N.A.	334*	4,584*	N.A.
All Languages	1959	1,315	7,927	18.9	63	1,231	2.9	6,817**	99,426**	237.3
	1970	1,347	19,653	41.7	103	8,495	18.0	8,133	121,506	258.0
	1971	1,231	20,504	42.8	103	9,233	19.3	8,068	126,698	264.6

Sources: *Pechat' 1959*: 54, 128, 164; 1970: 95, 158, 188; 1971: 95, 158, 188.

NOTE: Totals for publications in language categories given in the sources do not always equal the totals for publications in all languages. Where the category "Other languages of the peoples of the USSR" is given in the source, the remainder are presumed to be in foreign languages and marked with an asterisk (*); otherwise, the total figure "All Languages" is marked with two asterisks (**) to indicate an unresolvable discrepancy.

[a] Includes all native speakers of the language.

Table 2.3

Electronic Media and Films in Ukrainian SSR

YEAR	RADIO					TELEVISION			MOVIES	
	No. Stations	No. Wired Sets (1,000)	Sets/100 Population	No. Wireless Sets (1,000)	Sets/100 Population	No. Stations	No. sets (1,000)	Sets/100 Population	Seats (1,000)	Seats/100 Population
1960	N.A.	7,203[a]	17.2[d]	4,431[a]	10.3[c]	N.A.	745[a]	1.7[c]	2,502[b]	5.0[d]
1970	N.A.	10,267[a]	21.6[d]	8,157[a]	17.2[c]	N.A.	7,167[a]	15.1[c]	5,157[b]	10.9[d]
1971	N.A.	10,825[a]	22.6[d]	8,288[d]	17.3[c]	N.A.	8,116[c]	17.0[c]	N.A.	N.A.

[a] *Transport i svyaz'*, 1972: 296–298.
[b] *Nar. obraz.*, 1971: 325.
[c] *Nar. khoz.*, 1972: 520, 528.
[d] Computed.
[e] *Televideniye i Radioveskkhaniye*, 1972: XII: 13, lists
14 TV "program centers" in the Ukraine in 1972.

Table 2.4

Selected Data on Education in Ukrainian SSR 1970–1971

Population: 47,878,000

		PER 1,000 POPULATION	% OF TOTAL
Ali schools[a]			
number of schools	29,900	.06	
number of students	8,404,000	175.5	
Newly opened elementary, incomplete secondary, and secondary schools			
number of schools	571		
number of student places	261,900	5.47	
Secondary special schools			
number of schools	755	·	
number of students	797,200	11.65	
Institutions of higher education			
number of institutions	138		
number of students	802,900	16.77	
Universities			
number of universities	8		
number of students			
total	101,046	2.11	100.0
day students	43,012	0.9	42.6
evening students	17,938	0.37	17.7
correspondence students	40,096	0.84	39.7
newly admitted			
total	18,700	0.4	100.0
day students	9,193	0.2	49.2
evening students	3,256	0.07	17.4
correspondence students	6,251	0.13	33.4
graduated			
total	16,172	0.34	100.0
day students	8,009	0.17	49.5
evening students	2,321	0.05	14.4
correspondence students	5,842	0.12	36.1
Graduate students			
total number	13,503	0.28	
in scientific research institutions	4,684	0.1	
in universities	8,819	0.18	
Number of persons with (in 1970) higher or secondary (complete and incomplete) education			
per 1,000 individuals 10 years and older	494		
per 1,000 individuals employed in national economy	668		
Number of workers graduated from professional-technical schools	286,200	5.98	

Source: *Nar. khoz. 1972:* 10, 108, 436–437, 516, 526, 527, 529.
[a] Regular schools and schools for adults as reported in *Narodne hospodarstvo.* 1970: 476, 481.

Galicia, indicating that Russian language schools tend to be considerably larger than their Ukrainian counterparts, reflecting either consolidation into 10-year schools or urban locations.[59] In Transcarpathia in 1969–1970 there were 614 Ukrainian schools with over 163,000 pupils (average 265 pupils), 15 Russian schools with 11,500 pupils (average 767), 70 Hungarian schools with 21,500 pupils (average 302), 12 Rumanian schools with 4,300 pupils (average 358), and, finally, 32 mixed schools.[60] In the highly urbanized, industrialized Dnepropetrovsk region, of a total of 1,529 general education schools, 1,255 taught in Ukrainian in 1970, but enrollment in Ukrainian schools was only one half of the total student enrollment. In the city of Dnepropetrovsk itself there were 35 Ukrainian schools.[61] A *samizdat* source, *Ukrainian Herald*, reported in 1972 that in 1966 in the city of Kiev there were 128,112 pupils in 150 Russian schools; and 38,299 in 57 Ukrainian schools. Among Russian schools identified by the source was school Number 57, with 1,600 pupils, in which were enrolled the children and grandchildren of Shelest, Shcherbitsky, Drozdenko, Paton, "and other elite." [62]

In 1967 Ukrainians constituted 61% of students in higher educational establishments of the Ukraine, with Russians 32%, Jews 3.8%, and others 3.2%.[63] In the west Ukraine, Ukrainians made up 83% of students in vocational and secondary specialized schools (out of a total 96,464) and 76% of students in higher educational establishments (of a total of 111,100). The faculty of Lvov University included 479 Ukrainians, 259 born in the west Ukraine. (Total number of faculty was not given.)[64] An earlier source asserted that at Lvov University 293 of 600 academic personnel were Ukrainians, 114 born in the west Ukraine.[65] (The area had about a 90% Ukrainian population in 1970.)

CULTURAL AND SCIENTIFIC INSTITUTIONS

No recent data are available on the nationality mix of scientific personnel in the Ukraine, but the share of Ukrainians among all scientific personnel in the USSR is known. In 1970, of 927,709 Soviet scholars, 100,215 were Ukrainian. Of total Soviet scholars, 224,490 held the advanced degree of Candidate of Science, 25,521 Ukrainian. Among the even more advanced Doctors of Science—23,616 in the USSR—Ukrainians numbered 2,235. These figures show some increase since 1950 in proportion of Ukrainians. In 1950, 14,692 of 162,508 scientific workers, 3,731 of 45,530 Candidates of Science, and 415 of 8,277 holding the doctorate degree were Ukrainians (4,948 Russians, 301 Georgians, and 246 Armenians were among those holding this degree).[66]

In 1960, latest year for which data are available for the Ukraine, there were 22,523 scientific workers of Ukrainian nationality in the republic, constituting 48.3% of all employed scientists. (In 1947 the percentage was 41.2.)[67] This represented almost two thirds of the Ukrainian scientists working in the USSR. Thirty-six% worked in other republics (in 1959 13.7% of Ukrainians lived outside the Ukraine).[68]

---

59 Oleksiuk, 1968: 742. In 1965–1966, 1,056 Ukrainian schools in the Ternopol province averaged 165 pupils apiece; 8 Russian schools, 576. In the Ivano-Frankovsk province, corresponding averages were 241 and 872 pupils per school.
60 *Radianska shkola*, 1970: VI: 45.
61 *Zoria* (Dnepropetrovsk) (February 7), 1970 (reporting trial of nationalist students), translated in *DSUP* (October), 1970: 4.
62 *Ukrayinskyi visnyk*, 1972: 60, 67.
63 "Delegation to Ukraine": 5.
64 Oleksiuk, 1968: 739–740.

65 Malanchuk, 1963: 598, 668.
66 *Nar. obraz.*, 1971: 270–271; cf. *Istoriya SSSR*, 1972: V: 110. By the end of 1973, according to a source published when this book was in press, Ukrainians numbered 120,373 scientific workers in the USSR (Soviet total 1,108,268), including 33,312 Candidates of Science (total 288,261) and 2,901 doctors (total 29,806). See *Vestnik statistiki* 1974: 4: 92.
67 *Vyssheye obrazovaniye v SSSR, Statisticheskii sbornik*, Moscow, 1961: 215, cited in Solovey, 1963: 258. As this book was in press, *Vestnik statistiki* 1974: 4: 93, reported that there were 154,121 scientific workers employed in the Ukrainian SSR at the end of 1973, of whom 78,044 were Ukrainian by nationality. They included 22,191 Candidates of Science (republic total 42,044) and 1,833 Doctors of Science (republic total 3,888).
68 Solovey, 1963: 78.

Table 2.5

Selected Data on Scientific and Cultural Facilities and Personnel in

Ukrainian SSR (1971)

Population: 47,878,000

Academy of Sciences		*Number of persons working*	
number of members	262	*in education and culture*	
number of scientific institutions		total	1,464,000
affiliated with academy	76	number per 1,000 population	30.6
total number of scientific workers	10,712		
		Number of persons working in science	
Museums		*and scientific services*	
number of museums	144	total	448,000
attendance	17,402,000	number per 1,000 population	9
attendance per 1,000 population	363		
		Number of public libraries	27,500
Theaters		number of books and magazines	
number of theaters	71	in public libraries	289,800,000
attendance	18,139,000		
attendance per 1,000 population	379	*Number of clubs*	25,700

Source: *Nar. khoz. 1972*: 106, 451, 525, 529.

National Attitudes

REVIEW OF FACTORS FORMING
NATIONAL ATTITUDES

In his 1972 address marking the fiftieth anniversary of the USSR, L. I. Brezhnev attributed survival of the nationality question in the USSR to "nationalistic prejudices, exaggerated or distorted national feelings," and to "objective problems" that arise "in a multinational state which seeks to establish the most correct balance between the interests of each nation . . . and the common interests of the Soviet people as a whole." [69] Both sets of factors contribute to attitudes in the Ukraine today. Perhaps the most important "prejudice" is the very concept that the Ukraine is a nation, not merely a subdivision of the Soviet people. National identity in East

Europe has centered around language, and the Ukrainians claim to be a nation because they speak and write—or would like to speak and write—Ukrainian. The Soviet stress on language assimilation and on the progressiveness of the Russian language, and the implication that those who refuse to become assimilated are somehow less progressive—even if they accept Marxism-Leninism and the current leadership of the CPSU—are sources of national dissatisfaction in the Ukraine.

Language by itself, isolated from other factors, does not necessarily lead to formation of national attitudes. Ukrainian, however, has become a language of modern culture, has established its capacity to serve as a tool of communication, and it is supported by the Ukrainian intelligentsia, who have a vested interest in its maintenance and development. Attempts to return it to the position of a dialect spoken by the uneducated, or even to assign it a secondary

69 Brezhnev, 1973: 11. Nationalist survivals, Brezhnev noted, are being encouraged by burgeois propagandists and politicians.

position, are resented by educated Ukrainians.

Another factor to take into consideration in formation of national attitudes is Ukrainian history. Soviet policy has been to eradicate all knowledge of past conflicts between Ukrainians and Russians or to present them in a distorted light. Pre-Soviet nationalists are portrayed as enemies of the Ukrainian people. Those achievements not attributed to Russia, such as the status of the Ukrainian language and culture in Austria, are passed over silently in textbooks, popular literature, and even scholarly works. Thus, because the Soviet regime has chosen to identify communism with Russia and to consider hostility to, or independence from, tsarist Russia as anti-Soviet, a familiarity with the Ukraine past may provide a source of national attitudes not only anti-Russian but anti-Soviet.

Sense of national identity among ethnic Ukrainians is strongest in the western areas, last to be incorporated into the Soviet Ukraine; it is less evident in the south and east. The Ukraine, however, has also developed a sense of *territorial* identity, shared by Ukrainians and non-Ukrainians alike. Thus, without regard to ethnic origin, inhabitants of the Ukraine may oppose such Soviet economic policies as the promotion of growth in Siberia and the Far East as being at the expense of their republic and detrimental to their interests. Brezhnev's "objective problems" are at work here. Although this territorial nationalism may be reinforced by language consciousness or a non-Russian or anti-Russian historical identity, it does not depend on them. It is just as natural for officials of the Ukrainian Gosplan or various ministries to advocate their own region's interests on grounds of economic rationality as it is for a convinced nationalist to interpret any Soviet action in favor of a non-Ukrainian region as motivated by an anti-Ukrainian bias. The Ukrainian first secretaries, whether ethnically Ukrainian or not, have shown that they enjoy those attributes of political statehood the Ukraine possesses, and top party and state officials in the Ukraine, whatever their origins, tend to take their power more seriously than intended by Moscow. In its territorial sense, the future of Ukrainian nationalism depends on leaders' ability to balance "nationalistic prejudices" with "objective problems."

Since so much of the Ukraine's history has been tied up with Poland, and to a smaller extent with Czechoslovakia and Hungary, the political status of these countries under communism is of great interest to Ukrainians. They may compare their lot with that of their western neighbors. Such a comparison is likely to produce critical attitudes toward present Soviet policy, especially if combined with a knowledge that in the past the Ukraine's history has been similar to that of Slovakia or Poland. This fact raises again the question of the historical factor in formation of national attitudes. A Ukrainian who knows nothing about the past will not see a contradiction in the fact that West Ukrainian peasants have been forced to collectivize while Polish peasants have not. Anyone ignorant of the decimation of Ukrainian party apparatus and cultural intelligentsia in the 1930s is likely to be less concerned by the arrests of 1972. The same applies to such events as the famine of 1933 or the armed struggles of the 1940s–1950s. As Karl W. Deutsch said. "Autonomy in the long run depends on memory. Where all memory is lost, where all past information and preferences have ceased to be effective, we are no longer dealing with a self-determining individual or social group." [70]

BASIC VIEWS OF SCHOLARS ON NATIONAL ATTITUDES

The Ukrainian national movement in the period of the Russian revolution and civil war (1917–1921), according to Richard Pipes, was rooted in a specific Ukrainian culture (language and folklore), historic tradition, and identity of interests among the well-to-do peasants of the Dnieper region. It was "a political expression of genuine interests and loyalties." While it enjoyed the support of a small but active group of intellectuals, it lacked sufficient strength outside what Pipes calls "the politically disorganized, ineffective and unreliable village." The fate of the Ukraine

---

70 Deutsch *et al.*, 1966: 128–129.

"was decided in the towns, where the population was almost entirely Russian in its culture, and hostile to Ukrainian nationalism." [71]

Both Western and Soviet writers on the contemporary Ukraine note that the village has given way to the city. The Soviet regime has transformed the Ukraine into an urban and industrial area. In 1964 an American political scientist of Ukrainian descent, Yaroslav Bilinsky, concluded that by the 1960s the Ukraine had "matured into a sociologically balanced nation," capable of self-rule despite the Soviet policy of "scattering educated Ukrainians into all corners" of the Soviet Union.[72]

In 1972 V. V. Pokshishevsky, professor of geography in Moscow, noted that the city, not the village, was now the "carrier of the ethnos" in the USSR. While the city produces an assimilationist tendency, it also stimulates "a sharpening of ethnic awareness." Specifically, Pokshishevsky cited the increase of the Ukrainian element in Kiev, which he explained by the city's attraction of Ukrainians from all over the Ukraine and by "further consolidation of the Ukrainian nation and a strengthening of ethnic consciousness. . . . It may be supposed that some Kievans, after some hesitation whether to consider themselves Ukrainian, later did so with absolute conviction; more children of mixed marriages have also declared themselves Ukrainian." [73]

On the other hand, in another work, John A. Armstrong of the University of Wisconsin, author of *Ukrainian Nationalism, 1939–1945* (New York: Columbia, 1955, 2nd ed. 1963), classified Ukrainians as "younger brothers" of the Russians, considering them still relatively low in social mobilization, and also close to Russians in major cultural respects. Armstrong expected Ukrainians to become objects of extremely intensive assimilationist efforts by the Soviet regime. The success of the regime, Armstrong thought, would depend on its improving the position of "submerged social strata, particularly the peasantry." [74] Evidently Armstrong took the view that the peasantry is the principal

group maintaining a separate Ukrainian identity and improvement of its economic and social position would facilitate assimilation to Russian nationality.

Various Western writers have connected emergence of national dissent during the 1960s with the republic's socioeconomic transformation. Tibor Szamuely, former Hungarian Communist scholar who emigrated to England in the early 1960s, wrote that the "old, romantic, peasant style and anti-Semitic" nationalism in the Ukraine "has been replaced by the modern, ideological nationalism of an industrialized, urbanized and literate society." [75] In a later article, Szamuely expressed the view that nationalism in the Ukraine (unlike the civil rights movement in Russia) fused "intellectual and peasant together." The resistance movement growing rapidly in the Ukraine in the last 10 years, subject to "far harsher repression than the Russian civil rightists," is "an openly nationalist movement, aiming at national independence for their country and therefore enjoying support that far transcends the ranks of the intelligentsia." [76]

Following the long tradition of the Ukrainian liberal intelligentsia, Ivan L. Rudnytsky, historian from the University of Alberta, has stressed historical factors forming political attitudes of Ukrainians. In a study published in 1963, Rudnytsky approvingly quoted two earlier Ukrainian figures, M. Drahomanov (1841–1895) and V. Lypynsky (1882–1931), who explained national differences between Russia and the Ukraine in terms of different political experiences in the past, especially the Ukraine's association with the West (Poland).[77] In a 1972 article, Rudnytsky argued again that contemporary Ukrainian national identity depends heavily on historical tradition. In particular, he states that annexation of the west Ukraine as a result of World War II has strengthened

---

71 Pipes, 1964: 149.
72 Bilinsky, 1964: 83.
73 Pokshishevsky, 1972: 116, 118–119.
74 Armstrong, 1968: 14–15, 18, 32.

75 Szamuely, 1968: 16–17. Similarly, a prominent Soviet writer of liberal persuasion, the late Ilya Ehrenburg, reportedly told Werth: "These people (it's never happened in the Ukraine before) deplore the old Ukrainian anti-Semitism, and those new Ukrainian nationalists are liberals . . . their sympathies lie with Western culture." Werth, 1969: 200–201.
76 Szamuely, 1972: 3–4.
77 Rudnytsky, 1963: 207.

Ukrainian nationalism in the USSR. The west Ukrainians, whose cultural and religious ties had been with Central Europe, helped bring about a "psychological mutation" of the east Ukrainian population. The dissent of the 1960s, he said, cannot be explained without taking into account this west Ukrainian factor. The Ukrainians are no longer engaged in a conflict with Poland, while the existence of a Soviet sphere of influence in Eastern Europe has added to Russian concerns, thereby easing the Russian pressure on the Ukraine. Communist Eastern Europe, especially its Ukrainian minorities, provides a previously nonexistent link with the outside world for the Ukrainian intelligentsia. Finally, Rudnytsky believes that emergence of the Communist bloc had deprived the USSR of its ideological legitimacy (indirectly reinforcing Ukrainian nationalism), because nothing in Marxism-Leninism requires the Ukraine to be inferior in status to the independent states of Eastern Europe.[78]

Vernon V. Aspaturian,[79] an American political scientist, and Robert Conquest,[80] a British author, have also argued that retention of separate political identity by the East European Communist countries has subverted legitimacy of the USSR as a multinational state. This may have been partly encouraged by some features of the Soviet constitution. As Pipes noted, "by placing the national territorial principle [national republics] at the base of the state's political administration," the Communists gave "constitutional recognition to the multinational structure of the Soviet population. . . . This purely formal feature of the Soviet Constitution may well prove to have been one of the most consequential aspects of the formation of the Soviet Union."[81]

Language as an attitudinal factor and the linguistic assimilation allegedly practiced by the Soviet regime and bitterly resented by Ukrainian dissenters have been prominently featured in *samizdat* materials coming out of the Soviet Union. Still, Walker Connor, a scholar of nationalism, considers the essence of the nation to be "psychological, a matter of attitude rather than a fact," arguing that language is a symbol, not the real issue, in contemporary Ukrainian unrest. As a method of asserting non-Russian identity, Ukrainians wage a campaign for national survival in terms of right to employ Ukrainian in speech and writing. Connor thinks that the nation would exist even if Ukrainian were replaced by Russian, just as the Irish nation has survived despite the virtual disappearance of Gaelic.[82] Similarly, Alexander Werth wrote in 1969 that nationalism was rising and might one day loosen the Ukraine's bonds with Moscow, but he doubted that Ukrainian would ever become *the* language of the Ukraine.[83]

In one of the few empirical studies of factors forming national attitudes in the Ukraine, L. M. Drobizheva, a Soviet Russian scholar, reported higher incidence of "nationalist" attitudes among those Ukrainians who read periodicals and books in Ukrainian only than among those who read in Russian only or in Russian and Ukrainian. Among the former, 80.7% approved of people of different nationalities working together and 77.1% approved of mixed marriages. Among the latter, corresponding figures were 90.9% and 87.1%[84] Drobizheva seems to have concluded that "nationalist attitudes" are modified by inducing non-Russians to read more in Russian rather than in their own language; she recommended that more Russian language publications and broadcasts be made available.

Soviet writers on national attitudes in the Ukraine argue that sources of national antagonism have been eradicated in the USSR and tensions which may develop are due essentially to tenacity of bourgeois survivals. Ukrainians, like all other Soviet nationalities, they assert, are Soviet patriots first of all, and their attitudes derive from and reflect the socialist system in the country and the triumph of the ideology of Marxism-Leninism. As discussed earlier, however, Brezhnev admitted recently that certain "objective problems" arise from the need to reconcile the interests of individual nations with those of the country as a

78 Rudnytsky, 1972: 244–248.
79 Aspaturian, 1966.
80 Conquest, 1971.
81 Pipes, 1964: 296–297.

82 Connor, 1972: 338.
83 Werth, 1969: 202.
84 Drobizheva, 1969: 77–78.

whole.[85] As if to illustrate Brezhnev's points, Petr Shelest, first secretary of the Ukrainian CP from 1963 to 1972, was recently criticized for treating the Soviet Ukraine's economic achievements in isolation from those of the entire Soviet Union and for attributing them to the Ukrainians alone rather than to all Soviet people, in his book *Ukrayino nasha Radians'ka* [*Our Soviet Ukraine*], published in 1970 (100,000 copies).[86]

RECENT MANIFESTATIONS OF NATIONALISM

Since Stalin's death, a major controversy in the history of Ukrainian nationalism and dissent has centered around its connection with earlier nationalism. Armed guerilla struggle against Soviet rule ceased in the western Ukraine in the early 1950s, but at the end of the decade the KGB was still arresting members of what it considered secret nationalist organizations.[87] Although it is impossible to establish direct links between those arrested in 1958–1961 and members of the OUN underground, there are indications that some at least were familiar with the latter's literature. A group established in 1964, the "Ukrainian National Front," regarding itself as a continuation of the OUN, in 1965–1966 "published" an underground journal, *Fatherland and Freedom*.[88]

The second phase in the history of Ukrainian dissent requiring the attention of the KGB came in 1965–1966, when various members of the Soviet Ukrainian literary and academic intelligentsia were arrested and tried in Lvov and Kiev.[89] Arrests of intellectuals in 1965 prompted the distinguished literary critic Ivan Dzyuba to write a long memorandum to P. Shelest, Ukrainian CP first secretary, and V. Shcherbitsky, prime minister of the Ukraine, protesting the arrests and Soviet treatment of the Ukrainian problem.[90] Vyacheslav Chornovil, a young TV journalist, compiled a collection of documents, testimonies, letters, and trial accounts which found their way to the West, where they were published first in Ukrainian and then in English.[91] Chornovil was soon arrested and tried while Dzyuba, although able to publish very little, managed to remain free.

Between 1966 and 1972 numerous arrests and trials became known abroad. Valentyn Moroz, an instructor in history, jailed from 1965 to 1969, was rearrested in 1970, after nine months of freedom and sentenced to a total of 14 years of prison, camp, and exile for writing nationalist essays, including "The Chronicle of Resistance" and "Amid the Snows." (His earlier work, "A Report from the Beria Reservation," was published in English by Browne, 1971.) Moroz was tried for the second time in late 1970.[92]

In 1969 the KGB arrested a group of students and instructors in Dnepropetrovsk. They were accused of disseminating nationalist propaganda and slandering the nationality policy of the CPSU, in a letter addressed to Kiev officials. They were tried in 1970 and all three Dnepropetrovsk papers published long articles against them.[93]

---

85 Brezhnev, 1973: 11.

86 "*Pro seriozni nedoliky ta pomylky odniei knyhy* [unsigned editorial]," *Komunist Ukrayiny*, 1973: IV: 77–82; specific reference is on p. 80. Shelest's other errors were said to include his failure to see benefits for the Ukraine in the area's annexation by tsarist Russia and his excessive stress on the originality and peculiar features of Ukrainian culture and history. *Ibid.*: 78, 80.

87 Three such organizations were uncovered in 1958–1961 in the western Ukraine: the United party for the Liberation of the Ukraine in 1958; the Ukrainian Workers and Peasants party, known also as the Jurists Group, allegedly active in 1959–1960 and its members tried in 1961; and the Ukrainian National Committee, whose 20 members were tried in Lvov in 1961. Two were executed, the rest receiving sentences of ten or more years in prison.

88 Browne, 1971: 227–234; for a brief analysis see Szamuely, 1968.

89 Browne, 1971: 97–171; *Chornovil Papers, passim.*

90 Dzyuba, 1968. A second English edition exists, and the work has recently been published in Italy. Dzyuba was born in 1931 in the Donbass.

91 *Lykho z rozumu*, 1968; *Chornovil Papers*, 1968. Chornovil was born in 1938 in the Cherkassy province of the eastern Ukraine.

92 *Svoboda* (August 21), 1971 and (January 12), 1972. Moroz was attacked by name in the Kiev paper *Radianska Osvita* (August 14), 1971. For a review of his ideas, see *Radio Liberty Dispatch* (October 22), 1970, and Luckyj, 1972. The Moroz affair caused a variety of protests, as shown by *Ukr. Visnyk*, No. 6.

93 The letter signed by "Creative Youth of Dnepropetrovsk" and containing a critique of conditions in Dnepropetrovsk, was published together with the newspaper accounts of the trial in *Molod' Dnipropetrovska v borot'bi proty rusyfikatsii* (Munich: Suchasnist, 1971).

A new wave of arrests came in January 1972, with several sentenced to long prison terms. One, Zinovia Franko (granddaughter of the great Ukrainian writer, Ivan Franko, 1856–1916), recanted and was released. With these arrests, the KGB attempted to associate the arrested intellectuals with émigré Ukrainian nationalist organizations, whose emissary Yaroslav Dobosh, a Belgian student of Ukrainian origin, had allegedly contacted them during his journey to the Ukraine in December 1971.[94]

No systematic analysis of the demands and programs of Ukrainian dissenters exists, but a British scholar, J. Birch of the University of Sheffield, has reviewed some of the best-known documents. The early organizations of 1958–1961 desired the "national liberation and establishment of an independent, sovereign Ukraine," and the secession of the Ukraine from the USSR. They advocated democratic methods to accomplish these goals and declared they would dissolve themselves if the Ukrainian people rejected their program. Other authors demanded transformation of the USSR in accord with principles of Marxism-Leninism and abandonment of such methods of Russification as (1) resettlement, (2) discrimination against Ukrainians in the educational system, and (3) relegating Ukrainian culture to a provincial role. There have also been various proposals for political reforms, including abolition of the KGB and censorship, release of all political prisoners, and right to establish political parties. National discrimination against other ethnic groups, specifically anti-Semitism, has been condemned, and a demand presented for "equal rights for minorities inside the Ukraine."[95]

Ivan Dzyuba's program has best been summarized by himself: "I propose . . . one thing only: *freedom*—freedom for the honest, public discussion of national matters, freedom of national choice, freedom for national self-knowledge, self-awareness, and self-development. But first and last comes freedom for discussions and disagreement."[96]

Whether or not there is a connection between old and new nationalism is still unresolved. The relationship between dissenters such as Dzyuba and the party leadership under Shelest is another puzzling problem. Commentators have noted that Ukrainian nationalism was treated relatively leniently in the later years of Shelest's rule. Dzyuba, for example, had been able to work in a publishing house even after his critique of Soviet nationality policy had been published in the West. Indeed, it was reported that the Dzyuba memorandum had been circulated among provincial party secretaries, by the Ukrainian Central Committee, for comment. Shelest's fall came two months after Dzyuba's expulsion from the Writers Union (and shortly after his arrest), and Shelest's protégés in the party have suffered demotions.[97] During his tenure in Kiev, Shelest identified himself with at least one proposal originally presented by Dzyuba. In 1968 he demanded that new college textbooks should be prepared by Ukrainian publishers, "first of all, in the Ukrainian language."[98] A special publishing house for college textbooks was established soon thereafter, issuing both Ukrainian and Russian university texts in science, engineering, and the humanities.[99]

The chairman of the Ukrainian Writers Union, Oles' Honchar, who had begun his career in the 1940s as an orthodox writer, said that in Ukrainian schools the native (i.e., Ukrainian) language was receiving less attention than foreign languages (he did not compare its status with that of Russian). In 1968 he published a novel, *Sobor*, which criticized the neglect of Ukrainian historical monuments and traditions. He depicted as a particularly "negative hero" a local party official who, lacking any re-

94 Dobosh was arrested at a border station but released after several months in prison and an act of public repentance broadcast over the Ukrainian TV network. See Radio Free Europe Research, 1331, March 14, 1972; *Radianska Ukrayina*, June 3, 1972; Visti z Ukrayiny, May 4, 1972; CDSP, XXIV: 22: 6. There is much on the arrests of 1972 in *Chronicle of Current Events* October 15, 1972: No. 26. See also *Index* 1972: 3–4: 120–123, 160, 166.
95 Birch, 1971: 20–34.

96 Dzyuba, 1968: 213.
97 "Struggle in the Kremlin," *Soviet Analyst* (June 8), 1972: 2–6; Radio Liberty dispatch (November 29), 1972; *Radianska Ukrayina* (January 27), 1973 (on dismissal of first secretary at Poltava).
98 *Literaturna Ukrayina* (September 6), 1968.
99 *Molod' Ukrayiny* (October 24), 1969; *Radianska Ukrayina* (September 6), 1970.

spect for or understanding of the national past, was ready to order the destruction of an old Cossack church. At first the Honchar novel was favorably reviewed; the line soon changed, and it was condemned. Honchar lost his position several years later, but has continued to write in his more customary orthodox vein.[100]

It is not easy to distinguish between dissent punishable by the KGB and that tolerated and expressed in the official media. Many arrested in 1965 and 1972 had been writing for the press, and in this sense their activities were not illegal. Officially tolerated dissent has expressed itself in concern for the Ukrainian language, its purity from foreign terms, protection of specifically Ukrainian linguistic features from Russian forms, and so on. Related to this was the defense of the Ukrainian language in the educational reform debate in 1958–1959, when Khrushchev proposed making Ukrainian and other republican languages elective subjects in Russian schools.[101]

---

[100] "Sobor," *Vitchyzna*, 1968, No. 1.

[101] There was a great deal of opposition to this proposal. The status of Ukrainian has been of particular concern to the Writers Union, which debated the problem at its congress of 1966. Bilinsky, 1968: 147–184, reviews Ukrainian assertiveness in the post-Stalin era.

REFERENCES

Armstrong, 1968
John A. Armstrong, "The Ethnic Scene in the Soviet Union: The View of the Dictatorship," in Erich Goldhagen, ed., *Ethnic Minorities in the Soviet Union* (New York: Praeger, 1968), 3–49.

Aspaturian, 1960
Vernon V. Aspaturian, *The Union Republics in Soviet Diplomacy: A Study of Soviet Federalism in the Service of Soviet Foreign Policy* (Geneva: Droz, 1960).

Aspaturian, 1966
Vernon V. Aspaturian, *The Soviet Union in the World Communist System* (Stanford: Hoover Institution, 1966).

Bilinsky, 1964
Yaroslav Bilinsky, *The Second Soviet Republic: The Ukraine after World War II* (New Brunswick, N. J.: Rutgers University Press, 1964).

Bilinsky, 1968
Yaroslav Bilinsky, "Assimilation and Ethnic Assertiveness Among Ukrainians of the Soviet Union," in Erich Goldhagen, ed., *Ethnic Minorities in the Soviet Union* (New York: Praeger, 1968), 147–184.

Birch, 1971
J. Birch, *The Ukrainian Nationalist Movement in the USSR Since 1956* (London: Ukrainian Information Service, 1971).

Bociurkiw, 1972
Bohdan R. Bociurkiw, "The Orthodox Church and the Soviet Regime in the Ukraine, 1953–1971," *Canadian Slavonic Papers*: Summer 1972: XIV, 2: 191–212.

Brezhnev, 1973
"The Fiftieth Anniversary of the Union of Soviet Socialist Republics, Address by L. I. Brezhnev, December 21, 1972," *New Times* (Moscow) (1973): I: 4–23.

Browne, 1971
Michael Browne, ed., *Ferment in the Ukraine: Documents by V. Chornovil, I. Kandyba, L. Lukyanenko, V. Moroz, and Others* (New York: Praeger, 1971).

Bruk, 1972
S. Bruk, "Natsional'not' i iazyk v perepisi naseleniya 1970 g.," *Vestnik statistiki* (1972): V: 42–54.

Chizhikova, 1968
L. N. Chizhikova, "Ob etnicheskikh protsessakh v vostochnykh raionakh Ukrainy," *Sovetskaia etnografiia* (1968): I: 18–31.

Chornovil Papers, 1968
Chornovil Papers, compiled by Viacheslav Chornovil (New York and Toronto: McGraw-Hill, 1968).

Connor, 1972
Walker Connor, "Nation-Building or Nation-Destroying?" *World Politics* (April 1972): XXIV: 3: 319–355.

Conquest, 1971
Robert Conquest, *The Nation Killers: Soviet Deportation of Nationalities* (New York: Macmillan, 1971).

Deutsch, 1963
Karl W. Deutsch, *The Nerves of Government* (New York: Free Press, 1963).

Drobizheva, 1969
L. M. Drobizheva, "O sblizhenii urovnei

kulturnogo razvitiia soiuznykh respublik," *Istoriia SSSR* (1969): 3: 61–79.

DSUP
Digest of the Soviet Ukrainian Press (New York: Prolog, 1957–).

Dzyuba, 1968
Ivan Dzyuba, *Internationalism or Russification? A Study in the Soviet Nationalities Problem* (London: Wiedenfeld & Nicolson, 1968).

Hodnett and Potichnyj, 1970
Grey Hodnett and Peter J. Potichnyj, *The Ukraine and the Czechoslovak Crisis* (Canberra: Australian National University, 1970).

Hooson, 1972
David Hooson, "The Outlook for Regional Development in the Soviet Union," *Slavic Review* (September 1972): XXXI: 3: 535–554.

Kozlov, 1972
V. I. Kozlov, "Etnicheskie osobennosti formirovaniia gorodskogo naseleniia v SSSR," in Iu. L. Pivovarov, ed., *Problemy sovremennoi urbanizatsii* (Moscow: Statistika, 1972), 142–156.

Kurman and Lebedinsky, 1968
M. V. Kurman and I. V. Lebedinsky, *Naselenie bolshogo sotsialisticheskogo goroda* (Moscow: Statistika, 1968).

Litviakov, 1969
P. Litviakov, ed., *Demograficheskie problemy zaniatosti* (Moscow, 1969).

Luckyj, 1972
George S. N. Luckyj, "Polarity in Ukrainian Intellectual Dissent," *Canadian Slavonic Papers* (1972): XIV: 2: 269–279.

Lykho z rozumu, 1968
Viacheslav Chornovil, *Lykho z rozumu,* 3rd ed. (Paris: PIUS, 1968).

Malanchuk, 1963
V. Malanchuk, *Torzhestvo leninskoyi natsionalnoyi polityky* (Lvov: Knyzhkovo-zhurnalne vydavnytstvo, 1963).

Malanchuk, 1972
Valentyn Malanchuk, "Dvi kontseptsii mynuloho i suchasnoho Ukrayiny," *Zhovten'* (1972): V: 110–121. Other parts of this long work appeared in *Zhovten'* (1972): I, III, IV.

Nar. obraz., 1971
Narodnoye obrazovaniye, nauka i kul'tura v SSSR: Statisticheskii sbornik (Moscow: Statistika, 1971).

Narodne hospodarstvo 1970
Narodne hospodarstvo Ukrayinskoyi RSR v 1970 rotsi, Statystychnyi shchorichnyk (Kiev: Statystyka, 1971).

Naseleniye, trudovye resursy, 1971
D. I. Valentei and I. F. Sorokina, eds., *Naseleniye, trudovye resursy SSSR* (Moscow: Mysl, 1971).

Oleksiuk, 1968
M. M. Oleksiuk et al., eds., *Torzhestvo istorychnoyi spravedlyvosti* (Lvov: Lvivskyi Derzhavnyi Universytet, 1968).

Pipes, 1964
R. Pipes, *The Formation of the Soviet Union: Communism and Nationalism 1917–1923* (Cambridge: Harvard University Press, 1964).

Pivovarov, 1972
Iu. L. Pivovarov, "Sovremennaia urbanizatsiia: sushchnost, faktory i osobennosti izucheniia," in Iu. L. Pivovarov, ed. *Problemy sovremennoi migratsii* (Moscow: Statistika, 1972), 9–32.

Pokshishevsky, 1972
V. V. Pokshishevsky, "Urbanization and Ethnogeographic Processes," *Soviet Geography: Review and Translation* (February 1972): XIII: 2: 113–120.

Rudnytsky, 1963
Ivan L. Rudnytsky, "The Role of the Ukraine in Modern History," *Slavic Review* (June 1963): XXII: 2: 199–216.

Rudnytsky, 1972
Ivan L. Rudnytsky, "The Soviet Ukraine in Historical Perspective," *Canadian Slavonic Papers* (Summer 1972): XIV: 2: 235–250.

Seton-Watson, 1967
Hugh Seton-Watson, *The Russian Empire 1801–1917* (Oxford: Oxford University Press, 1967).

Solovey, 1963
Dmytro Solovey, *Ukrayinska nauka v kolonialnykh putakh* (New York: Prolog, 1963).

Soviet Ukraine, 1970
Soviet Ukraine, Chief Editorial Board: M. P. Bazhan et al. (Kiev: Editorial Office of Ukrainian Soviet Encyclopedia, Academy of Sciences of Ukrainian SSR, n. d. [but 1970]).

Swoboda, 1971
Victor Swoboda, "The Ukraine," in George Schopflin, ed., *The Soviet Union and Eastern Europe: A Handbook* (New York: Praeger, 1971).

Szamuely, 1968
Tibor Szamuely, "The Resurgence of Ukrainian Nationalism," *The Reporter,* May 30, 1968, 15–18.

Szamuely, 1972
Tibor Szamuely, "The Future of Soviet Dissent," *The Spectator* (London), July 22, 1972, as reprinted in *America, The English Section* (Philadelphia), December 21, 1972, 3–4.

Transport i svyaz', 1972
    Transport i svyaz' SSSR (Moscow: Statistika, 1972).
Ukraina, Terazniejszość i przeszłość, 1970
    Ukraina, Teraźniejszość i przeszłość, Mieczyslaw Karas and Antoni Podraza, eds. (Kraków: Uniwersyete Jagiellonski, 1970).
Ukraine: A Concise Encyclopaedia, 1963
    Ukraine: A Concise Encyclopaedia, vol. I, Volodymyr Kubijovyc, ed. (Toronto: University of Toronto Press, 1963) (also vol. II).
Voloboi and Popovkin, 1972
    P. V. Voloboi and V. A. Popovkin, *Problemy teryorialnoyi spetsializatsii i kompleksnoho rozvytku narodnoho hospodarstva Ukrayinskoi RSR* (Kiev: Naukova Dumka, 1972).

Werth, 1969
    Alexander Werth, *Russia: Hopes and Fears* (London: Barrie & Rockliff, 1969).
Yizhakevych, 1966
    H. P. Yizhakevych, "Vzayemodiya bratnikh mov yak vyiav neporushnoyi druzhby narodiv," *Internatsionalne vykhovannia trudiashchykh* (Kiev: Naukova dumka, 1966), 165–179.
Zuban', 1967
    O. K. Zuban', *Borot'ba Komunistychnoyi partii Ukrayiny za rozvytok narodnoyi osvity (1945–1952 rr.)* (Lvov: Lvivskyi Derzhavnyi Universytet, 1967).
Z'yizd Pys'mennykiv, 1967
    V [Fifth] *Z'yizd Pys'mennykiv Radianskoyi Ukrayiny* (Kiev, 1967).

3 | BELORUSSIA and THE BELORUSSIANS

Jan Zaprudnik

General Information

TERRITORY

The territory of Soviet Belorussia[1] encompasses 80,134 square miles, nearly 1% of the USSR. It is the sixth largest Soviet republic. Bordering on Poland in the west, Lithuania and Latvia in the northwest, the Russian SFSR in the north and east, and the Ukraine in the south, its territory stretches 350 miles from south to north and about 400 miles from west to east. Belorussia's main administrative centers are Minsk (the capital, 1972 population 1 million), Brest, Grodno, Vitebsk, Mogilev, and Gomel. Since establishment of the Belorussian SSR on January 1, 1919, its territory has changed dramatically as a result of historical claims, military conflict, and political manipulations, and also because of the expressed desire of Belorussians to be included in the

republic. Large territories including the cities of Vitebsk, Mogilev, and Gomel were ceded to the BSSR by the RSFSR during the 1920s. The greatest changes resulted from the Soviet Union's participation in the Molotov-Ribbentrop pact which divided Poland in 1939. Much of the formerly Polish territory was incorporated into the BSSR, nearly doubling its size. The Bialystok region was returned to Poland in 1945, but the rest has remained a part of Belorussia.

The latest territorial change occurred in 1964 when 8.7 square miles in the Manastyrshchyna *raion* of the Smolensk *oblast* were transferred from the Russian federation to Soviet Belorussia at the request of the local population.[2]

Belorussia lies in the western part of the East European plain. Its highest elevation is 1,135 feet above sea level and its lowest 279 feet above sea level. Three-fifths of its territory lies between 325 and 550 feet above sea level.[3] A chain of hills from the

---

[1] The English spelling of this name was derived from transliteration rules of the *Government Printing Office* (GPO) *Style Manual* (1967). The first syllable is pronounced to rhyme with "yell." In the United Nations and some scholary publications in the West, the name is spelled Byelorussia.

[2] *Zviazda* (Minsk) (December 25), 1964.
[3] For details see Astashkin, 1970: 12–15.

southwest to the northwest constitutes a watershed separating the rivers flowing north into the Baltic Sea (Western Dvina, Nieman) from those flowing south into the Black Sea (Pripet, Dnieper).

Most of the republic is covered by the deposits of ancient glaciers—clay, sands, gravel, and boulders. The soil is relatively poor and needs fertilizing. A large part of the territory is covered by marshes and bogs. One third is covered by forests, which play an important part in the republic's economy.[4] Belorussia has 3,000 rivers with a total length of over 31,000 miles, of which about 5,000 miles are navigable; 4,000 of the republic's 10,000 lakes are of considerable size.[5]

The climate is moderately continental and relatively wet because of the proximity of the Baltic Sea and the influence of Atlantic winds. The average yearly precipitation is 20 to 26 inches (in wet years up to 40 inches). Temperatures vary from an absolute low of −40°F. (January) to 95°F. (July). The growing season lasts 176 to 205 days.

Belorussia is rich in peat, rock salt, potassium salts, oil, coal, shale, dolomites, limestone, marl, kaolin, all sorts of clays, sands and gravel, and other building materials. Even diamonds have been found.[6] Many of these resources have been surveyed only in recent decades, dispelling the time-honored myth about the poverty of the Belorussian land.

ECONOMY

Belorussia specializes in agriculture and light industries. The structure of the republic's GNP in 1969 was as follows: industry, 45.7%; construction, 9.9%; agriculture, 29.8%; transportation, 4.0%; commerce, supply, and other forms of material production, 11.3%.[7]

Occupying nearly 1% of the Soviet Union's territory and having 3.7% of the total population, Belorussia in 1970 produced 18% of the USSR's tractors, 18% of

its motorcycles and scooters, 14% of its metal-cutting lathes, 15% of its bearings, 11% of its mineral fertilizers, 11% of its pianos, and 10% of its wrist watches, chemical fibers, and television sets.[8]

The main stress in development of nonmetallic branches of the republic's machine-building industry is on instrument making, radio and electric equipment, and electronics as well as chemical and oil refining industries (in 1972 5.8 million tons of oil were extracted in Belorussia).[9]

In per capita electricity production, Belorussia stands tenth among Soviet republics with 1,669 kw/hrs against an average of 3,052 for the entire Union.[10] In 1970 the production of electricity represented an increase of 1.8 times that of 1965.[11]

The Belorussian SSR, with 2.9% of the Union's arable land, produced 13.7% of potatoes, 22.4% of flax fiber, 6.3% of milk, and 5.6% of meat in the Soviet Union in 1970. The BSSR has 6.2% of the USSR's cows and 5.9% of its hogs. Of the 186,800,000 tons of grain produced in the USSR in 1970, 4.2 million were grown in Belorussia (mainly rye, wheat, barley, buckwheat, and oats).[12]

HISTORY

The name Belorussia in its present application is of relatively recent origin. During the second half of the nineteenth century and the beginning of the twentieth western parts of Belorussia and even the region of Minsk were referred to as "Litva" [Lithuania]. The Belorussian city of Brest is known to history as Brest-Litovsk. This is a terminological reflection of the historic fact that, between the thirteenth and the second half of the eighteenth century, Belorussia was at the center of the huge medieval empire known as the Grand Duchy of Lithuania (since 1569 in political union with the Kingdom of Poland).

4 Ibid.: 281, 317.
5 Ibid.: 347, 372.
6 Sovetskaya Belorussiya (July 1), 1967.
7 Marcinkievic, 1972: 25.

8 Nar. khoz. 1970: 70, 72; Marcinkievic, 1972: 23.
9 Planovoye khozyaistvo (Moscow), 1972: VII: 72. For oil production, see Zviazda (Minsk), November 10, 1972.
10 Nar. khoz. 1970: 105.
11 Vestnik statistiki, 1972: VIII: 76.
12 Nar. khoz. 1970: 155.

When in 1891 the Russian Brockhaus-Yefron, *Entsiklopedicheskii slovar,* had to explain the term *Belorussiya*, it stated vaguely: "Formerly, *Belorussiya* mainly embraced the principalities of Polotsk, Vitebsk, and Smolensk. Presently, *Belorussiya* includes mainly the Minsk, Mogilev, and the western part of the Smolensk *gubernias*." [13]

The origin and meaning of the name Belorussia have been variously explained as referring to the people's fair complexion, predominantly white attire, or freedom from Mongol domination in the thirteenth century. "From various explanations of the term," states the BSSR Academy's *History of the BSSR*, "the most plausible, we think, is the one interpreting *Bielaja Ruś* as a Sovereign and Free *Ruś*." [14]

The forebears of the Belorussians, East Slavic tribes of Kryvichy, Dryhavichy (Dregoviches), and Radzimichy, moved into the area from the west and southwest around the six century A.D., displacing or gradually assimilating the local East Baltic tribes.[15]

The beginnings of political organization in the Belorussian lands go back to the ninth century when, according to an ancient chronicle, one of Prince Riurik's men received the principality of Polotsk. This town, situated along the "Road from the Varangians to the Greeks" and connected by the West Dvina River with the Baltic Sea, soon became a major political and cultural center. "The main content of the political history of the Polotsk principality in the second half of the 11th and the first half of the 12th centuries was the struggle of the feudal nobility for political separation from Kiev." [16] During the thirteenth and fourteenth centuries, all Belorussian lands along with the larger part of the Ukraine and some Russian territories were incorporated into the Grand Duchy of Lithuania.

In 1385, because of military pressures by German Knights in the northwest and Tatars in the south, Lithuania concluded a dynastic union with Poland. The independence of the grand duchy, however, was preserved. In 1569, in the face of expanding Muscovy, the duchy entered into a political federation with Poland, ceding the Ukrainian territories to it. Now the duchy consisted of Belorussian and Lithuanian lands. Sharing with Poland a common king and parliament, it retained, however, its name, own government, finances, military forces, and legislation.[17] The Belorussian nobility, attracted by the privileges of the Polish *szlachta*, embraced Catholicism and the Polish language. The process of Polonization was accelerated by establishment of the Uniate Church in 1596. In 1697 Belorussian ceased to be official language of the Grand Duchy of Lithuania and was replaced by Polish.[18]

By three consecutive partitions of the Polish Commonwealth—in 1772, 1793, and 1795—Belorussia was incorporated into the Russian Empire. The annexation of Belorussia (or "reunification," as Soviet historians would have it) did not change its basic social structure of large landed estates and serf labor.

As late as 1834, 90% of the total population were peasants, two thirds belonging to landlords of predominantly Catholic belief and Polish culture.[19]

Throughout the nineteenth century and during the first two decades of the twentieth, Belorussia—viewed by tsarist officialdom as an inalienable part of Russia—remained, in the words of Premier Stolypin, an area of "economically weak Russian majority and economically strong Polish minority." [20]

The "economically strong Polish minority" was undermined somewhat after the anti-Russian uprisings of 1830 and 1863, which had strong repercussions on Belorussia. The clash between Orthodox Russian and Catholic Polish nationalism over Belorussia during the nineteenth century precipitated a vast number of historical,

13 *Entisiklopedicheskii slovar*, 1891: V: 231. See more in Zaprudnik, 1969: 7–19. *Gubernias* were tsarist administrative units roughly comparable to *oblasts* today.
14 *Historyja*, 1972: I: 175–176. See also Vakar, 1949: VIII:3.
15 Sedov, 1970: 191–192. The role of the Baltic substratum in formation of the Belorussian people is a lively issue in present historiography. A concise review of various approaches to the question are given by M. Ya. Grinblat, 1968: 20–39.
16 *Historyja*, 1972: I: 110.

17 *BielSE*, 1971: III: 234; *Historyja*, 1972: 229, 289.
18 *Historyja litaratury*, 1968: I: 411.
19 *Historyja*, 1972: I: 478.
20 Zaprudnik, 1969: 195. See also *Historyja*, 1972: I: 583ff.

ethnographic, and linguistic publications which contributed considerably to the development of Belorussian literature, national awareness, and political aspirations.

The roots of the modern Belorussian political revival lie in the 1863 uprising led by Kastus Kalinouski (1838–1864),[21] and the activities of Belorussian *Narodniks* in the 1870s–1880s. The *Narodniks* "most fully defined the essential traits of nationhood and on the basis of these proved the existence of an independent Belorussian nation." [22]

Through efforts of the Belorussian socialist *Hramada*, founded in 1903, and other Belorussian political parties, a Belorussian National Convention was convened in December 1917.[23] This led to proclamation on March 25, 1918, of the independent Belorussian Democratic Republic [*Biełaruskaja Narodnaja Respublika*]. These developments, combined with promptings of Belorussian sections of the Russian Communist party for Belorussian statehood, resulted in establishment of the Belorussian SSR.[24]

The Treaty of Riga, concluding the Russo-Polish war of 1919–1920, divided Belorussia between the USSR and Poland. Belorussians were allowed a certain measure of political and cultural freedom until 1927 by the Poles and until 1929 in the USSR. In September 1939 the USSR reannexed western Belorussia along with the western Ukraine.

The country was devastated by World War II, losing 25% of its population and immeasurable material wealth. According to agreements concluded at the Yalta conference, the republic became a founding member of the United Nations and began the task of rebuilding.

DEMOGRAPHY

In 1970 there were approximately 9 million people in Soviet Belorussia with the following breakdown according to nationality and in comparison with the 1959 census.[25]

	1970 (in thousands)	% of Total	1959 (in thousands)	% of Total
Belorussian SSR	9,002	100.0	8,056	100.0
Belorussians	7,290	81.0	6,532	81.1
Russians	938	10.4	660	8.2
Poles	383	4.3	539	6.7
Ukrainians	191	2.1	133	1.7
Jews	148	1.6	150	1.9
Other Nationalities	52	0.6	42	0.4

While the percentage of Belorussians has remained constant with respect to the rest of the population, the number of Russians, Ukrainians, and "Others" in the republic has increased. The number of Jews has decreased slightly, Poles even more substantially. The latter phenomenon is probably best explained by the progress of reassimilation among Belorussian Catholics. "The larger part of the Polish national group in the republic is of native (i.e. Belorussian) origin." [26]

Approximately 2 million Belorussians in the Soviet Union are estimated to live outside their republic.[27] Their numbers have increased since 1959:[28]

In 1970 the 9.1 million Belorussians were fourth largest group in the Soviet Union, after the Russians, Ukrainians, and Uzbeks. In 1959 they occupied third place, but then

21 Smirnov, 1963: 331–332.
22 Sambuk, 1972: 176.
23 Malashko, 1969: 90–91; Zaprudnik, 1966: IV: 218, 222ff.
24 Mienski, 1955: 5–33; V. Krutalevic, 1968: IX: 168–210.

25 *Izvestiya* (April 7), 1971; *Sovetskaya Belorussiya* (May 19), 1971.
26 Rakov, 1969: 130.
27 *Ibid.*: 127.
28 *Nar. khoz. 1970:* 18–21.

Republic	1970 (in thousands)	% of Total	1959 (in thousands)	% of Total
Russian SFSR	964	0.7	844	0.7
Ukrainian SSR	386	0.8	291	0.7
Kazakh SSR	198	1.5	106	1.2
Lithuanian SSR	45	1.5	30	1.1
Latvian SSR	95	4.0	62	2.9
Estonian SSR	19	1.4	11	0.9

dropped behind the Uzbeks who have had a higher birth rate.

In 1970, according to the census, out of 9 million Belorussians in the Soviet Union, 7,290,000 (80.9%) lived in their own republic. Unlike the Baltic states, where the percentage of those living in their own republic increased between 1959 and 1970, the percentage of Belorussians in the USSR dropped since it was 82.7% in 1959 (when 6,532,000 of the 7,913,000 Belorussians in the Soviet Union lived in Belorussia).[29]

Total population of the Belorussian SSR slipped from third place in the USSR in 1940 to fifth in 1970. This was due to (1) World War II losses (2.2 million killed, 380,000 deported to Germany or emigrating to Western Europe);[30] (2) a negative balance of migration—both internal to Ka-

zakhstan and Siberia, and external to Poland—with a loss between 1950 and 1964 of 1.2 million people, or 60% of the country's natural increase;[31] (3) a lower rate of natural increase in recent years (13.7 per 1,000 in 1940 versus 8.6 per 1,000 in 1970 with corresponding figures for the USSR, 13.2 and 9.2).[32] In spite of a reversal of the trend toward emigration since 1965, due to intensified economic development of the country,[33] it was not until 1971 that Belorussia regained its pre-World War II level of population.[34]

Traditionally an agricultural country, Belorussia still has a predominantly rural character,[35] as shown below.

In March 1971 the Communist party of Belorussia had a membership of 434,527, constituting 3% (up from 2% in 1956) of

	1970		1959	
	% Urban Population	% Rural Population	% Urban Population	% Rural Population
USSR	56	44	48	52
BSSR	43	57	31	69
Difference for BSSR	−13	+13	−17	+17

the total membership of the CPSU.[36] The latest available nationality breakdown of the CPB (379,221 members) is dated January 1968: Belorussians, 70% Russians, 18.5%; Ukrainians, 4.4%; Others, 7.1%.[37] There were 27,382 Belorussians in the Ukrainian CP in 1968.[38] The total number of Belorussians in the CPSU in 1973 was given as 521,544.[39] Clearly, Belorussians were underrepresented in the CPB whereas Russian representation was almost double its weight in the population.

Of 425 deputies elected in June 1971 to the Supreme Soviet of the BSSR, 296 (70%) were party members.[40] In local soviets of

31 Rakau, 1968: 186.
32 Nar. khoz. 1970: 50–51. According to Andrej Bahrovič, a Belorussian-American scholar, the total demographic loss for the BSSR between 1939 and 1959 was in the vicinity of 6 million people killed, deported, or unborn. See Bahrovic, 1962: 34.
33 Rakau, 1968: 86.
34 Zviazda (November 26), 1972.
35 Sovetskaya Belorussiya (May 19), 1971.
36 Duevel, 1971: tables II, III, IV.
37 Kommunist Belorussii, 1968: VIII: 36.
38 Radianska Ukrayina (Kiev) (June 30), 1968.
39 Problems of Communism (July–August), 1971: 20; Politicheskoye samoobrazovaniye, 1974: I: 59.
40 Cyrvonaja zmiena (Minsk) (June 17), 1971.

29 Nar. khoz. 1970: 15; Sovetskaya Belorussiya (May 19), 1971.
30 Rakov, 1969: 16.

the BSSR, 35,373 of 80,652 deputies (44%) were Communists.[41] The Belorussian SSR is represented in the CPSU Central Committee and the Central Auditing Commission (totaling 254 members) by 11 delegates (including one member of the military).[42]

Kirill T. Mazurov, a Belorussian, has been a full member of the CPSU's Politburo since 1965. He is also first deputy premier of the Soviet Union. The Belorussian Piotr M. Masherov has been first secretary of the CPB since 1965 and alternate member of the CPSU Politburo.[43] Mikhail V. Zimyanin, *Pravda*'s editor, is also a Belorussian.[44]

CULTURE

The basic features of Belorussian culture developed along with the process of consolidating Belorussian nationality. The Byzantine tradition of Christianity was an early powerful external factor in shaping spiritual and material culture. The great cathedral of St. Sophia in Polotsk was built almost simultaneously with the ones in Kiev and Novgorod[45] in the mid-eleventh century. The cities of Polotsk, Turau, Vitebsk, and Pinsk with their churches and monasteries became centers of literacy, education, and artistic creativity. The activities and writings of St. Euphrosyne of Polotsk,[46] St. Cyril of Turau,[47] and the highly developed and original architecture stand as best evidence of the achievements of medieval Belorussia.

In the sixteenth century "in the Grand Duchy of Lithuania Belorussian was the language of official business and legal procedures, as well as literary works and religious polemics." [48] The great humanist Francišak Skaryna from Polotsk (1485?–1540) translated the Bible into Belorussian

publishing lavish editions in Prague (1517–1519) and Vilna (1522–1525).[49] The Reformation and Counter Reformation evoked intense polemics in Belorussia, producing a flood of publications and keeping numerous printing houses busy. Education was spread throughout the country via a network of church schools. Vilna Academy, founded in 1579, became an important center of scholarship for the entire area.

Until the end of the sixteenth century Belorussians maintained their Orthodox faith. But the growth of Polish influence in the seventeenth and eighteenth centuries and the proselytism of the Jesuits changed the picture. By the end of the nineteenth century 25% of Belorussians were Catholics, but the advance of Christianity and the religious battles left intact many ancient pagan elements in the spiritual outlook of the masses. "Byełaya Ruś," observed the Russian ethnographer P. Bessonov in 1871, "preserved in its ceremonies, and in the songs accompanying them, echoes of the most ancient times as nowhere else among the Slavs." [50]

Folklore, social injustices, national oppression (the Belorussian language was prohibited between 1859 and 1905), and memories of a glorious past became basic ingredients of the national revival toward the end of the nineteenth century. The names of Francisak Bahusevic (1840–1900), Janka Kapala (1882–1942), Jakub Kołas (1882–1957), and Maksim Bahdanovič (1891–1917) and the newspaper *Naša Niva* [*Our Soil*] (1906–1915),[51] to which three of them contributed, are milestones in the development of Belorussian culture and national consciousness.[52] The monumental work of the academician Jaufim Karski (1861–1931), *Belorusy*, laid the scientific foundation for study of Belorussian.[53]

Great strides were made in Belorussian culture during the 1920s.[54] The terror of the 1930s, however, sharply reduced creative activities.[55]

41 *Sovetskoye gosudarstvo i pravo* (Moscow), 1972: XII: 163.
42 Duevel, 1971: Table IV.
43 Radio Liberty, CRD 334/69 (October 10), 1969, "Spravka o chlenakh Politburo i Sekretariata TsK KPSS."
44 *Who's Who in the USSR*, 1966: 993. See also Duevel, 1965.
45 Alekseyev, 1966: 194–196; *Historyja*, 1972: I: 138.
46 Nadson, 1969: 3–24.
47 Nadson, 1965: 4–15.
48 *BielSE*, III: 237.

49 See *Biełaruskaha knihadrukavannia*, 1968; *Zapisy*, 1970: 5, entirely devoted to F. Skaryna.
50 Grinblat, 1968: 248, 252.
51 Nadson, 1967: 184–206.
52 *Historyja litaratury*, 1968: V.
53 McMillin, 1967: 207–214.
54 Niamiha, 1955: 34–66.
55 Adamovich, 1958: 145–172; Krushinsky, 1953; Kabysh, 1958: 77–88.

Since the end of World War II, Belorussian culture has steadily developed in spite of difficulties and restrictions, building to a very large extent on achievements of past centuries.

EXTERNAL RELATIONS

External relations of the Belorussian SSR are concerned mainly with Belorussia's membership in the UN and UNESCO, and the approximately 2 million Belorussians living in the West.[56]

During the postwar decades, delegates from Soviet Belorussia took part in over 300 international conferences.[57] As of 1969 the BSSR had been signatory to more than 100 international treaties, agreements, conventions, and protocols.[58]. Belorussia, however, has no diplomatic representation of its own abroad with the exception of a permanent mission at the UN, thus lending credence to U.S. Secretary of State William P. Rogers' statement before the UN General Assembly that "Belorussia and the Ukraine are not separate states." [59]

In 1964 the Belorussian section of the All-Union Committee for the Return to the Homeland (established in 1955) was transformed into the Belorussian Society for Cultural Ties with Countrymen Abroad.[60] Since 1955 a Belorussian language weekly, *Hołas Radzimy* [*Voice of the Homeland*] has been published in Minsk (circulation, 6,750; with some texts in Russian, English, French, and German) and distributed abroad together with brochures and booklets in the *Voice of the Homeland* series.[61] In 1970 the Belorussian Society for Friendship and Cultural Ties with Foreign Countries maintained contacts with 271 "progressive organizations" in 53 countries.[62]

Belorussian language radio broadcasts, conducted by Radio Soviet Belorussia and Radio Moscow, are beamed to Western Europe, North America, and Latin America.[63] Radio Liberty and Radio Vatican broadcast in Belorussian.

About 200,000 Belorussians are in Poland. They have their own schools and a social-cultural society headquartered in Bialystok with a network of branches. Since 1956 they have published the weekly *Niva*, a magazine for children called *Zorka*, and yearly almanacs.

Media

LANGUAGE DATA

The Belorussian language came into use before the thirteenth century.[64] "In the Grand Duchy of Lithuania [14th–17th centuries] the Belorussian language was long used in official, diplomatic, and private correspondence, in municipal, regional and feudal courts." [65] During the course of the eighteenth and nineteenth centuries, it was replaced first by Polish and then in some areas by Russian. Scholarly studies of Belorussian began in the early nineteenth century.[66] The development of modern orthographic and grammatical norms occurred with late nineteenth-century publications,

especially with the weekly *Naša Niva* [*Our Soil*], published from 1906 to 1915.[67]

The first important modern grammar appeared in 1918.[68] Before the Soviet era, and outside the USSR after 1917, both Latin and Cyrillic alphabets were used, the latter gaining predominance.

Traditionally, language has played a significant role in developing and maintaining national consciousness. "Belorussia, my brothers, is where our language lives," Francišak Bahusevič, the "father" of modern Belorussian literature, declared in 1891.[69]

56 *BielSE*, II: 215. The figure "nearly one million" is mentioned in *BielSE*, II: 261.
57 *Sovetskoye gosudarstvo i pravo*, 1970: XIV: 41.
58 *BielSE*, I: 415.
59 *New York Times* (October 5), 1971.

60 *BielSE*, II: 215.
61 *BielSE*, III: 528.
62 *BielSE*, II: 215.
63 *East-West Digest*, 1972: 622–623.
64 Filin, 1972: 3.
65 *BielSE*, II: 226; Zurauski, 1967.
66 *Biełaruskaje*, 1967: 5.
67 Zurauski, 1968: II: 118ff.
68 *Ibid*.: 160ff.
69 Aleksandrovic et al., 1971: 221.

	IN BELORUSSIAN	IN RUSSIAN
Organs of CC of CPB, Supreme Soviet, and Council of Ministers of BSSR, daily, Minsk	*Zviazda* (97,500)	*Sovetskaya Belorussiya* (276,900)
Organs of CC of Komsomol of BSSR appearing five times a week, in Minsk	*Cyrvonaja zmiena* (69,150)	*Znamya yunosti* (408,300)
Organs of CC of Komsomol of BSSR and republic's Council of Pioneer Organization, weekly, in Minsk	*Pljanier Bielarusi* (366,050)	*Zor'ka* (1,090,100)

This attitude is typical of current efforts to maintain the native language as *sine qua non* for national survival.

According to the 1970 census, of 7,290,000 Belorussians in the BSSR, 6,571,000 (90.1%) indicated Belorussian as their native language (in 1959 the percentage was 93.2). Belorussian was also named as native language by 328,000 members of other nationalities of the republic. In addition, 606,000 people indicated Belorussian as a second language which they spoke fluently. In 1970 the total number of Belorussian speakers in the republic was 7,505,000, or 83.4% of the entire population.[70]

In 1970, 80.6% of all Belorussians in the USSR considered Belorussian their native language[71] (down from 84.2% in 1959; cf. Table 3.1).

The ability to speak Russian fluently as a second language was claimed by 49% of the Belorussians in the USSR (52.2% in BSSR and 35.4% outside the republic). A. Rakov, discussing results of the 1959 census, observed, however: "By finding themselves among natives of other republics which have distinctly specific conditions of life—social, economic, cultural, linguistic, and other differences—the Belorussians as well as any other national minority in the given republic will feel an especially strong Russian influence in respect to language and other aspects of culture. Among the Belorussians living outside of their republic only 30% consider Belorussian as their native language." [72]

LOCAL MEDIA

Literacy among those aged between 9 and 49 years has progressed as follows: 1897, 32%; 1926, 57.7%; 1939, 80.8%; 1959, 99.0%; and 1970, 99.8%.[73]

In 1971, 168 newspapers appeared in Soviet Belorussia (128 in Belorussian), as well as 111 periodical publications such as magazines, "notebooks" (containing mainly material for propagandists), bulletins, collections of scholarly articles, proceedings of learned societies, and so on. Of the 111 periodical publications, 27 were printed in Belorussian. The category of "periodical publications" comprises 29 magazines, 17 printed in Belorussian.[74]

Since some newspapers as well as periodicals are of limited circulation, a better perspective is obtained when the total year's circulations for Belorussian and Russian are compared.

Thus, the total circulation of Belorussian language newspapers in 1971 was 255,127,000 copies, while in Russian 444,982,000 copies were printed.[75] In the same year, total circulation of all other periodicals in the Belorussian language was 22,650,000; in Russian, 5,263,000.[76]

Belorussian is more widely used in local media. On the all-republic level, however, preference is given to Russian, as can be seen from the single-issue circulation figures for a set of parallel newspapers,[77] shown at the top of this page.

The two all-republic Belorussian newspapers, addressed especially to members of the intelligentsia and educators, have no

70 *Sovetskaya Belorussiya* (May 19), 1971. For details of 1959 census, see Rakov, 1969: 124–136.
71 *Izvestiya* (April 17), 1971.
72 Rakov, 1969: 128–129. Calculations based on 1970 census indicate this figure to be 41.1% for Belorussians living in other republics of the USSR, and this is the figure given in Table 3.1.

73 *Nar. obraz.*, 1971: 21.
74 *Pechat'* 1970: 158, 188.
75 *Ibid.*: 188.
76 *Ibid.*: 158.
77 *Letapis*, 1972: I: 43.

Table 3.1

Native and Second Languages Spoken by Belorussians
(in thousands)

Number of Belorussians residing	1959	1970	SPEAKING AS NATIVE LANGUAGE						SPEAKING AS SECOND LANGUAGE[a]	
			Belorussian 1959	1970	*% Point Change* 1959–1970	*Russian* 1959	1970	*% Point Change* 1959–1970	*Russian* 1970	*Other Languages of Peoples of USSR* 1970[b]
in Belorussian SSR	6,532 (100%)	7,290 (100%)	6,086 (93.2%)	6,571 (90.1%)	−3.1	442 (6.8%)	717 (9.8%)	+3.0	3,809 (52.2%)	326 (4.5%)
in other Soviet republics	1,381 (100%)	1,762 (100%)	578 (41.8%)	724 (41.1%)	−.7	770 (55.8%)	1,001 (56.8%)	+1.0	623 (35.4%)	331 (18.8%)
Total	7,913 (100%)	9,052 (100%)	6,665 (84.2%)	7,296 (80.6%)	−3.6	1,212 (15.3%)	1,718 (19.0%)	+3.7	4,432 (49.0%)	657 (7.3%)

[a] No data are available for 1959, since no questions regarding command of a second language were asked in the 1959 census.

[b] Including Belorussian, if not the native language.

Sources: For 1959 census, *Itogi SSSR, 1959*, Table 53; *Itogi, Belorusskaya SSR, 1959*, Table 53. For 1970 census, *Itogi 1970*: IV: 20, 192.

Table 3.2

Publications in Belorussian SSR

Language of Publication	Year	NEWSPAPERS[a]			MAGAZINES			BOOKS AND BROCHURES		
		No.	Per Issue Circulation (1,000)	Copies/100 in Language Group[b]	No.	Per Issue Circulation (1,000)	Copies/100 in Language Group[b]	No. Titles	Total Volume (1,000)	Books & Brochures/100 in Language Group[b]
Russian	1959	46	820	62.6	N.A.	N.A.	N.A.	744	7,601	580.4
	1971	40	2,576	135.0	12	145	7.6	2,135	15,882	832.6
Belorussian	1959	167	950	14.9	N.A.	N.A.	N.A.	571	9,499	149.3
	1971	128	1,598	23.2	17	819	11.9	419	9,814	142.3
Minority Languages	1959	0	0	0	N.A.	N.A.	N.A.	N.A.	N.A.	N.A.
	1971	0	0	0	0	0	0	1	7	N.A.
Foreign Languages	1959	0	0	N.A.	N.A.	N.A.	N.A.	N.A.	N.A.	N.A.
	1971	0	0	N.A.	0	0	N.A.	N.A.	N.A.	N.A.
All Languages	1959	213	1,770	22.0	19	365	4.5	1,317[c]	17,101[c]	212.3
	1971	168	4,174	46.4	29	964	10.7	2,598	26,212	291.5

Sources: *Pechat' 1959*: 54, 128, 164; *1971*: 95, 178, 188.
[a] 1970 figures do not include *kolkhoz* newspapers.
[b] Includes all native speakers of the language.
[c] Book totals given in *Pechat'* sometimes differ from totals in language categories. The indication is that books are published in other languages, but no data is given.

Russian language counterparts in the BSSR. They are *Litaratura i mastactva* [*Literature and Art*], a 16-page weekly illustrated tabloid (circulation 12,950) and *Nastaunickaja hazieta* [*Teachers' Newspaper*], a full-size four-page semiweekly (circulation, 68,507). Indicative of the drive toward Russification in rural areas is publication of the Russian language daily *Sel'skaya gazeta* [*Rural Newspaper*] (circulation 147,850) without a Belorussian language counterpart.[78]

A vast majority of scientific periodicals in the BSSR are published exclusively in Russian.[79] The relationship between Belorussian and Russian publishing in Minsk is illustrated by the circulation of *Vecherni Minsk* [*Evening Minsk*] of 1,450 in Belorussian and 185,300 in Russian.[80]

In book publishing the republic has shown steady progress, both in number of titles and total copies printed:

YEAR	NO. TITLES	NO. COPIES
1960	1,602	14,231,000
1965	1,931	23,016,000
1970	2,174	25,170,000

Following is the breakdown of Belorussian and Russian language titles for the same years:

In book publishing the Belorussian language has been losing ground to Russian since 1956, when 285 titles were printed in

YEAR	BELORUSSIAN TITLES	RUSSIAN TITLES
1960	425	1,177
1965	295	1,636
1970	428	1,746
1971	419	2,179

Belorussian versus 461 in Russian, as compared with 428 versus 305 in 1954.[81] In 1971 the total number of Belorussian books and brochures printed in the BSSR constituted 37.4% of book production in the republic.[82]

In 1968 the population had 1,200,000 radio receivers and 826,000 television sets for personal use in addition to those owned by institutions and collective farms for public use. In the same year there were 136 television sets per 1,000 urban population, 195 radio receivers per 1,000, and 169 loudspeakers per 1,000. Among the rural population there were only 28 television sets per 1,000 and 284 radio receivers and radio loudspeakers per 1,000.[83] (See Table 3.3 for summary totals for other dates.)

By 1968 the entire territory of the republic was covered by radio networks and

77% (inhabited by 84% of the population) by TV networks. Plans were adopted to complete television coverage for the republic by 1970. The foundation was being laid for color TV.[84]

In 1968 Belorussian radio had three programs totaling 18 hours of broadcasting.[85] Besides Radio Soviet Belorussia, two daily half-hour programs were maintained for countrymen abroad.[86] In 1967 a weekly Moscow-based half-hour radio program "Rodina" was broadcast in Belorussian for Western Europe and the Americas.[87]

Currently, Belorussian television is working on three channels totaling 11 hours of programming a day.[88] Only one channel, however, carries most of the programs of local origin; the other two are predominantly relay stations for Moscow programming. No data are available for either locally originated TV programs or for the

78 *Ibid.*
79 *Ibid.*: 32–43.
80 *Ibid.*: 51.
81 *Pechat'* 1954: 38; 1957: 44–45.
82 *Nar. obraz.*, 1971: 362; *Pechat'* 1970: 95.
83 Yeshin, 1970: 148–149.

84 Kokhonov and Mayevsky, 1968: 42, 50.
85 *Litaratura i mastactva* (November 15), 1968.
86 *Hołas radzimy*, 1968: 18; 1969: 12.
87 *Hołas radzimy*, 1967: 25.
88 Touscik, 1973: I: 60.

Table 3.3

Electronic Media and Films in Belorussia SSR

YEAR	RADIO					TELEVISION			MOVIES	
	No. Stations	No. Wired Sets (1,000)	Sets/100 Population	No. Wireless Sets (1,000)	Sets/100 Population	No. Stations	No. sets (1,000)	Sets/100 Population	Seats (1,000)	Seats/100 Population
1960	N.A.	1,258[d]	15.3[d]	633[a]	7.7[c]	N.A.	62[a]	0.8[c]	287[b]	3.4[d]
1970	N.A.	1,996[a]	21.9[d]	1,400[a]	15.4[c]	N.A.	1,111[a]	12.2[c]	638[b]	7.0[d]
1971	N.A.	2,148[d]	23.5[d]	1,545[d]	16.9[c]	N.A.	1,265[c]	13.8[c]	N.A.	N.A.

[a] Source: *Transport i svyaz'* 1972: 296–298.
[b] Source: *Nar. obraz.*, 1971: 325.
[c] Source: *Nar. khoz.*, 1972: 572, 578.
[d] Computed from data cited above ([b] and [c]).

Belorussian language's place in them. According to recent sources, about 70% of radio programs and about 20% to 25% of TV broadcasts are in Belorussian. A Belorussian language weekly, *Belorussian Television and Radio*, has a circulation of 150,000.[89]

EDUCATIONAL INSTITUTIONS

On June 23, 1972, a law was passed by the Supreme Soviet of the BSSR, "On the Complete Switch to General Secondary Education of the Youth of the Belorussian SSR." [90] In February 1972 *The Teachers' Newspaper* reported that 91.4% of former eighth-graders were continuing their education in the ninth grade.[91] In 1971 over 90% of Belorussia's teachers had received a higher education.[92]

There are no data on how many of the 10,783 schools in the BSSR use Belorussian or Russian as language of instruction; this is a closely guarded secret of Soviet nationality policy. There is evidence, however, that urban schools use the Russian language exclusively. The Canadian-Ukrainian author John Kolasky, who studied in the Ukraine in 1963–1965, reported upon his return to Canada that "there are no schools in Minsk with Belorussian as the language of instruction.[93] In 1972 this report was confirmed in the United States by a highly placed Soviet Belorussian official. On the other hand, statements asserting that Belorussian has been eliminated from secondary education are false. *The Annals of Printing in the BSSR*, containing the titles of textbooks for all subjects for all secondary school grades, include Belorussian titles.[94]

Since the latter half of the 1960s, instruction in BSSR schools has been conducted according to revised programs. Following are hours assigned for teaching the Belorussian and Russian languages and literatures:

In Schools with Belorussian as Language of Instruction

Grades	1	2	3	4	5	6	7	8	9	10
Belorussian language	12	7	7–6	5	3	3–2	2–1	2–1	—	—
Russian language	—	4–5	5–6	5	4–5	4	3	2	—	—
Belorussian literature	—	—	—	2–1	2–1	1–2	1–2	1–2	2	2
Russian literature	—	—	—	2	2	2	2	3	4	3

In Schools with Russian as Language of Instruction

Grades	1	2	3	4	5	6	7	8	9	10
Russian language	12	11	9	7	6	5	3	2	—	1
Belorussian language	—	—	3	3–4	2	2	2	2–1	—	—
Russian literature	—	—	—	2	2	2	2	3	4	3
Belorussian literature	—	—	—	1	1	1	1	1–2	2	2

Source: *Nastaunickaja hazieta*, April 8, 1970.

89 *Letapis*, 1972: I: 32.
90 *Narodnaja asvieta* (Minsk), 1972: VII: 6ff.
91 *Nastaunickaja hazieta* (February 3), 1972. This indicates a large number of incomplete secondary school graduates continuing in complete secondary schools.
92 *Nar. obraz.*, 1972: VII: 76.
93 Kolasky, 1968: 72.
94 *Letapis*, 1971: XI: 22; XII: 36; 1972: IV: 29; V: 27.

Table 3.4

Selected Data on Education in Belorussian SSR (1971)

Population: 9,142,000

		PER 1,000 POPULATION	% OF TOTAL
All schools			
number of schools	10,783	1.18	
number of students	1,863,000	203.8	
Newly opened elementary, incomplete secondary, and secondary schools			
number of schools	120		
number of student places	53,100	5.8	
Secondary special schools			
number of schools	130		
number of students	149,000	16.29	
Institutions of higher education			
number of institutions	28		
number of students	142,800	15.62	
Universities			
number of universities	2		
number of students			
total	22,412	2.45	
day students	12,434		55.4
evening students	3,174		14.1
correspondence students	6,804		30.3
newly admitted			
total	4,708	0.5	
day students	2,880		61.1
evening students	643		13.6
correspondence students	1,185		25.1
graduated			
total	3,444	0.38	
day students	2,063		59.9
evening students	405		11.7
correspondence students	976		28.3
Graduate students			
total number	2,793	0.03	
in scientific research institutions	1,369		
in universities	1,424		
Number of persons with (in 1970) higher or secondary (complete and incomplete) education			
per 1,000 individuals, 10 years and older	440		
per 1,000 individuals employed in national economy	594		
Number of workers graduated from professional-technical schools	58,600	6.41	

Source: *Nar. khoz. 1972*: 108, 437, 531, 539, 540, 542.

In its ratio of specialized secondary school students (161 students per 10,000 population), the Belorussian SSR is eighth among the union republics (the average for the USSR is 180 per 10,000 population).[95] The republic ranks eleventh in its ratio of college students (154 per 10,000 population; the USSR average is 188).[96]

Of the 28 higher schools [*vuzy*] in the BSSR in 1970–1971, six prepared specialists in industrial engineering and construction (42,313 students), one in transportation and communication (4,973 students), four in agriculture (19,160), two in economics and law (9,557), nine in education (51,045), four in medical studies and physical education (11,272), and two in arts and cinematography (1,714).[97]

Russian is used throughout the higher educational institutions of the BSSR with the exception of certain courses in philology and literature.

In 1971, of the approximately 140,000 students of higher education in the BSSR, 63.5% (88,942) were Belorussians (with Belorussians constituting 81% of the BSSR population). At the same time, of the 130,200 Belorussian students in the Soviet Union, 40,560 men and women were studying in other republics of the Union, mainly in the RSFSR (29,053) and Ukraine (6,705).[98]

CULTURAL AND SCIENTIFIC INSTITUTIONS

In 1970, 173 scientific institutions of the BSSR employed 21,863 scientific workers (425 doctors of science and 5,564 candidates of science).[99] No data are available as to their national composition, but an idea can be obtained from the following breakdown of the 18,618 BSSR pedagogical and scientific workers at the beginning of 1969: 48% Belorussians, 35.5% Russians, 7.8%

Jews, 6.2% Ukrainians, 2.7% other nationalities.[100]

The higher proportion of scientists of other nationalities can be accounted for by recent developmental trends in science and industry for which the republic had to invite specialists from other Soviet centers. In recent years, "a tendency has become evident toward a growth in the number of Belorussian scientists both in proportion to their total as well as among the category of the most qualified who have scientific degrees."[101] In 1960, among the doctors of science in the republic, Belorussians constituted 33%; in 1969, 41.3%. Among candidates of science the figures were 44% and 46.2% respectively.[102]

As to total number of Belorussian scientists in the USSR, their ranks grew from 2,713 in 1950 to 6,358 in 1960, 12,814 in 1965, and 18,968 in 1970.[103]

Belorussia has a high proportion of specialists in the humanities—over 29% of the scientific workers.[104] The fastest growing group of scientists are those in engineering, chemistry, physics, mathematics, and economics.[105]

In 1970 the Academy of Sciences of the BSSR employed 123 doctors and 888 candidates of science constituting 33.5% of academy scientific workers. This represents an increase over the previous year of 16 doctors and 74 candidates. Total number of academy employees increased by 998 from 1969 to 1970.[106]

Of 14 professional theaters, three perform in the Belorussian language, the rest in Russian. There are, however, numerous "people's theaters" where Belorussian is used widely. Attendance at professional theaters was 297.2 per 1,000 population in 1971.[107]

In 1970 the Belorussian Film Studio Bielaruśfilm produced 58 films, 12 full-length.[108] The Belorussian language occupies, however, an insignificant place in the

95 *Nar. obraz.*, 1971: 167; see also Composite Tables section in Appendix.
96 *Ibid.*:158.
97 *Nar. obraz.*, 1971: 170.
98 Computed from *Ibid.*: 197–204.
99 *Viesci AN BSSR*, 1972: VI: 36. See also *Nar. obraz.*, 1971: 257.

100 *Połymia*, 1969: IX: 178.
101 *Ibid.*
102 *Ibid.*
103 *Nar. obraz.*, 1971: 270.
104 *Połymia*, 1969: IX: 177.
105 *Ibid.*
106 *Viesci AN BSSR*, 1971: III: 142.
107 *Nar. khoz. 1972:* 451.
108 *Nar. obraz.*, 1971: 330.

film industry—though Belorussian writers and critics have been trying to change this in recent years.

In 1971 there were 49 museums in the republic, with total attendance amounting to 3,421,000, or 374 per 1,000 population.[109] There were 7,199 public libraries in 1971 with a total of 59.1 million books and magazines in circulation; 6,139 clubs were reported.[110]

National Attitudes

REVIEW OF FACTORS FORMING NATIONAL ATTITUDES

Until recently, many Western authorities agreed that the Belorussian language, culture, and even identity were weak and probably open to successful Russification. New studies and evidence, however, indicate that the process of Russification, though ongoing, is paralleled by a revival of Belorussian national consciousness.

Like other Soviet minorities, Belorussians seek to consolidate and strengthen a national identity within the Soviet system. The "scientific-technological revolution," acting as catalyst in formation of national attitudes, has been accompanied by a growth in the intelligentsia, urbanization, and influx of non-Belorussian specialists from other areas of the Soviet Union. The national psychology—nurtured by traditional literary images of Belorussia as a country of poor soil, sands, and marshes—was jolted by the progress of science and technology and the discovery in recent years of numerous natural resources, especially oil. Advances in the chemical industry have been particularly strong.

Although the Belorussian language and culture have been subtly or even overtly discriminated against by the party and by the Soviet government, official vilification and derision have never been in evidence as in western Belorussia, under Poland, before 1939 or in pre-1917 tsarist Belorussia. Official Soviet theoreticians attempt to explain that "it would be a great mistake to think that the rapprochement of nations under socialism means a process of 'de-nationalization' leading to the disappearance of nations." [111] On the contrary, "the existence of national differences is an inviolable fact," and will remain so for a long time. This requires a "careful attitude toward [national] languages and cultures." [112]

Since the level of urbanization is one indicator of modernization in general, it is clear that Belorussia, with 43% of the population living in cities, in many respects lags behind the RSFSR and Latvia, both with an urban population of 62%, as well as the USSR as a whole (with an average of 57%). On the other hand, urbanization also means Russification: for example, in 1959, 79% of Russian speakers in Belorussia lived in cities.[113] Thus, slowness to modernize may help preserve national identity.

Writers have constantly tried to maintain that the road to humanity lies "through one's own people." [114] "The road to universal international culture," wrote Maryna Barstok, a literary critic, "lies through a full and thorough development of one's own national and unique values. . . . There is no need to hasten artificially the slow, centuries-long process of the unification of national cultures and languages or to favor any one single language. The native language is the basis of a national culture. Only in his native language can a person fully reveal himself and express his most intimate feelings." [115] "When a work of art is saturated with national values," a Belorussian spokeswoman explained at the All-Union Symposium on Children's Literature

109 *Nar. khoz. 1972:* 451.
110 *Ibid.*: 542.
111 Karluk, 1972.
112 *Ibid.*
113 Rakov, 1969: 133.
114 Dziubajła, 1972: 243.
115 *Połymia*, 1968: IV: 203.

held in Minsk, "it reflects general human characteristics." [116]

This concern is not limited to writers. In January 1968 U. Stalmašonak, chairman of the Artists Union of Belorussia, said in his report to the Union's congress: "Mutual international influences should be organically coupled with the application of the traditions of a national culture. . . . Each art should have its own distinctions related to the particularities of national character and to the history and traditions of a people." [117]

However, Belorussian literature has been most pronounced on the subject of national values and consciousness. One of its essential characteristics has been described as an "active patriotic pathos—a singing love for Belorussia, her native language, and an interest in the history of the people." [118]

The idea of preservation and cultivation of national values is especially popular with young writers. Zenia Janiščyc spoke for many when she wrote, "We should not only listen to our times but also look more attentively into specific features of our national life and always feel our responsibility to literature and to our readers." [119]

What Janka Špakouski wrote of Piatrus Makal's poetry (b. 1932) could be said of many Belorussian writers and artists: "His national-political consciousness is growing sharper as well as his blood ties with the culture of his people." Spakouski quoted Makal:

Our children and grandchildren will
    recapitulate us—
Nations are not written off on pension.
You shall resound, my native language
As the word which cannot be thrown
    out of a song![120]

An important factor in maintenance and development of socialist Belorussia's "national consciousness" has been the territorial principle of Soviet cultural autonomy which associates cultural values and achievements with a given territory and, through a Marxian philosophical prism,

connects them with the working masses. In the case of Belorussia, whose upper strata had been either Polanized or Russified during most of the eighteenth and nineteenth centuries, cultural, scholarly, and scientific achievements are treated as an organic part of the people's past, for those achievements "were possible only as a result of interchange between the physical and the intellectual work." [121]

The same territorial principle works not only in respect to the past, but to the present (and future). It imparts Belorussian national attributes to persons and undertakings associated with the territory of the republic. Because they live and work in Belorussia, non-Belorussian members of the Academy of Sciences of the BSSR— I. N. Akhverdov, an Armenian, P. A. Alsmik, a Latvian, N. P. Bulygin, a Russian, I. S. Kravchenko, a Ukrainian, and so on—[122] are considered "Belorussian scientists." [123]

Belorussia's membership in the United Nations and the success of its athletes in international competitions, epitomized by Alexander Medved and Olga Korbut, have been used widely by the republic's media— both Belorussian and Russian—to emphasize achievements of the Belorussian socialist nation.

BASIC VIEWS OF SCHOLARS ON NATIONAL ATTITUDES

Although Belorussia has been aptly described as "the Western Gate" to the Soviet Union[124]—proven correct by both Napoleon and Hitler—there is a pronounced dearth of studies of her past and present in Western languages. One of the earliest attempts at a more or less systematic presentation of Belorussia for the English-speaking world was the "Subcontractor's Monograph," *Belorussia*, printed in 1955 by the Human Relations Area Files.[125] Despite the editors' good

116 *Litaratura i mastactva* (April 7), 1972 (speech by Esfir Hurevič, "For National Particularity").
117 *Litaratura i mastactva* (January 12, 16), 1968 (speech by art critic V. Smatau).
118 *Litaratura i mastactva* (November 22), 1968.
119 *Litaratura i mastactva* (February 26), 1971.
120 *Neman*, 1969: II: 173.

121 Biralo, 1971: 13.
122 *Neman*, 1972: XII: 16.
123 *BielSE*, I: 274, II: 10, 464; VI: 109.
124 *Połymia*, 1970: VIII: 162.
125 Subcontractor's Monograph, HRAF–19, Chicago–10, *Belorussia* (New Haven: Human Relations Area Files, 1955).

intentions, it is an inadequate compendium of miscellaneous data.

A principal source of information has been Nicholas P. Vakar's book *Belorussia: The Making of a Nation*, accompanied by *A Bibliographical Guide to Belorussia*.[126] Covering the entire history of Belorussia, the author emphasizes the last one hundred years, specifically the role of Belorussian nationalism in shaping political history. He concluded that Belorussian nationalism was heading "at home, toward complete dissolution in the Soviet sea; abroad, toward further crystallization of the nationalist doctrine." [127] Some years after the publication of his book, Vakar, in an attempt "to sum up the ambiguities and uncertainties of the Belorussian situation," wrote: "We cannot speak of either nationhood or extinction. The people have their special ethnic characteristics, but the trend is to preserve them merely for their historical and sentimental value." [128] Readable, including much interesting information, Vakar's writings are interspersed with factual errors and present a very personal point of view contested by recent evidence and other scholars.

A valuable study is by Anthony Adamovich, participant in the Belorussian literary life of the 1920s and survivor of the Stalinist purges. His book, *Opposition to Sovietization in Belorussian Literature (1917–1957)*, describes intense efforts during the years of NEP to create a national literature "that will be seen by centuries and nations." [129] After the tragedies of the 1930s and World War II, efforts were launched in the mid–1950s to return to the national values and goals of the 1920s. In January 1957, however, the Communist party of Belorussia condemned any " 'revision' of the dirty linen of the Belorussian nationalists with the purpose of finding something 'positive, valuable, or progressive' there." [130]

By the 1970s many of the 1957 restrictions had been lifted, and the rehabilitation of the past made considerable headway. The literary organization *Excelsior [Uzvyšsa]*, figuring prominently in Adamovich's *Opposition* as leading core of the Belorussian national front, was recently described in the following words:

> *Excelsior* was set up basically as a reaction to the creative and organizational structure of *Maladniak* [organization inspired by the Komsomol]. In spite of some mistakes of an idea-tional-esthetic nature which, by the way, were typical of all literary organizations, it is necessary to indicate rectitude and justification of the establishment of this union. The Excelsiorists addressed themselves to the classical national heritage, actively adopted achievements of foreign literatures, and generously drew on the treasury of Belorussian folklore. They endeavored to get rid of provincial confinement to create an art which would "be seen by centuries and nations." [131]

In conjunction with the above, note the very last sentence of Adamovich's book: "When sooner or later the brakes no longer hold, the regeneration of 'people's progress' in Belorussia will surely begin from where it left off—from the *Excelsior* movement, from the heights once won by the Belorussian national literary opposition against Sovietization."

A new monograph has been added to the scant literature on Belorussia in Western languages: Ivan S. Lubachko's book, *Belorussia Under Soviet Rule, 1917–1957*.[132] The principal conclusion runs contrary to Vakar's thesis about "complete dissolution" of Belorussian nationalism "in the Soviet sea." Lubachko states that in the post-Stalin era "national feeling became more intense than ever." Valuable details corroborating this view are in an article by A. Adamovich, "The Non-Russians," which reviewed the Soviet literary scene with an emphasis on Belorussian literature.[133]

Two main currents during the early 1960s are described in Stanislau Stankevich's monograph, *Belorussian Literature Under the Soviets*. With "at least 300

126 Vakar, 1956.
127 *Ibid*: 225.
128 Vakar, 1968: 226.
129 Adamovich, 1958: 86.
130 Adamovich, 1958: 73. Reference is made to an article in *Zviada* (January 12), 1957, entitled "For the Ideological Purity of our Literary Positions."

131 *Viesci AN BSSR*, 1972: VI: 56.
132 (Lexington, Ky.: University of Kentucky Press, 1972).
133 Adamovich, 1964: 100–129.

creatively active writers," Belorussian literature was characterized by prevalence of humanitarian themes as a natural reaction to Stalinist suppression and by an emphasis on national values and allegiance as defense against the slogan (1961) about inevitability of "merger of all languages into one language of the future Communist society." [134]

These tendencies remain very much alive. A recent survey of young Belorussian poets, noting "an unceasing influx of new forces into literature," acknowledged that "patriotic themes, as well as the theme of love, friendship, and nature have always been very attractive for young writers." [135] At the same time the reviewer chided the young for a major shortcoming: "lowering of civic and moral standards" (another term for *partiinost*).[136]

Soviet literature is quite extensive on the Belorussian socialist nation. It is uniform in basic theses and, in many cases, written collectively. Belorussia is pictured as a prosperous, highly industrialized nation, equal to other members of the Soviet family, marching merrily toward communism.[137] Under the surface, however, is a significant amount of revisionism concerning the national past, reflecting both attitudinal shifts and progress of historical scholarship and proving ideological nutrients for the national consciousness.

CURRENT MANIFESTATIONS OF NATIONALISM

Evidence of overt dissent or *samizdat* activity has been scarce. Only recently has it been reported that "in Belorussia there appears irregularly and with long intervals a periodical *Listok* [*Newsletter*] in Belorussian (this is known only from information brought by Jewish emigrants to Israel)." [138] In 1970 the *Chronicle of Current Events*

reported a demonstration in Minsk of students demanding "freedom of speech and of the press." [139] In 1972 oral reports reached the United States about a trial held in Minsk behind closed doors of members of the Kim circle, a group disenchanted with the Soviet political and economic system, caught on a plane to Moscow with some unidentified manuscripts. There is even less information about specific goals and national views of the dissidents.

Much more evident are indirect expressions of nationalist sentiment. M. Maserau (Masherov), first secretary of CPB, speaking to a conference of instructors of social science in February 1972, explained: "Special attention should be paid to the question of the struggle against relapse into nationalism and nationalistic views." [140] The main theoretical journal of the CPB, *Kommunist Belorussii*, directed at the beginning of the new 1972–1973 school year: "In the courses of the Party and the Komsomol education system it is necessary to unmask in detail the anti-Communist and anti-Soviet essence of bourgeois and revisionist views on the nationality question, to decisively debunk those who, in the morass of nationalist superstitions, are attempting to poison the atmosphere of friendship." [141]

Certainly, such rhetoric has a prophylactic purpose. There are, however, clear indications that the Belorussian intelligentsia are resisting the Russification drive and enjoying limited success in this endeavor.

B. Frejdkin, teacher of Belorussian in the city of Polotsk, recalled in 1965 how two years earlier his school had been "engulfed by the so-called 'epidemics of liberation' from the Belorussian language." As a result of a concerted effort by teachers, writers, and parents, supported by enthusiastic students, the tide, Frejdkin believed, had been turned back. The parents decided to make the teaching of Belorussian compulsory for all students.[142]

Similar efforts have been undertaken in

---

134 Stankevich, 1967: 12–14, 167.
135 *Maładosc'*, 1973: I: 131.
136 *Ibid.*: 133.
137 In 1972 the entire sixth issue of *Viesci AN BSSR* (Social Sciences Series) was devoted to achievements by Belorussia in major areas of national life.
138 *Homin Ukrainy* (Toronto) (October 21), 1972; reprinted in *Facts on Byelorussia* (New York), I: 40.

---

139 *Facts on Byelorussia*, I: 40.
140 *Ibid.*: 6.
141 *Kommunist Belorussii*, 1972: IX: 13.
142 *Litaratura i mastactva* (May 18), 1965; reprinted in *Naviny z Biełarusi* (New York.: Radio Liberty) (May 31), 1965.

other regions. V. Dajlida, principal of a high school in the Sluck district, suggested in the writers' journal, *Połymia*, that "the Belorussian language should be compulsory throughout the whole of Belorussia." [143] The language battle became a rallying cry for the Belorussian intelligentsia, especially writers and teachers. Attacked by official criticism for his war novels, the embattled Belorussian author Vasil Bykau was defended by a petition containing 65 colleagues' signatures, presented to the Central Committee of CPB. In a speech to the Fifth Congress of Belorussian writers, Bykau assured the audience that "so long as the writers were united on such vital matters [referring to solidarity of the 65 in defense of his creative freedom] and were prepared to declare themselves openly, the Belorussian people may rest assured about the future destiny of their literature." [144]

Much effort has gone into defense of the national language in the educational system. The curriculum has been revised and new textbooks introduced. An English language booklet, *Byelorussia*, published in Moscow in 1972, tells the reader that in the BSSR "in schools, where the teaching is in Russian, Belorussian is a compulsory subject." [145]

The battle for the national language has gone beyond the secondary school curricula, however. A case was reported in a literary newspaper (probably to provide an example) of how a certain M. Lazar of the Maladečna district refused to accept his passport because it was written only in Russian. The passport was exchanged.[146] The law says that passports be written in two languages, Belorussian and Russian.

At the Second Congress of Belorussia's Union of Cinematographers, held in Minsk in February 1967, the opinion was expressed that "the Belorussian cinema should be created by efforts of Belorussian actors." [147] The same idea was supported by several spokesmen and editorially by the newspaper *Literature and Art*.[148] However, the representative of government and party, B. Paulonak, chairman of the State Committee for Cinematography, "categorically" rejected pleas for national characteristics in the cinema: "Raising the question of creating a Belorussian cinema by Belorussian hands," he declared, "is not the solution to the problem of national art; this is, pardon me, something that smells of nationalism." [149]

A major campaign waged in recent years is to launch new periodicals and increase the circulation of existing ones. There have been attempts to use legal arguments to boost circulation. Kastus Cvirka, senior inspector of the State Administration for Dissemination of Printed Material, complained of "criminal attitudes" in institutional subscriptions to the Belorussian literary-artistic magazines, *Połymia*, *Małados ć*, and *Biełarus ́*. "It is self-evident that our Republic's literary-artistic magazines are destined for hundreds of thousands of readers. But, strange as it may seem, their circulation is still very small—a few thousand copies." [150] Cvirka suggested that to overcome existing obstacles "lists of publications not be considered as recommendations but compulsory and have the force of law."

Belorussia now has over 620,000 specialists with higher or secondary education; a little more than two thirds (68%) are Belorussians.[151] This percentage is somewhat low, for their weight in the republic's total population is more than four fifths (81%).[152] Nevertheless, the continual proportional growth of Belorussian intelligentsia might be an additional reason for the heavy concentration of party propaganda on the dangers of bourgeois nationalism.

Religion as well as language has strong roots among the population,[153] but without additional research it is difficult to ascertain

143 *Połymia*, 1966: IV: 163.
144 *Facts on Byelorussia*, I: 46.
145 *Byelorussia*, 1972: 7.
146 *Litaratura i mastactva* (August 23), 1966; reprinted in *Naviny z Biełarusi* (September 15), 1966.
147 *Litaratura i mastactva* (February 21), 1967.
148 *Litaratura i mastactva* (February 14), 1967.

149 *Litaratura i mastactva* (February 21), 1967; reprinted in *Naviny z Biełarusi* (March 15), 1967.
150 The circulations of *Połymia*, *Małados ć*, and *Biełarus ́* in July 1966 were, respectively, 5,812 (January 1973: 10,112), 7,833 (January 1973: 17,251), 11,394 (January 1973: 21,535). *Litaratura i mastactva* (July 8), 1966.
151 *Nastaŭnickaja hazieta* (Minsk) (February 17), 1973; *Planovoye khozyaystvo* (Moscow), 1972: VII 41.
152 *BSE*, V: 123.
153 *Facts on Byelorussia*, I: 7: 35–36.

the relationship between Belorussian national and religious values.

As seen above, there is a resurgence of national culture and consciousness in Belorussia. This is somewhat parallel to the continuing process of Russification. This apparent contradiction can perhaps be resolved by substituting present notions about single monolithic identification of a person with language, culture, and nationality with a more flexible concept of multiple adherence (bilingualism, multiculture, and binationalism—applying to the same person). The Belorussian situation may be an outstanding case of such multiple identity patterns.

REFERENCES

Adamovich, 1958
  Anthony Adamovich, *Opposition to Sovietization in Belorussian Literature (1917–1957)* (New York: Scarecrow Press, 1958).
Adamovich, 1964
  Anthony Adamovich, "The Non-Russians," in Max Hayward and Edward L. Crowley, eds., *Soviet Literature in the Sixties: An International Symposium* (New York: Praeger, 1964).
Aleksandrovič et al., 1971
  S. Ch. Aleksandrovic et al., compilers, *Biełaruskaja litaratura XIX stahoddzia* (Minsk: *Vyšejsaja škoła* Press, 1971).
Alekseyev, 1966
  L. V. Alekseyev, *Polotskaya zemlya* (Moscow: Nauka Press, 1966).
Astashkin, 1970
  N. D. Astashkin, *Prirodnyiye resursy BSSR* (Minsk: Navuka i tekhnika, 1970).
Bahrovic, 1962
  Andrej Bahrovič, *Zycharstva Biełaruskaje SSR u sviatle pierapisu 1959 hodu* [Population of Belorussian SSR in Light of 1959 Census] (Munich: Whiteruthenian Institute of Arts and Sciences, 1962).
Belorussia, 1972
  Belorussia (Moscow: Novosti Press Agency Publishing House, 1972).
Biełaruskaha knihadrukavannia, 1968
  Academy of Sciences of the BSSR, *450 hod biełaruskaha knihadrukavannia* [450 Years of Belorussian Bookprinting] (Minsk: Navuka i tekhnika, 1968).
Biełaruskaje, 1967
  Academy of Sciences of the BSSR, *Biełaruskaje movaznaùstva. Biblijahrafičny ùkazalnik (1825–1965hh.)* [Belorussian Linguistics: Bibliography, 1825–1965] (Minsk: Navuka i tekknika, 1968).
BielSE, 1971
  Academy of Sciences of the BSSR, *Biełaruskaja Savieckaja Encykłapiedyja* Minsk, 1969–).
Biralo, 1971
  A. A. Biralo, *Filosofskaya i obshchestvennaya mysl v Belorussii i Litvye v kontse XVII–seredine XVIII vv.* (Minsk: Belorussian State University Press, 1971).
CDSP
  Current Digest of the Soviet Press, published by Joint Committee on Slavic Studies.
Duevel, 1971
  Christian Duevel, "The Central Committee and the Central Auditing Commission Elected by the 24th CPSU Congress," part IV. *Radio Liberty* CRD 310/71, October 6, 1971.
Dziubajła, 1972
  P. K. Dziubajła, ed., *Šlachi razviccia biełaruskaj savieckaj prozy* [Roads of Development of the Soviet Belorussian Prose] (Minsk: Navuka i tekhnika, 1972).
East-West Digest, 1972
  East-West Digest (Richmond, Surrey, England: Foreign Affairs Publishing, 1972).
Facts on Byelorussia
  Facts on Byelorussia, News Bulletin, Jan Zaprudnik, ed. (New York: Queens College, SGS).
Filin, 1972
  F. P. Filin, *Proiskhozhdeniye russkogo ukrainskogo i belorusskogo yazykov* (Leningrad: Nauka Press, 1972).
Grinblat, 1968
  M. Ya. Grinblat, *Belorusy: Ocherki proiskhozhdeniya i etnicheskoy istorii* (Minsk: Navuka i tekhnika, 1968).
Historyja, 1972
  Academy of Sciences of BSSR, *Historyja Biełaruskaj SSR* (Minsk: Navuka i tekhnika, 1972).

Historyja Litaratury
Academy of Sciences of BSSR, *Historyja bielaruskaj dakastryčnickaj litaratury* [*History of the Belorussian Pre-Revolutionary Literature*] (Minsk: Navuka i tekhnika, 1969).

Itogi Belorusskaya SSR, 1959
Itogi Belorusskaya SSR, 1959 (Moscow: Statistika, 1960).

Itogi SSSR 1959
Itogi vsesoyuznoi perepisi naseleniya 1959 goda SSSR (Moscow: Gosstatizdat, 1962), summary volume and volumes on the 15 republics.

JBS
Journal of Byelorussian Studies (London, 1965–).

Kabysh, 1958
Simon Kabysh, "The Belorussians," *Genocide in the USSR* (New York: Scarecrow Press, 1958).

Karluk, 1972
A. Karluk, "Zblizennie i adzinstva nacyj" ["Rapprochement and Unity of Nations"], *Zviazda* (Minsk), October 21, 1972.

Kokhonov, 1967
F. L. Kokhonov and V. F. Medvedev, *Ekonomika Belorusskoy SSR* (Moscow: Ekonomika, 1967).

Kokhonov, 1968
G. M. Kokhonov and V. F. Mayevsky, compilers, *Nasha Respublika* [*Our Republic*] (Minsk: Bielarus Press, 1968).

Kolasky, 1968
John Kolasky, *Education in Soviet Ukraine* (Toronto: Martin, 1968).

Krushinsky, 1953
S. Krushinsky, *Byelorussian Communism and Nationalism* (New York: Research Program on USSR, 1953).

Krutalevic, 1968
V. Krutalevič, "Abviaščennie respubliki," *Połymia* (Minsk: 1968): 9.

Letapis, 1972
Letapis druku BSSR (Minsk: House of Book of BSSR, 1972): 1.

Litaratura i mastactva
Litaratura i mastactva [*Literature and Art*], published in Minsk.

Malashko, 1969
A. M. Malashko, *K voprosu ob oformlenii Odnopartiinoi sistemy v SSSR* (Minsk: Belorussian State University Press, 1969).

Marcinkievič, 1972
F. S. Marcinkievič, "Ekanamičnaje razviccio Biełarusi u sastavie SSSR" [Economic Development of Belorussia within the USSR], *Viesci AN BSSR, Sieryja hramadzkich navuk* [*News of the*

Academy of Sciences of the BSSR. Social Science Series], 1972.

McMillin, 1967
Arnold B. McMillin, "Academician Ja. F. Karski," *Journal of Baltic Studies* (1967): I: 3.

Mienski, 1955
J. Mienski, "The Establishment of the Belorussian SSR," *Belorussian Review* (Munich: Institute for Study of USSR, 1955).

Nadson, 1965
Alexander Nadson, "The Writing of St. Cyril of Turau," *Journal of Baltic Studies* (1965): I: 1.

Nadson, 1967
Alexander Nadson, "Nasha Niva," *Journal of Baltic Studies* (1967): I: 3.

Nar. khoz. 1970
Narodnoye khozyaistvo SSSR v 1970 godu (Moscow: Statistika, 1971).

Nar. khoz. 1972
Narodnoye khozyaistvo SSSR 1922–1972, Yubileinyi statisticheskii yezhegodnik (Moscow: Statistika, 1972).

Nar. obraz., 1971
Narodnoye obrazovaniye, nauka i kul'tura v SSSR: statisticheskii sbornik (Moscow: Statistika, 1971).

Niamiha, 1955
H. Niamiha, "Education in Belorussia before the Rout of 'National Democracy': 1917–1930," *Belorussian Review* (Munich) (1955): 1.

Pechat' 1959
Pechat' SSSR v 1959 godu (Moscow: Kniga, 1960).

Pechat' 1970
Pechat' SSSR v 1970 godu (Moscow: Kniga, 1971).

Politicheskoye, 1974
Politicheskoye samoobrazovaniye (Moscow: Pravda, 1974).

Rakau, 1968
A. Rakau, "Mihracyja i niekatoryja jaje prablemy u BSSR" [Migration of Population in BSSR and Some of Its Problems], *Połymia* (1968): 3. (Belorussian spelling for the author A. Rakov.)

Rakov, 1969
A. A. Rakov, *Naseleniye BSSR* (Minsk: Navuka i tekhnika, 1969).

Sambuk, 1972
S. M. Sambuk, *Revolutsionnyiye narodniki Belorussii* (Minsk: Navuka i tekhnika, 1972).

Sels. khoz., 1971
Selskoye khozyaystvo SSR (Moscow: Statistika, 1971).

Smirnov, 1963
A. F. Smirnov, *Vosstaniye 1863 goda v*

Litve i Belorussii (Moscow: Academy of Sciences of USSR, 1963).

Stankevich, 1967
Stanislau Stankevich, *Bielaruskaja padsavieckaja litaratura* [*Belorussian Literature under the Soviets*] (New York, 1967).

Touscik, 1973
A. A. Touscik, "Druk, telebacannie i radyjo-dziejsny srodak kamunistycnaha vychavannia" [The Press, Television, and Radio as an Effective Means for Communist Upbringing], *Viesci AN BSSR. Sieryia hramadzkich navuk* [News of Academy of Sciences of BSSR Series of Social Sciences], N.1. (Minsk, 1973).

Transport i svyaz', 1972
Transport i svyaz' SSSR (Moscow: Statistika, 1972).

Vakar, 1949
Nicholas Vakar, "The Name, 'White Russia,'" *American Slavic and East European Review* (October 1949): VIII: 3: 201–213.

Vakar, 1956
N. P. Vakar, *Belorussia: The Making of a Nation* (Cambridge: Harvard University Press, 1956).

Vakar, 1968
Nicholas P. Vakar, "The Belorussian People between Nationhood and Extinction," in Erich Goldhagen, ed., *Ethnic Minorities in the Soviet Union* (New York: Praeger, 1968).

Viesci AN BSSR, 1972
Viesci AN BSSR. Sieryja hramadzkich navuk [*News of Academy of Sciences of BSSR. Social Science Series*] (Minsk, 1972).

Yeshin, 1970
S. Z. Yeshin, *Razvitiye kultury v BSSR za gody Sovetskoy vlasti* (Minsk: Vyšejašaja škoła Press, 1970).

Zapisy, 1970
Zapisy (Munich: Whiteruthenian Institute of Arts and Sciences, 1970).

Zaprudnik, 1969
J. Zaprudnik, "Political Struggle for Byelorussia in the Tsarist State Dumas, 1906–1917," New York University, unpublished dissertation, 1969.

Žurauski, 1967
A. I. Zurauski, ed., *Historyja bielaruskaj litaraturnaj movy* [*History of Belorussian Literary Language*] (Minsk: Navuka i tekhnika, 1967): I.

Part II

THE BALTICS

Part II discusses the republics of Estonia, Latvia, and Lithuania which, while differing from each other, share critical historical experiences. They are the most Westward-looking of the republics, with strong Germanic and Polish influences reflected in their cultural and religious heritage. They also share a recent experience of independence, having been independent states from the end of World War I until just prior to World War II.

These three Baltic republics, tiny in size and population relative to the USSR as a whole, also share a higher level of economic and industrial development—characteristics that have attracted increasing numbers of Slavs into each republic.

4 | ESTONIA and THE ESTONIANS

Rein Taagepera

General Information

TERRITORY[1]

Ethnically, Estonian territory has remained the same at least since 1200 A.D. It includes the present Estonian SSR (17,000 square miles) and the Petseri district of the RSFSR Pskov *oblast* (which belonged to the independent Republic of Estonia of 1918–1940). Estonia is a quasi-peninsula the size of Denmark, separated from Sweden by the 150-mile-wide Baltic Sea, from Finland by the 50-mile-wide Gulf of Finland, and from Russia by the 20-mile-wide Peipsi Lake and the Narva River. Only the border with Latvia offers no natural barriers. Estonia extends 220 miles from east to west and 150 miles from north to south. Islands form 9% of the territory, and lakes occupy 5%.

Estonia consists of rather marshy plains, with the highest hills reaching up to 1,000 feet at most. Although the climate is softened by the presence of the sea, rye rather than wheat is the traditional cereal. Communication lines are well developed. With the exception of oil shale, there are few natural resources apart from phosphates, peat, and water.

Estonia is one of the Baltic republics which stand out by use of Latin script, past and present Western way of life, and high per capita national income. Their 1940 annexation by the Soviet Union has not been recognized by the United States. Estonia differs from the other Baltic republics because of its special ties with Finland (including similarities in language); a quasi-official socioeconomic "laboratory republic" for the Soviet Union, it is the world leader in oil shale technology and mining.

ECONOMY[2]

A skilled labor force is Estonia's main asset and, as a result, the republic is extensively industrialized in spite of a lack of natural resources. Per capita gross indus-

---

1 *ENE*, 1970: 2; Hooson, 1966: 232–250.

2 *ENE*, 1970: 2.

trial output (2,100 rubles in 1968) is higher than in any other Soviet area outside the RSFSR northwest (2,300 rubles) and center (2,200 rubles) and Latvia (2,100 rubles). Per capita national income follows the same pattern.[3] Estonia produces 75% of all Soviet oil shale, 6% of its oil instrumentation, 5% of its excavators, and 3% of its paper and cotton fabrics. Oil shale is used for electricity and as a basis for the chemical industry.

Agriculture is relatively efficient, with yields among the highest in the USSR, in spite of the northern climate and indifferent soil. Yet about 80% of agricultural income is from animal husbandry, with a Denmark-like emphasis on dairy farming and bacon. Agricultural production is small in the all-Soviet context. In fishing, Estonia's share is 3% of the Soviet total.

From 1960 to 1967, production and employment trends were the following. Industry's share of total production grew from 60.3% to 64.0%, while agriculture's share decreased from 20.9% to 18.4%. Collective farms' share of total employed population decreased from 17.5% to 11.0%; share of "production" workers and employees (including state farms) grew from 61.5% to 67.1%; share of "non-production" employees increased from 20.3% to 21.8%. Since 1967 "production" labor has remained at 67%, while collective farmers' share has further decreased to 9% and "non-production" labor has grown to 24% in 1971.[4]

HISTORY[5]

Man has inhabited Estonia for 10,000 years, and the Finnic forefathers of the present-day Estonians arrived 5,000 years ago.[6] The loosely organized Estonian counties resisted early Russian conquest attempts, but were subdued (and incidentally baptized) around 1220 by German knights who later joined the Teutonic Order. Gradually, serfdom was established and completed by 1500, under a German-speaking

nobility, clergy, and city elite tied loosely to the German Empire. This establishment's switch to vernacular-oriented Lutheranism in 1521 triggered printing of the first Estonian language book in 1535—barely 80 years after Gutenberg perfected the art. The German political rule started to crumble around 1560 and, after brief Russian and Polish penetrations, Sweden held all of Estonia during the seventeenth century.

Around 1710 Russia conquered Estonia, and its German establishment reachieved autonomous status which began to be restricted only around 1840. A Pietist movement during the eighteenth century effectively converted the Estonian peasants to Christianity for the first time. In 1802–1819 serfdom was abolished, and starting from 1849 land ownership by peasants became feasible in practice. This emancipation coincided with the start of industrialization, supplying an economic basis for an Estonian national awakening encouraged by romantic and nationalist trends elsewhere in Europe. Occasionally, the tsarist government supported this nationalism as a counterweight to the ruling Germans, but peasant goodwill was lost in an all-out Russification drive after 1880. By 1900 Estonia had emerged as a fully literate nation; its people were conscious of a separate identity, proud of their rapid economic and cultural progress, and demanded a voice in local politics and administration. Their vision of the future Russian Empire was along federalist lines with broad local autonomy.[7]

After the Russian February Revolution of 1917, Estonian autonomy became a reality. Under the twin pressure of Bolshevik takeover and threat of a German occupation, independence was declared in early 1918 by the non-Bolshevik leaders who had obtained 63% of the national vote in late 1917. After two years of fighting against the Soviets and the Germans, independence became real, and a democratic regime was inaugurated. A drastic land reform was carried out which helped agriculture, but industry was badly hurt by being cut off from its Russian markets. Cultural autonomy for ethnic minorities was established and pre-

3 Wagener, 1971: 24; Bush, 1970.
4 ESSR 1971: 239.
5 ENE, 1970: 2.
6 Uustalu, 1952; Kruus, 1935; Rei, 1970.

7 Raun, 1971.

served for the duration of the republic. World depression and the spread of fascism led to a "preventive dictatorship" in 1934 but a return to democracy started in 1938. The Communist vote, 37% in late 1917, dropped to less than 10% by 1920. After an abortive putsch attempt in 1924, the Communist party was declared illegal, and played hardly any role thereafter.[8] In 1938 most imprisoned members were released. Cultural development during independence was rapid, social legislation was among the most advanced in Europe, but living standards remained low compared to Scandinavia.

The 1939 Molotov-Ribbentrop pact gave the Soviet Union a free hand in Estonia, which had to abandon its previous stand of neutrality and accept a mutual assistance pact involving Soviet military bases on the Estonian coast. Suddenly, in June 1940, the Soviet army occupied all of Estonia. Due to the presence of these forces, the non-Communist parties were not in position to protest when their tickets were disqualified prior to subsequent elections. Nor were they prepared to demand a recount when the Communists announced a landslide in favor of their single ticket. Joining the Soviet Union was not a declared issue during this brief "People's Democracy" period, during which some local Communists talked about an "Outer Mongolian status" for Estonia. On orders by Stalin, and with the shadow of the 1937–1938 Stalinist purges at their backs, local Communists asked for incorporation into the Soviet Union in August 1940. Subsequently, Estonia suffered its share of Stalinist excesses, including forced collectivization of agriculture and mass deportations which by 1949 involved about 10% of the population.[9]

During the twilight of the 1941–1944 German occupation the government of the prewar Republic of Estonia reconstituted itself and went into exile in Scandinavia where it still exists. About 6% of the population also left and, with extremely few exceptions, remained in the West.

In 1950 native-born Communist leaders of Estonia were purged for alleged nation-alism, replaced by Estonians who had grown up in Russia. These "Yestonians," as they are called, still occupy all major government and party posts in Soviet Estonia.[10]

After Stalin's death most surviving deportees returned. Russification of the culture largely stopped, but denationalization of the country continued through a partly uncontrolled influx of Russian immigrants. The consumer goods situation in the cities improved, and during the 1960s the collective farmers' lives also improved markedly. Local autonomy increased in 1956, but decreased again during the 1960s. Industry has skyrocketed, with partly undesirable ecological and demographic results.[11]

DEMOGRAPHY[12]

A basic demographic factor in twentieth-century Estonia has been a low birth rate which led to practically zero population growth during independence. Under present conditions growth has occurred, but through massive immigration. The birth rate has been under 2.0% per year ever since 1915, and has been around 1.4% to 1.6% since 1963. (In comparison, the all-Soviet rate was over 2.5% until 1960.) Natural increase in Estonia was 0.4% to 0.6% throughout the 1960s, at a time when the all-Soviet natural increase dropped from 1.8% to 0.9%.[13] The number of ethnic Estonians increased by 0.3% per year.

Combined with the labor needs of an industry-worshipping regime, and with the easier and more "Western" living conditions in Estonia, the low natural increase has resulted in a continuous flow of mainly Russian-speaking immigrants. From 1959 to 1970 the ethnically Estonian population grew by 32,000 while the non-Estonian population grew by 127,000. Total population growth was relatively slower (13%) than the Soviet average (16%). The lack of mas-

8 Lipping, 1971; Nodel, 1971.
9 Rei, 1970:320; Uustalu, 1970:352; Parming, 1972.

10 Because their Russian accent changed "e" into "ye," people started to call them *jeestlased* (which might be translated as "Yestonians") instead of *eestlased* [Estonians] Cf. Taagepera, 1970.
11 Cf. Järvesoo, 1973.
12 Parming, 1972; *Itogi 1970*; *Horisont*, 1968; Taagepera, 1973.
13 *ESSR*, 1971.

sive immigration into higher-birth-rate Lithuania suggests that immigration is not deliberately organized for Russification purposes. But the Soviet authorities have not taken any measures to stem the flow with its visible denationalizing effects, despite efforts in this direction by the few home-grown Communist leaders.

From 1959 to 1970 the Estonians' share of the republic's population dropped from 75% to 68% while the Russians' share increased from 20% to 25%. If the present trend continues, Estonia would become ethnically less than half Estonian by the year 2000. The recent decrease in the Russian birth rate (which reduced the RSFSR rate *below* that of the Estonian SSR by 1968)[14] suggests that immigration trends into Estonia may change before Estonians are reduced to a minority in their own country. It should be emphasized that while the country is being denationalized through immigration, assimilation of individuals works rather in favor of Estonians: 62% of the offspring of mixed marriages in Tallinn has been reported opting for Estonian nationality;[15] there is much anecdotal evidence for Russian children picking up the Estonian language; and 6.1% of rural Russians declared a "non-Russian" everyday language in the 1970 census.

Urbanization has accelerated ever since 1950. By 1970, 65% of the population lived in cities and towns, compared to 56% in 1959 and 35% in 1939. This makes Estonia the most urbanized union republic; however, central and northwest RSFSR are even more urbanized (71% and 73%, respectively). Estonians formed 58% of the urban population and 88% of the rural population in 1970. Due to heavy migration of young people into the cities, the rural birth rate has fallen below the urban birth rate, which is rather unusual. Of the labor force 22% were employed in agriculture in 1968, compared to 27% for the USSR.

The elite are predominantly Estonian in the cultural field and strongly Russian in the political and special technology fields. To judge from distribution of decorations, communications and transport (especially civil aviation) are in Russian hands, while universities are run by Estonians. Estonians are strongly underrepresented in Communist party membership—on a Union-wide basis, 3% belonged to the party in 1965, compared to 6% of Russians and Georgians. On January 1, 1970, 52.3% of the members of the Communist party of Estonia were Estonians;[16] 4.0% of Estonians in Estonia were party members. In contrast, 7.7% of the Russians in Estonia were party members. The disparity between the skills and political power of Estonians is marked: with 68% of the republic's population, Estonians represent 76% of the "specialists," [17] but only 52% of party membership. The issue is further complicated by the existence of "Yestonians"—people of Estonia extraction who grew up in the Soviet Union while Estonia was not part of it. These semidenationalized people occupy most of the power positions and, as a group, may account for an appreciable fraction of the nominally Estonian party membership. Highest-ranking native Communists are presently Vice Premiers E. Tõnurist and A. Green and Third Party Secretary V. Väljas. Few ethnic Russians are among the power elite, and it remains to be seen who will replace the present Yestonian leaders when these old men die.[18]

At the other extreme of the social scale, Russian immigrants are also Estonia's "Puerto Ricans" (as an Estonian put it to a visitor from New York), doing the unskilled jobs shunned by Estonians, especially in construction.[19] Russians are a majority in northeast Estonia's oil shale region and a strong minority in the capital city, Tallinn.[20]

CULTURE[21]

In terms of culture, Estonia (along with most of Latvia) could be characterized as "Soviet Scandinavia." The similarity

---

14 K. Laas, in *Eesti Kommunist* (November), 1971.
15 Terentjeva, 1970.

16 Institut Istorii Partii pri TsK KP Estonii, *Nekotorye Voprosy Organizatsionno-Partiinoi Raboty* (Tallinn: Eesti Raamat, 1971): 74.
17 *Nõukogude Õpetaja* [*Soviet Teacher*] (July 22), 1972:2.
18 Cf. Taagepera, 1970. On the term "Yestonian," see the section on history, note 10.
19 Taagepera, 1968.
20 In 1970 Tallinn was 55.7% Estonian and 35.0% Russian (*Itogi 1970*:IV:320).
21 Vardys, 1970; Taagepera, 1973; Nirk, 1970.

starts with racial characteristics, a largely common history, use of Latin script, and predominance of Lutheranism as the traditional religion. It continues with present tastes in applied art and architecture. Some Russians characterize the area as the "Soviet 'Abroad' " [*Sovetskaya zagranitsa*], a chunk of the West within the Union, to which the Moscow youth flocks for holiday as a substitute for Stockholm and Paris.

Apart from Iceland, Estonia may be the smallest nation of the world with a modern culture expressed through its own language. There are drawbacks—sometimes one has the feeling that every tenth Estonian is busy translating—but Estonians can read everything ranging from Homer and Shakespeare to Segal's *Love Story* and graduate-level physics texts in their own language. The Russian language does not represent an indispensable link to the rest of the world; their contemporary artistic and literary evolution goes abreast with the Russian, sometimes preceding it. Estonian composers like A. Pärt and J. Rääts have been in the forefront of dodecaphonal music in the USSR.[22] The first Soviet jazz festival was held in Estonia, currently a bastion of pop music. Abstract art was practiced in Estonia at least as early as in Moscow and, possibly in contrast to Moscow, has by now acquired wide popularity (and probably snob appeal). Kafka, Ionesco, and Dostoyevsky were available to Soviet Estonians earlier than to the Russian reading public.

Of all aspects of contemporary Estonian culture, the theater has perhaps the greatest potential for a Soviet-wide and even wider impact. Paul-Eerik Rummo's *Cinderella Game* (1969) has been performed in New York (1971), although not yet in the USSR beyond Estonia.[23]

Contemporary prose includes Mrozek-style satire (A. Valton),[24] historical novels which combine literary quality with national appeal (J. Kross),[25] collective farm realism at its best (M. Traat), realistic descriptions of city life and work (Aimee Beekman),[26] and analysis of Stalinism (E.

Vetemaa).[27] In poetry, all modern trends and styles are represented, although some surrealist (A. Alliksaar),[28] mystical (U. Masing), and "hippy" (J. Isotamm)[29] poets have difficulties in getting published.

Present cultural activity is another stage in a constant evolution which started with the "national awakening" around 1860, caught up with contemporary West European developments early in this century, and continued unabated through independence and the Soviet period, except for a "historical gap" (a term used by young Soviet Estonians)[30] under Stalin. In the midst of this modernism, Estonia retains its authentic folk singers, with orally transmitted repertoire going back to the pre-Christian era—possibly the only ones in Europe. In resonance with the world-wide new interest in folk song, Estonia is delving with new pride into this heritage.

EXTERNAL RELATIONS[31]

Estonia has direct trade agreements with several East European Communist countries (East Germany, Hungary, Czechoslovakia) and also with Finland.[32] Like other European Union republics, it is a member of the International Radio and Television Organization, and occasionally its foreign affairs minister is part of the Soviet UN delegation. In the mid-sixties restrictions on tourism in and out of Estonia were relaxed, and it now involves hundreds of Estonians and thousands of foreigners (mainly Finns) per year. Estonia's student construction corps works each summer in People's Democracies, and its superb male chorus has visited Scandinavia repeatedly. A number of international scientific conferences have been held in Estonia, including a UNESCO symposium on oil shale.

Estonia's ties with Finland are of special interest. The languages are similar and Finnish TV can be seen in northern Estonia.

22 Olt, 1972.
23 Valgemäe, 1972.
24 For brief analyses of some of these works, see *Books Abroad*, 1973: XLVII: 394–396.
25 *Books Abroad*, 1972: XLVI: 142.
26 *Ibid.*, 1969: XLIII: 446.

27 *Ibid.*, 1968: XLII: 310.
28 *Ibid.*: 621.
29 *Ibid.*, 1972: XLVI: 329.
30 Grabbi, 1969.
31 See *Estonian Events* for details.
32 *Estonian Events* (December), 1972: no. 35; (February), 1971: no. 24; (February), 1968: no. 4.

Estonian-Finnish kinship feelings have become acceptable, and a direct shipline between Tallinn and Helsinki has operated since 1965. It is used mainly by Finns (who come often to Tallinn because of its cheap liquor). Cultural interaction has also become quite frequent. A high-rise hotel has been built in Tallinn by a Finnish company, with Finnish materials and labor, resulting in a number of intermarriages; the brides were allowed to emigrate to Finland.

Interaction with Estonian exiles (mostly in Sweden and North America) has also broadened. With most Estonians having relatives abroad, visits to and from Estonia have become frequent compared to those available to the Russian population, although the process of getting a visitor's visa remains extremely frustrating and often fruitless. Parcels sent by exiles were credited with visibly raising the consumption level in Estonia as far back as the late fifties. In a way, the exiles are a subculture part and parcel of Soviet Estonia in spite of the geographic and political separation. Sometimes their cultural activity induces the Soviets to allow more funds and leeway to Estonian culture at home, and their usually rigid anticommunism has not prevented contacts on human and cultural levels.

Among Soviet nations, contacts are predictably the most intense with the other Baltic republics, and mastering the Russian lingua franca may have facilitated them. Various cultural meetings are becoming so frequent that one might wonder whether a common Baltic cultural community is not in process of formation.[33] Contacts with nations further off are impeded by popular prejudice toward darker-skinned people and a tendency to consider them as Russians. But the cultural elite is consciously trying to overcome this barrier, especially with regard to Georgians and Armenians whose achievements they admire. As the largest, most developed Finnic nation within the Soviet Union, Estonia may represent an example to follow for the five Finnic-language autonomous republics within the RSFSR (Karelia, Komi, Mari, Mordva, Udmurt). Their linguists often defend dissertations in Estonia, and some cultural contacts exist.[34]

Media

LANGUAGE DATA

Estonian belongs to the Finno-Ugric language group and uses the Latin script. Finnish and Estonian are mutually about as intelligible as German and Dutch or French and Spanish, while Hungarian and Volga Finnic languages are unintelligible to an untrained Estonian, as are all Indo-European languages (including Latvian, Russian, and German). The language is characterized by many vowels and few consonants, elaborate declension of nouns and adjectives, rather long agglutinative words, lack of gender and article, and distinction between three different durations of stressed vowels and consonants. Through scholarly "linguistic engineering" during the last 50 years, new word roots and derivatives have been created to keep pace with modern developments; for example, instead of the Russian *lunokhod* [moon vehicle], Soviet Estonian press uses *kuukulgur*.

Estonian is also used by about 100,000 emigrants and exiles in the West, mostly in Sweden (22,000) and North America (40,000). They have newspapers, publishing houses, and organized youth education (including a college-level summer institute in Canada).

LOCAL MEDIA

Soviet Print Media

Of periodicals available for foreign subscription in 1973, 24 are in Estonian, 2 in Russian, and 8 mixed or double edition. Language distribution of local and special interest periodicals is similar. Total number of periodicals is higher than in any union republic except Russia and the Ukraine. Of

---

33 Cf. Vardys, 1970.
34 *Estonian Events* (February), 1971: no. 24:5; *Baltic Events* (June), 1973: no. 3:2.

Table 4.1

Native and Second Languages Spoken by Estonians

(in thousands)

| | Number of Estonians Residing | | SPEAKING AS NATIVE LANGUAGE | | | | | | SPEAKING AS SECOND LANGUAGE[a] | |
| | | | Estonian | | | Russian | | | | Other Languages of Peoples of USSR 1970[b] |
	1959	1970	1959	1970	% Point Change 1959–1970	1959	1970	% Point Change 1959–1970	Russian 1970	
in Estonian SSR	893 (100%)	925 (100%)	887 (99.3%)	918 (99.2%)	−0.1	6 (0.7%)	7 (0.8%)	+0.1	255 (27.6%)	6 (0.6%)
in other Soviet republics	96 (100%)	82 (100%)	54 (56.6%)	44 (53.7%)	−2.9	40 (41.8%)	37 (45.1%)	+3.3	37 (45.1%)	14 (17.1%)
Total	989 (100%)	1,007 (100%)	941 (95.2%)	962 (95.5%)	+0.3	46 (4.7%)	44 (4.4%)	−0.3	292 (29%)	20 (2%)

Sources: *Itogi Estonii, 1959*: tables 53, 54; *Itogi 1970*: IV: 20, 317.

[a] No data are available for 1959, since no questions regarding command of a second language were asked in the 1959 census.

[b] Including Estonian if not the native language.

books published in 1969, 19% were in Russian. (See also Table 4.2.)

Major newspapers (with circulation in 1968):[35] *Rahva Hääl* [*People's Voice*], 150,000; *Noorte Hääl* [*Voice of the Youth*], 115,000; *Sovetskaya Estonia* (in Russian) and *Molodezh Estonii* (in Russian) are typical Soviet 4-page dailies. *Edasi* [*Forward*], 86,000, local daily of the university city of Tartu, more intellectual and controversial, is in demand throughout Estonia although subscriptions are restricted to Tartu. Tallinn's *Õhtuleht* [*Evening Paper*] is popular for its buy-and-sell ads. *Sirp ja Vasar* [*Sickle and Hammer*] is the major cultural weekly (16 pages; circulation 54,000), combining ideological near-orthodoxy with moderate cultural nationalism. There are special weeklies for Estonians abroad (*Kodumaa* [*Homeland*]), teachers (*Nõukogude Õpetaja* [*Soviet Teacher*]), radio and TV news (*Raadioleht* [*Radio Paper*] and *Televisioon*), children (*Säde* [*Spark*], twice weekly), and sports (*Spordileht* [*Sports Paper*], thrice weekly). In 1972 Estonia had 43 newspapers, 28 (i.e., 65%) in Estonian.[36]

Major monthly journals: *Looming* [*Creative Work*] publishes original prose and poetry, a few translations, and cultural-social articles (about 160 pages per issue; circulation 5,000 in 1962, 16,000 in 1972). *Eesti Kommunist/Kommunist Estonii* (80 pages; 15,000 in Estonian, 5,000 in Russian) is relatively liberal compared to other republic party journals, and seems to miss few occasions to commemorate an Estonian Communist killed by Stalin. There are monthlies for nature and ecology (*Eesti Loodus* [*Estonia's Nature*], 37,000 in 1972); sports (*Kehakultuur* [*Body Cultivation*], twice monthly); teenagers (*Noorus* [*Youth*]); health (*N. E. Tervishoid* [*Sov. Est. Health Preservation*], every second month); pedagogy (*Nõukogude Kool* [*Soviet School*]); women (*Nõukogude Naine* [*Soviet Women*]); popular science (*Horisont* [*Horizon*], 50,000); pioneers (*Pioneer*); agriculture (*Sotsialistlik Põllumajandus* [*Socialist Agriculture*], twice monthly); technology (*Tehnika ja Tootmine* [*Technology and Production*], 17,000), small children (*Täheke*

[Starlet], 68,000); and language and literature (*Keel ja Kirjandus* [*Language and Literature*], 3,500).

The ESSR Academy of Sciences publishes five quarterlies including the Union-wide journal of Finno-Ugric studies (*Sovetskoe Finnougrovedeniye*). They use predominantly Russian and have a circulation of 900 each. An 80-page fashion quarterly (*Siluett*) with a 1.50 rubles price tag per issue has a 50,000 circulation in Estonian and 350,000 in Russian, suggesting Union-wide prestige.

A weekly paperback series (*Loomingu Raamatukogu* [*Library of Creative Work*], circulation 15,000 to 25,000) offers an excellent world-wide selection of classics and of current best-sellers.[37] Estonian pre-Soviet literature is available to a fairly large extent: works by social democrat (E. Vilde), liberal (A. H. Tammsaare), and even definitely conservative (K. A. Hindrey) authors, originally published during the independence period or earlier, have been republished. Some exile works (e.g., by M. Under and K. Ristikivi)[38] also have been reprinted. Typical printings of prose fiction are 20,000 to 35,000 copies for new works, and 50,000 copies for some pre-Soviet classics. Poetry and popular science printings range from 6,000 to 12,000 copies. There is a large variety of original and translated children's books, with printings of 30,000 to 60,000 copies.

Soviet Electronic Media[39]

As of 1973, the single TV program seems to be one quarter in Estonian and three quarters in Russian.[40] (Leningrad and central TV can also be seen in Estonia.) There are three parallel radio programs (including 3 hours of stereo daily), with Es-

---

35 *ENE*, 1970:2. No later figures have been found for individual newspapers, except for *Sirp ja Vasar* (55,500 in 1973).

36 J. Käbin, in *Eesti Kommunist* (November), 1972: no. 11: 7–12.

37 Some 1972 translations: E. Segal, *Love Story*; E. O'Neill, *Long Day's Journey into Night*; L. J. Peter and R. Hull, *The Peter Principle*; I. Babel, *Maria*; P. Brook, *The Empty Place*; A. Camus, *Le mythe de Sisphe*.

38 *Books Abroad*, 1973: XLVII: 394.

39 *Rahva Hääl* (February 1, May 6), 1973.

40 In 1973, 1,100 hours of a total 3,500 broadcast on TV will be produced in Estonia. Scanning of programs in *Rahva Hääl* confirms that at least one half of the items are listed as originating in central and Leningrad TV or in central studios like "Lenfilm"; moreover, a few apparently locally produced items bear the label "in Russian."

tonian probably predominating.[41] There are over 300,000 TV sets and nearly 600,000 radio sets (in 1971, 291,000 and 537,000, respectively).[42] Availability of sets per 1,000 population (209 and 386, respectively, in 1971) is highest of all union republics. Locally originating color TV started in January 1973, with 4 hours per day and 800 receivers; 15,000 color sets were planned by the end of 1973.

Foreign Media

An undeterminable number of Western publications reach Estonia through exile letters, mail subscriptions (e.g., sports and science magazines paid for in the West reach subscribers in Estonia fairly regularly), and tourists. Estonian language exile literary publications command high prices on the black market, and exile books and newspapers are available in research libraries but require special permission. Foreign Communist newspapers are available. Of these, Finland's *Kansan Uutiset* is popular because it has the Finnish TV programs.

Finnish TV can be seen (and partly understood) in northern Estonia which seems to be the only part of the Soviet Union where any non-Communist TV is available. Due to self-censorship of Finnish media in matters which might offend the Soviet Union, Soviet Estonian authorities have come to accept this unique window through which neutral Western news reports (such as those on moon walks) reach Estonia directly. The BBC and Voice of America broadcasts (in Estonian and Russian) as well as Radio Liberty broadcasts (in Russian but not in Estonian) have listeners and are occasionally attacked in the press.

In addition to numerous East European films, some Western films are shown (*They Shoot Horses, Don't They?*, in 1973).

EDUCATIONAL INSTITUTIONS

"Estonian is the language spoken at all our schools, except for the few public schools and kindergartens where education

is carried on in Russian," says an English language Soviet Estonian source,[43] and it is largely true, except in regions with concentrated Russian immigration. Estonian children attend Estonian language schools, along with many mixed-marriage children and even some Russians (because of lack of Russian language facilities, and even because of what *Sovetskaya Estonia* has chided as snob appeal). Of Estonia's 757 general schools, 556 (i.e., 73%) use Estonian, 90 use Russian, and 60 are mixed.[44]

The same applies to the six institutions of higher education: Tartu State University (6,300 undergraduate students in 1971), Tallinn Polytechnical Institute (9,100), Estonian Academy of Agriculture (3,600), Tallinn Pedagogical Institute (2,100), Estonian State Art Institute (500), and Tallinn State Conservatory (360).[45] Language breakdown for the most prestigious (Tartu State University, founded in 1632) is the following.[46] In 1960, 89% of the students studied in Estonian language courses. In 1962, 90% of faculty had Estonian names. University press publications in 1958–1962 (over 200 books and course outlines) were 88% in Estonian and 7% in Russian. In 1970, 81% of 6,200 students were Estonian by nationality (compared to 84% in 1933, during Estonia's independence). In all higher education institutions, 82% of students were Estonians in 1960, with Tallinn Polytech probably the most multinational and Pedagogical Institute the most Estonian.

CULTURAL AND SCIENTIFIC INSTITUTIONS

The first Cybernetics Institute in the Soviet Union was founded in 1960 in Tallinn, Estonia.[47] "Estonia was chosen as an experimental republic for creating a general automatized planning and directing system."[48] The first econometric model in the USSR was constructed by Moscow

41 Impression based on program listings in *Rahva Hääl*.
42 *Nar. khoz. 1972*: 681, 690.
43 Reinop, 1967.
44 J. Käbin, in *Eesti Kommunist* (November), 1972: no. 11: 7–12.
45 *ESSR 1971*: 321. Total number of students is quite stable: 21,360 in 1965, 21,980 in 1971.
46 Künnapas, 1965; *Rahva Hääl* (August 21), 1970.
47 Kahk, 1965: 22.
48 Kahk, 1967: 10.

Table 4.2

Publications in Estonian SSR

Language of Publication	Year	NEWSPAPERS[a]			MAGAZINES			BOOKS & BROCHURES		
		No.	Per Issue Circulation (1,000)	Copies/100 in Language Group[e]	No.	Per Issue Circulation (1,000)	Copies/100 in Language Group[e]	No. Titles	Total Volume (1,000)	Books & Brochures/100 in Language Group[e]
Russian	1959	12	69	26.1	N.A.	N.A.	N.A.	179	696	263.6
	1971	7	123	32.9	2	202	54.0	674	2,004	535.7
Estonian	1959	55	518	56.4	N.A.	N.A.	N.A.	933	7,070	770.3
	1971	27	896	96.3	18	535	57.5	1,505	10,615	1,140.6
Minority Languages	1959	0	0	0	N.A.	N.A.	N.A.	5[b]	15	ca. 25
	1971	0	0	0	d	N.A.	N.A.	5[b]	75	146.1
Foreign Languages	1959	0	0	0	N.A.	N.A.	N.A.	(28)[c]	(169)	N.A.
	1971	0	0	0	5[d]	5	N.A.	(182)[c]	(368)	N.A.
All Languages	1959	67	587	43.3	19	222	16.4	1,145[c]	7,950	586.3
	1971	34	1,019	75.1	25	742	54.7	2,366[c]	13,062	963.2

Sources: Pechat' 1971: 97, 160, 189. Pechat' 1959: 58, 130, 165.

[a] 1971 figures do not include kolkhoz newspapers.

[b] This figure may include publication in non-Soviet languages.

[c] Book totals as given in Pechat' usually differ from totals in language categories. The indication is that books are published in other languages, but no data is given. Figures in parentheses are the presumed production of books in other languages based on this discrepancy.

[d] Denoted in source as "other languages of the world," not clearly Soviet or foreign.

[e] Includes all native speakers of the language.

Table 4.3

Electronic Media and Films in Estonian SSR

YEAR	RADIO					TELEVISION			MOVIES	
	Stations	Wired Sets (1,000)	/100 Population	Wireless Sets (1,000)	/100 Population	All Stations	Sets (1,000)	/100 Population	Seats (1,000)	/100 Population
1960	N.A.	81[a]	6.8[d]	272[a]	22.3[c]	N.A.	38[a]	3.1[c]	41[b]	3.4[d]
1970	N.A.	96[a]	6.9[d]	505[a]	36.8[c]	N.A.	277[a]	20.2[c]	79[b]	5.7[d]
1971	N.A.	99[d]	7.1[d]	536[d]	38.6[c]	N.A.	291[c]	20.9[c]	N.A.	N.A.

[a] *Transport i svyaz' SSR*, 1972: 296–298.
[b] *Nar. obraz.*, 1971: 325.
[c] *Nar. khoz.* 1972: 684, 690.
[d] Computed.

Table 4.4

Selected Data on Education in Estonian SSR

(1971)

		PER 1,000 POPULATION	% OF TOTAL
All schools			
number of schools	766	0.55	
number of students	212,000	152	
Newly opened elementary, incomplete secondary, and secondary schools			
number of schools	5	4	
number of student places	5,800		
Secondary special schools			
number of schools	37		
number of students	23,600	17.0	
Institutions of higher education			
number of institutions	6		
number of students	22,000	15.8	
Universities			
number of universities	1		
number of students			
total	6,297	4.5	
day students	4,322	3.1	68.6
evening students	0		
correspondence students	1,975	1.4	31.4
newly admitted			
total	1,391	1.0	
day students	1,007	0.7	72.4
evening students	0		
correspondence students	384	0.28	27.6
graduated			
total	859	0.6	
day students	668	0.48	77.8
evening students	0		
correspondence students	191	0.14	22.2
Graduate students			
total	536	0.39	
in scientific research institutions	246	0.18	
in universities	290	0.21	
Number of persons (in 1970) with higher or secondary (complete and incomplete) education			
per 1,000 individuals, 10 years and older	506		
per 1,000 individuals employed in national economy	660		
Number of workers graduated from professional-technical schools	5,000		

Source: *Nar. khoz. 1972: 108, 439, 681, 688, 689, 691.* January 1972 population for Estonia was 1,391,100 (*Ibid.*: 10).

economists for Estonia and reduced to manageable size by Estonian economists.[49] Computerized bookkeeping is being tested in Estonia for future Union-wide use.

Other Soviet "firsts" in Estonia include eradication of polio (1958), introduction of money wages for farm workers, and switching to *sovkhoz* self-management.

Of the researchers at the Cybernetics Institute, 90% are Estonians, including the institute head.[50] About 75% of paper authors in the physics-math journal of the ESSR Academy of Sciences in 1969 had Estonian names. Regarding the relative

number of scientific workers, Estonians (with 0.30% of the population) are about on a par with Russians, and are markedly surpassed in the USSR only by Georgians and Armenians.[51] Of all science workers active in Estonia, 84% are Estonians and 11% are Russians. Medical and agricultural research is almost completely in Estonian hands and so are the well-developed folklore and language studies. (The Institute of Language and Literature has a staff of 100.)[52] In social science and humanities, Russians occupy a number of key ideological positions.

Table 4.5

Selected Data on Scientific and Cultural Facilities and Personnel in Estonian SSR

(1971)

Academy of Sciences			
number of members	38	*Number of Persons Working*	
number of scientific institutions		*in Education and Culture*	
affiliated with academy	15	total	47,000
total number of scientific workers	811	number/1,000 population	33.8
Museums		*Number of Persons Working in Science*	
		and Scientific Services	
number of museums	44	total	18,000
attendance	995,000	number/1,000 population	13
attendance/1,000 population	715		
		Number of Public Libraries	816
Theaters		number of books and magazines	
number of theaters	9	in public libraries	9,158,000
attendance	1,252,000		
attendance/1,000 population	900	*Number of Clubs*	515

Source: *Nar. khoz. 1972*: 106, 451, 601.
    January 1972 population for Estonia was 1,391,000 (*Ibid.*: 10).

National Attitudes

REVIEW OF FACTORS FORMING
NATIONAL ATTITUDES

A basic factor for the Estonian nation is its language, which sets it apart from all neighbors except Finns, making gradual fusion (or expansion) difficult. Additional

factors are its semipeninsular location, and a power shift from Germans to Russians precisely at a time when assimilation to Germans was starting on a somewhat larger scale. Assimilation to Russians has been made especially difficult by differences in script and traditional religion, coupled with

49 *Eesti Kommunist* (August), 1969: no. 8: 24–29.
50 From list in Aben, 1970.

51 Kahk, 1965.
52 Ahven, 1970.

a feeling of superiority that every European nation seems to have toward its eastern neighbor. (The complementary feeling of cultural inferiority toward the western neighbor is also manifested by some Russians toward Estonians.)

The short period of independence helped Estonia to leapfrog German influence and make direct contact with Western Europe, demonstrating that they could manage without German or Russian tutelage. The generation is gone who had to still persuade themselves that they were "just as smart as any other people." The present-day Estonian takes this for granted, as he takes for granted being Estonian.

Attitudes toward Soviet rule are affected by various conflicting considerations. Advent of Soviet rule did away with independent statehood, rather than continuing tsarist Russian rule or taking over from the Germans or other foreigners. It is known in Estonia that an exile government exists and that the United States does not recognize annexation by the Soviet Union. But Soviet power is uncontested in Estonia. The influx of immigrants and foreign control are resented. Joining the Communist party was considered treason by many until 1956; since then feelings have been mixed. High average age and low number of 15- to 25-year-olds makes for caution rather than bravado. Even people who dislike the regime do not always enjoy the prospect of turbulent change.

BASIC VIEWS OF SCHOLARS ON NATIONAL ATTITUDES

The only known attempt at even a half-systematic inquiry of Estonian attitudes was carried out by a Swedish journalist of Estonian origin, A. Küng.[53] On a visit, he asked all Estonians he met: "What are the three best and three worst things about present-day Estonia?" While the inquiry lacked (and, given the conditions in the USSR, had to lack) the rigor normally demanded of opinion polls, his report is of interest because it is the only one available. On the positive side, nearly all respondents first

mentioned a vigorous educational and cultural development. Also frequently mentioned were improvements of rural living standards and industrial development. On the negative side, Russification came first. Also mentioned were shortage and poor quality of consumer goods and lack of freedom to travel abroad and to criticize power holders.

The subtitle of Küng's book is "A Study in Imperialism." This is the diagnosis of the situation in Soviet Estonia by an author who earlier criticized Swedish policies toward the Lapps, investigated the oppressed ethnic minorities world wide, and is openly critical of both the U.S. intervention in Vietnam and the "cold warriors" among Estonian exiles. He views Estonia as annexed to the Soviet Union against its will, exploited (although still wealthier than the exploiter), bossed around, threatened by slow genocide through foreign-imposed immigration, resigned exteriorly, and resentful deep inside. Similar views are presented by Uustalu[54] and most Western scholars.

Soviet views on Estonia are presented authoritatively in the *Soviet Estonian Encyclopedia*.[55] It is important to point out differences between these 1970 views and earlier ones. The Stalinist assertion of early medieval friendship and cooperation with Russians (under Russian leadership) has been reduced to the level existing in prewar "bourgeois" history.[56] The Russian conquest of Estonia in 1710 is no longer presented as an unmitigated boon to the Estonian people. While still calling the 1934–1937 dictatorship "Fascist," it is acknowledged that it "differed fundamentally from the German variety," and the term "dictatorship" is not extended to the post-1938 period. In June 1940 "bourgeois Estonia was forced to consent to the arrival of further Soviet army units, but President K. Päts temporized with forming a new government. Under such conditions the socialist revolution started." It is recognized that during the 1949 collectivization of agriculture the wealthier farmers "were dispersed and resettled in the interior regions of the USSR," and that "grave errors" were committed in the course

---

53 Küng, 1971.

54 Uustalu, 1970.
55 *ENE*, 1970: 2.
56 Kruus, 1935.

of the 1950 antinationalist campaign. The rapid economic and cultural development after 1956 is stressed.

Consensus between Western (almost entirely exile stock) and Soviet scholars on interpretation of Estonia's past and present has increased since the 1950s. Western scholars recognize the post-Stalin cultural and economic progress and have come to accept that 1934–1937 was indeed a dictatorial period, that industry suffered under independence, and that Swedish rule of the seventeenth century was not a golden age compared to the following Russian tsarist rule.[57] Increasingly, Soviet scholars are recognizing that Russian-dominated periods in history were not best for Estonians, that the independence period saw intensive cultural development, that the Soviet army was in Estonia during the 1940 "revolution," that Stalinist period was culturally an "historical gap," and that industrialization can be overdone from the ecological viewpoint. Strong disagreement persists regarding three issues: whether the July 1940 election results (93% for the Communist front) were blatantly falsified (there is agreement that no other parties were allowed to run); to what extent the population presently accepts communism and/or Moscow-centered rule; and whether Russian immigration represents a threat to the Estonian nation. There is little difference in degree of cultural nationalism between the Soviet Estonian cultural establishment and the exiles.

RECENT MANIFESTATIONS OF NATIONALISM[58]

Estonian cultural nationalism has become widely accepted by the regime (in contrast to Stalin's days). Demands to recognize dead and exile non-Communist writers culminated in 1968 and were largely successful.[59] Demands for purity of language from Russian loan words have been addressed by *Eesti Kommunist* (February 1970: 76) to party propagandists. Around 1968 demands

were made that music and art *must* be "national" (folklore-inspired) but such extremes have decreased since. The mammoth song festivals (attendance in 1969 was 250,000, one quarter of the Estonians) are a prime example of a cultural safety valve for nationalism: traditional Estonian songs predominate; visiting Finnish choruses get large ovations and Russian ones little; demonstratively, the public and choruses repeat a certain patriotic song after the close of the official program.[60]

Poems were published in 1967–1968 demanding less bossing by "Aunt Masha," attacking the language fusion doctrine, and declaring the precedence of nationality over ideology. But lately the tone has been subdued.

Economic nationalism is almost forced upon local officials by the excessive centralization. Often it is more localism than nationalism, indistinguishable from similar home rule demands made in Siberia and even in the Moscow *oblast*. Occasionally, the Soviet Estonian establishment has objected to immigration, and the desire to avoid problems on the home front has made First Secretary Käbin effectively shelter moderate nationalism from Moscow suspicions. Cooperation with other Baltic republics in culture and economics has increased beyond what was allowed in the 1950s, an expression of internationalism not adverse to nationalism.

Non-Nationalist Dissent

Estonia has been the focus of Union-wide quests for civil rights, which are not nationalist except to the extent that civil rights include national rights. In 1969 a "Union of Fighters for Political Freedom" led by navy officers was crushed in Tallinn. A quarter of the 31 people arrested were Estonians.[61] A widely circulated "Program of the Democratic Movement" could have been the work of the same group; it shows signs of non-Russian and probably Baltic authorship.[62]

---

57 Loit, 1971.
58 Taagepera, 1970; 1973.
59 There is no basic contrast between treatments in Nirk, 1970 (Soviet) and Mägi, 1968 (exile).

60 *Estonian Events* (August), 1969: no. 15:3.
61 *Khronika*, 1969:9; *New York Times* (October 24), 1969: 1.
62 *Khronika*, 1969:10; *Radio Liberty Dispatch* (May 20), 1970.

An earlier (1968) anonymous memo by "numerous members of the ESSR technological intelligentsia" also soft-pedaled the national issue and concentrated on all-Union problems of civil rights and rapprochement with the West.[63] Residents of Estonia have been arrested for sympathizing with Solzhenitsyn[64] and for protesting against the invasion of Czechoslovakia.[65] At a party organization meeting called to endorse the invasion, Tartu State University Communists refused to do so and a faculty member blurted out: "In the house of the hanged man one does not speak of rope." (He received a light reprimand because of his previous good record and the general atmosphere of the moment.)[66]

Hippy behavior (including wearing of crosses)[67] and New Leftist manifestations[68] are other forms of non-national protest, as is a poet publishing his esoteric verses in Sweden when he could not do it in Estonia.[69] Publishing of Jewish authors, shunned in the USSR and immediately after an anti-Jewish campaign,[70] has the same connotations. Consumer protest against shortage of goods is quite differently motivated, but quickly becomes anti-Russian when the shortage is seen as due to export to Russia or excessive purchasing by Russian tourists.[71] The sorest spot is the housing shortage, widely viewed as caused or worsened by preferential treatment given to Russian immigrants.

National Dissent

Even high Soviet Estonian officials are liable to crack jokes making fun of Russians and their alleged lack of culture.[72] In streetcars and other public places, according to numerous visitors, Russians are "routinely" cursed with decreasing concern for consequences. Students have repeatedly carried unorthodox slogans and chanted nationalist songs during officially organized demonstrations.[73] After the Czechs won a televised Soviet-Czech ice hockey match on April 20, 1972, several hundred Tallinn Polytech students shouted "We won!" and took to the streets.[74] Some were arrested and many more expelled. There are still flowers on the grave of Kuperjanov, a 1919 independence war hero who died fighting the Bolsheviks, although he has no relatives left.[75] The prevalent mood of Soviet Estonians the author has met is well expressed by a U.S. press quote: "If we were just left alone, we could do better." [76] The only exception argued that leaving the Soviet Union would cost Estonian scientists research grants. Many, however, are disturbed by the thought of a violent change of regime. Behind the friction between technocrats and intellectuals lurks a deeper cleavage: there are those who were deported around 1949 and those who helped to deport them. While obviously the latter have a vested interest in the regime's survival, the specter of potential white terror scares wider circles.[77] National communism aiming at a separate but Communist Estonian state seems a pre-

---

63 *Münchner Merkur*, 1968:306; *Frankfurter Allgemeine Zeitung* (December 18), 1968.

64 *Khronika*, 1971: 18.

65 *Frankfurter Allgemeine Zeitung* (October 9), 1968.

66 Private communication, directly checked by author with people attending the meeting.

67 Described in the poem "Ristilugu" ["The Cross Story"] by A. Siig, 1971—text and translation in *Estonian Events* (April), 1972: 31.

68 Taagepera, 1971.

69 *Estonian Events* (December), 1969: no. 17: 3.

70 *Estonian Events* (April), 1972 no. 31: 1; (August/October), 1972: nos. 21–22: 1.

71 This feeling is reflected in many private letters. Tourists interested only in shoes, sausages, and textiles are also scored in a Lithuanian short piece (by V. Žilinskaite) reproduced in *Sirp ja Vasar* (September 3), 1971. In a story by V. Ilus, *Looming* (November), 1968: XI: 1,656–1,664), the main motive of a Russian moving from Moscow *oblast* to Estonia is that "they have all sorts of sausages in the store. But we had only one type."

72 Personal observation. Sample: The Czechs wanted to create a ministry for maritime affairs. When reminded that their country is landlocked, they replied: "So what? After all, Russia does have a ministry for cultural affairs."

73 Sample slogans and ditties: "Yankees, Go Behind the Peipsi!" [i.e., into Russia]; "Out, out of this republic, you who eat Estonia's bread but do not speak Estonian language!" *Estonian Events* (October), 1969: no. 16: 2; (August), 1971: no. 27: 1.

74 For details see *Estonian Events* (December), 1972: 2.

75 Private communication by an eyewitness.

76 *Christian Science Monitor* (September 17), 1969.

77 Mati Unt, a young rather unorthodox Soviet Estonian writer, describes how a drunken "patriot" declares Unt personally responsible for, and fit to be executed because of, everything that has happened under Soviet rule, even while Unt was a small child (M. Unt, "Tühirand: Love Story," *Looming* [May], 1972: no. 5: 707).

ferable solution to some, besides seeming more realizable. Recent open attacks[78]

[78] A. Vader, *Eesti Kommunist* (May), 1972: no. 5: 3–12; A. Lebbin, *Eesti Kommunist* (May), 1971: no. 5: 37–47; translations of relevant passages in *Estonian Events* (August), 1972: no. 33: 6; (August), 1961: no. 27: 4. Three independent private communications agree the issue was discussed at a writers' party meeting around 1967, with some writers coming out in favor of the people's democracy proposal.

against the idea of an Estonian People's Democracy suggest that it is spreading. An underground democratic "Estonian National Front" has also been reported.[79] It demands a referendum on self-determination and in May 1972 published a voluminous first issue of an underground journal, "Eesti Demokraat."

[79] *Khronika*, 1972: 25.

REFERENCES

Aben, 1970
H. Aben, *1960–1970 ENSV TA Küberneetika Instituut* (Tallinn: ESSR Academy of Sciences, 1970).

Ahven, 1970
E. Ahven, *Institute of Language and Literature* (Tallinn: ESSR Academy of Sciences, 1970).

Baltic Review
Baltic Review, irregular (New York: Committees for Liberation of Estonia, Latvia, Lithuania); 38 issues from 1953 to 1971.

Books Abroad
Books Abroad: An International Literary Quarterly (U. of Oklahoma). Reviews regularly books in Estonian and several other USSR languages.

Bush, 1970
K. Bush, *Radio Liberty Dispatch*, April 1, 1970 (on incomes).

ENE, 1970
Eesti Nõukogude Entsüklopeedia [*Estonian Soviet Encyclopedia*] (Tallinn, 1970): II.

ESSR 1971
Narodnoye khozyaistvo Estonskoi SSR v 1971 godu (Tallinn: Statistika, 1972).

Estonian Events
Estonian Events, bimonthly newsletter edited by R. Taagepera (Irvine: University of California, 1967–1972). Title from 1973 on: *Baltic Events*.

Geography, 1964, 1971
Tartu State University, *Publications on Geography*; vols. IV (1964) and VII (1971) are in English.

Grabbi, 1969
H. Grabbi, "The Soviet Estonian Intellectual Scene in the Sixties," in Ivask, 1969: 73–74.

Hooson, 1966
D. Hooson, *The Soviet Union: Peoples and Regions* (London: University of London Press, 1966).

Horisont, 1968
Horisont, monthly, Tallinn: No. 4 (1968) focuses on demography.

Ilves, 1967
V. Ilves, *Soviet Estonian Film Art* (Series "10 Aspects of Estonian Life") (Tallinn: Eesti Raamat, 1967).

Itogi 1970
Itogi vsesoyuznoi perepisi naseleniya 1970 goda, vol. IV (Moscow: Statistika, 1973).

Itogi Estonii, 1959
Itogi vsesoyuznoi perepisi naseleniya 1959 goda: Estonskaya SSR (Moscow: Statistika, 1960).

Ivask, 1968
I. Ivask, "Recent Trends in Estonian Poetry," *Books Abroad* (Autumn 1968): XLII: 517–520.

Ivask, 1969
I. Ivask, ed., *First Conference on Baltic Studies: Summary of Proceedings* (Tacoma, Washington: Association for Advancement of Baltic Studies, 1969).

Järvesoo, 1969
E. Järvesoo, "Estonian Economy Since 1944: Policies, Structural Change and Standard of Living," in Ivask, 1969: 93–95.

Järvesoo, 1973
E. Järvesoo, "Progress Despite Collectivization: Agriculture in Estonia," in Ziedonis et al., 1973.

Jeret, 1967
Ü. Jeret, *Industry and Building in Soviet Estonia* (Series "10 Aspects of Estonian Life") (Tallinn: Eesti Raamat, 1967).

Journal of Baltic Studies

Journal of Baltic Studies, quarterly (New York: Association for Advancement of Baltic Studies, since 1970). (Up to 1971: *Bulletin of Baltic Studies*.)

Kahk, 1965
J. Kahk, ed., *Nõukogude Eesti teadus* (Tallinn: Eesti Raamat, 1965).

Kahk, 1967
J. Kahk, *Soviet Estonian Science* (Series "10 Aspects of Estonian Life") (Tallinn: Eesti Raamat, 1967).

Kartna, 1967
A. Kartna, *Soviet Estonian Art* (Series "10 Aspects of Estonian Life") (Tallinn: Eesti Raamat, 1967).

Khronika
Khronika tekushchikh sobytii [*Chronicle of Current Events*], underground bimonthly, Moscow.

Kodumaa, 1972
Kodumaa Publishers, *Estonia* (Tallinn, 1972).

Kõressaar and Rannit, 1965
V. Kõressaar and A. Rannit, eds., *Estonian Poetry and Language* (Stockholm: Publishing House Kirjastus Vaba Eesti, 1965).

Kruus, 1935
Hans Kruus, *Histoire de l'Estonie* (Paris: Payot, 1935).

Küng, 1971
A. Küng, *Estland: en studie i imperialism* (Stockholm: Aldus, 1971). An English translation exists in manuscript form.

Künnapas, 1965
T. Künnapas, "Tartu Riiklik Ülikool," in R. Taagepera, ed., *Eesti Uliõpilaste Seltsi Album XIV* (New York: Estonian Student Association EUS, 1965): 61–77.

Lipping, 1971
I. Lipping, "The Coup of December 1, 1924, in Estonia," in Šilbajoris et al., 1971: 60.

Loit, 1971
A. Loit, "The Good Old Swedish Times—Myth or Reality?", in Šilbajoris et al., 1971: 80–81.

Loogus, 1967
P. Loogus, *Social Security in Soviet Estonia* (Series "10 Aspects of Estonian Life") (Tallinn: Eesti Raamat, 1967).

Mägi, 1968
A. Mägi, *Estonian Literature* (Stockholm: Baltic Humanitarian Association, 1968).

Mets, 1967
E. Mets, *Soviet Estonian Agriculture* (Series "10 Aspects of Estonian Life") (Tallinn: Eesti Raamat, 1967).

Nar. khoz. 1972
Narodnoye khozyaistvo SSSR 1922–1972, Yubileinyi statisticheskii Yezhegodnik (Moscow: Statistika, 1972).

Nar. obraz., 1971
Narodnoye obrazovaniye, nauka i kul'tura v SSSR: statisticheskii sbornik (Moscow: Statistika, 1971).

Nirk, 1970
E. Nirk, *Estonian Literature* (Tallinn: Eesti Raamat, 1970).

Nodel, 1971
E. Nodel, "Strategy and Tactics of the Estonian Communist Party: 1917–1939," in Šilbajoris et al., 1971: 63–64.

Normet and Vahter, 1967
L. Normet and A. Vahter, *Soviet Estonian Music* (Series "10 Aspects of Estonian Life") (Tallinn: Eesti Raamat, 1967).

Olt, 1972
H. Olt, *Modern Estonian Composers* (Tallinn: Kodumaa, 1972).

Parming, 1972
T. Parming, "Population Changes in Estonia, 1935–1970," *Population Studies* (1972): XXVI: 53–78.

Pechat' 1959
Pechat' SSSR v 1959 godu (Moscow: Kniga, 1960).

Pechat' 1970
Pechat' SSSR v 1970 godu (Moscow: Kniga, 1971).

Peep, 1967
H. Peep, *Soviet Estonian Literature* (Series "10 Aspects of Estonian Life") (Tallinn: Eesti Raamat, 1967).

Pennar, 1968
Jaan Pennar, "Nationalism in the Soviet Baltics," in E. Goldhagen, ed., *Ethnic Minorities in the Soviet Union* (New York: Praeger, 1968): 198–217.

Raun, 1971
T. Ü. Raun, "Estonia and the Nationalities Problem in 1905," in Šilbajoris et al., 1971: 52.

Rei, 1970
August Rei, *The Drama of the Baltic Peoples* (Stockholm: Kirjastus Vaba Eesti, 1970).

Reinop, 1967
H. Reinop, *Education in Soviet Estonia* (Series "10 Aspects of Estonian Life") (Tallinn: Eesti Raamat, 1967).

Šilbajoris et al., 1971
R. Šilbajoris, A. Ziedonis, E. Anderson, eds., *Second Conference on Baltic Studies: Summary of Proceedings* (Norman, Okla.: Association for Advancement of Baltic Studies, 1971).

Soviet Literature, 1972
Soviet Literature (Moscow), August 1972 issue focuses on Estonia.

Taagepera, 1968
Rein Taagepera, "National Differences Within Soviet Demographic Trends," *Soviet Studies* (1968): XX: 478–489.

Taagepera, 1970
Rein Taagepera, "Nationalism in the Estonian Communist Party," *Bulletin* (Munich: Institute for Study of USSR, January 1970): no. 1: 3–15.

Taagepera, 1971
Rein Taagepera, "The Impact of the New Left on Estonia," in Šilbajoris et al., 1971: 53.

Taagepera, 1972
Rein Taagepera, "The Problem of Political Collaboration in Soviet Estonian Literature," paper presented at Conference on Baltic Literatures, Ohio State University, October 28–29, 1972.

Taagepera, 1973
Rein Taagepera, "Dissimilarities Between the Northwestern Soviet Republics," in Ziedonis et al., 1973.

Tauli, 1965
V. Tauli, "Johannes Aavik's Language Reform 1912–1962," in Kõressaar and Rannit, 1965.

Terentjeva, 1970
L. Terentjeva, "How Do Youths from Binational Families Determine Their Nationality?" *Zinatne un tehnika* (Riga) (August 1970): no. 8: 10–12. Translated in *Bulletin of Baltic Studies* (December 1970): no. 4, 5–11.

Uustalu, 1952
E. Uustalu, *History of the Estonian People* (London: Boreas, 1952).

Valgemäe, 1969
M. Valgemäe, "Recent Developments in Soviet Estonian Drama," *Bulletin* (Munich: Institute for Study of USSR, September 1969): IX: 16–23.

Valgemäe, 1972
M. Valgemäe, "Death of a Sea Gull: The Absurd in Finno-Baltic Drama," *Books Abroad*, 1972: XLVI: 374.

Valter, 1967
M. Valter, *Soviet Estonian Drama* (Series "10 Aspects of Estonian Life") (Tallinn: Eesti Raamat, 1967).

Vardys, 1970
V. S. Vardys, "The Role of the Baltic Republics in the Soviet Union," paper prepared for Conference on Influence of East Europe and Western Territories of USSR on Soviet Society, University of Michigan Center for East European Studies, 1970.

Wagener, 1971
H. J. Wagener, "Regional Output Levels in the Soviet Union," *Radio Liberty Research Paper*, 1971: 41.

Ziedonis et al., 1973
A. Ziedonis, R. Taagepera, M. Valgemäe, eds., *Problems of Mininations: Baltic Perspectives* (New York: Association for Advancement of Baltic Studies, 1973).

5 | LATVIA and THE LATVIANS

Frederic T. Harned

General Information

TERRITORY

The Latvian SSR is one of the youngest union republics of the USSR. It was incorporated into the Union, together with its neighbors, Estonia and Lithuania, in early August 1940. In the struggle for control of important Baltic trade routes, all major nations of Northern Europe have at some time attacked and conquered parts of that sea's eastern shore; Latvia and its capital Riga occupy the central position of the Baltic coast. Riga was founded by the German Teutonic Order in 1201 A.D.[1] For the past 800 years the Latvians have been less participants than prizes of war. Although at times they have fought ably, there have always been too few of them to stem the tide of conquest. Only in 1918, amid the chaos of the Russian Civil War, were the Latvians able to found their own independent state. They were able to maintain it for only twenty years.

Located between 55°40′ and 58°5′ north latitude,[2] the territory of the Latvian SSR coincides with that of the independent Republic of Latvia, with the exception of an area of 464 square miles on the northeastern border annexed to the RSFSR in 1945, and of cessions to the RSFSR and Estonia, totaling about 308 square miles, made between 1953 and 1957.[3] Its total area of 24,595 square miles, slightly smaller than Ireland, makes it the fourth smallest union republic. The 1,171-mile-long border of Latvia touches upon Estonia, the RSFSR, Belorussia, and Lithuania, and includes 307 miles of seacoast along the Baltic and the Gulf of Riga.[4]

Latvia's climate is relatively mild and moist, reflecting the influence of the Baltic Sea and the Atlantic Ocean. Its growing season extends roughly between April 15 and October 15, averaging 183 days per

---

1 Spekke, 1951: 135.

2 Rutkis, 1967: 14.
3 King, 1965: 10; *BSE*, 1953: XXIV: 318; *Yezhegodnik, 1957*: 147.
4 Rutkis, 1967: 155

94

year.[5] Annual rainfall averages 21.6 to 31.5 inches in different parts of the country.[6] The large majority of the land is a gentle rolling plain. Uplands, with a maximum elevation of 1,017 feet, are located in the east-central part and in the west.[7] Sixty% of the territory is used for agriculture, and 27% is in forests.[8] Latvia is rich in lakes and rivers. Chief among the latter are the Daugava (222 miles in Latvia; known in Belorussia as the Western Dvina), the Gauja, the Lielupe, and the Venta. The republic is, however, poorly supplied with mineral deposits. Primary mining products are sand and sandstone, gypsum, dolomite, limestone and clay.[9]

ECONOMY

Latvia entered a period of swift industrial growth and economic development in the second half of the nineteenth century when it was part of tsarist Russia. The Baltic coast soon became one of the most developed parts of the empire and was the only area achieving general literacy by 1897.[10] The port of Riga carried a significant portion of Russia's European trade. This tie, together with the German baronial class' influence and Latvia's trade partnership with Europe between the two world wars, has left a lasting Western imprint on the population. Economic growth was seriously impaired by World War I. Much of Latvia's industrial plant was destroyed or evacuated to Russia. The loss of its source of raw materials and of its markets, due to subsequent separation from the Soviet Union and the latter's autarchic policies, led the Latvian government to concentrate on development of the country as a source of high-quality agricultural products for the urban Western markets (on the model of Denmark). Since 1940 the Soviet government has concentrated on redeveloping the republic's industrial significance, due in part to its relatively skilled labor force, well-developed rail and

highway network, and proximity to major population centers.[11]

Nearly 38% of the Latvian labor force is employed in industry, making it the most heavily industrialized Soviet Union republic.[12] Key branches of industry are machine building and metalworking, which employed 33% of the industrial labor force in 1971. Light industry employed 23%, the lumber, cellulose, and paper industries, 13%, and the food industry, 13%.[13] With less than 1% of the USSR population, Latvia produces over half of the motorcycles, almost half of the telephones, one third of the trolley cars, more than one fourth of the railroad passenger cars, about one fourth of the radios and radio-phonographs, 19% of the refrigeration plants, 12% of the washing machines, and 4.3% of the agricultural machines made in the USSR.[14]

Traditionally, the Latvian peasant has lived on his own farmstead, with house located in the middle of his fields, rather than in a village, as was the pattern in central and southern Russia. When collectivization on the Russian model was forcibly accomplished between 1947 and 1950, losses and disruption were very great.[15] Thousands of "kulaks" were deported to Siberia. Grain production in 1950 was roughly half of what it had been in 1940. Meat production was down 35%; milk, 40%.[16]

Approximately 20% of the working population is employed in agriculture.[17] This

---

5 Rutkis, 1967: 109.
6 LME, 1969: II: 280.
7 Rutkis, 1967: 109.
8 King, 1965: 11, 13.
9 Rutkis, 1967: 23–24.
10 Soviet Union, 1969: 278.

11 Maciuka, 1972: 19–20. In 1938 approximately 6% of the Latvian population was employed in industry, including 1% in metalworking, vs. 17% and 5%, respectively, in 1966. Percentages computed from King (1965: 44), on the basis of 1935 population (Rutkis, 1967: 292), and from LME (II: 282) and LTS (1968: 307), on the basis of 1966 population (Rutkis, 1967: 296). King (1965: 69) notes that in 1950 production of the machine-building and metalworking industry was already 1,157% of that for 1940.
12 Nar. khoz. Latvii 1971: 38.
13 Ibid.: 76.
14 Nar. khoz. 1970: 70–79. Nar. khoz. Latvii 1971: 34–35.
15 Rutkis, 1967: 344–356. Isolated farmhouses have not disappeared, although authorities have continually pushed for resettlement of farmers into villages.
16 Widmer, 1969: 392–393.
17 Nar. khoz. Latvii 1971: 264–265.

includes 163,000 collective farmers and 14,000 workers and employees occupied primarily in *sovkhoz* work. As during the period of independence, animal husbandry remains the most important branch of agriculture. In 1970, 77% of the monetary income of Latvian *kolkhozy* was obtained from sale of animals and animal products (i.e., milk and eggs).[18] Cattle and hogs are the basic types of livestock. Crops include rye, barley, oats, wheat, flax, sugarbeets, potatoes, and fodder grasses.[19]

The Latvian ports of Riga, Ventspils [Vindau], and Liepaja [Libau] handle more than 40% of the Soviet foreign trade that travels via the Baltic. Riga's share in Baltic shipping is second only to that of Leningrad.[20] Winter routes can usually be maintained in Riga with the help of ice breakers, however, and the ports of Liepaja and Ventspils are essentially ice-free.[21]

In both level of productivity and standard of living, Latvia is among the leading Soviet republics. In 1970 per capita produced national income was 1,574 rubles, second only to Estonia and one third higher than the corresponding figure for the USSR as a whole.[22] The diet of the average Latvian includes considerably more protein and less cereal than that of the average Soviet citizen.

Of 15 union republics, Latvia ranks first in amount of useful living space for urban residents, first in hospital beds per 10,000 residents, second in doctors per 10,000[23] (at 36.2, one of the highest ratios in the world), first in number of radios, TVs, and radio loudspeakers per capita,[24] second in per capita trade turnover and proportion of population having a savings account, and fourth in sum of money saved per capita.[25] The consistently high showing in these indices demonstrates that in a general sense Latvia and its neighbor Estonia are among the most developed and economically favored parts of the Soviet Union.

HISTORY

Baltic tribes entered the territory of modern Latvia sometime during the last two millennia B.C. Over the centuries they pushed out or absorbed indigenous Finno-Ugric tribes of Estonians and Livs. The Latvian tribes of Sels, Latgallians, Semigallians, and Cours developed agriculture and metals, traded with the Romans in amber, and gained a reputation as sea pirates. By the latter part of the first millennium A.D., they had developed a system of fortresses to protect their lands from constant incursions by Vikings and Slavs. Eastern portions of the country may have been under tribute to Novogorod and Pskov at various times, but at others—as in a major battle between the Semigallians and the Princes of Polotsk in 1106—the Balts repulsed the Slavs.[26]

At the turn of the thirteenth century a new threat proved too much for the Latvian tribes. German ecclesiastics followed their merchants into the area. Bishop Albert founded the city of Riga in 1201 and the Order of the Brethren of the Sword the following year, which began to bring the Latvians the way of the cross in a very literal sense. The Semigallians and Cours fought back fiercely. In 1236 they united with Lithuanian forces to defeat the Order at the Battle of Saule [Siauliai].[27] The Germans

---

18 *LTS*, 1970: 220.

19 *Ibid.*: 171; *LME*: II: 284.

20 Rutkis, 1967: 473.

21 King, 1965: 17.

22 *Nar. khoz. Latvii 1971*: 56. Soviet calculation of national incomes excludes services and is thus not really comparable to Western figures. See R. Campbell et al., "Methodological Problems Comparing the US and the USSR Economies," in *Soviet Economic Prospects for the Seventies* (Washington, D.C.: Government Printing Office, 1973): 122–146.

23 *Nar. khoz. 1970*: 561; *LTS*, 1968: 350.

24 Latvia had a considerable number of radio receivers during the period of independence. The proportion of wave receivers (allowing a choice of channels) to loudspeakers (wire transmissions, no choice of channels) in the Baltic republics was roughly double that for the USSR as a whole as late as 1959 (F. Gayle Durham, *Radio and Television in the Soviet Union*, Research Program on Problems of International Communication and Security, Center for International Studies, M.I.T., 1965: 96), and is still significantly higher than the all-Union average. *Nar. khoz. Latvii*: 1972: 240.

25 *Nar. khoz. 1970*: 546, 563–564, 579; *Soviet Union*, 1969: 312–340. Figures for hospital beds are for 1966; others for 1970 and 1971.

26 *Latvia*, 1968: 15; Spekke, 1951: 112; Rutkis, 1967: 6; *Istoriya LSSR*, 1955: 30–32.

27 *Istoriya LSSR*, 1955: 35–36. Even Stalinist history does not claim Russian participation in the battle, although it does claim that the defenders were "inspired" by a Russian victory at Yuriev (Tartu) two years earlier.

reorganized into the Livonian Order of Teutonic Knights, which continued the struggle until the conquest of Latvia was completed in 1290. A decentralized state, the Livonian Confederation, was organized, and the Latvians were reduced to peasants and bound to the land in an early form of serfdom. The land-owning and governing class of German barons, created during this time, survived the later Polish, Swedish, and Russian conquests and remained in power until the Revolution of 1917–1918.

The Livonian Confederation endured internal dissension, peasant revolts, and incursions of the growing Russian and Polish-Lithuanian states until 1561 when, weakened by strife growing out of the Reformation (Lutheranism was especially active in the towns of Riga and Reval [Tallinn]) and the long Livonian war of Ivan IV, it was dissolved. Lithuania-Poland occupied eastern Latvia and defended it against the Russians. The Duchy of Courland was organized in the west; it recognized the suzerainty of the Polish crown but was in fact virtually autonomous.[28]

Throughout the sixteenth and seventeenth centuries, Latvia was exposed to the intellectual currents of the Reformation and Counter Reformation and to the influences of three different Western cultures— Swedish, Polish, and German. Livonia and Courland remained predominantly Lutheran. Latgale, in the east, held by Poland until the first partition of that country in 1772, was reconverted to Catholicism. Religious works were printed in the local language; German and Swedish scholars began to discover Latvian folksongs, customs, and traditions. The life of the peasant became increasingly harsh, however, as the rights of the barons and the requirements of statutory labor were extended, culminating in full serfdom after the Russian takeover.[29] Until that time, Riga served as a city of refuge for peasants fleeing the control of harsh landlords and the devastation of war. During this period the cities, while still predominantly German in character, gained in native population.

Sweden's control over Riga and Livonia was consolidated early in the seventeenth century. It was not broken until Peter I's victory in the Great Northern War, which once again devastated the countryside. This victory brought the province under the Russian crown in 1721. Peter welcomed the German barons into the service of the Russian state and allowed them to retain their privileges. The duke of Courland's widow became Empress Anna Ivanovna in 1730, and a later duke, Ernst Biron, exercised great power as a favorite of the empress.[30] Formal Russian control over Courland did not come until the third partition of Poland in 1795, but Russian influence had grown continuously throughout the century.

The end of the eighteenth century saw the rest of Latvia come under Russian control via the partitions of Poland, marking the end of three centuries of intermittent warfare and strife. Latvia did not become a major battlefield again until World War I. Soviet historians stress the great positive benefit of the peace, unity and opportunity for economic development which the unification with Russia afforded the people of Latvia.[31] Some credence must be granted this assertion, although the picture was by no means rosy. Serfdom prevailed, mitigated somewhat by the reforms of Alexander I in 1804 and 1816–1819.[32] There were famines and peasant revolts. The oppressions of the autocracy hindered, but did not stop, development of media, literature, and learning in the Latvian language.

The Russians governed Latvia in three separate units: the *gubernii* of Livonia (including part of Estonia) and Courland contained most of the country, but Latgale was administered as part of the Vitebsk *guberniya* and did not enjoy the same limited degree of autonomy as did the other two

28 Rutkis, 1967: 217.
29 Spekke, 1951: 188; *Istoriya LSSR*, 1955: 95.

30 Spekke, 1951: 255–256.
31 *Istoriya LSSR*, 1955: 114. There was some fighting in Latvia during the Napoleonic invasion. *Ibid.*: 124.
32 The decree of 1804 provided that peasants in Livland, Estland, and Courland could not be sold without also selling the land; the laws of 1816–1819 granted the peasants personal freedom requiring that their relations with the landlords be regulated by "free contracts." The peasants received no land, which led to reference to their new rights as "the freedom of the bird." This differed from the 1861 abolition of serfdom in Russia, when the state purchased land for the peasants and saddled them with a heavy repayment burden. Spekke, 1951: 290; *Istoriya LSSR*, 1955: 128.

provinces.[33] This autonomy, exercised by the local nobility, contributed to maintenance of a non-Russian culture in the region, but increasingly it was restricted in the latter half of the nineteenth century. Essentially, Alexander III abolished it, but by that time the Latvian National Awakening was in full swing.

The personal freedom (without land) granted to Latvian peasants in 1816–1819 allowed considerable movement to the cities and growth of manufacturing and trade.[34] Riga began to become a Latvian, rather than German, city.[35] The first Latvian language newspaper was published in 1822 in Jelgava. Latvian literature began to move away from its clerical and religious origins and to establish more secular concerns. The small but growing intelligentsia included men such as P. Balodis (1839–1918), educated in St. Petersburg, who had established ties with the growing radical movement in Russia.

In 1854 a group of Latvian students at the University of Tartu, in Estonia, founded a small intellectual circle which expanded into the movement known as the Young Latvians [*Mladolatyshi*] and became a major force in the growth of Latvian culture and national consciousness. In 1862, unable to publish at home, these men founded a Latvian newspaper in St. Petersburg. Although it lasted only three years, the *Petersburgas Avize* was uncompromising in its call for national rights and gained a significant readership in Latvia.[36] Among the leaders of the Young Latvians were such national heroes as Krisjanis Barons, who devoted his later life to a massive compilation of Latvian folksongs; Juris Alunans, poet and journalist; Krisjanis Valdemars and Atis Kronwalds, who worked as publicists and public speakers and assisted in formation of the Latvian Society of Riga. This society sponsored the first national gathering of the Latvians, a song festival in 1873.

In 1897 Riga had 48,000 industrial workers in a total population of 282,000.[37] The wealth of the country was increasing rapidly, and Latvians were sharing in it to a greater and greater extent. Many of the large landed estates of the German nobility were divided up and sold to the peasants. The growth of a successful entrepreneurial class drained much militancy from the Young Latvian movement. This created a vacuum, soon filled by a new generation of young intellectuals who became even more deeply influenced by socialist thought and teaching. These men came to be known as the "New Current" (*Jaunā Strava, Novotechentsy*) and were among the leaders of the growing revolutionary movement. One of them, Peteris Stuchka, later founded the Communist party of Latvia. Another, the poet Jānis Rainis, is acclaimed and claimed by both Communist and nationalist Latvians.

Social Democratic organizations were founded throughout Latvia in 1901 and 1902, at first primarily by Russians, then Latvians began to take on leading roles. In 1904 representatives of many groups, with a total membership of perhaps 4,000, met in Riga and organized the Latvian Social Democratic Workers' party. They worked closely with the Russian SD's, but insisted on a national principle of federation rather than a territorial one, as the Leninists wanted.[38] By late 1905, in the midst of the revolution, the party claimed 14,000 members. Lenin is said to have remarked that during the 1905 revolution the workers and SD's of Latvia "occupied one of the first, most important places in the struggle against autocracy." [39] Indeed, Soviet statistics indicate that Latvia was the most revolutionary part of the empire in terms of ratio of strikers to total number of workers.[40]

Nationalist and socialist currents remained strong after suppression of the 1905 revolution. They exploded under the impact

33 Rutkis, 1967: 216–217.
34 Soviet historians note that Riga had 54 capitalist manufacturing enterprises in either 1820 or 1830, depending on which source is consulted. See *Istoriya LSSR*, 1955: 142; *Vēsture*, 1967: 121. Neither book notes the date as an error, and neither gives a reference source.
35 Rutkis, 1967: 181.
36 Spekke, 1951: 307; *Istoriya LSSR*, 1955: 211; *Latvia*, 1968: 18.

37 Spekke, 1951: 308; Rutkis, 1967: 292. Spekke's figure of 148,000 must be an error, as this represents some 51% of Riga's total population at that time. Rutkis, 1967: 316, gives a figure of 61,000 industrial workers in Riga in 1935.
38 *Istoriya LSSR*, 1955: 262–268.
39 *Ibid.*: 281.
40 *Istoriya LSSR*, 1955: 281–282.

of the devastation caused by World War I, fought for three years on Latvian territory (the battle lines divided the country in half for much of the time), and the anarchy following Russia's February Revolution.

In 1917 provisional governmental and semigovernmental councils proliferated among Latvian rifle regiments in the Russian army (formed in 1915) and Latvian refugees scattered throughout Russia. Several cooperated to form the Latvian Provisional National Council on November 18, 1917. After the October Revolution, pro-Bolshevik groups proclaimed the establishment of Soviet power in occupied eastern Latvia, but left the country in the van of the German advance in the spring of 1918, in which all of Latvia was occupied. Enjoying limited recognition from the German occupation authorities, the Provisional Council and leaders from Courland, previously isolated from the rest of the country by the battle lines, united to form a pre-parliament, the Latvian People's Council, and to elect a provisional government under Kārlis Ulmanis in November 1918.

In 1919, following the collapse of Imperial Germany, Soviet troops, including major elements of the Latvian rifle regiments, returned to Latvia. They pressed hard against Latvian national forces from the east, as did freebooting German forces in the west. With assistance in the form of money and supplies from the Allies and military support from Estonia, the Latvians succeeded in driving both Soviet and German forces out of the country by early 1920. A peace treaty with Soviet Russia, in which the young Bolshevik government renounced all claims to Latvian territory, was signed in August of that year.

Many Latvians remained in Russia after creation of the Latvian republic. They played a disproportionately large role in the creation of the Soviet Union. The Red Latvian Rifles were one of the most reliable units available to the Bolsheviks. They played a significant role in the civil war battles, from the Ukraine to Siberia. Latvian Communists such as Roberts Eiche, Roberts Eidemanis, and Jānis Rudzutaks were widely influential, the last named as a Politburo member. Latvian Communists in the Soviet Union, however, were virtually annihilated during Stalin's purges. Soviet

historiography has consistently played down their significance.[41]

The Republic of Latvia carried out an extensive land reform during the 1920s. The degree of equality of access to land thus obtained is still in dispute between Soviet and Western authors.[42] The established parliamentary system provided extensive cultural autonomy, including schools and press, for the ethnic minorities. Political parties proliferated, with twenty-five represented in the 100-member *Saeima* [Parliament] in 1928.[43] Development of a stable government proved impossible, and in May 1934 Prime Minister Ulmanis dissolved the *Saeima* and established an authoritarian regime, corporate and national in character but not clearly fascist. Political parties were banned, a few leaders of extremist parties on both left and right were interred and/or prosecuted, and some restrictions were placed on the press, but there was no secret police and the courts remained relatively independent.[44] This regime remained in power until the Soviet occupation.

In 1939, after the Molotov-Ribbentrop pact with Germany, the Soviet Union forced the Baltic states to sign mutual assistance pacts allowing stationing of Soviet troops on their soil but guaranteeing noninterference in internal affairs. Nine months later, in June 1940, under threat of imminent Soviet attack, the government of Latvia was forced to resign in favor of one more "friendly" to the Soviet Union (in fact, hand-picked by Andrei Vyshinsky, special Soviet emissary to Latvia) and to allow entry of Soviet forces in unlimited numbers. New elections were proclaimed, in which only the Communist-backed list

---

41 Gērmanis, 1970: 6–12.
42 For a statistical assessment, see Rein Taagepera, "Inequality Indices for Baltic Farm Size Distribution, 1929–1940," *Journal of Baltic Studies* (Spring), 1972: III: 1: 26–34.
43 Spekke, 1951: 375.
44 *Ibid.*: 376; Von Rauch, 1970: 132–133; Rutkis, 1967: 242; Bilmanis, 1947: 154. Dependent upon agricultural exports, Latvia was significantly affected by the Great Depression. Apparently this factor hastened the end of democratic government there. The Ulmanis regime kept a balanced budget, but seemed successful in encouraging recovery and further developing the road network and supply of electric power. Latvia's economic situation improved considerably in 1936–1937. Bilmanis, 1947: 306, 333–337.

of candidates was allowed to stand. After a campaign in which the Communists denied any desire to Sovietize Latvia, the new parliament immediately requested incorporation into the Soviet Union.[45]

The new Soviet regime proclaimed the nationalization of property, dismantling much of the existing social system, but had little time to organize Soviet-style institutions before the Nazi invasion of June 1941. There was, however, time to plan and carry out deportations (on the night of June 14, 1941, more than 15,000 Latvians of all ages and in all walks of life were taken) and executions.[46] All major political leaders, including President Ulmanis and the commander of Latvian forces, J. Balodis, disappeared. Most estimates are that some 34,000 Latvians died or disappeared in 1940–1941. Additional deportations followed expulsion of Nazi troops from Latvia, in connection with reestablishment of Soviet control, elimination of nationalist guerillas who fought the Soviets actively until at least 1948, and the collectivization drive. There is no accurate way to calculate the losses inflicted on the nation by the war and by imposition of the Soviet system. There may easily have been in the neighborhood of 290,000 dead from military action, execution, or deportation. In addition to those killed or imprisoned, many more sought refuge in Western nations, from Sweden to Australia.[47]

DEMOGRAPHY

The population of Latvia, according to the 1970 census, was 2,364,127, an increase of 13% from 1959.[48] This rate of growth was about average for European peoples of the USSR. Much of that growth, however (58% according to data from one Soviet source[49], was achieved through immigration, mostly of non-Latvians, from other parts of the Union. Ethnic Latvians represented 62.0% of the republic's population in 1959, but only 56.8% in 1970. Russians increased from 26.6% to 29.8% of the population, and other Slavic peoples (Belorussians, Poles, and Ukrainians) from 7.2% to 9.0%. In 1935 ethnic Latvians had constituted over three quarters of the republic's population.[50]

The steady erosion of the ethnic nature of their country is of concern to many Latvians, both at home and abroad. Denationalization is strongest in the cities, where the Russian population tends to concentrate. Latvians constituted only 41% of the 1970 population of Riga, down from 45% in 1959.[51] Nearly 94% of Latvians in the USSR live in their republic, so that the Latvian portion of the republic population is not likely to be significantly reinforced by further concentration of the nationality in its homeland. That concentration is already one of the highest in the Soviet Union, exceeded only by that of the Georgians and the Lithuanians.

With the urban population making up almost two thirds (62%) of the total republic population, Latvia is one of the most highly urbanized parts of the Soviet Union. Riga, the capital, with over 700,000 inhabitants, is second only to Leningrad as largest city on the Soviet Baltic coast. The population is one of the most highly educated in the Soviet Union. Only Estonia has a larger proportion of specialists with higher or specialized secondary education.[52]

A major reason that immigration presents such a threat to the nation is its very low rate of natural population growth. While Latvia's birth rate of 14.5 births per 1,000 population is only marginally lower than the rate for the RSFSR (14.6), the death rate, at 11.6 per 1,000, is considerably higher, leaving a natural growth rate of only 2.9 per 1,000, lowest in the USSR (only a little over half the rate for the RSFSR). Two factors are at work here. First, there is a large number of the aged (17.3% of Latvia's population is over 60 years old, with only 28.7% under 20,

45 Tarulis, 1959: 253; Berzins, 1963: 90.
46 Rutkis, 1967: 253, 774.
47 Rutkis, 1967: 292–327; *Latvia*, 1968: 53–54; King, 1965: 86.
48 *CDSP*, 1971: XXIII: 16: 14.
49 *Sovetskaya Latviya* (June 23), 1971. Translated in *JPRS* #53732, "Translations on USSR Political and Sociological Affairs," series (August 2), 1971: 166: 73.

50 Rutkis, 1967: 292, 302. In 1970 the absolute number of Latvians in Latvia was smaller than in 1935!
51 Russians, Belorussians, and Ukrainians constituted over 50% of the population of Riga in 1970. *Itogi 1970*: IV: 283.
52 *Nar. khoz. 1970*: 234.

whereas corresponding figures for the USSR as a whole are 11.8% and 38%), reflected in a high death rate (life expectancy in Latvia is nearly equal to that of the U.S.).[53] Age structure of the USSR's ethnic Latvian population is even less favorable: fully 20% are over 60 years old, and only 26% are under 20.[54] Second, there is a cultural preference for smaller families, begun later in life.[55]

The Communist party of Latvia reported 127,753 members and candidate members on January 1, 1971,[56] or roughly 5.4% of the population, compared to the CPSU's 5.9%.[57] At the time of formation of the LSSR, the Latvian Communist party was minuscule, comprising less than 700 members and candidates as late as 1944.[58] After the war, party ranks were filled in large part by importation of cadres, both Latvian and non-Latvian, from other Soviet republics. But the party remained small in comparison to the population throughout the 1950s and 1960s.[59] Current data on the ethnic breakdown in the party are not published, but Western studies have indicated a clear preponderance of Russians at all levels.[60]

It is clear that non-Latvians or Latvians with long residence in Russia, considered Russified by Western writers and by some native Latvian Communists,[61] play a dis-

proportionate role in the top party leadership. Of the five secretaries of the CPL, First Secretary August Voss was raised in Russia, arriving in Latvia in 1945. Second Secretary N. Belukha, apparently in charge of cadres and party organization, is a Ukrainian and speaks no Latvian. Secretary for Propaganda A. Drizulis lived in Russia until he was 25, as did Industry Secretary E. Petersons. Agriculture Secretary R. Verro is an Estonian and does not speak Latvian. Chairman of the Council of Ministers was born in Belorussia; chairman of the Supreme Soviet was born in Moscow.[62] Slow promotion of native cadres and failure to encourage use of the Latvian language by party workers was a major concern of a group of Latvian Communists, nominally led by Deputy Premier E. Berklāvs, removed in a major purge of the CPL in 1959–1960.[63] Dominance of the political system by men with few ties to the local population continues to be a source of tension.

CULTURE

The beginnings of modern Latvian literature and culture are generally dated from the works of the poet Juris Alunans and the Young Latvian writers of the late nineteenth century. Publication of the national epic *Lačplesis* [*Bearslayer*] in 1888 was a milestone, coming only a few years after the Finnish *Kalevala* and the Estonian *Kalevipoeg*. Janis Rainis (1865–1929) is widely regarded as the greatest Latvian writer. His wife Aspazija (1868–1943) is also ranked highly in the West, although the Soviets have treated her less kindly.[64] Other major writers of this period include Rudolfs Blaumanis, Augusts Deglavs, and Andrievs Niedra.

In 1935, about 68% of the Latvian population adhered to the Evangelical Lutheran Church, 26% to Roman Catholicism.[65] Religious feelings reflected the country's historical development, with most Catholics

53 *Ibid.*: 50–51; *LTS*, 1971: 331. *Statistical Abstract of U.S.*, 1971: 53.
54 *Itogi 1970*: IV: 363.
55 *Vestnik statistiki* (June), 1971: VI: 23–24. Translated in *JPRS*, "Translations on USSR Political and Sociological Affairs" (August 17), 1971: 170. Another complicating factor is the divorce rate, one of the highest in the world (in 1970, 45 divorces were recorded for every 100 marriages). See *Nauka i tekhnika* (January), 1972: I: 4–7.
56 Voss report to XXI Congress CPL (February 25), 1971; *Sovetskaya Latviya* (February 26), 1971.
57 *Partiinaya zhizn'* (December), 1971: XXIV: 4; *Nar. khoz. 1970*: 7. A more informative figure is CP strength as a percent of *adult* population: Latvia—7.2%; USSR—9.0%. *Radio Liberty Dispatch*, "Major Turnover of Leading Party Cadres in Union Republics" (April 20), 1971: 9.
58 *Ocherki*, 1965: 92.
59 Widmer, 1969: 167.
60 Vardys, 1964: 9–10; King, 1968: 61–62; Trapans, 1963.
61 "Letter of 17 Latvian Communists," *Brivība* (Stockholm) (January), 1972: 1: 225: 5–8; *Congressional Record* (February 21), 1972. See also analysis of the "Letter" and of Soviet rebuttal in *Soviet Analyst* (London) (March 2), 1972: I: 1: 306; (April 13), 1972: I: 4: 4–6.

62 "Letter of 17 Latvian Communists"; see also biographical sketches of these men in *LME*.
63 King, 1965: 188–203; Berzins, 1963: 255–261; "Letter of 17 Latvian Communists": Widmer, 1969: 311–317.
64 Ekmanis, 1972: 44–70, *passim*; Rutkis, 1967: 509–510.
65 *Ibid.*: 616.

concentrated in Latgale, the eastern part of the country under Polish rule during the Reformation and Counter Reformation. The strength of religion today cannot be determined with any accuracy, given Soviet pressures against such expression. A survey conducted by A. I. Kholmogorov between 1964 and 1969, however suggests that roughly 10% of Latvians surveyed claimed to participate in religious holidays, as against 6.6% of the Russians and 28% of the Lithuanians resident in Latvia.[66] The implication is that religious beliefs are not as tenaciously held by the Latvians as by the neighboring Lithuanians, and not as closely tied to national identity.[67] The traditions and culture associated with religion, especially the achievement ethic of Lutheranism, strengthen the Western orientation of the Latvians and distinguish them from the Slavs whose culture was heavily influenced by Orthodoxy. Latvians tend to be disciplined and hard working. Cleanliness, orderliness, and making a good appearance are deeply rooted values.[68] The quality of Latvian and Estonian manufacturers is generally recognized as among the highest in the USSR. Latvian furniture and clothing products are in great demand throughout the USSR.

An old Latvian tradition, more national and folkloristic than religious, is celebration of Midsummer Day and its eve, called St. John's eve or *Janu Naktis*. This holiday was abolished by the Soviets in 1960, but its observance has continued. Since 1966 it received limited recognition in the official press (a photograph and some traditional songs are printed on the back page of *Cina*, the party's Latvian language daily), but Latvians are not given the day off from work. In 1973, and perhaps in other years, *Intourist*, Soviet Company for Travel in the USSR, sponsored the holiday for Latvian visitors from abroad. Signs of local observance were widespread in Riga.[69]

The folksong is a characteristic form and national songfests, held every five years, provide settings for demonstration of national feelings.[70] Most noted Latvian composers of both folk and classical music include Emēlis Melngailis and the brothers Jāzeps and Jānis Medins. The latter is well received by the Soviets even though he lived in Sweden from World War II until his death in 1966.[71]

Soviet Latvian writers awarded prizes by the Soviet regime include Vilis Lacis (chairman of the Council of Ministers from 1946 to 1959), Andrejs Upīts, and Jānis Sudrabkalns, but their work is generally considered poor quality in the West.[72] Today young writers in Latvia continue to be concerned with national or non-Soviet cultural values. There has been frequent criticism of these writers and of organizations responsible for their work in the party press, as well as some arrests.[73] (For information on Latvian literary journals and press, see section on media.)

The Latvian republic is regarded as one of high culture. Riga is a highly developed, well maintained metropolis with architectural and cultural features similar to those of other large European cities. Latvia has ten theaters, most located in Riga. They include Opera and Ballet Theater; Rainis, a drama theater; Russian Drama Theater; Youth Theater; and Komsomol Theater. Riga Cinema Studio produces films in both Latvian and Russian. Latvian Academy of Sciences (established in 1946) consists of 16 scientific institutions and personnel of 1,500 including 45 academicians. Latvia also has an Academy of Agriculture, Art Academy, and Stuchka Latvian State University. Latvian Public Library holds 3 million volumes (1967). Riga Museum of Fine Arts and the Museum of Latvian History are well known throughout the republic.[74]

---

66 Kholomogorov, 1970: 74–75. Significance of the figures is not clear, and they should be interpreted with caution. As additional evidence of the maintenance of religious feelings in Latvia, Rein Taagepera has reported an interview given by the Lutheran archbishop of Latvia in which he stated that 240 Latvian congregations own their own church buildings (*Estonian Events* [June], 1969: XIV: 5). In 1936 there were 325 Lutheran congregations in Latvia (Rutkis, 1967: 618).
67 Such identification has been given limited recognition by the Soviets. See *Newsletter from Behind the Iron Curtain* (June), 1971: 470.
68 Andersons, 1953: 79, 148.

---

69 Rutkis, 1967: 501; personal observations of F. Harned.
70 *Ibid.*: 501, 547.
71 *Glimpses of Latvian Culture*, 1971: 21–22.
72 Rutkis, 1967: 517–518.
73 Ekmanis, 1972: 60; *Estonian Events* (February), 1968: IV: 1, and (December), 1968: XI: 1; *Cina* (September 15), 1970 and (March 3) 1972.
74 *Nar. obraz.*, 1971: 334; *SSSR*, 1967: 591; *Nar. khoz.* 1970: 660, 674.

EXTERNAL RELATIONS

Unlike their neighbors, the Estonians and the Lithuanians, the Latvians have no unambiguous established external face to provide support for their national distinctiveness. Estonians in Tallinn can receive and understand the radio and television broadcasts of their Finnish cousins across the Gulf. The ethnic and linguistic tie reinforces their own national awareness of being non-Russian and non-Slav. The Catholic Lithuanians have the Church and can argue for religious policies on the model of those prevailing in neighboring Poland. The Latvians have no ethnic relatives except the Lithuanians and the role of Lutheranism as a national church is not clear. Although they received a great deal of German cultural influence, the memory of the Baltic barons and of German policies during the two world wars is still strong. Sweden is home for several thousand Latvian émigrés and serves as center for many political and intellectual activities, but it is ethnically and linguistically foreign. Great Britain gave Latvia some support in the struggle for independence, but on the whole the country is relatively isolated.

Their position as small, developed, Europeanized segment in a large, mostly Slavic state is shared by the two small neighbors. There was limited cooperation among the three Baltic states during the period of independence, but it was not carried very far. This was due in part to Lithuania's involvement in the dispute with Poland over Vilnius. The Soviets have allowed a slowly increasing amount of interrepublic cooperation among the three. For some purposes they treat the Baltic region (three republics plus the Kaliningrad *oblast*) as a unit, with Riga as the principal headquarters. This has contributed to the flow of Russian officials into Riga, however, and under Soviet conditions could be of only limited support at best in maintaining the distinctiveness of the region.

The Latvians, unlike some of the other nationalities, have a relatively large and nationally conscious émigré population, working to preserve and expand their national culture, maintaining contacts and communication with the homeland. They have also tried to make world opinion aware of the mode of Latvia's accession to the Soviet Union and the position of its people.

Latvian language periodicals are published in the West, with several publishing houses maintained by the émigrés. Latvians played a leading role in establishment of the Baltiska Institutet in Stockholm and the Association for the Advancement of Baltic Studies, headquartered in New York. Latvian national associations are in almost every city with a Latvian community, sponsoring special schools for children, cultural festivals, radio broadcasts, and news publications on developments in Soviet Latvia. Judging from reactions in the Soviet press, their influence is not inconsiderable. The authorities of Soviet Latvia make a special effort to reach emigrant co-nationals through special broadcasts and publications, as well as through encouraging tourism to the former homeland.[75]

Media

LANGUAGE DATA

Latvian and Lithuanian are the only surviving members of the Baltic group of Indo-European languages. They are distinct—in vocabulary, structure, and morphology—from the Germanic and Slavic languages of surrounding countries.[76] Books appeared in Latvian as early as the seventeenth century. The standard literary form was established during the National Awakening (second half of the nineteenth century) and the

---

[75] Personal conversations with a number of such tourists in June 1973 gave a clear impression that the effect of these programs is not necessarily favorable to the regime, among either tourists or their relatives and friends in Latvia.

[76] Estonian, a Finnic language, is even more foreign. Only a few words of Finnic origin have been incorporated into Latvian.

Table 5.1

Native and Second Languages Spoken by Latvians

(in thousands)

| Number of Latvians Residing | | | SPEAKING AS NATIVE LANGUAGE | | | | | | SPEAKING AS SECOND LANGUAGE[a] | |
| | | | Latvian | | | Russian | | | Russian | Other Languages of Peoples of USSR |
	1959	1970	1959	1970	% Point Change 1959–1970	1959	1970	% Point Change 1959–1970	1970	1970
in Latvian SSR	1,298 (92.7%)	1,342 (93.8%)	1,277 (98.4%)	1,316 (98.1%)	−0.3	19 (1.5%)	25 (1.9%)	+0.4	608 (45.3%)	4.4 (0.3%)
in other Soviet republics	102 (7.3%)	88 (6.2%)	54 (52.9%)	45 (51.1%)	−1.8	45 (44.1%)	40 (45.5%)	+1.4	38 (43.2%)	5.6 (6.4%)
Total	1,400 (100%)	1,430 (100%)	1,331 (95.1%)	1,361 (95.2%)	+0.1	64 (4.6%)	65 (4.5%)	−0.1	646 (45.2%)	10 (0.7%)

Sources: *Itogi 1959*: tables 53–55; *Itogi 1970*: IV: 20, 280; *Nar. khoz. 1972*: 32.

[a] No data are available for 1959, since no questions regarding command of a second language were asked in the 1959 census.

period of independence (1918 to 1940). The current system of orthography uses the Latin alphabet with certain diacritic marks.

In 1970 more than 95% of Latvians in the USSR, and more than 98% of those resident in Latvia, considered Latvian their native language (see Table 5.1).[77] By comparison, 97.9% of Lithuanians of the Soviet Union—marginally more concentrated in their own republic than are the Latvians—considered Lithuanian their native tongue. Similarly, almost 96% of Estonians, fewer of whom live in Estonia, considered Estonian their first language.[78] Thus, the loyalty of Latvians to their national language would appear to be slightly less than that of their neighbors, but it is well above that of the Ukrainians, Belorussians, or Armenians.

In 1970 more than half of the total population of Latvia (56.9%, including some 29,000 non-Latvians) claimed Latvian as a native language. An additional 8% claimed fluency in Latvian as a second language. Approximately two fifths of the population claimed Russian as a native language, and another one third claimed Russian as a second language. Thus, the proportions of the total population fluent in either one or the other were quite similar—64.9% for Latvian, 67.2% for Russian.[79]

Data from the 1970 census regarding native language by age indicates that, among all Latvians in the Soviet Union, those in their twenties and over 50 years old are most likely to claim Latvian as their native language. The following table summarizes the data:

Age Structure and Native Language of Latvians in USSR, 1970

Age Group (years)	No. Latvians	CLAIMING LATVIAN AS NATIVE LANGUAGE	
		No.	% of Age Group
0–10	215,689	207,889	96.4
11–15	94,056	90,808	96.5
16–19	64,234	62,254	96.9
20–29	179,944	176,048	97.8
30–39	202,149	197,477	97.7
40–49	170,654	166,619	97.6
50–59	133,817	131,625	98.4
60+	295,966	292,414	98.8
Total	1,429,844[80]	1,361,414	95.2

LOCAL MEDIA

Latvia achieved general literacy by the beginning of the twentieth century. Its population has been plentifully supplied with reading materials by the Soviet regime.

A total of 76 newspapers are published, 49 in Latvian and the rest in Russian (see Table 5.2). Their 1971 average circulation (1,297,000) amounted to 71.8 copies of Latvian newspapers per 100 inhabitants of

77 *Itogi 1970*: IV: 20, 280.

78 In 1970, 94.1% of Lithuanians in the Soviet Union lived in their own republic as did 93.8% of Latvians and 91.9% of Estonians in their respective republics. Figures for all three peoples represented increases over those for 1959. *CDSP*, XXIII: 16: 16–18.

79 *Itogi 1970*: IV: 280. For the urban population, the figures are 55% Latvian, 70% Russian; for Riga, 51% Latvian, 81% Russian. *Ibid.*: 281, 283.

80 Data for age groups is for Latvians in the Latvian SSR and other major regions of settlement; 94.9% of total number of Soviet Latvians is included in this listing, whereas the total given in the table is for all Soviet Latvians. *Itogi 1970*: IV: 360(*n*), 363.

Table 5.2

Publications in Latvian SSR

Language of Publication	Year	NEWSPAPERS[a]			MAGAZINES			BOOKS & BROCHURES		
		No.	Per Issue Circulation (1,000)	Copies/100 in Language Group[d]	No.	Per Issue Circulation (1,000)	Copies/100 in Language Group[d]	No. Titles	Total Volume (1,000)	Books & Brochures/100 in Language Group[d]
Russian	1959	25	194	29.5	N.A.	N.A.	N.A.	700	2,910	442.9
	1971	27	331	39.0	10	75	8.8	1,140	2,646	311.8
Latvian[b]	1959	75	632	48.4	N.A.	N.A.	N.A.	1,256	9,737	746.1
	1971	49	966	71.8	17[b]	1,019	75.8	1,169	12,625	938.9
Minority Languages	1959	0	0	0	N.A.	N.A.	N.A.	0	0	0
	1971	0	0	0	0	0	0	3	56	32.8
Foreign Languages	1959	0	0	0	N.A.	N.A.	N.A.	(21)[c]	(202)[c]	N.A.
	1971	0	0	0	0	0	0	(82)[c]	(289)[c]	N.A.
All Languages	1959	100	826	39.5	15	474	22.6	1,977[c]	12,849	613.8
	1971	76	1,297	54.9	27	1,094	46.3	2,394[c]	15,616	660.5

Sources: *Pechat'* 1959: 58, 129, 165; *Pechat'* 1971: 96, 159, 189.

[a] 1970 figures do not include *kolkhoz* newspapers.

[b] Includes journals appearing simultaneously in Russian and Latvian.

[c] Book totals as given in *Pechat'* sometimes differ from totals in language categories. The indication is that books are published in other languages but no data is given. Figures in parentheses are the presumed production of books in other languages based on this discrepancy.

[d] Includes all native speakers of the language.

the republic who considered Latvian their native language, and 39.0 per 100 Russian speakers.[81] The Russian speakers have, of course, the centrally published newspapers available as well.

Of the nine all-republic newspapers, most important are the two dailies, *Cina* [*Struggle*] (in Latvian, with 1970 circulation of 190,000) and *Sovetskaya Latviya* (in Russian, circulation 105,000), organs of the CC CP Latvia and the LSSR Council of Ministers; the Komsomol papers, *Padomju Jaunatne* [*Soviet Youth*] (circulation 157,000) and *Sovetskaya molodyozh* [*Soviet Youth*] (circulation 152,000); and *Literatūra un Māksla* [*Literature and Art*] (circulation 48,000), weekly organ of the Writers' Union as well as of other creative artists.[82] *Dzimtenes Balss* [*Voice of the Homeland*], weekly publication for Latvians abroad, is counted among the all-republic papers.

The eleven city newspapers include Latvian and Russian language pairs for the cities of Riga (and Jūrmala), Jelgava, Liepaja, Ventspils, and Rezekne; Daugavpils is served by a Russian paper alone. The 1970 circulation of *Rigas Balss* [*Voice of Riga*] was 78,000 in Latvian and 61,000 in Russian.[83]

Two thirds of the 27 magazines are in Latvian. In 1970 they had a total per issue circulation of 1,043,000, 93% in Latvian. Thus, Latvian language readers are far better supplied with locally produced journals than are Russian readers. Magazines published in Moscow are readily available in Latvia, which redresses the balance. The most important journals, with 1970 circulation figures, are *Padomju Latvijas Komunists* (16,300; also published in Russian as *Kommunist Sovetskoi Latvii*, circulation 5,100), party monthly; *Zvaigzne* [*Star*] (111,700), a popular fiction fortnightly; *Karogs* [*Banner*] (18,000), journal of the Writers' Union; *Veseliba* [*Health*] (162,000), Ministry of Health's journal of popular medicine; *Padomju Latvijas Sieviete* [*Soviet*

Latvian Woman] (169,700), political and literary journal for women published by the CC CP Latvia; and *Dadzis* [*Burdock*] (76,400), official satirical journal.

In book publishing, only Estonia publishes more titles per capita, or larger editions per capita, than does Latvia. However, the proportion of Latvian language books of all books published in Latvia has declined steadily from a high of 81% of new titles in 1945 to slightly over 50% in 1970.[84] Almost all the rest are published in Russian. In volume, Latvian books have consistently outnumbered the Russian by three or four to one. In 1970, nearly one quarter of the titles appearing in Latvian, encompassing over two fifths of the total volume, were translations from other languages, especially Russian.[85]

The Baltic republics are far better supplied with radio and television receivers than are the rest of the Soviet Union. In 1971 Latvia had more TV sets per 1,000 inhabitants than France had in 1969.[86] There was a radio or radio-phonograph for every third inhabitant. Wired loudspeakers constituted only 16% of the radio receiving points in Latvia, less than half of the all-Union average.[87] This supply of selector receivers, coupled with geographic position, suggests that the country has a high capacity for receiving foreign broadcasts. Radio Luxembourg, in particular, is a popular source of Western music.[88]

In 1968 Latvian SSR Radio broadcasts four separate programs, including one in stereo, for a total of 27 hours daily, in Latvian and Russian. A foreign service in Latvian and Swedish is also maintained.[89] Small local stations are in the cities of Jelgava and Rezekne, in 26 *raions*, and in many *sovkhozy*, *kolkhozy*, and large industrial establishments.[90] Amateur radio is popular. Organized and encouraged by

---

81 Computed from *Pechat'* 1971: 189; *Itogi* 1970: IV: 280.
82 *Preses Hronika* (December), 1970: 79–111. This is a monthly listing of publications in Latvia. Once a year it carries complete information on journals and newspapers.
83 *Ibid.*

84 *LTS*, 1971: 418. Latvian language books are published in larger editions, so that four fifths of all books in 1970 were in Latvian. This percentage has been increasing since 1965.
85 *Pechat'* 1970: 96.
86 202 vs. 201, or one set for every five persons. *Nar. khoz.* 1972: 628; *UN Statistical Yearbook*, 1970: 805.
87 Computed from *Nar. khoz.* 1972: *passim.*
88 Personal communication, June 1973.
89 *LME*, 1970: III: 119.
90 *Ibid.*

Table 5.3

Electronic Media and Films in Latvian SSR

YEAR	RADIO				TELEVISION			MOVIES	
	No. Stations	No. Wired Sets (1,000)	/100 Population	No. Wireless Sets (1,000)	/100 Population	No. Stations	No. sets (1,000)	/100 Population	Seats (1,000)	/100 Population
1960	N.A.	183	8.5	419	19.5	4	83	3.9	119	5.6
1970	N.A.	245	10.3	787	33.0	8	459	19.2	177	7.4
1971	N.A.	263	10.9	865	35.9	8	487	20.2	180	7.5

Sources: Televedeniye i radioveshchaniye, 1972: 12, 13; Pechat' i kulturno-prosvetitel'nye uchrezhdeniyz Latviiskoi SSR (Riga: Statistika, 1971), 24; Nar. khoz. 1972: 622, 628; Nar. khoz. Latvii 1971: 239, 358; Transport i svyaz' SSR, 1972: 296–298; Nar. obraz., 1971: 325.

DOSAAF, 30,000 amateurs, operating 300 stations, were registered in 1968.[91]

There were eight TV stations in Latvia in 1970, but only the one in Riga originated local programming. Two programs are available. TV Riga broadcasts approximately 5½ hours per day, roughly two thirds of local origin (in both Latvian and Russian), the rest from Moscow. Central television broadcasts about 14 hours per day. On TV Riga programming in Latvian averages just under 2 hours per day of the total 5 to 6 hours; on Central television all programming is in Russian.[92]

EDUCATIONAL INSTITUTIONS

General education in the republic is provided chiefly in unified eight-year schools. Abolition of Khrushchev's educational reforms in the early 1960s included a return to the Soviet standard of general seven-year education. Pressure from Baltic educators and writers, however, led to a decision to allow these three republics to resume the more traditional eight-year period.[93] Four-year primary schools are almost exclusively in rural areas, and their number has been halved since 1945.[94]

Official reference sources do not distinguish among these schools by language of instruction. One Western source estimated that Russian language general education schools enrolled about one third of all students in 1955–1956.[95] During the 1960s this proportion may have been reduced by the marked increase in schools with classes taught in both Latvian and Russian. There were 240 bilingual schools in 1967 of a total of 1,200, with almost one third of the country's schoolchildren enrolled.[96] Proportion of children of any given nationality attending the bilingual schools is not known. It may be presumed that they include many of the largest schools, especially in the cities, and that continued consolidation of rural schools has added to their number. In Latvian language schools, Russian is a compulsory subject, beginning in the second grade.[97]

Roughly two thirds of the graduates of eight-year schools continue their education in either general secondary or specialized secondary schools.[98] About one third of the students in these schools have a chance to go on to one of Latvia's ten higher educational institutions or *vuzy*.[99] In 1971 enrollment in Latvia's 55 specialized secondary schools was 38,600.[100]

Most important *vuzy* include Latvian State University, named for Peteris Stucka, at Riga; Riga Polytechnic Institute; Latvian Agricultural Academy; and other specialized institutes for medicine, pedagogy, music, and art.[101] Both Latvian and Russian tend to be used for teaching at these institutes, except for the university, where many courses are available in Latvian only.[102]

Latvia is well supplied with educated manpower. With Estonia, it tops the list of Soviet republics in specialists with higher or specialized secondary education working in the economy (78 per 1,000 inhabitants).[103] Only 55%, however, are Latvian.[104] Only 47% of the students in *vuzy* in 1970–1971 were Latvians, down from 64% in 1960–1961, whereas the Latvian share of the population had diminished merely from 62.0% to 56.8% during the same period.[105] When ranked by nationality, Latvians are sixth in the ratio of specialists

91 *Ibid.*: 116.

92 See schedules in *Sovetskaya Latviya* (July 23), 1972.

93 Vardys, 1967: 60–61; Bilinsky, 1968: 424; Pennar, 1971: 241.

94 *LTS*, 1971: 389.

95 Rutkis, 1967: 574.

96 *Izvestia* (January 5), 1967: 3. See also Vardys, 1967: 60; Pennar, 1971: 241.

97 *LME*, III: 160.

98 Computed from *LTS*, 1971: 391, 397. Many others continue in evening schools for working and rural youth. *Ibid.*: 392.

99 *Nar. khoz. 1972*: 629. In the USSR, the term *vuz*, plural *vuzy*, (*vyssheye uchebnoye zavedeniye* [higher educational institutions]) refers to such institutions as universities, technical institutes, agricultural academies, etc.

100 Computed from average class size and rate of *vuz* matriculation. *LTS*, 1971: 397; *Nar. obraz.*, 1971: 173.

101 For complete list, see Rutkis, 1967: 575–576; for enrollments, see *LTS*, 1971: 400.

102 Dreifelds, 1970: 4.

103 Computed from *Nar. obraz.*, 1971: 234.

104 Pennar, 1971: 249.

105 Computed from *Nar. obraz.*, 1971: 201; 88% of Latvian college students are in school in Latvia.

Table 5.4

Selected Data on Education in Latvian SSR (1971)

Population: 2,409,000

		PER 1,000 POPULATION	% OF TOTAL
All schools			
number of schools	1,137	.47	
number of students	358,000	149.6	
Newly opened elementary, incomplete *secondary, and secondary schools*			
number of schools	11		
number of student places	6,800	2.8	
Secondary special schools			
number of schools	55		
number of students	38,600	16.0	
Institutions of higher education			
number of institutions	10		
number of students	41,000	17.0	
Universities			
number of universities	1		
number of students			
total	8,641	3.59	
day students	3,879	1.6	44.9
evening students	1,724	0.72	20.0
correspondence students	3,038	1.26	35.1
newly admitted			
total	1,669	0.69	
day students	894	0.37	53.6
evening students	300	0.12	18.0
correspondence students	475	0.20	28.4
graduated			
total	1,250	0.5	
day students	767	0.32	61.4
evening students	213	0.09	17.0
correspondence students	270	0.11	21.6
Graduate students			
total number	914	0.38	
in scientific research institutions	325	0.13	
in universities	589	0.24	
Number of persons with higher or *secondary (complete and incomplete)* *education*			
per 1,000 individuals, 10 years and older	517		
per 1,000 individuals employed in national economy	661		
Number of workers graduated from *professional-technical schools*	15,400	6.39	

Source: *Nar. khoz. 1972*: 439, 619, 626, 627, 629.

with higher education to population.[106] Their ranking in proportion of students is lower; Latvians are eleventh among the nationalities in this study in ratio of *vuzy* students to population, and tenth in students in specialized secondary education.[107] Complete secondary education in Latvia is more thorough than in the other republics, entailing 11 years of study instead of the 10 years required elsewhere.

CULTURAL AND SCIENTIFIC INSTITUTIONS

The Latvian Academy of Sciences was founded in 1946. As of January 1970, it encompasses 14 research institutes organized into three divisions (physics and technical science, chemistry and biology, and social sciences), plus a general library. Its presidents have all been ethnic Latvians,

although K. Plaude, president since 1960, and both vice presidents spent the interwar years in the Soviet Union. The director of the Institute of History, A. Drizulis, also a secretary of the CC CP Latvia, was reared and educated in Russia. At the end of 1968, the academy had 23 full members and 25 corresponding members. Twenty of the former and 19 of the latter have Latvian surnames; the rest appear to be of Slavic origin.[108]

The 1971 production of the Riga Film Studio included 7 full-length films (6 features and 1 documentary) and 79 shorter films, cartoons, and newsreels. There are 1,172 movie houses and 129 mobile film units in Latvia. The average citizen goes to the movies 16 times per year, somewhat less than the average Soviet citizen (19 times).[109] Russian language and foreign films are shown with Latvian subtitles. This substitution for the Russian language occurs only in the Baltic republics and Kazakhstan.[110]

106 The first five, in order, are: Jews, Georgians, Armenians, Estonians, Russians. From *Nar. obraz.*, 1971: 240.

107 *Nar. obraz.*, 1971: 196. The comparatively low proportion of the Latvian population in corresponding age brackets should be considered.

108 *LME*: I: 411, 677; III: 42, 606, 761–763.

109 *Nar. obraz.*, 1971: 327, 330; *Nar. khoz. Latvii* 1972: 358–359.

110 Taagepera, *Estonian Events* (December), 1970: 23: 5, citing *Sirp ja Vasar* (September 4), 1970.

Table 5.5

Selected Data on Scientific and Cultural Facilities and Personnel in Latvian SSR (1971)

Population: 2,409,000

Academy of Sciences		*Number of persons working in*	
number of members	51	*education and culture*	
number of scientific institutions		total	81,000
affiliated with academy	16	number per 1,000 population	33.6
total number of scientific workers	1,558		
		Number of persons working in science	
Museums		*and scientific services*	
number of museums	54	total	27,000
attendance	2,717,000	number per 1,000 population	11.2
attendance per 1,000 population	1,128		
		Number of public libraries	1,511
Theaters		number of books and magazines	
number of theaters	10	in public libraries	16,643,000
attendance	2,203,000		
attendance per 1,000 population	914	*Number of clubs*	1,021

Source: *Nar. khoz. 1972*: 106, 451, 625.

Except for cinematography, publishing, and the electronic media, cultural affairs are guided by the Ministry of Culture. Its guidance includes budgetary allocations as well as controls over the "ideological and artistic quality" of dramatic, musical, and artistic works.[111] Museums, libraries, clubs, parks, and zoos are under the Ministry of Culture. V. Kaupuzh, a musician reared in independent Latvia, has been Minister of Culture since 1962.[112]

Ten professional theaters were operating at the end of 1970, including State Opera and Ballet Theater. Seven are located in Riga, and three in other cities. Four perform in Latvian only, two in Russian only, and four in both languages. Amateur theater has always been very popular. Best amateur companies are awarded the title of "People's Theaters." There were eighteen in 1969: thirteen Latvian, three Russian, and one (in Rezekne) with both Latvian and Russian companies.[113]

National Attitudes

REVIEW OF FACTORS FORMING NATIONAL ATTITUDES

The Latvians are a small people, ethnically distinct from their neighbors except for the Lithuanians. For centuries they have maintained this distinctiveness in spite of assimilative efforts by German and Russian overlords. Development of an intelligentsia in the latter half of the nineteenth century coincided with a period of rapid industrial growth resulting in formation of both nationalist and socialist-internationalist trends. During the Russian Civil War the Latvians became even more divided among themselves—pro-Communists against anti-Communists—than were the Estonians or Lithuanians. Establishment of the independent Latvian republic isolated most pro-Bolshevik Latvians, however, and Stalin's purges decimated Latvians living in the USSR. Few native Communists with strong local ties were left by the time Latvia became part of the Soviet Union.

Oriented toward west-central Europe by a heritage of Germanic culture, religion, alphabet, and historic trade ties, the Baltic peoples are the most Westernized portion of the Soviet population, serving as a major channel for introduction of Western ideas and fashions into the USSR.[114] Higher level of economic development and welfare—both at time of incorporation into the Soviet Union and at present—combines with this background to produce an environment in which Latvians may feel superior to the Russians and other Slavs.[115]

Incorporation of Latvia into the Soviet Union occurred within the lifetime of almost 60% of its present population.[116] Despite the fact that Soviet historiography has slowly eliminated references to the significant roles played by "changed international circumstances" (a euphemism for the Molotov-Ribbentrop pact) and the Red Army, Sovietization of Latvia was neither free nor voluntary. It led to deportation of most political leaders and a major portion of its mobilized and educated population, as well as to considerable emigration. This traumatic series of events left many Latvians with relatives in the West, and the Soviet regime has made unceasing efforts to counter and discredit the information and political activities of the exiles.[117]

The Soviet period of Latvian history has seen a continued large immigration of Russians and other Slavs into the republic. This has significantly reduced the predominance

111 *LME*, 1969: II: 580.
112 *Ibid*.: II: 56.
113 *Ibid*.: II: 708–709; 1970: III: 501; Rutkis, 1967: 552–553.
114 Rein Taagepera, 1973. For a Soviet viewpoint, see Vasili Askenov, *A Ticket To The Stars* (New York: Signet Books, 1963), *passim*.

115 King, 1968: 62. For a similar sentiment among Lithuanians, see *Soviet Analyst* (November), 1972: I: 18: 4.
116 *Sovetskaya Latviya* (June 23), 1971.
117 See *Cīna* (February 24), 1972, wherein the exiled Social Democratic leader Dr. Bruno Kalnins is accused of forging the "Letter of 17 Latvian Communists"; and Radio Liberty Dispatch, *Dissidents Among the National Minorities in the USSR* (August 29), 1972: 4.

of ethnic Balts in the population, especially in the cities. A great deal of this immigration was connected with reestablishment of heavy industry, and some natives have argued that a primary purpose of such industrialization was to provide for importation of Russians.[118] The small size and slow growth of the native contingent in the CPL have meant that political power was and continues to be exercised by Russians and imports of Latvian origin long resident in Russia who speak Latvian imperfectly. This leadership has resisted the tendency to become "renationalized" and to act as a buffer between Moscow and national Communists, as seems to have prevailed in Estonia.[119] They remain close to the Moscow line, perhaps influenced by the rise of one of their number, Arvids Pelshe, to chairmanship of the CPSU party Control Committee. The one attempt of native Communists to gain influence and speak out for republic and national interests was crushed in 1959.[120]

The attitudes of Latvians today toward the Soviet system in general and the future of their nation in particular are difficult to determine. Most information has to be gleaned from official publications, private communications, and reports of visitors. Latvian participation in *samizdat* has been relatively small, especially in comparison with the activities of Estonians, Lithuanians, and the Jewish population of Riga. The latter group has played a conspicuous role in the current Jewish awakening in the Soviet Union. Such sources do, however, provide many indications that the Latvians are concerned—perhaps increasingly so—about preservation of their national culture.

The leadership of the Latvian CP has frequently attacked any expression of nationalist feelings and "political immaturity," thereby demonstrating the persistence of such feelings. *Cīņa* criticized the Union of Writers and Artists in September 1970 for not giving sufficient attention to "ideological growth" of its members. The 1972 congress of the Latvian Komsomol also heard criticism of poor political

education work among young writers.[121] The existence of cultural nationalism and the desire of young Latvian writers to reevaluate those parts of their literary heritage denigrated by the Soviets has been documented by Rolfs Ekmanis of Arizona State University.[122]

Augusts Voss, first secretary of the CPL, has repeatedly castigated survivals of bourgeois nationalism among the population.[123] Publication of an official rebuttal—a highly inadequate one—to the so-called "Letter of 17 Latvian Communists" is evidence of the interest created by this letter when it was rebroadcast to Latvia by Radio Liberty.[124]

BASIC VIEWS OF SCHOLARS ON NATIONAL ATTITUDES

Rein Taagepera of the University of California at Irvine has written that "resistance to the regime has been sporadic, varied, and possibly slowly increasing in all Baltic republics." [125] He is less sanguine about the future of the Latvian nation, however, concluding that it is in greater danger of assimilation than its neighbors. This is due in large part to an ever increasing Russian population and lack of support and protection from its own party elite.

A major study of attitudes and social behavior in national relations was conducted between 1964 and 1969 by a group of Soviet scholars led by A. I. Kholmogorov. Data showed a strong trend toward growth of "international features" among the population of Latvia, but with some interesting variations; for example, although census

118 "Nationality Problems: Latvia," *Soviet Analyst* (March 2), 1972: I: 1: 4.
119 Taagepera, 1973: 7–9.
120 On the events of 1959, see section on nationalism.

121 *Cīņa* (September 15), 1970; (March 3), 1972. *Sovietskaya Latviya* (March 10), 1973, repeats criticism of this kind and connects it to nationalism. Translated in *FBIS* (March 19), 1973: FBIS–SOV–73–53: III: J2–J5.
122 Ekmanis, 1972: 59–60, 66.
123 See, for example, his articles in *Pravda* (March 20), 1971, and in *Politicheskoye samoobrazovaniye* (June), 1972. The latter was quoted in *Radio Liberty Dispatch* (August 20), 1972: 4. See also his speech to XXI Congress of CPL, *Sovietskaya Latviya* (February 26), 1971 (*FBIS* No. 55, Supp. 11, March 22, 1971, esp. pp. 60–61).
124 *Soviet Analyst* (April 13), 1972: I: 4: 4. Private communications in Riga in June 1963 indicate a belief that the "Letter" could have originated locally.
125 Taagepera, 1973: 9.

data show that a great many use Russian at work, only 7.4% of Latvians use Russian in the home.[126] Two thirds of those surveyed said they had friends among other nationalities, a figure significantly below the 86% average for non-Latvian residents of the republic.[127] Latvians reacted much less favorably to the idea of multinational work collectives than did the others, were less likely to have visited another Soviet republic, and showed a stronger preference for their national culture.[128]

Other Soviet studies, including one by the ethnographer L. Terent'eva, have pointed to a marked increase in frequency of mixed marriages in the city of Riga—from 30% in 1948 to 36% in 1963. Jānis Vitols reported that 38% of the marriages in Riga in 1970 were between people of different nationalities.[129] Apparently, publication of Terent'eva's results in the Latvian journal Zinātne un Tekhnika in 1970 caused a commotion, for that issue was withdrawn almost immediately from public circulation.[130] Kholmogorov's sample of several different parts of Latvia, however, indicated that Latvians were less prone to enter mixed marriages than were representatives of other nationalities. Slightly over 11% surveyed had made such marriages versus approximately a third of the Russian population.

Under Soviet law, children of such marriages have the opportunity to choose the nationality of either parent for their internal passport. In Riga the children of Latvian-Russian marriages showed a tendency to prefer Latvian registration 57% to 43%. Children of marriages between Latvians and members of other nationalities chose Latvian with even greater frequency.[131]

Such studies, though inconclusive, tend to show that nationalist feelings and particularism have not disappeared among the Latvians, although not manifested in illegal dissent as often as among the other Baltic peoples.

---

126 Kholmogorov, 1970: 119, 121.
127 Ibid.: 175.
128 Ibid.: 172, 180, 185.
129 Nauka i tekhnika (February), 1972: 32–35.
130 The article is translated, with commentary, in King, 1970. See also Terent'eva's article in Sovetskaya etnografya, 1969: III: 20–30.
131 Zinātne un tekhnika (August), 1970: VIII: 12.

RECENT MANIFESTATIONS OF NATIONALISM

As Anthony Astrakhan, former Moscow correspondent for the Washington Post, wrote in 1970, "Nationalism in Estonia and neighboring Latvia is easy for a visitor to sense but hard to document. What you see with your eyes is more a wish for cultural autonomy than a plan or dream of seceding from the Soviet Union.[132] This observation seems more true for Latvia than for Estonia, where the Khronika [Chronicle] has reported the existence of an organized national movement. Still, a number of Latvians have been involved in illegal dissent in recent years. Teataja, an Estonian émigré journal, reported the trial of seven young Latvian writers and literary critics in May-June 1968.[133] Soviet underground channels carried reports on the arrest of ten persons gathered at the grave of Jānis Čakste, first president of independent Latvia, on the 1969 anniversary of their declaration of independence, November 18.[134] In February 1971 three young Latvians were sentenced to prison terms for distributing anti-Soviet leaflets.[135]

It is possible that Latvians are among the self-styled "Democrats of Russia, Ukraine, and the Baltic States" who have authored two major pieces of samizdat literature. The Memorandum of this group, published abroad in December 1970, mentions Latvians among the "hundreds" imprisoned for advocating secession of their republic from the Soviet Union.[136]

Most important recent document emerging from Latvia is the "Letter of 17 Latvian Communists" (further referred to as Letter), which appeared in the West in January 1972. Although its authors are unknown, as are the channels by which it reached the West, this document is widely

---

132 Washington Post (December 11), 1970.
133 Cited in Estonian Events (December), 1968: XI: 1.
134 Anthony Astrakhan, Washington Post (December 11), 1970.
135 Latvian Information Bulletin (Latvian Legation, Washington, D.C.) (October), 1971: IV: 13.
136 Myroslav Prokop, 1971; "Translations on USSR Political and Social Affairs," JPRS (December 9), 1971: 193: 4.

held to be authentic.[137] In the *Letter*, the authors identify themselves as long-time party members, all born in Latvia. Most appear to have been former party undergrounders in bourgeois Latvia, who had become convinced that Leninism was being used consciously and deliberately as a screen for Great Russian chauvinism. They recall that at the June 1953 plenum of the Central Committee of the CPL, Russian domination of the Latvian party and its *apparat* was criticized as a distortion of Leninist nationalities policy. The "thaw" lasted only a short time, however (apparently reflecting Beria's attempt to gain power in the party by winning the support of non-Russian cadres),[138] and Russification was resumed "ever more obtrusively and purposefully." The *Letter* then describes several aspects of that policy: (1) Russian control of the second secretary and cadres secretary posts; (2) importation of both construction workers and permanent labor for large new factories; (3) location of major military bases and all-Union health resorts in Latvia; (4) Russian domination of many government departments (65% of doctors in the city health services are said not to speak Latvian, which causes "crude errors in diagnoses and the prescription of remedies"); (5) use of Russian for two thirds of all radio and television broadcasts; and (6) insistence on conducting meetings in Russian even if only one Russian is in the group. The authors conclude:: "Everything national is being eliminated. Forced assimilation is

being practiced. Peoples, cultures, and traditions do not have equal rights."

As one example of natives' attempts to resist this policy (others are implied but not described), the *Letter* recounts the Berklavs affair in 1959, when a majority of the Latvian Politburo members began to support him in opposing Russification. Khrushchev himself came to Latvia to oversee Berklavs' dismissal. In the purge that followed, CPL First Secretary J. Kalnberzins was kicked upstairs to chairman of the Presidium of the Supreme Soviet, and Premier V. Lacis was removed, as were two other Central Committee CPL secretaries, chairman of the republic trade union, editor of *Cīna*, first secretary and several other members of the Riga City committee, first and second secretaries of the Latvian Komsomol, and numerous other party and government officials. According to the *Letter*, "today only foreigners and those Latvians who have lived all their lives in Russia and appeared in Latvia only after the Second World War work in leadership positions." [139]

After the Voice of America broadcast to the USSR on the content of the *Letter*, both Russian and Latvian press organs of the CC CPL printed a rebuttal which failed to confront any of the major charges directly. Instead, it concentrated on accusing émigrés of forging the letter and countered with information not related to points raised in it.[140] The obvious inadequacy of the rebuttal points to the truth of the accusations, revealing the leadership's concern over survival of nationalism in Latvia.

---

137 *Brivība* (January), 1972: I: 2–4; *New York Times* (February 27), 1972; Duevel, 1972; *Soviet Analyst* (March 2), 1972: I: 1: 3–6.
138 Duevel, 1972.

139 For additional references to the Berklavs affair, see section on demography.
140 *Soviet Analyst* (April 13), 1972: I: 4: 4–6.

REFERENCES

Andersons, 1953
    Edgars Andersons, *Cross Road Country, Latvia* (Waverly, Iowa: Latviju Grāmata, 1953).
Berzins, 1963
    Alfred Berzins, *The Unpunished Crime* (New York: Robert Speller, 1963).

Bilinsky, 1968
    Yaroslav Bilinsky, "Assimilation and Ethnic Assertiveness Among Ukrainians of the Soviet Union," in Erich Goldhagen ed., *Ethnic Minorities in the Soviet Union* (New York: Praeger, 1968), 147–184.

Bilmanis, 1947
  Alfreds Bilmanis, *Latvia as an Indepen-
  dent State* (Washington, D.C.: Latvian
  Legation, 1947).
BSE Yezhegodnik 1957
  *Bol'shaya Sovetskaya Entsiklopediya,
  Yezhegodnik 1957 [Great Soviet Encyclo-
  pedia, 1957 Annual Supplement]* (Mos-
  cow: Bol'shaya Sovetskaya Entsiklo-
  pediya, 1958).
BSE 1953
  Bol'shaya Sovetskaya Entsiklopediya, 2nd
  ed. (Moscow: Bol'shaya Entsiklopediya,
  1953).
CDSP
  Current Digest of the Soviet Press, pub-
  lished by Joint Committee on Slavic
  Studies.
Dreifelds, 1970
  Juris Dreifelds, "Latvia Today," in Taage-
  pera, *Estonian Events* (August 1970):
  nos. 21–22: 4.
Duevel, 1972
  Christian Duevel, "Additional Light on
  the Beria Case," *Radio Liberty Research
  Report*, January 27, 1972.
Ekmanis, 1972
  Rolfs Ekmanis, "Soviet Attitudes toward
  Pre-Soviet Latvian Writers," *Journal of
  Baltic Studies* (Spring 1972): III: 1:
  44–70.
FBIS
  Foreign Broadcast Information Service,
  published by U.S. Department of Com-
  merce.
Gērmanis, 1970
  Uldis Gērmanis, "Zemgaliesu Koman-
  dieris," *Jauna Gaita* (Toronto) (1970):
  XV: 17: 3–17.
Glimpses of Latvian Culture, 1971
  Glimpses of Latvian Culture, pamphlet
  (Riga: Liesma, 1971).
Istoriya LSSR, 1955
  *Istoriya Latviiskoi SSR: Sokrashchennyi
  kurs* (Riga: Zinātne, 1955).
Itogi 1970
  *Itogi vsesoyuznoi perepisi naselenyia 1970
  goda*, vol. IV (Moscow: Statistika, 1973).
JPRS
  Joint Publications Research Service.
  Translations on USSR Political and Socio-
  logical Affairs (published by U.S. Depart-
  ment of Commerce).
Kholmogorov, 1970
  A. I. Kholmogorov, *Internatsional'nyye
  cherty Sovetskikh natsii* (Moscow: Mysl',
  1970).
King, 1965
  Gundar Julian King, *Economic Policies
  in Occupied Latvia* (Tacoma: Pacific
  Lutheran University Press, 1965).

King, 1968
  Gundar Julian King, "Management of the
  Economy and Political Power: The Lat-
  vian case," *Lituanus* (Winter 1968):
  XIV: 4: 54–72.
King, 1970
  Gundar Julian King, *The Tale of Three
  Cities*. Communication presented to
  Second Conference on Baltic Studies, San
  Jose, California, November 28, 1970.
Latvia, 1968
  Latvia (Washington, D.C.: American Lat-
  vian Association, 1968).
LME
  Latvijas PSR Mazā Enciklopēdija (Riga:
  Zinātne, 1967–1970).
LTS
  Latvijas PSR Tautas Saimniecība (Riga:
  Statistika, 1968 and 1971 [pub. date
  1972; title 1971]).
Maciuika, 1972
  Benedict V. Maciuika, "The Role of the
  Baltic Republics in the Economy of the
  USSR," *Journal of Baltic Studies* (1972):
  III: 1: 18–25.
Nar. khoz. 1970
  Narodnoye khozyaistvo SSSR v 1970 godu
  (Moscow: Statistika, 1971).
Nar. khoz. 1972
  *Narodnoye khozyaistvo SSSR 1922–
  1972, Yubileinyi statisticheskii yezhe-
  godnik* (Moscow: Statistika, 1972).
Nar. khoz. Latvii 1971
  *Narodnoye khozyaistvo Latviiskoi SSR v
  1971 gody* (Riga: Statistika, 1972).
Nar. obraz., 1971
  *Narodnoye obrazovaniye, nauka i kul'tura
  v SSSR: statisticheskii sbornik* (Moscow:
  Statistika, 1971).
Ocherki, 1965
  *Ocherki razvitiya gosudarstvennosti
  Sovetskikh pribaltiiskikh respublik
  [Sketches on Development of Soviet Bal-
  tic Republics]* (Tallinn: Eesti Raamat,
  1965).
Pechat' 1959
  Pechat' SSSR v 1959 godu (Moscow:
  Kniga, 1960).
Pechat' 1971
  Pechat' SSSR v 1971 godu (Moscow:
  Kniga, 1972).
Pennar, 1971
  Jaan Pennar et al., *Modernization and
  Diversity in Soviet Education, with
  Special Reference to Nationality Groups*
  (New York: Praeger, 1971).
Presses Hronika
  Latvijas PSR Preses Hronika. Monthly
  Publication of Committee on Press,
  Latvian PSR Council of Ministers.

Rutkis, 1967
J. Rutkis, ed., *Latvia: Country and People* (Stockholm: Latvian National Foundation, 1967).

Soviet Union, 1969
Soviet Union 50 Years: Statistical Returns (Moscow: Progress Publishers, 1969).

Spekke, 1951
Arnolds Spekke, *History of Latvia: An Outline* (Stockholm: M. Goppers, 1951).

Statistical Abstract of U.S.
U.S. Bureau of Census, *Statistical Abstract of United States* (Washington, D.C., 1971), 92nd ed.

Taagepera, 1973
Rein Taagepera, "Dissimilarities Between the Northwest Soviet Republics," in A. Ziedonis, R. Taagepera, M. Valgemäe, eds., *Problems of Mini-Nations: Baltic Perspectives* (New York: Association for Advancement of Baltic Studies, 1973).

Tarulis, 1959
Albert N. Tarulis, *Soviet Policy Toward the Baltic States 1918–1940* (South Bend, Ind.: University of Notre Dame Press, 1959).

Trapans, 1963
Andris Trapans, "A Note on Latvian Communist Party Membership 1941–1961," *Baltic Review* (April 1963): XXVI: 17–30.

UN Statistical Yearbook, 1970
United Nations Statistical Yearbook, 1970 (New York, 1971).

Vardys, 1964
V. Stanley Vardys, "Soviet Colonialism in the Baltic States: A Note on the Nature of Modern Colonialism," *Lituanus* (Summer 1964): X: 2: 5–23.

Vēsture, 1967
Latvijas PSR Vēsture, Saīsinats Kurss (Riga: Zinātne, 1967).

Von Rauch, 1970
Georg von Rauch, *Geschichte der baltischen Staaten* (Stuttgart: Kohlhammer, 1970).

Widmer, 1969
Michael Jean Widmer, *Nationalism and Communism in Latvia: The Latvian Communist Party Under Soviet Rule.* Unpublished Ph.D. dissertation, Harvard University, 1969.

6 | LITHUANIA and THE LITHUANIANS

Frederic T. Harned

General Information

TERRITORY[1]

The Lithuanian Soviet Socialist Republic is the southernmost and largest of the three Baltic republics incorporated into the Soviet Union in August 1940. Its 25,000-square-mile area is slightly less than the combined area of Belgium and the Netherlands. It is bordered by the Latvian SSR to the north, the Belorussian SSR to the east and south, the Kaliningrad *oblast* of the RSFSR in the west (formerly the Koenigsberg region of German East Prussia), and Poland to the southwest. The republic possesses some 60 miles of seacoast along the Baltic Sea, including the ports of Klaipeda (Memel) and Palanga. The capital is Vilnius (Russian, Vilna; Polish, Wilno).

Lithuania's history has been one of stubborn resistance to the encroachments of three powerful neighboring cultures—those of Germany, Poland, and Russia. Unlike their Latvian neighbors, the medieval Lithuanians successfully resisted German conquest and, in union with Poland, built a powerful empire. Russian pressure steadily reduced the size of their domain, and Polish influence their distinctiveness, until both were submerged in the partitions of Poland. When independence was reestablished in the aftermath of World War I, two major cities, Klaipeda and Vilnius, were in foreign hands.[2] Lithuania seized Klaipeda from Germany in 1923 and held it until 1939, but Vilnius remained under Polish control until the start of World War II.

Occupying the lower reaches of the Nemunas (Niemen) River basin, Lithuania is predominantly a relatively flat lowland, with many marshes, rivers, and glacial lakes. Highlands in the east and southeast reach a maximum elevation of 967 feet. Deciduous and fir forests cover 16% of the

---

1 *SSSR 1967:* 567–568; *Ekonomika Litvy 1970;* Simutis, 1942: 16–18; *LME, 1969:* II: 374–377.

2 The historic Lithuanian capital, Vilnius, had at times more Poles and Jews than Lithuanians in its population. The adjacent territories are predominantly Lithuanian although a large Polish minority still lives there.

republic's territory, 58% of which is used for agriculture.

Although Lithuania's latitude is roughly that of Moscow, the climate of the republic is considerably milder, due to moderating influence of the Atlantic air mass and the Baltic Sea. Mean annual temperatures range from 23°F. in January to 63°F. in July. Average rainfall, much of which falls in August, ranges from 23 to 31 inches per year. The ground is frozen for about four months of the year. The climate is excellent for raising livestock and growing flax.

Lithuania lacks fuel resources other than wood and peat. There is some iron ore, but primary resources are chalk, gypsum, limestone, sand, and clay. The Lithuanian seacoast has been known as a source of amber since the days of the Roman Empire.

ECONOMY

Unlike the other Baltic provinces, Lithuania remained economically underdeveloped during the tsarist period. Except for leather and metalworking, there was little industry because of lack of raw materials, absence of a large port, and proximity to Germany.[3] Lithuania's abundant timber supplied a growing lumber industry in Klaipeda, then part of Germany. Much land remained in large estates and was used primarily for cultivation of grain crops or flax and for horse breeding.[4] Dairying and swine and poultry raising were minimal.

Lithuania's industrial base, such as it was, was largely destroyed or dislocated during World War I. In the years that followed, the government of independent Lithuania pursued a consciously agrarian policy, encouraging production of high-quality meats, eggs, and dairy products. These industries showed significant growth during the interwar years, due in part to the very low level from which they began, forming the predominant share of the country's exports.[5] A thorough land reform improved distribution of land holdings and had a great economic impact, since 76% of the population depended on land for subsis-

tence.[6] Industrial production also expanded during the period, although at a slower rate. Primary industries included textiles, food and luxury goods, timber, clay, and stone products.[7] Klaipeda, reunited with the body of Lithuania in 1923–1939 and since 1945, remained the most industrialized area.

World War II and imposition of the Soviet system again substantially damaged Lithuania's economy. Agricultural output of important commodities such as rye, wheat, barley, sugar beets, and flax, declined markedly in 1939–1950 and even between 1950 and 1955.[8]

After the initial dislocation and disruption—in part conditioned by widespread guerilla warfare against the Soviets—Lithuania's economy began a period of remarkable growth and continuous industrialization. Although still trailing Latvia and Estonia in level of development, Lithuania has steadily gained on them, surpassing much of the rest of the Soviet Union. Whereas in 1939 only 22.9% of the population lived in cities, the 1970 census showed that urban population slightly exceeded rural population (50.2% to 49.8%). Estimates for 1971 placed 53% of the population in cities.[9] Lithuania led all union republics in growth rate of gross industrial product between 1940 and 1969. Official figures showed that this index grew twenty-eight-fold in the 29-year period, while the figure for the USSR as a whole was eleven-fold.[10] A 1972 report gave the volume of Lithuania's industrial output as 34 times higher than before the war, and electric power production over 90 times higher.[11]

Nineteen-seventy statistics list 28.5% of the working population as *kolkhozniki* or *sovkhoz* workers, and 27% as employed in industry.[12] The contribution of agriculture to the gross social product in 1970 was approximately half that of industry, again

---

3 Vardys, 1965: 21–22.
4 Simutis, 1942: 22, 66.
5 *Ibid.*: 51–65.

6 Taagepera, 1972a: 26–34; Sabaliunas, 1972: 4–5.
7 Simutis, 1942: 68–70.
8 Vardys, 1965: 154.
9 *Ekonomika Litvy*, 1970: 18; *Nar. khoz. 1972*: 594.
10 *Ibid.*: 421.
11 *Soviet Life* (November), 1972: 15.
12 Data is for *"kolkhozniki* taking part in work" of *kolkhozy*, plus *sovkhoz* workers. Members of kolkhoz families are not included. Even so, collective farm workers outnumber *sovkhoz* workers by almost two to one.

reflecting growth of the latter in Lithuania's economy.[13] Within the sphere of agricultural production, dairying and livestock remained the most important branches. Together, they accounted for almost 90% of the ruble payments to collective and state farms for agricultural produce in 1970.[14]

In 1965, 60% of Lithuania's total industrial production was accounted for by light industry, food, and fish, the earliest industries to be strongly developed.[15] Greatest growth during the 1960s, however, was experienced in heavy industry. Gross production of electrical energy in 1970 was nearly eight times the 1960 figure; chemical and oil refining, more than 13 times; machine-building and metalworking, almost six times; and construction materials, four times.[16] In the same period, percentage of industrial workers employed in machine-building and metalworking grew from 23% to 33%, and that of workers in light industry and food production dropped from 45% to 38%.[17]

Lithuania produces machine tools and instruments, automation equipment, electronic computers, radio and TV sets, refrigerators, and fishing trawlers.[18] With 1.3% of the USSR's population, in 1970 it produced 11.3% of its metal-cutting lathes, 5.5% of its socks and stockings, 4.8% of its fish, and 4.1% of its animal fats.[19]

Expansion of Lithuania's economy has corresponded with a growth in indicators of the standard of living. The republic led all union republics in growth of national income between 1960 and 1970; in savings per capita, it moved from ninth place to fifth during the same period. Lithuania's ranking in terms of per capita trade turnover advanced from fifth to third during the decade, so that now it trails only Estonia and Latvia, as is the case in terms of produced national income per capita. The republic ranked sixth among Soviet republics in doctors per 10,000 in 1971, up from eighth in 1966, and surpasses West

Germany, France, and Italy in this respect.[20] Emerging from many years of backwardness, Lithuania is rapidly assuming a leading position in the Union in terms of economic growth and development.[21]

HISTORY

By the beginning of the thirteenth century, the ancestors of the modern Lithuanians had established a feudal-noble social order, uniting loosely the several Baltic tribes under the leadership of five major families. These people had arrived in the region during the last two millennia B.C., and until the fourth century after Christ had occupied much of what is today Belorussia. The pressure of Slavic expansion had steadily forced them toward the north and west, where new threats confronted them: the Order of the Sword in Riga and the Teutonic Order in East Prussia. In part protected by a central position among the Baltic peoples, the Lithuanians avoided the respective fates of the Latvians (subjugation) and Old Prussians (annihilation), forming a unified monarchy under Mindaugas.[22] In 1236 the Lithuanians and Slavs defeated the Order of the Sword at Siauliai. Later, Mindaugas accepted Christianity in exchange for recognition by the Germans, reorganized into the Livonian Order, as king of Lithuania. Continued incursions by the Order led him to renounce his decision. Gediminas (1316–1341) organized the territory into a grand duchy, founding the city of Vilnius as capital in 1323.[23] Two sons succeeded him, extending Lithuania's power over Belorussia and most of the western Ukraine to the Black Sea. Thus, Lithuania became one of the largest empires of medieval Europe. Gediminas' grandson, Grand Duke Jogaila, was invited to marry the Polish queen and become king of Poland in 1385, on condition that he unite the two states.[24] In exchange for for-

13 *Ekonomika Litvy*, 1970: 47.
14 *Ibid.*: 185.
15 *Litva*, 1967: 315.
16 *Ekonomika Litvy*, 1970: 69. By contrast, growth of all industry was 303%, and light industry, 269%.
17 *Ibid.*: 101; *Nar. khoz. Litvy 1965*: 72.
18 *Soviet Life* (November), 1972: 15.
19 *Nar khoz. 1970*: 70–79.

20 *Soviet Life*: (November), 1972: 15.
21 *Nar. khoz. 1970*: 534, 563–564, 579; *Ekonomika Litvy*, 1970: 457; *Nar. khoz. 1972*: 515ff; *Nar. khoz. Latvii 1971*: 56.
22 *Gerutis et al.*, 1969: 45–46.
23 *Stukas*, 1966: 6.
24 *Vardys*, 1965: 5.

mal subordination, he named his cousin Vytautas grand duke of Lithuania in 1392. At this beginning stage of the Polish-Lithuanian union, the two states remained separate, under a common sovereign.[25] Together, Vytautas and Jogaila (called Jagiello by the Poles) soundly defeated the Teutonic Order at Tannenburg in 1410, ending the Germans' eastward expansion.[26]

The reign of Vytautas (1392–1430) marked the apex of Lithuanian power and territorial extent. He won a bloody victory over the Tatars at Vorksla in 1399, ending their westward expansion. His daughter was regent in Moscow and mother of Grand Duke Basil II.[27] During the same period, Catholicism became thoroughly entrenched as the national religion, opening the way to the influx of Western culture, received in Lithuania through Polish mediation. Its power and attraction led to an increase in Polish influence and gradual Polonization of the Lithuanian nobility.

Simultaneously, during the fifteenth and sixteenth centuries, Muscovy was growing stronger, eating away at the Lithuanians' empire. Steady pressure from the east, the extra burden of protecting the territories of Latgale and Courland won in the Livonian War (1558–1582), and end of the Jagiellonian dynasty led to the Union of Lublin (1572), binding Lithuania still more tightly to Poland.[28] Under this agreement, Lithuania maintained a separate executive and judicial system and currency, but the person of the grand duke was formally united with that of the Polish king, while previously the two titles could be held by different people.[29] Further, the diets of the two countries were prohibited from meeting separately.[30]

Within the Union of Lublin, Lithuania was almost completely engulfed by European culture.[31] The Renaissance attracted young nobility to European universities. The Polish language spread among members of the nobility, eventually becoming their first language and, in 1698, the official language of all state institutions.[32] The University of Vilnius was founded in 1579 by Jesuits, a major force in bringing Western culture to the masses through sermons in the vernacular.[33] Culturally, Lithuania was well on its way to becoming part of Poland, although enough of a sense of difference remained for the Lithuanian nobility to play a major role in preventing centralization of authority. Thus, they contributed to decline of the state, leaving it an easy prey for larger neighbors in the partitions of the eighteenth century.[34] Although submerged, the Lithuanian language and culture remained alive, preserved by the lower classes, until revitalized by the nascent intelligentsia in the nineteenth century.

In 1796 Russia occupied all of Lithuania except for Klaipeda, the coastline south of the city, and the area west to the Nemunas River, all of which fell to Prussia. These areas, together with Lithuanian-inhabited areas around Koenigsberg controlled by the Germans since the fifteenth century, were known as Lithuania Minor. It was here in the early eighteenth century, under the influence of Lutheran pastors and work at the University of Koenigsberg, that development of Lithuanian into a literary language began.[35] The work was picked up at the University of Vilnius in the beginning of the nineteenth century; historical, folkloristic, and linguistic researches commenced.[36] Ideas of romanticism and nationalism engendered by Europe's Age of Revolution were echoed at the university. Students founded secret societies and discussed revolutionary ideas, their activities leading to closing of the university (1832) as part of the tsarist reaction to the Polish-Lithuanian revolt of 1830–31.[37]

Unrest was not eliminated, however; the Poles and Lithuanians rebelled again in 1863. Tsarist figures show that most battles occurred in Lithuanian districts.[38] The revolt bore a social as well as national

25 *Ibid.*
26 Jurgela, 1948: 150–160.
27 Vardys, 1965: 4.
28 *Ibid.*: 5–6; Gerutis *et al.*, 1969: 78–80.
29 In practice, the titles of king and grand duke had been held by the same person, with few exceptions, since 1440 (Stukas, 1966: 14).
30 Stukas, 1966: 16.
31 Gerutis *et al.*, 1969: 83.

32 Stukas, 1966: 17.
33 Gerutis *et al.*, 1969: 86–89.
34 *Ibid.*: 99–103.
35 Stukas, 1966: 64, 101–105.
36 Gerutis *et al.*, 1968: 112–117.
37 *Ibid.*: 119–120.
38 *Ibid.*: 126.

character as grievances were expressed over emancipation of the serfs without ceding land and over impressment into the army. Afterwards the tsarist government sought to pacify the region by reducing Polish influence. Some improvement in the lot of the peasantry occurred vis-à-vis the Polish (or Polonized) landlords, and publication of Lithuanian books in the Latin alphabet (a vehicle for Polish influence) was banned.[39]

The latter measure had a decisively counterproductive effect, for Lithuanian books and periodicals in Latin were readily available in Lithuania Minor. The Church, led by Bishop Motiejus Valancius (1810–1875), refused to allow printing of religious books in Cyrillic. To supply the need, Valancius assisted in organization of a network of "book-carriers" who smuggled Lithuanian books and periodicals in the forbidden alphabet from Lithuania Minor. He also played a major role in creating a literate audience, earlier establishing a wide system of schools in parishes of his diocese.[40]

Patriotic and nationalist literature was soon spread throughout Lithuania by the book-carriers, who attained the status of folk heroes as cultural Robin Hoods.[41] First such newspaper to appear was *Ausra* [*Dawn*], published in 1883–1886 by Dr. Jonas Basanavicius, regarded as a patriarch of the nation.[42] *Varpas* [*The Bell*], founded by Vincas Kudirka (1858–1899), was more directly politically oriented, printing harsh criticisms of Russian and Polish activities. Many others followed. The press ban provided a cause, creating an underground communications network uniting representatives of the rising Lithuanian middle classes and intelligentsia. By the time the ban was revoked in 1904, a strong national movement had emerged.

Socialist ideas were also emerging. Vilnius was an important center for the Jewish *Bund*, the Polish Socialist party, and the Lithuanian Social Democrats.[43] As the Lithuanian proletariat was minimal, however, socialism remained more an intel-

lectual current and less a popular one than in neighboring Latvia. After centuries of gradual Polonization and blurring of distinctions between the two countries (both Poland and Lithuania consider Adam Mickiewicz [Adomas Mickevicius] a national poet), national identity remained the burning issue. As a result, during the Revolution of 1905, the Assembly of Vilnius demanded autonomy for Lithuania.[44] This was one of the first such appeals within the Russian Empire.

During World War I, all of Lithuania was occupied by Germany from September 1915 until the end of the war. The Germans allowed formation of a national council or *Taryba* at Vilnius in September 1917, hoping to use it to legitimate their planned annexation of the country. The council proved stubborn but realistic, cooperating when the pressure was on and resisting when it could. It proclaimed independence and perpetual union with Germany in December 1917 and unconditional independence in February 1918. In June it invited a German prince to become king of Lithuania, but withdrew the invitation in November 1918.[45] With the German surrender, the *Taryba* sought to form a provisional government in Vilnius. The Red Army, however, took the city in January 1919, proclaiming a Soviet regime under Vincas Mickivicius-Kapsukas. The Lithuanian nationalists retreated to Kaunas, where they began forming an army.

With financial and material assistance from Western states, and especially with inadvertent aid of the Bolsheviks, who had alienated the peasantry with premature attempts at collectivization, the Lithuanians succeeded in advancing to the Daugava by August 1919.[46] They also defeated a German army under Bermondt-Avalov in northern Lithuania in November 1919, but were unable to retake Vilnius, seized by Poland. The Soviets reoccupied Vilnius during an advance on Warsaw in 1920, abandoning it again after their defeat. A "rebellion," planned in Warsaw, left the city in Polish hands.[47] Trusting in the League of Nations, Lithuania sought the return of Vilnius through peaceful means. The League failed

---

39 *Ibid.*: 129–131.
40 Stukas, 1966: 61–64.
41 *Ibid.*: 77.
42 *Ibid.* See also Jurgela, 1948: 475–481, 488.
43 Gerutis *et al.*, 1969: 135.

44 Vardys, 1965: 7.
45 *Ibid.*: 13–14; Gerutis *et al.*, 1969: 152–160.
46 Vardys, 1965: 15.
47 *Ibid.*: 18.

to act, in part due to France's support of Poland, and the dispute over the city poisoned Lithuanian-Polish relations throughout the interwar period.

The Lithuanian Constituent Assembly convened in May 1920, adopting a constitution in August 1922.[48] The government was to be formed by a president elected by the parliament, or *Seimas*, and responsible to it. The 1922 elections returned too many different parties to the *Seimas* for a stable government to be formed. Center-right coalitions led by the Christian-Democrats held power until 1926, when they were dislodged by a Populist-Socialist coalition backed by parties of the German, Jewish, and Polish minorities. The leftist policies of this government and antagonism toward the Poles were key factors in leading Antanas Smetona, first president of the infant republic, a strong nationalist, to seize power in December 1926 and organize a dictatorial regime.[49]

Despite difficulties and short life, the democratic government was able to achieve effective land reform and institute public education, permitting the Catholic Church and national minorities to continue operating their own private school systems as well. Externally, the government seized Klaipeda from Germany in 1923, and the seaport was united with the hinterland for the first time in 700 years.

Smetona's nationalist regime was authoritarian and restrictive but not fascist, although the president had expressed admiration for Mussolini's theories. The regime was reluctant to use "arbitrary and excessive compulsion" against the opposition, which continued to exist, although hampered by press controls and a ban on opposition parties.[50] Economic and social policies tended to be conservative. Lithuania kept a balanced budget and took on little foreign debt. Investment was directed toward encouragement of agriculture rather than industrial development.[51]

Forced by Hitler's Germany to return Klaipeda in March 1939, the nationalist government lost so much support that it had to form a new cabinet which included Christian Democrats and Populists. This concession might have presaged a return to liberal politics,[52] but any such possibility was cut short by Soviet intervention. The details were similar in all three Baltic republics: imposition of "mutual assistance pacts" allowing introduction of the Red Army, complaints that the governments were anti-Soviet and not living up to the pacts, imposition of a new government hand-picked by a Soviet plenipotentiary, elections in which only the Communist slate was allowed, and new assemblies which "unanimously" voted for incorporation into the USSR.[53] In Lithuania's case the deal was sweetened by the return of Vilnius, which the Soviets had taken from Poland. Soviet policies in 1940–1941, however, which included nationalizations, deportations, and persecution of clergy, negated whatever good will might have been won by offering of the historic city. When the Nazis attacked Russia in June 1941, the Lithuanians rose up, hastening the Russians' retreat. Nationalist forces were in control of most major cities by the time the Germans arrived.[54]

Spurned in efforts to win recognition from the Nazis, Lithuanian nationalists turned to underground resistance and guerilla warfare, receiving widespread popular support.[55] The Nazi retreat did not end the struggle; guerilla warfare against the Soviets dragged on for eight more years until the power of the KGB troops and collectivization of the countryside ended it. Soviet sources estimated that 20,000 on each side died in the fighting.[56] Save for the OUN movement in the western Ukraine, the duration and scope of Lithuanian armed resistance to Soviet power was unequaled among Soviet nationalities since the Basmachi rebellion in Central Asia during the 1920s.

Supremacy of the Soviet system in Lithuania appears to have become generally accepted during the mid-1950s. The Lithuanians made the most of new circumstances, achieving a truly remarkable rate of economic growth during the 1960s. The local Communist regime is led by native Lithua-

48 Gerutis *et al.*, 1969: 193–199.
49 Vardys, 1965: 32–34; Sabaliunas, 1972: 6–8.
50 Vardys, 1965: 30–31, 38–39.
51 *Ibid.*: 26.

52 Sabaliunas, 1972: 8–9.
53 Tarulis, 1959: 145–256.
54 Vardys, 1965: 64–67.
55 *Ibid.*: 69.
56 *Ibid.*: 86. *Khronika* (July 2), 1971: 20, cites KGB sources as saying that 50,000 partisans died.

nians and seems to be allowed substantial autonomy from Moscow. Things have not, however, been entirely peaceful. There were major riots in Kaunas in 1956 during the Hungarian Revolution. Educational and cultural cadres were purged for nationalism in 1959,[57] and religious and nationalist dissent surfaced repeatedly during the early 1970s, including major demonstrations in 1972.[58]

DEMOGRAPHY

World War II and imposition of the Soviet system were demographically disastrous for Lithuania. The Nazis inflicted losses of 250,000 to 300,000 on the prewar population of approximately 3 million, including the majority of the nearly 200,000 Jews in the country. Emigration of the German and Polish populations meant a loss of another quarter of a million persons. Aside from these war losses, Soviet rule brought mass deportations in 1940–1941 and 1946–1950. An authoritative Western source estimated a loss of 500,000 persons liquidated, confined to camps, dispersed, or deported.[59] Despite a relatively high birth rate, Lithuania's population in 1959 was smaller than in 1939.

According to census results, population of the Lithuanian SSR on January 15, 1970, was 3,128,236. Of these, 80.1% were ethnic Lithuanians, 8.6% Russians, 7.7% Poles, and 1.1% Belorussians, making Lithuania one of the most homogeneous of Soviet republics. In sharp contrast to the other Baltic republics (and, incidentally, in all other European Soviet republics), the indigenous nationality increased as a percentage of total population between 1959 and 1970 (from 79.3% to 80.1%).[60] Total number of Lithuanians in the USSR increased by almost 15% during the decade of the 1960s (a rate higher than that for any other European nation in the USSR except the Moldavians), and they have shown a strong loyalty to the republic. The proportion of all Soviet Lithuanians living in the Lithua-

nian republic increased from 92.3% to 94.1% (again, largest percentage increase among Soviet Europeans), and a Soviet source indicated that, of the 50,000 net immigrants to the republic in 1959–1970, over half were Lithuanians returning from other Soviet republics.[61]

Although a majority of the population lived in cities as of 1970, among Lithuanians in the republic the rural population still held a slight edge: 54% to 46%. In 1959 only one third of Lithuanians were urbanized; traditionally, cities have contained large populations of other ethnic groups. In the past, these have been primarily Jews and Poles (especially in Vilnius) and Germans (in Klaipeda).[62] Russians became a major component of urban population after World War II. Urbanization of ethnic Lithuanians in the 1960s, however, has given them a dominant position in the great population centers of the republic. In Vilnius their percentage of the population increased from 33.6% to 42.8% in 1959–1970; in Kaunas, from 82% to 84%; in Klaipeda, from 55% to 61%. This trend may insure that these major cities will remain true national centers.[63]

Educational level rose markedly in the 1960s. Only 23% of the population aged 10 and over had even a partial secondary education in 1959; 38% did in 1970. Still, the level remained low by all-Soviet standards; corresponding averages for the USSR were 36% and 48%.[64] However, Lithuanian figures for the working population were higher and showed an even more significant growth than those for the population at large—from 25% to 48.6%.

A Soviet source blames "the joyless heritage of bourgeois Lithuania" for the relatively low proportion of people with

---

57 *Lituanus* (Summer), 1972: XVIII: 2: 6; Pospielovsky, 1972: 4.
58 See section on nationalism.
59 Vardys, 1965: 240–241.
60 See Comparative Tables section in Appendix.

61 P. Gaucas, *Mokslas ir Gyvenimas* [*Science and Life*] (June), 1971, cited in Taagepera, 1972b: 4.
62 Many Poles continue to live in the Vilnius area: 18% of city's population is Polish, and three surrounding rural *raions* publish newspapers in Polish. *Ekonomika Litvy*, 1970: 36; *Spaudos Metraštis*, 1971: I: 65–76.
63 *Ekonomika Litvy*, 1970: 36. See also Szporluk, 1971: 30.
64 *Nar. obraz.* (August), 1971: table 5. Lithuania has a relatively large aged population (15% of inhabitants were over 60 in 1970, versus 11.8% for the all-Soviet average), which may account for much of the difference.

more than secondary education. Indeed, the proportion of people so educated in Lithuania in 1939 was less than half that for Latvia and Estonia.[65]

Historically, the Communist party of Lithuania has had a relatively small following, although its leadership is predominantly native-born. The party was founded during World War I among Lithuanian refugees in Russia. During the interwar years membership never exceeded 2,000 and much was apparently drawn from national minorities living in Lithuania.[66] By 1959 the party had grown to 54,000 members, or 2% of the republic's population at that time. This was well below the 4% of the USSR population in the CPSU. In 1971, with 122,469 members (3.9% of the population), the CP Lithuania was still the second smallest, relative to population, among the European Soviet republic parties. The rank-and-file membership of the CP Lithuania has consistently contained a lower proportion of ethnic Lithuanians than does the general population. In 1961, 62% of the CPL membership was Lithuanian, versus 79% of the population. In 1972, if all Lithuanians in the CPSU were members of the CPL, they would still constitute only 76% of its membership, versus 80% of the population.[67]

On the other hand, ethnic Lithuanians have dominated the top leadership of the CPL since the Khrushchev years. Antanas Sniechkus has been first secretary of the party since 1936. Among current leaders of national Communist parties, only Mao Tse-tung has greater seniority. Although in the early Soviet years as much as 50% of the Central Committee of the Lithuanian party was non-Lithuanian, the number of Lithuanians at this level has consistently increased. The party bureau and secretariat elected in 1971 contained only one non-Lithuanian, the Russian second secretary Kharazov.[68] Western observers referred to the CPL as "Sniechkus' personal machine," noting that it is committed to developing Lithuanian culture.[69] Protection by top party leadership has undoubtedly contributed to maintenance of a more relaxed cultural atmosphere in the republic.

CULTURE

Although religious books were published in Lithuanian in the mid-sixteenth century, secular literature is generally agreed to have begun with Kristijonas Donelaitis (1714–1780), whose principal work, *The Seasons*, depicts the life of the Lithuanian peasant through the year's cycle.[70] Adam Mickiewicz (1798–1855) is widely considered the greatest Lithuanian poet. Although he wrote in Polish, his works evoked the Lithuanian spirit and countryside. The national awakening movement in the second half of the nineteenth century was fed by numerous poets and writers, among them Antanas Baranauskas (1835–1902) and Maironis (1862–1932). The fact that these two men and many other writers were also Catholic clergy attests to the very close identification of the Church with Lithuanian culture and intellectual development.[71]

In 1940 over 80% of the population of Lithuania, and 94% of the ethnic Lithuanians, were Catholic.[72] Most of the rest were Lutheran, living in the areas formerly controlled by Germany. The educational system in tsarist Lithuania was largely administered by the Catholic Church, and Catholic-oriented parties played a major role in the politics of independent Lithuania. Many churchmen supported the partisan warfare against the Soviets in the late 1940s. The establishment of Soviet power brought sharp persecution of both clergy and believers[73] but, despite all pressures, there is ample evidence that Catholicism remains strong. In 1972 the Soviet press indicated that a community of Lithuanians as far away as Kazakhstan continued to practice their beliefs.[74]

65 *Sovetskaya Litva* (May 11), 1971: 5.
66 Vardys, 1965: 112–113.
67 Vardys, 1964: 9–10, tables 2a, 2b. There are no data on number of Lithuanians in the CPL after 1961.
68 Vardys, 1965: 115–122; *Sovetskaya Litva* (March 6), 1971.

69 Vardys, 1965: 122; Taagepera, 1972c: 22.
70 Stukas, 1966: 105–106; *Litva*, 1967: 103.
71 Rimaitis, 1971: 1.
72 Vardys, 1965: 21–22, 213.
73 *The Church and State under Communism*, 1965.
74 *Kaz. pravda* (August 27), 1972, translated in FBIS Daily Report (September 14), 1972.

Catholicism and the impact of Western ideas and values represent one major aspect of Lithuanian culture brought to the country through Poland. The impact of Polish culture was especially strong on the upper classes, but traditional forms were preserved among the peasantry. As perhaps befits a nation only now in the full flood of modernization, distinctive folkloristic elements remain a second major strand in culture. The *daina*, a form of folksong shared by Lithuanians and Latvians, is considered a central part of the nation's creative heritage. Ceramics, woodcut, embroidery, and the working of amber are highly developed; pictorial art, sculpture, mosaics, and stained glass are popular forms. Of 296 contributors to a USSR photo exhibition touring the United States in 1970, a full 10% were Lithuanians.[75] Perhaps the most renowned Lithuanian artist is Mykolas Ciurlionis (1875–1911), whose work anticipated abstractionist and surrealist art.[76] Modern Lithuanian artists also experiment with abstract art and Western techniques, but are rarely allowed to exhibit them.[77]

Western critics have had relatively little praise for Soviet Lithuanian literature. Young writers such as J. Marcinkevicius, E. Miezelaitis, and R. Lankauskas, however, have received favorable attention, especially since 1960. Dramatists appear somewhat bolder than other writers in testing limits of permitted literary expression.[78] (See section on cultural institutions.)

Exemplifying twin elements of native tradition and Western influence, Lithuanian writers have described the character of the people as an interesting and complex mixture of Western activity and purposefulness with Eastern passivity. Lithuanians are said to be doggedly perseverant and inclined to resist authority passively, "except when authoritarianism exceeds reasonable limits." [79] Immanuel Kant has reportedly

written than the Lithuanian "knows no servility. He is accustomed to speak to his superiors on terms of equality . . . [he] is proud, but knows nothing of arrogance." [80] The Lithuanians are proud of their historical and cultural traditions, and capable of working patiently at problems despite obstacles. They are determined, realistic, and steady, placing a high value on moderation. Perhaps such traits are in part responsible for enabling them to make the most of the system thrust upon them.[81]

EXTERNAL RELATIONS

During independence, Lithuania was oriented to the West and regarded by the intelligentsia as a Western European country.[82] Its economy was consciously modeled on that of Denmark, and its major trading partners were Germany and Great Britain.[83] The ideology of the nationalist dictatorship had many similarities to the ideas of fascist Italy, although its application was more restrained.[84] Trade, religion, tradition, and intellectual currents all bound the country to the European world. In addition, beginning in the late nineteenth and early twentieth centuries, many Lithuanians had emigrated to the West, the great majority to America. These émigrés played an active role in the struggle for their homeland's independence. Lithuanian-Americans sought to win United States recognition of the young government, bought bonds to finance its armament, and some even returned to Lithuania to take part in the armed struggle. World War II brought about a new movement among Lithuanians abroad and renewed concern for the nation's future. The bitter partisan warfare against the Soviets deepened these ties; one of the last guerilla leaders was American-born.[85]

As of 1972, many of the roughly 2 mil-

75 Contributions listed in *Soviet Union Today*, brochure accompanying exhibition, published by Novosti Press Agency.

76 *Lituanus* (Winter), 1965: XI: 4: 5–24.

77 Private communications.

78 *Lituanus* (Fall), 1966: XII: 3: 25–43; Vardys, 1965: 197–214.

79 Stukas, 1966: 172–173.

80 *Ibid.*

81 For additional evaluations of the national character, see Simutis, 1942: 112 and Sabaliunas, 1972: 32.

82 Vardys, 1965: 89.

83 Simutis, 1942: 92.

84 Sabaliunas, 1972: 30–31.

85 Vardys, 1965: 86.

lion[86] Lithuanians outside the Soviet Union continue to work actively to maintain culture, language, and identity. Various organizations seek to keep the issue of Baltic independence alive before Western governments and the United Nations, to transmit materials to Lithuania, and to gather data about conditions there.[87] Repeated denunciations in the Soviet press testify to their continued influence.[88]

Unquestionably, the single most important external influence on Lithuania is the Catholic Church, which has long viewed itself as an outpost of Catholicism in the northeast, on the front lines against the worlds of Orthodoxy and Lutheranism. Accordingly, the tone and intensity of religious teaching has been especially strong, and Catholicism has become an important element of national identity.[89] The Soviets have repeatedly cited Radio Vatican and Radio Rome as disturbing influences in the re-

public.[90] Popular opposition to Soviet interference with work of the Church was widespread in 1971 and 1972, indicating the continuing significance of this Western influence.

Poland is another focus of particular importance for Lithuania. By tradition an ally, the primary conduit for Western culture and religion, in the nineteenth century Poland became the foil against which Lithuanian distinctiveness and national separateness had to be asserted. In the twentieth century Poland became an enemy in the conflict over Vilnius. Thus, the relationship is characterized by an approach-avoidance conflict, by ties of a shared religion and a resolute assertion of differences. The *modus vivendi* established between the Church and the Polish Communist regime draws attention as a possible model for Lithuania, which could be asserted in opposition to present Soviet policies.

Media

LANGUAGE DATA

Lithuanian is one of the oldest surviving Indo-European languages. Together with Sanskrit, it is considered an important tool in studying common roots of the Indo-European family. Among living languages, Lithuanian and Latvian are the only representatives of the Baltic group, distinct from both Germanic and Slavic groups. Lithuanian is written in the Latin alphabet with addition of certain diacritic marks.[91]

As indicated in Table 6.1, Lithuanians in the USSR as a whole and in the republic demonstrate a strong loyalty to their language, stronger than that of other European

peoples of the Soviet Union. Between 95.0% and 95.5% of Estonians, Latvians, and Moldavians cited the language of their nationality as native language in 1970; the figure for Lithuanians was 97.9%, a small increase from 1959. Conversely, only 1.5% of Lithuanians gave Russian as their native tongue, versus some 4% for the others. Undoubtedly, these figures are conditioned by the greater homogeneity of the republic, the larger concentration of Lithuanians, and the somewhat stronger protection from Russianizing pressures provided by the local regime.[92] Nearly a quarter of non-Lithuanians in the republic cited Lithuanian as either first or second language. A 1965 study

---

86 *The Marian* (Chicago: American Province of Congregation of Marian Fathers) (February 1), 1969: 27. Some 1,600,000 of these Lithuanians are in the U.S.A.
87 See Audenas, 1963, especially pp. 89–90; "Baltic Action Manual," 1971.
88 Benyušis, 1972.
89 Even the Soviets have recognized this phenomenon. See G. Ziminas in *Zhurnalist*, 1972: VII: 6–7.

90 *Sovetskaya Litva* (July 4), 1972; A. Sniechkus in *Zhurnalist*, 1972: XII: 11–12; report on article in *Partiinaya Zhizn'*, *New York Times* (March 8), 1970.
91 *Lituanus* (Winter), 1972: XVIII: 4: 60–61.
92 *Kommunist* (Litva), 1972: II: 42–47, translated in *JPRS*: No. 221: 47. Census results report only 20% of non-Lithuanian rural population as speaking Lithuanian. *Itogi 1970*: IV: 273–275.

Table 6.1

Native and Second Languages Spoken by Lithuanians

(in thousands)

	Number of Lithuanians Residing		SPEAKING AS NATIVE LANGUAGE						SPEAKING AS SECOND LANGUAGE[a]	
			Lithuanian		% Point Change	Russian		% Point Change	Russian	Other Languages of Peoples of USSR
	1959	1970	1959	1970	1959–1970	1959	1970	1959–1970	1970	1970[b]
in Lithuanian SSR	2,151 (100%)	2,507 (100%)	2,133 (99.2%)	2,494 (99.5%)	+0.3	3 (0.1%)	4.6 (0.2%)	+0.1	872 (34.8%)	18 (0.7%)
in other Soviet republics	175 (100%)	158 (100%)	141 (80.6%)	115 (72.8%)	−7.8	26 (15%)	27.4 (17%)	+2	85 (53.8%)	33 (20.9%)
Total	2,326 (100%)	2,665 (100%)	2,275 (97.8%)	2,609 (97.9%)	+0.1	29 (1.2%)	32 (1.5%)	+0.3	957 (35.9%)	51 (1.9%)

Sources: For 1959 census, *Itogi SSSR, 1959*: Table 53; *Itogi Litovskaya SSR, 1959*: Table 53. For 1970 census, *Ekonomika Litvy, 1970*: 35; *Nar. khoz. 1972*: 32.

[a] No data are available for 1959, since no questions regarding command of a second language were asked in the 1959 census.

[b] Including Lithuanian, if not native language.

in two rural *raions* showed that almost all non-Lithuanians knew the language.

A study of 1959 census data for several nationalities by Brian D. Silver showed among Latvians, Estonians, and others that usage of the national language was highest among older age groups and showed a definite downtrend in younger groups. For Lithuanians, highest retention of the national language was among people between 20 and 39.[93] Soviet statistics show that 84% of schoolchildren in the republic study in Lithuanian language schools.[94] These data suggest that the use of Lithuanian is likely to remain strong at least through the 1970s.

LOCAL MEDIA

In 1897, according to the Russian census of that year, 54% of the population of Lithuania was literate. This level of literacy, well above that of most of the empire, was attained largely through the work of Catholic schools. A major effort to eliminate illiteracy among the entire population did not come until the Sovietization of the country; Soviet statistics record that 77% of the population was literate in 1939, and 98.5% in 1959.[95]

Lithuania is one of the leading Soviet republics in publication of books, newspapers, journals per capita, although it lags noticeably behind Estonia and Latvia in this regard: 2,186 books and pamphlets were published in 1970, with a total press run of over 14 million, a ratio of over four books per inhabitant. Of these, nearly two thirds of the titles, and over 80% of the total copies, were published in Lithuanian. One fifth were translations from other languages. Divided into functional categories, nearly one third (712) were instructional materials or manuals related to production; 257 were fiction, including children's books, and 252 were reference materials.[96]

Ninety-one newspapers were published, the large majority in Lithuanian (74), but also in Russian (13) and 4 in Polish.[97] The 13 republic-level papers included official party government organs in each of the three languages (*Tiesa* [*Truth*], in Lithuanian with circulation of 251,992;[98] *Sovietskaya Litva*, in Russian with circulation of 66,295; *Czerwony Sztandar* [*Red Banner*], in Polish with circulation of 35,377) and the Komsomol organ in Lithuanian (circulation, 91,002) and Russian (14,113). Other republic-level organs appeared only in Lithuanian and included *Valstieciu Laikrastis* [*Peasant's Paper*] with circulation of 237,801; *Literatura ir Menas* [*Literature and Art*], cultural weekly with circulation of 31,500; and *Lietuvos Pionieris* [*Lithuanian Pioneer*], a twice-weekly paper for children 10 to 14 years of age, with circulation of 180,749.

Of five cities with daily newspapers, Kaunas, Panevežis, and Sauliai publish in Lithuanian only; Klaipeda publishes in Lithuanian and Russian (circulations 26,929 and 15,914, respectively); and an evening newspaper serves both Vilnius and Kaunas in the two languages (Lithuanian edition 27,947, Russian 29,412).[99]

Official sources disagree on the number of Russian language journals published in Lithuania. *Pechat' 1970* lists five, with total circulation of 6,000 copies per issue; but *Spaudos Metraštis*, the Lithuanian press chronicle, names only one, *Kommunist*, with a per-issue circulation of 34,500.[100] One journal, *Kobieta Radziecka*, an illustrated monthly for women, is in Polish. It is clear, however, that the overwhelming majority of journals are in Lithuanian. Major journals include *Komunistas* [*Communist*], party theoretical monthly, with circulation of 173,600; *Mokslas ir Gyvenimas* [*Science and Life*], Znanie society journal, with circulation of 194,700; and *Jaunimo Gretos* [*Ranks of Youth*], illustrated

93 Silver, 1972: 221–223. The above data are for all Lithuanians in the USSR; 1970 census data yield similar results for Lithuanians in their republic. *Itogi 1970*: IV: 380.
94 *Ekonomika Litvy*, 1970: 358.
95 *Nar. khoz.* 1972: 594.
96 *Pechat' 1970*: 96, 126–127. See also Table 6.2.

97 Three are published in *raions* near Vilnius, indicating that Lithuania's Polish population is concentrated in the city and environs.
98 All circulation figures are for 1970 unless otherwise indicated.
99 *Spaudos Metrastis*, 1971: I: 65–72.
100 *Pechat' 1970*: 159; *Spaudos Metraštis*, 1971: I: 65–72.

Table 6.2

Publications in Lithuanian SSR

Language of Publication	Year	NEWSPAPERS[a]			MAGAZINES			BOOKS & BROCHURES		
		No.	Per Issue Circulation (1,000)	Copies/100 in Language Group[e]	No.	Per Issue Circulation (1,000)	Copies/100 in Language Group[e]	No. Titles	Total Volume (1,000)	Books & Brochures/100 in Language Group[e]
Russian	1959	14	92	34.6	N.A.	N.A.	N.A.	351	2,283	857.4
	1970	13	188	59.2	5	6	1.9	631	2,067	652.0
	1971	12	151	47.5	5	6	1.9	421	1,635	515.8
Lithuanian	1959	105	799	37.1	N.A.	N.A.	N.A.	1,691	10,203	472.0
	1970	74	1,876	75.2[d]	23	1,432	57.4[d]	1,412	12,014	481.6[d]
	1971	72	1,590	63.7[d]	24	1,489	59.7[d]	1,351	12,163	487.6[d]
Minority Languages	1959	8[b]	19	6.7	N.A.	N.A.	N.A.	N.A.	N.A.	N.A.
	1970	0	0	0	0	0	0	1	1	N.A.
	1971	0	0	0	0	0	0	3	146	N.A.
Foreign Languages (Polish)	1959	N.A.	N.A.	N.A.	N.A.	N.A.	N.A.	N.A.	N.A.	N.A.
	1970	4	45	20.3	1	33	14.9	c	c	c
	1971	4	50	22.5	1	37	16.7	c	c	c
All Languages	1959	127	910	33.6	18	427	15.7	2,137[c]	12,810	472.4
	1970	91	2,109	67.5	29	1,471	47.1	2,186[c]	14,612	467.1
	1971	88	1,791	56.7	30	1,532	48.4	1,884[c]	14,484	457.5

Sources: *Pechat' 1959*: 56, 129, 165; *1970*: 96, 159, 188.

a 1970 figures do not include kolkhoz newspapers.

b This figure may include publication in non-Soviet languages (Polish).

c Book totals as given in *Pechat'* sometimes differ from totals in language categories. The indication is that books are published in other languages, but no data is given

d 1970 and 1971 Lithuanian language group data for ethnic Lithuanians giving Lithuanian as native language only, as given in 1970 census reports.

e Includes all native speakers of the language.

Table 6.3

Electronic Media and Films in Lithuanian SSR

YEAR	RADIO				TELEVISION				MOVIES	
	No. Stations	No. Wired Sets (1,000)	Sets/100 Population	No. Wireless Sets (1,000)	Sets/100 Population	No. Stations	No. sets (1,000)	Sets/100 Population	Seats (1,000)	Seats/100 Population
1960	N.A.	167[a]	5.9[d]	330[a]	11.8[c]	N.A.	21[a]	.7[c]	79[b]	2.8[d]
1970	45[e]	189[a]	5.9[d]	699[a]	22.1[c]	2	453[a]	14.3[c]	179[b]	5.6[d]
1971	45[e]	200[d]	6.2[d]	772	24.1[c]	2	502[c]	15.7[c]	N.A.	N.A.

[a] Source: Transport i svyaz' SSR, 1972: 296–298.
[b] Source: Nar. obraz., 1971: 325.
[c] Source: Nar. khoz., 1972: 572, 578.
[d] Computed from data cited above ([b] and [c]).
[e] Estimated. One major station in Vilnius and at least one local station in each raion.

literary monthly for young people with circulation of 135,800.[101]

Radio communications developed fairly early. A station in Kaunas began broadcasting in 1926 and one in Klaipeda in 1936.[102] Partly as a result of this early development, radio receivers have been in relatively good supply for some time. In 1971 the republic ranked third in the Soviet Union, behind Latvia and Estonia, in number of broadcast receivers per capita, with one for every four inhabitants.[103] These receivers exceeded the number of wired loudspeakers by a factor of more than four to one, a pattern distinguishing the Baltic republics from the rest of the USSR.[104] Radio Vilnius, major station in the republic, broadcasts three separate programs, a total of 26 hours per day, in four languages.[105] In addition, editorial boards operate in all of the republic's 44 *raions*, broadcasting local news through the wired radio network.[106]

Television broadcasting began in 1957 with the opening of a station in Vilnius. In 1972 this was still the only station in the republic originating local programming, although there is a second "auxiliary" station in Kaunas.[107] In 1971 Lithuania had over 500,000 TV sets, or 16 for every 100 inhabitants. In the Soviet Union this ratio was exceeded only by Estonia, Latvia, the RSFSR, and the Ukraine.[108]

EDUCATIONAL INSTITUTIONS

Lithuania is the only Baltic republic where teaching in general education schools is also in a language (Polish) other than Russian or that of the titular nationality.[109] The following table compares the language of instruction of students in elementary, eight-year, and general secondary schools with the corresponding nationality's percentage in the republic.

LANGUAGE OF INSTRUCTION	% OF STUDENTS	% OF NATIONALITY IN REPUBLIC
Lithuanian	84	80.1
Russian	12	8.5
Polish	4	7.7

Students who begin their education in Lithuanian suffer no discrimination at higher levels; university instruction is "almost exclusively in Lithuanian," and the vast majority of students in the republic's *vuzy* (83.5% in 1970–1971)[110] are Lithuanians.[111] Over 95% of Soviet Lithuanians attending *vuzy* do so in the republic—a figure higher than the percent of all Lithuanians living in the republic, and highest for any Soviet nationality.[112] The twelve *vuzy* include the university at Vilnius, now named for V. Kapsukas (with a 1970–1971 enrollment of 15,700); pedagogical institutes in Vilnius and Siauliai; the Kaunas Polytechnical Institute, second largest school in the republic with 14,900 students; and specialized academies for agriculture, veterinary medicine, art, physical culture, and medicine.[113]

Total 1969–1970 enrollment in Lithuania's *vuzy* was 55,700, the republic ranking sixth in the USSR for *vuzy* students per 1,000 inhabitants (17.8). In the ratio of *technikum* (schools for specialized secondary education) students to population, Lithuania ranked first in the USSR with 20.7 per 1,000 inhabitants.[114]

CULTURAL AND SCIENTIFIC INSTITUTIONS

The Lithuanian Academy of Sciences included twelve scientific and research institutes in 1971. It has received wide recognition for its work in mathematics, cybernetics, and the physics of semicon-

101 For discussion of cultural press in Lithuania, see *Lituanus* (Spring), 1966: XII: 1: 21–32.
102 Gerutis, 1972: 255.
103 *Nar. khoz.* 1972: 604.
104 *Transport i svyaz'*, 1972: 296, 298. See also Table 6.3.
105 *Litva za polveka*, 1967: 408.
106 *Ibid.*
107 *Televedeniye i radioveshchaniye*, 1972: XII: 13.
108 *Nar. khoz.* 1972: 604.
109 Russian is taught as a subject in all schools, beginning in the first year.

110 This is an acronym for *vysshiye uchebnyye zavedeniya* [higher educational institutions].
111 *Lituanus* (Winter), 1972: XVIII: 4: 60–61; percentage was computed from figures in *Nar. obraz.*, 1971: 197ff.
112 *Nar. obraz.*, 1971: 197ff.
113 It is an interesting comment on the future of Lithuania that the enrollment in Kaunas Polytechnical is more than twice that of the agricultural and veterinary schools combined.
114 *Ekonomika Litvy*, 1970: 462–463.

Table 6.4

Selected Data on Education in Lithuanian SSR (1971)

Population: 3,202,000

		PER 1,000 POPULATION	% OF TOTAL
All schools			
number of schools	3,432	1.1	
number of students	581,000	181.4	
Newly opened elementary, incomplete secondary, and secondary schools			
number of schools	45		
number of student places	20,900	6.53	
Secondary special schools			
number of schools	79		
number of students	65,900	20.6	
Institutions of higher education			
number of institutions	12		
number of students	58,200	18.2	
Universities			
number of universities	1		
number of students			
total	15,826		
day students	7,466		47.1
evening students	2,885		18.2
correspondence students	5,495		34.7
newly admitted			
total	2,870		
day students	1,610		56.0
evening students	500		17.4
correspondence students	760		26.4
graduated			
total	1,727		
day students	912		53.0
evening students	381		22.0
correspondence students	434		25.1
Graduate students			
total number	1,020	0.32	
in scientific research institutions	409		
in universities	611		
Number of persons with (in 1970) higher or secondary (complete and incomplete) education			
per 1,000 individuals, 10 years and older	382		
per 1,000 individuals employed in national economy	496		
Number of workers graduated from professional-technical schools	16,600	5.18	

Source: *Nar. khoz 1972*: 108, 438, 594, 603, 605.

ductors.[115] Roughly 70 other scientific organizations are attached to the various ministries, government authorities, and schools. In 1971 there were a total of nearly 9,000 scientific workers in the republic,[116] over 85% ethnically Lithuanian, 7.4% Russian, and 3.8% Jewish.[117]

Eleven professional theaters in Lithuania include an opera and ballet theater in Vilnius and in Kaunas, puppet and drama theaters in the same cities, and drama theaters as well in Klaipeda, Panevezhis, and Šiauliai. Vilnius also has a Russian Dramatic theater.[118] Lithuanian playwrights such as Juozas Grušas and Kazys Saja have produced works employing modern Western dramatic techniques and dealing with themes of alienation and tension in Soviet society.[119]

Feature films have been produced by the Lithuanian Film Studio since 1952, and several have won prizes in international competition.[120] Thirty new films playing in the cinemas of Vilnius and Kaunas were reviewed in *Sovetskaya Litva* in a seven-week period in early 1973. One was produced in Lithuania, three in Western Europe, and the rest in Eastern Europe, other Soviet republics, the central studios of Mosfilm and Lenfilm (Moscow and Leningrad), and North Korea.[121] Most are dubbed or subtitled in Lithuanian.[122]

Prominent among Lithuania's 33 museums are the Lithuanian SSR Museum of Art in Vilnius, the Čiurlionis Art Museum in Kaunas, and museums in the historic castles of Vilnius and Trakai. Palanga is the home of a unique museum of amber and artistic works.[123]

---

115 *Litva za polveka*, 1967: 401–402.
116 Among them, 182 Doctors of Science and 2,710 Candidates of Science.
117 *Ekonomika Litvy, 1970*: 368, 370.
118 *Litva za polveka*, 1967: 426.
119 Bronius Vaskelis, "Contemporary Lithuanian Drama," *Lituanus* (Fall 1967): XIII: 3: 11–16, 27.

120 *Litva za polveka*, 1967: 415–416; Butkus, 1964: 82–83.
121 *Sovetskaya Litva* (February 14, 20; March 6, 13, 20, 27; April 2), 1973.
122 Private communication.
123 *Litva za polveka*, 1967: 412–414.

Table 6.5

Selected Data on Scientific and Cultural Facilities and Personnel in Lithuanian SSR (1971)

Population: 3,202,000

Academy of Sciences		*Number of persons working in*	
number of members	30	*education and culture*	
number of scientific institutions		total	103,000
affiliated with academy	12	number per 1,000 population	32
total number of scientific workers	1,285		
		Number of persons working in science	
Museums		*and scientific services*	
number of museums	33	total	31,000
attendance	3,253,000	number per 1,000 population	9.7
attendance per 1,000 population	1,016		
		Number of public libraries	2,498
Theaters		number of books and magazines	
number of theaters	11	in public libraries	19,515,000
attendance	1,387,000		
attendance per 1,000 population	433	*Number of clubs*	1,493

Source: *Nar. khoz. 1972*: 106, 451, 601.

National Attitudes

REVIEW OF FACTORS FORMING NATIONAL ATTITUDES

Lithuania, like the other Baltic republics, Latvia and Estonia, is a small, Westernized, highly cultured nation bordering on territories of far larger, more powerful peoples. Unlike Latvia and Estonia, Lithuania possesses a long history of independence, and even of former imperial greatness. The Soviets have not tried to ignore or suppress the historical past when the grand dukes of Lithuania dealt as equals with the princes of Muscovy, but have chosen to interpret it in the light of the "great friendship" theory of Russian-minority relations. The role of the grand duchy in stopping the Germans is particularly stressed. The Lithuanian-Polish uprisings of 1830 and 1863 have not been purged of their "national-liberation" character, even in official sources, although, of course, the class element is emphasized, and the revolts are said to have been directed against the tsar rather than Russia.[124] As a result, Lithuania's history remains a source of national pride and distinctiveness.[125]

More recent history, especially the long partisan war against the Soviets in the aftermath of World War II and the massive deportations accompanying establishment of Soviet power, remains part of the personal experience of most Lithuanians today. The trial testimony of Simas Kudirka, the sailor who sought asylum in the United States in November 1970, vividly expressed the scale and impact of these repressions, which must have left few Lithuanian families untouched.[126]

Their language also appears to be a factor of particular pride for Lithuanians. The frequency with which both Western and Soviet sources point to the preservation of a great many ancient words and forms in the language and to its importance as a research tool unique among living languages indicates that it is held to have special value as a national symbol.

The ties to Western civilization inherent in Catholicism also remain an integral part of Lithuanian culture. The unrest among Lithuanian Catholics is simultaneously both a religious and a national expression. Soviet restrictions on training of priests and interference in their work are major issues in themselves. They were central issues cited in the trials of priests in 1971 and 1972 and in the "Chronicle of the Lithuanian Catholic Church." [127] But it is worthy of note that these documents and protests concern themselves only with religious repressions in Lithuania, not with those against Catholics in Latvia or Belorussia, and that their authors refer to themselves as "Catholics of Lithuania." [128] Circumstantial evidence points to religious motives behind the attempted defection of Kudirka and the Kaunas riots in May 1972.[129]

BASIC VIEWS OF SCHOLARS ON NATIONAL ATTITUDES

Scholarly evaluations are not yet available concerning the signs of widespread dissent and unrest in Lithuania which surfaced with particular vigor in 1970–1972. The evidence, however, is abundant and unmistakable. *Samizdat* documents began appearing in 1968 and have grown in frequency and scope.[130] The underground *Khronika tekushchikh sobytii* carries a regular section for "Events in Lithuania"; two issues of a separate "Chronicle of the Lithuanian Catholic Church" reached the West in November

---

124 *Litva*, 1967: 72.
125 See Zimanas (in *Pravda*, January 24, 1969) attacking "incorrect views of the history of one's people" as an expression of bourgeois nationalism.
126 Anatole Shub, *Boston Globe* (August 7), 1971; *Khronika* (July 2), 1971: 20.

---

127 Taagepera, 1973: 2.
128 *Survey* (Summer), 1972: XVIII: 3: 237–240.
129 Pospielovsky, 1972.
130 For list, see *Radio Liberty Research Bulletin* (February 15), 1973: 47–73.

1972.[131] Three self-immolations and an attempted fourth occurred in 1972, as did large-scale rioting. Of three known attempts to hijack airplanes in the Soviet Union in 1969–1970, two, including the only successful one, were made by Lithuanians.[132]

Beginning roughly in the mid–1960s, Soviet sources in Lithuania have repeatedly admitted that nationalism has "still not been fully eradicated in our society."[133] citing several different causes of dissatisfaction. A prominent one is foreign media. Voice of America, Radio Vatican, Madrid, and Radio Rome were all cited in 1972 as broadcasting "lying propaganda" to the republic to "evoke feelings of national exclusiveness." Young people are cited as particularly susceptible to such efforts.[134] Tourists are accused of smuggling anti-Soviet literature, including works by "bourgeois nationalists," into the republic.[135]

The intimate connection between religious and nationalist dissent has been explicitly recognized by Soviet commentators. In 1970 the Vatican was accused of engaging "in a number of hostile acts aimed at stirring up religious and nationalist activities in Lithuania."[136] The Church has been accused of using "the large body of priests for ideologically influencing the people's emotions and intellects."[137]

The rapid economic development of the country under the Soviets has apparently left many Lithuanians unconvinced that the Soviet system is, after all, a good thing. Rather, according to official sources, it has contributed to national pride, providing a cover for nationalist attitudes. According to V. Stanley Vardys of the University of Oklahoma, *Komunistas* in 1966 published an article in which the author "scolded the youth for preferring republic needs to those of the Soviet Union, for claiming that it was the Lithuanian ability, not the 'help from the brotherly nations' that accounted for the re-

public's progress." Ideas of "national communism" were seen as a new incarnation of "bourgeois" nationalism.[138]

G. Zimanas, editor of *Tiesa*, repeated the warning in 1969, asserting that the party must oppose camouflaging bourgeois nationalism by presenting it as an endeavor to strive for the flourishing of the republic.[139] Zimanas elaborated further on the problem in 1972:

> We must refute such inimical inventions as . . . yes, the peoples of the Baltic have achieved certain successes, but the source of these achievements is solely the abilities and talents of the peoples, which Soviet power could not suppress. According to this same logic everything that is good in the Baltic arises exclusively from the national qualities of the Baltic peoples, and the "policy of Moscow" bears responsibility for everything that is unsatisfactory.
>
> It happens that a person praises the achievements of the republic and at the same time, willingly or unwillingly, advocates separatism.[140]

Western scholars such as Benedict Maciuika of the University of Connecticut have also seen evidence that Lithuanians have developed the ability and willingness to use the system for their own ends:

> There is mounting evidence, suggesting that although parts of the political-institutional framework have been adopted, it is being used *not* exclusively for the USSR interests as the regime would want it, but to further the interests of one's *own* national group. It has been realized by many in Lithuania that the Soviet system can be used, albeit only with difficulty and very circumspectly, to serve the welfare of one's own nation [emphasis in original].[141]

Maciuika concludes that political socialization of Lithuania "is really far from completed," and not likely to be completed "in the foreseeable future." Vardays concluded in 1965, on the basis of continuous party discussions and attention to the problem, that

---

131 Taagepera, 1973.
132 "Violations," 1972: 62–63.
133 *Komunistas*, 1972: X: 1–7, translated in *JPRS*: CCC: 36–40.
134 Sniečkus, in *Zhurnalist*, 1972: XII: 11–12; Benyušis, 1972.
135 Benyušis, 1972.
136 Article by Barkauskas, a secretary of the CC CP Lithuania in *Partiinaya zhizn'*, reported in *New York Times* (March 8), 1970.
137 Benyušis, 1972.

138 Vardys, in *Res Baltica*, 1968: 129.
139 *Pravda* (January 24), 1969.
140 Zimanas in *Zhurnalist*, 1972: VII: 6–7.
141 Maciuika, 1972.

nationalism is felt to have a broad basis and is feared as a "dangerous social force" Subsequent years have made it clear that this concern is well placed.[142]

RECENT MANIFESTATIONS OF NATIONALISM

Protest in Lithuania has taken many forms, ranging from refusals to speak or understand Russian, participation in *samizdat*, and attempted defections such as that of Kudirka,[143] to airplane hijackings[144] and self-immolations on public streets and squares.[145] The speed and regularity with which information on events in Lithuania has been reaching underground circles in Moscow suggest that the dissent movement is well organized and relatively widespread. Further evidence that nationalist organizations do exist in Lithuania is provided in the *Khronika* report that a Liudvikas Simutis, born in 1935, was sentenced in December 1971 to 25 years of strict regime for being an active member of an underground "Movement for the Freedom of Lithuania." [146]

The demonstrations in Kaunas on May 18–19, 1972, and the petition campaigns[147] against religious persecution are direct evidence of the scale of dissent. On May 14, a Sunday afternoon, in a city square in Kaunas, Romas Kalanta, a 19-year-old student and Komsomol member who had expressed interest in becoming a priest, made a speech protesting Soviet oppression, then poured gasoline over himself and set fire to it. He died in a hospital several hours later. His burial was set for May 18, and many young people gathered at the home of Kalanta's parents, where the body was laid out well before the appointed time. Special

security agents carried the body to a hearse via a rear exit, and the mourners were unable to keep up with the car as it sped away to the cemetery. Angry at this deception, they went instead to the site of the immolation, where the crowd soon grew to a size of several thousand, a great many young people.[148]

The crowd in the square became boisterous; witnesses report shouts of "Freedom for Lithuania" and singing of national songs. Violence erupted when police tried to disperse the throng. At least one policeman was killed or seriously injured when hit with a rock.[149] Clashes with the police continued throughout the city for the rest of the day, and reports indicate that fires broke out in several areas, including one in the city headquarters of the Communist party.[150]

Demonstrations began again at about 3:00 A.M. on May 19. Toward 5:00 P.M., military units, presumably of the MVD, were brought in, and succeeded in quelling the disorders. Sources indicate that between 400 and 500 people were detained by the police. Many were released soon afterward, but an estimated 200 were kept in prison for 15 days or more.[151] Soviet sources tried to present the disruptions as the work of a small group of "hooligans," and eight young people were convicted on such charges in October.[152]

In contrast to the drama of the events in Kaunas, Catholic dissent has been quieter, more persistent, and more enduring. Apparently, it involves more people. Letters to Soviet and Church authorities began appearing in underground channels in 1968, at first signed only by individual priests or groups of clergymen, protesting strict limits on the number of new priests that could be trained[153] and other harassing restrictions on the Church. Arrests of priests began in

---

142 Vardys, 1965: 249–250.
143 For details, see *Lituanus* (Fall), 1972: XVIII: 3.
144 See "Violations," 1972: 62–63; *New York Times* (October 18, 21), 1970 and (January 20, February 1), 1971.
145 *Khronika* (July 5), 1972: XXVI: 22–24.
146 *Khronika* (May 20), 1972: XXV: 34.
147 Petition campaigns and protests have been reported throughout Lithuania, from Klaipeda in the west to Zarasai in the east, and from Akmene in the north to Varena in the south. Most major cities are represented, as are numerous small towns and rural areas.

148 *Time* (July 31), 1972: 27–28; *New York Times* (May 26), 1972; *Khronika* (October 15), 1972: 17–20; July 1972 issue of "ELTA" published by Supreme Committee for Liberation of Lithuania, based in New York City.
149 *Khronika*, 1972: 27.
150 *Time* (July 31), 1972: 28.
151 *Khronika*, 1972: XXVII: 19; *New York Times* (June 14), 1972.
152 *New York Times* (October 4), 1972; FBIS Daily Reports (October 5, 17), 1972.
153 According to one such letter, only five or six new priests are ordained each year, whereas death claims around thirty. See "Violations," 1972: 34.

1970, however, apparently bringing the laity into the protest movement. In August 1971 Father Jouzas Zdebskis, a priest who had signed one of the earlier letters,[154] was arrested and accused of "systematically" teaching the catechism to children. He was tried and convicted in November. Before his trial, 2,000 members of his parish signed an open letter to the Soviet government protesting the action and demanding his release.[155]

About a month later another petition was circulated, signed by 1,190 parishioners in a different *raion,* protesting removal of their priest.[156] In December 1971 sentencing of Father Bubnys of Raseinai *raion* (between Kaunas and Siauliai) brought another appeal, signed by 1,344 parishioners.[157]

None of these petitions received an official reply. The silence provoked a far more massive effort. In January 1972 a stack of identical petitions signed by over 17,000 Catholics from all over Lithuania was received in the West. This appeal was addressed to Kurt Waldheim, Secretary General of the United Nations, with the request that he pass it on directly to CPSU General Secretary Brezhnev. The signatures included full names and addresses, and frequently telephone numbers, of signers.[158] Organizers of the appeal noted that even more signatures would have been obtained but for the interference of the militia and the KGB.[159]

Local petitions and protests continued to appear throughout 1972. In the spring the first issue of *Chronicle of the Lithuanian Catholic Church* appeared.[160] In reporting on events and persecutions in all parts of Lithuania, this document reveals the extent of the underground communications effort. Moscow *Khronika* reported that three editions of this journal had appeared by October 1972; two were received in the West in November.[161] Lithuanian émigré sources indicated that a copy of the fourth edition was received in April 1973.[162]

The import of all this activity is difficult to assess. It seems clear that a great deal of the Catholic dissent would die down if the Soviet state would live up to guarantees expressed in its Constitution and implied in its propaganda. But the Kaunas riots and the continuously expressed concern of the Soviet Lithuanian regime over nationalism imply that, particularly among youth, national pride remains widespread and demands more scope than the Soviet regime is willing to allow. Lithuanians are proud of their heritage, progress, culture, and ties to the West. Their distinctiveness has in part been sheltered by their domination of the leading positions in the republic party and government. But in 1973, Snieckus, first secretary of the CPL, turned seventy years old; whether his "machine" can continue without him, and how Moscow will respond to the unrest, remain open and crucial questions.

154 *Radio Liberty Research Bulletin* (February 15), 1973: 8.
155 *New York Times* (September 27), 1971.
156 *Radio Liberty Research Bulletin* (February 15), 1973: 8; *Survey* (Summer 1972): XVIII: 3: 237.
157 *Ibid.* [both sources].
158 *Christian Science Monitor* (December 7), 1972.
159 Text of the appeal is given in *Survey* (Summer), 1972: XVIII: 3: 237–240.

160 For a list of contents, see *Radio Liberty Research Bulletin* (February 15), 1973: 6–8.
161 *Khronika* (October 15), 1972: XXVII: 20; *Baltic Events* (February), 1973: I: 2.
162 Private communication. See also *Baltic Events* (June), 1973: III: 1.

REFERENCES

Audenas, 1963
    Juozas Audenas ed., *Twenty Years' Struggle for Freedom of Lithuania* (New York: ELTA Information Service, 1963).
Baltic Action Maunal, 1971
    Baltic Action Manual, publication of First Baltic Information Conference of North

America, New York, March 27–28, 1971.
Benyušis, 1972
    P. Benyusis, in *Sovetskaya Litva,* July 4, 1972: 2.
Butkus, 1964
    T. Butkus, *Take a Look at Soviet Lithuania* (Vilnius: Mintis, 1964).

Church and State Under Communism, 1965
  Church and State Under Communism,
  vol. IV (Lithuania, Latvia, and Estonia),
  Special Study by subcommittee of Com-
  mittee on Judiciary, U.S. Senate (Wash-
  ington, D.C.: Government Printing Office,
  1965).
Ekonomika Litvy, 1970
  *Ekonomika i kul'tura Litovskoi SSR v
  1970 godu. Statisticheskii yezhegodnik*
  (Vilnius: Statistika, 1971).
FBIS
  Foreign Broadcast Information Service,
  published by U.S. Department of Com-
  merce.
Gerutis *et al.*, 1969
  Albertas Gerutis *et al.*, *Lithuania*: 700
  Years, rev. 2nd ed. (New York: Manyland
  Books, 1969).
Itogi 1970
  Itogi vsesoyuznoi perepisi naseleniya 1970
  goda, vol. IV (Moscow: Statistika, 1973).
JPRS
  Joint Publications Research Service.
  Translations on USSR Political and Socio-
  logical Affairs (published by U.S. Depart-
  ment of Commerce).
Jurgela, 1948
  Constantine R. Jurgela, *History of the
  Lithuanian Nation* (New York: Lithua-
  nian Cultural Institute, 1948).
Khronika
  Khronika tekushchikh sobytii [*Chron-
  icle of Current Events*], underground
  bimonthly, Moscow.
Litva, 1967
  Litva, series *Sovetskii Soyuz: Geografi-
  cheskoe Opisanie v 22 Tomakh* (Moscow:
  Mysl', 1967).
Litva za polveka, 1967
  Litva za polveka novoi epokhi (Vilnius:
  Mintis, 1967).
LME
  Latvijas PSR Mazā Enciklopēdija (Riga:
  Zinātne, 1967–1970).
Maciuika, 1967
  Benedict V Maciuika, "Die Russifizierung
  Litauens seit 1959: Versuch einer Quan-
  titativen Analyse" ["Russification of
  Lithuania since 1959: An attempt at a
  Quantitative Analysis"], *Acta Baltica*
  (1967): VII: 289–302.
Maciuika, 1972
  Benedict V. Maciuika, "The Apparat of
  Political Socialization in Soviet Lithua-
  nia: Evaluation of Structure and Per-
  formance," paper delivered to Third
  Conference on Baltic Studies of AABS,
  Toronto, Canada, May 11, 1972.
Nar. khoz. 1970
  Narodnoye khozyaistvo SSSR v 1970 godu
  (Moscow: Statistika, 1971).

Nar. khoz. 1971
  *Narodnoye khozyaistvo SSSR 1922–1972:
  Yubileinyi statisticheskii yezhegodnik*
  (Moscow: Statistika, 1972).
Nar. khoz. Latvii 1972
  *Narodnoye khozyaistvo Latviiskoi SSR v
  1971 godu* (Riga: Statistika, 1972).
Nar. khoz. Litvy 1965
  *Narodnoye khozyaistvo Litovskoi SSR v
  1965 godu* (Vilnius: Statistika Litovskoye
  otdeleniye, 1971).
Nar. obraz., 1971
  *Narodnoye obrazovaniye, nauka i kul'tura
  v SSSR: statisticheskii sbornik* (Moscow:
  Statistika, 1971).
Pechat' 1959
  Pechat' SSSR v 1959 godu (Moscow:
  Kniga, 1960).
Pechat' 1970
  Pechat' SSSR v 1970 godu (Moscow:
  Kniga, 1971).
Pospielovsky, 1972
  Dimitry Pospielovsky, "The Kaunas Riots
  and the National and Religious Tensions
  in the USSR," *Radio Liberty Research
  Bulletin*, May 31, 1972: 127–172.
Res Baltica, 1968
  Adolf Sprudzs and Armin Rusis, eds., *Res
  Baltica* (Leyden: Sitjthoff, 1968).
Rimaitis, 1971
  J. Rimaitis, "Religion in Lithuania,"
  pamphlet (Vilnius: Gintaras, 1971).
Sabaliunas, 1972
  Leonas Sabaliunas, *Lithuania in Crisis:
  Nationalism to Communism, 1939–1940*
  (Bloomington: Indiana University Press,
  1972).
Silver, 1972
  Brian David Silver, *Ethnic Identity
  Change Among Soviet Nationalities: A
  Statistical Analysis*, unpublished Ph.D.
  thesis, University of Wisconsin, 1972.
Simutis, 1942
  Anicetas Simutis, *The Economic Recon-
  struction of Lithuania After 1918* (New
  York: Columbia University Press, 1942).
SSSR, 1967
  *Soyuz Sovetskikh Sotsialisticheskikh Res-
  publik 1917–1967* (Moscow: Sovetskaya
  entsiklopediya, 1967).
Stukas, 1966
  Jack J. Stukas, *Awakening Lithuania*
  (Madison, N.J.: Florham Park Press,
  1966).
Szporluk, 1971
  Roman Szporluk, "Dissent and the Non-
  Russian Nationalities," paper prepared
  for Conference on Dissent in Soviet
  Union, McMaster University, Hamilton,
  Ontario, October 22–23, 1971.
Taagepera, 1972a
  Rein Taagepera, "Inequality Indices for

Baltic Farm Size Distribution, 1929–1940," *Journal of Baltic Studies* (Spring 1972): III: 1: 26–34.

Taagepera, 1972b
Rein Taagepera, "Dissimilarities Among the Northwestern Soviet Republics," paper presented at plenary session of Third Conference on Baltic Studies, Toronto, May 11–14, 1972.

Taagepera, 1972c
Rein Taagepera, *Estonian Events*, December 1972: 35.

Taagepera, 1973
Rein Taagepera, *Baltic Events* (February 1973): I: 36.

Tarulis, 1959
Albert N. Tarulis, *Soviet Policy Toward the Baltic States 1918–1940* (South Bend, Ind.: University of Notre Dame Press, 1959).

Transport i svyaz', 1972
Transport i svyaz' SSSR (Moscow: Statistika, 1972).

Vardys, 1964
V. Stanley Vardys, "Soviet Colonialism in the Baltic States: A Note on the Nature of Modern Colonialism," *Lituanus* (Summer 1964): X: 2: 5–23.

Vardys, 1965
V. Stanley Vardys ed., *Lithuania Under the Soviets* (New York: Praeger, 1965).

"Violations," 1972
"The Violations of Human Rights in Soviet-Occupied Lithuania: A Report for 1971"; Lithuanian American Community, 405 Leon Ave., Delran, N. J. 08075, February 16, 1972.

Part III

THE
TRANSCAUCASUS

The Transcaucasus is a relatively small but populous area consisting of the republics of Armenia, Georgia, and Azerbaidzhan. Located at the crossroads of Europe and Asia, between the Black Sea and the Caspian Sea, the area has historically been subject to expansionist pressures from Iran, Turkey, and Russia. After the 1917 revolution in Russia the three republics experienced a brief period of independence, terminated by the Red Army's victory. With formation of the USSR in the early 1920s, the republics were combined in a single Transcaucasian Soviet Federation of Socialist Republics. In 1936 they became separate union republics.

Despite geographical similarities and shared historical experiences, there are great differences among the three republics, and attitudes of enmity and mistrust have often prevailed. Azerbaidzhan differs from the other republics in its Moslem population and closeness to Turkey, which has a similar language and culture, and Iran, with a large Azeri population. It has a fragmented political history and a lower level of development than the other republics. (For indicators of development, see the Comparative Tables section in the Appendix.)

Armenia and Georgia, by contrast, pride themselves on an ancient Christian culture and a long history of independent statehood. They are among the most highly developed nations in the USSR. They too, however, are very different from each other. Their churches, languages, and cultures differ, and their relationship has often been one of rivalry. No major Georgian diaspora is comparable to the world-wide dispersion of Armenians, and nothing in Georgian history parallels the Turkish persecution of Armenians.

7 | ARMENIA and THE ARMENIANS

Mary K. Matossian

General Information

TERRITORY

Historic Armenia is an upland, or "mountain island," wedged between the mountain structures of Anatolia and Iran and higher than either. It does not quite extend to the Black Sea on the west or the Caspian Sea on the east; to the north are the Pontus and Lesser Caucasus mountains; to the south are the Eastern Taurus Mountains out of which flow the Tigris and Euphrates rivers. Approximate area of the Armenian upland is 100,000 square miles; its average elevation, 5,000 feet above sea level. Today, Soviet Armenia occupies only 11,175 square miles on the northern rim of the historic Armenian homeland in one of the most mountainous parts of the region. The lowest point in Soviet Armenia is 1,279 feet above sea level; over 70% of the republic is over 4,921 feet high.[1] The land is studded with extinct volcanos, volcanic rock, and volcanic soils.

Highest peak in the Armenian upland is Mount Ararat (according to the Bible, site of the landing of Noah's Ark), 16,945 feet high. It is located in Turkish territory but clearly visible from Yerevan, capital of Soviet Armenia. Mount Ararat, called by Armenians "Mother of the World," is the most important geographic symbol of their identity. The highest peak within the territory of Soviet Armenia is Mount Aragats (Alagöz), which is 13,410 feet.

Lake Van, 1,460 square miles in area, is the largest lake in the Armenian upland. In Soviet Armenia the largest lake is Sevan, 497 square miles, home of a famous salmon-trout, the *ishkhan,* and currently being developed as a summer resort.

The climate of Soviet Armenia varies according to altitude, but is generally hot and dry in summer and cold in winter. The weather is mildest in the Araxes Valley around Yerevan, where the best season is autumn (mild, warm, and sunny). In the highlands winter lasts for six months and the temperature may fall to −40°; many peaks remain snow-covered all year round. Annual rainfall ranges from 10 to 35 inches in different parts of the republic.[2]

Only 12% of Soviet Armenian territory is

---

[1] *Armeniya,* 1966: 314–315.

[2] *Ibid.*: 318.

covered with trees and shrubs. This de-forestation has been a basic cause of soil erosion. Many believe that the Armenian up-land was original home of the grapevine, and viticulture is an important activity in Soviet Armenia. There are many rich soils in Armenia, but cultivation is hindered by presence of surface stones and lack of water.

The principal known energy resource of Soviet Armenia is hydroelectric power. The country is also rich in metals (copper, molybdenum, aluminium, lead, zinc, mer-cury, gold, silver, iron, chrome) and min-erals, especially building stone (tufa, marble) and limestone (for cement).

ECONOMY

In 1969[3] industry accounted for over two thirds of the ruble value of production in Armenia. From 1913 to 1969, the value of industrial production increased 162 times, second highest growth rate in the Soviet Union. Much of this advance occurred in the 1930s; since then the rate has slowed considerably. Between 1950 and 1960 indus-try in eight other republics grew faster than in Armenia. In 1960–1969 Armenian indus-try grew by 238%, well above the USSR average (209%), but below that of five other republics.[4]

Nonferrous metallurgy is one of the most important branches of industrial produc-tion. The republic is a major source of molybdenum, aluminum, and rare metals such as selenium and tellurium, also boast-ing significant deposits of gold and silver.[5] The chemical industry developed markedly during the 1960s and has become a major branch. Machine-building and metalwork-ing employed over one third of the indus-trial labor force, accounting for one fifth of

the total industrial production in 1969.[6] A new automobile plant was built in Yerevan in that year.[7]

Armenia is one of the Soviet Union's most important centers for scientific re-search and production of calculators, computers, and measuring instruments em-ploying semiconductor electronics. The food industry is also significant through produc-tion of wines, cognac, fruit preserves, and juices.[8]

The products of Soviet Armenia are exported to the United States, England, France, West Germany, and other developed countries. The republic's specialized econ-omy is heavily dependent on exports to other Soviet republics or abroad. Over 95% of the products of machine-building indus-tries are exported, as are 90% of fruit and vegetable products and 70% of wines and liqueurs.[9] Armenian cognac is prized throughout the USSR.

While under Ottoman and Persian rule, the Armenian people's energies could not be channeled into political or military activity, and the best lands were in Moslem hands. Consequently, Armenians became mer-chants and artisans, coming to excel in these activities, growing richer than their Moslem neighbors. Armenians have always admired hard work and business acumen while Moslems had more aristocratic, less bourgeois values.

Although Soviet rule has brought major changes in the structure of Armenian eco-nomic activity, indicators of the standard of living suggest that the republic is still better off than most of its Caucasian and Central Asian neighbors, approaching the higher standards of the European Soviet republics. In 1970 Armenia ranked second among Soviet republics in savings per capita and eighth in trade turnover (among the non-European republics, only Kazakh-stan had higher per capita turnover).[10] Only Georgia and three European republics ex-

3 According to *Sovetskaya Armeniya* (1970: 46), the "gross social product" of the republic was as follows: industry, 67.9%; agriculture, 11.9%; con-struction, 12.7%; transport and communication, 1.8%; and trade, supply, and "other categories," 5.7%.
4 Lithuania, Belorussia, Moldavia, Kirgizia, and Kazakhstan all had higher rates of industrial growth. *Ekonomika Litvy*, 1970: 421.
5 *Armeniya*, 1966: 119–123.

6 *Sovetskaya Armeniya*, 1970: 132. This source omits data on the role of chemistry and light metals in the overall industrial picture, although other sources attest to their significance.
7 *BSE*, 1970: 229; *Armeniya za 50 let*, 1970: 96, 106.
8 *Armeniya*, 1966: 128–139.
9 *Ibid.*: 128, 139.
10 *Nar. khoz.* 1970: 563–564, 579.

ceeded Armenia in ratio of doctors to population.[11]

HISTORY

The Armenian upland had its first period of prosperity in the third millennium B.C. before arrival of the Armenians. The inhabitants, who worshipped the Mother Goddess, may have been among the first to use bronze, viticulture, and the wheel. This flourishing culture was broken up by invaders, probably Indo-Europeans, at the end of the third millennium.[12]

Urartu (cf. Ararat) was first state in the Armenian upland; it lasted from 880 to 590 B.C. The people spoke Hurrian, a language akin to the Japhetic languages of the Caucasus (e.g., Georgian), and used a cuneiform script. Well-planned citadel towns and irrigation systems were features of this state. Eventually, it fell to the Medes and the Armenians, who arrived in the sixth century B.C., or perhaps earlier.

The first united Armenian state was organized by the Artaxid dynasty, ruling from 190 to 1 B.C., followed by the Arsacid dynasty, which lasted until 428 A.D. Under the Artaxids, Armenian became the language of all social classes in the area. The state records were kept in Greek and Iranian, however, and the religion was a mixture of Greek and Iranian pagan elements. Under Tigranes the Great (95–55 B.C.), Armenian power reached its height, extending over most of modern Syria and Lebanon. By 55 B.C. the Romans had brought the Armenians under their control.

In 301 A.D. the Arsacid king Tiridates III adopted Christianity as state religion under the inspiration of the nobleman St. Gregory the Illuminator. To this day Armenians refer to their church as "Gregorian," regarding it as apostolic. Since the six century A.D. they have been separate from both Roman and Eastern (Byzantine Greek) churches. Although Armenian political power has been evanescent, the Armenian Church has been a strong independent institution, able to preserve Armenian ethnic identity under

foreign domination. Furthermore, Christian culture has made it easy for Armenians to identify with Western civilization and import Western ideas and practices.

The Armenian people played an important role in the Byzantine Empire as fighters, administrators, and scholars. Many Byzantine emperors were Armenian. Meanwhile, the Armenian upland became a disputed border area between the Byzantines and, in succession, Arabs, Persians, and Turks. The Armenian Bagratid dynasty established a prosperous state, with Ani as capital, in the upland in the tenth century but it fell to the Seljuk Turks in the mideleventh century.

Another Armenian principality arose in the southeastern corner of Anatolia, Cilicia, a fertile land adjoining northern Syria. After it was retaken from the Arabs by the Byzantines, Armenians colonized it (late 10th and early 11th centuries). The Armenian rulers of Cilicia cooperated with the Crusaders. The area became known as "Lesser Armenia" and had a large Armenian population until the massacres of 1915 by the Turks. But a succession of Mongol, Mamluk, and Ottoman Turk invasions brought down the state of Cilicia by the end of the fourteenth century.

The Armenian upland became the scene of struggle between Ottoman Turks and Persians; finally, it was divided between them in 1639, with the Turks getting the larger share. Present-day Soviet Armenia was constituted from the Persian share of the upland. For Armenians the twelfth to eighteenth centuries was a period of cultural darkness under the shadow of Islam, and especially of the newly converted Central Asian nomads.[13]

The Russians conquered Persian Armenia in 1828. Little was done to develop the economy of this backward area, and enterprising Armenians moved to Tbilisi in Georgia where many prospered. Armenians profited from the educational and cultural institutions of tsarist Russia. Glad to be under the protection of a Christian ruler, they vigorously resisted the Russification campaign of the late nineteenth and early twentieth centuries. They also had to cope with secular Turkish nationalism, both

---

11 *Nar. khoz.* 1972: 515, *passim.*
12 Lang, 1970: 67–70.

13 *Ibid.*, 1970: 67–70, *passim.*

within the Caucasus (in Azerbaidzhan) and in the Ottoman Empire.

When eastern Armenia passed from Persian to Russian rule in 1828, there was no immediate change in Armenian political attitudes; they had merely exchanged one master for another. For western Armenians, however, decline of Ottoman power in the nineteenth century was an opportunity to improve political status, and involved a revival of assertive attitudes. Armenian political resistance was first organized in Erzurum in 1880. In 1890 the Armenian Revolutionary Federation (Dashnaktsutiun) was founded to unify the growing revolutionary nationalist movement in both western and eastern Armenia.[14]

The Ottoman government could count on support of Turks and Kurds in the empire to help suppress the richer Armenians, envied and resented for their wealth. In 1894–1896 an estimated several hundred thousand Armenians were massacred in eastern Turkey. Worse was to come. During World War I, when Ottoman and tsarist armies were fighting on the Caucasian front, the Ottoman government feared a "stab in the back" from the resident population. Consequently, in 1915 it adopted a policy of "deportation" of Armenians to remote areas —a euphemism for genocide. About 1.5 million Armenians perished from enforced hardship or were killed by Turks and Kurds.[15]

At the end of the nineteenth century secular Armenian nationalist parties appeared, all with a left-wing flavor on socioeconomic issues. Of these, the Dashnaktsutiun was most important. Today this party is the center of anti-Soviet activity in the Armenian diaspora.

During 1918–1920 there was an interregnum between tsarist government control and effective control by the Bolshevik government in Transcaucasia. The eastern Armenians enjoyed a brief period of national independence; a republic was formed led by the Dashnaktsutiun. During this period Turkish power was resurgent, and Georgians and Azerbaidzhani Turks abandoned their alliance with the Armenians in the spring of 1918. But, although American relief supplies saved many who were starving in 1919, no effective Allied military aid was available. In December 1920 the Russians reappeared, this time wearing helmets with a red star. In view of the Turkish threat, this was not an entirely unwelcome event. The principal Dashnak leaders who did not flee eastern Armenia were arrested or killed.[16]

An Armenian Soviet Republic was proclaimed in November 1920. It became part of the Transcaucasian Soviet Federation which joined the Soviet Union in December 1922. In 1936 the federation was dissolved and Armenia became a separate union republic.[17] During the 1920s Soviet authority was extended to every remote corner of eastern Armenia. The Communist party of Armenia recruited a sufficient membership, mostly from young males of the better educated urban population. The policy of *korenizatsiya* ("rooting" the new institutions through recruitment of native cadres) was followed systematically, so that the personnel, high and low, of all institutions were Armenians. The Armenian SSR attracted able Armenians from other parts of the USSR who had left when eastern Armenia appeared too remote and unpromising an area. Economic reconstruction began, but new development was limited. A network of state schools was extended throughout the country, and enrollment grew fast. Yerevan State University was reorganized in 1923; the language of instruction was Armenian.

Collectivization was forcibly resisted. Guerilla forces retreated to the mountains and, ultimately, to Persia. The climax of resistance came in the summer of 1931, but its end came early in 1932. Famine prevailed from 1931 to 1934.

Leader of Soviet Armenia from May 1930 to July 1936 was an outstanding young Armenian named Aghasi Khanchian. Born in Van in Turkish Armenia in 1901, he took refuge with his family in eastern Armenia in 1915. During the Great Purge of 1936–1938, he and a generation of able young Armenian Communist leaders were executed.

The 1930s were a period of rapid industrial growth, and there were numerous opportunities for advancement. Many ac-

14 Gidney, 1967: 24–40.
15 *Ibid.*: 56–57.

16 Hovannisian, 1967, 1971; Kazemzadeh, 1951.
17 *BSE*, 1947: 1914–1971.

quired a college education and a good job, but the people profiting most were offspring of the intelligentsia. Women enrolled in higher education and entered the skilled labor market in larger numbers. Armenia escaped the devastation of World War II and these trends continued during the post-war period.

The post-Stalin thaw in Soviet Armenia permitted expression not so much of resistance to violations of individual rights as resistance to denial of rights of the Armenian nation. Since 1965 nationalist sentiment has been openly expressed, but directed more against Turks than Russians (see later in this chapter).[18]

DEMOGRAPHY

Although Armenians speak an Indo-European language, physically they resemble more the pre-Indo-European population of the upland depicted on Hittite and Urartian friezes. The typical individual is of medium height, distinguished by a round head with broad forehead, dark hair and dark eyes with thick dark eyebrows and eyelashes.[19]

As of January 1970, total population of the Armenian SSR was 2,491,873 persons, with 88.6% Armenians. This represents a threefold increase under Soviet rule. The rate of average natural increase in Armenia is 19.5 per 1,000 compared to 9.8 per 1,000 in the USSR generally. Soviet Armenia is the most ethnically homogeneous of all the Soviet republics; however, only 56% of Armenians in the USSR live there. This figure is smaller than that for any other republican nationality. The majority of Soviet Armenians outside of the Armenian SSR are in Soviet Georgia and Azerbaidzhan.[20]

In Soviet Armenia mean density of population is 281 persons per square mile, seven times mean density of the USSR. But 45% of the population lives in the Ararat Valley, constituting only 6.5% of the republic's territory.

From 1959 to 1970 urban population grew 68% and rural, 15%. In 1970, 60% of the population was urban, as opposed to 50% in 1959. Yerevan, the capital, had 767,000 inhabitants; Leninakan had 164,000; and Kirovakan, 107,000.

Most Armenians prefer to live in Yerevan, where the climate is relatively mild and life is more dynamic. Rapid economic development in the 1960s increased the number of jobs in Yerevan and its population is 95.3% Armenian.

As of January 1, 1969, blue- or white-collar employees and their families constituted 76% of the republic's population (compared with 12.7% in 1926 and 31.2% in 1939) In 1926 independent peasants and artisans were in a majority (76.2%); by 1939 collective farmers and collectivized artisans held the majority (63.4%).

Of total number of persons in blue- and white-collar jobs in 1971 (870,000), distribution among branches of the economy was as follows:[21]

Industry	182,000	or	32%
Construction	106,000		12%
Agriculture	96,000		11%
Transport	56,000		6%
Communication	12,000		0.013%
Health	42,000		0.05%
Education	100,000		11%
Science	35,000		0.04%

Women constituted about 40% of the total labor force in 1968.

In January 1971 the Communist party of Armenia had a total of 130,353 members and candidates, ranking fifth among Soviet republics in ratio of party size to population. No recent data are available on percentage of Armenians in the republic party, but it may be presumed high, since in January 1972 a total of 223,372 Armenians were in the CPSU. Armenians trailed only Georgians and Russians in terms of relative size of party representation.[22]

---

18 Matossian, 1962.
19 Lang, 1970: 37; Aslanyan, 1971: 81.
20 Of 3,559,000 Armenians in the USSR, 1,351,000 live in other Soviet republics. Of these, 484,000 (35%) live in Azerbaidzhan, 452,000 (33%) in Georgia, and 299,000 (22%) in the RSFSR. *Nar. khoz. 1972:* 500, 569, 581.

21 "Rabochiye i sluzhashchiye zanyatye v norodnom khozyaistve" ["Workers and Employees in the Economy"]. This figure does not include collective farmers, who numbered 105,000 in 1971. *Nar. khoz. 1972:* 662–663.
22 See Comparative Tables section in Appendix.

CULTURE

At the start of the fifth century A.D. St. Mesrop Mashtots invented the unique Armenian alphabet, which uses the Greek alphabet as a base, and Armenian literature began. The Armenian Church was responsible for organization and conservation of this literature, comparable to Byzantine Greek literature. In addition, Armenian folk singers kept alive a strong oral tradition. Of particular interest is the epic of *David of Sasun*, probably originating in the eighth or ninth centuries A.D. in the same period and region as the Byzantine epic of *Digenis Akrites*. Gradually, the language of written literature and of the Armenian Church, *Grabar*, became more and more divergent from colloquial speech, the language of oral tradition. In the nineteenth century a written literary language closer to colloquial Armenian, *Ashkharabar*, was developed by the secular intelligentsia.[23]

Arts in which Armenians have excelled are architecture and music. In the sixth and seventh centuries A.D. they played a major role in solving the problem of building a dome over a square building (involving use of pendentives). Folk music was little appreciated until collected by Komitas (Solomon Solomonian, 1869–1935) and developed by Aram Khachaturian (b. 1903) and Alan Hovhannes (b. 1911).

Two outstanding modern artists are Hovhannes Aivazovsky (1817–1900) and Martiros Sarian (b. 1880). There have been many competent writers in Soviet Armenia, but none has achieved the international reputation of the American-Armenian, William Saroyan (b. 1908).

The two great centers of learning in Soviet Armenia are Yerevan State University (founded 1921) and Armenian Academy of Sciences (founded 1943). Armenia has a national symphony, string quartet, song and dance ensemble, and opera house.

Families are traditionally patriarchal and patrilocal. Extended households have always been common, and even today extended family ties appear strong. In rural areas of Soviet Armenia brides are still expected to be virgins; in Yerevan, women

do not usually go to restaurants. And, as elsewhere in most of the Middle East, presentable foreign female visitors are the object of considerable male attention in Yerevan, where *machismo* is prized. Family control over behavior of members is strong, particularly in the case of women. In general, the traditional wedding ritual has been maintained and parental consent for a marriage is considered necessary. Only the intelligentsia of Yerevan depart from these age-old patterns.[24] In this ethnically homogeneous population, marriage between Armenians and non-Armenians is very rare.

Traditional dress has disappeared from all but a few remote localities and Yerevan theatrical productions. Old-fashioned housing is rapidly being replaced by modern Soviet-style apartments and village settlements.[25] But traditional Armenian foods predominate everywhere in Soviet Armenia: shish kebab, rice, yogurt, bulghour, stuffed vegetables, pastries, and local wines. (These are also traditional in Georgia, Azerbaidzhan, and most of the Middle East.)

The Armenian Apostolic Church has long been a central element in the culture. By tradition, every child born of Armenian parents is considered a member of the Armenian Church. Subsequently, some join the Roman or Protestant churches. There is little reliable data on number of adherents of the Armenian Church in Soviet Armenia.[26] In the diaspora social life of the various Armenian communities centers around the church.

Prior to the 1930s the Soviet regime had merely seized most of the property (including the parish schools) of the Armenian Church, but in the 1930s a campaign of active persecution was conducted. The clergy has been molested in various ways and atheist propaganda is distributed. Today the younger generation shows little interest in church activities, although it is widely regarded as a symbol of Armenian nationalism. Echmiadzin, world center of the Armenian Church near Yerevan, is allowed to hold religious services and train

---

23 *Armeniya*, 1966: 65.

24 Matossian, 1968: 185–197; Ter-Sarkisiants, 1972.
25 *Armeniya* 1966: 96–98.
26 Vazgen I, patriarch of the Soviet Armenian Church, estimated that half of the Armenians in the republic are believers, but there is no hard evidence to corroborate this figure. *New York Times* (December 18), 1971: 6.

a few clergymen under close surveillance. The *Catholicos* (head of the church) was allowed to visit his flock in the diaspora; but a visit to the United States scheduled for the spring of 1973 was cancelled. Echmiadzin's financial support comes largely from contributions in the diaspora; support from within Soviet Armenia appears slight.

A 1971 *New York Times* article suggests that Soviet authorities allowed the Soviet branch of the Armenian Church to flourish under the leadership of Catholicos Vazgen as a means of increasing the moral authority of Echmiadzin among the more than 1.5 million Armenians abroad. In return, the church makes concessions to the government at times, including pro-Soviet material in its services.[27]

EXTERNAL RELATIONS

The Turks and Armenians still regard each other with deep animosity, even among widely scattered Armenian émigré populations. Armenians regard Georgians as rivals, unduly favored by Stalin and the Soviet authorities. The history, fine arts, and customs of Georgians and Armenians are remarkably similar, but neither ethnic group will admit this. Armenians respect the bravery and fighting spirit of Russians but like to think of themselves as more clever. (The above judgments are impressionistic; there are no reliable studies of the subject.)

The most important ties of Soviet Armenians abroad are with the diaspora. Consequently, in international politics, the Armenians are growing more optimistic. This is apparent in the efforts of Soviet Armenians to reach out to Armenians in the diaspora, and vice versa. About 1.7 million Armenians are outside the Soviet Union.[28] Largest single group is in the United States (400,000); there are 200,000 in Iran, 180,000 in Lebanon, 120,000 in Syria, 120,000 in Turkey (still!), and 170,000 in France, to mention only major concentrations.

Because of emphasis on business skill in Armenian culture, many Armenians in the diaspora have become wealthy, and a few are multimillionaires (Calouste Gulbenkian, Kirk Kerkorian, Alex Manougian, for example). With revival of ethnicity in the United States, the Armenian community has made vigorous efforts to keep alive knowledge of the Armenian language, literature, music, dance, and other customs. Even the most vigorously anti-Soviet Armenian party in the diaspora, the Dashnaktsutiun, takes pride in the constructive work going on in Soviet Armenia. For many Armenians are once again thinking in continents and feeling in centuries.

Armenia is the only Soviet area which has actively sought immigration of its nationality from outside the USSR.[29] According to estimates, the country has attracted several tens of thousands, mainly from the Middle East, but also from the United States and Europe.

Media

LANGUAGE DATA

Armenian is an independent branch of the Indo-European family. It is a *satem*[30] language, as are the Baltic, Slavic, Albanian, and Indo-Iranian languages, but the consonant system of Armenian resembles that of Georgian and other languages of the

Kartvelian group. This may be the result of the original merging of Armenians with the Hurrian-speaking people of Urartu. Armenian is written in a unique script invented in 406 A.D. Soviet authorities have made

---

27 See *New York Times* (December 8), 1971: 6, which reports a sermon honoring establishment of Soviet power in Armenia on November 29, 1920.

28 *Armeniya za 50 let*, 1970: 290.
29 Only similar case in Soviet history is the effort of Birobidzhan to attract Jewish immigrants. Goldberg, 1961, *passim*.
30 An Indo-European language family in which in prehistoric times palatal stops became palatal or alveolar fricatives.

Table 7.1

Native and Second Languages Spoken by Armenians

(in thousands)

	No. Armenians Residing		SPEAKING AS NATIVE LANGUAGE						SPEAKING AS SECOND LANGUAGE[a]	
			Armenian		% Point Change	Russian		% Point Change	Russian	Other Languages of Peoples of USSR[b]
	1959	1970	1959	1970	1959–1970	1959	1970	1959–1970	1970	1970
in Armenian SSR	1,552 (100%)	2,208 (100%)	1,540 (99.2%)	2,204 (99.8%)	+0.6	11 (0.7%)	5 (0.2%)	−0.5	514 (23.3%)	26 (1.2%)
in other Soviet republics	1,235 (100%)	1,351 (100%)	965 (78.3%)	1,049 (77.6%)	−0.7	222 (17.9%)	265 (19.6%)	+1.7	357 (41.2%)	187 (13.8%)
Total	2,787 (100%)	3,559 (100%)	2,505 (90%)	3,253 (91.4%)	+1.4	233 (8.3%)	270 (7.6%)	−0.7	1,071 (30.1%)	214 (6.0%)

Sources: For 1959 census, *Itogi SSSR*, 1959: Table 53; *Itogi Armyanskoi SSR*, 1959: Table 53. For 1970 census, *Itogi 1970*: IV: 20, 303.

[a] No data are available for 1959, since no questions regarding command of a second language were asked in the 1959 census.

[b] Including Armenian, if not the native tongue.

changes in the orthography but do not attempt to replace the alphabet. Almost all of the 1.7 million Armenians outside the USSR speak Armenian.

In the USSR some 3.25 million Armenians regard Armenian as their native tongue. Within the Armenian SSR the proportion of Armenians giving Armenian as native language increased from 99.2% in 1959 to 99.8% in 1970. In 1970 only 23.5% of Armenians in the republic claimed to be fluent in Russian, although, almost necessarily, more must have had some knowledge of the language.

The 1970 census data do not provide evidence of substantial Russification. In 1957 a visiting American scholar found that an Armenian family of scientists spoke Russian at home habitually. In 1971 a Soviet Armenian scholar asserted that in 1957 this was not unusual but currently it was disappearing. He stated also that the more educated families used Armenian as native tongue.[31] There has been a negligible drop in use of Armenian as a first language among Armenians in the USSR outside of Soviet Armenia: from 78.3% in 1959 to 77.6% in 1970.

LOCAL MEDIA

Largest collection of Armenian manuscripts in the world (25,000) is housed in the famous Matenadaran in Yerevan, open to accredited scholars. Armenia is third in the USSR (after Estonia and Latvia) in number of library books per capita.[32]

There are 71 newspapers published in the Armenian SSR (including 61 published in Armenian). Average circulation is 1,221,000 copies, about 1.1 million in Armenian. Twenty-nine magazines are published, including 17 in Armenian, with total circulation of 513,000 copies (over 496,000 in Armenian).

The two major newspapers are *Sovetakan Hayastan* [*Soviet Armenia*], organ of the Armenian Communist party, appearing six times weekly, and *Avangard*, organ of the Komsomol, appearing three times weekly. The two major Russian newspapers are

Kommunist, organ of the Armenian Communist party, appearing six times weekly, and *Komsomolets*, organ of the Central Committee of the Leninist Young Communist League of Armenia, appearing three times weekly.

Among principal periodicals in the Armenian SSR are:

Hayastani Ashkhatavorui [*Working Woman of Armenia*], journal of the Central Committee of the Armenian Communist party, published in Armenian and popular among women;

Hayastani Gyukhtntesutyun [*Armenian Agriculture*], journal of the Central Committee of the Communist party, published in Armenian;

Garun [*Spring*], combined journal of the Komsomol and the Union of Writers of the Armenian SSR, which publishes fiction, moral problems for the younger generation, and translations, in Armenian;

Leninyan Ugiov [*Along Lenin's Way*], politically oriented journal of the Central Committee of the Armenian Communist party, in Armenian;

Literaturnaya Armeniya [*Literature of Armenia*], journal of the Armenian SSR Union of Writers, which publishes fiction, in Russian;

Pioneer, journal of the Komsomol and Pioneers of the Armenian SSR, which publishes fiction for 10–15-year-olds, in Armenian;

Sovetaken Arvest [*Soviet Art*], published jointly by the Ministry of Culture of the Armenian SSR and State Committee for Cinematography of the Armenian SSR, in Armenian;

Sovetaken Hayastan [*Soviet Armenia*], published in Armenian by Armenian Committee of Cultural Relations with Compatriots Abroad;

Sovetaken Grakanutyun [*Soviet Literature*], journal of Armenian SSR Union of Writers, published in Armenian; and

Vozni [*Hedgehog*], satirical journal published fortnightly in Armenian.[33]

The first radio station was inaugurated in Yerevan in 1926, and the first TV station in 1956. In 1968 Soviet Armenia had one

31 Personal observations by M. Matossian.
32 Aslanyan, 1971: 93.

33 *Europa Yearbook*, 1972: 1281.

Table 7.2

Publications in Armenian SSR

Language of Publication	Year	NEWSPAPERS[a]			MAGAZINES			BOOKS & BROCHURES		
		No.	Per Issue Circulation (1,000)	Copies/100 in Language Group[e]	No.	Per Issue Circulation (1,000)	Copies/100 in Language Group[e]	No. Titles	Total Volume (1,000)	Books & Brochures/100 in Language Group[e]
Russian	1959	2	30	40.4	N.A.	N.A.	N.A.	142	800	107.8
	1971	3	56	72.8	12	17	22.1	218	1,613	2,098.1
Armenian[b]	1959	57	303	19.6	N.A.	N.A.	N.A.	997	6,069	393.4
	1971	61	1,132	51.3	17	496	22.5	840	8,663	392.4
Minority Languages	1959	5[c]	14	9.5	N.A.	N.A.	N.A.	19	32	21.9
	1971	7	33	15.9	0	0	0	23	57	27.5
Foreign Languages	1959	0	0	0	N.A.	N.A.	N.A.	(10)[d]	(174)	N.A.
	1971	0	0	0	0	0	0	(28)[d]	(205)	N.A.
All Languages	1959	64	347	19.6	22	984	56	1,168[d]	7,075	400.2
	1971	71	1,221	49.0	29	513	20.6	1,109[d]	10,538	422.9

Sources: *Pechat' 1959*: 58, 130, 165; *Pechat' 1971*: 96, 160, 189.

Note: The 1971 Russian language group data was obtained from 1970 census data as follows:

1. Aggregating number of minority people whose native language is not that of their minority.
2. Subtracting number of non-Armenian native speakers of Armenian.
3. Adding number of non-Armenian-speaking Armenians and number of Russian-speaking Russians to this.

The result is a maximum limit on number of native speakers of Russian—76,879 people. The 1970 census data indicates that 537,825 inhabitants of Armenia are fluent in Russian as second language. If total of both native speakers and those fluent in Russian as second language is considered as the Russian language group in 1971, newspaper copies per 100 equals 9.1; magazines, 2.8; and books, 262.4.

The minority language group equals the sum of minority peoples whose native language is that of their minority. Armenians and Russians were not considered.

[a] 1971 figures do not include *kolkhoz* newspapers

[b] Some of these are published in both Russian and Armenian languages.

[c] This figure may include publications in non-Soviet languages.

[d] Book totals as given in *Pechat'* sometimes differ from totals in language categories. The indication is that books are published in other languages, but no data is given. Figures in parentheses are the presumed production of books in other languages based on this discrepancy.

[e] Includes native speakers of the language.

Table 7.3

Electronic Media and Films in Armenian SSR

YEAR	RADIO					TELEVISION			MOVIES	
	No. Stations	No. Wired Sets (1,000)	/100 Population	No. Wireless Sets (1,000)	/100 Population	No. Stations	No. sets (1,000)	/100 Population	Seats (1,000)	/100 Population
1960	N.A.	139[a]	7.3[d]	204[a]	10.7[c]	N.A.	38[a]	2.0[c]	61[b]	3.2[d]
1970	N.A.	228[a]	9.0[d]	374[a]	14.7[c]	N.A.	243[a]	10.4[c]	131[b]	5.1[d]
1971	N.A.	267[d]	10.2[d]	388[d]	14.9[c]	N.A.	284[c]	10.9[c]	N.A.	N.A.

[a] Source: *Transport i svyaz' SSR*, 1972: 296–298.
[b] Source: *Narodnoye obrazovaniye, kul'tura i nauka v SSSR*, 1971: 325.
[c] Source: *Nar. khoz. 1972*: 572, 578.
[d] Computed from data cited above ([b] and [c]).
[e] See text for 1968 figures.

TV and two radio stations broadcasting in Armenian, Russian, Azerbaidzhani, Turkish, and Kurdish for domestic audiences, and a radio station broadcasting in Armenian and Arabic to Near Eastern audiences outside the USSR.[34] Armenian language publications brought in from abroad to Soviet Armenia enjoy some attention.

EDUCATIONAL INSTITUTIONS

In the nineteenth century Armenians had little opportunity for higher education. In Ottoman territory principal opportunities were in American missionary schools. By 1914 these schools had enrolled 2,500 college students and 4,500 high school students, the majority Armenians.[35] In the Russian Empire main places for advanced education for Armenians were Lazarevskii [Lazarian] Institute in Moscow (opened in 1815); Echmiadzin Seminary (opened in 1837); and Nersesian School in Tbilisi (opened in 1824).

In the latter part of the nineteenth century the Russian government began organizing a network of state schools in eastern Armenia, while the Armenian Church developed a network of parish schools in both western and eastern Armenia. The Armenians were quicker to seize educational opportunities than their Moslem neighbors for, as Christians, they identified with the "advanced" civilization of Western Europe and welcomed Western learning as their own. The cumulative effect of this in the Soviet Union is that Armenians have an extraordinarily high proportion of college students per capita. Among the 17 major nationalities of the USSR, they ranked third after the Jews and Georgians, with 23 college students per 1,000 population.[36]

In 1938 study of the Russian language became obligatory in secondary schools and higher educational institutions. In 1946 Russian became mandatory in the second grade, and in 1957 in the first grade of all schools. Soviet Armenians appear to have a reading knowledge of Russian, but in 1971

very little Russian was spoken in Yerevan.[37]

The overwhelming majority of the educated are Armenians taught in Armenian language schools. In the city of Yerevan, among employed persons only, 810 men and 815 women out of 1,000 have at least an incomplete secondary education.

Among the union republics, Armenia holds first place for number of students per 10,000 population.[38] Armenians living in Georgia and Azerbaidzhan come to Yerevan to study.[39] In 1969–1970 there were 53,355 students in the higher educational institutions of Soviet Armenia: 96% Armenians, 2.5% Russians, and less than 1% each Azerbaidzhanis, Kurds, and other nationalities;[40] 62.8% of Armenians in all Soviet higher educational institutions were studying in Armenia (a figure slightly higher than the percentage of Soviet Armenians living in Armenia).[41]

CULTURAL AND SCIENTIFIC INSTITUTIONS

A branch of the All-Union Academy of Sciences was founded in 1935. Eight years later, in 1943, it was converted into the Armenian SSR Academy of Sciences. The work of the academy, especially in the fields of astrophysics, stellar astronomy, physics of elementary particles, and chemistry of silicates and polymers, has made Yerevan—where the large majority of Armenian research institutes are located—a major scientific center. One of the largest, most important archives of ancient Middle Eastern manuscripts, both Armenian and non-Armenian, is also located in the city.

Of 17 major Soviet nationalities, only the Jews have a higher ratio of scientific workers to population than the Armenians.[42] Nearly one half of the Armenian scientific workers are employed outside the republic, but they still dominate the local scientific establishment. Of 11,577 scientific workers in Armenia in 1969, 94% were Armenians, 3.6% Russians, and 0.6%

---

34 *BSE*, 1970: 238.

35 Matossian, 1962.

36 See all-Union Comparative Tables section in Appendix.

37 Personal observation by M. Matossian.

38 Aslanyan, 1971: 667.

39 *Armeniya*, 1966: 101.

40 *Sovetskaya Armeniya*, 1970: 352.

41 *Ibid.*; *Nar. obraz.*, 1971: 196.

42 See Comparative Tables section in Appendix.

Table 7.4

Selected Data on Education in Armenia (1971)

		PER 1,000 POPULATION	% OF TOTAL
All schools			
number of schools	1,542	0.59	
number of students	667,000	255.9	
Newly opened elementary, incomplete secondary, and secondary schools			
number of schools	68		
number of student places	39,400	15.1	
Secondary special schools			
number of schools	63		
number of students	48,600	18.6	
Institutions of higher education			
number of institutions	12		
number of students	54,900	21.1	
Universities			
number of universities	1		
number of students			
total	11,912		
day students	7,193		60
evening students	2,713		23
correspondence students	2,006		17
newly admitted			
total	2,192		
day students	1,542		70
evening students	324		15
correspondence students	326		15
graduated			
total	1,876		
day students	1,121		60
evening students	414		22
correspondence students	341		18
Graduate students			
total number	1,135	0.44	
in scientific research institutions	554		
in universities	581		
Number of persons with (in 1970) higher or secondary (complete and incomplete) education			
per 1,000 individuals, 10 years and older	516		
per 1,000 individuals employed in national economy	697		
Number of workers graduated from professional-technical schools	16,200	6.22	

Source: *Nar. khoz. 1972*: 108, 439, 656, 664, 665, 667; 1972 (January) population for Armenian SSR was given as 2,606,000 (*Ibid.*: 12).

Jewish, with other nationalities making up smaller fractions of the total.

Theaters for drama are in Leninakan, Goris, Kirovakan, Artashat, and other regional centers. Yerevan boasts the largest number of theaters, including one for opera and ballet, a state drama theater, a Russian drama theater, and a puppet theater.

Armenians are prominent in Soviet scien-

tific and artistic elites, constituting a particularly skilled work force. Aram Khachaturyan is among the greatest living composers. Leading figures in music and literature have already been mentioned.[43] In addition, Victor Hambartzumian has been president of International Society of Astrophysicists. Tigran Petrosian preceded Boris Spassky as world chess champion.

Table 7.5

Selected Data on Scientific and Cultural Facilities and Personnel in Armenia (1971)

1972 Population: 2,606,000

Academy of Sciences		*Number of persons working*	
number of members	89	*in education and culture*	
number of scientific institutions		total	100,000
affiliated with academy	35	number per 1,000 population	38
total number of scientific workers	2,286		
		Number of persons working in science	
Museums		*and scientific services*	
number of museums	34	total	35,000
attendance	1,495,000	number per 1,000 population	13.4
attendance per 1,000 population	573.7		
		Number of public libraries	1,266
Theaters		number of books and magazines	
number of theaters	14	in public libraries	11,193,000
attendance	1,714,000		
attendance per 1,000 population	657.7	*Number of clubs*	1,146

Source: *Nar. khoz. 1972*: 106, 451, 663.

National Attitudes

REVIEW OF FACTORS FORMING
NATIONAL ATTITUDES

The Armenians emerged as a historical group in the middle of the sixth century B.C., playing an active role in Near Eastern politics until the end of the fourteenth century A.D. During this period they were not distinguishable from neighbors. Although officially Christian in religion, they were as warlike as other contemporary Christian peoples; indeed, they constituted the backbone of the Byzantine military forces. Writ-

ten literature, beginning in the early fifth century A.D., and scientific work were on a par with the Byzantine Greeks.[44]

A decisive change in national attitude came about as a result of conquest of the area by nomadic peoples from Central Asia: Seljuk Turks, Mongols, and Ottoman Turks. From the fifteenth to eighteenth centuries Armenians were a subject people under Moslem domination,[45] excluded from mem-

43 See preceding section on culture.
44 Personal observations of M. Matossian.
45 See section on history earlier in this chapter.

bership in the ruling class, and hence from military and administrative activities. Although monks preserved manuscripts of culture, there was little creativity during these centuries. By necessity, Armenians learned to practice the defensive tactics of a subject people: outward humility and simplicity combined with shrewdness. They lost the assertive attitudes of conquerors and rulers.

Ever since the massacres by the Turks during World War I (see section on history), the Armenians have been a "captive ally" of the Russians—captive not only by the overwhelming fact of Soviet power, but by the presence of a third involved party, the Turks. There are Turks in Turkey at the border of the Soviet Union; there are Turks within the Soviet Union (79,000 in 1970); there is a Turkish and Azeri (a people close to the Turks) minority within Soviet Armenia itself.[46]

This is still the most decisive force in shaping national attitudes. In the summer of 1971 a taxi driver in Yerevan told an American visitor, "If the Red Army wanted men to fight the Turks, I would volunteer." This is a relatively mild statement of Armenian feeling.[47]

Another distinctive characteristic has been the prohibition against polygamy, and strict disapproval of sexual promiscuity in general. Of course Armenian girls, rather than boys, and Armenian women, rather than men, have been zealously guarded as a matter of family honor. Nor have husbands and wives had equal status in the family. The husband has had the strong position, by custom, as in Turkish families. Main difference between Armenians and Turks has been the interaction between husband and wife. In the Armenian family they have not lived in entirely separate spheres or dwelt in segregated apartments. The typical Armenian family has probably a more intense "emotional system," more supportive of its members, than the Turkish family. Perhaps for this reason Armenians have demonstrated a higher energy output, and achieved more successes, in occupations open to them.[48]

Whereas 2.2 million Armenians live in Armenia, some 3 million live outside its borders—1.35 million in the USSR and 1.7 million outside the USSR.[49] Contact with this diaspora, larger by one third than the population in Armenia itself, is a powerful factor influencing attitudes. Armenia is the only union republic with such a large proportion of its nationality in the diaspora. Education of youth outside the republic in the language and culture of their people is a natural concern of the national-minded intelligentsia.

BASIC VIEWS OF SCHOLARS ON NATIONAL ATTITUDES

Almost all Western scholarship has been concerned with ancient and medieval history and culture of Armenians. Authors analyzing the nationalist movement, massacres, and crisis of 1915–1920 have treated Armenians as victims of other people's national attitudes, not their own. No study of Armenian national attitudes by any Western scholar would meet contemporary tests of validity and reliability. In a book by M. Matossian, *The Impact of Soviet Policies in Armenia*, tenuous conclusions drawn aroused no great controversy. Politically active Armenians know each other's attitudes and see no particular reason to subject them to scientific analysis for the benefit of *odars* (non-Armenians).

Soviet scholars argue that Armenians are grateful to the Russians for "saving" them from the Terrible Turk, the Corrupt Persian, and Poverty and Backwardness. The amount of credit they give to the Armenians themselves for the progress made in Soviet Armenia depends on shifting political winds. In a recent authoritative work dealing with Armenian-Russian relations,[50] it has been asserted that tsarist Russia's chief contribution to Armenians was to put them in contact with creative Russian culture and those currents from advanced Western culture coming into Russia. It cites many eastern Armenian writers, scholars, scientists, artists, and military leaders who bene-

---

46 See earlier section on demography.
47 Personal observations by M. Matossian.
48 Cf. *Armeniya*, 1966: 86–108. This is a tentative hypothesis of M. Matossian.

49 See Table 7.1 and earlier sections on demography and on external relations.
50 *Armeniya za 50 let*, 1970: 21–31.

fited from these contacts. The book does not portray Russian rule before 1917 as generally liberating, but as better than that of Turks and Persians. This can be considered a plausible position.

John Armstrong's thesis on "mobilised diaspora" nationalities can be only applied partly to Armenians since, paradoxically, they have both a very homogeneous republic of their own and a large population outside their borders. The Armenian diaspora, however, displays some of the characteristics outlined by Armstrong, such as concentration in certain sections of the economy and high levels of education and skill.[51] Armenians have contributed a number of prominent Soviet political leaders (e.g., Anastas Mikoyan), as well as inventors and scientists (e.g., Artem Mikoyan, the brothers L. A. and I. A. Orbeli, N. M. Sisakyan, A. A. Arzumanyan, Yu. Arutyunyan).[52]

RECENT MANIFESTATIONS OF NATIONALISM

There are indications that nationalist feeling has grown stronger in recent years. A violent outbreak on April 24, 1965, in Yerevan marked the fiftieth anniversary of the Turkish massacres of 1915. Planned public memorials became the occasion for spontaneous demonstrations.[53] Part of the fallout from this was the replacement of the then secretary of the Communist party of Armenia, Y. N. Zarobian, by A. E. Kochinian. In 1966 a collection of documents dealing with the 1915 massacres was published in Yerevan[54] A monument to victims was also erected in the capital. In the summer of 1971 a major exhibit on Armenian-Turkish relations, including the massacres, was prominently displayed in the state historical museum.

Another manifestation of nationalism has been the interest shown in Yerevan in the Karabakh region, an autonomous region under Azerbaidzhan administration possess-

ing a concentration of Armenian population. In 1971 two scholarly articles, one on Karabakh folklore and another on "Soviet construction in Karabakh, 1920–1925" appeared in the Lraper [Vestnik], Social Sciences Division, Academy of Sciences, Armenian SSR.[55] Eventual incorporation of Karabakh into Soviet Armenia may be a goal of the Yerevan leadership.

Principal new development in nationalist expression is more active Soviet courtship of the diaspora. In 1970 a Soviet Armenian anniversary volume devoted a special chapter to the diaspora,[56] giving a detailed account of Armenian cultural organizations, the press, and creative individuals in the various diaspora communities. Most interesting was the conciliatory attitude toward various Armenian political parties abroad. The book criticized the Hunchak party for its "petty bourgeois and nationalist" character, but cited its services in rallying support in the diaspora for Soviet Armenia and fighting the Dashnak party. The Ramgavars,[57] characterized as "big merchants, millionaires" with "bourgeois-nationalist ideology," were congratulated for efforts to preserve Armenian culture abroad, support of repatriation of Armenians to Soviet Armenia, and their struggle against the Dashnaks. The Armenian compatriotic (fellow townsmen) societies, Armenian General Benevolent Union, and Gulbenkian Foundation were also cited for generous financial support of activities in Soviet Armenia. In return, it was noted that Soviet Armenia continues to accept repatriates from the diaspora as well as to grant scholarships to Armenians from the diaspora (360 in 1968–1969) to study in higher educational institutions in Yerevan.

This courtship of the diaspora was exemplified in publication, by a Soviet Armenian scholarly journal, of an article about Armenian studies in the United States, written by a respected Armenian-American scholar, Professor Nina Garsoyan of Columbia Uni-

51 Armstrong, 1968: 8–9, 12–14.
52 Armeniya, 1966: 102; J. Turkevich, Soviet Men of Science (Princeton, N.J.: Van Nostrand, 1963), passim.
53 Matossian, 1967: 65–69.
54 Nersisian, 1966.

55 Lraper (May), 1971: V: 20–25; (August), 1971: 8.
56 Armeniya za 50 let, 1970: 282–334.
57 The Ramgaver (democratic) party originated as a coalition of several revolutionary parties in Turkish Armenia. According to a personal communication, it conducts cultural, charitable, and informational activities among Armenians in the diaspora and "keeps an open mind" about Soviet Armenia.

versity, and translated into Russian.[58] A year later, 1972, an attack on Western studies of Soviet ethnic minorities appeared in the same journal.[59] Pipes, Kolarz, and others were taken to task, but the work on Soviet Armenia by M. Matossian was not mentioned.

Assertive nationalist attitudes have remained much the same throughout the twentieth century, but only in the last eight years have they been openly expressed in Soviet Armenia. The active campaign to develop ties between Soviet Armenia and diaspora amounts to a new level of nationalist activity. The "typical" patriotic Armenian, both inside and outside the Soviet Union, would probably prefer an independent state, but accepts Armenian membership in the Soviet Union as an unavoidable necessity at present.

According to Armenian émigrés and émigré organizations in the United States, there has recently been a heightened awareness of national problems among the intelligentsia in the republic. Special concern was aroused as the result of an incursion of Azeris into Armenian territory. The Azeris, a Turkic agricultural people, sustain a high fertility ratio, migrating into areas from which more ambitious Armenians are moving for better opportunities, usually in the cities. An Armenian planner related that special efforts were being undertaken by authorities to locate new sophisticated industries in such areas to reverse outflow of young Armenians and create an inflow.

In the first months of 1973, the central Soviet leadership manifested concern about nationalism and economic slackness by appointing Russians to two major positions and removing Armenians who had occupied them. In January Arkady R. Rakosin replaced General Kevork Badamiants as head of the state security agency; in March Pavel B. Anisimov was appointed second secretary of the Armenian CP, replacing A. Ter-Gazaryants. Mr. Anisimov, who had no previous connection with Armenia whatever, had been appointed by the Armenian Central Committee in the presence of a special emissary from Moscow.[60] In an analysis of speeches of party leaders during the December 1972 jubilee celebrations, a Western writer concluded that seven of the first secretaries of republican parties had "deviated" from the Brezhnev line on national policy. One was the Armenian first secretary.[61]

---

[58] *Lraper* (October), 1971: 10.
[59] M. M. Hakopian, "Against the Falsification of the National Politics of the Communist Party of Soviet Union," *Lraper* (July), 1972: 7.

[60] *Armenian Reporter* (Flushing, N.Y.) (April 12), 1973.
[61] Paul Whol, *Christian Science Monitor* (February 6), 1973.

REFERENCES

Armeniya, 1966
  Armeniya, series Sovietskii Soyuz: Geograficheskoy opisaniye v 22 tomakh (Moscow: Mysl', 1966).
Armeniya za 50 let, 1970
  Akademiya nauk Armianskoi SSR, *Sovetskaya Armeniya za 50 let* (Yerevan, 1970).
Armstrong, 1968
  J. Armstrong, "The Ethnic Scene in the Soviet Union: The View of the Dictatorship," in E. Goldhagen, ed., *Ethnic Minorities in the USSR* (New York: Praeger, 1968): 3–49.
Aslanyan, 1971
  A. A. Aslanyan et al., *Soviet Armenia* (Moscow, 1971).

BSE, 1947
  Bol'shaya Sovetskaya Entsiklopediya, 1st ed. (Moscow: Bol'shaya Sovetskaya Entsiklopediya, 1947).
BSE, 1970
  Bol'shaya Sovetskaya Entsiklopediya, 34th ed. (Moscow: Bol'shaya Sovetskaya Entsiklopediya, 1970).
Charanis, n.d.
  P. Charanis, *The Armenians in the Byzantine Empire* (Lisbon: Gulbenkian Foundation, n.d.).
Der Nersessian, 1970
  Sirarpie Der Nersessian, *The Armenians* (New York: Praeger, 1970).
Ekonomika, 1967
  Armenian SSR, Central Statistics Ad-

ministration, *Ekonomika i kul'tura Armenii* (Yerevan, 1967).

Ekonomika Litvy 1970
Ekonomika i kul'tura Litovskoi SSR v 1970 godu. Statisticheskii yezhegodnik (Vilnius: Statistika, 1971).

Europa Yearbook, 1972
Europa Yearbook (London: Europa, 1972).

Gidney, 1967
James B. Gidney, *A Mandate for Armenia* (Kent, Ohio: Kent University Press, 1967).

Goldberg, 1961
B. Z. Goldberg, *The Jewish Problem in the Soviet Union: Analysis and Solution* (New York: Crown, 1961).

Grabill, 1971
Joseph L. Grabill, *Protestant Diplomacy and the Near East: Missionary Influence on American Policy, 1810–1927* (Minneapolis: University of Minnesota Press, 1971).

Hakopian, 1972
M. M. Hakopian, "Against the Falsification of the National Politics of the Communist Party of the Soviet Union," *Lraper* (July 1972): 7.

Hovhannisian, 1967
Richard Hovhannisian, *Armenia on the Road to Independence* (Berkeley–Los Angeles: University of California Press, 1967).

Hovannisian, 1971
Richard Hovannisian, *The Republic of Armenia*, vol I (Berkeley–Los Angeles: University of California Press, 1971).

Itogi 1959
Itogi vsesoyuznoi perepisi naseleniya 1959 goda SSSR (Moscow: Gosstatizdat, 1962).

Itogi 1970
Itogi vsesoyuznoi perepisi naseleniya 1970 goda, vol. IV (Moscow: Statistika, 1973).

Itogi Armyanskoi SSR, 1959
Itogi Armyanskoi SSR, 1959 (Moscow: Statistika, 1960).

Katz, 1973
Zev Katz "The New Nationalism in the USSR," *Midstream* (February 1973): 3–13.

Kazemzadeh, 1951
Firuz Kazemzadeh, *The Struggle for Transcaucasia* (New York, 1951).

Lang, 1970
David M. Lang, *Armenia, Cradle of Civilization* (London: George Allen & Unwin, 1970).

Matossian, 1962
Mary Matossian, *The Impact of Soviet Policies in Armenia* (Leiden: Brill, 1962).

Matossian, 1967
Mary Matossian, "The Armenians," *Problems of Communism* (September-October 1967): XVI: 5: 65–69.

Matossian, 1968
Mary Matossian, "Communist Rule and the Changing Armenian Cultural Pattern, in Erich Goldhagen, ed., *Ethnic Minorities in the Soviet Union* (New York: Praeger, 1968): 185–197.

Nar. khoz. 1970
Narodnoye khozyaistvo SSSR v 1970 godu (Moscow: Statistika, 1971).

Nar. khoz. 1972
Narodnoye khozyaistvo SSSR 1922–1972, Yubileinyi statisticheskii yezhegodnik (Moscow: Statistika, 1972).

Nar. obraz., 1971
Narodnoye obrazovaniye, nauka i kul'tura v SSSR: statisticheskii sbornik (Moscow: Statistika, 1971).

Nersisian, 1966
M. G. Nersisian, ed., *Genotsid armyan v Osmanskoi imperii: Sbornik dokumentov i materialov* (Yerevan, 1966).

Pechat' 1959
Pechat' SSSR v 1959 godu (Moscow: Kniga, 1960).

Pechat' 1971
Pechat' SSSR v 1971 godu (Moscow: Kniga, 1972).

Sovetskaya Armeniya, 1970
Sovetskaya Armeniya za 50 let. Sbornik statisticheskikh materialov (Yerevan, 1970).

Ter-Sarkisiants, 1972
A. E. Ter-Sarkisiants, *Sovremennaya sem'ya u Armyan* (Moscow: Nauka, 1972).

8 | GEORGIA and THE GEORGIANS

Richard B. Dobson

General Information

TERRITORY[1]

The Georgian Soviet Socialist Republic occupies an area of 26,757 square miles in Transcaucasia, bordering on the Russian SFSR to the north, the Azerbaidzhan SSR to the east, the Armenian SSR and Turkey to the south, and the Black Sea to the west. Within its borders are Abkhazian Autonomous Republic (capital: Sukhumi), Adzhar Autonomous Republic (capital: Batumi), and South Ossetian Autonomous District (capital: Tskhinvali).

Georgia is divided into three principal geographic regions: Greater Caucasus Mountains, stretching from Black Sea to the Caspian and forming remarkable ridges of longitudinal and transverse ranges; South Georgian Highlands, a high plateau extending into Turkey and Armenia; and the central region of intermountain basins, extending latitudinally, distinguished by a gentle relief. Several peaks of the central part of the Greater Caucasus range are taller than Mont Blanc, highest peak of the Alps.

This diversity is reflected in the climate, warm and humid in the western region, where annual rainfall is heaviest in the USSR (40–98 inches), and warm but drier in the inland regions. In the Caucasian uplands cool subalpine conditions prevail, while above the timberline climate is cold and alpine. Georgia has some rich mineral reserves, including coal at Tkibuli and Tkvarchili and manganese at Chiatura, as well as much water power from its mountain rivers.

ECONOMY

Abolition of serfdom in Georgia (1864–1871) and completion of railway lines linking Baku, Tbilisi, and the Black Sea ports of Batumi and Poti in the 1870s and 1880s spurred development of industry and trade. Baku oil began to pass through Batumi to the world market, and exploitation of the

---

[1] *Narody Kavkaza*, 1962: II: 207–211; Javakhishvili and Gvelesiani, 1964; Davitaya, 1972.

Tkvibul coal deposits was under way. Manganese mining, initiated in Chiatura in 1879, provided one third to one half of world export of the mineral early in this century; Georgia remains a major source today. But, despite this economic development, Georgia remained mainly an agrarian region. Whereas before World War I industry accounted for 41% of the value of total production in the Russian Empire, its share in Georgia amounted to only 13%.[2]

The present structure of the Georgian economy is shown in the following data (based on actual prices, 1970):[3]

Branch of Economy	"Total Social Product" (%)[4]	National Income (%)
Industry	59.4	39.0
Construction	10.6	10.9
Agriculture	20.6	34.7
Transportation and communications	2.6	3.1
Commerce, material-technical supplying	6.8	12.3
Total economy	100.0	100.0

Industrial production accounts for nearly three fifths of the "total social product" and two fifths of the national income. In 1970, 34% of the workforce were employed in industry, construction, transportation, and communications, while 38% were employed in agriculture and lumbering. An additional 24% were engaged in nonmaterial production.[5]

Notwithstanding a dearth of tillable land, the economy continues strongly dependent on agricultural production and the industrial processing of produce. Subtropical crops requiring a good deal of heat and moisture, notably tea and citrus, are grown on large plantations in the western region near the Black Sea. Grapes and a wide

variety of fruits are for the most part produced in the eastern regions: Kakheti, Kartli, and upper Imereti. Tea is Georgia's most important crop, accounting for 94–95% of all high-quality tea grown in the USSR. Almost 45% of the value of total industrial production is produced by the food-processing branch. Aromatic tea, high-grade tobacco, citrus and canned fruit, wines and brandies, tung and other vegetable oils, cheeses, and mineral waters are among the many products of Georgia's food industry.[6]

Georgia also has major heavy industrial facilities. Indeed, it ranks third in metallurgical production among the union republics. It produced 783,000 tons of pig iron, 1,411,000 tons of steel, and 1,205,000 tons of rolled metal in 1970. The center of this production is the gigantic Rustavi steel mill complex, not far from Tbilisi, built following World War II. Dashkesan iron ore is the main raw material for these mills, while coal from the greatly expanded mining complex in Tkibuli and Tkvarchili serves as principal source of fuel. Along with the metallurgical industry, the chemical and machine-tool industries have also been developing. The latter, centered in Tbilisi, produces metal-cutting lathes, motor vehicles, tractors, electric locomotives, agricultural machinery, and many other products.[7]

Georgia has a well-developed, unified power system whose many hydroelectric plants produce more than 8,000 million kilowatt hours of power annually. Its light industry, specializing in production of fabrics, clothes, and leather footwear, and its mountain and coastal health resorts, attracting people from all over the Soviet Union, are also economically significant.

There is a sizeable private sector in agriculture and, judging by press reports, party decisions, and eyewitness reports, illegal or semilegal dealings have been prevalent too. Small garden plots, though only a small fraction of farm acreage, produce about 40% of Georgia's $1.2 billion agricultural

2 Javakhishvili and Gvelesiani, 1964: 52–53; Davitaya, 1972: 48–50.

3 "Gruzinskaya," BSE, 1972: VII: 372.

4 This is a Soviet unit for measuring the performance of the Soviet economy, not identical to any Western measure. For further information on this subject, see R. W. Campbell, M. M. Earle, Jr., H. S. Levine, and F. W. Dresch, "Methodological Problems Comparing the U.S. and USSR Economies," Soviet Economic Prospects for the Seventies (Washington, D.C.: Government Printing Office, 1973): 122–146.

5 "Gruzinskaya," BSE, 1972: VII: 372.

6 Davitaya, 1972: 81, 86–87; Gugushvili, Gruzinskaya SSR: kratkii istoriko-ekonomicheskii ocherk, 1971: 143–158. See also Gugushvili, Gruzinskaya SSR: Sel'skoye khozyaistvo, 1971. Almost all citrus fruit produced in the USSR is grown in Georgia.

7 Davitaya, 1972: 79–81; Gugushvili, Gruzinskaya SSR: industriya, 1971.

output, according to Western estimates.[8] A recent Soviet press account reveals that only 68% of grapes produced in Georgia are sold to state procurement agencies, as compared with 88% in Azerbaidzhan and 97% in Armenia.[9] Widespread speculation and illegal trade, subjects of much public discussion, have been the object of First Secretary E. Shevardnadze's extensive cleanup campaign, but it is impossible to ascertain the value of commerce involved in illegal operations.

Indices of standard of living for 1970 give an impression of highly uneven development. The republic ranks exceptionally high in ratio of doctors to population, 36.8 for every 10,000 inhabitants.[10] The supply of useful living space per urban resident places Georgia third among the USSR republics. Per capita trade turnover, however, is relatively low, exceeding only the figures for Moldavia, Azerbaidzhan, and four of the five Central Asian republics. The republic's produced national income has grown by only 102% between 1960 and 1971, third lowest rate in the USSR.[11]

Soviet 1970 data on savings accounts paint a very interesting picture. Every fourth inhabitant of Georgia has such an account, whereas the USSR average is every third. Average size of an account, at 1,016

rubles, is largest in the Union, far outstripping the average (581 rubles). As a result, Georgia trails only Estonia and Armenia in savings per capita, although these are considerably less evenly distributed among the population than in Estonia and somewhat less so than in Armenia.[12]

HISTORY

The national identity and culture of Georgians, one of the oldest national groups in the Soviet Union, has been shaped by a long turbulent history. Between the twelfth and seventh centuries B.C., the various Georgian tribes settled in the Caucasus began to unite.[13] First state to come into being in western Georgia was the kingdom of Colchis (6th century B.C.) on the Black Sea coast, whose rise coincided approximately with that of the Achaemenid Persian Empire and establishment of Greek colonies on the east coast of the Black Sea. In the third century B.C. the kingdom of Kartli (or Iberia), founded in eastern Georgia with its capital in Mtskheta, succeeded in uniting the main provinces of eastern, western, and southern Georgia into a single state.[14]

In the second half of the first century A.D. the kingdoms of Colchis and Kartli were conquered by the Romans, who dominated the coastal area for some time. Not long after Emperor Constantine proclaimed Christianity official religion of the Roman Empire (then centered in Constantinople), Christianity was established as official religion in eastern Georgia (ca. 330) and later (ca. 520) in western Georgia.[15] Henceforth, like the Armenians, the Georgians became an outpost of Christianity in the East, affiliated with the great centers of orthodox Christianity, distinguished from the cultures of Zoroastrian Persia and the later Islamic world.

In the early sixth century (523), Persian

8 Hedrick Smith, "Soviet Georgia Goes Own Way, Does Well," *New York Times* (December 16), 1971: 10. "Western economists estimate," Smith observes, "that from such lucrative crops as grapes for Georgian wines and cognacs and citrus and other fruits, or flowers that can fetch a ruble apiece . . . when flown to Moscow in winter, Georgian farmers earn more than $400 million a year on their private plots alone."
9 S. Davitaya, "Reflections Engendered by Meetings in the Mountains: Paradoxes of Orchards and Vegetable Gardens," *Izvestia* (March 23), 1973, in *CDSP* (April 18), 1973: XXV: 12: 9–10. It is reported that in recent years privately grown and marketed produce comprises more than 99% of total volume of trade in collective farm markets in major cities. G. Davarashvili, "From the Collegium of the Georgian Republic Ministry of Trade: Are the Municipal Markets Collective Farm Markets or Not?" *Zarya vostoka* (October 14), 1973, abstracted in *CDSP* (November 28), 1973: XXV: 44: 20.
10 *Nar. khoz.* 1922–1972: 515ff; *Statistical Abstract of the United States*, 1971: 799–800.
11 *Nar. khoz.* 1970: 579, 546; *Nar khoz.* 1922–1972: 360. The seemingly low rate of trade turnover may be a result of extensive private dealings, not reflected in the official statistics.

12 *Nar. khoz.* 1970: 563–564.
13 Georgians call themselves *Kartveli* and their homeland *Sakartvelo*, land of the Georgians. Both of these names are derived from *Karti*, as the kindred Georgian tribes were called.
14 On these early kingdoms and their culture, see Lang, 1966.
15 On the adoption of Christianity, see *ibid.*: 91–95.

Sassanids extended their domination into the Kartlian kingdom. Though regaining independence toward the end of the century, first eastern and then western Georgia were soon overrun by the Arabs. By the end of the ninth century, with termination of Arab domination, Georgians entered a period of economic, cultural, and political progress. King Bagrat, adoptive son of David III, managed to break the resistance of feudal lords and independent princes, bringing nearly all Georgian lands under his control. In 1080 the kingdom fell to the Seljuk Turks. King David IV (1089–1125), who bears the epithet "the Restorer," carried out a successful campaign against the Turks between 1120 and 1122 to reunite the lands.

Georgia attained its greatest heights during the reign of Queen Tamara (1184–1213), great granddaughter of David the Restorer. By the end of her reign it had become the strongest state in the Transcaucasus, including all of Armenia in addition to Georgia proper. This was a period of economic advance and cultural flowering. Towns were thriving centers of handicraft manufacture and trade, and the population of Tbilisi, including suburbs, exceeded 100,000. A caravan route linking Europe with India passed through the country. Science and philosophy flourished and high standards were achieved in Georgian art, jewelry, church architecture, and literature. Exemplifying the latter is Shota Rustaveli's classic poem, *The Knight in the Tiger's Skin*, dedicated to Queen Tamara.[16]

Soon thereafter the main force of Genghis Khan's army invaded the country (1235). Mongol hegemony over most of the country lasted until the fourteenth century. For a short time thereafter, liberated and reunified, Georgia recovered its international standing and began a brisk trade with the city-states of northern Italy. But between 1386 and 1403 eight invasions of Tamerlane's hordes reduced the country to ruins. In 1453 the capture of Constantinople by the Ottoman Turks prevented Georgia from maintaining direct relations with Western Europe, and feuding between the king and his powerful vassals led to disintegration of the unified Georgian state by the end of the fifteenth century.

Early in the sixteenth century Georgia found itself a battlefield between two neighboring powers, Turkey and Safavi Iran. After a long struggle, the Georgians, led by Irakli II and Solomon I, managed to reestablish independent states in the middle of the eighteenth century. Seeking allies to bolster Georgia's position vis-à-vis Turkey and Iran, Iraki II at the end of 1782 asked Catherine II of Russia, whose borders extended almost as far south as the Great Caucasian Range, to place the kingdom of Kartli-Kakhetia under Russian protection. The following year a treaty of friendship was signed between the two states. In 1795 Georgia sustained yet another disastrous invasion by Iranian troops, when Shah Agha Mohammed attacked the kingdom of Kartli-Kakhetia and burned Tbilisi. Then, for a variety of reasons, Emperor Paul I decided to annex the kingdom. Under a decree issued by his successor, Alexander I, on September 12, 1801, the kingdom of Kartli-Kakhetia was joined to the Russian Empire. The other Georgian lands were incorporated as a result of the Russo-Turkish wars later in the century.[17]

With incorporation of Georgian lands within the Russian Empire, internal and external commerce increased, and Russian and European intellectual currents began to penetrate the intelligentsia which was taking shape. The first Georgian newspaper, *Sakartvelos gazeti* [*Georgian Gazette*], was published between 1819 and 1822, and a Russian paper, *Tiflisskiye vedomosti* [*Tiflis News*], appeared in 1828, with a supplement in Georgian.[18] In the 1860s the *Tergdaleuli* socioliterary movement manifested itself.[19] Ilya Chavchavadze (1837–1907), Georgian poet and essayist, was in the forefront of this movement, which united many

16 Javakhishvili and Gvelesiani, 1964: 40–41. See also Lang, 1966.

17 Almost the whole of western Georgia was gained by Russia by 1811; Poti, Akhaltsikhe, Akhalkalaki, and ten districts of Samtskhe-Saatabago were incorporated in 1828–1829; and Adzharia, including Batumi and the Artvini district, was joined to Russia in 1878. On the initial treaty and the tsars' decisions to annex Georgia, see Lang, 1962: 37–41, and his more ample account in *The Last Years of the Georgian Monarchy, 1658–1832* (New York: Columbia University Press, 1957). See also the major study by Allen, 1932.

18 Lang, 1962: 63.

19 *Tergdaleuli* means, literally, "one who has drunk from the Terek water," referring to those who passed through the gorge of the Terek River on the way to and from Russian universities.

young intellectuals influenced by critical thought of the Russian intelligentsia (in particular, Belinsky, Herzen, Chernyshevsky, and Dobrolyubov).

Mesame Dasi (so-called "Third Group"), organized by young radicals in 1892, became the first Marxist political group in Georgia.[20] Among its leaders were Nikolai Chkheidze, who was to become Menshevik president of the Petrograd Soviet in 1917, and Noe Zhordaniya, future president of independent Georgia. In 1898 the militant wing of *Mesame Dasi* gained the adherence of a former student of the Tbilisi Theological Seminary—Josef Dzhughashvili, the future Stalin.[21]

Unlike many other national movements, as Pipes observes, "The Georgian movement became from its very inception closely identified if not completely fused with Marxian socialism." [22] In the First Duma six of seven Georgian deputies were Social Democrats, and in the more conservative Second Duma, two of three. Social Democrats, overwhelmingly Menshevik in affiliation, played an active role. Following the abdication of Nicholas II, they emerged as the leading political force, predominating in the newly established local soviets. After the Bolshevik coup in October 1917, Georgian Menshevik leaders still avowed allegiance to the Russian Provisional Government. Only after the Bolsheviks signed the Treaty of Brest-Litovsk, in which Transcaucasian territories were ceded to the Axis powers, did leaders declare Georgia's independence, enter into a short-lived Transcaucasian Federation, and then establish a sovereign republic in May 1918. Leaders entered into alliances with European powers (in turn, Germany and Great Britain) and attempted to carry out a socialistic reform program. Independent Georgia was recognized by 22 countries.

In May 1920 Soviet Russia signed a treaty with Georgia recognizing her independence and renouncing all interference in her affairs.[23] On February 16, 1921, however, the 11th Red Army, headed by Sergo Ordzhonikidze, invaded Georgia from Azerbaidzhan (ostensibly to aid the Bolsheviks who were leading a popular revolt) and placed the country under Communist rule. A Soviet-Turkish treaty was signed in March 1921, establishing the present borders between the two countries. The policy favored by Stalin—merging of Georgia into a Transcaucasian Socialist Federated Soviet Republic—provoked strong opposition among Georgian Communist leaders, who feared excessive centralization and Great Russian domination. Stalin emerged triumphant.[24] The Transcaucasian SFSR (which included Armenia, Azerbaidzhan, and Georgia) was formed in 1922 and entered into the USSR. It lasted until December 5, 1936, when the Georgian SSR was formally established as a constituent unit of the USSR.

During the years of Stalin's rule and Beria's administration of the secret police, both men had close ties with compatriots in key positions of the Georgian Communist party (GCP). Following Stalin's death, the Georgian apparatus appeared to be an important source of support for Beria. For that reason, an extensive purge of the apparatus was carried out by rivals (with execution of Georgian officials, including Beria himself). Vasily Mzhavanadze was then appointed first secretary of the GCP and remained in power for 19 years.

In 1972 Eduard Shevardnadze, who had served as minister of internal security in GSSR for seven years, was appointed first secretary of the party organization in Tbilisi and, two months later (September 30), of the GCP as a whole. The deposed Mzhavanadze was also removed from his position as candidate member of the Politburo. The 44-year-old Shevardnadze began a wide-

---

20 Later, Chavchavadze and his confreres became known as *Pirveli Dasi* [*First Group*] to distinguish them from the more radical *Meore Dasi* [*Second Group*] founded in 1869 by Giorgi Tsereteli (1840–1915), prolific and versatile poet and publicist, and Niko Nikoladze. Both of these circles were more moderate than *Mesame Dasi*. Lang, 1962: 109–111, 122–129.

21 On Stalin's childhood and youth, see Bertram Wolfe, *Three Who Made a Revolution* (New York: Dial Press, 1961), and Adam Ulam, *Stalin* (New York: Viking Press, 1973). A valuable source on *Mesame Dasi* and politics of young radicals of this period is Noe Zhordaniya, *Moya zhizn'* (Stanford, Calif.: Hoover Institute, 1968).

22 Pipes, 1964: 17.

23 For background and constitution of Georgia, see Kandelaki, 1953: 191–209, and the account by Avalishvili, 1940.

24 Before his final stroke, Lenin was giving much attention to the "Georgian question," reconsidering national policy in view of the highhanded methods used by Stalin and Ordzhonikidze. See Pipes, 1964: 266–293.

ranging purge of his predecessor's adminis-
·tration, accused of a tolerant disposition
toward corruption, private trade, and speculation, as well as bureaucratic inefficiency.
Prominent private dealers were arrested,
and the easy-going atmosphere appeared to
have changed.[25]

DEMOGRAPHY

The population of the republic was
4,686,000 in 1970, as compared with
4,044,000 in 1959, 3,540,000 in 1939, and
2,601,000 in 1913.[26] The percentage increase between 1959 and 1970 (15.9%)
was almost identical to the rate for the
USSR as a whole during this period.[27] In
1940 the birth rate exceeded the death rate
by slightly more than 18 per 1,000. Although the birth rate declined sharply during the war, by 1945 it began to rise again.
Between 1950 and 1963 the rate of natural
increase averaged about 16 per 1,000, approximately the same as the all-Union
mean.[28] As of 1969 the birth rate in
Georgia was 18.7 per 1,000, while the rate
of mortality was a low 7.5. The resultant
rate of increase (11.2 per 1,000) was only
slightly higher than the USSR average (8.9
per 1,000).[29]

Georgia is among the most densely populated regions of the USSR. In 1926, on the
average, there were 98 persons per square
mile in the republic, whereas by 1969 the
number had increased to 176. The great
majority of the population is concentrated
in low-lying regions where good agricultural
lands and industrial centers are located;
about nine tenths lives at less than 3,280
feet above sea level in an area with less
than half of the republic's territory. In 1959

mean population density of this area was
290 persons per square mile.[30]

During the Soviet period, the urban population of Georgia increased more than
threefold (from 666,000 in 1913 to
2,241,000 in 1970) while the rural population grew by only 27% (from 1,935,000 to
2,447,000). At present, slightly more than
half of the population is living on the land
or residing in small settlements.[31]

Simultaneously, great changes in occupational structure have occurred. As a result
of planned industrialization, the number of
people working in industry increased about
twentyfold between 1926 and 1959, and the
proportion of industrial and state farm
workers (including members of their families) rose from 6.9% to 46.7% of the
population during the same period. Meanwhile, the share of office workers (including
members of their families) grew apprecia-
bly, rising from 7.6% to almost a quarter
of the population. Collective farmers (along
with family members) comprise 28% of the
population in 1970.[32] The fact that more
than a third of the workforce is employed in
agriculture reflects the economic importance of labor-intensive crops (especially
tea, viticulture, and citrus fruits).[33]

Along with expansion of educational
facilities, number of specialists employed in
the economy has risen sharply (from 67.100
in 1941 to 324,900 by 1970). Those with
higher education numbered 185,400 in
1970, compared to 33,900 in 1941.[34] On a
number of indices—including number of
individuals with complete or incomplete
secondary education per 1,000 (over age
10) or with higher education—Georgia

25 *Pravda* (September 30), 1972; *New York Times*
(December 9), 1972: 9; *Soviet Analyst*, I: 17: 2–3,
II: 2: 2.
26 Davitaya, 1972: 58; Dzhaoshvili, 1968: 8.
27 Bruk, 1972: 334, table 1.
28 Davitaya, 1972: 58; Dzhaoshvili, 1968: 19.
29 In recent years, the rate of natural increase in
Georgia has been higher than that of the European
republics (except Moldavia), but lower than that
of the Central Asian republics, Kazakhstan, and
neighboring Azerbaidzhan, where the rate of increase was 22.3 per 1,000 in 1969. Bruk, 1972:
345–346.

30 Davitaya, 1972: 65.
31 *Ibid.*: 58; Dzhaoshvili, 1968.
32 Close to 65% of all of Georgia's industrial
workers and office employees are concentrated in
three major industrial centers: Tbilisi-Rustavi industrial complex (specializing in ferrous metallurgy, chemicals, engineering, building materials,
food processing, and light industries); Zestafoni-
Chiatura complex (center of electro-metallurgical
and mining industries); and Kutaisi-Tkibuli complex (important for coal mining, engineering, and
light industries). Davitaya, 1972: 64, 82. Figures
for 1970 from *Itogi 1970*: V: 10.
33 *Ibid.*: 236.
34 *Sovet. Gruziya po leninskomu puti*, 1970: 123;
Nar. obraz., 1971: 234. More than half (52%) of
the total number of specialists were women in
1970. In 1968, 78% were of Georgian nationality.

ranks first among the constituent republics of the USSR.[35]

Georgians have continued to maintain numerical predominance in the population (see Table 8.1). Between 1926 and 1939 their share declined from 66.8% to 61.4%, mainly as a consequence of a massive influx of Russians, whose share increased correspondingly from 3.6% to 8.7%. Subsequently, the Georgians have increased in relative as well as absolute numbers. In 1959 they made up 64.3% of the population, whereas at the time of the latest census they numbered 3,131,000, constituting 66.8%. In 1970, 9.7% were Armenian and 8.5% Russian (for other nationalities, see Table 8.1). Although Armenians and Russians have decreased in relative terms, Azerbaidzhani increased from 3.8% in 1959 to 4.6% in 1970.

Many minorities are associated with specific regions. The Abkhazians and Ossets are concentrated principally in administrative units bearing their names. The Abkhazians, related to the ancient Heniochi, belong to the northwestern or Adyghe-Circassian group of Caucasian peoples, while the Ossets are descendants of the medieval Alans, an Indo-Iranian people connected with the Samatians.[36] Armenians reside principally in the southeast areas of the republic, while Azerbaidzhanis tend to live in plateau regions of eastern Georgia.[37] Another minority group, the Adzhars, a people of Georgian stock who adopted Islam during centuries of Ottoman rule and differ in some aspects of culture from the Georgians proper, are found mainly in the Adzar Autonomous Republic.[38]

As of January 1, 1971, the Communist party of Georgia had 286,084 members and 10,291 candidate members.[39] It is worthwhile to examine members' social charac-

teristics to draw inferences about which groups are most involved in the political system and to see what types of people leaders have considered most desirable for inclusion in the party. With respect to age, it is striking that, whereas in 1940 more than four fifths of the membership was under 40 years of age (and slightly more than 40% were 30 or under), in 1970 membership was composed predominantly of older persons—60% were 41 years of age or older.[40] The leadership, in particular, has aged: whereas in 1958 more than 78% of the secretaries of province, city, and district party committees were under 40 years of age, by 1973 this index had dropped to 24%.[41]

Statistics on educational attainment of members reveal that the party has had much success in recruiting highly trained personnel, whose share of the membership far exceeds representation in the population as a whole. In 1940 nearly 12% of the membership had complete or incomplete higher education; in 1970 this group accounted for slightly more than 30% of the membership.[42] Strength of the party among highly trained academic and research personnel is reflected in the fact that in 1970 of 942 doctors of science 406 were party members.[43] In 1973 almost all (99%) party officials are reported to have obtained a higher education.[44] A large yet gradually declining proportion of members (47.6% in 1970) are employed in nonmanual occupations.[45] At present, about three fourths of the membership is composed of Georgians,

---

35 The number of people in Georgia possessing a complete or incomplete secondary education per 1,000 (over age 10) rose sharply from 165 to 554 between 1939 and 1970. The latter figure puts Georgia in first place on this index, well ahead of the all-Union average (483). (In last place, according to the latest census, was Lithuania, with 382.) As of 1970, 58 per 1,000 in the Georgian republic have a higher education. Bruk, 1972: 353; Davitaya, 1972: 68.
36 Lang, 1966: 20.
37 *Narody Kavkaza*, 1962: II: 213.
38 Lang, 1966: 20.
39 "Gruzinskaya," *Yezhegodnik*, 1971: 128.

40 *Komm. partiya Gruzii v tsifrakh*, 1971: 96, 267. In 1970 only 14% of the membership was 30 or under.
41 Report, Plenary Session, GCP CC, "Party Leadership Should Measure Up to Today's Tasks," *Zarya vostoka* (February 28), 1973, translated in *CDSP* (April 25), 1973: XXV: 13: 6.
42 *Komm. partiya Gruzii v tsifrakh*, 1971: 96, 267.
43 *Ibid.*: 267; *Komsomol Gruzii v tsifrakh i faktakh*, 1971: 77.
44 Report, Plenary Session, GCP CC, "Party Leadership Should Measure Up to Today's Tasks," *CDSP* (April 25), 1973: XXV: 13: 6.
45 *Komm. partiya Gruzii v tsifrakh*, 1971: 93, 221, 242, 264. Fifty-two percent of party members were employees in 1940, whereas only 17.2% of the population as a whole were so classified in 1939. In 1960, 48.1% of members were employees, whereas at the time of the census in 1959, 24% of the population was placed in this category. Dzhaoshvili, 1968: 44.

Table 8.1

Population of Georgian Republic by Nationality

NATIONALITY	1897 Absolute No.	%	1926 Absolute No.	%	1939 Absolute No.	%	1959 Absolute No.	%	1970 Absolute No.	%
Georgians	1,310,307	68.3	1,788,186	66.8	2,173,574	61.4	2,600,588	64.3	3,130,741	66.8
Armenians	177,012	9.2	307,018	11.5	414,182	11.7	442,916	11.0	452,309	9.7
Russians	—	—	96,085	3.6	307,988	8.7	407,886	10.1	396,694	8.5
Azerbaidzhanis	109,529	5.7	143,951	5.4	187,621	5.3	153,600	3.8	217,758	4.6
Ossets	71,501	3.7	113,298	4.2	148,680	4.2	141,178	3.5	150,185	3.2
Greeks	38,540	2.0	54,054	2.0	84,960	2.4	72,938	1.8	89,246	1.9
Abkhazians	59,481	3.1	56,847	2.1	56,640	1.6	62,878	1.5	79,449	1.7
Jews	12,182	0.6	30,159	1.1	42,480	1.2	51,582	1.3	55,382	1.2
Ukrainians	101,044	5.3	14,356	0.5	46,020	1.3	52,236	1.3	49,622	1.1
Others	39,827	2.1	72,739	2.8	77,878	2.2	53,091	1.3	64,972	1.3
Belorussians	—	—	540	—	N.A.	—	5,152	0.1	N.A.	N.A.
Total	1,919,423	100.0	2,677,233	100.0	3,540,023	100.0	4,044,045	100.0	4,686,358	100.0

Source: Dzhaoshvili, 1968: 48. Itogi 1970: IV: 13.

Table 8.2

Membership of Communist Party of GSSR by Nationality

(as of January 1)

| NATIONALITY | ABSOLUTE NOS. | | | | % | | | | % OF POPULATION |
	1940	1960	1965	1970	1940	1960	1965	1970	1970
Georgians	62,842	153,391	184,725	220,868	70.7	73.5	74.5	76.1	66.8
Abkhazians	1,042	2,778	3,500	4,230	1.2	1.3	1.4	1.4	1.7
Ossets	4,080	7,214	8,340	9,606	4.6	3.5	3.4	3.3	3.2
Armenians	11,256	20,070	22,448	23,352	12.6	9.6	9.0	8.0	9.7
Azerbaidzhani	1,973	3,689	4,981	6,268	2.2	1.8	2.0	2.2	4.6
Russians	4,789	13,715	15,371	16,044	5.4	6.6	6.2	5.5	8.5
Ukrainians	579	2,412	2,565	2,787	.6	1.1	1.0	1.0	1.1
Others	2,390[a]	5,315[b]	6,445[c]	7,036[d]	2.7	2.6	2.5	2.5	4.4
Total	88,951	208,584	248,375	290,191	100.0	100.0	100.0	100.0	100.0

Sources: Party membership figures are derived from *Kom. partiya Gruzii v tsifrakh*, 1971: 94, 221, 243, 265.

[a] Including 877 Greeks, 644 Jews, and 869 others.
[b] Including 2,126 Greeks, 1,830 Jews, and 1,359 others.
[c] Including 2,814 Greeks, 2,076 Jews, and 1,555 others.
[d] Including 3,234 Greeks, 2,128 Jews, and 1,674 others.

who have increased their share over the years (see Table 8.2). Armenian representation has been decreasing relative to other nationalities, while Azerbaidzhanis have been consistently underrepresented.

CULTURE

Although no institution through the ages has been more central to cultural life than the Georgian Orthodox Church, it is difficult to determine from published sources the place of the Church and Orthodox creed in Georgian culture today. Incorporated into the Russian Holy Synod in 1811, the Georgian Church declared its renewed independent status in 1917 following abdication of the Russian emperor.[46] It was not recognized by the Russian Orthodox Church until 1943. Incorporation of Georgia within the Soviet Union resulted in confiscation of church property, closing of churches, and a strident atheistic campaign. Georgia's Communist-supported "Militant Godless" organization reported 101,586 members, forming 1,478 cells, in 1931; by 1938 membership had increased to 145,413, representing 4% of the population, an all-Union record.[47] How many Georgians remain devoted to the Church is not known. In the early 1960s it was reported that the Church had 7 bishops, 105 priests, 80 parishes, 3 monasteries, and 1 convent, as well as a publishing house whose only regular publication is an annual liturgical calendar.[48]

Georgian literature is known to date back many centuries, although no examples of writings from the pre-Christian period exist

46 Lang, 1962: 177–179, 195.

47 Kolarz, 1961: 100–104.
48 Elie Melia, "The Georgian Orthodox Church," in Marshall *et al.*, 1971: 235–236.

today.[49] A renowned example from the twelfth- and thirteenth-century classical period is Shota Rustaveli's epic *The Knight in the Tiger's Skin*.[50] The thirteenth-century writer Sulkhan Saba Orbeliani is known for his collection of parables and fables, *The Wisdom of Fiction*, as well as his book *Travel in Europe*, the first important example of Georgian documentary prose. Outstanding among the more recent nineteenth-century writers are Ilia Chavchavadze (1837–1907), Akaky Tsereteli (1840–1915), Alexander Kazbeghi (1848–1893), and Vazha Pshavela (1861–1915). Major contributions to literature in this century were made by Niko Lordkipanidze and Leo Kiacheli, prominent pre-revolutionary writers. Well-known poets include Galaktion Tabidze, a "People's Poet of Georgia," Georgi Leonidze, Irakly Abashidze, Alexander Gomiashvili, Grigol Abashidze, Alexander Abasheli, Sandro Shanshiashvili, and Simon Chikovani. Konstantin Gamsakhurdia, author of historical novels, has won acclaim, as have writers Mikhail Javakhishvili and Shalva Dadiani. Not a few writers—including the highly talented poets Paolo Yashvili and Titsian Tabidze—perished in the purges of 1937–1938.[51] In the estimation of some scholars, the quality of literary work has suffered from imposition of political controls.[52] Though socialist realism continues to be the ideologically prescribed style, Georgian literature at its best continues to display much creativity and verve, as well as stylistic features of the national literary tradition.

The dramatic heritage also stretches back through the ages. A revival of the theater, in which Georgi Eristavi played a prominent role, occurred in the nineteenth century, and early in this century there were several theaters in Georgia. There are now more than 20 regular theaters and about 30 amateur folk theaters, as well as Rustaveli Theatrical Institute in Tbilisi for training actors, stage directors, and other specialists. Kote Mardzanishvili is considered an outstanding director of the Soviet period. Together with Sandro Akhmeteli, he is largely responsible for techniques used today. Vakhtang Chabukiani is preeminent master of classical dance.

Extant psalms of the eighth, ninth, and tenth centuries testify to a long tradition of musical composition, revealing that even at that time Georgians had their own system of musical transcription. Georgian folk songs have been appreciated by leading Russian composers (including Glinka, Tchaikovsky, and Ippolitov-Ivanov). Drawing on this folk tradition, composer Zakhari Paliashvili wrote the operas *Abesalom and Eteri*, *Daisi*, and *Latavra*. Music owes much to operatic and symphonic works of Dmitri Arakishvili, comic opera of Viktor Dolidze, *Keto and Kote*, choral compositions of Niko Sulkhanishvili, and scores of Meliton Balanchivadze. Today musicians are trained in the Tbilisi Conservatory and various groups—including Quartet of Georgia, Vocal Ensemble Shvidkatsa, State Song and Dance Ensemble, State Symphony Orchestra, and State Folk Dance Ensemble—have gained wide recognition.

One form of the fine arts having a long tradition is metal-chasing, dating back to the second millennium B.C. and reaching its highest stage in the tenth to twelfth centuries. Closely associated with metal-chasing is gold enameling. Especially noteworthy are works of the brothers Bek and Beshken Opizari done during the reign of Queen Tamara. Extant gold icon covers and book bindings, massive crosses and vessels and enameled decorations reveal the consummate skill of artists of that era. Work of this kind is still being carried on by such artists as Irakly Ochiauri, Dmitry Kipshidze, Koba Guruli, and Guram Gabashvili.

Professional easel painting, graphic arts, and sculpture developed in the nineteenth century. Since then paintings by Niko Pirosmanishvili have gained fame. Realistic artists of the older generation include Grigory Maisuradze, Gigo Gabashvili, Alexander Mrevliashvili, Mose Toidze, and sculptor Yakov Nikoladze. Lado Gudiashvili has been granted the honorific title of

49 For a review of scholarly work on Georgian folklore, see Barnov, 1972. Unless otherwise noted, the review of culture given here is based on material in the following: *Georgian Soviet Socialist Republic*, 1968: 63–70; Gugushvili, *Gruzinskaya SSR: kul'tura*, 1971; Davitaya, 1972: 67–73.

50 According to one source, "not only during the feudal period, but also down to our century, at first handwritten, and since the 18th century, printed copies of this poem were considered the most important part of a Georgian bride's dowry." Davitaya, 1972: 68.

51 "Georgian Soviet Socialist Republic," *McGraw-Hill Encyclopedia of Russia and the Soviet Union*, 1961: 195.

52 Lang, 1962: 257.

People's Artist of Georgia for his paintings. Modern sculpture is best exemplified by works of Nikoloz Kandelaki, Valeryan Topuridze, Shota Mikatadze, and Elguya Amashukeli.

The large group of gifted film makers includes Mikhail Chiaureli, Nikoloz Shengelaya, Siko Dolidze, Leo Esakia, David Rondeli, Revaz Chkheidze, and Tengiz Abuladze. Among films gaining renown outside Georgia are *Lurja Magdany* (produced by T. Abuladze and R. Chkheidze), which won prizes at Cannes and Edinburgh in 1956, *Foster Children* and *Supplication* (produced by T. Abuladze), and Revaz Chkheidze's film *A Soldier's Father*. The latter owes its great international success in part to the acting of the late Sergo Zakariadze, awarded first prize for best male role at the Fourth International Film Festival in Moscow in 1965. *The Wedding* by the young director Mikhail Kobakhidze won three prizes at the International Film Festival in Oberhausen in 1965 and the Grand Prix for best short film at Cannes in 1966.

EXTERNAL RELATIONS

Linguistically, the Georgian people are distinguished from major neighboring nationalities (see section on language). Although the overwhelming majority of Georgians are concentrated within the republic there are also somewhat more than 90,000 scattered throughout the USSR, and groups have settled in Turkey and Iran. Along shores of the Black Sea in Turkey live one of the Kartvelian tribes related to the Georgians—the Lazes. Although there are no reliable data on number of Georgians living in these neighboring countries, it has been estimated that more than 330,000 Georgians and Lazes live in Turkey, and probably some tens of thousands of Georgians inhabit regions of northern Iran.[53] Moreover, a Georgian colony was established by émigrés in Paris in 1921, and other small groups are found in other countries of Western Europe and in the Western hemisphere. Georgians in Paris and Munich have played leading roles in publicizing the republic's culture and political aims.

Historically, Georgians have been in contact with European countries via the Black Sea and the Mediterranean, although such contact was interrupted by various invasions, especially those of the Tatars, and by capture of Constantinople by the Turks. Because of a shared Christian faith, leaders have tended to look to Christian kingdoms of Europe and, later, to the Russian tsar for support against the hostile Islamic powers, Turkey and Iran. Since incorporation of Georgia within the Soviet Union, contacts with the Western world have been impeded, while those with other peoples within the USSR have been strengthened.

In 1946 a society was established to make connections with other "friendship societies," receive delegations from abroad, and dispatch informational material on Georgia. Since then, the number of foreigners visiting the country has greatly increased, especially during the 1960s. In 1969 about 50,000 foreign tourists and a large number of official delegations visited the republic.[54] Meetings between Georgian and foreign scientists have become more frequent, and cooperative ventures have been undertaken.

Media

LANGUAGE

Georgian belongs to the Ibero-Caucasian group of the Caucasian family of languages which, despite some linguistic borrowings, is distinct and separate from the Indo-European, Turkish, and Semitic families. Although its origin continues to be a subject of controversy, it is reasonably well established that the modern Georgian, Svanian, and Mingrelo-Laz languages trace their descent from Old Kartvelian. None of

---

53 Dzhaoshvili, 1968: 49–50.

54 Gugushvili, *Gruzinskaya SSR: kul'tura*, 1971: 182. Most tourists were from other Communist countries. Evidently, only a small fraction of these visitors are received by the Georgian Society of Friendship and Cultural Ties (abbreviated GODUKS), since the same source states (p. 185) that in 1969 this organization received more than 3,000 visitors.

Table 8.3

Native and Second Languages Spoken by Georgians

(in thousands)

No. Georgians Residing			SPEAKING AS NATIVE LANGUAGE						SPEAKING AS SECOND LANGUAGE[a]	
			Georgian			Russian			Russian	Other languages of the peoples of USSR
	1959	1970	1959	1970	% Point Change 1959–1970	1959	1970	% Point Change 1959–1970	1970	1970[b]
in Georgian SSR	2,601 (100%)	3,131 (100%)	2,588 (99.5%)	3,122 (99.4%)	–.1	12 (0.4%)	13 (0.4%)	0	629 (20.1%)	21 (0.7%)
in other Soviet republics	91 (100%)	114 (100%)	67 (73.4%)	71 (62.3%)	–11.1	23 (25.3%)	32 (28.1%)	+2.8	62 (54.4%)	11 (9.6%)
Total	2,692 (100%)	3,245 (100%)	2,655 (98.6%)	3,193 (98.4%)	–.2	35 (1.3%)	45 (1.4%)	+.1	691 (21.3%)	32 (1.0%)

Sources: For 1959 census, *Itogi SSSR, 1959*: table 53; *Itogi, Gruzinskaya SSR, 1959*: table 53; for 1970 census, *Itogi 1970*: IV: 20, 253.

[a] No data are available for 1959, since no questions regarding command of a second language were asked in the 1959 census.

[b] Including Georgian, if not the native language.

these languages related to Georgian is currently used by more than a few thousand
individuals. Old Georgian and classical Armenian, which developed in proximity,
have certain structural similarities and may
share a common Anatolian, possibly Hurrian, origin. Georgians have two kinds of
written language—an ancient ecclesiastical
(*khutsuri*) script and a modern form
derived from it. Ancient literary sources
attribute creation of the Georgian alphabet
to the time of Alexander the Great.[55]

In 1970 almost all Georgians resident in
the GSSR claimed Georgian as native
tongue, compared with only 62% of those
living outside of the republic (see Table
8.3). Naturally, knowledge of Russian is
much more common among the latter
(82.5%) than among the former (20.5%).
Nevertheless, Georgians do not face the
same danger of losing a large part of their
national group through Russification as do
some other Soviet nationalities (e.g., the
Ukrainians), since about 3.5% live outside
the republic.

Further information can be gleaned from
1970 census data. In Table 8.4, the nationalities are rank-ordered according to quantitative strength of attachment to their
native language. Almost all Georgians, Russians, Azerbaidzhanis, and Abkhazians in
the GSSR regard their nationality's language as native tongue, compared with
70% to 85% of the Armenians, Jews, Ossetians, Kurds, and Tatars and decidedly
fewer (65% to 40%) of the Assyrians,
Ukrainians, Belorussians, and Greeks.
Knowledge of Russian is prevalent among
the nationalities, except for Georgians and
Azerbaidzhanis. Other languages (notably,
Georgian) are not so widely known by those
not native speakers, but appear to have
been mastered by considerable numbers of
some peoples of the Caucasus (Armenians,
Assyrians, Ossetians, Kurds). In the census
more than 100,000 people of non-Georgian

nationality gave Georgian as native language, and an additional 164,000 non-
Georgians reported mastery of Georgian as
a second language.[56]

LOCAL MEDIA

In 1971, 126 newspapers (excluding
kolkhoz editions) with an average circulation of 2,984,000 per issue were published
regularly in the republic (see Table 8.5)[57]
Of these papers, 107 were in Georgian, 11
in Russian, and 8 in languages of other
minorities. More than 80% were in Georgian. Average 1971 circulation (2,532,000)
resulted in a high saturation rate: 78.7
copies per 100 inhabitants of the GSSR
considering Georgian as native language.
Most important newspapers are *Zarya vostoka* [*Eastern Dawn*], appearing six times
weekly in Russian, and the Georgian language *Akhalgazdra Komunisti* [*Young Communist*] and *Komunist*, published three and
six times weekly, respectively, in Tbilisi.

According to one source, 95 journals and
periodicals, including 80 in Georgian, were
published in the republic in 1968. The
yearly printing ran to 12,199,000—
11,587,000 in Georgian.[58] Data presented
in Table 8.5 are based upon a more
restrictive definition of a magazine and,
consequently, the figures are much lower:
22 journals, with combined circulation of
823,000, are published; of these, 18 appear
in Georgian. Magazines dealing with literature and the arts include two publications
of the Georgian SSR Union of Writers:
Mnatobi [*Luminary*] in Georgian and
Literaturnaya Gruziya [*Literature of Georgia*] in Russian; *Ziskari* [*Dawn*], joint publication of the Writers Union and the
Komsomol: *Drosha* [*Banner*], published under the auspices of the Central Committee
of the Georgian Communist party; and
Sabochota khelovneba [*Soviet Art*], journal

55 Lang, 1966: 22–27, 76–78; *Narody Kavkaza*,
1962: II: 212. It is likely that Svanian split off
from Old Kartvelian in the second millennium
B.C., becoming the language of the Svans, inhabitants of the Caucasian highlands; Laz and
Migrelian are subdivisions of the ancient Colchian
or Tzanic tongue, once spoken extensively around
the eastern end of the Black Sea. Lang estimates
that now Svanian speakers number no more than
25,000 (p. 23).

56 *Zarya vostoka* (May 8), 1971: 1. See much more
detailed data on nationalities' languages in *Itogi
1970*: IV: 253–257 (table 15).
57 According to another source, 145 newspapers,
including 125 in Georgian, were printed in 1968 in
the GSSR. Annual circulation was about 518 million—430 million in Georgian. Gugushvili, *Gruzinskaya SSR: kul'tura*, 1971: 75.
58 *Ibid.*

Table 8.4

Languages of Population of Georgian SSR, by Nationality[a]

Census Data,1970

NATIONALITY[b]	NO. (IN THOUSANDS)	% CONSIDERING NATIONALITY'S LANGUAGE AS NATIVE TONGUE			% WITH FLUENT KNOWLEDGE OF SECOND LANGUAGE (OF SOVIET PEOPLES)	
	1970	1959	1970	Difference	Russian	Other
Georgian	3,131	99.5	99.4	—0.1	20.1	0.7
Russian	397	99.5	99.4	—0.1	—	12.6
Azerbaidzhani	218	98.3	97.6	—0.7	16.5	6.2
Abkhazian	79	95.8	97.2	+1.4	59.3	2.4
Armenian	452	82.3	84.8	+2.5	35.5	13.7
Jewish[c]	55	72.3	80.9	+8.6	26.1	7.7
Ossetian	150	86.3	79.1	—7.2	25.3	28.2
Kurd	21	85.4	79.0	—6.4	28.2	31.0
Tatar	6	70.9	71.2	+0.3	51.3	14.5
Assyrian	6	63.4	64.6	+1.2	34.5	26.3
Ukrainian	50	56.4	59.0	+3.6	47.9	13.8
Belorussian	6	49.6	50.2	+0.6	41.1	13.4
Greek	89	44.8	40.2	—4.6	36.9	23.5
Others	26	—	—	—	—	—
Entire population	4,686	94.7	94.3	—0.4	21.5	5.0

Source: *Zarya vostoka* (May 8), 1971: 1.

[a] Nationality and languages were determined in the census by personal declaration of respondents. Children's nationality was determined by parents' declaration.

[b] Nationalities are ranked according to strength of nationalities' attachment to native language in 1970 (i.e., percentage considering own nationality language as native tongue).

[c] The figures on Jews are ambiguous, since the majority of Georgian Jews consider Georgian their native tongue. See *Itogi 1970*: IV: 253.

of the Ministry of Culture of the GSSR. More specialized periodicals in the same area include *Dila* [*Morning*], illustrated magazine aimed at children between the ages of 5 and 10, and *Pioneri* [*Pioneer*], similar magazine for children 10 to 15, both joint publications of the Georgian Komsomol and Pioneer organizations, as well as *Niangi* [*Crocodile*], satirical magazine published fortnightly under the auspices of the Central Committee of the Georgian Communist party. *Metsniereba da*

tekhnika [*Science and Technology*] is a popular science monthly published under the auspices of the Georgian Academy of Sciences. *Sakartvelos kali* [*Georgian Woman*] is a women's magazine issued by the party's Central Committee, as is the more strictly political journal *Sakartvelos komunisti* [*Communist of Georgia*].[59]

---

[59] Information on periodicals from *Europa Yearbook, 1972*, I: 1,293. All are monthlies, published in Georgian, unless otherwise noted.

Table 8.5

Publications in Georgia

Language of Publication	Year	NEWSPAPERS[a]			MAGAZINES			BOOKS & BROCHURES		
		No.	Per Issue Circulation (1,000)	Copies/100 in Language Group[e]	No.	Per Issue Circulation (1,000)	Copies/100 in Language Group[e]	No. Titles	Total Volume (1,000)	Books & Brochures/100 in Language Group[e]
Russian	1959	17	200	38.8	N.A.	N.A.	N.A.	455	2,415	468.8
	1971	11	330	63.3	1	4	0.8	656	2,982	572.2
Georgian	1959	90[b]	741	27.5	N.A.	N.A.	N.A.	1,593	9,832	364.9
	1971	107[b]	2,532	78.7	18[b]	800	24.9	1,666	13,995	435.3
Minority Languages	1959	16[c]	56	6.4	N.A.	N.A.	N.A.	104	231	26.6
	1971	8	122	12.8	3	19	2.0	103	153	16.1
Foreign Languages	1959	0	0	0	N.A.	N.A.	N.A.	(39)[d]	(332)[d]	N.A.
	1971	0	0	0	0	0	N.A.	(61)[d]	(459)[d]	N.A.
All Languages	1959	123	997	24.7	23	221	5.5	2,191[d]	12,810	316.8
	1971	126	2,984	63.7	22	823	17.6	2,486[d]	17,589	375.3

Sources: *Pechat' 1959*: 56, 129, 164.
Pechat' 1971: 96, 159 188.

[a] 1971 figures do not include *kolkhoz* newspapers.
[b] Some publications appeared in both Russian and Georgian languages.
[c] This figure may include publications in non-Soviet languages

[d] Book totals as given in *Pechat'* sometimes differ from totals in language categories. The indication is that books are published in other languages, but no data is given. Figures in parentheses are the presumed production of books in other languages based on this discrepancy.
[e] Includes native speakers of the language.

Table 8.6

Electronic Media and Films in Georgia

| YEAR | RADIO | | | | | TELEVISION | | | | MOVIES | |
	No. Stations	No. Wired Sets (1,000)	/100 Population	No. Wireless Sets (1,000)	/100 Population	No. Stations	No. sets (1,000)	/100 Population	Seats (1,000)	/100 Population
1960	N.A.	320[a]	7.6[d]	526[a]	12.6[c]	N.A.	52[a]	1.2[c]	179[b]	4.2[d]
1970	N.A.	393[a]	8.3[d]	891[a]	18.8[c]	N.A.	464[a]	9.8[c]	312[b]	6.5[d]
1971	N.A.	406[d]	8.4[d]	910[d]	19.0[c]	N.A.	513[c]	10.7[c]	N.A.	N.A.

[a] Source: *Transport i svyaz' SSSR*, 1972: 296–298.
[b] Source: *Nar. obraz.*, 1971: 325.
[c] Source: *Nar. khoz. 1922–1972*: 572, 578.
[d] Computed from data cited above ([b] and [c]).

Recent data indicate that there are 910,000 wireless radio receivers and 513,000 television sets in the republic, constituting, respectively, 19.0 and 10.7 broadcast receivers per 100 persons (see Table 8.6). On the average, there are about 40 hours of central broadcasting each day. Central radio broadcasting averages 30 hours daily, divided into three programs; languages are Georgian, Russian, and Azerbaidzhanian. Since 1971 two TV programs (in Russian and Georgian) have been transmitted each day. TV shows in color are transmitted from Tbilisi three times a week, and relay facilities make it possible for viewers to pick up TV broadcasts from Moscow and, by means of the "Intervidyeniye" and "Evrovidyeniye" systems, from countries of Europe and other continents. Radio programs are also broadcast locally outside of the capital.[60]

EDUCATIONAL INSTITUTIONS

In the academic year 1962–1963, universal eight-year education was achieved in the republic.[61] In 1971 Georgia had 4,521 general education schools with a total enrollment of somewhat more than 1 million students. Of 4,258 general education schools in 1965–1966, 2,962 used Georgian as language of instruction, while 287 used Russian, 242 Armenian, 194 Ossetian, 162 Azerbaidzhani, 39 Abkhaz, and an additional 372 were bilingual.[62] In 1971 there were 100 specialized secondary schools in which 52,000 students were enrolled, as well as 18 institutions of higher education with a combined student body of 89,000. Tbilisi State University, founded in 1918, is largest of these institutions with an enrollment of 16,000.[63] Lenin Polytechnical Institute is largest academic institution for training engineers and technicians. The country's academic center is Vake District of Tbilisi where seven institutions of higher education are located and 4,000 students reside.

Georgians are heavily represented among students enrolled in specialized secondary schools and institutions of higher education. In the academic year 1969–1970, they made up four fifths of the students of specialized secondary schools in the GSSR (see Table 8.8). In the same year, Georgians constituted 82.6% of the college students, while Russians made up 6.8%, Armenians 3.6%, Ossets 2.3%, Abkhazians 1.6%, Azerbaidzhani 0.5%, and other nationalities 2.6%.[64] Twenty-seven of every 1,000 Georgians aged 10 or older in the Soviet Union were enrolled in institutions of higher education in 1969–1970, whereas the all-Union average was 19.[65]

Georgian is reported to be very frequently used as the language of instruction at higher schools, even at technological colleges. Russian is used less than in almost any other republic. Graduates of universities are mostly assigned to work in the republic to provide national cadres of intelligentsia. Yet some prominent scientists and academicians in the main Soviet centers outside Georgia are of Georgian origin (e.g., D. Gvishiani, deputy chairman, Committee for Science and Technology, USSR Council of Ministers, and Professor V. Chkhikvadze, until recently director, Institute of State and Law, USSR Academy of Sciences).[66]

CULTURAL AND SCIENTIFIC INSTITUTIONS

The Academy of Sciences, Georgian SSR, founded in 1941, became one of the largest centers of scientific research in the Soviet Union. Its six branches encompass 44 scientific institutions, including 38 for research.

60 Gugushvili, *Gruzinskaya SSR: kul'tura,* 1971: 174–175; "Gruzinskaya," *BSE,* 1972: VII: 381.
61 Gugushvili, *Gruzinskaya SSR: kul'tura,* 1971: 19–20.
62 *Ibid.*: 20.
63 *Nar. obraz.,* 1971: 164.

64 Gugushvili, *Gruzinskaya SSR: kul'tura,* 1971: 29.
65 Thus, among the nationalities Georgians had strongest relative representation in institutions of higher education. There was no doubt, however, a great proportion of Jews among the college students. At the other extreme, only 11 Moldavians of every 1,000 were attending a higher school. Bruk, 1972: 354.
66 *Nauchno-tekhnicheskaya revolyutsiya i sotsial'nyi progress* (Moscow: Politizdat, 1972): 49–69; V. Chkhikvadze et al., eds., *The Soviet State and Law* (Moscow: Progress Publishers, 1969). Also, from Zev Katz' interviews with Georgian émigrés.

Table 8.7

Selected Data on Education in Georgia (1971)

Population: 4,189,000

		PER 1,000 POPULATION	% OF TOTAL
All schools			
number of schools	4,521	1.1	
number of students	1,045,000	249.5	
Newly opened elementary, incomplete *secondary, and secondary schools*			
number of schools	102		
number of student places	41,100	9.8	
Secondary special schools			
number of schools	100		
number of students	52,700	12.6	
Institutions of higher education			
number of institutions	18		
number of students	89,200	21.3	
Universities			
number of universities	1		
number of students			
total	16,331		
day students	8,665		53
evening students	5,370		32.8
correspondence students	2,296		14
newly admitted			
total	2,666		
day students	1,586		59.4
evening students	915		34.3
correspondence students	165		6.1
graduated			
total	2,460		
day students	1,413		57.4
evening students	610		24.7
correspondence students	437		17.7
Graduate students			
total number	1,376	0.33	
in scientific research institutions	717		
in universities	659		
Number of persons with (in 1970) higher or *secondary (complete and incomplete)* *education*			
per 1,000 individuals, 10 years and older	554		
per 1,000 individuals employed in national economy	711		
Number of workers graduated from *professional-technical schools*	22,000	5.3	

Source: *Nar. khoz. 1922–1972*: 108, 438, 569, 576, 577, 579.

Table 8.8

National Composition of Students Enrolled in Specialized Secondary Schools and Institutions of Higher Education of Georgian Republic

	SPECIALIZED SECONDARY SCHOOLS		INSTITUTIONS OF HIGHER EDUCATION	
Academic year	*1960–1961*	*1969–1970*	*1960–1961*	*1969–1970*
Total number of students	26,252	50,649	56,322	90,121
Nationality				
Georgians	21,175	40,829	43,237	74,473
Russians	1,749	3,787	5,390	6,061
Armenians	1,250	2,420	3,596	3,285
Azerbaidzhani	188	320	448	412
Abkhazians	353	676	799	1,447
Ossets	608	886	967	2,109
Ukrainians	290	430	419	466
Others	639	1,301	1,466	1,868

Source: *Komsomol Gruzii v tsifrakh i faktakh*, 1971: 71.

Altogether, there are 200 scientific research institutes in Georgia, plus 18 institutions of higher education.[67] The number of academic research cadres [*nauchnyye rabotniki*] has grown rapidly, increasing from 3,513 in 1940 to 9,137 in 1960 and 20,160 in 1970.[68] Although data on national composition of this group are not available, it may be estimated that about four fifths are Georgians.

Among the most important scientific institutes are A. M. Razmadze Mathematical Institute, Georgian Institute of Physics, Institute of Earth Mechanics, Institute of Cybernetics (first of its kind in the USSR), P. G Melikishvili Institute of Physical and Organic Chemistry, Vakhushti Institute of Geography, Institute of the Biochemistry of Vegetation, and numerous others.[69]

Historical studies are pursued in I. A. Dzhavakhishvili Institute of History, Archeology, and Ethnography and Institute of Eastern Studies, while economic research is done largely by the academy's Institute of Economics and Law and Institute of Economics and Economic Planning under the Georgian Gosplan. Principal serial publications on economics and law, respectively, are the monthly journals *Sakartvelos sakhalkho meurneoba* and *Sabochota samartali*.[70] Regular publications of Georgian Academy of Sciences are *Soobshcheniya AN GSSR* (in Georgian and Russian); *Matsne* (or *Vestnik*), organ of the Division of Socal Sciences, appearing in Russian and Georgian; and *Metsniyereba da takhnika*

---

67 Gugushvili, *Gruzinskaya SSR: kul'tura*, 1971: 41–42; *Nar. obraz.*, 1971: 249.

68 *Ibid.*: 247. Throughout the USSR were 18,433 "scientific workers" of Georgian nationality in 1970. The great majority, no doubt, were in the GSSR. *Ibid.*: 270–271.

69 A concise overview of research activities of these and other scientific institutions is given in "Gruzinskaya," BSE, 1972: 375–378.

70 *Ibid.*: 380–381.

(in Georgian only).[71] In addition, there are numerous scholarly societies and professional unions.[72]

As of 1971 the republic had 3,640 public libraries, housing more than 23 million copies of books and magazines. Major libraries include Karl Marx State Library, Tbilisi University Library, Central Library of the Academy of Sciences, and Ya. Go-

gebashvili Republic Library for Public Education in Tbilisi, as well as republic libraries of Adzhar and Abkhaz ASSR.

In the same year there were more than 2,000 officially sponsored clubs and 75 museums in the republic. Most famous is S. Dzhanashia State Museum of Georgia, located in the capital, renowned for its collection of Georgian art.

Table 8.9

Selected Data on Scientific and Cultural Facilities and Personnel

in Georgia (1971)

Population: 4,189,000

Academy of Sciences		*Number of persons working in*	
number of members	108	*education and culture*	
number of scientific institutions		total	182,000
affiliated with academy	41	number per 1,000 population	38
total number of scientific workers	4,438		
		Number of persons working in science	
Museums		*and scientific services*	
number of museums	75	total	50,000
attendance	2,886,000	number per 1,000 population	10
attendance per 1,000 population	603		
		Number of public libraries	3,640
Theaters		number of books and magazines	
number of theaters	22	in public libraries	23,010,000
attendance	3,248,000		
attendance per 1,000 population	678	*Number of clubs*	2,122

Source: *Nar. khoz. 1922–1972*: 106, 451, 575.

National Attitudes

REVIEW OF FACTORS FORMING
NATIONAL ATTITUDES

In the face of repeated threats to national survival, Georgians have managed to preserve and develop their culture through the ages. This strong cultural tradition, with awareness of a long and turbulent history

and continued geographical concentration, contributes to the Georgians' sense of collective identity in modern times. Moreover, because of devotion to Christianity, they have traditionally felt a sense of affinity with Christians in Europe, as well as with Russians. For the same reason, they sharply distinguished themselves from neighboring Islamic peoples—Iranians, Ottoman Turks, and Azeri Turks—regarded as enemies. Their perception of themselves as surrounded by hostile, culturally alien Moslem peoples may explain in some

---

71 *Ibid.*: 381.
72 Names and addresses of some are given in Khutsishvili, 1969: 42–43.

measure the absence of a strongly anti-Russian separatist movement during the nineteenth and early twentieth century.

To understand the Georgians, one cannot overlook the fact that the most famous Georgian in this century was Josef Dzhugashvili, known as Stalin. It seems strange, as historian of the Stalinist period Roy Medvedev observes, that in Georgia and Azerbaidzhan, where the mass repression of 1937–1938 was probably worse than in other republics, the most persistent efforts are being made to restore the cult of Stalin.[73] Yet Stalin may be seen both as a particular example of the kind of response some Georgians make to the Soviet system and as a national symbol of Georgian achievement. It is perhaps not fortuitous that Stalin, representative of a small non-Slavic people, should have been so obsessed with power and the virtues of Russian culture, eventually becoming a Great Russian chauvinist.[74] Though an active proponent of the dominant Russian culture, Stalin was nonetheless regarded as a great *Georgian* by many countrymen.[75] The riots erupting in Tbilisi in 1956 appear to have been, in part, a Georgian nationalist response to initiation of destalinization. So closely were people identified with Stalin that an attack upon him was regarded as an attack upon themselves.[76] The Stalin museum is still maintained at his birthplace in Gori, a factory continues to bear his name, and one traveling north of Tbilisi on the Georgian-Military Road is likely to see painted (in Russian) on the bare rock "Glory to the Great Stalin!"[77]

During the Stalinist era, certain Georgian

nationals attained great prominence and power. Sergo Ordzhonikidze, Stalin's right-hand man until his death in 1937, served on the Politburo, occupying the post of people's commissar for heavy industry. Abel Yenukidze was secretary-general of the Central Executive Committee (before 1937 supreme legislative body of the USSR) and Lavrenti P. Beria (member of the Mingrelian minority in Georgia) became head of the Soviet secret police after playing a leading role in the party organization in the Transcaucasian region. From his own experience in Russia between 1943 and 1947 as well as interviews with émigrés, F. Barghoorn concludes that "there was considerable resentment among Russians against Stalin, Beria, and other Georgians in high places and that this animosity was probably shared by many non-Russians, particularly Armenians."[78] Stalin and Beria, in particular, have been blamed for strengthening nationalism in the republic. For instance, a 1956 Komsomol report states:

> As a result of Beria's sway, which could have arisen only under conditions of the cult of the individual, nationalist elements tried to impose upon Georgian young people a feeling of national exclusiveness, to enclose them within a narrowly national frame. The Georgian YCL did not sharply and consistently oppose pernicious nationalist influences on youth, exercised unsatisfactory guidance over ideological work and did a poor job of bringing up young people in a spirit of proletarian internationalism, of friendship of peoples.
>
> The Georgian YCL Central Committee underestimated the fact that the Stalin cult had taken deep root in the consciousness of young people, and that it had acquired especially exaggerated proportions and a nationalist coloring in the Republic.[79]

In the post-Stalin period, influence of Georgians at the center of the party has subsided, and there is now no prominent

73 Medvedev, 1972: 344.

74 Lenin called attention to this when he was examining the behavior of Stalin, Ordzhonikidze, and Dzerzhinsky in relation to leading Georgian Communists branded as nationalists for resistance to central control. See Pipes, 1964: 282–287.

75 A number of Georgians have expressed this sentiment to the author.

76 On the 1956 riots, see Lang, 1962: 264–266. During the disorders, 106 persons are said to have been killed, and 200 wounded. Several hundred more were subsequently deported to labor camps in Siberia.

77 Personal observation in 1969. Other foreign travelers told the author that, though not "officially" sanctioned, this slogan is a regular feature on the road; they reported seeing portraits of Stalin prominently displayed in barber shops and at border check points in the late sixties.

78 Barghoorn, 1956: 49–50.

79 "Eliminate Shortcomings and Mistakes in the Ideological Upbringing of Young People," *Zarya vostoka* (October 2), 1956, in *CDSP*: VIII: 41: 23, as cited in Jeffrey W. Hahn, "Political Socialization in the USSR: The Komsomol and the Educational System," Ph.D. dissertation, Duke University, 1971, reproduced by University Microfilms: 409.

Georgian in the Soviet leadership. Taken as a group, however, they are highly educated, always overrepresented within the CPSU. At present, Georgians are more heavily represented in the CPSU than any of the other union republic nationalities.[80]

Although Georgians have played an active role in the official political system, they are also reported to engage in illicit activity. They are reputedly clever businessmen and frequently come under attack for such socialistically unprincipled initiative. E. A. Shevardnadze, now first secretary of the Georgian Communist party, has repeatedly scored this well-known phenomenon. As he declared on one occasion, "One is literally consumed with shame upon seeing persons who were born in Rustaveli's homeland, which poets have compared with paradise, wandering about, literally for months at a time, in the markets of Vladivostock, Khabarovsk, Moscow, Leningrad, Kharkov, and Kiev, selling fruit from the soil of Georgia, fruit they never raised."[81]

References to such commercial dealings have appeared often in the Soviet press, especially in the wake of Shevardnadze's appointment, since there has been a concerted effort to crack down on such malefactors.[82] For instance, a recent decision of the Central Committee of the GCP stated that during 1972 "administrative organs registered more than 1,200 cases of motor transport being used for personal gains." In some cases, vehicles were used for weeks at a time for illegal transport of produce to far-off regions; in another case, it was discovered that an ostensibly empty railway car was, in fact, loaded with a thousand tons of produce for sale in a distant market.[83] The amount of power and wealth which some private businessmen may acquire is seen in the case of Lazishvili, reputedly a millionaire, who created and "owned" an extensive network of underground factories manufacturing various consumer goods. He was also reportedly a "king-maker," who exercised great influence

over such leading Georgian Communists as Gegeshidze and Mzhavandze.[84]

The February 1973 plenary session, GCP, brought to light "serious violations of the Leninist principles of the selection and placement of cadres in the past, when officials were appointed to executive positions not on the basis of their business and moral qualities but through wire-pulling, acquaintances, and family ties and according to the principles of personal loyalty." Consequently, "schemers, bribetakers and extortionists managed by dishonest means to make their way even into executive positions. It was in that [recent] period [under Mzhavanadze] that it was possible to 'order' a Minister's chair for the notorious schemer Babunashvili, when it seemed that his chair as director of the Tbilisi Worsteds Combine was cramping his style. . . . As is known," the report continued, "private ownership has become widespread in the republic in recent years. This applies, for instance, to the illegal construction of *dachas* and individual homes. Flagrant, outrageous violations have been discovered in the Abkhaz Autonomous Republic, in Mtskheta, Gardabani, Telavi, Khashur, and Makharadze Districts and in other districts."[85] The ex-

---

80 See Table A.11 in the Appendix.
81 *CDSP* (July 26), 1972: XXIV: 26: 10.
82 See, for instance, "Widespread Speculation in Agricultural Products in Georgian SSR," *JPRS: Translations on USSR Political and Sociological Affairs* (December 7), 1972: CCCVIII: 27–31.
83 "Georgian Party Denounces Illegal Use of Motor Vehicles," *JPRS* (same series as above) (January 11), 1973: CCCXVIII: 14–16.

84 Chianurov, 1972: 3–4. Soon after being appointed first secretary of the Georgian Communist party, E. A. Shevardnadze had Lazishvili arrested. "Soviets Find Underground Factory Net," *Christian Science Monitor*, Eastern ed. (March 14), 1973: 3.
85 "Party Leadership Should Measure Up to Today's Tasks," *Zarya vostoka* (February 28), 1973; translated in *CDSP* (May 16), 1973: XXV: 13: 6. The report suggested that such corruption was very extensive: "In an atmosphere of lack of principle, nepotism, mutual backscratching and toadyism, as well as the complete absence of control on the part of the Party agencies, primary Party organizations and economic executives, bribetakers ruled the roost in the Tbilisi Municipal Telephone Network Administration, the Tbilisi State Medical Institute, the inspection group of the Ministry of Everyday Services to the Population, the medical commissions of the Ministry of Social Security, Tbilisi Passenger Station No. 3, the Borzhomi and Akhaltsikhe Trucking enterprises, the Adzhar Supply Administration, the Adigeni District and Khashuri Railroad Hospitals, the Batumi Motor Vehicle School, the Kutaisi Food Trade Organization, the Rustavi Metal Structurals Plant and the Tbilisi Synthetic Goods Factory, in the systems of the Georgian Republic Grape and Fruit State Farms and Winemaking Industry Trust, the Ministry of Agriculture, the Ministry of State Farms, etc. The Party organizations and executives of the higher departments involved supposedly failed to notice that these people were living beyond their means,

tent of such private enterprise and corruption must be taken into account in any study of factors sustaining national attitudes in Georgia. Since it is presumably in the interest of private operators to escape central state controls, they are viewed by the authorities as a dangerous element which may contribute to pressure for national autonomy.

BASIC VIEWS OF SCHOLARS ON NATIONAL ATTITUDES

"Compared with their Russian and Moslem neighbors," D. M. Lang notes, "the Georgians stand out by their proud, often flamboyant bearing, which is based on a conviction of the superiority of their own culture and achievements. It has been said, in fact, that in Georgia, every peasant is a prince, or behaves like one." [86]

Many have called attention to these traits. Though commonly seen as a free, uninhibited, hospitable people, Georgians are believed to be proud defenders of a code of honor with keen sense of family and kinship ties and deeply ingrained national consciousness. W. E. D. Allen, who has written extensively on Georgians, sees in them an "aesthetic irresponsibility," an indomitable love of life joined with strong devotion to a code of honor enabling them to fight fiercely and heedlessly against foreign invaders without succumbing to the sense of inferiority which domination may induce.[87]

In the eyes of Laurens van der Post, Georgians evince a "largeness of gesture and personality," personal warmth and impulsiveness—in short, a characteristically "Mediterranean" nature. Sense of nobility is combined with love of style—a concern with the fine gesture, a certain courtliness of manner, and individualistic elegance in dress.[88] Yet others perceive "Eastern" traits—for example, a patriarchal protective regard for their women, perhaps fostered by centuries of Arab and Persian rule.[89]

Some typical Georgian behavioral and cultural traits are looked upon with disfavor by the authorities. Official sources have portrayed them as "clearly determined to preserve as much of their own way of doing things as possible—which includes a notorious addiction to private enterprise of all kinds." [90] Discussion in the GCP plenary session of December 1972 called attention to evidence of considerable corruption and "a tolerant attitude toward vestiges of the past, toward remnants of private-ownership psychology, personal enrichment, and money-grubbing." [91] At a meeting of the GCP *aktiv* (April 1973), speakers "condemned the distortion of the fine folk traditions of Georgian hospitality as displayed in the holding of lavish weddings, nameday celebrations and funeral feasts, all frequently accompanied by drinking bouts. It was noted that instances in which the arrival of inspection commissions and brigades 'from above' is accompanied by interminable welcoming feasts should be combatted." [92]

A Western commentator (H. Smith, *New York Times*) recently reflected on such traits, concluding, "Georgia's easy style of commerce is matched by the lively temperament of its people, with their love of song, drink and poetry, their limitless hospitality, their immense cultural pride." "In the Soviet systems," Smith observed, "Georgians are mavericks. Their movie industry indulges in experimental pantomimes and caricatures. Their museums dare to show abstract paintings, frowned upon elsewhere, along with national treasures . . . [and] also

---

had acquired houses and *dachas*, had bought automobiles and were leading an idle existence. Furthermore, these people were encouraged in every way and received job promotions. For example, in Telavi and a number of other districts in the republic, there was an 'active competition' as to who would build the best-looking house with the greatest number of extravagances." Further reports on corruption and illegality in the GSSR are in *CDSP* (August 29), 1973: XXV: 31: 5–7, 9; *CDSP* (November 28), 1973: XXV: 44: 1–6.
86 Lang, 1966: 27–28.
87 Cited in Van der Post, 1965: 105.

88 *Ibid.*
89 Barghoorn, 1956: 50.
90 "Dissidents among the National Minorities in the USSR," *Radio Liberty Research Bulletin* 16 (August 30), 1972; CRD 224/72, 16: 4–5.
91 Report of Plenary Session of GCP CC, "On the Tasks of the Republic's Party Organization," *Zarya vostoka* (November 4), 1972, as abstracted in *CDSP* (December 20), 1972: 24.
92 "Intensify Ideological-Political Work," *Zarya vostoka* (April 27), 1973, in *CDSP* (May 16), 1973: XXV: 16: 6.

pictures of Stalin in the early stages of his career." Repeatedly conquered by foreigners through the ages, they "have learned to romanticize their defeats and find ultimate defense in preserving their culture and their language.

"Toward outsiders," he also noted, "Georgians display a sense of superiority. When a foreigner observed to a Georgian that Georgians seemed to live better than people in Russia, he readily agreed. 'The Russians have no taste,' he said." [93]

RECENT MANIFESTATIONS OF NATIONALISM

Little information on Georgian nationalist sentiments and behavior is available in the West. *Samizdat* documents revealing nationalist tendencies, such as those written by Ukrainians, Jews, Tatars, and Russians, have not surfaced, if they are circulated at all. Yet, not infrequently, discussions of national deviations appear in the official press. For instance, a report on the February 1973 plenary session of the GCP stressed that with a weakening of party control in recent years "ideological-political work suffered considerably. A half-baked nationalism raised its head in some places in the republic; things came to such a pass that attempts were made to rehabilitate émigré writers who are hostile to us." [94]

Another example is the official censure following April 1972 publication of *A Historiography of the Bourgeois-Democratic Movement and the Victory of the Socialist Revolution in Georgia (1917–1921)* by U. I. Sidamonidze, senior staff member, Institute of History, Archeology, and Ethnography, Georgian Academy of Sciences. The book was severely criticized in a Bureau of the Tbilisi City Party Committee decree for "white-washing" Georgian Menshevik leaders, anti-Leninist appraisal of the period of Georgian independence, and general nationalist tendencies. The author represented the Georgian declaration of independence as a

"progressive act." [95] Sanctions were taken against not only Sidamonidze, who was reprimanded and may be deprived of his doctor's degree, but a wide number of individuals, including the book's editor, director and party secretary of the publishing house Metsniereba, director and party secretary of the institute, officials in Institute of Party History, Georgian CP Central Committee, and others involved. Yet, as Duevel points out in an analysis of the "Sidamonidze affair," the measures of punishment meted out were quite lenient—everyone implicated incurred only a reprimand or public rebuke. In view of the gravity of the charges leveled, and the fact that more than once in recent years the party had called for greater control over "distortions" in historical writings, he suggests that "the growth of nationalist sentiments has gone so far as to permeate the republic's ruling elite, which has tried to shield the national-minded Georgian scholars from Moscow's wrath." [96] Though such an inference is speculative, there is no doubt that the party is having difficulty in keeping in line various scholars inclined to "revise" Georgian history.[97]

At an April 1973 meeting of GCP *aktiv*, numerous manifestations of nationalism were brought to light. It was asserted that "in Abkhazia a half-baked 'theory' according to which responsible posts should be filled

---

93 Hedrick Smith, "Soviet Georgia Goes Own Way, Does Well," *New York Times* (December 16), 1971: 10.

94 *Zarya vostoka* (February 28), 1973; translated in *CDSP* (April 25), 1973: XXV: 13: 6.

95 *Zarya vostoka* (April 27), 1972; "A Georgian Historian's Ideological Errors," in *CDSP* (May 31), 1972: XXIV: 18: 5, 30.

96 Duevel, 1972: 2, 6.

97 The need for increased ideological vigilance and resolute combating of any manifestations of nationalist and chauvinist tendencies has been stressed repeatedly. See, for instance, "Tbilisi Party Body Reacts to Criticism," *CDSP* (April 12), 1972: XXIV: 11: 8–10. Another historical work attacked for revisionism about the same time was A. Menabde, *Nekotorye voprosy razvitiya Gruzinskoi natsional'noi gosudarstvennosti* (Tbilisi: Metsniereba, 1970). Again in February 1974 a party report castigated "manifestations of a politically dangerous tendency, under the guise of restoring historical objectivity, to depart from a Party appraisal of the activity of N. Zhordania, the Menshevik leader, double-dyed national chauvinist and inveterate enemy of Soviet Georgia, and others. There have even been some attempts to cast doubts on such historic events as Georgia's annexation to Russia." "Bring the Organizational and Political Work of the Capital's Party Organization up to the Level of Today's Tasks. Speech by E. A. Shevardnadze," *Zarya vostoka* (February 8), 1974: abstracted in *CDSP*: XXVI: 8: 3.

only by representatives of the indigenous nationality had gained a certain currency" while elsewhere certain executives "urged the Adzhar Party organization to reject proposals to set up a Georgian Steamship Line, to build new factories and plants and to develop resorts and tourism, basing their advice on the premise that this would lead to the migration of people from other republics." Literary works by certain Ossetian writers were criticized, purportedly because they "still betray elements of the idealization of outmoded traditions and the glorification of moribund attributes of antiquity." Evidently alluding to Georgians, the official report also stated that "in the union republics there may be not only local nationalism but also local chauvinism with respect to the smaller nations and nationalities." It was stressed that those "comrades who waste their time and energy on investigating such problems as whose civilization is older or how many sentences mention Azerbaidzhan or Georgia in, let us say, 'The History of Soviet Mathematics,' are stirring up trouble and acting against the traditional friendship of peoples and their mutual understanding and mutual respect." [98]

The continued sensitivity and significance of national relations is also stressed in discussions of social research. At a conference on concrete sociological research organized by Higher Komsomol School near Moscow in early 1970, it was recommended that a Georgian not interview an Armenian because the individual's ethnic sentiments would influence the validity of the inquiry.[99] At the same conference, one lecturer compared "Russification" [obruseniye] of northern peoples such as the Kalmyks and Chukchi with the process of "consolidation" [ukrupneniye] of Georgians who exercise cultural influence on the Adzhar, Abkhaz, Ossetian, and other minority peoples within the republic. Several seminar participants protested that what may be regarded as "consolidation" from the Georgians' point of view is seen as "assimilation" by the smaller peoples.[100]

One example of growing nationalism in the Georgian SSR is presented by Georgian Jews who have preserved much of their heritage under Soviet rule. They attach great importance to family ties, and even the young are religious. Their national aspirations appear to be expressed clearly in a desire to emigrate to Israel, and in the last few years thousands have been permitted to do so. It is estimated that about one third of Soviet Jews who have left for Israel are from Georgia.[101] The strong devotion of these Jews to community is evidenced by their insistence on living in the same neighborhood in Israel (which makes their absorption into the Israeli culture more difficult). The emigrants report that local Georgians, unlike Russians, do not regard their desire to leave the country with hostility. Rather, since they are nationalistic and proud of their traditions, Georgians understand the Jews' aspiration to live in a country of their own.[102]

According to Jewish émigrés from Georgia, there has been a considerable national resurgence among Georgians in recent

peared studying interpersonal relations of the ethnically mixed work force of a machine-tool manufacturing plant in Tbilisi (surveyed in early 1967). It was found that "about 24% of the informants have interpersonal contacts only with members of their own nation. Interpersonal associations with members of the same nations were marked by a higher level of intensity" (i.e., greater number of activities shared with friends). Nearly three quarters of informants had close friends outside their national group, though such relations were less "intense." Although researchers did not give a detailed breakdown showing to what extent members of specific nationalities associate with those of their own nationality or others, they note that intensity of interpersonal relations is highest among Georgians and lowest among Russians, concluding that ethnic identity continues to be a significant determinant of interpersonal relations, but positing that multinational work groups contribute to fostering crossnational personal ties. Vacheishvili and Menabdishvili, 1972: 27, plus Table 2 on p. 21. National composition of work force was 50.8% Georgians, 27.5% Russians, 10.4% Armenians, 4.9% Ossets, 3.7% Ukrainians (Table 1, p. 20).

101 If this estimate is correct, around 40% of the Georgian Jews have already left the country. At the time of the 1970 census, there were 55,000 Jews in Georgia; Itogi 1970: 17.

102 From Zev Katz' personal reports and talks with émigrés. A number of press reports have detailed difficulties in Georgian Jews' adaptation to Israeli society stemming from strong religiosity, clannishness, and economic position. Terence Smith, "Angry Soviet Georgians in Israeli Port City Await Improvements," New York Times (July 19), 1973.

98 "Intensify Ideological-Political Work," *Zarya vostoka* (April 27), 1973: translated in *CDSP* (May 16), 1973: XXV: 16: 5.

99 Radio Liberty Audience Research, *Background Report* No. 8–73: 3.

100 *Ibid.*: 4. Although little empirical research on ethnic relations has been published, a report ap-

years. The ideological crisis following the anti-Stalin campaign was especially severe, strengthening the trend toward a keener national consciousness. Georgians, proud of a 3,000-year-old history and culture, are better educated, better dressed, and better fed than Russians. They adhere to a way of life in which honor, chivalry, and ancient tradition are of great importance, and some clearly regard Russians and their materialistic ideology as inferior. Yet opinions are divided regarding the future of the republic. Some argue for independence, pointing to the period of 1918–1921; others think their country is doing well within the Soviet system and argue for more autonomy. Altogether, discussions about such matters are reportedly confined to small groups of the nationally conscious.[103]

---

[103] From Zev Katz' personal reports and talks with émigrés.

REFERENCES

Allen, 1932
  W. E. D. Allen, *A History of the Georgian People: From the Beginning Down to the Russian Conquest in the Nineteenth Century* (London: Kegan Paul, Trench, Trubner and Co., 1932).
Avalishvili, 1940
  Zourab Avalishvili, *The Independence of Georgia in International Politics 1918–1921* (London: Headley Brothers, 1940).
Barghoorn, 1956
  Frederick C. Barghoorn, *Soviet Russian Nationalism* (New York: Oxford University Press, 1956).
Barnov, 1972
  G. D. Barnov, "Gruzinskaya fol'kloristika 1960-kh godov" [Studies of Georgian Folklore in the 1960s], *Sovetskaya etnografiya* (1972): 6.
Bruk, 1972
  S. I. Bruk, "Ethnodemographic Processes in the USSR (On Materials from the 1970 Census)," Part I, *Soviet Sociology* (Spring 1972): X: 331–374.
CDSP
  Current Digest of the Soviet Press, published by Joint Committee on Slavic Studies.
Chianurov, 1972
  Ya. A. Chianurov, "Georgia and Her Party Leaders," *Radio Liberty Dispatch*, November 27, 1972.
Davitaya, 1972
  F. F. Davitaya, ed., *Soviet Georgia* (Moscow: Progress Publishers, 1972).
Duevel, 1972
  Christian Duevel, "Nationalist Rumblings in Georgia," *Radio Liberty Dispatch*, May 10, 1972.
Dzhaoshvili, 1968
  V. Sh. Dzhaoshvili, *Naseleniye Gruzii:*

Ekonomiko-geograficheskoye issledovaniye [Population of Georgia: An Economic-geographical Study] (Tbilisi: Metsniereba, 1968).
Europa Yearbook, 1972
  Europa Yearbook, 1972 (London: Europa Publications, 1972).
Georgian SSR, 1968
  Georgian Soviet Socialist Republic (Moscow: Novosti, 1968).
"Gruzinskaya," 1972
  "Gruzinskaya Sovetskaya Sotsialisticheskaya Respublika," *Bol'shaya sovetskaya entsiklopediya* (1972): VII.
"Gruzinskaya SSR," *Yezhegodnik*, 1971
  "Gruzinskaya Sovetskaya Sotsialisticheskaya Respublika," *Yezhegodnik bol'shoi sovetskoi entsiklopedii* 1971 (Moscow: Soviet Encyclopedia, 1971): 128–133.
Gugushvili, *Gruzinskaya SSR*, 1971
  P. V. Gugushvili, ed., *Gruzinskaya SSR* (subtitle) (Tbilisi: Merani, 1971).
  The books listed below were published under the auspices of Institute of Economics and Law, Georgian SSR Academy of Sciences, editor P. V. Gugushvili, on occasion of 50th anniversary of establishment of Soviet power in Georgia:
  Gruzinskaya SSR: kratkii istoriko-ekonomicheskii ocherk [Georgian SSR: A Short Historical-economic Outline].
  Gruzinskaya SSR: kul'tura [Georgian SSR: Culture].
  A. L. Gunia, *Gruzinskaya SSR: industriya* [Georgian SSR: Industry].
  M. K. Kakhetelidze and B. A. Khasia, *Gruzinskaya SSR: sel'skoye khozyaistvo* [Georgian SSR: Agriculture].
  A. G. Nutsubidze and R. P. Kharbedia, *Gruzinskaya SSR: material'noye blag-*

osostoyaniye naroda [*Georgian SSR: The People's Material Well-being*].

Itogi 1959
Itogi vsesoyuznoi perepisi naseleniya 1959 godu SSSR (Moscow: Gosstatizdat, 1962).

Itogi 1970
Itogi vsesoyuznoi perepisi naseleniya 1970 goda (Moscow: Statistika, 1973).

Itogi, Gruzinskaya SSR, 1959
Itogi Gruzinskaya SSR, 1959 (Moscow: Statistika, 1960).

Javakhishvili and Gvelesiani, 1964
Aleksandra Javakhishvili and Giorgi Gvelesiani, eds., *Soviet Georgia: Its Geography, History, and Economy* (Moscow: Progress Publishers, 1964).

JPRS
Joint Publications Research Service. Translations on USSR Political and Sociological Affairs (published by U.S. Department of Commerce).

Kaloyev, 1971
B. A. Kaloyev, *Osetiny (istoriko-etnograficheskoye issledovaniye)* [*The Ossets: An Historical-ethnographic Study*] (Moscow: Nauka, 1971).

Kandelaki, 1953
Constantin Kandelaki, *The Georgian Question Before the Free World* (Paris, 1953).

Khutsishvili, 1969
Giorgi Khutsishvili, *Georgia: Short Gazetteer-Guide* (Tbilisi: Sabchota Sakartvelo, 1969).

Kolarz, 1961
Walter Kolarz, *Religion in the Soviet Union* (New York: Macmillan, 1961).

Kom. partiya Gruzii v tsifrakh, 1971
Ye. G. Kurtsikidze et al., comps., *Komunisticheskaya partiya Gruzii v tsifrakh (1921–1970 gg.) (Sbornik statisticheskikh materialov)* [*Communist Party of Georgia in Figures, 1921–1970: A Collection of Statistical Materials*], (Tblisi: Central Committee of the Communist Party of Georgia, 1971).

Komsomol Gruzii v tsifrakh i faktakh, 1971
A. I. Kakuliya and An. A. Rogava, *Komsomol Gruzii v tsifrakh i faktakh* [*Komsomol of Georgia in Figures and Facts*] (Tbilisi: Central Committee, Komsomol of Georgia, 1971).

Lang, 1962
David Marshall Lang, *A Modern History of Soviet Georgia* (New York: Grove Press, 1962).

Lang, 1966
David Marshall Lang, *The Georgians* (London and New York: Thames & Hudson and Praeger, 1966).

Marshall *et al.*, 1971
Richard H. Marshall et al., eds., *Aspects of Religion in the Soviet Union, 1917–1967* (Chicago: University of Chicago Press, 1971).

Medvedev, 1972
Roy A. Medvedev, *Let History Judge: The Origins and Consequences of Stalinism*, Colleen Taylor trans., David Joravsky, ed. (New York: Knopf, 1972).

Menabde, 1970
Akakii Menabde, *Nekotoryye voprosy razvitiya Gruzinskoi natsional'noi gosudarstvennosti* [*Some Problems Pertaining to Development of Georgian Statehood*] (Tbilisi: Metsniereba, 1970).

Nar. khoz. 1970
Narodnoye khozyaistvo SSSR v 1970 godu (Moscow: Statistika, 1971).

Nar. khoz. 1922–1972
Narodnoye khozyaistvo SSSR 1922–1972: Yubileinyi statisticheskii yezhegodnik (Moscow: Statistika, 1972).

Nar. obraz., 1971
Narodnoye obrazovaniye, nauka i kul'tura v SSSR: statisticheskii sbornik (Moscow: Statistika, 1971).

Narody Kavkaza, 1962
B. A. Gardanov et al., *Narody Kavkaza*, vol. II in the series *Narody mira: etnograficheskiye ocherki* [*Peoples of the Caucasus* in the series *Peoples of the World: Ethnographic Outlines*] (Moscow, 1962).

Natmeladze and Sturua, 1968
M. V. Natmeladze and N. I. Sturua, eds., *Istoriya Gruzii* [*History of Georgia*], vol. III (Tbilisi: Sabchota Sakartvelo, 1968).

Ocherki istorii KPG, 1971
D. G. Sturua et al., eds., *Ocherki istorii kommunisticheskoy partii Gruzii, 1883–1970* [*Outline of History of Communist Party of Georgia, 1883–1970*] (Tbilisi: Central Committee, Communist Party of Georgia, 1971).

Pechat' 1959
Pechat' SSSR v 1959 godu (Moscow: Kniga, 1960).

Pechat' 1970
Pechat' SSSR v 1970 godu (Moscow: Kniga, 1971).

Pipes, 1964
Richard Pipes, *The Formation of the Soviet Union: Communism and Nationalism 1917–1923*, rev. ed. (Cambridge: Harvard University Press, 1964).

Statistical Abstract of the United States, 1971
U.S. Bureau of the Census, *Statistical Abstract of the United States* (Washington, D.C.: Government Printing Office, 1971).

Transport i svyaz' SSSR, 1972
    Transport i svyaz' SSSR (Moscow: Statistika, 1972).
Vacheishvili and Menabdishvili, 1972
    A. Sh Vacheishvili and E. S. Menabdishvili, "Ethnic Relations in the Social Structure of an Industrial Work Force,"
Soviet Sociology (Summer 1972): XI: 3–30.
Van der Post, 1965
    Laurens Van der Post, *Journey into Russia* (London: The Reprint Society, 1965).

9 | AZERBAIDZHAN and THE AZERBAIDZHANIS

Frank Huddle, Jr.

General Information

TERRITORY

Although the area populated by Azerbaidzhanis has not historically been one political unit, it is geographically compact. Outside the USSR, Iranian Azerbaidzhanis occupy the provinces [*ustan*] of east and west Azerbaidzhan, an area the size of Scotland. The Soviet republic of Azerbaidzhan has an almost equal area—33,425 square miles. In addition, two small autonomous territorial units. Nakhichevan ASSR and Nagorno-Karabakh Autonomous Region, lie within administrative purview of the Azerbaidzhan SSR.

Soviet Azerbaidzhan is bordered on the north by the mountainous Daghestan ASSR, on the northwest by Georgia, on the southwest by Armenia and a small piece of Turkey, on the south by Iran, and on the east by the Caspian Sea. In relief, the republic resembles an amphitheater, with mountains on all but the eastern side. Numerous rivers finger their way down from the mountain regions, creating valleys which gradually flatten out into the Kura

Araksin Depression. This below-sea level region, roughly 100 by 50 miles in size, constitutes the core of the amphitheater and is itself cut in half by the Dura, the republic's principal river.

The climate reflects principal features of Azerbaidzhan's relief. Generally, the plains have a dry subtropical climate: hot and dry in the summer, with a warm drizzly fall, a chilly winter, and an unpredictable spring. For the seaside towns of Baku, the capital, and Lenkoran, the January and August average temperatures are 39°F. and 78–79°F. Average yearly mountain temperatures fall about 1°F. per 300 feet of elevation. Thus, Istisu, at roughly 6,600 feet elevation, has a January average of 21°F. and an August average of 56°F. Lowland rainfall varies from 5 to 15 inches except near Lenkoran on the southern Caspian coast where the rainfall, 38 inches yearly, equals or surpasses that of the high mountains.[1]

The republic's substantial natural re-

1 *Azerbaidzhan*, 1971: 28–35, 281–286.

sources include the much-depleted oil supplies, gas deposits, and the largest iron
deposits in the Caucasus at Dashkesan.
There are also commercially useful deposits
of aluminum, copper, lead, zinc, sulfur,
pyrites, molybdenum, cobalt, and building
materials (cement, marble, and tufa).

ECONOMY

Oil and oil-related industries have dominated the Azerbaidzhani economy since
about 1871 when oil (hitherto collected
from fifty-foot-deep, hand-dug pits) was
first extracted by modern methods. In the
1870s drilling spread rapidly and by 1883
Baku oil could be shipped to foreign markets on the new Transcaucasus railroad. At
the turn of the century the Baku fields enabled Russia to produce nearly 50% of the
world's oil.

Foreign enterprises profited heavily from
the oil boom. Nobel, principal force behind
the early drilling, developed the Russian
market, supplying it with oil from Azerbaidzhan, while the Rothschilds handled the
sale and transport of kerosene to Europe.
The labor supply also had a foreign tinge,
with Russians performing skilled labor,
Iranians unskilled, and Armenians handling services.

From 1903 on the oil industry suffered
from labor unrest, peaking in 1905 with
Armenian-Russian-Azerbaidzhani conflicts
and the general turmoil of revolution. After
1905, despite ongoing construction of the
Baku-Batum pipeline, the decline continued
as foreign competition and world production of oil increased sharply. The 1906
decree fixing royalties at 35% hurt the
Azerbaidzhani industry further as did allo-
cation of scarce tank cars to refineries in
proportion to output, a policy which forced
refineries to produce at a financial loss to
ensure themselves cars.[2] Unquestionably,
the end of the oil boom aggravated labor
difficulties, encouraging rural Azerbaidzhan
to remain largely agricultural.[3]

From before World War I to the 1940s oil

production grew steadily but slowly.[4] In the
1930s the Baku fields still pumped 75–80%
of Soviet oil, but between 1950 and 1960
Azerbaidzhan's percentage of Soviet oil production plummeted from roughly one half
to one seventh while the vast Ural-Volga
region's percentage rose to 70. Azerbaidzhani production remains steady today at
7% of the USSR total.

With the republic's dominant industry
relatively stagnant, there have been numerous recriminations in recent years. In 1969,
upon taking office, Aliyev, first secretary of
the party, made a free-wheeling attack upon
the economy. "Even the oil industry [is]
failing to meet its delivery quotas . . . and
some factories are barely operating at one-
third efficiency."[5] Three years later Aliyev
pointed out that "the desired results in the
discovery and exploitation of new oil . . .
have not been achieved."[6] Attempts to expand marine drilling, modernize the industry, and increase more rapidly production
of oil-industry equipment have encountered
similar delays. The plethora of complaints
raised by Aliyev and others includes shortage of specialists in geology and engineering, employee turnover, disinterest of youth,
poor labor discipline, lags in drilling, poor
work by builders of drilling platforms, and
failure of industrial suppliers.[7]

Today, diminishing reserves, high expenses and technological problems of off-
shore drilling, and need for more pipelines
prevent expansion of the oil industry despite
the generally fine quality of Baku oil. The
Soviet response has been diversification,
especially into oil-related industries. Thus,
in 1967 Azerbaidzhan manufactured 46%
of the USSR's oil equipment,[8] and natural
gas exploitation has increased to 19 billion
cubic feet per year.[9] Mining and ferrous
metallurgy have also grown; 1971 steel output amounted to 730,500 tons, of which
steel pipe production was 459,100 tons.[10]

---

2 U.S. Department of Commerce, *Trade Information
Bulletin*: 1,263: 2.
3 For accounts of the 1900–1910 period, see Akhundov, 1955, and Larin, 1909.

4 1913: 7.7 million tons; 1940: 22.2 million tons;
1971: 19.2 million tons. *SSSR i soyuznye respubliki*,
1972: 146.
5 *Bak. rab.* (August 7), 1969.
6 *Bak. rab.* (March 14), 1972: 2–4. Translated in
JPRS (April 20), 1972: 235.
7 *New York Times* (August 12), 1969; *Bak. rab.*
(October 20), 1970 and (March 11), 1971; *Pravda*
(January 2), 1973: 2ff.
8 *BSE*, 1970: I: 258.
9 *SSSR i soyuznye respubliki*, 1972: 146.
10 *Ibid.*

Mining is concentrated in the Dashkesan district, which has the largest iron mines in the Caucasus, rich deposits of alunite, and other minerals. Other mining products include molybdenum, lead, zinc, sulfur, and precious metals. Another major export of Azerbaidzhan is cement, now exported to thirty countries; 1971 production was 1,455,000 tons.[11]

Although agricultural output has more than tripled since 1913 (official all-Union average increase is 312%), agricultural cash crops cannot substitute for the oil industry's sluggishness. Cotton leads the way, representing 40–50% of agricultural income,[12] but the unspoken assumption is that its future is limited by the following factors: (1) constricted area of the flat Kura basin, which has a suitable climate; (2) competition from long-fibered Central Asian cotton; and (3) lack of mechanization in the industry. As of 1971, "only 13% of cotton harvesting jobs are done by mechanization."[13]

Value of 1972's agricultural products exceeded the 1966–1970 average by 23%,[14] but Aliyev, in November 1972, labeled grain cultivation, vegetable growing, viticulture, and stock breeding as lagging. Production figures for 1971 were 608,000 tons of grain, 420,700 of vegetables, and 316,200 of wine, with 4,447,900 sheep and goats.[15]

Nearly all economic indicators suggest that Azerbaidzhan leads only the Moslem republics (and sometimes Moldavia) in standard of living and level of industrialization. Moreover, the republic ranks last in tempo of growth and per capita trade turnover.[16]

As mentioned earlier, these difficulties were acknowledged in 1969–1970, and attributed to problems of labor discipline and low technological levels. They continue.

"The majority of our enterprises work erratically: in the first 10 days they produce 10–15% of [the month's] products, but in the last 10 days more than 50%."[17] Production plans in 1972 for leading industries —oil, steel, cement—were not fulfilled.[18]

Other indicators confirm this story. In ratio of doctors to population, Azerbaidzhan ranks tenth with 25.1/10,000, but some rural areas have only 4 to 5 per 10,000.[19] The republic ranks next to last in ratio of savings accounts to population and eleventh in per capita savings (102.4 rubles).[20]

In view of the decline of oil reserves, limited amount of arable land, and low level of technology, Azerbaidzhan will probably continue to fall behind, although the 1971–1975 Five-Year Plan calls for a 46% increase in industrial production and a 33% rise in real income.[21]

HISTORY

The territory of Azerbaidzhan, ancient Media, has suffered many invasions: Cyrus in the sixth century B.C., Alexander in 330 B.C., and the Sassanids in 226 A.D. Four and a half centuries later powerful Moslem invaders subjugated and converted much of Azerbaidzhan, while from the tenth to twelfth centuries many Turkic tribes migrated into Azerbaidzhan, mixing with the indigenous population and creating a new Turkic language, Azerbaidzhani.[22] During the thirteenth and fourteenth centuries the country was relatively untouched by Mongol invasions.

The Turkish element grew steadily. By the fifteenth century, "Azerbaidzhan was inhabited by a people of Irano-Turkish origin, speaking a mixture of the two languages."[23] The region's Shiite sect of Islam linked the Azerbaidzhanis more closely with Iran, however, than with their Turkish kin.

Two centuries later Peter the Great defeated Persia, annexing the Derbent and Baku regions by the Treaty of 1724. Though Nadir Shah regained these territories for

---

11 *Ibid.*
12 The 1962–1963 bumper crop of 431,000 tons exceeded the plan by 20%, but climatic conditions were very favorable. The 1966–1970 average was 328,000 tons.
13 *Bak. rab.* (March 11), 1971.
14 *Bak. rab.* (December 29), 1972.
15 *SSSR i soyuznye respubliki*, 1972: 151. There are 1,574,800 cattle, and only 121,000 pigs. Georgia, for example, has six times as many pigs and this hints that Moslem prohibitions are lingering on (though not so strongly as in Central Asia).
16 See *Nar. khoz. 1970:* 534, 579. For Azerbaidzhan, 1970 economic output was 164% of 1960. USSR average was 197.7%. Trade turnover per capita was 397 rubles in 1970. USSR average was 639 rubles.

17 *Bak. rab.* (March 11), 1971: 13.
18 *Vyshka* (November 26), 1972: 1–2.
19 *Nar. khoz.* 1972: 515ff.
20 *Ibid.*
21 *Soviet Life* (September), 1972: 8.
22 Also referred to as "Azeri."
23 Kazemzadeh, 1951: 5.

Persia a dozen years afterward, they were lost once and for all in the early nineteenth century when Russia's drive into the Caucasus wheeled east. The 1813 Treaty of Gulistan ceded the Azerbaidzhan khanate to Russia, a decision confirmed by the 1826 rematch in which, notwithstanding early defeats of Ermolov, the Russians conquered Yerevan, Nakhichevan, and Tabriz. Tabriz was retained by the Persians, but the 1828 Treaty of Turkmanchai confirmed the other conquests.

Throughout the nineteenth century, Russian influence in rural domestic policy was that of an outsider, allowing mullahs sway over the masses.[24] Until the 1870s few documented economic or social changes took place; the country remained Islamic, agrarian, and isolated from the West.

In the late nineteenth century, the conjunction of several factors encouraged national consciousness: Turkish revival of national feeling; the rise of anticlericalism in the Islamic world; Sunni-oriented Jadidism; political and cultural weakness of Persia, Azerbaidzhan's traditional cultural mentor; and the first real presence of foreign enterprises. These developments prompted those with education and political sophistication to compete with the mullahs and Begs for political and cultural control. Though the newly arisen oil industry employed comparatively few Azerbaidzhanis,[25] this became, with the Azerbaidzhani publishing industry in Baku, a prime breeding ground in Russia for the Moslem Left. In 1875 members of the intelligentsia drawn from landed and industrialist groups began to print literature in the Azerbaidzhani language. For the period 1875–1917, 60 of the 172 periodicals put out by Russian Moslems came from Baku.[26]

The revolution of 1905, continued influx of foreigners, and especially the 1905 race riots[27] embittered many. Hümmet, a Mos-

lem Marxist organization founded in 1904 during the labor unrest, gained membership in this atmosphere,[28] but by 1907 Russian agents had destroyed it. Four years later, under the leadership of Mehmed Emin Rasulzade, the hardier Musavat party crystalized from right-wing remnants of Hümmet and found encouraging models in the 1908 Constitution Movement in Iran, the Young Turks, and the 1909–1911 Tabriz revolts. At first socialist, the party soon became an Islamic/modernist party with little formal ideology and a program of Moslem unity, independence of Moslem states, and promotion of Moslem trade.

World War I hit the country hard, especially in urbanized areas, like Baku, dependent on food imports.[29] By 1917 the split had widened further between Baku—with a large, active, dissatisfied, somewhat alien proletariat sympathetic to a revolutionary ideology—and the hinterland, populated by farmers and favorably inclined toward the Musavat.

In the October 1917 elections the Musavat drew the largest vote but withdrew soon after, allowing Shaumian, a Bolshevik, to become chairman of the Baku Soviet government. Between November 1917 and March 1918 the Musavat moved right and began to regard the Bolsheviks as anti-Azerbaidzhani. A harsh winter, famine, and bread riots exacerbated these feelings and on March 30, 1918, full-scale ethnic riots broke out.

In April 1918 the Transcaucasian Republics separated from the Soviets, but this unstable alliance of convenience fell apart almost immediately, and by May an independent Azerbaidzhan existed. With Ottoman troops advancing and the hinterland under Musavat control, the Bolsheviks, though isolated, held Baku until September when Turkish troops entered the city.[30] The Turks' brief but unpopular control ended

---

24 Baku and the oil fields were "in many respects treated as a semi-colonial area. Here, the government's main concern was keeping order and exploiting the oil reserves." Suny, 1972: 8.
25 Azerbaidzhanis made up 11.1% of office workers, 16.1% of skilled workers, and 54% of unskilled. See Aliyarov, 1967: 35.
26 Among the Russian-Moslem centers of this period, Baku was first and Kazan second in publishing journals.
27 Between the Armenians, Azerbaidzhanis, and Russians.

28 Its membership was limited, however, to the urban intellectual elite.
29 Food prices rose 100% or more in 1917 while wages rose perhaps 60%. Kazemzadeh, 1951: 32. Another estimate says that between 1913 and 1918 real wages fell 80%. Dubner, 1931: 52.
30 Soon after, 26 Bolshevik commissars were executed after being captured in an attempt to escape from Baku. Shaumian and his compatriots remain Azerbaidzhan's most celebrated martyrs of the revolution.

with the November 1918 armistice and British occupation of Baku.

From this moment, the Azerbaidzhan national state faced problems surmountable only with Allied help. Agrarian production had fallen to one fourth of the prewar level, oil "could be pumped but not marketed," the question of land reform split the country-side along class lines, and an obvious and well-organized Bolshevik "fifth column" remained in Baku.[31]

While the Azerbaidzhan delegation to Versailles got short shrift from an unsympathetic Wilson, the government passed from one crisis to another as the Bolsheviks gained in strength both internally and externally. On April 28, 1920, Baku fell without a shot as the government, riven to the last by dissension between those conciliatory and those nonconciliatory to the Bolsheviks, capitulated to Baku Communists and the arrival of the 11th Red Army.

"The introduction of Soviet rule into Baku was accompanied by severe repressive measures." [32] Ordzhonikidze, foreshadowing his future political style, executed Prime Minister Khan Khoiskii, breaking with the lenient policy shown elsewhere to nationalist leaders in the border regions.

"Actual power in Azerbaidzhan was wielded by the Kavburo[33] and by the local Communist party organs run by Ordzhonikidze and his appointees." [34] Under his guidance, the Azerbaidzhan Communist party approved the new constitution for the Transcaucasian SFSR; in 1922 this federation composed of Georgia, Armenia, and Azerbaidzhan entered the USSR. In December 1936 this arrangement was liquidated and each republic entered separately into the USSR.

With political control a dead issue after March 1920,[35] the Soviets concentrated more concern on economic and cultural transformation of the Azerbaidzhan SSR. Agricultural growth was steady, and collectivization followed the pattern of other republics, with 1929 a key year. Literacy,

perhaps the key to steady technological development, rose spectacularly. In Baku, in 1927, 68.1% of deputies elected to the soviets were illiterate; by 1959, 97% overall literacy had been achieved.[36]

This rise in Soviet-taught literacy coincided with a decline of Islam, hitherto the dominant force in the traditional rural life of Azerbaidzhan. Up to 1928 the Soviets fought the religion principally by co-opting the Islamic modernists who preached a modernization of Islam and by directing the attack against Ashara, a nonorthodox flagellation ceremony condemned by reformists. From 1924 to 1928 Islam was discouraged with gradually increasing success.[37] The frontal assault began in 1928, waxing in the early 1930s as the League of Militant Godless' membership rolls suggest—3,000 in 1930, 67,000 in 1931.

As Islam withered away, parallel problems with nationalism declined. Sultan Galiyevism,[38] never the strong force that it was among Bashkirs and Tatars, continued into the 1930s. "Former zealots of the Hümmet who had turned communist, headed by Khanbudagov, splintered into a faction which demanded the expulsion of the Russian colonists and workmen settled in Moslem Transcaucasia and the replacement of 'Europeans' by Turkic nationals." [39] A first purge swept away the strongly nationalist followers of Khanbudagov, a second removed most of the old Hümmet members, and the third purge, directed by Bagirov in 1937–1938, swept away many top officials including G. M. Musabekov, former chairman of the Council of Commissars of Transcaucasia, and Husein Rakhmanov, secretary of the Central Committee and chairman of the Council of Ministers of Azerbaidzhan.[40]

Since the war the republic's life has been relatively tranquil, with slow, steady economic growth and diversification and a gradual erosion of traditional Islamic life.[41]

---

31 This is drawn from Pipes' account (1964: 207). See also Kazemzadeh, 1951, and Kharmandarian, 1969, a significant Soviet contribution.
32 Pipes, 1954: 228.
33 Caucasian Bureau of the Bolshevik party.
34 *Ibid.*: 229.
35 The Allies were busy elsewhere and Russia's neighbors, Turkey and Persia, were weaker than ever. See *Diplomats*, 1963: 172–209.

36 *Nar. obraz.*, 1971: 22.
37 See Hadjibeyli, 1959: 20ff., for very lucid account.
38 See chapter on the Tatars in Part V.
39 Bennigsen and Lemercier-Quelquejay, 1967: 157.
40 See Medvedev, 1971: 205, 344; Conquest, 1968: 245–246; and *Bak. rab.* (May 27), 1956, for accounts of purges and rehabilitation.
41 See section on culture for more details, and material on national attitudes for recent developments.

DEMOGRAPHY

In the 1960s the population of Azerbaidzhan rose dramatically, from 3,697,700 in 1959 to 5,177,100 in 1970. Earlier censuses in 1913 and 1939 found 2,339,200 and 3,205,200 respectively.[42] The increase between 1959 and 1970 was 38.4%, about 2.5 times that of the USSR as a whole. Broken down by nationalities, the data show that (within the republic) Azerbaidzhanis increased by 51.4% while Russians grew by 1.8%.[43]

In 1970 urban population, rising steadily since the nineteenth century, barely overtook the rural. Nonetheless, population in the countryside grew by 32.1% during 1959–1970, and continuing rural growth should create tensions "since the natives of Transcaucasia are reluctant to go farming in Kazakhstan or Siberia," [44] and it is questionable whether Azerbaidzhan's industry and urban enterprises will absorb these new labor reserves.

Demographic data for Azerbaidzhan, as for other Moslem republics, suggest that the high birth rate–low death rate situation will continue. Percentage of married women aged 16–19 is roughly double the USSR average,[45] and 46.2% of the population is 15 or under.

Population density varies within the republic with about one half of the urban dwellers in Baku alone.[46] By region, the density ranges from 60.6 per square mile in Lenkoran to 3 per square mile on the Apsheron peninsula, with higher regions less densely populated.[47]

Data on occupational structure are fragmentary. Of course, the numbers employed who have technical training is increasing From 1959–1968 the absolute number of workers and white-collar employees almost doubled. The most complete breakdown is given for 1959, when of 80% employed in the sector of material wealth,[48] 26.5% were working in industry, building, and transport, 49.6% in agriculture.[49] It is significant that women constitute 40% of the occupational force though the statistics do not necessarily imply that all jobs are equally open to men and women.

Available data on the Communist party of Azerbaidzhan have some curious aspects.[50] There has been a constant rise in membership, percentage of women members, and percentage of those with higher and middle education. All categories exhibit an almost uncanny, steady increase.

Apparently, some efforts have been made to increase the role of the titular nationality in the party. In 1959 137,533 party members were 54% Azerbaidzhani, 19% Armenian, and 17% Russian. Population percentages were 67.5%, 12%, and 13.6%, respectively. This imbalance can be explained in part by the large, well-educated Armenian and Russian minorities living in Baku;[51] 1970 figures show a smaller imbalance; Azerbaidzhanis constituted 66.5% of the party, Armenians 13.4%, and Russians 12.4%

An examination of party membership by occupation shows that since 1956 there has been a steady rise in percentage of workers and a corresponding drop in number of "employees and others." This is not surprising since the 20th Congress of the Communist party (1956) directed the party to induct more workers.

The party membership is aging slightly,

---

42 Census enumerators do not seem to have undercounted women, always a problem in Moslem areas (F. Huddle).

43 National growth rate was 25.6/1,000 in 1960; for the USSR it was 9.6/1,000. Before 1940 growth rate for the republic was 14.7/1,000. *Azerbaidzhan*, 1971: 77.

44 *Survey* (Autumn), 1971: 22.

45 *Itogi*, 1970: II: 263, 265.

46 Proportion of Azerbaidzhanis in Baku rose from 36.8% (1959) to 46.3% (1970); 1970 percentages for other nationalities in Baku were: Russians, 27.7%; Armenians, 16.4%; Jews, 2.4%; Tatars, 2.19%. *Bak. rab.* (May 21), 1971.

47 Of population, 80% lives at less than 1,640 feet above sea level. Density is 27 per square mile while, overall, it is 22.8 per square mile. *Azerbaidzhan*, 1971: 81.

---

48 In Soviet sources, this phrase is apparently used to refer to production and handling of goods as opposed to services.

49 In 1967 there were 1,139,000 workers and white-collar employees—292,000 in industry, 90,000 in construction, 128,000 in transport and related industries, and 156,000 in agriculture. *BSE*, 1970: I: 249.

50 This and the following data are from *Kompartiya Azerbaidzhana*, 1970.

51 Of 236,674 party members, 133,405 lived in cities (January 1970 enumeration) and 49,625 had completed higher education. *BSE*, 1970: I: 249.

but there has been a rapid increase in the under-20 category.[52] In 1967 those 40 and under made up 53.7% of the party; in 1970 they constituted 52%.

Women are badly underrepresented in the party, especially when one considers that they are 40% of the labor force. Nonetheless, Moslem Azerbaidzhan had 48,758 female party members (19.5%) in 1970 while the USSR had 20.9%. Female membership in the Azerbaidzhani party has fluctuated considerably from a low of 4.1% in 1921 to a wartime peak of 30.1%.[53]

CULTURE

Azerbaidzhan presents two cultural worlds: one urban in which Islam and its traditional customs, art, and literature have largely died; the other rural and isolated in which women still wear black shawls and Moslem values have more than historical significance.[54] But, in sum, Islam lingers on more as a source of tradition than as an actively worshipped religion.[55] While such Moslem customs persist as circumcision, religious proverbs,[56] naming of children with Allah's attributes, and early marriage for women, the five pillars of faith are no longer observed. Zakat [alms] is forbidden,[57] public prayer is quite rare, Ramadan (month of fasting) conflicts with work schedules and is effectively discouraged, and Hajj is limited to a handful of token pilgrims allowed to visit Mecca. The fifth pillar, Shahada, profession of belief in Allah and his prophet Mohammed, "is made by the believer in his heart, and thus eludes the control of the authorities." [58]

Links with the Shiite cultural centers in

Iran have been severed since 1913, and the Soviets assert that "only old people still note [the Shiite festivals of] Kurban-Bairam and Muharran." [59] Yet, though the Koran is not available in bookstores, several conditions suggest that both the specific Shiite practices and general Moslem ones are still followed. The press has made numerous references to youth clinging to outdated traditions and religious customs, and as recently as 1963 "500 Azeri Shi'is assembled in Ashkhabad for the penitential festival of Ashura." [60] Nonetheless, "formal Islam has withered under the pressure of militant atheism." [61] In 1970 Azerbaidzhan had only 16 mosques, two in Baku.

Accompanying Islam's decline is the disappearance of many traditional customs. European "franji" fashions reached Baku in the late nineteenth century and now dominate the urban and more accessible rural areas. The veil [chaudar] is illegal and its replacement, the head scarf, is not universal. Non-Islamic holidays, such as Nohroz, Persian festival of the new year, and harvest festivals are still celebrated, and the official stance seems to be to regard these as substitutes for Moslem holidays. Traditional food is still eaten by most, and such Turkish specialties as pilau, dolma, and flat cakes are popular.

The role of women is a conglomerate of Soviet-encouraged employment equality and remnants of many Moslem customs. In rural areas girls often abandon school for arranged marriages, women are usually left at home, and many "have the status of a servant while the men engage in wild drinking bouts." [62]

Traditional art and literature have been largely replaced by Socialist Realism and somewhat out-of-date Western artistic movements. Pictorial artists have to thread a narrow course and what is acceptable is not always clear. For example, Makhmud Tagiyev's much praised My Baku looks like a 1906 Fauvist work with an industrial touch.[63] Some frequent complaints are that

52 *Kompartiya Azerbaidzhana*, 1970: 47–48. In 1965 there were 177 members 20 and under; in 1970, 1,363. The increase has had little statistical impact since this category remains small compared to the party as a whole.
53 *Ibid.*
54 *Vyshka* (July 17), 1972; *Syracuse Herald-American* (December 6), 1970. 11.
55 *New York Times* (December 13), 1972.
56 Frequently, Soviet sources quote the proverb "first it is necessary to build up the inside of the mosque and then the outside" to show that Islam is hostile to cooperative enterprise.
57 But begging does exist both here and in Central Asia. Personal observation of F. Huddle.
58 Bennigsen and Lemercier-Quelquejay, 1967: 179.

59 *Azerbaidzhan*, 1971: 89.
60 Bennigsen and Lemercier-Quelquejay, 1967: 179.
61 *New York Times* (December 13), 1971; Hadjibeyli, 1959.
62 *Vyshka* (July 17), 1972.
63 *Soviet Life* (September), 1972: 12–13, has a nice reproduction.

"the Union of Artists is still exercising poor control over artists in the applied genre," [64] that painters (not Tagiyev) copy the worst Western models of modern art, and that art does not combat vestiges of the past lingering in people's minds.

A number of works by Azerbaidzhani composers have been performed abroad. Amirov's symphonic "mugums" are well received and Hadjibekov's opera *Leila and Madzhnun* is frequently performed. In sum, however, "the music of Azerbaidzhani composers is less strongly original and less professional than that of Armenian and Georgian composers." [65] Today, Stalinist criticism and demands for "something I can whistle" and muted, and music, especially traditional music, is praised.

The most impressive artistic tradition is in literature. Nizami (1141–1209) and Fizuli (1498–1558), two Azerbaidzhanis who wrote in Persian, are still revered. In the nineteenth century satirists Mirza Vazekh, Kasumbek Zabir, and Sayid Shirva were widely read in Turkey,[66] as was playwright Fath 'Ali Akhudzade (1812–1878), whose work has been translated into many languages. His skillful plays are acceptable to the establishment today—especially such productions as *The Alchemist*[67] with the big losers believing in the old ways and *The Attorneys* depicting venal Moslem courts. Of the twentieth-century writers, perhaps most significant are versatile poet and playwright Samed Vurgun (1906–1956), epic novelist Mirza Ibragimov, and playwright Dzhafar Dzhabardi.

EXTERNAL RELATIONS

The republic has had significant historical ties with Iran and Turkey. Since 1920 Turkey's relationship with Azerbaidzhan

has been confined largely to serving as haven for a small number of exiles.[68] During World War II "Turkish army officers, many of them born and raised in the Caucasus or Azerbaidzhan, were denied permission by the Turkish government to volunteer for the German armed forces." [69] In the postwar period there has been little direct contact, although Turkish Prime Minister Demirel visited Baku in 1966, "receiving a rousing welcome which amounted to a political demonstration." [70] Turkish-Soviet relations, improving since 1953, are now cordial.

From 1909 to 1914 and from 1941 to 1946 Iranian Azerbaidzhan was controlled by Russia. World War II occupation was prolonged by one year when a separatist movement supported by Soviet troops (Azerbaidzhanis, for the most part) controlled the region.[71] U.S. diplomatic pressure and lack of grassroots support spelled failure for the separatists, despite considerable popular animosity to the Teheran government.[72] Since 1946 all has been quiet with little contact and the Soviets have "reinforced the Iranian frontier with a complicated system of electric wires and barbed wires." [73]

The Soviet Union and Iran have had "correct relations" in recent years. Soviet influence there has increased slightly since the all-time low in the post-Mossadegh period. Azerbaidzhan's ties with coreligionists in the Central Asian republics are aided

---

64 *Bak. rab.* (April 28), 1972: 2ff. Translated in *JPRS Translations on USSR Political and Sociological Affairs* (May 25), 1972: 250.

65 Olkhovskii, 1948: 264.

66 The early twentieth-century satirical journal *Molla Nasreddin* was highly praised in Turkey and is remembered today.

67 This play has interesting similarities with Ben Jonson's masterpiece of the same name, although there is no clear evidence of a direct relationship. A translation by Guy le Strange is in *The Journal of the Royal Asiatic Society* (1886): 103–123.

68 Mostly former Pan-Turanists and intellectuals from Central Asia and the Caucasus. Munich also has a contingent which in the past has reportedly been encouraged by western intelligence agencies.

69 Vali, 1971: 172; Hostler, 1957: 171–177.

70 Vali, 1971: 179.

71 "Soviet writers treat this as a spontaneous movement on the part of the people in which the Soviet Government played no part whatever." *Historians of the Middle East*, 1962: 385. (See Ivanov, 1952.) Best Western and Persian accounts are Avery, 1965; Lenczowski, 1949; Rostow, *Middle East Journal* (Winter), 1956; and Pasyān, 1948.

72 The government has always discouraged the Azerbaidzhani language and often has neglected the area's economic needs. Perhaps the most specific grievance is that Iranian Azerbaidzhan gets little return on the taxes it pays to Teheran.

73 Medvedev, 1971: 247. Several informants have reported that the Iranian border with Central Asia is less tightly guarded and that Turkmen wander back and forth in certain areas.

by increasing use of Russian, but the historical and economic links are not strong.

Azerbaidzhan is also used by the Soviets as a showpiece in dealings with the Middle East and Third World, and occasional delegations visit Baku.[74]

Media

LANGUAGE DATA

Azerbaidzhani, Osman, and Turkmen belong to the southern branch of Altaic languages. Since the relationship of Azerbaidzhani to Osman Turkish is about as close as Danish to Norwegian, Turks and Azerbaidzhanis can communicate with careful speech. They can read each other's prose without much difficulty in spite of the different alphabets (Cyrillic and Latin, respectively) and twentieth-century divergences in lexical borrowings.

Among Turkish languages, Azerbaidzhani is next to Osman and Uzbek in number of native speakers, with roughly 4.3 million in the USSR, 100,000 in Iraq, and 4 million in Iran.[75] All dialects are mutually intelligible, though heavy Russianization of the technical vocabulary of Soviet Azerbaidzhani would not be well understood in Iran.

The USSR's Azerbaidzhanis enjoy a well-adapted Cyrillic alphabet, much more suitable than Arabic for this vowel-harmony language.[76] In 1922 the USSR dropped Arabic script for Azerbaidzhani and, after 15 years of Latin script, switched to Cyrillic in 1937. As far as phonetic fit is concerned, the present alphabet is one of the most successful for a Turkic language.[77] Within the USSR the Academy of the Azerbaidzhani Language has handled technical language problems and "issued normative rulings to preserve the purity of the language." [78] Of course, Russian loan words (e.g., *pivo* [beer], *poyezd* [train]) are numerous, while the Arabo-Persianized form of the language, spoken in Iran and written everywhere before 1920, has faded away.

Azerbaidzhani is gaining strength. From 1959 to 1970 the percentage of Azerbaidzhanis speaking their native language rose from 97.6% to 98.2%[79] and of these in 1970 only 16.6% spoke Russian as a second language.[80] In recent years various measures have been taken to ensure use of Russian. In 1970 teaching of Russian was introduced everywhere in the republic from the first grade on, and several steps have been taken to improve language teaching[81] and make language learning more popular.

The resilience of Azerbaidzhani is all the more surprising when one considers that "the language of commerce, politics, and

74 For a typical example see *Bak. rab.* (May 5), 1972. See also *JPRS* (June 6), 1972: 254, which describes Aliyev's reception of a delegation of the Syrian Committee of Afro-Asian Solidarity. *Survey* (January), 1968, has an article by Geoffrey Wheeler which in part analyzes Third World–Moslem–Russian contacts.

75 The published volumes for Iran's most recent census (1966) do not include ethnic background or native language materials. Iran, in general, discourages Azerbaidzhani. See *Iran Census* of 1966. On Azeris, see Cottam, 1964; Avery, 1965; and Lenczowski, 1949.

76 Arabic script is not well equipped to indicate short vowels and rounded vowels, both plentiful in Azerbaidzhani.

77 Perhaps the principal graphemic shortcoming is that "the Azeri language has acquired a form in which it is wholly impossible to incorporate many Russian and international terms in their Russian form. Sometimes cases of overcompensation for Russian changing of h to g in foreign names occurs. Thus we get Holan Heights and Hunnar Jarring." Nissman, *RLD* (February 11), 1971.

78 Householder and Mansour, 1965; Menges, 1968.

79 Including 98.9% of the Azerbaidzhanis living in Azerbaidzhan SSR.

80 See Table 9.1 for details. Note especially that only 27.2% of Azerbaidzhanis living outside their titular republic claim Russian as second language.

81 *Uchitelskaya gazeta* (July 18), 1972, criticizes the poor language laboratory facilities and says that "at present there are only two people in the entire republic with an academic degree in the methodology of teaching Russian." See *Bak. rab.* (December 8), 1972: 4, and (January 6), 1973 for articles documenting positive response to feedback on language education techniques.

Table 9.1

Native and Second Languages Spoken by Azerbaidzhanis

(in thousands)

No. Azerbaidzhanis Residing			SPEAKING AS NATIVE LANGUAGE						SPEAKING AS SECOND LANGUAGE[a]	
			Azerbaidzhani		% Point Change 1959–1970	Russian		% Point Change 1959–1970	Russian 1970	Other Languages of Peoples of USSR 1970[b]
	1959	1970	1959	1970		1959	1970			
in Azerbaidzhan SSR	2,494 (100%)	3,777 (100%)	2,446 (98.1%)	3,741 (98.9%)	+0.8	20 (0.79%)	28 (.75%)	−0.04	564 (14.9%)	56 (1.5%)
in other Soviet republics	445 (100%)	603 (100%)	424 (95.1%)	567 (94.1%)	−1.0	16 (3.7%)	29 (4.8%)	+1.1	164 (27.2%)	53 (3.8%)
Total	2,940 (100%)	4,380 (100%)	2,870 (97.6%)	4,301 (98.2%)	+0.6	36 (1.2%)	57 (1.3%)	+0.1	727 (16.6%)	109 (2.5%)

Sources: *Itogi 1959*: tables 53, 54; *Itogi 1970*: IV: 20, 263.

[a] No data available for 1959, since no questions regarding command of a second language were asked in the 1959 census.

[b] Including Azerbaidzhani, if not the native language.

advancement in Russian," [82] that Russian is continually promoted, and that pupils who go on to secondary education often move to Russian schools. But, between the fifth to eighth and ninth to eleventh years, the drop in attendance at schools in the republic is from 319,000 to 72,000, and those who do not continue are less exposed to the Russian language, which may help account for the persistence of Azerbaidzhani.

LOCAL MEDIA

In 1971 the Azerbaidzhan SSR published 115 newspapers with total circulation of 2,192,000. Ninety-one were in Azerbaidzhani (Azeri), though by far the most important party organ, *Bakinskii rabochii*, was in Russian. Average circulation of Azerbaidzhani newspapers was 1,781,000, yielding the low saturation figure of 47.7 copies per 1,000 native speakers.[83] Other than *Bakinskii rabochii*, the most significant newspapers are *Aberbaichan Kanchlari* [*Youth of Azerbaidzhan*], appearing thrice weekly, and ·*Kommunist*, issued six times weekly. Both are in Azerbaidzhani.

The republic prints 29 magazines, including 23 in Azerbaidzhani, comprising 97% of the total circulation of 950,000.[84] *Azerbaidzhan*, devoted to both local and international literature, has expanded rapidly in recent years,[85] printing 66,323 copies per month in early 1973. Typical recent issues include the works of foreign writers such as Robert Burns, a selection of contemporary Third World literature, some Russian pieces, and dozens of short compositions by Azerbaidzhanis. All material is in Azerbaidzhani, and the tone is quite sophisticated.

Considerably smaller is *Literaturnyi Azerbaidzhan*, journal of the Azerbaidzhan SSR Union of Writers, entirely in Russian.[86] While there are numerous technical journals, especially ones relating to the oil industry, the most widespread science magazine is *Elm ve Khayat* [*Science and Life*], an Azerbaidzhani version of *Popular Science*. *Kend Khayaty* [*Country Life*] is a technical journal devoted to advanced agricultural techniques. Other well-known journals include *Azerbaichan Gadyny* [*Women of Azerbaidzhan*], popular illustrated; *Azerbaichan Kommunisti* [*Communists of Azerbaidzhan*], political; *Kirpi* [*Hedgehog*], satirical fortnightly published by the *Kommunist* newspaper; and *Pioner*, a youth magazine.[87]

Since, in terms of circulation, 81% of newspapers and 97% of magazines are in Azerbaidzhani, one might conclude that news, especially international news,[88] is less available to Azerbaidzhani readers than non-news subjects.

In 1971 the sluggish book industry put out 430 Russian and 802 Azerbaidzhani titles, with copies printed amounting to 1,971,000 and 9,889,000 respectively.[89] These totals are small relative to those of other republics; Azerbaidzhan's 2.38 books printed per capita surpasses only Tadzhikistan and Belorussia. Libraries, however, are adequately stocked, with 21,164,000 books.

Electronic media enjoy relatively greater popularity and, while number of sets per capita (14.8 radios per 100; 10.1 television sets per 100)[90] is lower than Georgia's, they have considerable impact. The high birth rate and low median age mean that adults have a higher number of radios per capita than the figures imply. Also, Azerbaidzhan does not have to cope with Georgia's diversity of languages. Sitting at home and listening to the radio evenings is a national

---

82 *New York Times* (December 13), 1972. The article also notes that major public speeches are delivered in Russian.

83 These figures are from *Pechat' 1971*: 96, 159, 188. For other data see *Europa Yearbook*, 1972: I: 1,284, or *Nar. obraz.*, 1971: 370.

84 Much larger figures are given in other sources than *Pechat'*, but these seem to define "magazine/journal" differently.

85 1964 circulation was 14,300; 1968 was 25,300; 1970, 50,000; 1973, 66,323. In addition, the price was recently lowered from 50 to 25 kopecks. Data taken from individual issues.

86 Circulation is only 3,820 though many writers are Azerbaidzhanis. This suggests that only a small number of Azerbaidzhani native speakers read Azerbaidzhani and Russian literature in Russian.

87 All are in Azerbaidzhani; published monthly unless otherwise noted.

88 *Bakinskii rabochii* has most of the international news.

89 *Pechat' 1971*: 96. In 1963, 976 Azerbaidzhani titles were published and 8,357,000 copies were printed. *SSSR v tsifrakh*, 1968: 375.

90 *Nar. khoz. 1972*: 585, 591.

pastime.[91] Two radio programs are broadcast from approximately 7:30 A.M. to midnight in Russian, Azerbaidzhani, and Armenian, featuring a mix of popular Azerbaidzhani melodies and classical music. In addition, the USSR has not jammed the Iranian and Turkish state radios since 1964, and Azerbaidzhanis receive their programs well.

Since 1956 TV viewers have had two programs. The first, televised from 9:55 A.M. to 12:00 or 1:00 P.M. and from 5:30 P.M. to midnight, is mostly in Azerbaidzhani with, occasionally, sizeable amounts in Russian.[92] Favored subjects are news, films, and concerts. The second program, relayed from Moscow and entirely in Russian, operates from 10 A.M. to 1:00 P.M. (sometimes through the afternoons) and from late afternoon to about 1:00 A.M. No foreign programs can be received; the nearest Turkish relay station, in Erzurum, is much too far away.

The cinema lags behind, with Azerbaidzhan ranking last among Soviet republics in movie attendance per person and last in number of seats in movie theaters per capita.[93] The 2,004 stationary and mobile theaters have 215,000 places—140,000 in cities and 75,000 in rural areas. In 1971 attendance was 57 million.[94]

EDUCATIONAL INSTITUTIONS

Since 1959 the republic has had obligatory eight-year education, and in 1966 educational policy makers felt confident enough to shift the emphasis to universal secondary education.

Still, in 1972, 23% of those enrolled in eight-year schools left without completing

their studies, and 60% of girls in the Akhsuiansk, Dzhalilabadsk, Kelbadzharsk, Lachinsk, and Leriksk districts received no secondary education at all.[95] A sharp drop in enrollment still occurs between the fifth and eighth year and between the ninth and eleventh year, with only 21.6% of rural students continuing beyond the eighth year.[96] These difficulties notwithstanding, the 1970 literacy rate in the republic was 99.8 for men and 99.5 for women.

In 1970–1971 school facilities were used by 1,503,000 students, with 71,000 in 79 special secondary establishments and 100,000 in higher institutions (see Table 9.4).[97] Recent breakdowns by nationality or language are not available,[98] but figures for women show that they constitute 33% of Azerbaidzhani students and 37% of the republic's students.[99]

Though there are complaints about teacher shortages and unfulfilled construction plans,[100] the number of students in higher institutions has increased rapidly— from 36,000 in 1960 to 100,000 in 1970.

In 1971 Kirov University, the Azerbaidzhan state university, had 11,530 students at its 12 faculties.[101] Besides an observatory and 30 laboratories, the university has a library of 1,500,000 books and since 1955 has published *Uchenye Zapiski* [*Scholarly Notes*] on many subjects. Its faculty has included such eminent scholars as philologist Ya. Marr, orientalist V. V. Bathold, and chemist Mamedaliev.

---

91 The legacy of an illiterate past often lingers on after literacy. Oral expression is still preferred, especially among elder people, and Azerbaidzhan does not have the great literary tradition of its neighbors. Throughout the Near East, printed media are weaker than audio-visual.

92 See *Bak. rab.* for sample schedules. With a special adapter it is now possible to listen in two languages. This could be important in promoting future bilingualism.

93 Azerbaidzhanis see 11 movies per capita per year; the USSR average is 19 per year. *Nar obraz.*, 1971: 327.

94 *BSE, Yezhegodnik*, 1972: 102.

---

95 *Bak. rab.* (November 5), 1972.

96 *Nar. obraz.*, 1971: 82–83.

97 *Nar. khoz.* 1972: 592. See also *Bak. rab.* (November 5), 1972, for later estimate. Figures given in *Nar. obraz.*, 1971: 38, are somewhat lower, but those on p. 27 are more inclusive and higher.

98 See *Nar. obraz.*, 1971: 196, for total number of Azerbaidzhanis in higher education and special secondary schools (listed by nationality but not by republic).

99 In 1960 figures were 28% and 34%, respectively. In Azerbaidzhan SSR, Russian women were 51% of the Russian school population. For the Armenian community in Azerbaidzhan the figure is 49%. *Nar. obraz.*, 1971: 200. See also *New York Times* (December 13), 1971; *Bak. rab.* (March 14), 1972; and Aliyev's speech of March 1971.

100 There have also been charges of nepotism, indifference, poor language training, and widespread cheating on entrance exams.

101 It had about 600 graduate students. For a full breakdown, consult *Nar. obraz.*, 1971: 164. See also Table 9.4.

Table 9.2

Publications in Azerbaidzhan SSR

Language of Publication	Year	NEWSPAPERS[a]			MAGAZINES			BOOKS & BROCHURES		
		No.	Per Issue Circulation (1,000)	Copies/100 in Language Group[e]	No.	Per Issue Circulation (1,000)	Copies/100 in Language Group[e]	No. Titles	Total Volume (1,000)	Books & Brochures/100 in Language Group[e]
Russian	1959	19	213	33.0	N.A.	N.A.	N.A.	283	2,243	347.7
	1971	13	339	56.5	4	18	3.0	430	1,971	328.5
Azeri	1959	87	466	18.9	N.A.	N.A.	N.A.	837	7,890	320.8
	1971	91[b]	1,781	47.7	23[b]	921	24.7	802	9,889	264.8
Minority Languages	1959	10[c]	41	N.A.	N.A.	N.A.	N.A.	9	38	N.A.
	1971	11	72	10.6	2	11	1.6	12	72	10.7
Foreign Languages	1959	0	0	0	N.A.	N.A.	N.A.	(15)[d]	(115)	N.A.
	1971	0	0	0	0	0	0	(28)[d]	(283)	N.A.
All Languages	1959	116	720	19.5	18	157	4.2	1,144[d]	10,286	278.2
	1971	115	2,192	42.8	29	950	18.6	1,269[d]	12,216	238.7

Source: *Pechat' 1971*: 160, 189.

[a] 1970 figures do not include kolkhoz newspapers.

[b] Figure includes periodicals published in both Azerbaidzhani and Russian editions.

[c] This figure may include publication in non-Soviet languages.

[d] Book totals as given in *Pechat'* usually differ from totals in language categories. Indication is that books are published in other languages, but no data is given. Figures in parentheses are the presumed production of books based on this discrepancy.

[e] Includes all native speakers of the language. 1970 language groups:

Azerbaidzhani—Number of Azerbaidzhanis speaking Azerbaidzhani natively =3,734,100.

Russian—Total number native Russian speakers (estimate 600,000).

Table 9.3

Electronic Media and Films in Azerbaidzhan SSR

YEAR	RADIO					TELEVISION			MOVIES	
	No. Stations	No. Wired Sets (1,000)	Sets/100 Population	No. Wireless Sets (1,000)	Sets/100 Population	Total No. Stations	No. sets (1,000)	Sets/100 Population	Seats (1,000)	Seats/100 Population
1960	N.A.	330[a]	8.3[d]	482[a]	12.1[c]	N.A.	68[a]	1.7[c]	126[b]	3.1[d]
1970	N.A.	450[a]	8.6[d]	758[a]	14.5[c]	8	493[a]	9.4[c]	215[b]	4.1[d]
1971	N.A.	464[d]	8.7[d]	788[d]	14.8[c]	N.A.[e]	539[c]	10.1[c]	N.A.	N.A.

[a] Source: *Transport i svyaz' SSR,* 1972: 296–298.
[b] Source: *Nar. obraz.,* 1971: 325.
[c] Source: *Nar. khoz.,* 1972: 572, 578.
[d] Computed from data cited above ([b] and [e]).
[e] Two TV stations originating programming were in Azerbaidzhan in 1972.

Table 9.4

Selected Data on Education in Azerbaidzhan SSR (1971)

		PER 1,000 POPULATION	% OF TOTAL
All schools			
number of schools	4,775		
number of students	1,503,000	282.	
Newly opened elementary, incomplete secondary, and secondary schools			
number of schools	106		
number of student places	35,300	6.6	
Secondary special schools			
number of schools	78		
number of students	70,600	13.2	
Institutions of higher education			
number of institutions	13		
number of students	100,000	18.8	
Universities			
number of universities	1		
number of students			
total	11,530		
day students	4,835		41.9
evening students	2,930		25.4
correspondence students	3,765		32.66
newly admitted			
total	2,316		
day students	1,062		45.8
evening students	553		23.8
correspondence students	701		30.2
graduated			
total	1,878		
day students	911		48.5
evening students	456		24.2
correspondence students	511		27.2
Graduate students			
total number	1,885	0.4	
in scientific research institutions	1,235		
in universities	650		
Number of persons with (in 1970) higher or secondary (complete and incomplete) education			
per 1,000 individuals, 10 years or older	471		
per 1,000 individuals employed in national economy	674		
Number of workers graduated from professional-technical schools	32,300	6.0	

Source: *Nar. khoz. 1972*: 108, 438, 581, 589, 590, 592.

Among other respected higher institutions are Azizbekov Institute of Oil and Chemistry, with students from oil-producing regions of Russia as well as from the Middle East; Akhundov Institute of Languages; Lenin Pedagogical Institute; Hadjibekov Conservatory; and N. Narimanov Medical Institute. About 1,000 foreign students study at Azerbaidzhan's higher institutions.

CULTURAL AND SCIENTIFIC INSTITUTIONS

The Azerbaidzhan Academy of Sciences, founded in 1945, embraces 31 affiliated institutions with 3,691 workers.[102] Its publications include *Izvestia* (in Russian and Azerbaidzhani), *Doklady*, and *Azerbaidzhanskii khimicheskii zhurnal*.

Overall, Azerbaidzhan has more than 130 scientific research institutions manned by 16,600 scientific workers.[103] Primary concerns are geologic mapping and physical

geography, such petrochemical problems as oil composition analysis and extraction techniques, synthetic rubber technology, and semiconductor work in physics. Perhaps best known and most respected is the Institut Nefti i Khimii [Oil and Chemistry Institute] in Baku,[104] with a library of 100,000 books, seven facilities, and a branch in Sumgait.

Azerbaidzhan's scientific establishment is behind neighboring Georgia, which has 25% more doctors of science and scientific workers.[105] First Secretary Aliyev criticized the scientific establishment in March 1971, calling for "elimination of the obscurity characteristic of their plans" and citing "shortcomings in the training of scientific cadres."

Cultural facilities (38 museums, 12 theaters, and 2,004 public libraries) are concentrated in Baku. This is hardly surprising since Baku is home of at least nine higher educational facilities, most of the intelligentsia, and half of the republic's urban population.

---

102 Most recent creation, in 1971, was a Social Science Center.
103 *Azerbaidzhan*, 1971: 94.

104 American experts, however, have been critical of Baku's applied technology. Ebel, 1961: 31, 54ff.
105 *Nar. obraz.*, 1971: 245. For a 1963 breakdown of scientific workers and doctors by nationality, see Nadzhafov, 1970: 173.

Table 9.5

Selected Data on Scientific and Cultural Facilities and Personnel in Azerbaidzhan SSR (1971)

Population: 5,326,000

Academy of Sciences		*Number of persons working in*	
number of members	93	*education and culture*	
number of scientific institutions		total	163,000
affiliated with academy	31	number per 1,000 population	30.6
total number of scientific workers	3,691		
		Number of persons working in science	
Museums		*and scientific services*	
number of museums	38	total	39,000
attendance	1,053,000	number per 1,000 population	7
attendance per 1,000 population	197.7		
		Number of public libraries	3,015
Theaters		number of books and magazines	
number of theaters	12	in public libraries	23,590,000
attendance	1,367,000		
attendance per 1,000 population	256.7	*Number of clubs*	2,214

Source: *Nar. khoz. 1972*: 106, 451, 589.

National Attitudes

REVIEW OF FACTORS FORMING NATIONAL ATTITUDES

Perhaps the most important factor in formation of national attitudes is that traditionally Azerbaidzhan was Moslem and tied to the Near East, especially Persia, until the twentieth century. National identity was heavily dependent on a Persian cultural heritage and a Persian (Shiite) sect of Islam. Even the traditional pilgrimages were more often made to Iran (to Ardabile or Meshad) than to Mecca. The literate read and wrote in Persian until the late eighteen hundreds and foreign travelers would refer to Azerbaidzhanis as Persians (or occasionally Tatars).[106]

From 1875 to 1920 Turkish influence grew, but it was cut off before establishing deep roots. Russia, not previously linked to Azerbaidzhan, has been most powerful source of influence ever since. The result is that the republic has a truncated Near Eastern history with a Russian-Soviet capstone. Party-oriented intellectuals are aware of this unstable combination and compensate by overemphasizing the cultural tradition of the past 100 years and treating the earlier national history as independent of Iran. Turkishness is stressed, but an independent Azerbaidzhani Turkishness, distinct from that of Turkey or Central Asia. In fact, however, the people, in contrast to Georgians and Armenians, do not have a single national, historical, or cultural tradition clearly their own.

In the early twentieth century, Islam was still the dominant political and social force outside Baku; for the previous ten centuries it had wielded an overwhelming influence on all Azerbaidzhanis. Today, it lingers in many lesser forms—limited role of women, positive attitude toward individual enterprise, early marriage of women, preference for sons, resistance to change, low intermarriage with Christians, choice of names, and many other customs.

As Islam disappears, the external orientation may be more and more toward Turkey, the linguistic and ethnic relative. The Azerbaidzhanis of Iran are firmly separate and the Iranian government has as little interest as the Soviets in formation of a national Azerbaidzhani state. Educated Azerbaidzhanis are once again adrift, cut off politically from Iranian Azerbaidzhanis, separated from Turkey by a different history and religious denomination, and not yet prepared to be a totally cooperative part of the USSR.[107]

Economics has significantly changed the national attitude. Azerbaidzhanis now have a true urban proletariat, a large number of workers with specialized training, and an industrialized, diversified economy. Half of the country is urbanized; the capital city Baku constitutes one quarter of the republic's population. Women are an important factor in the labor force, and education is universal. The steady rise of real income and moderate increase of consumer goods have probably kept abreast of rising expectation. This economic progress has defused nationalism to some degree. Language has also affected attitudes. Use of the Cyrillic alphabet, importation of Russian vocabulary, and mandatory use of Russian in certain situations have slowly directed Azerbaidzhan toward bilingualism, encouraging the people to identify modernization with Russian culture and values. In view of the weak literary-historical tradition, it was not unreasonable to expect that the Azerbaidzhani language would lose strength; yet, startlingly, it gained between 1959 and 1970.[108]

Demographic influences will be increasingly important in the future. If rapid rural growth continues, the population squeeze may raise tensions and underemployment problems, forcing large-scale migrations to the city.

---

106 Kazemzadeh, 1951: 329.

107 Personal observation.
108 See earlier section.

BASIC VIEWS OF SCHOLARS ON
NATIONAL ATTITUDES

Unlike their "cunning" Armenian and "flamboyant" Georgian neighbors, Azerbaidzhanis have been little stereotyped or even described by travelers and scholars. Rather, a diffuse, generalized picture emerges of a stolid Turk with a patina of Russian-Soviet values rather than Ataturk's. Writers like W. E. D. Allen, with much to say about Georgians, talk of Baku and its hinterland without commenting on the people.[109] Perhaps this testifies to the lack of a dynamic Azerbaidzhani national tradition in the eyes of Western observers.

Soviet publications and modern Western journalists provide us with a sketchy picture of the people, who appear taciturn, with strong family ties, reacting neither negatively nor positively to change. Like other Transcaucasians, Azerbaidzhanis have been accused of evading financial *ukases* (decrees) of the state. In recent years there have been numerous citations of bribery (to get jobs and university admission),[110] violation of price listings, and "absence of order in the farmers' markets where marketeers and speculators operate freely." [111]

A man interviewed by the *New York Times* boasted that "as a taxi driver he collects a minimum of 20 rubles to meet the State quota for a State owned taxi, and pockets the rest." A bribe or a friend was needed to get the job. Bribery for better medical service is also documented.[112] Nonetheless, taken all in all, Azerbaidzhani wheeling and dealing cannot match that of the Georgians.[113]

Especially in the countryside, traditionalism persists—in continuance of private enterprise, limited roles and early marriages for women, reluctance to migrate, and passive resistance to state employment.[114]

---

109 Allen and Muratoff, 1953; Marvin, 1884.
110 *New York Times* (August 12), 1969 and (December 13) 1971. See also *Bak. rab.* (August 7), 1969, and (November 5, February 11), 1972, for examples.
111 *Bak. rab.* (August 7), 1969.
112 *New York Times* (December 8), 1971.
113 See chapter on Georgia.
114 *Pravda* (June 26), 1972, had a particularly illustrative article on this passive resistance. *JPRS* (August 22), 1972: CCLXXVI: 14–17.

Above all, Islamic customs color rural activities, and even atheistic urbanites still discuss the effects of Islam on society.

R. N. Frye observes that Azerbaidzhanis enjoy listening to Istanbul Turkish and being reminded of their Turkishness.[115] Foreign observers have also noted the (male) penchant for backgammon, coffeehouses, and radio—all suggestive of Turkey or Iranian Azerbaidzhan.[116]

Such fragmentary evidence suggests that many people would prefer a regional autonomy permitting more individual enterprise, certain Islamic customs, and a degree of Turkish fraternity.

RECENT MANIFESTATIONS OF
NATIONALISM

In recent years no outbreaks of nationalism have been documented by Western sources, Russian official media, or *samizdat*. Feelings have expressed themselves only in continuing passive resistance to religious and social change on the Soviet mode. The evidence suggests that the Azerbaidzhani historical and cultural legacy is at best mildly conducive to future nationalistic activity. This heritage is most visible in the negative attitude toward cooperative enterprise, full equality for women, atheism, and the multinational state. In the next decade some nationalistic trends are possible, but hardly inevitable.

If nationalism is posited as an active force, we can explain why it has not surfaced by the following arguments: (1) *samizdat*, for the most part, originates in Baltic, Moscow, Leningrad, and Ukrainian intellectual circles representing the mainstream of current Soviet thought; (2) neighboring Daghestan has had nationalistic revolts (1968) but does not have *samizdat*; (3) Azerbaidzhan is a heavily controlled border area, cut off from its Iranian and Turkish compatriots and distant from the rest of the USSR; (4) there is a strong but still latent sense of Turkishness which Turkey cannot encourage; the citizenry, particularly the isolated rural

---

115 Personal interview, May 12, 1973. Frye is Aga Khan Professor of Persian Studies at Harvard University.
116 Numerous personal interviews.

folk, do however label themselves as "Turkis" and respond well to foreigners who speak Osman Turkish (Turkish Prime Minister Demiral was exceptionally well received in 1966); and (5) Aliyev, first secretary of the Communist party and former chief of the security police, found it necessary to remove more than 50 senior government-party officials upon taking office and has sharply criticized the republic's lack of educational, economic, and cultural progress. This house cleaning may have forestalled a nationalistic outbreak.

To shift to the other side and regard Azerbaidzhani nationalism as historically weak, likely to dwindle or disappear in an era of stability, economic progress, and skillfully controlled education, we can state that:

1. Azerbaidzhanis were passive during the long religious crises of the early 1950s while the Kirgiz defended their national tradition vigorously.[117]
2. The Shamil question never meant much in Azerbaidzhan.[118]
3. Refugee movements and VOA broadcasts of the 1950s had little influence.[119] *Azerbaychan*, a monthly review serving as the organ of the Azerbaidzhan National Association, faded after its manager, Fatalibeili, was murdered in 1954.

The noted writer Mehmet Rasulzade, who broadcast for VOA, died in 1955 and could not be replaced with a man of similar stature. And United Caucasus, organ of Committee for Caucasian Independence, was defunct by the early 1960s and always dependent during its life on Western intelligence agency backing. In addition, there is very little, if any, contact between Azerbaidzhan exiles in Turkey, Western Europe, and the United States and their relatives and friends in the USSR.

4. There is no outside "model" for the Azerbaidzhani since Iranian Azerbaidzhan is firmly controlled by Teheran. Soviet Azerbaidzhanis are dimly aware that brethren in Iran have not prospered economically.
5. Nationalism, if it exists, is expressed through a distinctive life style and national pride rather than by political agitation.[120]

Historically, the country has not been unified. Its culture and religion were imported from Iran; its language and ethnic background are Turkish. Twentieth-century influences have been overwhelmingly Russian. Azerbaidzhan in the twentieth century might have joined the Third World's nationalistic movements, but it has been cut off from sources of cultural and national feeling, passively pressured to conform to an anti-Islamic, anti-Near Eastern model, economically transformed and improved, and skillfully guided.

---

117 Bennigsen and Lemercier-Quelquejay, 1967: 215, 216.
118 For full account of the Shamil question consult Tillett, 1969. The author does not, however, try to evaluate the impact of the controversy on Daghestan and Azerbaidzhan. See also Laqueur, 1958: 415–444.
119 Also, they broadcast only 15 minutes a day. Personal communication with Azerbaidzhanis in United States and Turkey by F. Huddle.

120 See "Review of Factors Forming National Attitudes."

REFERENCES

Akhundov, 1955
    Fath 'Ali Akhundzade, *Sochineniya* (Baku: Azer. Gosizdat, 1955).
Aliyarov, 1967
    S. S. Aliyarov, "Chislennost', professional'nyi i natsional'nyi sostav bakinskogo proletariata v period pervoi mirovoi voiny," *Uchenyye zapiski Azerbaidzhanskogo gosudarstvennogo universiteta imeni S. M. Kirova, Seriya istorii i filosofskikh nauk*, Nos. 1, 2 (Baku, 1967).
Allen and Muratoff, 1953
    W. E. D. Allen and Paul Muratoff, *Caucasian Battlefields* (Cambridge: Cambridge University Press, 1953).
Arif, 1971
    Mehmed Arif, *Istoriya Azerbaidzhanskoi literatury* (Baku: Elm, 1971).

Avery, 1965
Peter Avery, *Modern Iran* (New York: Praeger, 1965).

Azerbaidzhan, 1971
Azerbaidzhan, Sovetskii soyuz (series), geograficheskoye opisaniye v 22x tomax (Moscow: Mysl', 1971).

Azerbaidzhan v tsifrakh
Azerbaidzhan v tsifrakh (various years) (Baku: Gosizdat, 1964–1970).

Azerbaidzhanskaya SSR, 1967
Azerbaidzhanskaya SSR, 50 letiyu velikogo oktyabrya (Baku: Statistiki, 1967).

Azerbaijan SSR, 1972
Azerbaijan Soviet Socialist Republic (Moscow: Novosti, 1972).

Bak. rab.
Bakinskii rabochii (Baku).

Bennigsen and Lemercier-Quelquejay, 1967
Alexandre Bennigsen and Chantal Lemercier-Quelquejay, *Islam in the Soviet Union* (New York and London: Praeger and Pall Mall Press, 1967).

BSE, 1970
Bol'shaya Sovetskaya entsiklopediya, 1st ed. (Moscow: Bol'shaya Sovetskaya entsiklopediya, 1970).

BSE, Yezhegodnik, 1972
Bol'shaya Sovetskaya entsiklopediya, Yezhegodnik (Moscow: Bol'shaya Sovetskaya entsiklopediya, 1972).

Campbell, 1968
Robert W. Campbell, *The Economics of Soviet Oil and Gas* (Baltimore: Johns Hopkins Press, 1968).

Conquest, 1968
Robert Conquest, *The Great Terror* (New York: Macmillan, 1968).

Cottam, 1964
Richard W. Cottam, *Nationalism in Iran* (Pittsburgh: University of Pittsburgh Press, 1964).

Curtis, 1911
William Elroy Curtis, *Around the Black Sea* (New York: Hodder & Stoughton, 1911).

Diplomats, 1963
Gordon Craig and Felix Gilbert, eds., *The Diplomats* (New York: Atheneum, 1963) paperback.

Dubner, 1931
A. Dubner, *Bakinskii proletariat v gody revolyutsii (1917–1920 gg.)* (Baku, 1931).

Ebel, 1961
Robert Ebel, *The Petroleum Industry of the Soviet Union* (New York: American Petroleum Institute, 1961).

Economic History of Iran, The, 1971
Economic History of Iran, The, Charles Issawi, ed. (Chicago: University of Chicago Press, 1971).

Europa Yearbook, 1972
Europa Yearbook (London: Europa Publications, 1972).

Hadjibeyli, 1959
Djeyhun Hadjibeyli (Khadzhibeili), *Anti-Islamistkaya propaganda i yeye metody v Azerbaidzhane* (Munich: Institute for Study of USSR, 1959).

Historians of the Middle East, 1962
Historians of the Middle East, Bernard Lewis and P. M. Holt, eds. (London: Oxford University Press, 1962).

Hostler, 1957
Charles W. Hostler, *Turkism and the Soviets* (London: George Allen & Unwin, 1957).

Householder and Mansour, 1965
Fred W. Householder and Lofti Mansour, *Basic Course in Azerbaijani* (New York: Mouton, 1965).

Itogi 1959
Itogi vsesoyuznoi perepisi naseleniya 1959 goda SSSR (Moscow: Gosstatizdat, 1962).

Itogi 1970
Itogi vsesoyuznoi perepisi naseleniya 1970 goda, vol. IV (Moscow Statistika, 1972–1973).

Ivanov, 1952
M. S. Ivanov, *Ocherk istorii Irana* (Moscow: Gosstatizdat, 1952).

JPRS
Joint Publications Research Service. Translations on USSR Political and Sociological Affairs (published by U.S. Department of Commerce).

Kazemzadeh, 1951
Firuz Kazemzadeh, *The Struggle for Transcaucasia (1917–1921)* (New York, 1951).

Kharmandarian, 1969
S. V. Kharmandarian, *Lenin i stanovleniye zakavkazskoi federatsii 1921–1923* (Yerevan: Izd-vo Aiastan, 1969).

Kompartiya Azerbaidzhana, 1970
Kommunisticheskaya Partiya Azerbaidzhana v tsifrakh (Baku: Azerbaidzhan Gosstatizdat, 1970).

Laqueur, 1958
Walter Laqueur, ed., *The Middle East in Transition* (New York: Praeger, 1958) [especially Geoffrey Wheeler, "Recent Soviet Attitudes toward Islam": 370–378; H. Carrère d'Encausse, "The Background of Soviet Policy in the Middle East": 388–398; and Paul Henze, "The Shamil Problem": 415–444].

Larin, 1909
Yurii Larin, *Rabochiye neftyanogo dela* (Moscow, 1909).

Lenczowski, 1949
George Lenczowski, *Russia and the West in Iran: 1918–1948* (Ithaca: Cornell University Press, 1949).

Mamedov, 1960
Shadabek F. Mamedov, *Mirza Fatali Akhundov* (Moscow: Znaniye, 1960).

Marvin, 1884
Charles Marvin, *The Region of the Eternal Fire* (London: W. H. Allen, 1884).

Medvedev, 1971
Zhores A. Medvedev, *The Medvedev Papers* (London: Macmillan, 1971).

Menges, 1968
C. Menges, *The Turkic Languages and Peoples* (Wiesbaden: Harrassowitz, 1968).

Nadzhafov, 1970
A. Nadzhafov, *Sblizheniye kul'tur sotsialisticheskikh natsii* (Baku: Azerbaidzhan Gosizdat, 1970).

Nar. khoz. 1970
Narodnoye khozyaistvo SSSR v 1970 godu (Moscow: Statistika, 1971).

Nar khoz. 1972
Narodnoye khozyaistvo SSSR 1922–1972, Yubileinyi statisticheskii yezhegodnik (Moscow: Statistika, 1972).

Nar. obraz., 1971
Narodnoye obrazovaniye, nauka i kul'tura v SSSR: statisticheskii sbornik (Moscow: Statistika, 1971).

Olkovskii, 1955
A. V. Olkovskii, *Music under the Soviets* (New York: Praeger, 1955).

Pasyān, 1948
Najaf Pasyān, *Marg būd bar gasht ham būd* (Teheran, 1948)

Pechat' 1970
Pechat' SSSR v 1970 godu (Moscow: Kniga, 1971).

Pipes, 1964
Richard Pipes, *The Formation of the Soviet Union: Communism and Nationalism 1917–1923*, rev. ed. (Cambridge: Harvard University Press, 1964).

Rasulzade, 1938
Mehmed Rasulzade, *Das Problem Aserbeidschan* (Berlin: Verlag Zeitschrift Kurtulusch, 1938).

RLD
Radio Liberty Dispatch (Munich)

SSSR i soyuznye respubliki, 1972
SSSR i soyuznye respubliki (Moscow: Statistika, 1972).

SSSR v tsifrakh 1968
TSSU SSSR, *SSSR v tsifrakh v 1968 godu* (Moscow: Statistika, 1969).

Suny, 1972
Roger G. Suny, *The Baku Commune 1917–1918* (Princeton, N.J.: Princeton University Press, 1972).

Tillett, 1969
Lowell Tillett, *The Great Friendship* (Chapel Hill: University of North Carolina Press, 1969).

Transport i svyaz' SSR, 1972.
Transport i svyaz' SSR (Moscow: Statistika, 1972).

Vali, 1971
Ferenc A. Vali, *Bridge across the Bosporus* (Baltimore: Johns Hopkins University Press, 1971).

Vyshka
Russian language newspaper, CC CP Azerbaidzhan (Baku).

Wheeler, 1960
Geoffrey Wheeler, *Racial Problems in Soviet Muslim Asia* (London: Oxford University Press, 1960).

Part IV

CENTRAL
ASIA

This part includes chapters for the five republics in Central Asia, as that area is defined in this study. (Some specialists would disagree with inclusion of Kazakhstan, regarding it as a transitional area between Central Asia and Siberia rather than as part of Central Asia in the strict sense of the word.) The five nationalities have much in common—ethnic origin, Islamic religion, many historical developments, position of women, demographic and occupational patterns, and, except for the Tadzhiks (whose language is in the Iranian group), Turkic languages, so that they are often able to understand each other's speech.

To help the nonspecialist reader, it may be useful to explain some historical-geographic terms related to Central Asia.

Turkestan: Historically, refers to area of the republics of Tadzhikstan, Turkmenistan, Uzbekistan, and Kirgizstan. Often used also to include Kazakhstan.

Bukhara (also spelled Bokhara): Leading Central Asian city-state until modern times and seat of the khanate of Bukhara, major Central Asian political force in the past five centuries. In prerevolutionary Russia, Bukhara was not administratively part of Turkestan. The label "Bukhara" applies to any area directly controlled by the emir of the Bukharan khanate.

Khiva: Central Asian khanate, a large oasis and environs, rivaling Bukhara throughout the seventeenth to nineteenth centuries, also separate from Turkestan. It was much smaller, less diverse, and less populated than Bukhara, but kept its independence until 1920.

Kokand: One of three khanates in nineteenth-century Central Asia. It has a much shorter history than Bukhara or Khiva, disappearing after 1875. Now the term refers only to the city of Kokand.

Kara-Kalpak: Autonomous region of the Uzbek SSR populated by the Kara-Kalpaks, a distinct Turkish subgroup.

10 | KAZAKHSTAN and THE KAZAKHS

Zev Katz

General Information

TERRITORY

Kazakhstan is second among union republics in territorial size (1,048,305 sq. mi.). It is as large as all of Western Europe. From the mountainous Chinese border in the east, it stretches to the Caspian Sea and the Urals in the west, extending from the Kirgizian steppe in the south through the deserts of Central Asia to the marshes and vast forests of Siberia in the north.[1]

Kazakhstan is generally thought of as a land of endless flat steppe, but the country has also pinewood-covered mountain ranges with peaks up to 16,000 feet high, rocky and hilly deserts, and huge dry plateaus. It is crossed by major rivers like the Irtysh (which empties into the Arctic Ocean) and has landlocked basins with rivers disappearing into the deserts or into huge salt lakes (the Syr'-Darya, for example). Major rivers serve as important transportation routes; others are navigable only in the spring.

Lowlands in the northwestern part of Kazakhstan stretch from the border with Siberia to the edge of the Caspian Sea. Lowest point in the USSR (Batyr canyon, 433 feet below sea level) is here. North of the Caspian Sea, the Kazakh border passes just east of the lower Volga and Volgograd (formerly Stalingrad). Following south, along the Caspian coast, hilly areas jut out onto the Mangyshlak Peninsula. During the 1960s, large oil and gas deposits were discovered here, and the town of Shevchenko was developed. In the southern Ural region, the Kazakh border runs south of the industrial towns of Magnitogorsk and Chelyabinsk, in which immense deposits of iron and copper ores have been discovered. Open-pit mining is carried on in the vicinity of Sarbai and Rudny.[2]

To the east, the border follows along western Siberia and passes south of Omsk,

---

1 *SSSR*, 1967: 538–539; *MSE*, 1959: 351. The area is given as 2,756,000 sq. km. (1,064,097 sq. mi.). There have been several minor territorial transfers between Kazakhstan and its neighbors. *BSE Yezhegodnik*, 1971: 133.

2 Shabad, 1951: 334–364; *Kazakhstan*, 1970, *passim*; *SSSR*, 1967: 533–536.

from which the vast Turgai plateau stretches southward. This is the "virgin lands," formerly steppe, with center in Tselinograd (formerly Akmolinsk). Further, to the southeast, the Kazakhstan border passes through a plateau, cutting across the Altai Mountains where it becomes the Sino-Soviet frontier. In this plateau area is a heavy concentration of coal mining and industry (mainly around Karaganda and Ust' Kamenogorsk).

In the south, Kazakhstan borders on the Turkmen, Uzbek, and Kirgiz union republics. From east to west, the border passes south of the capital of Alma-Ata and north of Frunze, capital of the Kirgiz SSR, and Tashkent, capital of the Uzbek SSR. Then it passes through the Kzyl-Kum desert to reach the Aral Sea. From the west coast of the Aral Sea, the boundary extends in a southwesterly direction, along the Uzbek and Turkmen borders, to the Caspian Sea.

In general, the southeastern parts of the republic are mountainous plateaus while the northern and western parts are flatlands. The rivers supply hydroelectric power. About two thirds of available land is used for pasturage. Black earth is suitable for intensive agriculture in the north. Kazakhstan holds first place in the USSR for proven mineral resources such as chrome, lead, tin, silver, copper, and phosphorus. It also has large deposits of gold, nickel, bauxite, and many other minerals.

The climate is extreme. Summers are very hot in the south and in the north, along the Siberian border, winters are cold and windy. Temperatures range from −49°F. in the north to +113°F in the southern deserts. Average temperatures in January are −4°F. in the north and +23°F. in the south; in July, +68°F. and +86°F., respectively.[3] Growing season in the "virgin lands" lasts for 110–140 days; it is even longer in the south. At Tselinograd annual rainfall is 12 inches, one half during the summer months. At Kzyl-Orda, to the southwest, it is five inches.[4]

The republic is subdivided into 18 provinces, including the capital city, Alma-Ata, as a separate administrative unit. The prov-

inces vary in size and population—from more than 1.5 million persons in the province of Karaganda to 0.25 million in the recently established (1970) Turgai province.[5]

ECONOMY

During the First Five-Year Plan (1929–1933), Kazakhstan became third in the USSR (after the RSFSR and the Ukraine) in overall production and it remains in this position today. It is first in the Soviet Union in production of lead, electricity, and coal, and second in copper and tin. By 1970 overall industrial production was 146 times higher than in 1913, whereas ratio for the USSR as a whole was 92 times.[6] Of working age population, 91% (up from 75% in 1959) were employed in the economy or studying. (This figure excludes housekeeping and private farming.) In 1970 the strength of the labor force was approximately 5.5 million: 4.7 million workers and employees, 0.8 million collective farmers.[7]

Major industries are related to first-stage processing of the republic's natural resources. Sokolovsk-Sarbai ore-refining works (near Rudny), Pavlodar aluminium plant, and Karaganda metal works are typical examples. Kazakhstan is also a major producer of chemicals, especially fertilizers, but basically supplies energy and raw materials to industries located outside its borders: for example, Kazakh coal and ores meet a major part of the needs of heavy industry concentrated in the Russian Urals. Chemicals supply fertilizer factories in other Central Asian republics. Electricity, coal, ores, grain, and oil are exported to burgeoning new industrial areas in Siberia. And, as expected, Kazakhstan is a major supplier of such agricultural products as grain, meat, wool, cotton, and fruit to other parts of the USSR, at the same time depending on importing finished products from other republics. From the RSFSR alone it

---

3 MSE, 1959: 351–353.
4 Kazakhstan, 1970: 41–42, 370.

5 BSE, Yezhegodnik, 1971: 133; Nar. khoz. 1970: 31.
6 Perevedentsev, 1972: 32; Kulichenko, 1972: 234, says 132 times; BSE, Yezhegodnik, 1971: 134.
7 Sovetskii Kazakhstan, 1971: 3; BSE, Yezhegodnik, 1971: 134.

imports half of its needs in woolen and cotton goods, 87% of its watches, and so on.

Trade between Kazakhstan and the rest of the USSR reflects some of the patterns of economic relations between colonial (or underdeveloped) countries and highly developed metropolitan countries. It also fits the classic Marxist (and Leninist) definition of colonial attitudes.[8] Most manufactured goods are neither owned nor produced by Kazakhs. A Soviet survey undertaken in a major newly developed mining town in northern Kazakhstan near the Russian Urals indicated that only 2% of a population of 100,000 were Kazakh. Similarly, only 2% of people employed at the town's ore-concentration complex were Kazakh, but only 10% of Kazakhs were unskilled. One fourth of enrollment in local boarding schools was Kazakh. The author suggested that low representation was due to the fact that this was not a traditional area of Kazakh settlement and people from all over the USSR were imported to work in local mines. This does not explain, however, why non-Kazakhs occupied most important positions in the town. A similar pattern is typical of many new developments in northern Kazakhstan, including those in the "virgin lands" area.[9]

The "virgin lands" fulfill a crucial role in the USSR economy and that of the Kazakh SSR in particular. Until the beginning of the "virgin lands" campaign in 1954, grain harvests in Kazakhstan had been very small. In 1955 the republic produced over 5 million tons of grain, and in 1958 production shot up to 22 million tons, 40% of all grain marketed in the USSR. (Most of the grain is marketed, because the republic's sparsely settled *sovkhozy* do not withhold much for their use, unlike *kolkhozy*, which have large peasant populations with large numbers of livestock to feed.) Grain output has varied: some years have yielded disastrously small harvests due to bad weather and grave mismanagement. Yet in 1972, a year of bad weather, the yield was highest ever—an estimated 27 million tons, or

nearly half as much grain as marketed by all other regions of the USSR together.[10]

During the ninth Five-Year Plan (1971–1975), industrial production in Kazakhstan is scheduled to grow 59%, as compared with 47% for the USSR as a whole. Coal production is slated to increase from 61.5 million tons in 1970 to 90 million tons in 1975 (46%). Production of oil is scheduled to increase from 13 to 30 million tons (130%). Steel output in 1975 will be more than twice that of 1970, and shoe production will increase from 28 million pairs to 35 million (25%). Total production of grain, at 2.5 million tons in 1940, grew to 22 million in 1970 and is to reach the *yearly average* of 25 million by 1975. This amounts to approximately one ninth of total Soviet grain needs. In 1970 electric energy production amounted to about 35 billion kwh, more than the total for a developed country the size of Switzerland. Per capita production was a little lower than in France but higher than in Italy.[11]

Kazakhstan's produced national income increased by 214% between 1960 and 1970, sixth fastest growth rate in the Soviet Union. Indicators of standard of living also advanced significantly during the decade, but not enough to raise the country's ranking among union republics. Savings per capita in 1970 were nearly four times as high as in 1960 (139.58 vs. 35.26 rubles per capita), but Kazakhstan slipped from seventh to ninth place, with a ratio less than half that of Estonia, the thriftiest republic. Trade turnover per capita in 1970 was 557 rubles, more than half that of Estonia (956 rubles) but almost 150 rubles less than that of the RSFSR.[12] In both respects Kazakhstan ranked first among Central Asian republics. In ratio of useful urban living space per urban inhabitant, the country's 12 square yards per person ranked tenth among the republics, but

---

8 *SSSR*, 1967: 540–544; Nove and Newth, 1967: chs. III, IV; Kulichenko, 1972: 230–237; *Nar. khoz. Kazakhstana*, 1968: *passim.*
9 Ye. Dvornikov, "52 Nationalities in a Kazakh Mining Town," *Soviet Life* (October), 1972: 40–43.

10 *Nar. khoz. 1970*: 309–311; 1972 yields from *Radio Liberty Dispatch* (October 25), 1972.
11 Kulichenko, 1972: 237; *Nar. khoz. 1970*: 101, 105, 184, 199, 242, 246, 310; *Soviet Life* (December), 1972: 18, 20.
12 Traditionally, Kazakhs have tended to invest their wealth in personal and domestic ornamentation or in livestock rather than placing it in banks. *Nar. khoz. 1970*: 534, 536, 546, 564, 579.

ahead of all Central Asia except Turk-menia.[13] As can be seen, the overall picture is mixed: some features of an under-developed economy parallel with rapid development.

HISTORY

The Kazakhs emerged in the fifteenth century, a mixture of Turkic tribes who had appeared there in the eighth century and Mongols settled in Central Asia since the thirteenth century. Consequently, they speak a Turkic language and are Moslem by religion, but facial features and much of their way of life are Mongolian. They were organized into tribal-feudal *ordas* [hordes]. Around 1456 a number of these tribes broke off from the declining Golden Horde to form three distinct *ordas*—Great, Middle, and Little—and occupy the territory of present-day Kazakhstan. These groups fought among themselves and with other Asian peoples.

Pressed by the dungans (Moslem Chinese), Khan Abulkhair, leader of the Little Horde, submitted in 1731 to the Rus-sians, pressing eastward into Siberia and Central Asia. Fighting between the Kazakhs and Kalmyks (another nomadic group) weakened both groups and eased extension of Russian control. From 1783 through 1797, however, the Little Horde rose against the Russians. In 1830 the Russians built a fort at Akmolinsk (now Tselinograd) and began to settle their people in the area. The Kazakhs rebelled again under Kenesary Kasymov in 1835. The Russians suppressed this rebellion also, and Kasymov was killed in fighting with the Kirgiz in 1847. The Russian push continued, and in 1853 the Russians built the fortress Verny, the modern Alma-Ata.[14]

By the turn of the century, modernization was under way. A nationalist movement began to develop, led by intellectuals such as Ali Bukeikhanov and Ahmed Baitursun. Although the great majority of Kazakhs re-mained nomadic tribesmen, a considerable number had already begun to cultivate crops and settle on the land. Under the im-pact of Russian capital, spurred by foreign investment and drive, the first modern workshops, factories, railways, and roads were built. In 1910 *Aykan*, first Kazakh newspaper, was published, followed in 1913 by *Kazakh*. In 1913 there were 36,000 workers in Kazakhstan. Few were Kazakhs, however; almost all modern institutions were operated by Europeans (e.g., Russians, Ukrainians, Germans, Jews). For the most part, Kazakhs continued to be ruled by the tribal-feudal nobility, to listen to Moslem mullahs, and to work as herdsmen and peasants. Nevertheless, disintegration of the feudal system had begun. The Kazakh pop-ulation diminished by 9% between 1902 and 1913. By 1914 the number of Russian and Ukrainian settlers in the Kazakh coun-try reached more than 1 million. In some provinces one third of the land was handed over by the tsarist government to the settlers.[15]

At first, it seemed that the Kazakhs would escape World War I, for they were not con-scripted into the tsarist army. Soon, how-ever, they were caught up in war and dis-ruption. In 1916 the tsarist government ordered callup of all males for auxiliary army duty. Kazakhs responded with a gen-eral rebellion under Amangeldy Imanov and Abdulghaffar, directed against Slav settlers in the republic. Although soon suppressed, the revolt caused strong national feelings and desire for liberation from Russian dom-ination, which came into the open in 1917. After the February 1917 revolution in Rus-sia, Kazakhs led by Ali Bukeikhanov de-manded full autonomy and created a national government, adopting the name of Alash Orda. In many cities and areas of Kazakhstan, pro-Bolshevik revolutionary committees and soviets were created, but Great Russian Whites and Orda became predominant. Much fighting was of an eth-

13 *Nar. khoz. 1970:* 10, 546.
14 Bennigsen and Lemercier-Quelquejay, 1967: 6–7. In their opinion, "between the 16th and 18th cen-turies . . . nomad Kazakh tribes . . . had superficially embraced Islam." Also, they list four hordes. But see *SSSR*, 1967: 536; Wheeler, 1964: 20–26; *MSE*, 1959: 354; Pipes, 1964: 84.

15 *MSE*, 1959: 354; Bennigsen and Lemercier-Quelquejay, 1967: 14–15, 24, 46; Pipes, 1964: 81–82; Coates, 1951: chs. 3–4.

nic character, pitting Kazakhs and Kirgiz against Slavic settlers, both Whites and Bolsheviks. In 1919–1920 the Red Army defeated the Whites in Central Asia. Weakened by struggles with the Whites and faced with the growing strength of the Reds, the majority of Alash Orda forces were compelled to recognize Soviet power. Yet some remained active against the Reds into the early 1920s. Dzhangildin, Kazakh chief allied with the Bolsheviks, and Akhmed Baitursun, nationalist leader become communist, were among the new Kazakh Soviet leaders.[16]

On July 10, 1919, Lenin signed a decree creating a revolutionary committee for the "Kirgiz" (Kazakh) territories. On August 26, 1920, an "Autonomous Kirgiz" (Kazakh) Soviet Socialist Republic, within the framework of the RSFSR, was established.[17] it became a union republic (a member of the Soviet Union formally equal to the RSFSR) with acceptance of the Stalin constitution in 1936. From the beginning of its history, leading personnel of the Kazakhstan republic have been almost entirely foreign; Kazakh Bolsheviks were extremely rare. At first, the capital was in Orenburg, Russian Urals; then it was moved to Kzyl Orda, and in 1929 to Alma-Ata, the present site.

During the five years (1916–1920) of general fighting and national social upheaval, the country suffered losses in both population and livestock. Many Kazakhs left with their herds for neighboring Chinese Sinkiang and Afghanistan. Of those remaining, having lost cattle to Slav settlers, White forces, and Red commissars, about 1 million died of starvation during the 1921–1922 famine.[18]

---

16 Pipes, 1964: 51, 81–86, 172–174; Wheeler, 1967: 46–47; BSE, 1953: 332–334; Bennigsen and Lemercier-Quelquejay, 1967: 71–72, 93, 96–97.
17 SSSR, 1967: 538; Pipes, 1964: 172–174; for a record sympathetic to the Soviet version of events, including details on Stalin's role, see Coates, 1951: ch. 5. In order to prevent confusion in their dealings with the Kazakhs and the Russian-Ukrainian Kozaks (Cossacks) living in the southeast of European Russia, Russians referred to Kazakhs as Kirgiz. They called the original Kirgiz tribes Kara-Kirgiz. The Kazakh republic was called Kirgiz until 1925.
18 Pipes, 1964: 172–175; SSSR, 1967: 537–539; BSE, 1953: 335–338; Coates, 1951: ch. 5.

In 1927 Soviet authorities began a series of major moves in Kazakhstan which completely changed its character. Large semi-feudal estates were abolished, with assets transferred to herdsmen and state farms. Collectivization began in 1929 and was completed by 1937, very late in comparison with other areas in the USSR. Forced collectivization caused decimation of herds. The authorities had to proceed cautiously in the outlying mountainous areas but, despite their efforts, Kazakhs continued to migrate abroad with their herds.

Since the end of the 1920s many new projects have been implemented in line with the Five-Year Plans. From the begining, the dual and contradictory character of Soviet modernization has been apparent. On the one hand, it meant economic development, cultural revolution, better health and communication services, and higher standard of living—at least for part of the population. On the other, it meant further centralization in Moscow's hands: loss of autonomy, forcible and sometimes bloody settlement of Kazakh nomads on the land through collectivation, and massive influx of European settlers. Ultimately, this series of events was responsible for changing the way of life, making the Kazakhs a minority in their own republic.

Some top leaders tried to oppose this process and were purged by Moscow for "bourgeois nationalism." Baitursunov was removed in 1925. Ryskulov, who criticized Soviet power for not fulfilling its promises to the Moslems, and other Kazakh Bolshevik leaders of the early period—even opponents of Alash Orda—disappeared in 1927–1928.[19] In the purges of 1937–1939, 18 Kazakh leaders were executed, including Kulumbetov, Eskarev, and Dasvokazov (respectively, chairman of the Executive Committee, deputy prime minister, and secretary of the party in Alma-Ata).

The dual process of modernization and colonialization was speeded up during World War II, when major industrial enterprises, along with large groups of residents

---

19 Among victims of the 1928 purge were also Seyfullin, Mendeshev, and Sadvakasov. See Bennigsen and Lemercier-Quelquejay, 1967: 106–107, 113, 157–160; Conquest, 1967: 95–96.

(Russians, Jews, Germans, Chechens, etc.), were evacuated (or, in some cases, exiled) from western parts of the USSR to Kazakhstan.[20] During World War II, Z. Shayakhmetov, a Kazakh, was appointed first secretary of the Kazakh Communist Party. But by 1954 a Russian, P. Ponomarenko, was appointed in his place, because Kazakhs were again resisting such a large influx of foreigners, this time within the framework of the "virgin lands" campaign, aimed at cultivating the immense steppe of the north. Kazakhstan was also chosen as site for the Soviet equivalent of Cape Kennedy, a cosmodrome for Soviet space launchings. Due to great difficulties encountered with these development projects, Khrushchev sent L. Brezhnev to Kazakhstan (where he was second secretary of the party in 1954 and first secretary in 1955–1956). By now, whole areas in northern Kazakhstan are inhabited mainly by Slavs.[21]

After tensions connected with the "virgin lands" policy eased, Kazakhs were again appointed to important positions in the republic. The present first secretary, D. Kunayev, is a Kazakh. Member of the all-powerful Politburo of the CPSU, he is first Kazakh to reach this level.[22]

DEMOGRAPHY

In population, Kazakhstan is a distant third among the USSR republics, after the RSFSR and the Ukraine. In 1971 it had more than 13 million inhabitants, 5.3% of total population of the Soviet Union.[23] Between 1913 and 1940 the population increased by only about 10% (from 5,565,000 to 6,054,000). Since many non-Kazakhs settled in the republic during that period, the Kazakh population must have diminished. During the next 30 years, 1940–1970, population of the republic more than doubled. Urban population grew from 10% of the total in 1913 to 51% in 1970. (This com-

pares favorably with overall figures for the USSR: 18% in 1913 and 56% in 1970.)

Kazakhstan has several major cities. The capital, Alma-Ata, had a population of 753,000 in 1972.[24] Karaganda, major mining and heavy industry center, had more than half a million inhabitants. Semipalatinsk is now a city of a quarter of a million. Tselinograd (formerly called Akmolinsk), capital of the "virgin lands," town of only 30,000 in 1939, had a population of 200,000 in 1971.[25]

Ethnic Composition of Population

Kazakhstan is unique among the republics in that the Kazakhs, titular nationality, are neither a majority nor a plurality in their homeland. In 1970, with a population of 4,161,000, they amounted to little more than 32% of the republic's total, while 5,500,000 Russians made up more than 42%. Kazakhstan ranks second to the Ukrainian SSR in number of Russians living within its borders; together with Ukrainians (930,000 or 7.2%) and Belorussians (198,000 or 1.5%) they made up an absolute majority of the population. Kazakhs view them as a single ethnic group: European and Slav.

Despite development efforts of the 1930s, by 1940 only 177,000 persons worked in industry and communications in the republic. After World War II, however, a modern industrial population emerged; workers in industry and communications numbered 625,000 in 1960 and more than 1 million by 1970. Most of the growth in urban population and industrial labor force resulted from immigration of non-Kazakhs; most Kazakhs remained in rural areas and agricultural sectors of the economy.[26]

The large non-Kazakh immigration has been compensated somewhat by the high Kazakh natural population growth. In 1940 the rate of natural increase was 19.5 per 1,000 population. In 1960, as a result of a sharp drop in the death rate (due to wide

20 On mass deportation of entire Soviet nationalities, see Conquest, 1967, 1970.

21 SSSR, 1967: 539–540.

22 D. Lewitsky, "Soviet Political Elite" (Stanford, Calif.: Stanford University, 1970), unpublished manuscript.

23 BSE, Yezhegodnik, 1971: 133.

24 On Alma-Ata and other cities, see Kazakhstan, 1970.

25 Nar. khoz. 1970: 9–10, 37–44, 50–51; "Sovetskii Kazakhstan," 1971: 1, 3; SSSR, 1967: 533–536; on Karaganda, see Coates, 1951: 125–127.

26 Nar. khoz. 1970: 159; see section of this chapter on the economy.

introduction of modern medicine), it rose to 30.5 per 1,000. In 1970 the rate was down to 17 per 1,000 population, following an influx of foreigners and a drop in the birth rate of the Kazakhs themselves. Yet it remained almost double the average for the Soviet Union (9 per 1,000 population).[27] Between 1959 and 1970 alone, total number of Kazakhs in the USSR (including those outside Kazakhstan) increased from 2,723,000 to 4,161,000. Their percentage of the republic's population rose from 29.8% to 32.4%, while the percentage of Russians dropped by 0.4%.

During 1959–1970 number of Kazakhs outside the country also rose—from 899,000 to 1,138,000. Almost all Kazakhs outside Kazakhstan live in two republics: the Russian SFSR (478,000) and Uzbekistan (549,000). Together, they make up about one fifth of all Kazakhs.

The 840,000 Germans "resettled" from Volga German Autonomous Republic in 1941–1942 are the largest exiled ethnic group in Kazakhstan. They comprise 6.3% of the population and almost half of all Germans in the USSR (1,846,000). The 284,000 Tatars who, while officially rehabilitated, have not been allowed to return to the Crimea, are second largest population-in-exile in the republic. There are also 35,000 Chechen and 22,700 Chuvash.[28] During skirmishes on the Sino-Soviet border, many Uigurs from Sinkiang crossed into Kazakhstan, and their number has risen from 60,000 in 1959 to 121,000 in 1970. There are also 208,000 Uzbeks in Kazakhstan; 80,000 Koreans, 60,000 Poles, 55,000 Azeris, and 27,000 Jews complete the picture.[29]

By 1970 almost 40% of the population was under 15 years old, and 60% under 30: a very young age structure, much younger than average for the USSR. However, the 0–4 age bracket has decreased by 4% since 1959, due to a leveling off of the birth rate and an influx of European settlers. The above-55 age bracket has increased to 12% of the population. These trends will probably continue during the 1970s.

In 1970, 48% of the population of Kazakhstan were males. Females outnumbered males up to age 44, except in the age group 20–24. Above 45, women outnumber men heavily. This is to be expected in a generation which survived both the war and Stalin's purges (for ages 50 to 70 there are almost two women for every man); the disproportion between sexes is greater in most other parts of the USSR. In 1970 the ratio of married people in Kazakhstan was higher than in 1959. In 1970 the ratio of married women was higher in the republic than in the USSR as a whole (620 per 1,000 population vs. 579 per 1,000). But for men the Kazakh ratio is lower than that for the USSR (608 per 1,000 vs. 722 per 1,000). This may be a result of better balance of the sexes in Kazakhstan than elsewhere. Also, marriages of young Kazakhs are made more difficult by traditional customs of bride payment [kalym] and arranged unions.[30]

Distribution of Kazakhs in Kazakhstan (1970)

Results of the 1970 census corroborate extreme differences in ethnic makeup of various parts of Kazakhstan, as shown in Table 10.1. The table indicates that as a consequence of settlement by Russians (Europeans) as well as of modernization and urbanization, the country comprises three ethnically and economically distinct areas: (A) the traditionally Kazakh south and west; (B) the predominantly Slav settled and modernized northeast;[31] and (C) the industrial and administrative towns and cities, where Europeans are a great majority and traditional Kazakh culture is little in evidence.

Area A is composed of eight provinces, from Semipalatinsk in the southeast through Taldy-Kurgan, Dzhambul, Chimkent, and Kzyl-Orda provinces in the traditional Kazakh south to the western provinces of Gur'yev, Ural'sk, and Aktyubinsk. In all these provinces, Kazakhs are a majority of the rural population (up to

---

27 *Nar. khoz. 1970*: 50–51; Census Data, 1970: 14, 16; *Nar. khoz. Kazakhstana 1968*: 6–8.
28 "Sovetskii Kazakhstan," 1971: 25–26; Conquest, 1971: chs. 4, 5, 12.
29 "Sovetskii Kazakhstan," 1971: 25–26; *Nar. khoz. 1970*: 19.

---

30 Census Data, 1970: 14–15; "Sovetskii Kazakhstan," 1971: 20–22; *Nar. khoz. 1970*: 13–14.
31 Table 10.1.

Table 10.1

Kazakhs by Percentage in Population and Knowledge of Russian in Provinces of Kazakh SSR (1970 Census)

PROVINCE (Ranked by % of Kazakhs in Total Population)		% OF KAZAKHS IN POPULATION	KNOWLEDGE OF RUSSIAN AS SECOND LANGUAGE[a]
1	Kzyl-Orda	A (total)[b]	70.76	27.22
		B (rural)[c]	92.74	19.19
2	Gur'yev	A	62.47	28.97
		B	91.72	16.64
3	Urals	A	49.33	40.76
		B	65.88	37.87
4	Aktyubinsk	A	47.52	42.09
		B	65.03	35.89
5	Chimkent	A	47.17	25.48
		B	60.98	20.08
6	Semipalatinsk	A	43.65	43.74
		B	59.83	35.94
7	Taldy-Kurgan	A	41.28	35.95
		B	56.75	32.48
8	Dzhambul	A	40.71	38.42
		B	56.20	33.86
9	Alma-Ata	A	35.59	36.12
		B	40.97	34.05
10	Turgai	A	32.47	39.35
		B	39.21	35.48
11	Pavlodar	A	25.17	60.08
		B	37.33	55.80
12	East Kabakhstan	A	23.17	46.13
		B	44.17	41.30
13	Kolchetav	A	22.69	58.30
		B	26.68	54.82
14	Tselinograd	A	18.68	62.66
		B	24.99	55.69
15	Karaganda	A	18.59	58.75
		B	50.15	45.25
16	Kustanai	A	15.47	61.98
		B	22.69	59.72
17	North Kazakhstan	A	14.95	61.43
		B	20.77	59.01
18	Alma-Ata (city)	A	12.09	80.79

Source: Calculated from *Itogi 1970*: 223–252.

[a] This is taken as an index of "Russification" since the percentage of Kazakhs who declared Russian as their native language is very small.

[b] A: In total population.

[c] B: In rural population.

93% in Kzyl-Orda) and between one third and two thirds of total population.

Alma-Ata typifies towns and cities included in area C. Kazakhs are only 12.5% of its population, and they have the highest percentage of Russian speakers in the republic (88.5% as native and second language combined).

So far there is no detailed breakdown by nationality of the population of other cities from the 1970 census. Fragmentary evidence from other sources upholds the non-Kazakh character of many cities in the republic.[32]

The influence of the Russianized capital is also felt in the Alma-Ata province. Alone among southern areas, it has less than half the Kazakh population in rural areas. There is no total correlation between Slav majorities and modernization, however, since such areas as Gur'yev province in which oil and gas fields were recently developed still have a large Kazakh majority.[33]

Composition of Communist Party

In 1924 only 8% of CP membership in Kazakhstan was Kazakh, while Russians and Ukrainians together made up 66%. Kazakh participation reached its height, 53%, in 1933–1936. Due to influx of refugees during World War II, it decreased to 32% in 1943 and by 1960 had risen only slightly, to 36%.

In 1965 there were about 450,000 party members in Kazakhstan, about 40% Kazakhs. By 1971 the party had grown to 575,000 members, but data on the national breakdown for this year are not available. The Komsomol had 1.2 million members in 1971.[34]

Although Kazakhs are a minority in the party, their proportion is higher than their relative weight in the republic's population (32.5%) in 1970. In 1965 there were 36 Communists per 1,000 population, less than the average for the USSR. The Kazakhs also

have more representation in the Kazakh Supreme Soviet than their proportion in the population would entitle them to have (about 40% to 32.5%, respectively).

A study of the Kazakh party in 1955–1964 showed that "Kazakhs were numerically overrepresented among the Party elite of the republic . . . half of all *obkom*, *gorkom*, and *raikom* [province, city, and district] secretaries were Kazakh, though they comprised only 36% of the party membership and 30% of the population." [35]

In 1933, 38% of party members were workers; by 1941 only 28%. For the same periods, percentages for agricultural workers decreased from 52% to 36%, while those for white-collar workers and specialists increased from 10% to 36% (and to 44% by 1946). Despite official demands to increase the proportion of workers and peasants in the party, white-collar workers and members of the intelligentsia have remained in the majority.[36] Although party and governmental organizations are usually headed by Kazakhs, inevitably they have Russian deputies. This appears to be a pattern in the USSR republics.[37]

CULTURE

Historically and culturally, Kazakhs are part of the larger group of Central Asian Moslems, which includes the Uzbeks, Turkmen, and Kirgiz peoples. Together, they amount to 20 million of more than 30 mil-

---

32 See section on economy.

33 *Itogi 1970*: 223–252.

34 See D. Kunayev's report to 13th Congress of Communist Party of Kazakhstan, *Kaz. pravda* (February 25), 1971; also in *FBIS*, Sov–71–49–5 (March 12), 1971. *BSE, Yezhegodnik*, 1971: 134.

35 At a party conference in Kazakhstan in 1925 local committees were rebuked for holding back peasant recruitment. Cited in Rigby, 1968: 396–397; the study is a Ph.D. thesis by J. W. Cleary, Australian National University, Canberra, 1967. See also *SSSR*, 1967: 540; *BSE, Yezhegodnik*, 1971: 134.

36 Rigby, 1968: 143, 228, 233, 269, 280–281; *SSSR*, 1967: 540.

37 D. Kunayev, Kazakh first secretary of the party, is assisted by V. Mesyats as second secretary. In 1971 B. Ashimov was chairman of the Council of Ministers, I. Slazhnev was one of his two first deputies. Niyazbekov was chairman of the Presidium of the Supreme Soviet, and A. Chasovnikova was his deputy. Z. Kamalidenov was first secretary of the Komsomol; second secretary was A. Semenchenko. *BSE, Yezhegodnik*, 1971: 133–134. For a discussion of problems arising in work of local soviets, see Aimbetov, Baimakhanov, and Imashev, 1967, *passim*.

lion Moslems[38] in the USSR. As part of the Central Asian world, the Kazakh people share in a history of 2,500 years and a civilization which reached heights long before the Russian state and culture appeared. Soviet-Moslem historians, writers, and poets have stressed links with the Moslem world. During the 1950s and 1960s, contacts with other Moslem peoples were encouraged by Soviet authorities.[39]

Kazakhstan has a strong oral tradition. During the eighteenth century, *akyns* [folk poets] roamed throughout the land. By the nineteenth century both Russians and Kazakhs had begun collecting Kazakh folklore. The poet and humanist Abai Kunanbayev, generally regarded as founder of modern Kazakh national literature and language and a "representative of realistic-democratic art," lived during this period. He translated many Russian literary works into Kazakh, which his Soviet biographies stress. In 1913 S. Kobeyev wrote the first Kazakh novel, *Kalym*, condemning the system of bride payment. During the twentieth century *akyns* devoted poems to the Kazakh national rebellion against tsarist Russia in 1916 and later to the victory of Soviet power in Central Asia.[40]

In the 1920s and 1930s national art was modernized under Soviet direction. A number of poets, novelists, playwrights, and composers appeared. In 1925 the first professional theater was established in Kzyl-Orda; later, it was transferred to Alma-Ata. Among the best-known playwrights and writers were M. Auezov, S. Mukanoz, and C. Musrepov.

Music tradition began with folk melodies played on the *dombra*, Kazakh national instrument, by the *akyns* during recitations of poetry. First musical drama was created in 1934 by E. Brusilovsky, Russian composer, who also wrote two major Kazakh operas and several symphonic pieces based on Kazakh melodies. Later, composers such as A. Zhubanov and M. Tulebayev appeared.[41]

EXTERNAL RELATIONS

Kazakhstan's territorial position and size contribute to the amorphous quality of its external relations. To the south, understandably, connections with the rest of the Moslem world remain strong. To the east, the situation is greatly influenced by China and developments in Sino-Soviet relations. In the north, impact of the European immigrants living in the new areas of settlement is important.

Identification with Islam is strong. Although Kazakh Moslems are unable to travel to Mecca, they often make journeys to the different Moslem shrines of Soviet Central Asia. Official Soviet attitude to Islam has varied since 1917 but, in general, Soviet-sponsored modernization has eroded the traditional social patterns of Islam (extended family and seclusion of women, for example).[42]

Until the Sino-Soviet confrontation on the Sinkiang border, Kazakhstan had no great strategic significance to the Soviet Union.[43] Now, however, it is militarily vital. Peking claims that approximately 20,000 square miles of territory in eastern Kazakhstan is rightfully China's. (The Chinese nuclear complex in Sinkiang is not far from this frontier.) Because of rising Sino-Soviet tension, Soviet military development in Kazakhstan has increased greatly in recent years. Soviet armed forces rose from 14 under-strength divisions in 1965 to 36 divisions in 1969, with shortrange and long-range nuclear missiles. (Total strength of Soviet forces on the Sino-Soviet border is now one-half million. Reportedly, these troops face a total of up to 1 million Chinese military and paramilitary troops.)

Baikonur has become the major Soviet space center. Concentration of Soviet military and technological personnel in this area has enhanced Russification of the republic.

38 *Nar. khoz. 1970:* 15–17; Critchlow, 1972: 18. For a list of Moslem nationalities in the USSR, see Wheeler, 1967: 74.
39 Bennigsen and Lemercier-Quelquejay, 1967, 1971; Kolarz, 1967: *passim.*
40 *MSE,* 1959: 357–358; Bennigsen and Lemercier-Quelquejay, 1967: 37, 46–47; Coates, 1951: 139–140.
41 For a review of Central Asian music, see Allworth, 1967.

42 Nevertheless, Islam was and is much stronger in the traditionally settled areas of Central Asia than in Kazakhstan.
43 Traditionally, nomadic Kazakhs moved across the Chinese border and back to Russia. This was still the case during 1920–1940. See Allen S. Whiting, *Sinkkiang: Pawn or Pivot* (East Lansing: Michigan State University Press, 1958).

The relations of Kazakhstan with the RSFSR, its giant neighbor, are colored by a great influx of Russians and a tight web of economic relations. The "virgin lands" in the north are predominantly settled by Russians and other Europeans in large, highly mechanized state farms (*sovkhozy*). In Tselinograd province, proportion of Kazakhs to Slavs is 1: 3. In Karaganda province, only one fifth of the population are Kazakhs;

three fifths are Slavs. In Kustanai province, ratio is 2: 7.[44] Even names of towns and new settlements in these areas are Russian —for example, Rudny, Tselinograd, Pavlodar, Petropavlosk, and Semipalatinsk. In the new settlements intermarriage of Kazakh elite with Russians is also common.[45] Precise data are not available on possible tensions between Kazakhs and Russians in these areas.

Media

LANGUAGE DATA

Kazakh belongs to the family of Turkic languages, as do the languages of three of the four other Central Asian republics— namely, Kirgiz, Turkmen, and Uzbek. (Tadzhik is a member of the Iranian branch of Indo-European.) Kazakh was written in Arabic script until the early 1930s, when Arabic was supplanted by the Latin alphabet. A decade later, as part of the Russification effort, the Latin alphabet was replaced by the Cyrillic (i.e., Russian) alphabet, now the script of all but five official languages of the 15 union republics. The Cyrillic alphabet is used throughout the Central Asian republics.

Table 10.2 shows that of 5,299,000 Kazakhs living in the USSR in 1970, a full 98% considered Kazakh their native language. The percentage is especially high— 98.8% for Kazakhs living on their own territory; for Kazakhs living outside their republic (mostly in the RSFSR and the Uzbek SSR) it was 94.6%. A comparison with data from the 1959 census shows this percentage has been declining somewhat.

Data in Table 10.2 show that members of the Kazakhs nationality for whom Kazakh is not the native language are overwhelmingly native speakers of Russian. There is little assimilation to other languages, even for those residing outside their own republic.[46]

Data on bilingualism have become available only with the 1970 census. They show that over 2 million, or fully two fifths of the Kazakhs, speak Russian as second language. Bilingualism with "other languages of the peoples of the USSR" includes command of Kazakh as second language.

There is a positive correlation between Kazakh-Russian ratio and language indicators for Kazakhs. Naturally, the higher the percentage of Russians (Europeans) in an area, the higher the knowledge of Russian by Kazakhs. In Alma-Ata, 6.7% of Kazakhs declared Russian as native and 80.8% knew Russian as second language— highest percentage by far in the republic. In Tselinograd, the "virgin lands" area, where Kazakhs are less than 19% of the population, almost two thirds (62.7%) know Russian as second language; the same is true of Kustanai province (62%). In Chimkent province, traditionally settled by Kazakhs, only 1 in 4 Kazakhs knew Russian. There are significant differences between urban and rural Kazakhs; the latter have less knowledge of Russian and are more rooted in the Kazakh language. In the same Chimkent area, only 1 of 5 rural Kazakhs knows Russian.[47]

Two more points, not shown in Table 10.2, should be mentioned. First, only a negligible number of non-Kazakh nationals are native speakers of Kazakh. In 1959 total number of people speaking Kazakh natively anywhere in the Soviet Union was 3,579,633; a comparison with Table 10.2 shows that only 16,901 were not of Kazakh

44 "Sovetskii Kazakhstan," 1971: 25–26.
45 *Soviet Life* (December), 1972; 32–33. See also Bennigsen and Lemercier-Quelquejay, 1967: 193–195, and section of this chapter on demography.
46 See sources cited in Table 10.2.

47 Table 10.2; *Itogi 1970*: IV: 223–252.

Table 10.2

Native and Second Languages Spoken by Kazakhs

(in thousands)

No. Kazakhs Residing			SPEAKING AS NATIVE LANGUAGE							SPEAKING AS SECOND LANGUAGE[a]		
			Kazakh		% Point Change 1959–1970	Russian		% Point Change 1959–1970		Russian 1970	Other Languages of Peoples of USSR[b] 1970
	1959	1970	1959	1970		1959	1970				
in Kazakh SSR	2,795 (100%)	4,234 (100%)	2,773 (99.2%)	4,186 (98.9%)	−0.3	21 (0.8%)	47 (1.1%)	+0.3		1,762 (41.8%)	22 (0.5%)
in other Soviet republics	827 (100%)	1,065 (100%)	790 (95.6%)	1,007 (94.6%)	−1.0	23 (2.8%)	40 (3.8%)	+1.0		476 (41.8%)	71 (6.7%)
Total	3,622 (100%)	5,299 (100%)	3,563 (98.4%)	5,193 (98.0%)	−0.4	44 (1.2%)	87 (1.6%)	+0.4		2,216 (41.8%)	93 (1.8%)

Sources: *Itogi 1959* and *Itogi, Kazakhskaya SSR 1959*: tables 53, 54; *Itogi 1970*: IV: 20, 223.

[a] No data are available for 1959, since no questions regarding command of a second language were asked in the 1959 census.

[b] Including Kazakh, if not the native language.

nationality. In 1970 only 13,691 non-Kazakhs living in Kazakhstan spoke Kazakh natively.[48] The 1970 data on bilingualism show that command of Kazakh as a second language is, similarly, low among non-Kazakh nationalities: only 100,033 non-Kazakhs spoke Kazakh as second language in 1970, while fluent knowledge of Russian as second language was reported by 3,416,119 people living in Kazakhstan (including 1,739,367 Kazakhs). Thus, non-Kazakh, non-Russian nationality groups opt overwhelmingly for Russian as second language. When there is a shift to another language, it is also to Russian.[49]

Second, there is a sizeable group of Kazakhs living outside the USSR borders, in neighboring Sinkiang province of the People's Republic of China. A figure given for this group in the early sixties was 500,000.[50]

LOCAL MEDIA

Kazakhs, like other Central Asian peoples, did not achieve mass literacy or a press of their own until the twentieth century. Given this backwardness, their achievements in communications media have been striking. Even so, in comparison with the other nationalities of the Soviet Union they are still far behind.[51]

In 1971 there were 360 newspapers published in the republic, 135 of them in Kazakh. Twelve of the 25 magazines were in Kazakh. Thus, the Kazakh share in these types of printing media was higher than their percentage of total population. Of 2,096 book titles, 654 were published in Kazakh. In terms of circulation, however, more than half of the books printed were Kazakh. In print media per 100 population, Kazakhs scored very low, approximately half as well as Latvia.[52]

Of republican newspapers, most influential and widely read is *Kazakhstanskaya pravda*, published in Russian in Alma-Ata.

Its Kazakh counterpart is *Sotsialistik Kazakstan*. Both are official organs of party and government. Two thirds of newspapers are *raion* [county] publications and usually appear in both Russian and Kazakh. Among the most important and popular periodicals are the literary journals *Zhuldyz* [*Star*] in Kazakh and *Prostor* [*Spaciousness*] in Russian, both published by the Union of Writers. Journals are highly diversified, including *Russkii yazyk v Kazakhskoi shkole* [*Russian Language in Kazakh School*] and *Zhurnal mod* [*Fashion Magazine*], both in Russian. Local Komsomol papers are *Leninskaya smena* [*Leninist Rising Generation*], in Russian, and *Leninshit zhas* (*Leninist Youth*], in Kazakh. Party monthlies are *Kazakstan kommunist*, in Kazakh, and *Partiinaya zhizn' Kazakhstana* [*Party Life of Kazakhstan*], in Russian. For resident Germans a daily newspaper *Freundschaft* [*Friendship*] is published in Tselinograd.

The usual pairs of local newspapers in Russian and (in this case) Kazakh are also published in the provinces. Kaztag is the Kazakh news agency. Among publishing houses are *Zhazhushy* [*Writer*] and *Kainar* [*Spring*], the latter specializing in agricultural subjects. The major Soviet publishing houses also have branches in Kazakhstan. (For example, *Nauka* [*Science*], which publishes on scientific topics in Moscow, has a subdivision in Alma-Ata.)[53]

Kazakhstan does not rank high in electronic media. In 1971 there were 18 wireless sets and 12 television sets per 100 population; in Latvia, there were 36 and 20, respectively; 40% of all radio outlets in the republic are wired.[54] Still, for a Central Asian republic, one wireless for every five persons and one television set for every eight may be regarded as high, especially since the average Kazakh family is much larger than the average Latvian family, for example.

Television channels include Central Television, a channel relayed by satellite, and one program from Alma-Ata. Roughly half of the Alma-Ata broadcasts are in Kazakh. The rest, and all programming on other channels, is in Russian.[55]

---

48 *Itogi 1970*: IV: 223.
49 See sources in Table 10.2.
50 Klaus Mehnert, *Peking and Moscow* (New York: Putnam, 1963).
51 *Nar. khoz. 1972*: 556; see also section on Kazakh history.
52 See Table 10.3.

53 *Europa Yearbook*, 1972: I: 1,296.
54 See Table 10.4 and sources.
55 *Kaz. pravda* (January 6), 1973: 4.

Table 10.3

Publications in Kazakh SSR

Language of Publication	Year	NEWSPAPERS			MAGAZINES			BOOKS & BROCHURES		
		No.	Per Issue Circulation (1,000)	Copies/100 in Language Group[d]	No.	Per Issue Circulation (1,000)	Copies/100 in Language Group[d]	No. Titles	Total Volume (1,000)	Books & Brochures/100 in Language Group[d]
Russian	1959	230	1,174	25.8	N.A.	N.A.	N.A.	947	7,536	165.7
	1971	216	2,736	41.7	13	538	8.2	1,324	11,769	179.5
Kazakh	1959	142	623	22.4	N.A.	N.A.	N.A.	767	8,054	289.2
	1971	135	1,495	35.6	12	1,442	34.3	654	13,083	311.5
Minority languages	1959	7[a]	27	1.4	N.A.	N.A.	N.A.	63	122	6.3
	1971	7	51	2.3	0	0	0	88	304	13.5
Foreign languages	1959	0	0	0	N.A.	N.A.	N.A.	(16)[c]	(160)	N.A.
	1971	(2)[b, c]	(33)	N.A.	0	0	0	(30)[c]	(113)	N.A.
All languages	1959	379	1,824	19.9	17	544	5.9	1,793[c]	15,872	173.4
	1971	360[b, c]	4,315	32.4	25	1,980	14.4	2,096[c]	22,309	173.6

Source: *Pechat'* 1959, 1971: 95; *Soviet Kazakhstan*, 1972: 31.

[a] Some may be in non-Soviet languages.
[b] Two newspapers, 1970, not accounted for—may be foreign language.
[c] Totals as given in *Pechat'* sometimes differ from totals in language categories. The indication is that books are published in other languages, but no data is given. Figures in parentheses are the presumed production of books in other languages based on this discrepancy.
[d] Includes all native speakers of the language.

Table 10.4

Electronic Media and Films in Kazakh SSR

YEAR	RADIO					TELEVISION				MOVIES	
	No. Stations	No. Wired Sets (1,000)	Sets/100 Population	No. Wireless Sets (1,000)	Sets/100 Population	No. Stations	No. sets (1,000)	Sets/100 Population		Seats (1,000)	Seats/100 Population
1960	N.A.	963[a]	10.3[d]	1,294[a]	12.8[c]	N.A.	95[a]	0.9[c]		448[b]	4.8[d]
1970	N.A.	1,825[a]	13.8[d]	2,314[a]	17.7[c]	N.A.	1,450[a]	11.1[c]		1,080[b]	8.2[d]
1971	N.A.	2,007[d]	14.9[d]	2,425[d]	18.0[c]	N.A.	1,645[c]	12.2[c]		N.A.	N.A.

[a] *Transport i svyaz'* SSSR, 1972: 296–298.

[b] *Nar. obraz.,* 1971: 325

[c] *Nar. khoz.* 1972.

[d] Computed.

In 1965 Kazakhstan had 15 committees and regional editorial boards for radio and television broadcasting, occupying fourth place in the USSR. There were 45.7 hours of television broadcasting per day (third in USSR), including 40 hours of local programs (a very high rate), with 11 hours locally produced. The Alma-Ata area had 13 hours of broadcasting per day, Tselinograd 3 hours, the Semipalatinsk area 1 hour, and the Pavlodar area 0.2 hours.[56] Broadcasting was in Russian and Kazakh; comprehensive and detailed breakdowns are presently unavailable.

In assessing effect of media in Kazakhstan, exposure to Russian media from neighboring European areas of the RSFSR and from Siberia must be taken into consideration. Since Kazakh is a Turkic language, Kazakhs may be able to make out broadcasts in other languages of the same family from neighboring Soviet and foreign areas. *Kazakhstanskaya pravda* publishes the schedule of Frunze radio in Kirgizistan, indicating a significant audience in Kazakhstan.

A film studio has produced such films as *The Songs of Abai*, *Dzhambul*, and *Botagoz*, as well as documentary films on Kazakhstan. Together with the RSFSR, Kazakhstan holds first place in the union for cinema attendance per capita (22 per year) and first place for cinema attendance in the countryside (23 per year).[57]

EDUCATIONAL INSTITUTIONS

Kazakhstan has a modern network of cultural and educational facilities including more than 10,000 schools with 3.3 million pupils.[58] By 1970 there were some 44 institutions of higher learning in the republic with about 200,000 students. Half of this enrollment figure represents part-time study. In Alma-Ata 12 institutions of higher learning are functioning, among them Kazakh State University with 10,000 students. With 19 college students per 1,000 population Kazakhs rank fifth as an

ethnic group in the USSR. They rank twelfth (15.5/1,000) among the union republics.[59]

In 1970, while the Kazakh ethnic group amounted to 4.35% of the total Soviet population, percentage of Kazakh graduate students was only 1.7%. Number of specialists with a higher education was 1.4%, and those with secondary education even less (1%). Among Soviet scientists only 0.8% were Kazakh, and among those with the doctoral degree, 0.7%. At advanced levels, they were far from an appropriate proportion in the USSR as a whole or even in their own republic; at the undergraduate level, however, the position of Kazakhs as an ethnic group is higher than that of Kazakhstan as a republic, as noted above.[60]

In 1970 there were 738,000 specialists with higher and/or specialized secondary education (professionals and semiprofessionals). In ratio of such specialists to population (57.5/1,000), Kazakhstan dropped from eighth place in 1960 to ninth in 1970 among the union republics. About 100,000 specialists were Kazakh professionals (with higher education). Kazakhs occupied tenth place among the union republican nationalities in number of specialists per 1,000 of their own ethnic group.[61]

General standard of education of the population rose after World War II as a result of the educational progress in the republic as well as immigration of a more educated population from the European USSR. In 1939 only 83 per 1,000 population had had more than a six-year education. By 1970 this number had risen to 470, almost equaling the USSR average.[62]

Major effort has been devoted to implementing general secondary education. Both Russian and Kazakh are used in the schools. At the primary level in rural areas settled mainly by Kazakhs, language of instruction is Kazakh, while in urban areas Russian predominates in schools, partly because the majority of the population is non-Kazakh

56 *Problemy televideniya i radio*, 1971: 209, 233, 240–241.
57 *Nar. khoz.* 1970: 674, 677; *SSSR*, 1967: 544; Coates, 1951: 145–146.
58 *Nar. khoz.* 1972: 567

59 *Nar. khoz. 1970*: 690, 694; Arutyunyan, 1972: 12–13; cf. on elites in Central Asia: Critchlow, 1972; Coates, 1951; *Nar. obraz.*, 1971: 233–234.
60 "The Intellectual Potential of Soviet Asians," RFE Research, USSR Nationalities (August 9), 1972; *Nar. obraz.*, 1971: 158, 196–197.
61 *Nar. obraz.*, 1971: 233–234.
62 *Vestnik statistiki*, 1972: I: 88–89; *Nar. khoz. 1970*: 25.

Table 10.5

Selected Data on Education in Kazakh SSR (1971)

Population: 13,470,000

		PER 1,000 POPULATION	% OF TOTAL
All schools			
number of schools	10,101		
number of students	3,296,000	244.7	
Newly opened elementary, incomplete secondary, and secondary schools			
number of schools	171		
number of student places	99,900	7.4	
Secondary special schools			
number of schools	198		
number of students	223,400	16.6	
Institutions of higher education			
number of institutions	44		
number of students	200,500	14.9	
Universities			
number of universities	1		
number of students			
total	10,082		
day students	5,240		52.0
evening students	1,281		12.7
correspondence students	3,561		35.3
newly admitted			
total	2,064		
day students	1,193		57.8
evening students	246		11.9
correspondence students	625		30.3
graduated			
total	1,460		
day students	836		57.3
evening students	163		11.1
correspondence students	461		31.6
Graduate students			
total number	2,551	.2	
in scientific research institutions	1,079		
in universities	1,472		
Number of persons with (in 1970) higher or secondary (complete and incomplete) education			
per 1,000 individuals, 10 years and older	468		
per 1,000 individuals employed in national economy	654		
Number of workers graduated from professional-technical schools	116,900	8.7	

Source: *Nar. khoz. 1972:* 108, 438, 556, 565, 567.

and partly because study of Russian is seen by Kazakh parents as a means of upward social mobility for their children.

At higher levels (college and secondary special schools), language of instruction is Russian, unless there is a special reason to use Kazakh. For example, Kazakh is used in Kazakh language and literature departments or at schools of education training teachers for Kazakh-speaking schools. According to reports from recent expatriates, there has been pressure from the intelligentsia for more instruction in Kazakh, especially at technical and medical colleges.[63]

CULTURAL AND SCIENTIFIC INSTITUTIONS

Kazakhstan has a network of 36 research institutes organized within Kazakh Academy of Sciences (established in 1945). In 1970 there were 7,905 Kazakh scientific

workers, more than 1.5 per 1,000 Kazakhs. Although this is a considerable achievement for Kazakhs in view of their recent degree of illiteracy, it is lower than the USSR average and about one third of the ratio for Georgians or Armenians.[64]

There are 25 theaters in the republic. Most prominent are in Alma-Ata: Abai Opera and Ballet Theater, Auezov Drama Theater (Kazakh), Lermontov Drama Theater (Russian), Dzhambul Philharmonic Hall, and Youth Theater. There are also provincial theaters in such cities as Tselinograd, Dzhambul, and Kustanai. Rate of theater attendance, however, at 251 per 1,000 population per year is lowest in the USSR.[65]

In 1971 about half a million people were working in cultural and educational institutions. Approximately 125,000 were employed in science-related work in the republic. The major institution of culture and entertainment is the Ministry of Culture which operates regional and urban houses of culture, various centers, village clubs, and reading rooms. Trade unions

---

63 Author's personal experience in Kazakhstan and talks with recent émigrés. See also *Russkii yazyk v Kazakhskoi shkole* (Moscow, pediodical), *passim*; G. Maksimov, article in *Vestnik statistiki*, 1972: 6: 16–23.

64 *Nar. obraz.*, 1971: 196.
65 *Ibid.*: 334–336.

Table 10.6

Selected Data on Scientific and Cultural Facilities and Personnel in Kazakh SSR (1971)

Population: 13,470,000

Academy of Sciences		*Number of persons working in*	
number of members	109	*education and culture*	
number of scientific institutions		total	498,000
affiliated with academy	36	number per 1,000 population	36
total number of scientific workers	3,172		
		Number of persons working in	
Museums		*science and scientific services*	
number of museums	30	total	124,000
attendance	1,167,000	number per 1,000 population	9
attendance per 1,000 population	86.6		
		Number of public libraries	7,901
Theaters		number of books and magazines in	
number of theaters	25	public libraries	69,798,000
attendance	3,382,000		
attendance per 1,000 population	251	*Number of clubs*	7,288

Source: *Nar. khoz.* 1972.

operate a network of cultural institutions and holiday houses. Apart from this, there are branches of the creative arts organizations (Writers' Union, Theater Performers' Union, etc.) and of voluntary cultural organizations such as *Znaniye* [Knowledge]. These arrange lecture series, exhibitions, and symposia. Other administrative agencies (apart from the Ministry of Culture) as well as collective farms and local agencies operate cultural institutions. In 1970 Kazakh Znaniye Society organized 730,000 lectures, attended by 38 million people. The trade unions operated 10,581 groups for arts and crafts, including amateur choirs, drama circles, musical groups, ballet circles, and special children's groups.[66]

National Attitudes

REVIEW OF FACTORS FORMING NATIONAL ATTITUDES

Removed at some distance from the political pressures China had exerted on Mongols to the east and Russians had exerted on the Golden Horde to the west, and only partly exposed to cultural influences of oases to the south, Kazakhs retained a nomadic way of life longer than most Central Asian pastoral tribes. But Russian conquest of Central Asia began in the 1860s. It had several causes, principally a need for cotton to replace the supply cut off by the American Civil War, a desire to protect Russian settlers and trade in Central Asia from nomadic raids, and competition with British expansion in the area (especially after the first Afghan war [1839–1840]).[67] The Russian colonization and modernization which followed led to attempts by authorities to Russianize the Central Asians, including Kazakhs.

The Russian system of administration disrupted traditional culture in several important ways. Imposition of a money tax pushed Kazakhs further away from family self-sufficiency and barter toward dependence on external markets. Russian-instituted registration in a single county interfered with yearly migration patterns, necessary to obtain good pasturage. Also, new Russian settlements blocked immigration routes. The Russian administrative system was totally foreign to Kazakh culture; it furthered breakdown of the tribal system as well as of the traditional political structure. This, together with a change from communal to personal land tenure, led to partial adoption of Russian values and weakening of kinship responsibilities. Many poor people were forced out of the pastoral way of life into the settlements.[68] From the late nineteenth century on, conflict between Russian settlers and Kazakh nomads became the most characteristic feature of life on the steppe.

Kazakhstan was accorded full status as a union republic in 1936. Agricultural collectivization, under the direction of zealous Russian officials, was traumatic for the Kazakh nomadic families, with thousands forced into collective farms. Those who resisted were killed or deported, and tribal leaders were impoverished, exiled, or killed. At the same time mining and industry were developed in regions that had previously been pasture lands or winter quarters for the tribes. Before and during World War II, many thousands of Ukrainians, Volga Germans, Poles, Crimean Tatars, and other nationality groups were deported to Kazakhstan. There was also an influx of Russian administrators, agitators, technicians, and "fraternal helpers" during this period.

As a consequence of these and other ongoing social processes (e.g., modernization, urbanization), three demographically and culturally distinct "Kazakhstans" have developed:[69]

66 *Ibid.*: 301–317.
67 Allworth, 1967; Richard A. Pierce, *Russian Central Asia, 1867–1917* (Berkeley: University of California Press, 1960). A valuable source for later material is Bacon, 1966.

68 Bacon, 1966: 98–99.
69 See section on demography.

1. Traditional Kazakh areas where extended families (now organized into *brigades*) and village culture still flourish.
2. "Virgin lands" to the north and east, inhabited mainly by Russian and other European settlers, living on large mechanized state farms where Slav peasant culture is predominant.
3. Industrial and administrative towns and cities, where Russians and other Europeans are in the majority and modern city culture is the norm.

Islam is the strongest traditional force in Kazakhstan, responsible for two major non-Soviet features: patriarchal rule and inferior status of women.[70] Among Soviet Moslems these traditions affect life style, not the religious dogma and practice known to the Central Asian south, to which they are indifferent. Islam remains a major inhibitor of sovietization, hindering intermarriage and other forms of social interaction.[71]

BASIC VIEWS OF SCHOLARS ON NATIONAL ATTITUDES

Attitudes vary among the groupings within the Kazakh population: the older, traditional, mostly rural person perceives things differently from the Soviet-educated young worker or from a member of a new elite. In turn, there may be a subdivision in attitudes within the latter, depending on whether the individual is a professional, *nachalnik* (in position of authority), scientist, and so on.

Western and Soviet scholars have developed theories pertaining to Central Asian or Islamic peoples in the USSR, rather than to Kazakhs in particular. Since such views center around the Uzbeks, Turkmen, Kirgiz, and Tadzhiks, regarded as the core people of Islamic Central Asia, they will be re-

viewed in sections devoted to these nationalities. For Kazakhs, following theories of the Western writer Geoffrey Wheeler,[72] it may be useful to differentiate between national (ethnic) consciousness and nationalism (aimed at separation and independence). The former develops with education and, one may add, with modernization in general. The latter also develops but remains latent in absence of proper preconditions: effective nationalist leaders and slackening of Soviet antinationalist repression.

Wheeler points out several specific factors which influence Central Asian attitudes. The Central Asian republics are landlocked and contiguous to the core Russian territories. The Soviet authorities developed Central Asia to a level much higher than that achieved in the former Asian and African colonies of European countries. Artificially induced concepts of nationhood were administered by the Soviets in small dosages to replace clan and tribal loyalties. At the same time, massive European colonization created a strong demographic base for the Soviet system.

Wheeler concludes that it is reasonable to assume there is an undercurrent of resentment against continued alien rule and regimentation; but also that the people would not be able (and would be most unlikely to attempt) to break free from the political, economic, and cultural strait jacket in which they are confined, unless there were some prospect of its deliberate or involuntary loosening by Moscow as a result of internal or external pressure.[73]

One may question other conclusions reached by Wheeler, however. He argues that "no coherent desire for separation was *ever* expressed by the Moslems of Central Asia," a statement hardly squaring with events of 1916–1921 or later in the 1920s in Kazakhstan and elsewhere in Central Asia. He also denies that there is "direct

---

70 Bennigsen and Lemercier-Quelquejay, 1967: 184–192. Kazakh and Kirgiz women have traditionally higher status in their societies than women of other Central Asian nationalities. Bacon, 1966: 204–205.

71 Cf. *Lit. gaz.* (January 24), 1973: 11.

72 Wheeler, 1964: 151–154.

73 *Ibid.* See also Bacon, 1966; Togan A. Zaki Velidi, *Turkestan Today* (unpublished English translation, Houghton Library, Harvard University). Views of other Western theorists (Kolarz, Bennigsen and Lemercier-Quelquejay, Nove and Newth, Rakowska-Harmstone, etc.) about the situation in Central Asia are discussed in chapters dealing with other Moslem nationalities.

evidence of the existence of Uzbek or other particularist national consciousness in Central Asia." But in Uzbek and Kazakh literature, there is ample evidence of such national consciousness.[74]

According to recent émigrés from the USSR,[75] some young elite in Central Asia, including Kazakhstan, argue that the optimal solution would be independence. When confronted with arguments questioning the viability of an independent Kazakhstan or Kirgizia, for example, they point to the existence of small states such as Luxembourg or Upper Volta. Some quote "Benelux" as an example of a confederation of small independent states. The great majority of the intelligentsia, however, argue that they should utilize to the full existing rights and opportunities within the USSR framework. In their opinion, this has not been done so far. Yet full utilization would give the local nationals (Kazakhs, in this case) a real measure of autonomy as a union republic.[76]

Soviet views of Kazakh relations with Russia (the USSR) have fluctuated, as seen from the way in which Kazakh history has been treated. Initially, Soviet historians presented the extension of Russian domination over the Kazakhs as a conquest. The version that Khan Abulkhair asked for Russian protection was dismissed, and any suggestion that the Kazakhs had willingly accepted Russian rule was rejected. Soviet historians argued that working people suffered from a "double yoke" of Kazakh feudal rulers and tsarist imperial domination. In 1937, however, the official Soviet version changed to the "lesser evil" theory. The Russian tsarist yoke was a lesser evil compared to British imperialism's attempts to expand into Central Asia. Soon, however, the version was again changed to another, according to which the Kazakhs accepted

Russian rule willingly. Abulkhair was presented as a wise statesman who had fulfilled the will of the people.[77]

Similarly, Kenesary Kasymov, leader of the anti-Russian revolt of 1835–1845, was at first presented by Soviet historians as a great legendary fighter for national liberation. Since the 1940s, however, he has been portrayed as leader of a reactionary struggle for restoration of feudalism, leading the people astray from the inevitable progress resulting from association with Russia. Only certain minor peasant uprisings of Kazakhs against Russians are now treated as progressive.

Until the 1940s Soviet historians wrote that the Kazakhs were worse off as a result of the Russian tsarist conquest, suffering both from their own feudal lords and from the Russian economic exploitation and suppression of their culture. Since then, however, stress has been on progressive economic development and positive influence of Russian intelligentsia on Kazakhs resulting from incorporation of Kazakhstan into Russia.

Initially, Soviet historians depicted relations between Kazakhs and tsarists as typical of those between an oppressed people and imperialist colonialists. Kazakhs, who had lost their independence and been subjugated by foreigners, hated them and during their rebellions killed all the Russians they could. Later, Soviet historians wrote that the hatred was reserved for tsarism only. The Kazakhs and the Russian working people, they maintained, had always been friendly and fought together against tsarism.[78]

According to current official Soviet theories, Kazakhs were originally only an ethnic group [*narodnost'*]. A recent authoritative book stresses that only "with the victory of the October Revolution were conditions created for the consolidation of the Kazakh ethnic group into a socialist *nation*." This became possible largely "as a result of the help provided to the Kazakh

---

74 Wheeler, 1964: 150–152. See also Allworth, 1967; Olaf Caroe, *Soviet Empire: The Turks of Central Asia and Stalinism*, 2nd ed. (New York: St. Martins, 1967).

75 Based on the authors' talks with émigrés in 1970–1973 in Austria, Israel, Germany, and the United States.

76 Z. Katz, "The New Nationalism in the USSR and Its Impact on the Jewish Problem," *Midstream* (February), 1973.

77 Tillet, 1967: 38–45; Bennigsen and Lemercier-Quelquejay, 1967: 218–220; Heer, 1971, *passim*. Soviet historiography also applies this theory to the other Islamic republics of Central Asia.

78 Tillet, 1967: 38–45; Bennigsen and Lemercier-Quelquejay, 1967: 218–220; Heer, 1971, *passim*.

people by the developed nations, *first and foremost by the Russian people*." The usual Soviet thesis of "the worker-peasant alliance" was given an interesting twist. The same source explains that "the development of economic, political, and cultural ties with the more highly developed Russian nation was a condition for involving the Kazakh people in the Russian proletarian movement . . . [and] facilitated the creation of an alliance of the working class of Russia with the Kazakh peasantry." [79]

RECENT MANIFESTATIONS OF NATIONALISM

The situation must be creating serious national tensions. Though direct evidence of this is limited, there is evidence that other ethnic groups in the USSR react with anger at sight of Russians settling en masse in new towns in their areas and running things as if at home.[80] A partial explanation for lack of expression of nationalist tensions can perhaps be found in the relatively small size of the Kazakh intelligentsia, source for most written dissent, and its limited weight in the republic's cultural organizations.[81]

Recently, there have been indications of nationalist dissatisfaction. A 1972 session of the Kazakhstan Writers' Union demanded that "a timely and firm rebuff should be given to any nationalist epidemics, no matter in what form they appear and from whom they derive." The works of "some literary and art figures" were criticized for "enthusiasm and distortion in the direction of long past events and history" which at times lacks "thorough class and party reference points." [82] These are frequent code phrases for criticizing national or ethnically centered works. *Sotsialistik Kazakhstan* has published a letter criticizing use of bad spelling on Kazakh language signs in Alma-

Ata,[83] literal translations from Russian, and even Russian words when Kazakh equivalents were available.

Of dissent, only isolated cases are known, and those involved were non-Kazakhs. In October 1971 Nahum Shafer, candidate of science and professor at Pavlodar Teachers College, was sentenced to 18 months' imprisonment for writing and distributing "anti-Soviet materials." Five other faculty members were also accused as "cooperators." [84] A descendant of a Russian revolutionary family, M. Yakubovich, who spent many years in camps near Karaganda and lived after his release in an invalid home in that city, undertook a long campaign to clear his name. He denounced the political trials under Stalin and secured a personal interview with Mikoyan in May 1967. In April 1968 the Karaganda KGB attempted to prepare a case against him but charges were dropped on instructions from Moscow.[85]

Kazakhstan has also been the scene of nationalist dissent among Crimean Tatars and Meskhetians, as well as of Christian religious dissent.[86] Among recent Jewish and German émigrés there are also former residents of Kazakhstan.

The bulk of the population has not been drawn into the cities where they could have become involved in such manifestations of dissent. In rural areas, however, ethnocentrism has been expressed through maintenance of traditional customs and attitudes, even by party members and local officials. In November 1972 *Kazakhstanskaya pravda* criticized widespread misappropriation and stealing of *kolkhoz* or state livestock for personal gain. Of 17 names mentioned in the article, all but four were Kazakh.[87] This cattle-raiding activity is a strong part of Kazakh traditional pastoral culture, as is Moslem religion and seclusion of women. These customs have forestalled official attempts at Russification—in particular, socialization of the population in

---

79 Kulichenko, 1972: 227–230. The alliance had to be that of the *Russian working class* with the *Kazakh* peasantry, since there was no Kazakh working class to speak of. Workers in Kazakhstan were mostly Russian.

80 Mowat, 1971, *passim*. See also Fedoseyev, 1972: 232–235, who gives a list of "nationalist manifestations."

81 See section on educational institutions.

82 Isinaliyev, in *Pravda* (October 8), 1972: 2.

---

83 *Radio Liberty Dispatch* (January 7), 1971.

84 *Chronicle of Current Events*, 1971, XXII: 22.

85 Peter Reddaway, ed., *Uncensored Russia* (New York: American Heritage Press, 1972); *Chronicle of Current Events, passim*.

86 *Kaz. pravda* (August 27), 1972, attacked a dissident Lithuanian priest resident in Kazakhstan.

87 *Kaz. pravda* (November 10), 1972: 2.

party doctrine. A survey conducted by the sociological group at the Lenin District party committee in Alma-Ata indicated that among many of the 490 respondents (students in the party system of education), "interest is going down." Some 25% in the lower party schools and 13% in other schools were found to have already studied the material presented. They were bored and felt their time was being wasted. About 5% of the students had not had enough education to absorb the material. Many of the 129 instructors in the system were considered unfit for their work.[88]

As elsewhere in the USSR, malfunctioning of services is a major problem and constant source of dissatisfaction. The author's perusal of *Kazakhstanskaya pravda* for one day chosen at random brought to light several examples. Workers at Pavlodar tractor factory were complaining about heavy traffic jams which resulted in late arrivals and broken-down motor vehicles. Their many complaints to the public transportation agency had been of no avail. A mining town in north Kazakhstan had not been able to obtain local mail service, medical services, or cultural facilities, because of jurisdictional differences between two district authorities. In Semipalatinsk a number of ships were unable to leave the river port because of lack of spare parts or because "the grain supply agency refused to release grain from the elevators." Despite urgent directives from Moscow, irrigation facilities in Kazakhstan were not mechanized, and yields from these areas were low. (This remains the case.) Irrigation specialists were working in head office in cities instead of on the farms where the work needed to be done. Many tenants in state-owned flats had not paid rent for years. The housing agency did nothing about it, however, since the local mayor, police chiefs, and other officials were among those in arrears. As a result, a large public debt had accumulated, making it impossible to go on with maintenance expenses.[89]

This type of dissatisfaction is reflected in a controversial Russian language novel set in northern Kazakhstan, *Other Dawns* [*Drugiye zori*]. Its main character is an inefficient, ruthless careerist who mismanages a mining complex, causing unnecessary hardships for miners and other workers. His inadequacy is not recognized by Soviet authorities, who do not suffer from the consequences. First published in *Prostor*, the novel was praised by the authorities. Eventually, it was criticized by the *nachalniks* and "labor aristocrats" of the Rudny mining and refining complex, by no means disinterested parties. Later, the novel was condemned by the deputy minister for ferrous metallurgy and the Kazakh Writers' Union.[90]

Nationalism and Stalinism have been prime problems in the cultural scene. Much Kazakh literature during the first period of Soviet power was devoted to Stalin. The exaggerated and slavish poems of Dzhambul, for decades presented as "the Kazakh national bard," after whom one of the main cities in the republic is named, are a well-known example. As a result, much of his poetry can hardly be popular today. Also, Kazakhs have not such a strong classical literature to fall back on as have the Russians.[91]

Another unsettled cultural issue relates to personalities oppressed during Stalin's regime. One such person was the late E. Bakmakhanov, major historian who refused to accept the arbitrary twists of Soviet historiography and failed—in the words of a Central Committee decision of 1951—"to reveal the deeply progressive significance of the annexation of Kazakhstan to Russia." He had also insisted on a progressive interpretation of the nineteenth-century Kenesary rebellion against Russian rule, after the party had changed its opinion and regarded the uprising as reactionary. He was duly purged, but reappeared in 1956 and again became the highest ranking Kazakh historian until his death in 1966.[92]

---

88 *Ibid.* (May 11), 1972: 2, the article "V zerkale sotsiologicheskogo analiza," by T. Dautov, chief of the sociological group and head of the philosophy department at the local medical school, and M. Voyevodina, district party secretary.
89 *Kaz. pravda* (May 11), 1972.

90 "Komu svetyat 'Drugiye zori,' " *Kaz. pravda* (May 11, October 17), 1971: 3; *Mizan*, 1971: II: 104.
91 Coates, 1951: 140.
92 Tillet, 1967: 43–45; cf. *BSE*, 1953; Bennigsen and Lemercier-Quelquejay, 1967: 218–222; in *ibid.*, see also pp. 215–217 on denigration of the national epics of the Central Asian peoples in 1951–1954 and their opposition to it.

REFERENCES

Aimbetov, Baimakhanov, and Imashev, 1967
A. Aimbetov, M. Baimakhanov, and M. Imashev, *Problemy sovershenstvovaniya organizatsii i devatel'nosti mestnykh sovetov* (Alma-Ata: Nauka, 1967).

Allworth, 1967
Edward Allworth, ed., *Central Asia: A Century of Russian Rule* (New York and London: Columbia University Press, 1967).

Allworth, 1971
Edward Allworth, ed., *Soviet Nationality Problems* (New York: Columbia University Press, 1971).

Arutyunyan, 1972
Yu V. Arutyunyan, "Sotsial'no-kulturnyye aspekty razvitiya i sblizheniya natsii v SSSR," *Sov. etnog.*, 1972: III: 3–19.

Bacon, 1966
Elizabeth Bacon, *Central Asians under Russian Rule: A Study in Culture Change* (Ithaca: Cornell University Press, 1966).

Bennigsen, 1971
A. Bennigsen, "Islamic or Local Consciousness Among Soviet Nationalities?", in Allworth, 1971: 168–182.

Bennigsen and Lemercier-Quelquejay, 1967
A. Bennigsen and Chantal Lemercier-Quelquejay, *Islam in the Soviet Union* (New York and London: Praeger and Pall Mall, 1967).

Bruk, 1972
S. Bruk, "Natsional'nost' i yazyk v perepisi naseleniya 1970 g.," *Vestnik statistiki*, 1972: V: 42–54.

BSE, 1953
Bol'shaya Sovetskaya Entsiklopediya 2nd ed. (Moscow: Bol'shaya Sovetskaya Entsiklopediya, 1953), vol. XIX.

BSE, Yezhegodnik, 1972
Bol'shaya Sovetskaya Entsiklopediya, Yezhegodnik (Moscow: Bol'shaya Sovetskaya Entsiklopediya, 1972).

Caroe, 1967
Olaf Caroe, *Soviet Empire: The Turks of Central Asia and Stalinism*, 2nd ed. (New York: St. Martin's Press, 1967).

Census Data, 1971
"Census Data: Age, Education, Nationality," *Digest* (1971): XXIII: 4: 14–18.

Coates, 1951
W. P. and Zelda Coates, *Soviets in Central Asia* (New York: Philosophical Library, 1951).

Conquest, 1967
Robert Conquest, *Soviet Nationalities Policy in Practice* (New York: Praeger, 1967).

Conquest, 1971
Robert Conquest, *The Nation Killers* (London: Macmillan, 1971).

Critchlow, 1972
James Critchlow, "Signs of Emerging Nationalism in the Moslem Soviet Republics," in Dodge, 1972.

Digest
Current Digest of the Soviet Press.

Dodge, 1972
Norton T. Dodge, ed., *Soviets in Asia* (Mechanicsville, Pa.: Cremona Foundation, 1972).

Dvornikov, 1972
Yevgeni Dvornikov, "Fifty-Two Nationalities in Kazakh Mining Town," *Soviet Life* (October 1972): 40–43.

Europa Yearbook, 1972
Europa Yearbook (London: Europa Publications, 1972).

FBIS
Foreign Broadcast Information Service, published by U.S. Department of Commerce.

Fedoseyev, 1972
P. N. Fedoseyev et al., eds., *Leninizm i natsional'nyi vopros v sovremennykh usloviyakh* (Moscow: Izd. polit. lit., 1972).

Feliforov, 1969
N. Feliforov, *O Leninskom printsipe nauchnogo upravleniya* (Alma-Ata: Kazakhstan, 1969).

Heer, 1971
Nancy W. Heer, *Politics and History in the Soviet Union* (Cambridge: MIT Press, 1971).

Itogi 1970
Itogi vsesoyuznoi perepisi naseleniya 1970 goda, vol. IV (Moscow: Statistika, 1973).

Kazakhstan, 1970
Sovetskii Soyuz (series), *Kazakhstan* (Moscow: Mysl', 1970).

Kaz. pravda
Kazakhstanskaya pravda [*Kazakhstan Truth*].

Kolarz, 1967
Walter Kolarz, *Russia and Her Colonies* (Hamden, Conn.: Shoestring Press, 1967).

Kulichenko, 1972
M. I. Kulichenko et al., eds., *Mnogonat-*

sional'noye sovetskoye gosudarstvo (Moscow: Izd. Polit. Lit., 1972).

Mowat, 1971
Farley Mowat, *The Siberians* (Boston: Little Brown, 1971).

MSE, 1959
Malaya Sovetskaya Entskilopediya (Moscow: Bol'shaya Sovetskaya Entsiklopediya, 1959).

Nar. khoz. 1970
Narodnoye khozyaistvo SSR v 1970 godu (Moscow: Statistika, 1971).

Nar. khoz. 1972
Narodnoye khozyaistvo SSSR 1922–1972, Yubileinyi statisticheskii yezhegodnik (Moscow: Statistika, 1972).

Nar. khoz. Kazakhstana 1968
Narodnoye khozyaistvo Kazakhstana v 1968 godu (Alma-Ata: Kazakhstan, 1970).

Nar. obraz., 1971
Narodnoye obrazovaniye, nauka i kul'tura v SSSR: statisticheskii sbornik (Moscow: Statistika, 1971).

Nove and Newth, 1966
Alec Nove and J. A. Newth, *The Soviet Middle East: A Communist Model for Development* (New York: Praeger, 1966).

Pechat' 1959
Pechat' SSSR v 1959 godu (Moscow: Kniga, 1960).

Pechat' 1970
Pechat' SSSR v 1970 godu (Moscow: Kniga, 1971).

Perevedentsev, 1972
Victor Perevedentsev, "Drawing Together," *Soviet Life*, October 1972.

Pipes, 1964
Richard Pipes, *The Formation of the Soviet Union: Communism and Nationalism 1917–1923*, rev. ed. (Cambridge: Harvard University Press, 1964).

Pipes, 1967
Richard Pipes, " 'Solving' the Nationality Problem," *POC* (September-October 1967): 125–131.

POC
Problems of Communism.

Problemy televideniya i radio, 1971
Problemy televideniya i radio (Moscow: Isskustvo, 1971).

Rakowska-Harmstone, 1972
T. Rakowska-Harmstone, "Recent Trends in Soviet Nationality Policy," in Dodge, 1972: 7–18.

Rigby, 1968
T. H. Rigby, *Communist Party Membership in the USSR, 1917–1967* (Princeton, N.J.: Princeton University Press, 1968).

Shabad, 1951
Theodore Shabad, *Geography of the USSR* (New York: Columbia University Press, 1951).

Sov. etnog.
Sovetskaya etnografiya [*Soviet Ethnography*].

"Sovetskii Kazakhstan," 1971
"Sovetskii Kazakhstan: Biografiya rosta," *Kaz. pravda* (June 9, 1971): 1, 3.

SSSR, 1967
Soyuz Sovetskikh Sotsialisticheskikh Respublik 1917–1967 (Moscow: Sovetskaya entsiklopediya, 1967).

Tillet, 1967
Lowell R. Tillet, "Nationalism and History," *POC* (September-October 1967): XVI: 36–45.

Transport i svyaz' SSSR, 1972
Transport i svyaz' SSSR. Statisticheskii sbornik (Moscow: Statistika, 1972).

Vestnik statistiki
Vestnik statistiki (Moscow, monthly).

Wagener, 1968
H. Wagener, "The RSFSR and the Non-Russian Republics: An Economic Comparison," Radio Liberty Research, CRD 399/68 (1968).

Wheeler, 1964
Geoffrey Wheeler, *The Modern History of Soviet Central Asia* (New York: Praeger, 1964).

Wheeler, 1967
Geoffrey Wheeler, "The Muslims of Central Asia," *POC* (September-October 1967): XVI: 72–80.

11 | KIRGIZISTAN and THE KIRGIZ

Allen Hetmanek

General Information

TERRITORY

The Kirgiz SSR, created as a separate administrative-territorial unit in 1924,[1] is located in the northeastern portion of Soviet Central Asia. In the east, it borders on the Sinkiang-Uigur Autonomous Region of China, in the west on the Uzbek SSR, in the south on the Tajik SSR, and in the north on the Kazakh SSR.[2] The area of Kirgizistan is 76,100 square miles. Capital of the republic is Frunze, whose 1970 population was 430,618.[3]

Kirgizistan has a continental climate. Temperatures vary with altitude. Summers are hot and dry in the valleys, mean temperature in July ranging between 63° and 81°F.[4] At the higher mountain elevations, however, there is a perpetual cover of snow. Winter is moderately cold in the valleys and extremely cold at higher altitudes. In January mean temperature is 22°F. in Frunze

and Przhevalsk but somewhat higher in Osh and Dzhalalabad.[5]

Precipitation varies with altitude and exposure to prevailing winds, rising from four inches a year in the western Issyk Kul Basin and the southwestern portion of the republic to 35 inches a year on the slopes of the Fergana range.[6]

Kirgizia is rich in natural resources. Minerals include the largest antimony and mercury reserves in the USSR as well as deposits of coal, natural gas, zinc, gold, arsenic, uranium, tin, lead, and oil.[7] Hydroelectric power resources exceed those of any republic except for the RSFSR, Tajikistan, Kazakhstan, and Georgia.[8] There are 25 million acres of mountain pasture and meadows in Kirgizistan, while 7–8% of the republic's area is suitable for cultivation. Forests cover 3–4% of the area.[9]

Kirgizistan is located entirely within the

---

1 Shabad, 1951: 371; Park, 1957: 99.
2 Shabad, 1951: 371.
3 Itogi 1970: IV: 290.
4 BSE, Yezhegodnik 1972: 460.

5 Otorbayev and Ryazantsev, 1970: 243.
6 BSE, 1973: 460.
7 Otorbayev and Ryazantsev, 1970: 87.
8 Ibid., 32.
9 USSR 72, 1972: 62.

mountain region of eastern Central Asia. The greater part of its area (85%) is situated at an altitude of more than 5,000 feet above sea level.[10] The western Tien Shan, one of the world's highest mountain systems, occupies the northern and central portions of the republic. In the south is the northeastern part of the Pamir-Alay system. Amidst the mountains are a number of valleys, most notably the Chu and Talas River valleys and the Lake Issyk Kul Basin in the north and the eastern portion of the Fergana valley in the south.

In Kirgizistan altitude determines settlement pattern, ethnic distribution, land use, and economic activity. The relatively small portion of the republic located below 3,000 feet accounts for 70% of the population and 80% of the agriculture. In the Chu and Talas River valleys and the Issyk Kul Basin to the north, the population is predominantly Slavic and agriculture of the European type is practiced, while in the Fergana valley a large Uzbek population carries on its traditional pursuit of cotton raising. The portion of the republic lying above 3,000 feet contains only 30% of the population, primarily Kirgiz pastoralists.[11]

ECONOMY

Kirgizistan, together with the rest of Central Asia, is less developed industrially than the western republics of the USSR. While per capita industrial production of the RSFSR amounted to 5,671 rubles in 1965, that of Kirgizistan was 968 rubles, only one sixth as great. Even two of Central Asia's republics outranked Kirgizia in this important economic index in 1965, relegating it to thirteenth place among the 15 union republics.[12]

While its relative standing remains low, the republic has made significant strides in industrialization since the pre–World War II era. At the present time 40 branches of industry are represented, with one, the nonferrous metallurgical industry, considered of all-Union significance. Other branches

of industry are power; production of construction materials; extraction of coal, petroleum, and natural gas; woodworking; manufacture of woolen, cotton, and silk textiles; refining of sugar; and meat canning.[13]

There are two industrial centers in the republic. One is located in northern Kirgizistan, primarily in Frunze. This center accounts for two thirds of total industrial production. The other center, located in the southwestern portion, accounts for the remaining one third.[14]

In 1969, 30% of the national income was derived from agriculture.[15] Livestock husbandry, traditional occupation of the Kirgiz, is the most important agricultural activity, presently accounting for over half of the total value of Kirgizistan's agricultural production.[16] While sheep raising produces over 60% of the income derived from livestock husbandry, cattle, pigs, and horses are also raised.[17] Among the valuable industrial crops are cotton, sugar beets, tobacco, opium poppies, and hemp. Food and forage crops include winter and spring wheat, corn, barley, rice, potatoes, fruits, and nuts.[18]

Roles of ethnic Kirgiz in the economy differ substantially from those of the predominantly European non-Kirgiz population.[19] Thus, of total agricultural labor force in 1959, 75% were Kirgiz and only 25% non-Kirgiz. In more highly skilled agricultural occupations such as tractor driver, combine operator, and machinist, Kirgiz formed only a minority of the workers, while in the unskilled category "occupations in agriculture with no designation of speciality," they were the great majority. Among industrial and other nonagricultural workers, the non-Kirgiz predominated, numbering 81.7% of the total. The Kirgiz, on the other hand, made up only 19.3% of the nonagricultural labor force. The Kirgiz constituted only 20.2% in managerial and

10 Krader, 1963: 21.
11 Ibid.
12 Holubnychy, 1968: 73.

13 Otorbayev and Ryazantsev, 1970: 87.
14 Ibid.: 88.
15 Kirgizistan v tsifrakh, 1971: 192.
16 Otorbayev and Ryazantsev, 1970: 105–111.
17 Ibid.: 99.
18 Ibid.: 99–104.
19 While predominantly European, the non-Kirgiz population includes non-Kirgiz Moslem groups such as Uzbeks and Tatars.

technical professions although their proportion of the total work force was almost twice that.[20]

HISTORY

A people called the Kik-Kun or Kirgiz lived in the area of the Yenisei River in Siberia as early as 201 B.C. The historian Bartol'd, moreover, writes of a Great Kirgiz State centered in Mongolia and eastern Turkestan in the ninth and tenth centuries. Historians and ethnographers disagree, however, about the connection between these Kirgiz of the distant past and those living in Central Asia today.[21] The first historical records establishing a predominant Kirgiz position in present-day Kirgizistan date back only to the early sixteenth century.

A tragic era in Kirgiz history opened in the late seventeenth century with conquest of their homeland by the Oirots, a Mongolian people from the Balkhash-Altai area. During the Oirot incursion, Kirgiz were forced to flee the Tien Shan Mountains into the Pamir and Alay ranges, the Fergana Valley, and Kashgar, whence they returned only after defeat of the Oirot Federation in the 1750s.[22]

Kirgiz independence was shortlived, however; in the early decade of the nineteenth century, their lands were taken by forces of the Kokand khanate. Although allowed considerable autonomy, Kirgiz were taxed heavily by Kokand, with alien Sarts settled on their lands.[23]

Russia began to extend its control over the Kirgiz in the mid-nineteenth century when termination of the Crimean War once again permitted diversion of Russian forces for the conquest of Central Asia. Initial Russian penetration into the area was achieved in 1855 when the chief *manap*[24] of the Bugu clan confederation

offered to accept Russian rule in exchange for assistance against his enemies.[25] In 1862 Pishpek, an important Kokand fortress, was taken by Russian forces.[26] The conquest was completed with the final defeat of Kokand in 1876.

Following its conquest by Russia, Kirgizistan became an area of Slavic agricultural resettlement. The movement began in 1866, and by 1911–1912 there were 87,000 migrants in present-day Kirgizistan and neighboring areas to the north.[27] Slavic colonization of Kirgiz territory led to significant constriction of grazing land, reduction in size of the nomads' flocks, and marked lowering of their standard of living. Kirgiz resentment over alienation of their land and wartime labor mobilization burst forth in major revolt in 1916; thousands of Russian settlers and Kirgiz were killed and perhaps 150,000 nomads fled for safety into China.[28]

The Bolsheviks established control over Kirgizistan in early 1918 after first seizing power in Tashkent, administrative center of Turkestan.[29] Initially, no separate administrative unit was established for Kirgiz; their land was distributed among various *oblasty*, or provinces, of the Turkestan Soviet Republic.

Soviet policy in this early period was openly colonialist. Virtually the entire administration was made up of Russians. Political parties constituted from among the indigenous population, such as Alash Orda, advocating creation of an autonomous Kazakh-Kirgiz republic, and Shuro-i-Islam, supporting Kokand autonomy, were dissolved.[30] As in the period before the revolution, Kirgiz lands were expropriated and handed over to Russian settlers.[31]

Confronted by popular revolt of the Basmachi,[32] the regime after 1919 turned to a

20 *Kirgiziya v tsifrakh*, 1963: 38–41; *Itogi, Kirgizskaya SSR*, 1959: 103–106.
21 Bartol'd, 1963: 475, 489–500.
22 Abramzon, 1963: 165.
23 Bartol'd, 1963: 535.
24 Manap was a term used in the 19th and early 20th centuries in northern Kirgizistan to denote the local Kirgiz leaders. They were referred to as great [*aga*], middle [*orto*], or minor [*chala*] *manaps* depending upon their position in the hierarchical leadership structure. See Abramzon, 1971: 158–159.

25 Bartol'd, 1963: 532.
26 *Ibid.*: 535.
27 Bartol'd, 1963: 323.
28 Malabayev, 1969: 39.
29 Zhantuarov, 1957: 98–101.
30 Kazakhbayev, 1966: 57–58.
31 *Pravda* (June 20), 1950.
32 The Basmachi revolt began in early 1918 when Irgash, commander of the Kokand Autonomous Government's vanquished military forces, formed a guerilla band to conduct military operations against the Bolsheviks. The insurrection suffered a severe setback in June 1922 when Enver Pasha, who for a time had united the movement into a single coordinated force, was killed. After this the Basmachi

more conciliatory policy in Turkestan. In Kirgizistan a land reform, introduced in 1920–1921, returned Kirgiz lands taken from them.[33] As part of delimitation of Central Asia in 1924, a Kirgiz Autonomous Oblast was created, with leading figures from the nationalist intelligentsia such as Qasim Tinistan-uulu brought into the administration.[34] Traditional Kirgiz culture with nomadic economy, clan-oriented society, and *manap* leadership was left substantially intact.[35]

Despite concessions by the Soviet regime, sharp differences between central authorities and Kirgiz intelligentsia remained, with conflict recurring at frequent intervals. In 1920, when native Communists from Kirgizistan and other portions of Turkestan sought to establish a separate Turkic Communist party and a Turkic republic with its own armed forces, Lenin objected and the plan had to be dropped.[36] An attempt by Abdukarim Sidik-uulu, chairman of the Semirech'ye Executive Committee, and other Kirgiz leaders to form a Kirgiz Mountain Oblast from regions of the Turkestan ASSR inhabited by Kirgiz was rejected in 1922 by higher party authorities.[37] The regime's interests clashed with those of Kirgiz intelligentsia again in 1925 when a group of leaders called The Thirty submitted a formal bill of grievances to the RKP-(b) Central Committee concerning conditions in Kirgizistan. The Thirty criticized conduct of official business in the Russian language, complained that insufficient native cadres were being trained to handle *oblast* affairs, advocated bringing educated people into the government regardless of social origin, opposed all measures of repression, and demanded ouster of Russian Communists from leading posts. The regime's response was to remove The Thirty

from official posts and exclude them from the party. Their leader, Abdukarim Sidik-uulu, was exiled.[38]

Another native faction within the leadership which clashed with Moscow's authority in this period was the so-called Ur-tokmok group, headed by K. Khudaykulov, head of the Kirgiz Koshchi [Poor Peasants'] Union, and D. Babakhanov, second secretary of the party organization. Apparently, this faction supported traditional Kirgiz leadership against Soviet attempts to displace and repress them. In February 1926, however, the Ur-tokmok leadership was excluded from the party; a year later, Khudaykulov and Babakhanov were put on trial and sentenced to prison.[39]

After 1928 a primary goal of Stalin's program for Kirgizistan was the denomadization and collectivization of the indigenous herdsmen. This agrarian revolution, initiated in 1927–1928, met with widespread opposition. Many slaughtered livestock or drove them across the border into China to escape turning them over to collective farms. The Basmachi movement, which had subsided, appeared once again in armed opposition to collectivization.[40] It was even alleged by regime spokesmen that Abdukarim Sidik-uulu, who had returned and was director of the Kirgiz State Planning Commission, organized a conspiratorial organization to oppose collectivization and overthrow the Communist regime in Kirgizistan with arms obtained from China and other foreign powers.[41] This opposition notwithstanding, the collectivization program was pressed forward; by 1933, 67% of peasant households had been collectivized.[42]

A second aspect of the drive for revolutionary goals was replacement of the greater part of the political and intellectual elite by persons deemed more responsive to and ideologically compatible with Stalinist leadership. Among state and party functionaries purged between 1933 and 1938 were three chairmen of the Kirgiz Council of Ministers—Abdrakhmanov, Irakayev, and Salikhov; three first secretaries of the

---

movement continued, but with a purely local character. It enjoyed somewhat of a revival after 1929 when the unpopular collectivization campaign swelled its ranks once again. Vakhabov, 1961: 288–289; Rywkin, 1963: 51–61.

33 This policy was not entirely successful, because many Kirgiz nomads remained on their land allotments only during the winter and when spring came abandoned the land and left for summer pastures with their flocks.

34 Altay, 1964: 101.

35 Kushner, 1929: 77–79, 88–112.

36 Zenkovsky, 1960: 244–248.

37 Kazakhbayev, 1966: 118–119.

---

38 Dzhunushev, 1966: 73–74.

39 Malabayev, 1969: 350–351.

40 *Ibid.*: 371–374, 393–394.

41 Zorin, 1934: 170–171.

42 Malabayev, 1969: 401.

Kirgiz party organization—Shakhray, Belot-skiy and Ammosov; and chairman of the Kirgiz Central Executive Committee—Urazbekov. The leading individual in the intelligentsia to be purged was Tinistan-uulu, a dominant figure in the republic's cultural and intellectual life. Also arrested were the writers Qarach-uulu, Kenesarin, Namatov, and Dzhamgirchinov.[43] The ranks of the new intelligentsia were decimated in the 1934–1939 period, while party membership declined by nearly 51%.[44]

Along with negative aspects of Stalinist policy, positive gains can be noted. Some industrialization was achieved, with substantial progress made in development of education and health care. In 1936 the Kirgiz achieved formal equality with other Central Asian peoples and higher status within the USSR when their autonomous republic was elevated to union republic status.[45]

DEMOGRAPHY

The population of Kirgizistan, according to the 1970 Soviet census, was 2,933,000.[46] This represents an increase of 42% for the 1959–1970 intercensal period, a higher rate of growth than for any other Soviet republic except the Uzbek, Tajik, and Turkmen SSRs.

Primary factor in the rapid rate of population growth between 1959 and 1970 was natural increase. The birth rate of the ethnic Kirgiz was approximately 40 per 1,000 in 1969 with an even higher rate obtaining in the earlier portion of the intercensal period.[47] The death rate, moreover, was low by Asian standards, and resulting rate of natural increase averaged 35–40 per 1,000 during the intercensal period.[48] The birth and natural increase rates of the sizeable Slavic population were moderate to low, bringing down the average natural increase for the republic.[49] Nevertheless, the latter was much higher than that of the European USSR, amounting to 30.8 per 1,000 in 1960 and 23.1 per 1,000 in 1970.

Together with natural increase, in-migration from other republics of the USSR and immigration from China contributed to the rapid rate of population growth during 1959–1970.[50] Indeed, the Kirgiz SSR received a larger volume of migrants during these years than any other Central Asian republic, save Uzbekistan.[51] The other areas of Central Asia, Kazakhstan, the Ural Region, and western Siberia supplied the great majority of the internal migrants into Kirgizistan in at least the first few years of the period.[52]

Urbanization has continued during the recent intercensal period, resulting in 58% growth in urban population to a 1970 figure of 1,097,000 (37.4% of the republic's total population). Unlike the situation in the USSR as a whole, this urban growth has not resulted in a decline of the rural population, which increased by 34% to 1,835,000 between 1959 and 1970.[53]

There were significant changes in ethnic composition of the Kirgiz SSR between 1959 and 1970 (see Table 11.1). While proportion of Kirgiz had been declining steadily, it increased during this period, rising from 40.5% to 43.8%.[54] Meanwhile, the proportion of Russians declined, marking a reversal in the long-term trend. From 1926 to 1959 proportion of Russians in the population had grown from 11.7% to 30.2%, but between 1959 and 1970 it declined from 30.2% to 29.2%.[55] Russians remain pre-

---

43 Altay, 1964: 97–107.
44 *Ibid.*: 97.
45 For more recent developments see section on nationalism.
46 *Sovetskaya Kirgiziya* (May 5), 1971.
47 Kadyraliyev, 1971: 30.
48 The Kirgiz population of the Kirgiz SSR increased by 53.5% between 1959 and 1970, or at a rate of 4% per annum. See Newth, 1972: 218. Although nearly all of this growth was natural increase, assimilation was a marginal factor.

49 The birth rate of Russians in Kirgizistan was 24 per 1,000 in 1959 and probably declined thereafter. See Yesipov, 1964: 116.
50 Estimates of net in-migration to Kirgizistan in 1959–1970 range from 100,000 (Sheehy, 1971: 10) to 210,000 (sum of Pokshishevsky's estimate for 1959–1967 and Newth's for 1968–1969; see Pokshishevsky, 1969: 70 and Newth, 1972: 206). The latter figure is probably too high while the former is for ethnic Russians only, thus omitting Uigurs who immigrated from China's Sinkiang Autonomous Region largely in 1962; Germans who came in from other regions of the Soviet East; and Belorussians and other groups.
51 Pokshishevsky, 1969: 70.
52 Obodov, 1965: 61.
53 *Itogi 1970*: I: 18–19.
54 *Sovetskaya Kirgiziya* (May 5), 1971.
55 *Ibid.*; Malabayev, 1969: 255.

Table 11.1

Ethnic Composition of Kirgiz SSR, 1959 and 1970

	1959		1970	
	No. (in 000s)	% of Total	No. (in 000s)	% of Total
Total	2,066	100.0	2,933	100.0
Kirgiz	837	40.5	1,285	43.8
Russians	624	30.2	856	29.2
Uzbeks	219	10.6	333	11.3
Ukrainians	137	6.6	120	4.1
Germans	40	1.9	90	3.1
Tatars	56	2.7	69	2.4
Uigurs	14	0.7	25	0.8
Kazakhs	20	1.0	22	0.8
Tadzhiks	15	0.7	22	0.7
Others	104	5.1	111	3.8

Source: *Itogi 1970*: IV: 14.

Table 11.2

Urban-Rural Distribution of Major Nationalities in Kirgiz SSR, 1970

	URBAN POPULATION		RURAL POPULATION		FRUNZE	
	No. (in 000s)	% of Total	No. (in 000s)	% of Total	No. (in 000s)	% of Total
Kirgiz	186	17.0	1,099	59.9	53	12.3
Russians	564	51.4	292	15.9	285	66.1
Uzbeks	120	10.9	213	11.6	27	6.3
Ukrainians	61	5.6	59	3.2	14	3.2
Others	166	15.1	172	9.4	52	12.1
Total	1,097	100.0	1,835	100.0	431	100.0

Source: *Itogi 1970:* IV: 286–290.

dominant in the cities of Kirgizistan, and especially in Frunze, the capital, as shown in Table 11.2.

Overall Communist party membership is 103,208 in Kirgizistan (1970): number of Kirgiz and Russians are approximately equal, 38,881 (37.7%) for the former compared with 38,847 (37.6%) for the latter.[56]

In 1959 the Kirgiz population, according to official classification, was composed predominantly of collective farmers. This class included 70% of Kirgiz within the Kirgiz SSR (see Table 11.3).[57]

---

[56] *Kommunisticheskaya Partiya Kirgizii*, 1971: 11.

[57] The social class statistics in this section were computed from percentages presented in Arutyunyan, 1971: 84. The collective farmer category includes a small number of private farmers and noncooperative artisans.

Table 11.3

Social Structure of Kirgiz in Kirgiz SSR, 1959

CLASS	NO.	%
Workers and Employees, Total	251,049	30
Workers	184,103	22
Employees	66,946	8
Collective Farmers et al.	585,782	70
Total	836,831	100

Source: Arutyunyan 1971: 84.

By comparison, only 23% of the predominantly European non-Kirgiz population was made up of collective farmers and their families.[58]

Second largest social group among the Kirgiz in 1959 were workers and employees (wage and salary earners) who, with their families, made up 30% of the Kirgiz population in the republic, as compared with 77% of the non-Kirgiz. The figures for employees or white-collar workers alone were 8% and 25%, respectively.

Comparable data from the 1970 census are not yet available. Data on the structure of the labor force, without breakdown by nationality or information on workers' families, indicate that in 1970 number of workers and employees was nearly twice that of 1959, while number of kolkhozniks declined only marginally.[59]

CULTURE

Literature

Prior to 1910, literature was entirely oral. The great literary monument of this era was the epic trilogy Manas, referred to as "the Iliad of the Steppe."[60] A prominent theme in nineteenth-century oral literature was the elegiac zar zaman [bad times]

motif, exemplified in the poem Zar Zaman by Aristonbek-uulu. This motif bewailed unfortunate effects of Russian colonization on the Kirgiz.[61]

The first published works by Kirgiz authors were Poem about an Earthquake by Moldo Kilich Mamirkan-uulu, published in 1911, and The History of the Kirgiz and The History of the Kirgiz Shadman by Osmanali Sidik-uulu, published in 1913 and 1914, respectively.[62] Sidik-uulu and Mamirkan-uulu were representatives of the jadid (Dzhadid) period of Central Asian literature which emphasized education, technical progress, and need for a national awakening.[63]

Leading figures of the early Soviet period were Qasim Tinistan-uulu, Sidik Qarachuulu, and Sidik-uulu. The poet-dramatist Tinistan-uulu, considered founder of Kirgiz Soviet literature by prominent literati, was a transitional figure. Although an early poem To the Alash was dedicated to the Kazakh and Kirgiz nationalist party, Alash-Orda, in 1930 he also co-authored a panegyric epistle to Stalin.[64]

Poetry has remained the primary genre in Kirgiz literature. Ali Tokombayev, author of the Bloody Years, a leading poet since the 1920s, has also written plays and novels.[65] Other prominent poets are Qurbanichbek Malikov and Temirqul Umetaliyev. The first work of prose (fiction) by the Kirgiz writer was the novela Adzhar, written in 1928 by Qasimali Bayalinov.[66] Tugelbay Sydykbekov has written several novels; two, Ken-Suu and Temir, deal with collectivization.[67] Most widely known Kirgiz writer of prose in the contemporary period is Chingiz Aytmatov who has written realistic, contemporary novellas, but has recently turned to folkloric and historical themes.[68]

Religion

The believers among the Kirgiz are Moslems, but many have retained elements of totemistic, demonological, and other pre-

---

58 Social class statistics for non-Kirgiz of the Kirgiz SSR are residuals, arrived at by subtracting data for the Kirgiz from that for the Kirgiz SSR for each category. The Kirgiz SSR social class data was presented in Itogi, Kirgizskaya SSR, 1959: 38.
59 Nar. khoz. 1972: 637–638.
60 Abramzon, 1971: 344–373.

61 Allworth, 1967: 406–408.
62 Toichinov, 1931: 211.
63 Bogdanova, 1957: 12.
64 Allworth, 1967: 414, 416–417.
65 Klimovich, 1959: 869.
66 Sydybekov, 1961: 305–307.
67 Ibid.: 414–432.
68 Literaturnaya gazeta (November 15), 1972.

Islamic beliefs.[69] In a recent survey conducted in rural Kirgizistan, 46.4% of the indigenous population questioned responded that they were believers.[70] On the other hand, only 29% of a sample of 487 Kirgiz polled in the urban center of Kok Yangak stated that they had retained their religious faith.[71] It is probable, however, that in neither case do these figures fully represent the extent of religious commitment, since data from another region of Central Asia indicate that many Moslems are reluctant to reveal they are religious to interviewers who are unbelievers or who have official status.[72]

The institutional structure of Islam in Kirgizistan consists of a small "official Mosque" and a much larger "unofficial Mosque," which functions illegally but is partially tolerated. The legal organization has 33 mosques, each with a registered *imam-khatib* and, in some cases, another functionary, all headed by the *kazi* of Kirgizistan, Maksud Ali Nazarbekov.[73] The "unofficial Mosque" is made up of unregistered Moslem congregations in almost every city, town, and village (an estimated 300 in the late 1950s), served by over 300 unregistered "itinerant" mullahs.[74] In recent years it has also included unlawful Moslem schools, Sufi ishans with their murids, or followers, various shrines of Moslem saints staffed by sheikhs, and a religious *samizdat*.[75]

Ethnology

Culture has undergone significant changes during the Soviet period, but many of the old mores retain deep roots. Although nomadism has been suppressed, many Kirgiz are transhumant shepherds, still spending a portion of the year away from their villages, pasturing their flocks in the mountains.[76] Clan and other kinship ties have weakened, but still play a role in conduct of funerals, memorial rites, and other ceremonials, in mutual aid practices, social organization, residential patterns, and even popular attitudes toward officials.[77] Many Islamic and pre-Islamic customs persist as illustrated by results of a recent survey at Kirgiz State University showing that, despite official condemnation of the practice, traditional funeral rites, generally conducted by a mullah, are considered a national custom by 68% of the students.[78] Most Kirgiz no longer live year-round in portable tent-like yurts, exchanging them for clay or adobe houses.[79] Home furnishings, clothing, and especially cuisine, however, retain many traditional elements in addition to those introduced from other cultures.[80]

EXTERNAL RELATIONS

The Kirgiz SSR has a foreign ministry, restricted largely to petty bureaucratic and ceremonial functions, the substantive conduct of foreign affairs being vested in the Foreign Ministry of the USSR. The foreign minister, S. Begmatova, is also deputy chairman of the Council of Ministers of the Kirgiz SSR.

Only a few Kirgiz are known to have served in Soviet diplomatic posts abroad. The foreign minister was a member of the Soviet Delegation at the 19th Session of the United Nations General Assembly. Z. Turdukulov was on the staff of the Soviet Embassy in Iraq, and T. Sarbanov served on the staff of the Soviet Embassy in Mexico.

Insofar as Kirgizistan is a Moslem, Asian, and until recently underdeveloped republic, certain affinities exist with the Third World, which are utilized in Soviet cultural diplomacy. Organizationally, this has often

---

69 Abramzon, 1971: 275–339.
70 Abdyldayev, 1970: 63.
71 Bazarbayev, 1967: 89.
72 Yesenbergenov, 1967: 202.
73 International Department, 1972: 16; Koichumanov, 1969: 341.
74 *Ibid*. The estimate of 300 congregations assumes that of 400 unregistered congregations in Kirgizistan of all faiths (Altmyshbayev, 1958: 34) three quarters, or the same proportion as among registered congregations, are Moslem.
75 Carrère d'Encausse, 1960: 21; Altmyshbayev, 1958: 34, 38; *Sovetskaya Kirgiziya* (October 21), 1959.

76 Krader, 1963: 24.
77 Abramzon, 1971: 189–207; Gardanov et al., 1961: 20.
78 Dorzhenov, 1968: 87.
79 Yurts are still used by shepherds when herding flocks in the mountains, as auxiliary summer residences and for ceremonial purpose.
80 Abramzon, 1971: 123–154, and personal observation.

been handled through Kirgiz Society for
Friendship and Cultural Relations with
Foreign Countries and Kirgiz Republican
Committee for Solidarity with Countries of
Asia and Africa, both parts of all-Union
mother organizations. Kirgiz (Chingiz
Aytmatov, G. Aytiyev, T. V. Usubaliyev, and
B. M. Mambetov) have served on Soviet
delegations abroad, as Soviet represen-
tatives at international conferences and ex-

hibitions, and in other similar roles.[81]
Delegations from Asian, African, and other
nations have visited the republic, and in
1971 an international seminar, "The Experience of Agrarian Reform in the Republics
of Central Asia and Its Significance for the
Liberated Countries," was held in Frunze
under Soviet sponsorship with representatives of 29 Asian, African, and Latin
American nations in attendance.[82]

Media

LANGUAGE DATA

Kirgiz is classified by Baskakov as belonging to the Kirgiz-Kypchak group of the
Eastern Hunish branch of the Turkic languages.[83] It is written in the Cyrillic script.
According to the 1970 census, Kirgiz is
spoken as native language by 1,435,000
Kirgiz or 98.8% of the total number of the
nationality (see Table 11.4). This is a
slightly higher proportion than in 1959.
Virtually all of the Kirgiz (99.7%) who
reside in the Kirgiz SSR consider Kirgiz
their native language, as do 92.1% of those
living in other republics of the USSR (see
Table 11.4). Russian is spoken as a native
language by 4,800 Kirgiz and as second language by 276,000 Kirgiz.

Outside the boundaries of the Soviet
Union, the Kirgiz language is spoken by
80,000 Kirgiz in China and 25,000 Kirgiz
in Afghanistan.[84]

LOCAL MEDIA

1971 the press consisted of 72 newspapers, 41 published in Kirgiz or in both
Kirgiz and Russian, 29 in Russian, and 2 in
other languages (see Table 11.5). Total
circulation of these newspapers was
944,000. Circulation of the Kirgiz and

mixed Kirgiz and Russian press was
597,000, or 46.3 copies per 100 Kirgiz
language native speakers, while that of the
local Russian language press was only
310,000, or 31.5 copies per 100 Russian language native speakers (see Table 11.5).
Many Russian language papers, moreover,
are mailed to the republic from outside.[85]

Although number of newspapers published declined between 1959 and 1971
from 98 to 72, overall circulation rose substantially. Circulation of the Russian language press grew by half during this period,
while that of the Kirgiz press soared to
nearly three times its 1959 level (see Table
11.5).

Most authoritative newspapers are *Sovetskaya Kirgiziya* and *Sovettik Kirgizstan*,
Russian and Kirgiz language organs of the
Central Committee, Communist party of
Kirgizistan, and Council of Ministers, Kirgiz SSR. Other leading press organs are
Kirgizstan Madaniyaty, newspaper devoted
to cultural and literary matters, and *Komsomolets Kirgizii* and *Leninchil Jash*, Russian and Kirgiz language organs of the
Komsomol organization of the republic.

There are 12 magazines published in the
Kirgiz SSR, with total circulation of
340,000 (see Table 11.5). This is more
than a threefold increase over 1959 circula-

81 Turgunbekov, 1969: 138–141.
82 Usubaliyev, 1971: 36.
83 Baskakov, 1969: 340.
84 *Ibid.*

85 There were 1,378,000 subscriptions to central
newspapers in Kirgizia in January 1973. This is one
and a half times the press runs of all republic
papers in Kirgizia. Kiosk sales are not included here.
Foreign newspapers and journals may also be received by subscription. *Sovetskaya Kirgiziya* (January 28), 1973: 4.

Table 11.4

Native and Second Languages Spoken by Kirgiz

(in thousands)

| No. Kirgiz Residing | | | SPEAKING AS NATIVE LANGUAGE | | | | | | SPEAKING AS SECOND LANGUAGE[a] | |
| | | | Kirgiz | | | Russian | | | | |
	1959	1970	1959	1970	% Point Change 1959–1970	1959	1970	% Point Change 1959–1970	Russian 1970	Other Languages of Peoples of USSR 1970[b]
in Kirgiz SSR	836.8 (100%)	1,285 (100%)	834 (99.7%)	1,281 (99.7%)	0.0	2 (0.2%)	3 (0.2%)	0.0	254 (19.8%)	10 (0.8%)
in other Soviet republics	132 (100%)	167 (100%)	122 (92.2%)	154 (92.1%)	−0.1	1 (0.8%)	2 (1.1%)	+0.3	21 (12.8%)	38 (22.5%)
Total	968.7 (100%)	1,452 (100%)	956 (98.7%)	1,435 (98.8%)	+0.1	3 (0.3%)	5 (0.33%)	0.0	276 (19%)	48 (3.3%)

Sources: *Sovetskaya Kirgiziya* (May 5), 1951; *Nar. khoz. 1972*: 32; *Itogi SSSR 1959*: table 53, *Itogi, Kirgizskaya SSR, 1959*: table 53.

[a] No data are available for 1959, since no questions regarding command of a second language were asked in the 1959 census.

[b] Including Kirgiz, if not the native language.

Table 11.5

Publications in Kirgiz SSR

Language of Publication	Year	NEWSPAPERS[a]			MAGAZINES			BOOKS & BROCHURES		
		No.	Per issue Circulation (1,000)	Copies/100 in Language Group[d]	No.	Per Issue Circulation (1,000)	Copies/100 in Language Group[d]	No. Titles	Total Volume (1,000)	Books & Brochures/100 in Language Group[d]
Russian	1959	44	162	22.2	N.A.	N.A.	N.A.	339	1,298	177.8
	1971	29	310	31.5	5	19	1.9	494	2,534	257.8
Kirgiz	1959	50	189	22.4	N.A.	N.A.	N.A.	389	2,805	333.1
	1971	41	597	46.3	7	321	24.9	446	3,787	293.4
Minority Languages	1959	4[b]	26	5.3	N.A.	N.A.	N.A.	10	22	4.5
	1971	2	37	5.6	0	0	0	8	5	0.8
Foreign Languages	1959	0	0	0	N.A.	N.A.	N.A.	0	0	0
	1971	0	0	0	0	0	0	(3)[c]	(36)	N.A.
All Languages	1959	98	377	18.2	10	104	5.0	738	4,125	199.7
	1971	72	944	32.3	12	340	11.6	951[c]	6,362	216.9

Sources: *Pechat'* 1959: 130, 165; *Pechat'* 1971: 96, 160, 189.

[a] 1971 figures do not include *kolkhoz* newspapers.

[b] This figure may include publication in non-Soviet languages.

[c] Book totals as given in *Pechat'* sometimes differ from totals in language categories. The indication is that books are published in other languages, but no data is given. Figures in parentheses are the presumed production of books in other languages based on this discrepancy.

[d] Includes all native speakers of the language.

tion of 104,000. Seven Kirgiz language magazines with circulation of 321,000 are published, as well as five Russian language magazines with circulation of 19,000. Number of copies of local magazines published per 100 persons of the appropriate language group is much higher for Kirgiz language than for Russian language publications (see Table 11.5), but it should be kept in mind that many Russian language magazines published outside the republic are read by residents of Kirgizistan, while no Kirgiz language magazines originate outside the republic. Among the leading magazines are *Kommunist*, organ of the Central Committee, Communist party, Kirgiz SSR; *Ala Too*, Kirgiz language organ of Union of Writers and Ministry of Culture, Kirgizistan; and *Literaturnyi Kirgizstan*, Russian language organ of Writers' Union of Kirgizistan and republic Komsomol organization. Other magazines are the youth publication *Jash Leninchi* [*Young Leninist*] and the very popular women's publication *Kïrgïzstan Ayaldarï* [*Women of Kirgizistan*].[86]

Only a handful of books were published by Kirgiz authors prior to the revolution, and these few works appeared in Ufa and elsewhere outside Kirgizistan in languages other than Kirgiz. By 1959, 738 different titles in 4,125,000 copies were issued in the republic; by 1971 this had grown to 951 titles in 6,362,000 copies (see Table 11.5). Approximately the same number of titles appeared in Kirgiz and Russian, but total number of copies of Kirgiz books published exceeded that of Russian language books substantially. Among leaders are Ala Too, Kïrgïzstan, Ilim, and Kirgiz State publishing houses.

The availability of early literary classics of Kirgiz and religious literature depends on character of the specific work. The first detailed transcription of the Kirgiz oral epic *Manas* appeared in the Soviet period and is generally available to, and read by, the Kirgiz.[87] Much other oral literature of the Kirgiz has been published during the Soviet period and is fully sanctioned. On the other hand, works of many anti-Russian and nationalistic writers of the prerevolu-

tionary and early Soviet period, such as Tinistan-uulu and Sidik-uulu, were confiscated in the 1930s and have not been republished.[88] Moslem religious works, such as the Koran and religious calendars, have been published in the Soviet Union, but number of copies printed does not satisfy the demand.[89] Religious *samizdat* is produced in Kirgizistan and elsewhere to help fill the gap.[90]

Electronic media are well developed. The population receives radio transmissions from Central Broadcasting Station (Radio Moscow) as well as from local stations. Broadcasts can be heard in both Russian and native languages of the area. Radio programs include news, music, literary programs, lectures, and broadcasts for children and schools.[91] Total radio sets numbered 678,000 in 1971; these included 325,000 wired sets or 10.6 per 100 inhabitants and 353,000 wireless sets or 11.5 per 100 inhabitants (see Table 11.6).

Telecasts are received from Moscow, Frunze, Tashkent, and Alma-Ata.[92] In 1966 there were only one television station and 10 relay transmitters in the republic.[93] Telecasts can be heard in the Kirgiz, Russian, Kazakh, and Uzbek languages.[94]

In 1966 only 35% of total population and 16% of the area of the republic could receive television transmissions,[95] a situation that changed sharply in the following five years, for television sets in 1971 numbered 364,000 or 11.8 per 100 inhabitants (see Table 11.6). Telecasts included films and dramatic productions, news, children's programs, educational and cultural programs, opera, concerts, ballet, and sports events.[96] Since a set usually serves about five people, it can be assumed that up to 60% of the population were able to watch television by 1971.

Kirgizistan has its own movie studio, *Kirgizfilm*.[97] There were 1,039 movie theaters and movie installations (1968)

86 Abramzon, 1958: 278.
87 Abramzon, 1971: 344.

88 Altay, 1964: 101–102.
89 Carrère d'Encausse, 1960: 10–13.
90 Altmyshbayev, 1958: 38.
91 UNESCO, 1964: 367.
92 Karakleyev, 1972: 343.
93 Psurtsev, 1967: 442.
94 Karakleyev, 1972: 343.
95 Psurtsev, 1967: 443.
96 *Sovetskaya Kirgiziya* (January 28), 1973.
97 Otorbayev and Ryazantsev, 1970: 255.

Table 11.6

Electronic Media and Films in Kirgiz SSR

YEAR	RADIO					TELEVISION			MOVIES	
	No. Stations	No. Wired Sets (1,000)	Sets/100 Population	No. Wireless Sets (1,000)	Sets/100 Population	No. Stations	No. Sets (1,000)	Sets/100 Population	Seats (1,000)	Seats/100 Population
1960	N.A.	202[a]	9.1[d]	157[a]	7.1[c]	N.A.	15[a]	.7[c]	101[b]	4.5[d]
1970	N.A.	306[a]	10.1[d]	328[a]	10.9[c]	11[e]	318[a]	10.6[c]	193[b]	6.4[d]
1971	N.A.	325[d]	10.6[d]	353[d]	11.5[c]	N.A.	364[c]	11.8[c]	N.A.	N.A.

[a] Source: *Transport i svyaz' SSR*, 1972: 296–298.

[b] Source: *Narodnoye obrazovaniye, kul'tura i nauka v SSSR*, 1971: 325.

[c] Source: *Nar. khoz.* 1972: 572, 578.

[d] Computed from data cited above ([b] and [c]).

[e] *Televedeniye i radioveshchaniye*, 1972: XII: 13.

with 193,000 seats (1970) in the republic.[98] They display locally made films as well as films produced in other USSR republics and foreign films.

EDUCATIONAL INSTITUTIONS

Educational advancement has been a major achievement of the Soviet regime in Kirgizistan where prerevolutionary level of education was extremely low. In 1971 there were 1,810 schools of all types in the republic with 999,000 students, or 259.9 students per 1,000 inhabitants (see Table 11.7).[99]

The elementary and secondary school systems are extensive. There were approximately 1,700 general educational schools at these levels in 1971, about 1,000 offering instruction in the Kirgiz language.[100] The number of pupils in such schools (1972) was 822,000, while the teaching staff numbered 41,800 (1971). There were also 36 specialized schools at the secondary level with 41,500 students (1971).[101] These secondary schools trained specialists in 101 fields.[102] Although eight-year education is now compulsory and the Ninth Five-Year Plan calls for universal ten-year education in the USSR by 1976, many Kirgiz pupils, particularly girls, leave school before completing the eighth grade.

The system of higher education consists of Kirgiz State University (13,370 students) and seven specialized institutes: Frunze Agricultural Institute, Frunze Medical Institute, Frunze Polytechnical Institute, Frunze Institute of Physical Culture and Sport, Frunze Women's Pedagogical Institute, Osh Pedagogical Institute, and Osh Branch of Frunze Polytechnical Institute.[103] These institutions train students in 78 different specialities; a total of 7,000 students graduated in 1972.[104] Total enrollment in higher education in 1971 was 48,900.[105] Language of matriculation is primarily Russian.[106]

CULTURAL AND SCIENTIFIC INSTITUTIONS

The primary center of scientific research is Kirgiz Academy of Sciences, established in 1954. In 1971 there were 18 scientific institutions affiliated with the academy, in which 1,232 scientific workers were engaged in various research activities.[107] In addition, there are a number of other research institutes, laboratories, and research stations not affiliated with the Academy of Sciences. In all, 30,000 persons or 9.7 per 1,000 of the population are employed in science and scientific services in Kirgizistan.[108]

Among cultural institutions located in the Kirgiz SSR are 6 museums, 6 theaters, 1,378 libraries, and 1,039 clubs.[109] A total of 95,000 persons are employed in culture and education in the republic, or 30 per 1,000 of the population.

National Attitudes

REVIEW OF FACTORS FORMING NATIONAL ATTITUDES

Among factors shaping national attitudes of the Kirgiz are the century-old Russian presence, the rise of national consciousness among the Kirgiz, their Islamic heritage, and regional ties. Perhaps most significant has been the Russian presence. Among the most relevant aspects of this presence, particularly in southern Kirgizistan, is that it was established by force and that force was

98 Ibid.; Nar. obraz., 1971: 325.
99 Nar. khoz. 1972: 642.
100 Lit. gaz. (May 1), 1972; Usubaliyev, 1971: 35.
101 Sovetskaya Kirgiziya (February 2), 1973; Lit. gaz. (May 1), 1972.
102 Nar. khoz. 1972: 642.
103 Otorbayev and Ryazantsev, 1970: 132, 177, 220.
104 Lit. gaz. (May 1), 1972; Sovetskaya Kirgiziya (February 2), 1973.
105 Lit. gaz. (May 1), 1972.
106 Sovetskaya Kirgiziya (February 2), 1962.
107 Nar. khoz. 1972: 106.
108 Ibid.
109 Vestnik statistiki, 1972: XII: 84–86.

Table 11.7

Selected Data on Education in Kirgiz SSR (1971)

		PER 1,000 POPULATION	% OF TOTAL
All schools			
number of schools	1,810	.59	
number of students	999,000	259.9	
Secondary special schools			
number of schools	36		
number of students	41,500	13.5	
Institutions of higher education			
number of institutions	9		
number of students	48,900	15.9	
Universities			
number of universities	1		
number of students			
total	13,370		
day students	6,268		47
evening students	1,054		8
correspondence students	6,048		45
newly admitted			
total	2,246		
day students	1,378		61
evening students	137		6
correspondence students	731		33
graduated			
total	2,154		
day students	922		43
evening students	289		13
correspondence students	943		44
Graduate students			
total number	750	.24	
in scientific research institutions	517		
in universities	233		
Number of persons with (in 1970) higher or secondary (complete and incomplete) education			
per 1,000 individuals, 10 years and older	452		
per 1,000 individuals employed in national economy	643		
Number of workers graduated from professional-technical schools	18,600	6.1	

Source: *Nar. khoz. 1972*: 108, 439, 631, 640, 642.

Table 11.8

Selected Data on Scientific and Cultural Facilities and Personnel in Kirgiz SSR (1971)

Academy of Sciences		*Number of persons working in*	
number of members	42	*education and culture*	
number of scientific institutions		total	95,000
affiliated with academy	18	number per 1,000 population	30
total number of scientific workers	1,232		
		Number of persons working in science	
Museums		*and scientific services*	
number of museums	6	total	30,000
attendance	543,000	number per 1,000 population	10
attendance per 1,000 population	177		
		Number of public libraries	1,378
Theaters		number of books and magazines	
number of theaters	6	in public libraries	11,853,000
attendance	1,301,000		
attendance per 1,000 population	423	*Number of clubs*	1,039

Source: *Nar. khoz. 1972*: 106 451, 638.

required at various intervals to maintain it. During the tsarist period the Russian presence had the character of colonialism and, although authorities differ about applicability of this term to the period of Soviet rule in Central Asia, at least some marks of colonialism have characterized this later period as well.[110]

While significant progress in economic, educational, and health fields has been attendant upon the Russian presence during the Soviet period, this progress has been made at the price of arbitrary rule from Moscow, movement of tens of thousands of Slavic migrants into the republic, and infiltration of Russian influence into the Kirgiz language and culture.

A second formative factor affecting national attitudes is modernization of loyalty patterns. Formerly, Kirgiz society, like other traditional societies, was atomized, with loyalty directed to extended family, clan subdivision, clan, and clan confederation.[111] National consciousness was weak and the Bugu, for example, were willing to submit to Russian rule in 1855 to gain Rus-

sian support against enemies from the Sary-bagysh confederation.[112] Even as late as the 1930s, clan loyalties were so firm that the Soviet regime was forced to compromise, initially creating soviets and collective farms on a clan basis.[113] Such kinship and regional loyalties tend to be transcended as processes of modernization take hold, transforming traditional societies while national consciousness develops.[114] Kirgiz society has been no exception. It would be an exaggeration to say that the people are no longer conscious of clan affiliations or that this consciousness no longer influences social behavior. National consciousness and loyalty to the nation have become more significant than clan affiliation, however, and today it is more important to a native that he is a Kirgiz and a Moslem than that he is affiliated with one or another clan or clan confederation.

A third factor is allegiance to Islam. Although somewhat less than half of the Kirgiz admit openly that they are believing Moslems, it is probable that many others privately adhere to Islam. It would appear, moreover, that many who are not religious

110 The case for and against applicability of the term colonialist to the period of Soviet rule in Central Asia is discussed in Nove and Newth, 1966: 113ff.
111 Bennigsen, 1971: 175–176.

112 Bartol'd, 1963: 532.
113 Malabayev, 1969: 352.
114 Smith, 1971: 94–95, 112.

feel part of the Moslem community and culture.[115]

Significance of the Islamic affiliation is manifold. First, it tends to separate the Kirgiz and other Moslem peoples from non-Moslem peoples, most importantly the Russians. In Islamic tradition, non-Moslems are categorized as *kafirs* or unbelievers, a term with negative connotations; marriage between Moslem girls and nonbelieving males is not permitted.[116] But Islam is not only a divisive force; it is a unifying force as well. At one time the adherents of Islam in Russia felt that they were all members of a single Moslem community to the virtual exclusion of any national consciousness. Although diverse national allegiances have developed among Soviet Moslems, the old bond of Islamic community survives. Indeed, in the opinion of Alexandre Bennigsen, the centripetal trends uniting Turkic and Moslem peoples are likely to prevail over centrifugal forces.[117]

If Islamic ties have been important to the Kirgiz, playing a role in their national attitudes, so have certain regional and ethnic ties within the broad Islamic community. There has long been a special relationship between Kirgiz and Kazakhs. Linguistic and cultural linkages are significant; in the pre-revolutionary and revolutionary period they cooperated in such political movements as *Ilyatiya* and *Alash-Orda*.[118] Even though divided into separate union republics during the greater part of the Soviet period, the two groups remain closely allied.

The Kirgiz have also had special relationships with other peoples of Central Asia, or Turkestan generally. Here again linguistic and cultural ties and common historical experiences play a role. The pan-Turkestani Shuro-i-Islamiya party had many adherents in Kirgizistan and in 1917, when the Turkestan autonomous government was formed in Kokand, there was a demonstration of support in Osh.[119] Despite national delimita-

tion of Central Asia and long separate existence of the Central Asian republics, these ties have not disappeared.

BASIC VIEWS OF SCHOLARS ON NATIONAL ATTITUDES

Leading Western authorities on the Soviet Moslems have written very little on Kirgiz national attitudes specifically, although they have discussed the problem as it relates to Central Asia or Soviet Islam generally. Two aspects of the question seem most relevant: relations between Moslems and Russians and national consciousness and nationalism among Soviet Moslem peoples.

There would seem to be substantial agreement among Western scholars in the field that tensions exist between Moslems and Russians in Central Asia. Thus Geoffrey Wheeler states that the great mass of Central Asian Moslems would like the Russians to leave their republics.[120] Bennigsen and Lemercier-Quelquejay also see friction between the two groups but feel it is limited to Moslem resistance against what they view as detrimental Russian influences on their literary heritage, history, and purity of language. They envision the possibility of more serious problems developing in the future, but also maintain that the Moslems feel a sense of satisfaction at achieving a higher level of material well-being, thanks to the Russians.[121]

When Central Asian specialists move from the problem of ethnic relations to that of national consciousness and nationalism, problems of definition become formidable. Both Wheeler and Bennigsen maintain, in later writings, that the Central Asian peoples have developed a national consciousness. Neither is certain, however about the precise character of this national consciousness. Bennigsen believes it is hypothetical whether centrifugal or centripetal trends will prevail among Soviet Moslems but thinks it most likely that either a regional Turkestan national consciousness or a broader pan-Turkic or pan-Islamic feeling

---

115 Dorzhenov, 1968: 87, and personal observation. In 1974, the author spoke with a half–Slavic Kirgiz Komsomol, educated in Russian–language schools, who nonetheless considered herself to be a Moslem.
116 Benningsen, 1955: 33. Although these divisive traditions have eroded to some extent, they still have considerable force in Central Asia.
117 Benningsen, 1971: 181–182, and personal observation.
118 Kutareva, 1947: 7; Chukubayev, 1967: 70.
119 *Lit. gaz.* (July 8), 1970.

120 Wheeler, 1968: 169.
121 Bennigsen and Lemercier-Quelquejay, 1967: 225–226.

is emerging.[122] Wheeler sees the possibility of a Turkic or Turkestan nation developing, but also feels that new nations might form on the basis of the present Soviet union republics or that there may be a reversion to prerevolutionary groupings.[123]

On the question of nationalism in Central Asia, Rywkin is quite correct when he maintains that most scholars in the field—specifically, he mentions Bennigsen, Pipes, Monteil, Kolarz, Carrère d'Encausse, and Laqueur—acknowledge its existence. He might have added such names as Caroe, Hayit, and Rakowska-Harmstone.[124] Geoffrey Wheeler, however, is a notable exception. While recognizing the existence of national consciousness in Central Asia, he sees none of the "characteristic signs of nationalism." Paradoxical as it may seem, the views of Wheeler and the other scholars are not necessarily in conflict. This is true because their concepts of nationalism differ. Wheeler sees it as a movement "having the positive aim of creating a nation-state enjoying a government exclusively its own," that is, the most restrictive concept utilized.[125] Rakowska-Harmstone defines it in a broader sense: a striving for political self-determination through movement of national elites into leading roles in their republics and participation in the all-Union decision-making process.[126] Benningsen and Lemercier-Quelquejay emphasize what might be called defensive nationalism (defense of the Moslems' national integrity). Although they also write of a desire for a greater political role in the USSR among Soviet Moslems, the French scholars feel that "the storm which will burst when the Moslem intelligentsia claims real independence is still beyond the horizon." [127] These latter scholars, and seemingly others as well, do not feel that nationalism must involve a movement for independence. Therefore, there is not necessarily a conflict between their affirmation of the existence of nationalism in Central Asia and Wheeler's denial of its existence.

In the Western literature on Central Asian national feeling, only two scholars have singled out the Kirgiz for special treatment. Elizabeth Bacon feels that, traditionally placing high value on independence, they are most prone to voice disapproval of unpopular policies of the Soviet regime.[128] Kolarz shared this view at least in part, writing that Kirgiz national opposition has been particularly vocal and attributing this to heavy in-migration into the republic making Russian predominance a definite possibility.[129]

Soviet scholars have also investigated various aspects of national relations in the Kirgiz SSR. Most work has been carried out by a small group of sociologists at Kirgiz State University in Frunze. The results of these studies reveal that "negative national attitudes" (as the term is used by Soviet sociologists) are held by a significant portion of the Kirgiz SSR population or of key elements in that population. Attitudes favoring intermarriage, for example, are viewed as positive by these sociologists yet, in a sample of 750 workers of various nationalities in Frunze, 27.5% did not favor their children and relatives entering into mixed marriages while 40% were indifferent; only 32.5% favored them.[130]

Although having friends of another nationality is considered a positive national attitude by Soviet sociologists, 22.7% of the sample polled in Kirgizistan revealed they had no such friends, a higher proportion than in three out of four other union and autonomous republics where similar studies were conducted.[131] Attitudes toward working with other nationalities were also studied, but only partial results of this poll were published. Of 440 workers on the predominantly Kirgiz Ala-Too Kolkhoz, 72% stated either that they preferred working in a collective of one nationality or refused to answer, while only 28% preferred working with other nationalities. On the Druzhba Kolkhoz, which has an ethnically mixed labor force, 39% favored working with other nationalities, 54% had no preference, and only 7% preferred working with one

122 Benningson, 1971: 180–182.
123 These prerevolutionary groupings are apparently the Uzbek-Tadzhik, Kazakh-Kirgiz-Karakalpak, and Turkmen groups which Wheeler felt were beginning to form in the later tsarist period. Wheeler, 1966: 41, 115.
124 Rywkin, 1963: 158.
125 Wheeler, 1966: 114–115.
126 Rakowska-Harmstone, 1971: 118.
127 Bennigsen and Lemercier-Quelquejay, 1967: 226–227.

128 Bacon, 1966: 213.
129 Kolarz, 1958: 64.
130 Izmailov, 1972: 88.
131 Tabaldiyev, 1971: 48.

nationality alone.[132] Perhaps the most significant poll on nationality attitudes, in view of the current drive conducted against "outmoded" customs, was taken among Kirgiz University students on attitudes toward traditional burial rites usually conducted by a mullah. A total of 68% of students queried stated that they considered these traditional rites a national custom of their people, revealing a marked divergence on this important question between the party and the future elite.[133] The findings of this poll are congruent with those of Kirgiz scholar Altmyshbayev that "nationalistic attitudes" are a vital force among the "backward portion of the intelligentsia of Kirgizistan" and particularly among the "backward portion of the youth." [134]

RECENT MANIFESTATIONS OF NATIONALISM

Despite the broad sweep of the Great Purge, which preceded the outbreak of World War II by only a few years, nationalism surfaced again during the war. At the Eighth Kirgiz Party Plenum in Frunze, on September 7 and 8, 1942, it was revealed that anti-Soviet nationalistic activity had been uncovered in the republic and that party members and, in some instances, former state and party officials were involved.[135] Some Kirgiz, moreover, were associated with the nationalistic, anti-Soviet Turkestan National Committee, which supported the Germans during World War II, and fought in the Turkic Legion organized among Soviet Moslem prisoners of war to assist the Wehrmacht against the Red Army.[136]

In the postwar period, the Kirgiz press presented evidence of continued tension between the native population and the Russians. Professor G. Nurov wrote in 1950 that there was a desire among Kirgiz intellectuals to represent the Russians "as the oppressors of the Kirgiz people." [137] In the

same year the leading Kirgiz writer Aaly Tokombayev was criticized for incorporating "pan-Islamic, pan-Turkic nationalist and anti-Russian ideas" in his newly published work *The Years of Bloodshed*. It was even charged that one Kirgiz writer had idealized the anti-Bolshevik Basmachi guerillas.[138]

With destalinization and moderation of some excesses of Stalinist nationality policy, there was greater possibility for articulation of national feeling among Kirgiz. It found expression in implementation of republic policy. In 1958 the Kirgiz language was made compulsory in Russian schools of Kirgizistan. A definite quota was established for Kirgiz in higher educational institutions.[139] Finally, the history of the republic was introduced into the schools. Except for the last-named measure, these innovations were declared "an infringement upon the rights of other nationalities" and revoked.[140] The removal of First Party Secretary I. C. Razzakov in May 1961 may have been in part connected with his approval of these measures.

Even with setbacks involved in revocation of these educational reforms, the nationally minded creative intelligentsia pressed for further concessions in the area of national rights. They strove particularly for freedom of expression in culture. The young Kirgiz poet Ramys Ryskulov even raised the demand for complete cultural freedom. In seeking the right to publish works of the great writer of the 1920s, Tinistan-uulu, Ryskulov called for a "pure art, free from the influence of Party policy." [141] His stand, moreover, was supported by the Kirgiz language newspaper *Leninchil Jash* [*Leninist Youth*].[142] In an article, "On the Crags of the Free Mountains," another poet, K. Mailikov, represented Qasim Tinistan-uulu and Sidik Qarach-uulu, both adherents of the Alash-Orda nationalist party, as founders of Kirgiz Soviet literature, despite an official ban against publication of their works.[143] Another literary figure whose rehabilitation

132 *Ibid.*: 47–48.
133 Dorzhenov, 1968: 87.
134 Altmyshbayev, 1958: 64.
135 *Partiya Kirgizii*, 1968: 201.
136 Hostler, 1957: 177–179.
137 Bennigsen, 1955: 33.

138 *Ibid.*
139 Razzakov, 1960: 48.
140 *Ibid.*
141 *Sovetskaya Kirgiziya* (September 19), 1961.
142 Adamovich, 1963: 143.
143 Malenov, 1960: 82.

was sought in this period of accentuated cultural nationalism was Moldo Kilich Mamirkan-uulu. The works of this pre-revolutionary writer had been banned by the Soviets because they idealized Kirgiz life prior to Russian rule, expressed fatalism and faith in the God of Islam, and in some instances praised the *manaps*. In 1957 literary historian M. K. Bogdanova urged at least partial rehabilitation of Mamirkan-uulu's works on the grounds that his philosophy included not only the "negative trend" described above but also a positive trend in that he praised innovation and encouraged the people to master new crafts and industries.[144]

Long an issue among the Kirgiz, restrictions on free exercise of national and religious traditions again became acute in 1970–1971, apparently as the result of a special resolution of the Central Committee, Kirgiz Communist party, condemning "obsolete customs" and of an official campaign to replace them with new "ideologically correct" ceremonies and rituals.[145] Among customs coming under attack were the elaborate festivities accompanying funerals, memorial rites, circumcisions, weddings, and so on. Insofar as many people, even from among the intelligentsia and students, viewed these practices not as "obsolete customs" but, to the contrary, as part of the national patrimony, official action against them was bound to arouse a nationalistic reaction, as even Kirgiz First Party Secretary Usubaliyev was forced to admit.[146]

Foremost in Usubaliyev's mind when he wrote of this nationalistic reaction was undoubtedly publication of the novella *The White Ship* by Chingiz Aytmatov. This work not only took a sympathetic view of those fostering "outworn" traditions of the people, but might be interpreted as a protest against party and state policy toward them.[147] That Aytmatov had taken a stand in favor of these traditions could not but concern Usubaliyev, for Aytmatov was not

only the best known Central Asian writer but recipient of the Lenin Prize.

A second issue is preservation and purification of the Kirgiz language. In recent years the regime has encouraged the spread of Russian and has widely employed the slogan that Russian is the second native language of the non-Russian nationalities of the USSR. The eminent academician K. K. Yudakhin, at a meeting of Kirgiz Academy of Sciences in 1972, however, expressed doubt as to correctness of this concept. The party organ *Sovetskaya Kirgiziya,* moreover, has found it necessary to argue against the allegation "of bourgeois writers" that Russian is an "enforced second language" in Kirgizistan.[148] Some Kirgiz, however, are not satisfied with limiting spread of the Russian language in Kirgizistan but wish to reduce those Russian influences that already exist. It has been revealed, for example, that the prominent writer T. Sydykbekov feels that the Kirgiz language is "contaminated with foreign terms," and that he is fighting for its "purification." [149]

While the Kirgiz struggle to preserve their cultural heritage has been a salient aspect of the nationality problem in recent years, another national initiative deserves attention. This involves an assertion of far-reaching constitutional rights by native constitutional lawyers for the Kirgiz people and republic. A claim, by Kirgiz doctor of juridical sciences K. Nurbekov, is that the Soviet state does not have the right to prosecute or take punitive action against one who advocates separation of a union republic from the Soviet Union.[150] A second claim asserted by the same Nurbekov is that Kirgiz SSR territory is inviolable and can be changed only with consent of the people; any forcible change against the will of the population is tantamount to annexation, constitutes an aggressive act, and violates the principle of self-determination.[151]

A final claim made by both Nurbekov and a second Kirgiz constitutional lawyer, Rafik Turgunbekov, asserts that the attempt by leaders to form a Kirgiz Mountain Oblast in 1922 constituted sovereign will of the

---

144 Bogdanova, 1957: 12.
145 Usubaliyev, 1971: 33. Usubaliyev renewed his criticisms in mid–1973, attacking writers who "glorify the past," resistance to learning Russian, and revival of religion. *Baltimore Sun* (July 6), 1973.
146 *Ibid.*; Gardanov et al., 1961: 20.
147 *The White Ship* was published in *Novy Mir*, 1970: 1.

148 *Sovetskaya Kirgiziya* (June 15), 1972.
149 *Sovetskaya Kirgiziya* (January 28), 1973.
150 *Sovetskaya Kirgiziya* (December 7), 1972.
151 Nurbekov, 1972: 14–15.

people, implying that refusal of the Soviet state to accede to this initiative contravened the sovereign will.[152] These concepts—that the people have a sovereign will independent of an in some instances contrary to that of the Soviet state, that the population of Kirgizistan has sovereign rights such as territorial inviolability which cannot be

---

[152] *Sovetskaya Kirgiziya* (December 7), 1972.

legally alienated by the Soviet state, and that advocacy of separation from the Soviet Union should not be punishable by law— are of much greater potential significance than the movement to protect the integrity of Kirgiz culture from State intervention and Russification. Unlike this latter movement, however, there is little evidence to indicate how widespread is the support for these legal positions.

REFERENCES

Abdyldayev, 1970
S. Abdyldayev, "Islam i zhenshchina," in V. Amanaliyev, chief ed., *Obshchestvennaya psikhologiya i religioznyye predrassudki* (Frunze: Illim, 1970).

Abramzon, 1958
S. M. Abramzon et al., *Byt kolkhoznikov Kirgizskikh selenii Darkhan i Chichkan* (Moscow: Izdatel'stvo Akademii Nauk SSSR, 1958).

Abramzon, 1963
S. M. Abramzon, "Kirgizy," in S. P. Tolstov et al., eds., *Narody Sredney Azii i Kazakhstana* II (Moscow: Izdatel'stvo Akademii Nauk SSSR, 1963).

Abramzon, 1971
S. M. Abramzon, *Kirgizy i ikh etnogeneticheskiye i istoriko-kul'turnyye svyazi* (Leningrad: Izdatel'stvo Nauka, 1971).

Adamovich, 1963
Anthony Adamovich, "Current Trends in Non-Russian Soviet Literature," *Studies on the Soviet Union* (1963): III 2: 59–145.

Allworth, 1967
Edward Allworth, ed., *Central Asia: A Century of Russian Rule* (New York and London: Columbia University Press, 1967).

Altay, 1964
Azamat Altay, "Kirgiziya During the Great Purge," *Central Asian Review* (1964): XII: 2: 97–107.

Altmyshbayev, 1958
A. Altmyshbayev, *Nekotoryye perezhitiki proshlogo v soznanii lyudey v Sredney Azii i rol' sotsialisticheskoi kultury v borbe s nimi* (Frunze, 1958).

Arutyunyan, 1971
Yu. V. Arutyunyan, *Sotsial'naya struktura sel'skogo naseleniya SSR* (Moscow: Izdatel'stvo Mysl', 1971).

Aytmatov, 1971
Chingiz Aytmatov, "Belyy Parakhod," *Novy mir* (January 1971): I: 31–100.

Bacon, 1966
Elizabeth E. Bacon, *Central Asia Under Russian Rule* (Ithaca: Cornell University Press, 1966).

Bartol'd, 1963
V. V. Bartol'd, "Kirgizy. Istoricheskiy ocherk," *Sochineniya*, II, Part 1 (Moscow: Izdatel'stvo Vostochnoy Literatury, 1963).

Baskakov, 1969
N. A. Baskakov, *Vvedeniye v izucheniye Tyurkskikh yazikov* (Moscow: Izdatel'stvo Vysshaya Shkola, 1969).

Bazarbayev, 1967
Zh. B. Bazarbayev, "Nekotoryye itogi izucheniya religioznosti naseleniya Karakalpakii," in A. I. Klibanov, chief ed., *Konkretnyye Isseledovaniya sovremennykh religioznykh verovanii* (Moscow: Mysl', 1967).

Bazarbayev, 1969
Sh. Bazarbayev, "Azïrkï Uchurdagi Diniy Kaldïklardïnkëë Bir Özgöchölüktörü Jönündö," in A. Isakbekova, ed., *Din jana Diniy Kaldïktar* (Frunze: Illim, 1969).

Bennigsen, 1955
Alexandre Bennigsen, "The Muslim Peoples of the Soviet Union and the Soviets. Part IV. The Political Problem," *Islamic Review* (July 1955): VII: 27–36.

Bennigsen, 1971
Alexandre Bennigsen, "Islamic or Local Consciousness among Soviet Nationalities," in Edward Allworth, ed., *Soviet Nationality Problems* (New York and London: Columbia University Press, 1971).

Bennigsen and Lemercier-Quelquejay, 1967
Alexandre Bennigsen and Chantal Lemer-

cier-Quelquejay, *Islam in the Soviet Union* (London and New York: Pall-Mall-Praeger, 1967).

Bogdanova, 1957
M. Bogdanova, *Antalogiya Kirgizskoy poezii* (Moscow: Gosudarstvennoye izdatel'stvo khudozhestvennoy literatury, 1957).

BSE, Yezhegodnik 1972
Bol'shaya Sovetskaya Entsiklopediya, Yezhegodnik 1973 (Bol'shaya Sovetskaya Entsiklopediya, 1973).

Carrère d'Encausse, 1960
Helene Carrère d'Encausse, "Organisation Officielle de l'Islam, en U.R.S.S.," *L'Afrique et L'Asie* (1960): LII: 4: 5–28.

Chukubayev, 1967
Abdukhan Chukubayev, *Klassovaya borba i obshchestvennaya mysl' v Kirgizii (1900–1917)* (Frunze: Izdatel'stvo Kyrgyzstan, 1967).

Dorzhenov, 1968
S. B. Dorzhenov, "K voprosu o ponyatii 'Musulmanin,' " in A. Taldybayev, ed., *O Nekotorykh ponyatiyakh teorii natsii* (Frunze: Ilim, 1968).

Dzhunushev, 1966
A. Dzhunushev, *Iz istorii obrazovaniy Kirgizskoi Avtonomoi Respubliki* (Frunze: Izdatel'stvo Kyrgyzstan, 1966).

Gardanov et al., 1961
V. K. Gardanov et al., "Osnovnyye napravleniya etnicheskikh protesessov u narodov SSSR," *Sovetskaya Etnografiya* (July-August 1961): IV: 9–46.

Hayit, 1956
Baymirza Hayit, *Turkestan im zwangisten Jahrhundert* (Darmstadt: Leske Verlag, 1956).

Holubnychy, 1968
Vsevolod Holubnychy, "Some Economic Aspects of Relations Among the Soviet Republics," in Erich Goldhagen, ed., *Ethnic Minorities in the Soviet Union* (New York: Praeger, 1968).

Hostler, 1957
Charles W. Hostler, *Turkism and the Soviets* (London: George Allen & Unwin, 1957).

International Department, 1972
International Department of Moslem Organizations in the USSR, *Moslems in the Soviet Union* (Moscow: Progress Publishers, 1972).

Itogi 1959
Itogi vsesoyuznoi perepisi naseleniya 1959 goda SSSR (Moscow: Gosstatizdat, 1962).

Itogi 1970
Itogi vsesoyuznoi perepisi naseleniya

1970 goda, vol. IV (Moscow: Statistika, 1972–1973).

Itogi, Kirgizskaya SSR 1959
Tsentral'noye Statisticheskoye Upravleniye, *Itogi vsesoyuznoi perepisi naseleniya 1959 goda: Kirgizskaya SSR* (Moscow: Gosstatizdat, 1963).

Izmailov, 1972
A. I. Izmailov, "Nekotoryye aspekty mezhnatsional'nykh brakov v SSSR," *Izvestiya Akademii Nauk Kirgizskoi SSR* (1972): IV: 87–89.

Kadyraliyev, 1971
S. Kadyraliyev, "O vozmozhnykh izmeneniyakh urovnya rozhdayemosti naseleniya Kirgizii," *Sbornik trudov aspirantov i soiskatelei. Kirgizskii Universitet. Seriya ekonomicheskikh nauk. Vypusk* (1971): VIII: 28–32.

Karakleyev, 1972
K. K. Karakleyev, ed., *Kirgizstan v bratskoi sem'ye narodov* (Frunze: Izdatel'stvo Kyrgyzstan, 1972).

Kazakhbayev, 1966
Abdukair Kazakhbayev, ed., *Ocherki istorii Kommunisticheskoi Partii Kirgizii* (Frunze: Kyrgyzstan, 1966).

Kirgiziya v tsifrakh, 1963
Kirgiziya v tsifrakh (Frunze: Gosudarstvennoye statisticheskoye izdatel'stvo, 1963).

Kirgiziya v tsifrakh, 1971
Kirgiziya v tsifrakh (Frunze: Gosudarstvennoye statisticheskoye izdatel'stvo, 1971).

Klimovich, 1959
L. I. Klimovich, *Khrestomatiya po literature narodov SSR* (Moscow: Gosudarstvennoye uchebno-pedagogicheskoye izdatel'stvo Ministertva prosveshchemiya RSFSR, 1959).

Koichumanov, 1969
K. I. Koichumanov, "Nekotoryye osobennosti ateisticheskoi propagandy v Kirgizii," *Voprosy istorii partii Kirgizii.* Vypusk (1969): V: 333–355.

Kolarz, 1958
Walter Kolarz, "The Nationalities under Khrushchev," *Soviet Survey* (April-June 1958): 57–65.

Kommunisticheskaya Partiya Kirgizii, 1971
Kommunisticheskaya Partiya Kirgizii. Kratkiy spravochnik (Frunze: Kyrgyzstan, 1971).

Kommunisticheskaya Partiya Kirgizii v rezelyutsiakh i resheniyakh, 1968
Kommunisticheskaya Partiya Kirgizii v rezolyutsiakh i resheniyakh, Part II (Frunze: Kyrgyzstan, 1968).

Krader, 1963
Lawrence Krader, *Peoples of Central Asia*

(Bloomington: Indiana University Publications, 1963).

Kushner, 1929
P. I. Kushner, *Gornaya Kirgiziya* (Moscow: Izdatel'stvo Kommunisticheskogo universiteta trudyashchikhsya vostoka, 1929).

Kutareva, 1947
V. E. Kutareva, *Osnovnyye etapy grazhdanskoi voyny v Kirgizii* (Frunze: Izdatel'stvo Kirgizskogo filiala Akademii nauk SSR, 1947).

Malabayev, 1969
D. M. Malabayev, *Ukrepleniye sovetov Kirgizii v periode stroitelstva sotsializma* (Frunze: Ilim, 1969).

Malenov, 1960
B. Malenov, "Nashe oruzhiye-Leninskii printsip partiinosti literatury," *Literaturnyi Kirgizstan* (1960): II: 80–84.

Nar. khoz. 1967
Narodnoye khozyaistvo SSSR v 1967 godu (Moscow: Statistika, 1968).

Nar. khoz. 1970
Narodnoye khozyaistvo SSSR v 1970 godu (Moscow: Statistika, 1971).

Nar. khoz. 1972
Narodnoye khozyaistvo SSSR 1922–1972, Yubileinyi statisticheskii yezhegodnik (Moscow: Statistika, 1972).

Nar. obraz., 1971
Narodnoye obrazovaniye, nauka, i kultura v SSSR (Moscow: Statistika, 1971).

Newth, 1972
J. A. Newth, "The 1970 Soviet Census," *Soviet Studies* (October 1972): 200–222.

Nove and Newth, 1966
Alec Nove and J. A. Newth, *The Soviet Middle East: A Communist Model for Development* (New York: Praeger, 1966).

Nurbekov, 1972
K. Nurbekov, "Ravnaya sredi ravnykh," *Literaturnyi Kirgizstan* (April 1972): 4.

Obodov, 1965
D. I. Obodov, "Kratkaya kharakteristika sovremennoy migratsii naseleniya i trudovykh resursov Kirgizskoi SSR," in Akademiya Nauk Kirgizskoi SSR. Institut Ekonomiki, *Naseleniye i trudovyye resursy Kirgizskoi SSR* (Frunze: Ilim, 1965.

Otorbayev and Ryazantsev, 1970
K. O. Otorbayev and S. N. Ryazantsev, eds., *Sovetskii Soyuz: Kirgiziya* (Moscow: Mysl', 1970).

Park, 1957
Alexander G. Park, *Bolshevism in Turkestan, 1917–1927* (New York: Columbia University Press, 1957).

Pogorelsky, 1935
P. Pogorelsky, "Sotsialicheskaya rekon-

struktsiya zhivotnovodstvogo khozyaistvo Kirgizii," *Revolyutsionnyi vostok* (June 1935): VI: 41–58.

Pokshishevsky, 1969
V. V. Pokshishevsky, "Migratsii naseleniya v SSSR," *Priroda* (September 1969): IX: 67–75.

Psurtsev, 1967
N. D. Psurtsev, *Razvitiye svyazi v SSSR* (Moscow: Izdatel'stvo Svyaz', 1967).

Rakowska-Harmstone, 1971
Teresa Rakowska-Harmstone, "The Dilemma of Nationalism in the Soviet Union," in John W. Strong, ed., *The Soviet Union under Brezhnev and Kosygin* (New York: Van Nostrand–Reinhold, 1971).

Razzakov, 1960
I. P. Razzakov, *Intelligentsiya sovetskogo Kirgizistana v borbe za osushchestvleniye reshenii XXI S'yezda KPSS* (Frunze: Kirgizgosizdat, 1960).

Rywkin, 1963
Michael Rywkin, *Russia in Central Asia* (New York: Collier Books, 1963).

Shabad, 1951
Theodore Shabad, *Geography of the USSR* (New York: Columbia University Press, 1951).

Sheehy, 1966
Ann Sheehy, "The Andizhan Uprising of 1898 and Soviet Historiography," *Central Asian Review* (1966): XIV: 2: 139–150.

Sheehy, 1971
Ann Sheehy, "Soviet Central Asia and the 1970 Census," *Mizan* (1971): XIII: 1: 3–15.

Smith, 1971
Anthony D. Smith, *Theories of Nationalism* (London: Duckworth, 1971).

Sydykbekov, 1961
T. Sydykbekov et al., *Ocherki istorii Kirgizskoi sovetskoi literatury* (Frunze: Izdatel'stvo Akademii nauk Kirgizskoy SSR, 1961).

Tabaldiyev, 1971
A. Tabaldiyev, "Aktual'nyye voprosy sotsiologicheskogo issledovaniya natsional'nykh otnosheniy v SSSR," *Nauchnyye doklady vysshey shkoly. Filosofskiye nauki* (February 1971): II: 43–52.

Tillett, 1969
Lowell Tillett, *The Great Friendship* (Chapel Hill: University of North Carolina Press, 1969).

Toichinov, 1931
I. Toichinov, "Kirgizskaya literatura," *Literaturnaya entsiklopediya* (1931): V: 211–212.

Transport i svyaz', 1972
Transport i svyaz' SSSR (Moscow: Statistika, 1972).

Turgunbekov, 1969
Rafik Turgunbekov, *Stanovleniye i razvitiye suverennogo gosudarstva Kirgizskogo naroda* (Frunze: Ilim, 1969).

UNESCO, 1964
UNESCO, *World Communications* (Amsterdam, 1964).

Usubaliyev, 1971
T. Usubaliyev, "XXIV s'yezd KPSS i internatsional'noye vospitaniye trudyashchikhsya," *Kommunist* (1971): XLVIII: 16: 26–39.

USSR 72, 1972
USSR 72 (Moscow: Novosti, 1972).

Vakhabov, 1961
Mavlyan Vakhabov, *Formirovaniye Uzbekskoi sotsialisticheskoi natsii* (Tashkent: Gosudarstvennoye izdatel'stvo Uzbekskoi SSR, 1961).

Wheeler, 1966
Geoffrey Wheeler, *The Peoples of Soviet Central Asia* (Chester Springs, Pa: Dufour Editions, 1966).

Wheeler, 1968
Geoffrey Wheeler, "The Problem of the Nationalities," *Studies on the Soviet Union* (1968): VII: 4: 99–110.

Yesenbergenov, 1967
Kh. Ye. Yesenbergenov, "Ob izuchenii religioznykh verovanii Karakalpakov," in A. I. Klibanov, ed., *Konkretnyye issledovaniya sovremennykh verovanii* (Moscow: Mysl', 1967).

Yesipov, 1964
N. Yesipov, "Chto vliyayet na uroven' rozhdayemosti?", *Nauchnyye doklady vysshey shkoly. Ekonomicheskiye nauki* (1964): I: 5: 114–119.

Zenkovsky, 1960
Serge A. Zenkovsky, *Pan-Turkism and Islam in Russia* (Cambridge: Harvard University Press, 1960).

Zhantuarov, 1957
S. V. Zhantuarov, *Oktyabr'skaya revolyutsiya i grazhdanskaya voina v Kirgizii* (Frunze, 1957).

Zorin, 1934
A. Zorin, "10 Let sovetskoy vlasti," *Revolyutsionnyi vostok* (June 1934): VI: 166–195.

12 | TURKMENISTAN and THE TURKMEN

Aman Berdi Murat

General Information

TERRITORY[1]

With 187,200 square miles (2.2% of the USSR), the Turkmen SSR is fourth largest union republic. Only the RSFSR, Kazakhstan, and the Ukraine are larger. Turkmenistan is the southernmost Soviet republic. It borders on Iran to the south, Afghanistan to the southeast, Uzbekistan to the northeast, and Kazakhstan to the northwest. In the west, its nearly 500-mile coastline on the Caspian Sea includes the port city of Krasnovodsk, called "the Gateway to Central Asia." Ashkhabad is the capital of the republic.

Far from any ocean, Turkmenistan has a continental climate with an abundance of light and warmth. Summers are long, dry, and hot; *average* temperatures in July often exceed 90°F. Winters are short but intense, with temperatures occasionally falling below −25°F.

Turkmenistan is driest region in the Soviet Union. Average annual rainfall is only 3 to 4 inches. Four fifths of the total area is covered by the Kara Kum Desert, fourth largest in the world.[2] The republic has nearly 300 days of sunshine per year, which has a restricting effect on the life cycle and on man's activity. In no other republic is the problem of water, or the lack of it, as crucial.

The few rivers and small streams flowing from neighboring Iran and Afghanistan into Turkmenistan include the Murgab (220 miles) and the Tedzen (186.4 miles). They are used extensively for irrigation, mainly for cotton growing. The Atrek River, which flows along or inside the Turkmen border for 87 miles, is the only one reaching the basin of the Caspian Sea. The longest Central Asian river, the Amu Darya, flows through Turkmen territory for 620 miles along the eastern portions of the Kara Kum Desert, constituting the most important

---

1 Ovezov, 1967: 7–9, 20–21, 52–62; *Turkmenistan,* 1969: 9–59, 92–118, 126–151; Freikin, 1957: 7–79.

2 There are also uplands and mountain ranges in the south, reaching a maximum elevation of 10,000 feet.

irrigation source. The manmade Kara Kum Canal runs from the Amu Darya in the southeast to just west of Ashkhabad. The Kara Kum Canal is navigable for approximately 250 miles of its 534-mile course. With its extension, it is expected to further ease the acute water shortage, to benefit the planned agricultural and industrial expansion in the west (oil and natural gas), and to link the republic with principal waterways of the Soviet Union via the Caspian Sea.

Turkmenistan is rich in natural resources. The Kara Kum Desert appears to be a treasure store of oil, gas, sulphur, potassium, coal, lead, barite, viterite, magnesium, bromine, iodine, and other minerals. Oil and gas are first, both in magnitude of deposits and in importance to the national economy. In explored oil and gas deposits, Turkmenistan takes second place in the USSR (in oil after the Tatar ASSR; in gas after west Siberia).

ECONOMY

As a part of Russian Turkestan, Turkmenistan was one of the least developed areas of tsarist Russia, supplying raw materials, primarily cotton, for expanding Russian industry. Today, Turkmenistan remains above all a source of raw materials, but oil, gas, and minerals play a major part in this production. In 1967 Turkmenistan ranked third among Soviet republics in production of both gas and oil.[3] The growth of industrial production in 1940–1950 and 1960–1970, however, was slowest of any union republic except Azerbaidzhan.[4] More recently the growth rate has risen, equaling the USSR average in 1965–1970. Expanded exploitation of the country's large oil, natural gas, and other mineral deposits and major efforts at increasing irrigation promise continued future advances.

In 1970 the republic, with 2.2% of the territory and 0.9% of the population of the USSR, produced 4.1% of its oil, 6.5% of its gas, 10.5% of its cotton fiber, and 1.3% of its vegetable oils.[5] Some processing of Turk-

menia's resources is done at home—notably petrochemicals at Krasnovodsk, chemical fertilizers at Chardzhou, and sulphur at Kara Bogaz-Gol. Other than oil machinery and chemical manufacture, there is relatively little heavy industry in the republic, but significant amounts of cotton, wool, and silk fabrics, furniture, cement, and glass are produced. The Ninth Five-Year Plan includes construction of a new oil-machinery plant at Ashkhabad and several light industry combines.[6]

Increased irrigation and reclamation, agricultural mechanization, and growth in production of mineral fertilizers have brought a major expansion in Turkmen agricultural output since 1966. Cotton remains by far the most important crop; in 1970, 60% of the irrigated land area was devoted to it, including major areas opened for irrigation by the Kara Kum Canal. Turkmenistan is second largest cotton producer in the USSR after Uzbekistan. In 1973 it produced over 1 million metric tons of cotton. Lesser but still significant crops include grains, silk, fruits, and vegetables.

Livestock accounts for two fifths of the gross output of Turkmen agriculture. Sheep and goats constitute the bulk of the herds; most important variety is karakul, from which "Persian lamb" fur is obtained.

Occupational structure of Turkmenistan is given in Table 12.1. Industrial workers constitute one of the smallest percentages of the labor force of any Soviet republic. Uzbekistan is the only other republic in which number of *kolkhozniki* increased between 1965 and 1971.

Table 12.1

Occupational Structure of Turkmenistan

	1965	1971
Workers and employees	390,000	498,000
in agriculture	28,000	32,000
in construction	61,000	82,000
in industry	80,000	93,000
Kolkhozniki	217,000	254,000

Source: *Nar. khoz. 1972*: 674–675.

---

3 *Turkmenistan, 1969*: 94–95.
4 *Nar. khoz. 1970*: 139–140.
5 *Ibid.*: 70–73.

6 *Nar. khoz. 1972*: 673.

HISTORY

Tradition traces Turkmen origins from the Oguz group of Turkic peoples, though other peoples have also been assimilated into the modern nation.[7] Beginning in the seventh and eighth centuries, the Oguz Turks migrated from their ancient homelands in eastern Asia into western Asia and the Middle East, where different branches later established the vast Seljukid and Ottoman empires. Linguistically, Turkmen remain more closely related to the Turks of Anatolia and Azerbaidzhan than to their neighbors in Soviet Central Asia.[8]

The vast Turkish migration was occasioned primarily by Chinese and Mongolian pressures and collapse of the Türküt Empire in the eighth century A.D. Apparently, Oguz-Turkmen tribes settled to the north of the Syr-Darya and Aral Sea about this time. In the tenth and eleventh centuries, following Arab conquest of Central Asia and subsequent conversion of many peoples there to Islam, the Oguz-Turkic tribes pressed south against Iranian frontiers and into the Middle East. Two brothers, Chagri and Togril Bek, established the Seljukid Empire in the southern part of modern Turkmenia in 1040 A.D., with its capital at Mary (Merv). In 1055 Togril entered Baghdad, establishing his line as protectors to the caliphate, with a concomitant right to conquer all Moslem territories in the caliph's name. Alp Arslan, nephew of Togril, defeated a Byzantine army at Malazgird in 1071, opening the way into Anatolia for the Ottoman Turks' conquest of Asia Minor, where they established an empire that lasted until 1918.[9] Osman, leader of another tribe of Oguz Turks, succeeded the Seljukids as head of the Turks in Anatolia in 1299. His dynasty, the Ottomans, proceeded with the conquest of Asia Minor. Another two Turkmen successor states moved into the Caucasus and Iran in the fourteenth and fifteenth centuries, laying the basis for the modern Azerbaidzhani nation.[10]

Oguz-Turkmens remaining in Central

Asia established themselves in Khorasan and Khorezm in the eleventh and twelfth centuries, forming the nucleus of the future Turkmen nation. Merv, ancient capital of the Seljukids (Mary in modern Turkmenistan), became an important political, economic, and cultural center.

During the Mongolian invasion and conquest, the northern Turkmen in the area of Mangyshlak peninsula and Khorezm fell under Batu and the Golden Horde. Southern Turkmenistan became part of the Timurid Empire in the fourteenth and fifteenth centuries and was later divided among the successor states of Khiva, Bukhara, and Persia. Many Turkmen retained independence by defending themselves and allying themselves to one or another of the conflicting parties. Their military skills and pastoral culture contributed greatly to independence, but they did not succeed in forming a lasting state of their own. Tribal clan and family loyalties predominated.[11] From the sixteenth century onward, their territories began to take on a clearly definable shape in the vast desert areas of modern Turkmenistan and on the northern edges of Iran and Afghanistan. On the eve of the Russian advance in the second half of the nineteenth century Turkmen tribes of Transcaspia were in the process of unifying under a central government led by the most powerful Teke-Turkmen tribes.[12] However, the political situation remained unstable up to the second half of the nineteenth century as the Russians advanced into Central Asia. British rivalry with Russia in the region added to its instability.

The Russians, throughout their penetration into Central Asia, encountered stiffest resistance and suffered biggest losses at the hands of the Turkmen.[13] During the reign of Peter the Great, the first Russian military expedition from the Caspian to Khiva in 1717 under Bakovich-Cherkassy was annihilated by Turkmen cavalry; the defeat caused the delay of the Russian advance by over a century. The final assault on Turkmen territories began only after conquests of Tashkent, Bukhara, and Khiva (1865–1878) and was not completed until 1884–1885. Thus, Turkmenistan was last

---

7 Krader, 1963: 58; Wheeler, 1966: 17–18.
8 Krader, 1963: 34; Benzing and Menges, 1959: 1–10.
9 Bartol'd, 1963: II: 1: 544–623; Cahen, 1968: 1–50, 72–84.
10 Sumer, 1967a, 1967b.

---

11 Bacon, 1966: 49–50; Wheeler, 1964: 43, 65.
12 König, 1962: 162.
13 Wheeler, 1966: 36.

Central Asian territory to come under Russian control. Greatest battle of the campaign was the Turkmen defense of the fortress of Goek-Tepe in 1881, resulting in Russian massacre of the garrison.[14] General Kuropatkin completed the conquest by occupying Merv and the Tedzhen and Murgab river valleys in 1884–1885.[15] An Anglo-Russian border treaty of 1895 established the present border between Russian Turkmenistan and Iran and Afghanistan, leaving a considerable Turkmen population in the latter two countries.

The "provisional status" decree of the tsarist government in 1890 placed all of the Transcaspian Oblast (Turkmenistan) under sole authority of the military governor of Transcaucasia and until 1898 the territory was governed separately from other Central Asian lands because of its strategic location vis-a-vis Afghanistan. Tsarist policies encouraged Russian settlement, resulting in impoverishment of natives and loss of many pastures and farm lands to colonists. Like other Central Asians, Turkmen were allowed only very limited representation in the dumas created after the 1905 revolution; unlike the others, they did have some limited access to military service. In general the area was treated like a colonial territory. Tsarist colonial rule did, nonetheless, bring the beginnings of modernity: a railroad was built through the territory and the Turkmen settlement of Ashkhabad was established as a tsarist fortress, railroad station, and administrative center of the Transcaspian region.

Turkmen participated in the general uprising of 1916 against tsarist rule in Central Asia. Led by Dzhunaid Khan, Turkmen overthrew the ruling Hanof Khiva, establishing themselves in power in 1918. Nationalist dissatisfactions were a strong force in this movement. Tsarist and later Soviet authorities responded with harsh military action to quell the rebelling populace.

The collapse of tsarist authority in the 1917 October revolution left a power vacuum in Turkmenistan. Several different groups and factions contended for ascendancy. Among the Turkmen, there were tradition-oriented raiders such as Dzhunaid

Khan, and representatives of a nascent nationalist intelligentsia such as Oraz Serdar, Hadji Murat, and Ovezbayev, who formed a Provisional Turkmen Congress in Ashkhabad.[16] Among Russian settlers in the area, three major divisions formed: the "Whites," primarily former tsarist administrators and military officials; a revolutionary group centered primarily around workers and employees of the Central Asian Railway, at first led by social revolutionaries; and a small group of Bolsheviks acting on the basis of instructions from the Tashkent soviet.[17]

The Whites formed a Provisional Government of Transcaspia (Turkmenistan) in mid-1917, resisting any concessions to the nationalist Turkmen until Bolshevik pressure forced them into a loose alliance in the summer of 1918. The railroad workers formed a soviet in Ashkhabad soon after news of the October revolution arrived; Bolsheviks succeeded in gaining leadership of the soviet by the end of the year. The Bolsheviks made overtures to the Turkmen, but refused to give them a strong voice in the leadership. When in February 1918 the Turkmen congress sought to form an army based on a nucleus of Turkmen cavalry units of the old tsarist army, the Tashkent soviet dispatched Red Army units to Ashkhabad to suppress them.[18] The Bolsheviks maintained an uneasy dictatorship in Ashkhabad until June 1918, when it collapsed under opposition from Turkmen, provisional government, and social revolutionaries in the soviet. The Whites and the Turkmen congress then came together to form a Transcaspian government which, with limited British assistance, held off the Bolsheviks until July 1919.[19] In Khiva the "Young Khivans," an Uzbek liberal modernist group, appealed to Tashkent for assistance against Dzhunaid Khan. A Red Army detachment drove him into the desert in January 1920. In September 1920, the emirate of Bukhara came to an end, opening the way for communist domination in both former Hanates. Dzhunaid Khan and Oraz

---

14 *Ibid.*
15 Krader, 1963: 104.

16 Wheeler, 1964: 111.
17 Turkestan, including Turkmenia, was virtually cut off from Russia from December 1917 until late 1919 by the Dutov rebellion in the southern Urals. Zenkovsky, 1960: 231; Doemming, 1969: 39–51.
18 Wheeler, 1964: 113.
19 Pipes, 1964: 18–181; Allworth, 1967: 228–236.

Serdar fought on in the desert for some years, as part of the Turkmen Basmachi resistance movement.[20]

At first Soviet Russia recognized the sovereignty of the "People's Republics" in Khiva (Khorezm) and Bukhara, with control over most of Turkestan. By 1923–1924 they had succeeded in infiltrating and removing the "Young Khivan" and "Young Bukharan" native cadres from power, reorganizing both states into "socialist republics" and establishing the supremacy of Soviet Russia over them. In 1924 the Bukhara and Khorezm (Khiva) republics were forced to agree to their own dismemberment and establishment of Uzbek and Turkmen SSRs on their territory. On October 27, 1924, the national-state demarcation in Central Asia and the creation of the Turkmen SSR was declared. An All-Turkmen Constituent Congress of Soviets was held in Ashkhabad in February 1925; an embryonic Turkmen Communist party was organized, and the Turkmen SSR was formally accepted into the USSR on May 13, 1925.[21]

Soviet sources have admitted the continued existence and activity of nationalist organizations in Turkmenistan through the 1920s and 1930s. Collectivization was especially traumatic, meaning in part forced settlement of nomads on collective farms. Thus harsh Soviet policies resulted in open rebellion in 1928–1932; two ministers of the government were charged with supporting the rebels and seeking establishment of an independent Turkmenian state under British protection.[22] The 1930s saw emergence of a national opposition movement, Turkmen Azatlygi (Turkmen Freedom); Aitakov, chairman of the Turkmen Supreme Soviet, and Atabayev, chairman of the Turkmen Soviet government, were accused of protecting national resistance movements and executed in 1937–1938. The "purges" (mass persecution) which followed took a heavy toll of Turkmen party and government leaders and creative intelli-

gentsia.[23] As late as 1948 the first secretary of the Turkmen CP, Batyrov, indicated that communism was not yet completely accepted by the natives.[24]

DEMOGRAPHY[25]

Central Asia has the highest rate of population growth in the Soviet Union, and Turkmenistan is typical of the pattern. Population grew from 1,516,375 in 1959 to 2,158,880 in 1970, or 42.4%. Among Soviet republics, only Tadzhikistan (46.4%) and Uzbekistan (44.8%) had higher growth rates for the period. The great bulk of the increase is attributable to natural growth rather than immigration; in 1969 Turkmenistan's birth rate was 34.3 per 1,000 inhabitants (second only to Tadzhikistan) and its death rate was one of the lowest; as a result, the republic's net natural growth rate in 1969 was 27.3 per 1,000. One reason is that the republic has a youthful population: according to the 1970 census, nearly half of the population (46.4%) are under 15 years of age, and nearly two thirds (65.5%) are 29 years old or less.

The great majority of inhabitants added to the republic during 1959–1970—roughly three out of four—were Turkmen. Total Slavic element in the population (Russians, Ukrainians, Belorussians) fell to 16.3% in 1970.

Turkmenistan is home for only about half of the ethnic Turkmen population. Significant minorities live elsewhere in the USSR (primarily in Central Asia) and in neighboring Middle Eastern countries; 1970 data for the USSR and 1967 estimates for other countries giving an overview of distribution of ethnic Turkmen are shown in Table 12.3.

---

20 Pipes, 1964: 181; Wheeler, 1964: 111; Ellis, 1963; Nepesov, 1950. For short description of the Basmachi movement, see chapter 22 on Kirgiz, section on history, note 32.
21 Amanov, 1970: 11–30; Abayeva, 1968: 13–32; *Istoriya Turkmenskoi SSR*, 1957: II: 249–258.
22 Kolarz, 1967: 293; Nepesov, 1950: 196–223, 299–356.

23 Neposov, 1950: 348–356; Hughes, 1964 (reprinted). This book by the American Negro poet contains a section on travels in Turkmenistan at the time of the purges. Hughes attributes the initial disillusionment with communism of his traveling companion, Arthur Koestler, to the purges. Otherwise, the book is replete with the poet's first-hand observations of Turkmen society.
24 Berdimurat, 1951: 213–217, 231–234; Kolarz, 1967: 295.
25 Data in this section are from *Itogi Turkmenskoi SSR*, 1959: 130, and *Itogi 1970*: IV: 308–309.

Table 12.2

Population of Turkmenistan 1959–1970

NATIONALITY	NO.		% OF TOTAL		INCREASE %
	1959	1970	1959	1970	1959–1970
Total population	1,516,375	2,158,880	100.0	100.0	42.4
Turkmen	923,724	1,416,700	60.9	65.6	53.4
Russians	262,701	313,079	17.3	14.5	19.5
Uzbeks	125,231	179,498	8.3	8.3	43.3
Kazakhs	69,552	68,519	4.6	3.2	−1.5
Tatars	29,946	36,457	2.0	1.7	21.7

Sources: *Itogi Turkmenskoi SSR*, 1959: 130; *Itogi 1970*: IV: 308–309.

Table 12.3

Geographical Distribution of Ethnic Turkmen

Turkmen SSR	1,416,700
Elsewhere in USSR (Uzbekistan, Tadzhikistan, Azerbaidzhan, Armenia)	108,600
Iran	450,000
Afghanistan	450,000
Iraq	200,000
Turkey	80,000
Other countries (Jordan, Syria, Tibet)	82,000
Total (approximate)	2,800,000

Sources: M. V. Khidirov and T. Nepesov, "Problems of Ancient and Medieval Turkmen Literary History" (in Turkmen), *Sovet Edebiaty*, 1972: VI: 112–128; S. Bruk, "Chislennost' i rasseleniye narodov mira," *Narody mira* (Moscow: 12d. Akademii Nauk SSSR, 1962): 408.

Historically, urbanization has been high in comparison to other Central Asian republics. This has been due in part to the extensive desert areas and the consequent oasis culture of the region, as well as to a tendency of Slavic settlers to locate in the cities. Rate of urbanization in 1959–1970, however, did not keep pace with that of the rest of the USSR. The urban portion of the population increased only from 46% to 48%, and the republic dropped from sixth to eleventh place in urbanization among Soviet republics. All other Central Asian republics showed a greater percentage gain in urban population than did Turkmenistan.

Still, urbanization of the indigenous nationality proceeded at a higher rate in 1959–1970. In Turkmenistan this also means that ethnic Turkmen are settling down beside Uzbeks, who have long represented a major part of the urban population. In 1970, 31.7% of ethnic Turkmen in Turkmenistan were urbanized, as opposed to 26.3% in 1959. They constituted 43% of the republic's urban population, versus 34.7% in 1959, whereas the Russian share decreased from 35.4% to 29%. In Ashkhabad, capital of the republic, percentage of Turkmen advanced from 30% to 38%; although the city is still 42.8% Russian, non-Slavic ethnic groups now compose a majority of the population. The trend is toward an end to Russian domination of this Asian city and a marked strengthening of the native element.

CULTURE

Turkmenistan is a region of ancient settlement. Archeological discoveries in the area date from both ancient and medieval times. A rich discovery at Anau, five miles east of Ashkhabad, dates back to the third and fourth centuries B.C.; Nisa, ancient capital of the Parthian Empire, lies buried in ruins on the western outskirts of Ashkhabad. Turkmen, as part of a vast Turkic migration, entered the area in the sixth to eighth centuries. Their dominance of the region can be dated from their adoption of Islam and from the end of the Iranian Samanid rule in the tenth century.

Expansion of the Oguz Turkmen into Persia, Transcaucasia, and Anatolia in the eleventh century and contact with Islamic culture in Baghdad inspired a major advance of Oguz-Turkmen culture and literature. Turkmen share this heritage with the Turks of Anatolia and Azerbaidzhan, giving the achievements of Oguz literature a distinct place among Turkic peoples and the Islamic world.

To this common heritage belong such major epics of the eleventh to sixteenth centuries as *Oguz-Nama*, about the legendary Oguz Khan, mythical predecessor of all Turks, and *Korkut Ata*, eleventh-century Turkmen epic. Important pieces of romantic folklore such as *Kör Ogli*, *Kissa-i-Yusuf*, and *Seyid Battal* are also part of this heritage, although originating in places outside the present Turkmen habitat. The Oguz were in close contact with Iranian culture throughout their history; many literati wrote in Persian, official language of Bukhara until 1920. The modern Turkmen literary language dates from the eighteenth century. Most outstanding name in classical Turkmen literature is that of the poet-philosopher Makhtumkuli (1733–1782).[26]

Up until the revolution, a great many Turkmen were pastoral nomads, although a large part had turned to a more settled agricultural existence in the oases in the eighteenth and nineteenth centuries. They tended nonetheless to keep to the portable *yurt* of the nomads rather than building more permanent housing. Tribal organizations and loyalties remained very strong. Turkmen were warlike in the past, struggling for survival and independence, often hiring out as mercenaries to different principalities of the region.[27]

Establishment of the Turkmen SSR and the Soviet system there brought a greater unity to the Turkmen tribes, exerting a positive effect on consolidation of a sense of nationhood and on modernization of culture and literature. The Arabic alphabet used by the Turks for a millennium was replaced by Latin in 1928–1929 and by Cyrillic in 1940. A major purpose of these changes was to enhance distinctions between Turkmen and other Turkic peoples and to increase the influence of Russian culture.[28]

Modernization brought difficult troubled times but has now taken hold. As elsewhere in Central Asia, introduction of a Western system of general and higher education, advance of the Turkmen literary language, emancipation of women, formation of a national intelligentsia, and adoption of Western art have not displaced traditional culture, but have been absorbed into it. Turkmen culture has retained much of its earlier form and characteristic values. Islam and its traditions have been strong among Turkmen, and there is evidence that practice of Moslem observances has been widely preserved since the revolution.[29] Despite the sweeping progress of Westernization, Islam and more strictly national traditions continue to be vital forces among Turkmen.

EXTERNAL RELATIONS

Most important of Turkmenistan's external relations are with other Central Asian peoples; the Soviet Union as a whole; and those foreign countries with Turkmen diasporas, especially Iran, Afghanistan, Iraq, and Turkey.

During the Stalinist period, direct cultural relations among Central Asian and Turkic peoples were restricted and inhibited by accusations of "Pan-Turkism" or "Pan-Islamism." At the same time, Russian cultural influence was favored.

In the post-Stalin era, both party line and advances in communication and mass media encouraged a drawing closer [*sblizheniye*] of peoples and increased cultural interchange. As a result, Turkmen have improved their awareness of other Central Asian and Turkic peoples—with whom they share a common past, cultural heritage, and Islamic religion—as well as of other Soviet peoples. Although subject to strict regulation, this development is nonetheless significant. Establishment of a Central Asian economic region in 1922–1934 and

---

26 Bacon, 1966: 144; Kolarz, 1967: 293; Makhtumkuli, 1960.
27 Bacon, 1966: 50–53; *Istoriya Turkmenskoi SSR*, 1957: I: 2: 65–105.

28 Kolarz, 1967: 293–294.
29 Bacon, 1966: 143.

1963–1965, recent discussions of its revival, advance of general education, jointly conducted research on history and culture, and joint literary conferences and art events have contributed to growing inter-relationships and a sense of common identity among Central Asian peoples. Furthermore, in recent years, cultural and scholarly conferences of Turkic-speaking peoples of the USSR have contributed to revival of cultural relations among Turkic peoples, disrupted during the Stalin era. Noteworthy is the All-Union Conference of Soviet Turkologists, held in Baku in 1966 to commemorate the 40th anniversary of the First Baku Congress of Turkologists. The conference resumed joint planning of cultural and linguistic development of Turkic peoples, initiating publication of a joint bimonthly, *Sovetskaya Turkologiya*.

Recent years have also witnessed a growing Turkmen interest in friendly relations with neighboring Middle Eastern countries and with Turkmen diasporas inhabiting those countries. Nearly half of the ethnic Turkmen live in the Middle East; close to 1 million are in Iran and Afghanistan, just south of the borders of the TSSR. Many Turkmen crossed the border to escape the tsarist conquest and later the harsh Soviet rule.

Until lately Turkmenistan was one of the most restricted areas of the Soviet Union. Not only were foreign tourists barred from entering the Turkmen SSR, but Turkmen themselves, on both sides of the border, could not cross it. Communication with Turkmen abroad is still confined largely to an infrequent exchange of letters and visits between relatives and to listening to radio broadcasts in Turkmen from across the border. Recently, however, Soviet Turkmen writers, journalists, and occasionally official Soviet delegations have visited countries on the other side of the border. Berdi Kerbabayev, best-known Turkmen writer, reported on his journey to Turkey in successive articles in the Soviet Turkmen press. His conversations with Turkish writers and intellectual circles and his rediscovery of monuments and proofs of a common Turkmen-Turkish past were of great interest to Turkmen society. There are the Turkmen societies for friendship and cultural exchange with the foreign countries, Turkmen branches of Soviet societies for friendship and cultural exchange with Afro-Asian countries, Arab countries, India, Vietnam, and others, and eventual exchange of official delegations, scholars, and artists.

Radio Liberty beams programs to Soviet Central Asia in the Turkmen language. Because of the great distance involved, weak transmitters, and Soviet jamming, these programs reach their intended listeners only on a relatively weak second hop. A 30-minute program is transmitted four times a week, giving news, news analysis, and comments on internal Turkmen problems.

Foreign printed media are not available to the general public, limited in use to persons with special permission in Turkmen state library and libraries of Turkmen Academy of Sciences, party, and other institutions. Turkmen books and other printed media are available in the West. In recent years a number of foreign books, mostly novels from the Third World, have been printed in Turkmen translation. There is a limited exchange of books between Turkmen state library in Ashkhabad and Columbia University Library, and similar exchanges with other American and Western universities and libraries.

Media

LANGUAGE DATA

Turkmen belongs to the southwestern group of Turkic languages, as do Azerbaidzhani, Kashgai (southern Iran), Anatolian Turkish, Balkan Turkish, and Crimean Tatar. In the fourteenth century the Turkmen used a literary language which soon came under the influence of the Central Asian literary Turkish, Chagatai, related to

Table 12.4

Native and Second Languages Spoken by Turkmen

(in thousands)

No. Turkmen Residing			SPEAKING AS NATIVE LANGUAGE						SPEAKING AS SECOND LANGUAGE[a]	
			Turkmen			Russian			Russian	Other Languages of Peoples of USSR[b]
	1959	1970	1959	1970	% Point Change 1959–1970	1959	1970	% Point Change 1959–1970	1970	1970
in Turkmen SSR	924 (100%)	1,417 (100%)	919 (99.5%)	1,407 (99.3%)	−0.2	5 (.5%)	9 (0.6%)	+0.1	210 (14.8%)	7 (0.5%)
in other Soviet republics	78 (100%)	108 (100%)	72 (92%)	101 (93.4%)	+1.4	2 (2.3%)	3 (2.8%)	+0.5	25 (25.3%)	13 (11.8%)
Total	1,002 (100%)	1,525 (100%)	990 (98.9%)	1,508 (98.9%)	0	7 (.7%)	12 (0.8%)	+0.1	235 (15.4%)	20 (1.3%)

Sources: *Itogi Turkmenskoi SSR, 1959*: tables 53, 54; *Itogi SSSR 1959*: table 53; *Nar. khoz. 1972*: 32; *Itogi 1970*: IV: 20, 306.

[a] No data are available for 1959, since no questions regarding command of a second language were asked in the 1959 census.

[b] Including Turkmen, if not native language.

the modern Uzbek and Kazakh languages. In the eighteenth and nineteenth centuries the Turkmen literary language again came into use, persisting until after formation of the Turkmen SSR. During the Soviet period Turkmen developed a literary language based on living Turkmen dialects.[30]

Turkmen employed the Arabic alphabet until 1928–1929, when a Latin alphabet more closely adapted to Turkmen phonemes was introduced. In turn, this alphabet was arbitrarily replaced by a modified form of Cyrillic alphabet in 1940.[31]

As indicated in Table 12.4, Turkmen display the typical Central Asian pattern of high retention of native language; 98.9% of Turkmen in the USSR and 99.3% of those in the Turkmen SSR consider Turkmen as native language. In the republic, those citing Russian as native tongue are concentrated in the cities, as are those who give Russian as second language of fluency. The former group includes roughly equal numbers of men and women, mostly descendants of mixed marriages, but those citing Russian as second language are predominantly male.[32] Even in the cities 97.9% of Turkmen gave national language as their own.

Turkmen is native language of 65.5% of the population, and Russian is first language of 17.1% of the republic. Of members of other nationalities in the country, 46,999 gave Russian as their tongue, and only 6,100 Turkmen. Uzbeks, Baluchis, and Kurds, however, cited Turkmen more often than Russian. Baluchis, Kurds, and Iranians in the Turkmen SSR listed Turkmen as second language more often than Russian, which may indicate a tendency among these Moslem groups to assimilate with Turkmen.

LOCAL MEDIA

Print Media

Mass media in Turkmenistan showed considerable growth in the 1960s. Per issue circulation of both newspapers and magazines more than doubled between 1959 and 1971. This growth can be attributed, in part, to growth of the Turkmen intelligentsia and continued spread of education in the republic, increasing numbers of immigrants, especially those coming to work in the booming oil and gas industries, easing of the paper shortage, and an official policy of promoting use of Russian.

Most important daily newspapers are *Sovet Turkmenistani* (in Turkmen) and *Turkmenskaya Iskra* [*Turkmen Spark*], in Russian, official organs of the Communist party and government of the republic. *Mugallimlar Gazyeti* [*Teachers' Gazette*], with 1972 circulation of over 21,000, and its Russian equivalent, *Uchitel'skaya Gazeta*, appear three times a week. Both are pedagogical papers aimed at teachers and educators. The Turkmen literary biweekly *Edebiyat & Sungat* [*Literature and Art*] is widely read in intellectual circles, reflecting current literary politics, popularizing both classic and modern works, and discussing problems of literature and language. This newspaper initiated a heated argument concerning language in the early 1960s, only to have it cut short by executive order.

Other newspapers include *Yash Kommunist* [*Young Communist*] and *Komsomolets Turkmenistana*, organs of the Young Communist League, and the Turkmen language organ of the Young Pioneers, *Mydam Tayyar* [*Always Ready*]. There are more than 40 local newspapers in the cities and *raions* of the republic. The two minority language papers are in Kazakh and Uzbek.

The quality of the press is not high even by Soviet standards. At a 1971 conference of republic ideological workers, the media were criticized as not meeting aesthetic demands of readers, not informing them properly, and being dry and uninteresting.[33]

Of magazines published in Turkmenistan, the following are among the most significant:

Sovet Edebiyati [*Soviet Literature*], in Turkmen, monthly, with 1973 circulation of 20,670 and *Ashkhabad*, in Russian, bi-monthly, with 1973 circulation

---

30 Kolarz, 1967: 294–295.
31 Wurm, 1954; Baskakov, 1960; Bazin, 1959: 308–317.
32 *Itogi 1970*: IV: 306–311.

---

33 *Sovet Turkmenistani* and *Turkmenskaya Iskra* (June 29), 1971.

Table 12.5

Publications in Turkmen SSR

Language of Publication	Year	NEWSPAPERS[a]			MAGAZINES			BOOKS AND BROCHURES		
		No.	Per Issue Circulation (1,000)	Copies/100 in Language Group[d]	No.	Per Issue Circulation (1,000)	Copies/100 in Language Group[d]	No. Titles	Total Volume (1,000)	Books & Brochures/100 in Language Group[d]
Russian	1959	21	96	31.3	N.A.	N.A.	N.A.	183	493	161
	1971	11	180	48.9	8	17	4.6	186	994	270
Turkmen	1959	54	251	27.1	N.A.	N.A.	N.A.	441	2,830	305.9
	1971	34	588	41.6	8	271	19.2	275	3,950	279.5
Minority Languages	1959	3[b]	4	1.4	N.A.	N.A.	N.A.	N.A.	N.A.	N.A.
	1971	2	7	1.9	0	0	0	N.A.	N.A.	N.A.
Foreign Languages	1959	0	0	0	N.A.	N.A.	N.A.	(3)[c]	(3)[c]	N.A.
	1971	0	0	0	0	0	0	(6)[c]	(929)[c]	N.A.
All Languages	1959	78	351	23.1	9	91	6	627[c]	3,326	219.3
	1971	47	775	35.9	16	288	13.3	467[c]	5,015	232.3

Sources: *Pechat' 1959*: 58, 130, 165; *Pechat' 1970*: 97, 160, 189; *Pechat' 1971*: 97, 160, 189.

[a] 1971 figures do not include *kolkhoz* newspapers.

[b] This figure may include publication in non-Soviet languages.

[c] Book totals as given in *Pechat'* sometimes differ from totals in language categories. The indication is that books are published in other languages, but no data is given. Figures in parentheses are the presumed production of books in other languages based on this discrepancy.

[d] Includes native speakers of the language.

of 4,900. These literary and sociopoliti-cal journals are published by the Writers' Union and are widely read by the intelligentsia.

Sovet Turkmenistaninin Ayallari [*Women of Soviet Turkmenistan*], in Turkmen, monthly, with 1973 circulation of 91,000. Political and literary magazine published by the Communist party. *Tokmak* [*Beetle*], in Turkmen, monthly, with 1972 circulation of 106,000, is a popular satirical journal.

Turkmenistan Kommunisti, in Turkmen, with 1973 circulation of 9,900, monthly theoretical and political organ of the Central Committee, Turkmen Communist party.

Book publishing was almost nonexistent in prerevolutionary Turkmenistan. Today the republic boasts two publishing houses with modern printing facilities and trained personnel. Over 118 million books have been issued since 1923, 5,015,000 in 1971 alone. A broad range of works are included: textbooks, scholarly works, propaganda brochures, atheistic works, and classics of Turkmen literature and Communist ideology. A 45-volume edition of Lenin's collected works has been published in Turkmen translation. First volume of the Turkmen encyclopedia is in print.

But the state of publishing is far from satisfactory. Annually, the Turkmenistan publishing house fails to fulfill its plan both in number of books and volumes. In May 1969, at the Second Congress of Turkmen Cultural Workers, the house was criticized for achieving only 69.3% of its 1968 plan.[34] Frequent complaints of shortages of paper and trained personnel are aired. Readers also complain that works of classical Turkmen literature and folk epics are not obtainable in bookshops.[35] The demand for books dealing with the Turkmen heritage is growing rapidly; nearly half of the novels published in 1967–1972 dealt with historic and historic-revolutionary themes.[36]

Electronic Media and Films

Radio and television broadcasting has also developed rapidly during the past decade; number of receiving sets has reached a point at which most Turkmen have access to them. Radio broadcasts from Ashkhabad cover the territory of the republic; television can be received in only about 80% of populated areas, but the Ninth Five-Year Plan (1970–1975) foresees construction of additional relay lines to reach areas near the Afghan border. At present, there are TV studios in Krasnovodsk, Nebit-Dagh, and Chardzhou, as well as in the capital.

Central studios in Ashkhabad broadcast three radio and three TV programs daily, including programs delivered by the Orbita and Vostok satellite systems. The Turkmen language is extensively used, predominating in programs of local origin. The goal is basic communication with the audience. According to one Soviet Central Asian author, "Daily information on the decisions of the Communist Party and the Soviet government . . . intended for every section of the population must be presented in their mother tongue, in that language in which the propaganda is most understandable and intelligible to them."[37]

The only film studio, Turkmenfilm, produces a few films and news chronicles of indifferent quality every year. In 1971–1972 it was criticized for not producing films glorifying the working class and contemporary life. Most popular foreign films available to the Turkmen audience originate in India or other Near Eastern countries.

EDUCATIONAL INSTITUTIONS

As elsewhere in Soviet Central Asia, education has made tremendous progress in the past half century in the Turkmen SSR. Literacy is now universal.[38] Although still somewhat low in comparison with other parts of the Soviet Union, education indicators in Turkmenistan are far above those

34 *Sovet Turkmenistani* and *Turkmenskaya Iskra* (June 29), 1971.
35 *Kniga,* 1965: 1.
36 Azimov, 1972: 3–15.

37 Khanazarov, 1963.
38 *Nar. khoz. 1972:* 669.

Table 12.6

Electronic Media and Films in Turkmen SSR

YEAR	RADIO					TELEVISION			MOVIES	
	No. Stations	No. Wired Sets (1,000)	Sets/100 Population	No. Wireless Sets (1,000)	Sets/100 Population	No. Stations[e]	No. Sets (1,000)	Sets/100 Population	Seats (1,000)	Seats/100 Population
1960	N.A.	150[a]	9.2[d]	182[a]	11.2[c]	N.A.	6[a]	0.4[c]	82[b]	5.0[d]
1970	N.A.	247[a]	11.1[d]	347[a]	15.6[c]	N.A.	186[a]	8.4[c]	143[b]	6.4[d]
1971	N.A.	260[d]	11.3[d]	376[d]	16.4[c]	N.A.	230[c]	10.0[c]	N.A.	N.A.

[a] Source: *Transport i svyaz' SSR*, 1972: 296–298.

[b] Source: *Nar. obraz.*, 1971: 325.

[c] Source: *Nar. khoz.* 1972: 572, 578.

[d] Computed from data cited above ([b] and [c]).

[e] See text for other years. *Problemy televideniya i radio*, 1971: 243, lists three TV studios in Turkmenistan in 1965.

Table 12.7

Selected Data on Education in Turkmen SSR (1971)

Population: 2,293,000

		PER 1,000 POPULATION	% OF TOTAL
All schools			
number of schools	1,653	.72	
number of students	585,000	255.1	
Newly opened elementary, incomplete secondary, and secondary schools			
number of schools	51		
number of student places	35,800	15.6	
Secondary special schools			
number of schools	29		
number of students	28,900	12.6	
Institutions of higher education			
number of institutions	5		
number of students	29,200	12.7	
Universities			
number of universities	1		
number of students			
total	10,124	4.4	
day students	5,298		52
evening students	1,049		10
correspondence students	3,777		38
newly admitted			
total	2,119	0.9	
day students	1,218		57
evening students	216		10
correspondence students	685		32
graduated			
total	1,470	0.6	
day students	894		61
evening students	109		7
correspondence students	467		32
Graduate students			
total number	620	.3	
in scientific research institutions	385		
in universities	235		
Number of persons with (in 1970) higher or secondary (complete and incomplete) education			
per 1,000 individuals, 10 years and older	475		
per 1,000 individuals employed in national economy	682		
Number of workers graduated from professional-technical schools	7,800	3.4	

Source: *Nar. khoz. 1972*: 108, 439, 669, 676, 677, 679.

in other Middle Eastern countries. Within Soviet Central Asia, Turkmenistan compares favorably with the other republics. It is first in ratio of people with higher and secondary education to the republic's adult population, and Turkmen trail only Azerbaidzhanis and Tatars, among Soviet Moslems, in ratio of scientific workers to population.[39]

The country has five higher educational institutions, including the state university and specialized schools for agriculture, medicine, pedagogy, and polytechnical studies; four are located in Ashkhabad.[40] The 28,000 students in these institutions in 1969–1970 amounted to 135 students per 10,000 inhabitants of the republic, a lower rate than for the Soviet Union as a whole. The rate for students in specialized secondary schools (130 per 10,000), however, was near the mean for Central Asia.

CULTURAL AND SCIENTIFIC INSTITUTIONS

The Turkmen Academy of Sciences was established in 1951. Centered in Ashkhabad, it now has 20 research institutes and many laboratories, experimental stations, and museums. Its work has been especially related to desert studies and oil and gas technology. Turkmenistan has a total of 56 scientific institutions with over 3,000 workers. More than half are said to be Turkmen.[41]

Four of the republic's six theaters are located in Ashkhabad. These include the Turkmen Academic Drama Theater, Russian Drama Theater, Turkmen Opera and Ballet Theater, and State Philharmonic.[42]

---

39 See tables A.5 and A.7 in Appendix.
40 *Turkmenistan*, 1969: 88, 173.

41 *Turkmenistan*, 1969: 89.
42 *Ibid.*: 173; *Europa Yearbook, 1970*: 1,314.

Table 12.8

Selected Data on Scientific and Cultural Facilities and Personnel in Turkmen SSR (1971)

Population: 2,293,000

Academy of Sciences		*Number of persons working in*	
number of members	43	*education and culture*	
number of scientific institutions		total	68,000
affiliated with academy	16	number per 1,000 population	29.7
total number of scientific workers	727		
		Number of persons working in science	
Museums		*and scientific services*	
number of museums	7	total	15,000
attendance	438,000	number per 1,000 population	6.5
attendance per 1,000 population	191		
		Number of public libraries	1,133
Theaters		number of books and magazines	
number of theaters	6	in public libraries	6,666,000
attendance	749,000		
attendance per 1,000 population	326.6	*Number of clubs*	733

Source: *Nar. khoz. 1972*: 106, 451, 675.

National Attitudes

REVIEW OF FACTORS FORMING NATIONAL ATTITUDES

Turkmen national attitudes have been powerfully affected by the transformation and modernization of society in the past half century. The Soviet regime has wrought radical changes in the political, economic, sociocultural, and intellectual life of the republic and its people. These changes have brought tensions and problems as well as the benefits of modernization. In a short half century, Turkmen have overcome inherited backwardness and consolidated a modern nation. Political reality of the Turkmen SSR serves as an expression of that nationhood. Growing industrialization and formation of a native working class, reorganization and expansion of irrigated agriculture, and emergence of a national intelligentsia have all played a part in formulation and expression of Turkmen attitudes.[43]

Writings and official statements issued during celebration of the 50th anniversary of formation of the USSR (1972) underlined the sovereignty of the Turkmen SSR, especially in regard to its right to establish direct relationships and to conclude agreements with foreign countries.[44] They also stressed the voluntary membership of union republics, and equality in sharing responsibility and power in overall planning and budget allocations. All this implies a sense of dissatisfaction with the degree of centralized USSR control. In the late 1960s and early 1970s, Turkmen authorities demanded that priority in funding be given to industrial projects which satisfy the republic's economic needs, in opposition to the prevailing line stressing overall division of labor. Apparently, there is consider-

able resentment over the fact that the bulk of Turkmenistan's large cotton production is shipped as raw material to Russian textile industries, and that Turkmen gas and oil is piped to other areas in disregard of Turkmenistan's own demands. There are clear manifestations that the intelligentsia is seeking a return to the 1920s' policy of "korenizatsiya," or Turkmenization, of party and government apparata, and to broadening social functions of the Turkmen language.[45]

Throughout history, the advance of culture in Central Asia has depended above all on irrigated agriculture. In this way, Soviet achievements in reconstruction and expansion of irrigated lands (particularly, construction of the Kara-Kum Canal) have profoundly affected the life of the rural Turkmen population. No other single Soviet measure has found such a wide degree of support and appreciation among Turkmen. At the same time, utilization of much newly opened land for cash-crop cotton production has raised new economic problems, increasing the importance of Turkmenistan in overall economy of the USSR. This may be a factor in Turkmen demands for greater economic diversification.

The Turkmen experience with the Central Asian Economic Region (1962–1965) fostered closer economic and cultural cooperation with other Central Asian republics and peoples. Revival of the region, now under consideration, would serve as organizational basis for coordination and common planning and for formulation of common attitudes. In combination with the existing trend toward greater cultural interchange and joint scholarly research, such a move could increase the regional particularism of Central Asia, reinforcing the bonds of the shared Islamic culture and a common heritage.

Effectively sealed off from the outside world during the past half century, Turk-

43 *Ocherki*, 1970: 469.
44 Begenchova, 1972: 38–42; Kiselyev, 1972: 74–81. See also *Turkmenistan kommunisti*, 1972: 12; *Izvestiya AN Turkmenskoi SSR*, serii *obshchestvennykh nauk*, 1972: 6.

45 Durdiyev, 1971: 10–17.

men have shown strong interest in renew-
ing outside contacts, especially with Turkmen minorities in Iran and Afghanistan.
These governments have been reluctant to
allow such contacts, but the exchange of
letters, publications, radio broadcasts, and
occasional visits has been growing.

BASIC VIEWS OF SCHOLARS ON NATIONAL ATTITUDES

There is basic agreement among both
Soviet and non-Soviet scholars that modernization of Soviet Central Asia during the
past half century has exerted a major effect
on the lives and attitudes of inhabitants.
There is less agreement, however, on the
nature of this effect. Soviet scholars have
generally stressed "flourishing" of the republics, giving little attention to negative
aspects or to results not consistent with the
party line.

Most Western scholars have dealt with
Turkmenistan only in the larger Central
Asian context. As such, many have seen
evidence of a general concern for native
cultural values and a resistance to Russification that, while lacking organizational
context and limited in written expression, is
nonetheless persistent and pervasive.
French scholars Alexandre Bennigsen and
Chantal Lemercier-Quelquejay, for example, have written:

> Soviet authors describe as "national-
> ism" the various manifestations of the
> resistance of the Moslems to Russian
> influence. This resistance is certainly
> an expression of discontent, but as far
> as is known it never takes the form of
> systematic opposition to communism
> or of demand for greater freedom. For
> the present, it is mainly a question of
> the negative reaction of self-defence—
> of defence of their literary heritage, of
> their history, of the purity of their
> language. . . .
>
>   Yet there is every reason to believe
> that the "nationalism" of the Moslems,
> from being purely defensive, could be-
> come insistent. Certain signs in the be-
> haviour of Moslem intellectuals afford
> ground for supposing that demands of
> this kind are in the air. Administra-
> tively, Moslems are stipulating larger

representation for their nations, to be
followed by a greater and more real
share of responsibility and power.[46]

Elizabeth Bacon, writing in 1966, argued
that traditional culture in Central Asia has
shown considerable tenacity even as it has
adapted to new conditions and borrowed
foreign elements: "The Central Asian
peoples have not lost their sense of ethnic
identity, nor are they likely to become
merged with the Russian people." [47] She
observed the persistence of old patterns in
occupations and social organization, and the
continuing strength of religious belief.
Further, she notes that the new intelligentsia acts as a buffer against Russianization
rather than as an agent for it:

> Soviet leaders appear doomed to dis-
> appointment in their hope that the in-
> telligentsia they had educated would
> lead the masses toward Russianiza-
> tion. The most highly educated Central
> Asians are also the most skilled in
> communicating the cultural values of
> their own ethnic group to those around
> them. Party members and administra-
> tors are inclined to react according to
> the values of their own culture rather
> than work toward Russianization.[48]

Jan Myrdal, son of the famed Swedish
sociologist, has provided a highly informative and personal account of travels in
Turkmenistan in 1960 and 1965. He also
saw potential conflict between native demands for continued social and political
growth and centralist insistence on maintaining controls:

> The conflict is not—as in Soviet pro-
> paganda it sometimes seems to be—a
> conflict between socialists and "bour-
> geois nationalists." I don't even think
> it is a conflict which has yet attained
> any clear organizational form, though
> it is already finding its reactive ideo-
> logical expressions and in the future
> can find its organizational. Nor is it a
> conflict which necessarily imperils the
> Union. Rather it is a conflict between
> those groups which for their own tech-
> nological and privilege-preserving rea-
> sons pursue a policy which is making

---

46 Bennigsen and Lemercier-Quelquejay, 1967:
225–226.
47 Bacon, 1966: 202.
48 *Ibid.*

the Union into a formal shell around a centralized "Russian" state, and those who want to see the Union realized. But if official policy continues to follow the same course as at present, then its result will be centrifugal and separatist movements.[49]

RECENT MANIFESTATIONS OF NATIONALISM

The Turkmen actively resisted imposition of tsarist and later Soviet rule. The last uprising took place in 1931 in the Kara Kum, as a response to the collectivization policy. It was suppressed by Soviet power; the rebelling herdsmen were forcibly resettled on cotton-growing *kolkhozy*. During the 1930s a large number of Turkmen party, government, and cultural leaders were accused of nationalism, "Pan-Turkism," or assisting the Basmachi and purged. Among them were premier of the TSSR government, Gaygisiz Atabay, and president of the republic's Supreme Soviet, Nedirbay Aytakov. Their posthumous rehabilitation included erection of memorials in the center of Ashkhabad. In his documentary novel *Gaygisiz Atabay*, Berdi Kerbabayev, the oldest and leading writer of Soviet Turkmenistan, noted that in those years "not hundreds, but thousands fell as victims of lawlessness," and that "although Atabay disappeared from the eyes, he always lived forth in the hearts of his people." [50]

Another group of intellectuals was accused of nationalism after 1948, including the historian Gayip Nepesov, criticized for *The Victory of Soviet Rule in Northern Turkmenistan 1917–1936*.[51] The book depicted Dzhunayd Khan and other leaders of the resistance in too positive a fashion for Soviet authorities. Nepesov was forced to rewrite the work and publish under a different title.[52]

In recent times, manifestations of nationalism have been restricted primarily to activities within established institutions of the Turkmen SSR. The so-called "Babayev affair" in 1958–1959 is a prominent example. The first secretary of the Central Committee of Turkmenistan's Communist party, Suhan Babayev, and the secretary of the Central Committee for Ideological-Cultural Affairs, Nurdzemal Durdiyeva, together with other leaders, argued that all leading posts should be occupied by Turkmen, and that officials of other nationalities should be appointed only when no candidates could be found among Turkmen cadres. The second secretary of the CC CPT, Grishayenkov, and other Russians, supported by the CC CPSU, opposed this demand. Consequently, Turkmen leaders were deposed and the entire party and government apparatus reshuffled. Babayev and his supporters were expelled from the party.[53]

The problem underlying this conflict remains unresolved. Intellectuals are now demanding greater self-government and an increased role for Turkmen in political, economic, and cultural life. Official Soviet propaganda has sought to discredit these aspirations as manifestations of "bourgeois nationalism" resulting from Western "bourgeois propaganda."

The present first secretary of the CC CP of Turkmenistan, Muhammetnazar Gapurov, condemned the rise of nationalism among students and intellectuals in his speech at the 24th party congress in Moscow April 1971, and again in the 11th Plenum, CC, CP, Turkmenia, in March 1973. Referring to events at the Polytechnical Institute, he stated: "There have been shortcomings and neglect in the international education work among students and professorial-teaching personnel of the institute. Under the influence of various concoctions of bourgeois propaganda . . . individual teachers and students at institutions of higher learning permit the occurrence of unhealthy, politically unsound statements." [54]

Gapurov also noted "shortcomings" in

---

49 Myrdal and Kessle, 1971: 213–214.
50 Kerbabayev, 1965: 454–455.
51 Nepesov, 1950.
52 Nepesov, 1958.

53 For more on the Babayev case, see the Soviet Turkmen papers, *Sovet Turkmenistani* and *Turkmenskaya iskra* (December 16), 1958, and subsequent issues.
54 The speech by M. Gapurov was reported in *Sovet Turkmenistani* and *Turkmenskaya iskra* (March 4), 1973.

atheistic propaganda. Survival of Islam as
a way of life and connection of Islamic
customs and traditions of Turkmen with
Central Asian culture are special concerns
of party officials. Gapurov speaking at the
Turkmen CC March Plenum in 1973,
stated, "The steady and persistent struggle
against the bearers of survivals of the past
is a necessity. Due to its peculiarity and
specific role, the Islamic cult cannot be
seen by us without anxiety. Islam, as is the
case with all religions, often poses in the
role as the 'preserver' of reactionary
national customs and traditions, it awakens
feelings of national exclusiveness, and
serves as a refuge for nationalism." [55] In
accord with recent party decisions, the
Soviet Turkmen press has called editorially
for reinforcement of "internationalist education" of youth and for struggle "against
the remnants of nationalism." [56]

Among dissidents the case of Annasoltan
Kekilova stands out, the first of its kind in
Central Asia to become known in the West.
A poet, daughter of the renowned writer
and scholar Aman Kekilov and niece of the
writer Shali Kekilov, she was committed to
a mental hospital as a result of her criti-

cisms of conditions in Turkmenistan. The
case came to light through a petition sent by
her mother to the Central Committee vouch-
ing for her sanity and pleading for her release. A copy of the petition, made available
to Western newsmen, was reported in the
New York Times and other newspapers.[57]

According to these reports (confirmed by
confidential sources), the poet criticized
shortcomings in her republic in a 56-page
illustrated report, addressed to the CC
CPSU in Moscow, and in a letter to the
party's 24th Congress (April 1971). Harassed by party officials, she lost her job, and
her works were banned from publication
and circulation.[58] Kekilova decided to renounce Soviet citizenship and emigrate.
Embarrassed Soviet authorities in Turkmenistan committed her to a hospital in an
attempt to force her to sign a statement
saying that she had forwarded her report
to the CC CPSU "while under nervous tension."

As the recent drive against nationalism
shows, this is only one illustration of widespread national discontent and self-asser-
tion in the republic.

---

[55] *Sovet Turkmenistani* and *Turkmenskaya iskra*
(March 4), 1973.
[56] Editorials in *Sovet Turkmenistani* (April 6, May
16), 1973.

[57] See *New York Times* (September 28), 1971; *The
Economist* (October 9), 1971; and the Turkish
newspaper published in Ankara, *Devlet* (December 27), 1971.
[58] Her poetry had been published in the Russian
language periodical, *Ashkhabad*, 1971: 2.

REFERENCES

Abayeva, 1968
Dina M. Abayeva, *Razvitiye obshchest-
vennogo ustroistva Turkmenskoi SSR
(1924–1964)* (Ashkhabad: Ylym, 1968).
Allworth, 1967
Edward Allworth, ed., *Central Asia: A
Century of Russian Rule* (New York:
Columbia University Press, 1967).
Amanov, 1970
Oraz B. Amanov, *Turkmenistan SSR
Yokari Soveti [Turkmenistan SSR Sup-
reme Soviet]* (Ashkhabad: Turkmenistan,
1970).
Azimov, 1972
P. Azimov, "Science in Soviet Turk-
menia," *Izvestiya akademii nauk Turk-

menskoi SSR*, Social Sciences Series
(Ashkhabad, 1972): VI: 3–15.
Bacon, 1966
Elizabeth Bacon, *Central Asians under
Russian Rule: A Study in Culture Change*
(Ithaca: Cornell University Press,
1966).
Bartol'd, 1963
V. V. Barthol'd, Sochineniya, II, 1:
Ocherki istorii Turkmenskogo naroda
(Moscow, 1963): 544–623.
Baskakov, 1960
N. A. Baskakov, *The Turkic Peoples of
USSR: The Development of Their Lan-
guages and Writing* (Oxford: Central
Asian Center, 1960).

Baskakov, 1967
N. A. Baskakov, "The Present State and Future Development of Alphabets for the Turkic National Languages of the USSR," *Voprosy yazykozhaniya* (1967): V. For an English summary see *Central Asian Review* (1968): XVI: 2: 97–109.

Bazin, 1959
Louis Bazin, "Le Turkmene," in *Philologiae Turcicae Fundamenta Tomus Primus* (Aquis Mattiacis Apud Franciscum Steiner, 1959): 308–317.

Begenchova, 1972
O. Begenchova, "Turkmenistan SSR Is a Sovereign State within the USSR," *Turkmenistan Kommunisti* (Ashkhabad, 1972): VIII: 38–42.

Bennigsen and Lemercier-Quelquejay, 1967
Alexandre Bennigsen and Chantal Lemercier-Quelquejay, *Islam in the Soviet Union* (New York and London: Praeger and Pall Mall Press, 1967).

Benzing and Menges, 1959
Johannes Benzing and Karl Heinrich Menges, "Classification of the Turkic Languages," in *Philologicae Turcicae Fundamenta Tomus Primus* (Aquis Mattiacis Apud Franciscum Steiner, 1959): 1–10.

Berdimurat, 1951
Aman Berdimurat, "Die Nationalitätenprobleme in der UdSSR unter besonderer Berucksichtigung Turkistans," (Doctoral Dissertation, Law Faculty, University of Munich, 1951).

Cahen, 1968
Claude Cahen, *Pre-Ottoman Turkey* (New York: Taplinger, 1968).

Doemming, 1969
Gerd von Doemming, *Transcaspia 1917* (Central Asian Research Center, London, 1969): XI: no. 1: 39–51.

Durdiyev, 1971
T. Durdiyev, "From the History of the Turkmenization of the State Apparatus of the Turkmen SSR," *Izvestiya akademii nauk Turkmenskoi SSR* (Ashkhabad, 1971): V: 10–17.

Ellis, 1963
C. H. Ellis, *The Transcaspian Episode, 1918–1919* (London: Hutchinson, 1963).

Europa Yearbook, 1970
Europa Yearbook, 1970 (London: Europa Publications, 1970).

Freikin, 1957
Z. G. Freikin, *Turkmenskaya SSR, Ekonomiko-geograficheskaya kharakteristika*, 2nd ed. (Moscow: Gos. Izdat., 1957).

Hughes, 1964
Langston Hughes, *I Wonder As I Wander* (New York: Hill and Wang, 1964), reprinted.

Istoriya Turkmenskoi SSR, 1957
Akademia nauk Turkmenskoi SSR, *Istoriya Turkmenskoi SSR* (Ashkhabad: Izd. Akademia nauk Turkmenskoi SSR, 1957), 2 vols.

Itogi 1970
Itogi vsesoyuznoi perepisi naseleniya 1970 goda, vol. IV (Moscow: Statistika, 1973).

Itogi SSSR 1959
Itogi vsesoyuznoi perepisi naseleniya 1959 goda SSSR (Moscow: Gosstatizdat, 1962).

Itogi Turkmenskaya SSR, 1959
Itogi vsesoyuznoi perepisi naseleniya 1959 goda, Turkmenskaya SSR (Moscow: Statistika, 1963).

Kerbabayev, 1965
Berdi Kerbabayev, *Gaygisiz Atabay* (Ashkhabad: Turkmenistan, 1965).

Khanazarov, 1963
K. Kh. Khanazarov, *Friendship of Nations and National Languages in the USSR* (Tashkent: Akademia nauk Uzbek SSR, 1963).

Kiselyev, 1972
D. S. Kiselyev, "Some Methodological Problems of National-State Relationship in the USSR," *Izvestiya akademii nauk Turkmenskoi SSR*, Social Sciences Series No. 1 (Ashkhabad, 1972).

Kniga, 1965
Kniga Sovetskogo Turkmenistana: Svodnaya bibliografiya 1920–1960 (Ashkhabad, 1965): 1.

Kolarz, 1967
Walter Kolarz, *Russia and Her Colonies* (Hamden, Conn.: Shoestring Press, 1967).

König, 1962
Wolfgang König, *Die Achal-Teke* (Berlin: Akademie-Verlag, 1962).

Krader, 1963
Lawrence Krader, *Peoples of Central Asia* (Bloomington: Indiana University Press, 1963).

Makhtumkuli, 1960
Makhtumkuli, *Sbornik stat'ei o zhizni i tvorchestve poeta* (Ashkhabad, 1960).

Myrdal and Kessle, 1971
Jan Myrdal and Gun Kessle, *Gates to Asia: A Diary from a Long Journey* (New York: Pantheon Books, 1971).

Nar. khoz. 1970
Narodnoye khozyaistvo SSSR v 1970 godu (Moscow: Statistika, 1971).

Nar. khoz. 1972
  Narodnoye khozyaistvo SSSR 1922–1972, Yubileinyi statisticheskii yezhegodnik (Moscow: Statistika, 1972).
Nar. obraz., 1971
  Narodnoye obrazovaniye, nauka i kul'tura v SSSR: statisticheskii sbornik (Moscow: Statistika, 1971).
Nepesov, 1950
  Gayib Nepesov, Pobeda sovetskogo stroya v severnom Turkmenistane (1917–1936) (Ashkhabad: AN USSR, Turkmen Branch, 1950).
Nepesov, 1958
  Gayib Nepesov, Veliki Oktyabr i Narodniye Revoluitsü v Severnomi vostochnom Turkmenistane (Ashkhabad: Turkmengosizdat, 1958).
Ocherki, 1970
  Ocherki istorii filosofskoi i obshchestvenno-politicheskoi mysli v Turkmenistane (Ashkhabad: Ylym, 1970).
Ovezov, 1967
  Balysh Ovezov, The Kara Kum in Flower (Moscow: Progress Publishing, 1967).
Pechat' 1959
  Pechat' SSSR v 1959 godu (Moscow: Kniga, 1960).
Pechat' 1970
  Pechat' SSSR v 1970 godu (Moscow: Kniga, 1971).
Pechat' 1971
  Pechat' SSSR v 1971 godu (Moscow: Kniga, 1972).
Pipes, 1964
  Richard Pipes, The Formation of the Soviet Union: Communism and Nationalism 1917–1923 (Cambridge: Harvard University Press, 1964), especially chapter, "Soviet Conquest of the Muslim Borderlands."
Sumer, 1967a
  Faruk Sumer, Oguzlar (Turkmenler) (Ankara, 1967)
Sumer, 1967b
  Faruk Sumer, Kara-Koyunlular (Ankara: Turkish Historical Society, 1967).
Televideniye i radioveshchaniye, 1972
  Televideniye i radioveshchaniye, 1972 (monthly, Moscow).
Transport i svyaz' SSSR, 1972
  Transport i svyaz' SSSR (Moscow: Statistika, 1972)
Turkmenistan, 1969
  Turkmenistan, Sovetskii soyuz series, Geograficheskoye opisaniye v 22 tomakh (Moscow: Mysl', 1969).
Wheeler, 1964
  Geoffrey Wheeler, The Modern History of Soviet Central Asia (New York: Praeger, 1964).
Wheeler, 1966
  Geoffrey Wheeler, The Peoples of Soviet Central Asia (London: Bodley Head, 1966).
Wurm, 1954
  Stefan Wurm, Turkic Peoples of the USSR (Oxford: Central Asian Research Center, 1954).
Zenkovsky, 1960
  Serge A. Zenkovsky, Pan-Turkism and Islam in Russia (Cambridge: Harvard University Press, 1960).

13 | UZBEKISTAN and THE UZBEKS

Donald S. Carlisle

General Information

TERRITORY

The Uzbek SSR was created in 1925 as a result of the Moscow-initiated "national delimitation" of borders. This far-reaching measure divided the former tsarist colony of Russian Turkestan into a number of sub-units with boundaries corresponding approximately to the distribution of the major Central Asian nationalities.[1] These state boundaries have remained essentially unchanged, although there has been some transfer of territory between republics. The capital of Uzbekistan was originally the ancient city of Samarkand, but in 1930 Tashkent became the capital.

Uzbekistan is a landlocked area encompassing 173,000 square miles. It borders the Turkmen SSR to the west, the Kazakh SSR to the north, and the Kirgiz and Tadzhik republics on the east and southeast. Only on its southwest boundary does Uzbekistan border on non-Soviet territory, for there it briefly touches Afghanistan.[2]

Uzbekistan has a hot dry climate and little rainfall; large stretches of land are steppe or desert.[3] Lack of water has drawn the settled population to cluster along the major rivers, and the bulk of the republic's population is concentrated in the Tashkent, Samarkand, and Bukharan oases, and in the Ferghana Valley.

Five major regions can be identified in Uzbekistan:[4]

The *northeast area* includes the Tashkent oasis, as well as the valley of the Angren River, which has undergone major development in the Soviet period. The "Hungry Steppe," where extensive efforts have been made to irrigate and develop inhospitable land, is also part of this region.

The main component of *eastern Uzbekistan* is the rich fertile Ferghana Valley, major cotton-producing center and citrus- and rice-producing area.

---

1 Park, 1957: 87–108.
2 *Uzbekistan*, 1967: 9.

3 *Ibid.*: 17–56.
4 *Ibid.*: 119.

Main focus of *central Uzbekistan* is the
Zeravshan valley and river. The region
includes the Samarkand and Bukharan
oases, and there is intensive cotton cultivation.

Southern Uzbekistan, which for a short
stretch of territory borders Afghanistan,
is the republic's most underdeveloped
area. Brought into the Uzbek SSR in 1925
from the Bukharan state, this region
shows the least effects of Soviet modernization efforts. This territory has the
strongest historical and cultural ties with
the Tadzhiks and Iranians.

The *northwest region* is also a backward
less-developed area. It includes the
Khorezm oasis as well as territory bordering on the Aral Sea. This region,
center of the former Khivan khanate,
was absorbed into the Uzbek SSR from
the short-lived Khorezm state in 1925. The
area also includes the Kara-Kalpak ASSR,
where cattle are important as well as
cotton.

ECONOMY

Uzbekistan is the world's third largest
producer of cotton after the United States
and China, and it is the USSR's chief source
of that crop. As Soviet academician Fers-
man observed during the 1930s:

> Whoever has made many trips to
> Central Asia knows that practically the
> whole of its attention is focused
> throughout the year on cotton: on
> planting, watering or harvesting it.
> When cotton-picking begins in au-
> tumn, when state-farm workers and
> collective farmers scatter over the
> fields in bright, colourful groups, and
> when new harvesting machines glisten
> in the sun, you begin to realize Central
> Asia's tremendous importance for the
> light industries of our country and why
> everything in Central Asia must really
> centre around cotton.[5]

The Uzbek republic also holds first place
in Soviet production of tractors for cotton
sowing, cotton cleaning equipment, karakul fur, and rice.[6]

Growth has been impressive; in 1940 in
the Uzbek SSR 2.3 million acres were sown
to cotton, while by 1971 the figure had risen
to nearly 4.2 million acres. Production of
raw cotton was 1,386,000 tons in 1940 and
4,511,000 tons in 1971.[7]

About 128,000 acres are sown to rice
today, double the 1960 acreage.[8] Before the
revolution 70% of the arable land was
sown to cereals and 20.3% to technical
crops. In 1965 cereals made up 37% and
technical crops (mostly cotton) nearly half
of sown acreage, while fodder, rice, grapes,
and fruit comprised the remainder.[9]

Impact of the Soviet regime on the Uzbek
economy began to be felt fully in the era
of the Five-Year Plans. The interval between
1926 and 1939 brought a major surge in
number of industrial and white-collar jobs
(see Table 13.1). An additional thrust to
Uzbekistan's development came with the
onset of World War II; the evacuation of
industry and personnel to the East during
this period accelerated modernization of
Central Asia.[10]

In 1970 469,000 persons in the labor
force were classified as industrial workers:
139,000 were involved in light industry and
an additional 132,000 were in machine
building and metal working associated with
growing, harvesting, transporting, and
transforming the cotton crop.[11] The overwhelming weight of the agricultural sector,
however, is still apparent; in 1970,
1,439,000 persons were employed on *sovkhozy* and *kolkhozy.*

Recent gas strikes in Uzbekistan have
contributed to the increasing importance
of Central Asia as a source of fuel and
power. Prospects are good for the republic's
petrochemical industry; both phosphorus
and nitrogenous fertilizer industries are
emerging. The engineering industry produces 68% of spinning and 100% of roving
machines made in the USSR. Prospects for
heavy metallurgy are poor, however, because of lack of iron ore in the region; iron
must be imported from Kazakhstan.[12]

---

5 Quoted in Vitkovich, 1954: 12.
6 *Uzbekistan,* 1967: 83–118.

7 *Ibid.:* 108; *Nar. khoz.* 1972: 546.
8 *Nar. khoz.* 1970: 87.
9 *Uzbekistan,* 1967: 108.
10 *Ekonomicheskaya istorii,* 1966; Rywkin, 1963:
ch. 4.
11 *Nar. khoz.* 1970: 199–204.
12 Conolly, 1967: 349.

Table 13.1

Changing Occupational Structure of Uzbek SSR

(%)

	1913[a]	1926	1939	1959	1963
Workers and Employees, Total	5.0	19.8	32.2	57.1	59.4
Workers			19.3	39.8	41.4
Employees			12.9	17.3	18.0
Peasants in Kolkhoz and Cooperative Artisans			64.9	42.6	40.54
Individual Peasants and Non-cooperative Artisans		80.2	2.9	0.3	0.06
Peasantry	74.6				
City Bourgeoisie	6.0				
Rural Bourgeoisie	13.0				
Others	1.4				

Source: R. Kh. Abdushakurov, *Torzhestvo leninskoi teorii perekhoda otstalykh stran k sotsializmu i kommunizmu minuya kapitalizm* (Tashkent, 1972): 143.

[a] Statistics for 1913 apply to Russian Turkestan, which was considerably larger than Uzbekistan today. The source cited, however, does not clarify the point.

HISTORY

Turkestan, from which the Uzbek SSR emerged in 1925, has an ancient history. It endured the impact of successive waves of Turco-Mongolian peoples as they swept across its steppe and desert-oasis regions. Its inhabitants have repeatedly been exposed to alien influences while absorbing and transforming the cultural legacy left by the last wave of intruders. In the eighth and ninth centuries it fell under the influence of Moslem culture and religion.[13] During the medieval period Arabic civilization flowered, and Tamerlane ruled his empire from the capital at Samarkand.[14] Bukhara became a center of learning and religious focus of the region. With a shift in trade routes in the fifteenth and sixteenth centuries, this Central Asian Islamic civilization entered a long period of decline and decay. The overall political order disintegrated, replaced by feuding local principalities. Subsequently, the Bukharan emirate and the Khivan and Kokand khanates crystallized as the major political units in constant competition and conflict. In the nineteenth century Russia expanded into Turkestan.

13 Caroe, 1967: chs. 2–4.
14 *Istoriya Samarkand*, 1970: 1. In 1969 Samarkand celebrated its 2,500th anniversary.

Turkestan was mainly a water-poor, desert-oasis region. The eastern region, center of the Kokand khanate, was partly encircled by mountains and included the rich Ferghana Valley. In Ferghana rice fields were cultivated, grapes and citrus were abundant; in the surrounding foothills nomads wandered through the seasons with their flocks. With the exception of Ferghana, however, and scattered oases watered by major rivers and their tributaries, the land was ill adapted to agriculture. Consequently, along these waterways and in surrounding villages [*kishlaks*] interlaced by the irrigation system, the bulk of the settled native population was concentrated, then as today. This created what one scholar has called an "oasis psychology," which he contends facilitated Russian conquest in the nineteenth century:

The isolated and scattered oases had caused the settled *dekkhans* [native peasants] to become fragmented into little-connected and often self-supporting districts, preventing the development of any "national" or regional unity. The fragile system of irrigation canals rendered agriculture, which formed the only substantial foundation for existence in the region, extremely vulnerable, voiding not only the possibility of active resistance, but even the willingness to engage in a struggle.

Innumerable nomadic invasions during the millennium of Central Asian history had conditioned the sedentary inhabitants of the oasis region to the inevitability of conquest, resulting in their fatalistic acceptance of domination by alien usurpers.[15]

Systematic Russian conquest took place between 1865 and 1884. On June 17, 1865, the city of Tashkent surrendered to the tsarist General Cherniayev and by 1868 the emirate of Bukhara was defeated. On August 12, 1873, the Khivan khan signed a peace treaty imposed by Russia. After several military encounters Russia conquered Kokand and on February 19, 1876, the khanate was abolished. By 1884 the last resistance of the local Turkmen tribes was overcome.[16]

The nineteenth-century tsarist conquest brought a visible Russian presence to the cities, "new towns," in which Russians congregated, springing up alongside "old towns," the ancient native quarters. By the turn of the twentieth century, Russian rule seemed secure. Railroad construction linked Russian Turkestan with central markets, and expansion of the area sowed to cotton reflected the Russian impact and their growing economic interest in the region. Lenin, in his critique of imperialism, would refer to Turkestan as Russia's colony and its "cotton appendix."

Russification was not pressed, and the tsars seemed tolerant of Moslem customs and religion. Nevertheless, immigration of Slavic peasants into the region, especially after 1906, had a heavy impact. Many natives—in particular, the nomadic Kirgiz and Kazakhs—had cause for resentment, very strong in Turkestan's rural regions on the eve of World War I. In 1916 tensions exploded when tsarist officials ordered a native callup to assist in the war effort. The 1916 native rebellion was labeled by one scholar "the most violent expression of popular dissatisfaction in the history of Russia between the revolution of 1905 and 1917." [17] Although the revolt was most

violent in Kazakh and Kirgiz areas, Samarkand, Tashkent, and Ferghana also had local revolts.[18]

The 1916 rebellion was more in the nature of a peasant *jacquerie* than a sustained revolt, and by early 1917 it appeared contained by Russian power. However, 1917 brought revolution to Petrograd and Moscow, and the Russian communities in Tashkent, Samarkand, and other cities of Turkestan were drawn into its vortex. After a short period of rule by local moderates and Mensheviks who supported the Provisional Government, the more radical Russians staged a *coup*. Led by railway workers and soldiers garrisoned in Tashkent, Bolsheviks and Left Social Revolutionaries seized power in November 1917, proclaiming a Soviet regime. The great mass of the native population appeared unaffected by, and unconcerned with, these events. Except for ineffective efforts by the small native intelligentsia to seize an opportunity to increase local autonomy, and later to achieve national independence, the Moslems appeared "passive observers" of the unfolding revolutionary drama.[19]

But they were not to remain passive for long. There was a fierce native reaction to the direct intervention and attack on the Moslem religion that followed seizure of power by the Russian-dominated Tashkent Soviet. Excursions into the *kishlaks* by armed Soviet forces in search of food and booty triggered what was both a national conflict and a "holy war." In the aftermath of Soviet military crushing of an emerging native government at Kokand, which had demanded autonomy and later independence, native resistance gathered momentum. The insurrection was especially strong in Ferghana. Native recruits streamed to the anti-Communist war operations of the "Basmachi," as armed opponents of the Soviet regime were labeled.[20] One Soviet writer observed:

The fight against the Basmachi was a fight with an entirely new, distinct and unique opponent. The Basmachi were

15 Zenkovsky, 1967: 225.
16 Carrere d'Encausse, 1971: 131–150; Pierce, 1960: 17–45.
17 Pipes, 1964b: 84.

18 Sokol, 1954: 72–166.
19 Park, 1957: 9–34; Zenkovsky, 1967: 225–237; Pipes, 1964b: 86–93.
20 Caroe, 1967: ch. 7.

made up of partisan detachments, exclusively on horseback. They were elusive and often dissolved in the neighboring villages literally before the eyes of our troops, who would immediately undertake a general search of the villages but without any results.[21]

Thus, the Bolsheviks were confronted with the difficult task of suppressing what was to become a recurrent phenomenon in the twentieth century: partisan war and guerilla tactics.

As Bolshevik fortunes in the civil war improved, Moscow was able to pay greater attention to Turkestan and dispatched troops to assist in crushing the native rebellion. In November 1919 a Turkestan commission sent by Lenin arrived on the scene. Soon thereafter, Frunze and Red Army forces also arrived, and in 1920–1921 the military tide was turned and the Basmachi in Ferghana basically undermined. Frunze and the Red Army were essential in crushing the Basmachi and securing Soviet rule. During the 1920s, however, Moscow sought to shape a pattern of rule resting on more than naked force. A version of the New Economic Policy (NEP) was introduced in Turkestan. The Bolsheviks sought to shape a nationality policy reflecting the NEP spirit. The policy approved was based on the norm that native culture within a socialist framework would be "national in form, socialist in content." Both "Great Russian chauvinism" and "bourgeois nationalism" were attacked by the regime as likely to alienate the population and to complicate Moscow's pattern of local control.[22] In 1924–1925 a "national delimitation" in Turkestan was declared. This entailed disappearance of Turkestan as a unit and in its place creation of separate national republics for the major ethnic groups, all still contained within a centralized Soviet state. It was a crucial step, enhancing Moscow's image on the local scene and partially neutralizing nationalist agitation for real independence. It also struck a blow against the Pan-Turkic movement which claimed the various ethnic

groups of Central Asia were not separate nationalities, but essentially one people united by common Islamic and Turkic bonds.[23]

The era of Five-Year Plans brought an end to Soviet toleration of quasi-nationalist tendencies, terminating the limited compromise with Moslem traditional society. The post–1928 industrialization-collectivization drive allotted to Uzbekistan the major role in assuring the USSR's "cotton independence" of foreign imports.[24] This marked the end of the Uzbek NEP. Moscow's directives, Russian personnel, and Slavic ways became dominant in Uzbekistan. The Russian presence, and eventually the heavy hand of Stalin himself, was felt in every sector of Uzbek life. The uneasy alliance of Moscow with the national Communist native elite was abruptly terminated in the Great Purge of 1937–1938. Such key figures as Faizulla Khodzhaev, chairman of the Uzbek *Sovnarkom*, and Akmal' Ikramov, first secretary of the Uzbek CP, were brought to Moscow, tried publicly, and sentenced alongside Bukharin in the show trial of March 1938.

In the years preceding World War II, and in the postwar period, Uzbekistan built canals, produced cotton, unmasked "nationalists," and glorified Stalin and local Stalinists. In the person of Usman Yusupov, first secretary of the Uzbek CP from 1937, and his associates, Moscow found successors to those like Khodzhaev and Ikramov who had been more nationally inclined and less subservient to Stalin. Uzbek history was rewritten, and Khodzhaev and Ikramov, prominent in Uzbek life at least since 1925, disappeared from the historical record except as "enemies of the people."

Like other republics after 1953, the Uzbek SSR embarked on partial destalinization during the Khrushchev era. Some victims of the "cult of personality" such as Ikramov and Khodzhaev have since been rehabilitated.[25] And the Uzbek SSR has continued to produce cotton. The most disastrous event in the recent period has been the

---

21 Cited in Pipes, 1964b: 179. See also Shamagdiev, 1961: 79–112.
22 Park, 1957: 115–203.

23 Caroe, 1967: 143–149; Park, 1957: 92–93.
24 Iskhakov, 1960: 49–60; Rywkin, 1963: 65–67; Caroe, 1967: 162–172.
25 For a discussion of rehabilitation of both men, see my analysis in *Kritika*: VIII: Nos. 2, 3.

Tashkent earthquake of 1966 which destroyed portions of that city.[26] These have since been reconstructed.[27]

DEMOGRAPHY

Although Uzbekistan is somewhat smaller in area than neighboring Turkmenistan, it has nearly six times the population—over 12 million. Among Soviet republics, only the RSFSR, the Ukraine, and Kazakhstan have larger populations. Uzbekistan's primarily agricultural character is reflected in the fact that, after more than four decades of telescoped industrial development, only 36% of the population is classified as urban.[28] Still, the republic's capital, Tashkent, reflects the effects of that growth; its population in 1971 was estimated at almost 1.5 million. The 18 other large urban centers are of more moderate size; except for Samarkand (272,000), all have fewer than 200,000 inhabitants. Six cities are over 100,000 in population, while the remaining 11 fall below that figure.[29]

National Composition of Population

Census data allow us to construct a broad picture of the ethnic composition of Uzbekistan: Table 13.2 shows how this pattern has changed over more than four decades. In 1926 Uzbeks comprised 66% of the population and Russians only 4.7%. Indeed, if one excluded the Tadzhiks (the Tadzhik ASSR was part of Uzbekistan at that time), the weight of Uzbeks would be substantially greater. One Soviet source, using such a calculation, stated that Uzbeks made up 76.1% of the population in 1930

and Russians, 5.6%.[30] Census figures for 1939 reflect the traumatic far-reaching changes unleashed during the Five-Year Plans. Table 13.2 draws attention to the influx of Russians who helped direct and manage the modernization process in that period. By 1939 Russians made up 11.5% of the Uzbek SSR's population, and Uzbeks had fallen to 65%.

By 1959 Russian share of the population had advanced to 13.5% (over 1 million) and the Uzbeks had decreased to 61%. The 1970 census gives a figure of 1,496,000 Russians, 12.5% of the total. During 1959–1970, the extraordinary rate of population growth raised the Uzbek component by 2.5 million, to 64% of the republic's population. Thus, statistics show that, unlike Kirgiz and Kazakhs, Uzbeks remain "masters of their own house," at least in demographic terms. Like Tadzhikistan, Uzbekistan does not appear to have been a target area for large-scale Slavic settlement. The climate and general environment have made the Uzbek SSR less attractive for influx of Slavs than the Kirgiz and Kazakh SSRs.

There have always been a substantial number of Tadzhiks and Kazakhs in Uzbekistan. Thus, the present large Tadzhik and Kazakh groupings in the Uzbek SSR are not unusual. Of particular note, however, is the large change in Tatar population over the years. The increase from 28,000 in 1926 to 147,000 in 1939 would appear related to influx of Volga Tatars during the Five-Year Plans. They were the source of more skilled cadres and workers for accelerating economic development. Subsequent rise to a population of 448,000 Tatars by 1959 indicates still another process, however. It is likely that post war transfer of Crimean Tatars to Central Asia and Stalin's liquidation of their republic account for this later increase of Tatars in Uzbekistan. Table 13.2 also shows a marked increase in Jews between 1939 and 1959. While there is an ancient Central Asian Jewish community, the 45,000 increase between 1939 and 1959 is perhaps due to movement of European Jews during the Nazi-Soviet war and perhaps even after 1945.

Unfortunately, Soviet statistical sources

26 The earthquake occurred on April 26. On April 27 both L. I. Brezhnev and A. N. Kosygin were in Tashkent. On May 9, 1966, there was another severe quake. For further information, see *Pravda* (May 15), 1966: 3. On May 31 *Komsomelskaya pravda* published the poem by A. Voznesensky, "Help Tashkent."

27 For more recent developments in Uzbekistan's history, see the section of this chapter on national attitudes.

28 *Pravda Vostoka* (April 28), 1971: 2.

29 *Nar. khoz. 1970*: 12.

30 Gosudarstvennaya Planovaya komissiya UzSSR, *Raiony UzSSR v Tsifrakh* (Samarkand, 1930): 43.

Table 13.2

National Composition of Uzbek SSR

	1926[a]		1939[b]		1959[c]		1970[c]	
	No.	%	No.	%	No.	%	No.	%
Total Uzbek SSR	5,297,457	100.0	6,271,259	100.0	8,261,000	100.0	11,960,000	100.0
Uzbeks	3,475,340	66.0	4,081,096	65.0	5,044,000	61.1	7,734,000	64.0
Russians	246,521	4.7	727,331	11.5	1,114,000	13.5	1,496,000	12.5
Tatars	28,401	0.5	147,157	2.3	448,000	5.4	578,000	4.8
Kazakhs	106,980	2.0	305,416	4.8	407,000	4.9	549,000	4.6
Tadzhiks	976,728	18.1	317,560	5.1	314,000	3.8	457,000	3.8
Jews	37,834	0.7	50,676	0.8	95,000	1.2	103,000	0.9
Kirghiz	90,743	1.7	89,044	1.4	93,000	1.1	111,000	0.9
Turkmen	25,945	0.5	46,543	0.7	55,000	0.7	71,000	0.6
Ukrainians	N.A.	N.A.	70,577	1.1	93,000	1.1	115,000	1.0
Kara-Kalpaks	26,563	0.5	181,420	2.8	168,000	2.0	230,000	1.9
Koreans	N.A.	N.A.	72,944	1.2	142,000	1.7	151,000	1.3
Others	282,393	5.3	110,495	4.3	288,000	3.5	365,000	3.0

[a] W. Medlin et al., 1971: 255.
[b] I. R. Mullyadzhanov, *Narodo naseleniye Uzbekskoi SSR*
(Tashkent, 1967): 177.
[c] *Pravda Vostoka* (April 28), 1971: 2.

do not provide adequate information regarding relative distribution of Russians, Uzbeks, and other ethnic groups in the labor force. Consequently, it is not possible to judge with total accuracy Russian-native composition among workers and employees, or ethnic breakdown of specific professional groups. Some information is available, though, and a picture can be obtained of nationality composition in some areas. Between 1939 and 1959 the working class in the Uzbek SSR grew from 526,645 to 1,218,221. In 1939 native population comprised 36.5% of the working class; by 1959 it had grown to 43.1%. During this period Russian workers increased from 188,591 to 308,425, while number of Uzbeks advanced from 200,997 to 525,519. The important role of Tatars in the Uzbek SSR is evident from relevant statistics. Among the working class in 1939 there were 29,004 Tatars; by 1959 the figure rose to 110,239. The 1959 figure for Tadzhik workers was 37,872; for Kazakh workers, 48,963.[31]

The key role of Slavs, especially Russians, in the Uzbek economy is strongly suggested by 1961 statistics on those employed who had a secondary specialist education. At that time 42% were Slavs while 37% of all such specialists were Russians. Uzbeks made up only 32%.[32]

Composition of Uzbek Communist Party and Supreme Soviet

The Uzbek Communist party has grown at a rapid rate since 1949. Table 13.3 shows growth pattern of the party as well as its changing class composition based on members' social origins. As in the USSR as a whole, recruitment efforts in the 1950s and 1960s produced a social class profile not at all congruent with the social structure of the Uzbek SSR as a whole. Table 13.3 traces that profile through time, illustrating the essential nature of the Communist party as an elite organization, which overrepresents the privileged and educated sectors of the population. In 1967, 41.4% of the Uzbek party fell into the "employee" category, and only 29.9% could claim a worker status as social origin. Though Uzbekistan was still funda-

31 Senyavskii and Tel'pukhovskii, 1971: 335–336.

32 *Sredneye obraz.*, 1962: 74.

Table 13.3

Changing Size and Social Composition of Uzbek Communist
Party, 1949–1967

YEAR	PARTY SIZE	SOCIAL ORIGINS (%)		
		Worker	Peasant	Employee
1949	132,918	22.9	29.9	47.3
1953	142,654	21.5	30.7	47.8
1958	173,104	21.7	30.0	48.3
1961	223,937	25.4	30.2	44.4
1965	314,279	28.7	29.3	42.0
1967	353,841	29.9	28.6	41.4
1968[a]	392,749	N.A.	N.A.	N.A.
1972[b]	438,335	N.A.	N.A.	N.A.

Source: *Kommunisticheskaya partiya Turkestana i Uzbekistana v tsifrakh (sbornik statisticheskikh materialov 1918–1967)* (Tashkent, 1968).

[a] Ellen Mickiewicz, *Handbook of Soviet Social Science Data* (New York: Free Press, 1973): 162.

[b] *BSE, Yezhegodnik*, 1972: 174.

mentally an agricultural region, peasants comprise only 28.6% of the Uzbek Communist party membership as of 1967.

Table 13.4 presents nationality statistics. By 1961 Uzbeks made up a substantial portion of the party (51.2%), and the figure rose to 53.3% as of January 1967. In 1961, 22.6% of the Uzbek CP were Russians, and by 1967 the figure had declined to 21.5%. The weight of Russians increases as one moves closer to the key centers of power. In 1949 Russians constituted 39% of the Uzbek Central Committee. In 1952 the figure was 36% but by 1961 it had declined to 28%.[33] In 1966, however it rose again to 31%. Of the Uzbek Central Committee members chosen at the 1971 Uzbek party congress, 34% were Russians.[34]

There are data on the number of Uzbeks among party workers and secretaries at various levels. As of January 1969, among workers of the Uzbek Central Committee and the provincial, city, and district committees [*obkoms, gorkoms*, and *raikoms*], Uzbeks held slightly more than one half of the

posts: 1,381 of a total of 2,635 "party workers." Specific data are available on number of Uzbek *apparatchiks* (full-time employees of the party organization, or *apparat*). As of January 1969, in the *apparat* of the Central Committee, Uzbeks held 69 of 149 posts (46.3%). In the *apparat* of the *obkoms*, they held 230 of 524 positions (43.8%). Of a total of 1,962 *apparatchiks* of *gorkoms* and *obkoms*, there were 1,082 Uzbeks (55.1%).[35]

Most important decision-making center of the Communist party, and of the Uzbek republic, is the bureau of the Central Committee. In 1949, of 14 full members, 9 were Russians and 5 Uzbeks;[36] in 1952 the figures were 9 and 6. On the 1971 Uzbek Central Committee bureau were 6 Russian and 5 Uzbek full members.[37]

The central party secretariat is the mainspring of the political system; there is overlap between its composition and that of the Central Committee bureau. In 1971 all five party secretaries were full members of the bureau. The first party secretary was Sharaf Rashidov, an Uzbek (born 1917).

33 Ethnic distribution calculated from Central Committee list in *Kommunisticheskaya partiya Uzbekistana*, 1968: 714–736.

34 Calculated from the Central Committee list in *Pravda Vostoka* (February 18), 1971: 1.

35 Nishanov, 1970.

36 *Pravda Vostoka* (March 6), 1949: 1.

37 Calculated from the bureau listed in *Pravda Vostoka* (February 18), 1971.

Table 13.4

National Composition of Uzbek Communist Party, 1949–1967

YEAR (%)	UZBEK	KARA-KALPAK	RUSSIAN	TATAR	KAZAKH	TADZHIK	JEW	KIRGIZ	UKRAINIAN	TURK-MEN	BELO-RUSSIAN	OTHERS
1949	58,035	2,121	36,094	6,345	6,285	3,380	4,036	683	4,901	444	488	10,106
(%)	(43.7)	(1.6)	(27.2)	(4.8)	(4.7)	(2.5)	(3.04)	(0.5)	(3.7)	(0.3)	(0.4)	(7.6)
1953	66,246	2,980	36,287	8,308	6,264	3,768	4,691	484	4,759	470	494	7,903
(%)	(46.4)	(2.1)	(25.4)	(5.8)	(4.4)	(2.6)	(3.3)	(0.3)	(3.3)	(0.3)	(0.4)	(5.5)
1961	114,680	4,477	50,702	12,145	8,807	6,706	5,884	1,498	6,642	898	726	10,772
(%)	(51.2)	(2.0)	(22.6)	(5.4)	(3.9)	(2.9)	(2.6)	(0.7)	(3.0)	(0.4)	(0.3)	(4.8)
1965	163,982	5,591	70,248	17,152	14,092	8,609	6,944	2,077	8,911	1,215	1,056	14,402
(%)	(52.2)	(1.8)	(22.3)	(5.4)	(4.6)	(2.7)	(2.2)	(0.7)	(2.8)	(0.4)	(0.3)	(4.6)
1967	188,571	6,354	76,214	19,358	15,674	9,943	7,167	2,371	9,577	1,420	1,171	16,021
(%)	(53.3)	(1.8)	(21.5)	(5.5)	(4.4)	(2.8)	(2.0)	(0.7)	(2.7)	(0.4)	(0.4)	(4.6)

Source: *Kommunisticheskaya partiya Turkestana i Uzbekistana v tsifrakh (sbornik statisticheskikh materialov 1918–1967).* (Tashkent, 1968).

Since 1929 all first party secretaries have been Uzbeks, (Ikramov, Yusupov, Niyazov, Mukhitdinov, Rashidov), while the second party secretary has been Russian. In 1971 the latter post was held by F. G. Lomonosov. Of the remaining three party secretaries, two were Uzbeks, and one was Russian.[38]

While the Uzbek Supreme Soviet is much less of a key decision-making institution than the central party organs, it is nonetheless important, at least in a formal sense, as the major legislative body of the republic. At a minimum, it has a symbolic function and can be checked to ascertain what ethnic groups are represented in its membership. Table 13.5 shows the breakdown of changing national composition of the Uzbek Supreme Soviet between 1947 and 1967. During this period percent of Uzbeks among deputies to the Supreme Soviet grew from 62% to almost 67% while the comparable figures for Russians decreased from 20.8% in 1947 to 15.7% in 1967. If one were to add the Ukrainian figure to the

---

38 *BSE, Yezhegodnik*, 1972: 174.

Russian figure for 1967, percent of Slavs reached 19%.

Comparison of these figures with those presented in Table 13.4 on ethnic representation in the Uzbek Communist party shows that in 1967 Uzbeks were more poorly represented within party ranks than within the Supreme Soviet. According to the 1970 census, Uzbeks comprise 64% of the Uzbek SSR's population and Russians 12.4%. Only 53.3% of the Uzbek CP were Uzbeks in 1967, however, while 21.5% were Russians.

Intermarriage

Intermarriage rates suggest that assimilation and "denationalization" are very slow processes. Relevant data appear in Table 13.6. Covering the period 1960 through 1965, the table shows that only 1.1% of all births to Uzbek women in 1960 involved a father of different nationality. In 1965 the comparable figure was 1.5%. The same tendency against intermarriage is exhibited by

Table 13.5

Composition of Deputies to Uzbek Supreme Soviet, by Nationality, 1947–1967

(%)

NATIONALITY	1947	1951	1955	1959	1963	1967
Uzbeks	62.4	63.8	65.64	73.2	70.5	66.81
Russians	20.8	21.4	21.66	14.0	14.0	15.72
Kara-Kalpaks	2.5	2.9	2.0	2.65	2.5	2.18
Ukrainians	3.2	2.5	3.0	2.0	9.8	3.27
Jews	2.0	0.4	N.A.	0.45	N.A.	N.A.
Tatars	1.5	0.4	N.A.	0.45	0.8	1.74
Armenians	1.5	1.2	1.5	1.5	0.87	0.84
Tadzhiks	3.0	2.4	1.4	2.0	1.9	2.40
Kazakhs	1.2	2.5	2.0	1.8	3.93	3.93
Kirgiz	0.2	N.A.	N.A.	0.45	0.4	0.65
Uigurs	0.5	N.A.	1.0	N.A.	N.A.	N.A.
Others	1.2	2.5	1.8	1.5	1.9	2.4
Total %	100.0	100.0	100.0	100.0	100.0	100.0
Total No. Deputies	(400)	(412)	(424)	(444)	(458)	(458)

Source: Akademiya Nauk Uzbekstoi SSR, *Sovety deputatov trudyashchikhsya Uzbekskoi SSR v tsifrakh (1925–1969)* (Tashkent: Izdatel'stvo "Fan" Uzbekskoi SSR, 1970): 79.

Table 13.6

Offspring of Mixed Marriages in the Uzbek SSR

(% of those born with father of different nationality)

NATIONALITY OF MOTHER	1960	1963	1965
Uzbek	1.1	1.0	1.5
Russian	22.0	22.5	22.8
Ukrainian	67.6	52.6	65.6
Belorussian	70.3	56.9	59.8
Kazakh	3.6	3.7	9.7
Armenian	17.4	19.1	23.1
Tatar	26.1	22.6	28.1
Jew	10.5	9.1	11.0
Tadzhik	10.7	8.9	7.9
Kirgiz	4.5	5.5	4.1
Turkmen	4.4	4.2	15.4
Kara-Kalpak	6.5	6.0	21.2
Others	16.8	16.5	19.3

Source: Nishanov, 1970: 302–303.

other Eastern nationalities in the Uzbek SSR, although less marked among Kirgiz and Kazakhs. It is in sharp contrast to the Slavic population. As the table shows, Ukrainians and Belorussians have by far the highest rate of women marrying outside their group. During 1960, in 70% of births to Belorussian women, the father was not Belorussian; and the comparable figure for Ukrainians was 67%. In 1965 Ukrainian and Belorussian figures were still extremely high. Figures for Russian women fluctuated between 18% and 23% during this same period. There was probably considerable intermarriage among Slavs. Since we do not have figures on Uzbek males, and it is not possible to say with assurance who they were marrying, it is clear the Uzbek women did not marry non-Uzbeks.

CULTURE

Islam and Islamic culture have deep roots in Uzbekistan. Not only as a religion but as a pattern for living, Islam shaped the lives of Central Asian peoples for centuries before the coming of the Russians. Both Samarkand and Bukhara—especially the former—contain ancient monuments bearing witness to the Moslem civilization that once flourished in the region.[39] At the beginning of the thirteenth century, Samarkand was plundered and devastated by the hordes of Genghis Khan.

In the late fourteenth century, Tamerlane made Samarkand his capital and began to restore and beautify the city. It was in this period that the major mosques, *medreses*, and mausoleums were constructed. Samarkand was also site of the observatory of Ulugh-bek, descendant of Tamerlane, who was both ruler and famous astronomer.

By the nineteenth century, if not before, Islam was sustaining an insulated, self-oriented culture, frozen in the past. It was on the defensive in the face of tsarist conquest and Russian impact. The mullahs and *ishans* who served Islam in Turkestan were fanatical devotees of the old ways and their interpretation of the ancient culture was narrow. The age-old tradition of local poets still flourished in the nineteenth century, and the oral tradition remained strong.[40]

By the late nineteenth century a new reform-minded Moslem intelligentsia began to emerge in Turkestan. The reformist movement, called *dzhadidism (djadidism)*, sought to change the educational system, carrying on a struggle to modernize education and adopt from the West those modernizing features that would further rebirth of a revitalized Islam.[41] It met with fierce resistance from the conservative religious elite. Many dzhadidist intellectuals, after efforts to modernize education and create a literary language, also embarked on political activities. During the revolution native political figures such as Bekbudi, Munavar Kari, and Abdul Fitrat could claim both political and literary reputations.[42]

The dzhadidist nationalists fought for revitalized Moslem culture, rejecting Russian influence and labeling Russians imperialists and colonialists, especially in view of suppression of the 1916 native revolt. During the early Soviet period, some participated in anti-Soviet organizations. Soon

39 Aleskerov, 1967.
40 Allworth, 1964: ch. 3.
41 *Ibid.*: chs. 4, 5; Zenkovsky, 1967: 6.
42 Allworth, 1967: ch. 13.

they were eased out of positions of influence; by the late 1920s and early 1930s, they had been suppressed and silenced. Those who survived until 1937, like the writers Fitrat and Cholpan, were purged in the years 1937–1938.

While there has been limited toleration of Uzbek folklore and traditional music during the Soviet period, there has also been a sustained effort to root out "past remnants." The major thrust from above has been to impose European, especially Russian, norms in the realm of culture and literature.[43] The campaign for "women's liberation," directed at the Moslem practice of female seclusion—which took extreme forms in Turkestan—has had many positive consequences, although the cost in assaulting local mores has also been great. Efforts to ignore the region's ancient heritage, to disparage the "feudal period," have borne less fruit and are less rational from a modernization perspective. In literature also, Uzbekistan, no less than the rest of the USSR, had to conform to "socialist realist" standards. Russian writers were imposed as essential models. Raw realism as a literary norm contrasted with the ancient Central Asian tradition of flowery poetic themes and images.[44]

Recent trends suggest some measure of toleration by the Soviet regime of efforts to search for cultural roots in an ancient past. The regime, however, must be acutely conscious of possible political ramifications and anti-Russian implications of too deep a native commitment to pre-Russian heritage; it is reluctant to sanction too strong an embracing of a cultural heritage that suggests all good things did not begin with the Russian conquest during the nineteenth century.

Regarding dzhadidist reformists Fitrat and Bekbudi, who had been purged, the Soviet leadership continued to take negative posture. There is no inclination to reinstate them as cultural and national heroes. Too deep an exploration of cultural roots of either an ancient or national character by present-day intellectuals is not encouraged by Moscow nor its local representatives in Uzbekistan.

In 1941 Friday was replaced by Sunday as official day of rest in the Uzbek SSR; also "Bazaar Day" was officially shifted from Friday to Sunday.[45] These moves had important implications for cultural identification.

Today the Spiritual Directorate for Sunni Moslems of Central Asia and Kazakhstan has headquarters at Tashkent. The Spiritual Directorate is authorized to publish a small number of works of a religious character. In 1947 it brought out a Koran in Arabic, and another edition was published at Tashkent in 1964. In addition, each year the Central Asian Directorate publishes 10,000 copies of a religious calendar consisting of 12 pages printed in Arabic characters.[46]

In Bukhara is the Miri-i-Arab *medrese*, a religious school for training Moslem religious functionaries for all of the USSR. Originally founded in 1535, the school was closed after the revolution, but opened again in 1952.[47]

EXTERNAL RELATIONS

Turkestan was once the territory across which major caravans moved on the route between Eastern and Western worlds. In the fifteenth and sixteenth centuries, Europe became a maritime civilization and Central Asia was subsequently bypassed. This shift in trade patterns was a major factor in Turkestan's isolation for centuries, reinforcing decay of the magnificent Islamic civilization that once flourished there. Nevertheless, contact with the Middle Eastern world remained alive into the nineteenth century. It declined thereafter, ending completely for a time following the Bolshevik revolution.

During tsarist rule in Turkestan, Bukhara and Khiva carried on foreign relations even though their independence was compromised by Russian rule in the region. The process of closing off Russian Turkestan was completed by absorption of these areas into the territorial pool from which the 1925 national delimitation produced Soviet republics. Since that time no foreign relations have been carried on directly by the Central

43 *Ibid.* ch. 14; Kary-Niyazov, 1955.
44 Allworth, 1967: ch. 14; Kary-Niyazov, 1955.

45 *Pravda Vostoka* (May 27, June 24), 1941.
46 Bennigsen and Lemercier-Quelquejay, 1967: 173.
47 *Ibid.*

Asian peoples. Under Stalinism, and especially after World War II, Central Asia was sealed off from the rest of the Moslem world. While during the tsarist period Russian Moslems had been able to perform the religious duty of a trip to Mecca, this option was no longer available during the Stalinist period.

In the post-Stalin period, the borders of Central Asia were partially opened to visitors from the outside world. The importance of the Uzbek SSR as a showcase increased as the USSR, in the mid-1950s, began to court Moslem states of the Middle East. As part of the effort to establish a new image in the Afro-Asian world, Soviet modernization accomplishments in Central Asia have been held up as a relevant model. The "noncapitalist development path," pioneered in the Soviet republics of Central Asia, is presented to these new states as an example of "building socialism." The republics of Soviet Central Asia have become a "beacon of socialism in the East," wrote an Indian historian who studied in the Uzbek SSR, adding:

> A study of the Soviet techniques and methods of social transformation, their results, and the reactions and responses of the people to them is certainly bound to be quite interesting and illuminating for all the newly-liberated Afro-Asian countries who are undertaking a vast process of social change in their march forward along the path of independent national development.[48]

Hardly a volume is published in the Uzbek SSR that does not devote some attention to the Central Asian republics' role as development models. Indeed, some books are devoted solely to this theme.[49]

Today Samarkand and Bukhara are major tourist attractions, drawing not only Moslems but Westerners, and Tashkent serves to illustrate the rapid industrial advance and modernization achievements of the Soviet model. Tashkent is also an important center for international meetings and conferences, and students from Middle Eastern countries such as Syria have been trained there under the Soviet foreign aid program. Nehru, Ayub Khan, and African leaders have visited the Uzbek SSR, and in

1963 Castro also made a trip to the region. Of Tashkent's new role in external affairs, one writer noted:

> Quite a large number of young specialists from many Afro-Asian and Latin American countries are being trained at Tashkent. The city of Tashkent has become a meeting place of writers, orientalists, cinematographers, public health workers, plant-breeders and cooperators of the whole world. Tashkent was host to the first conference of Afro-Asian writers held in October, 1958. Here too, the international trade union seminar, symposium on sanitary education sponsored by the UN, the conference dealing with diseases in tropical countries, the session of the UNESCO Consultative Committee on the Study of Arid Zones and the international seminar of women of Asian and African countries on women's education were held.[50]

In May 1972 Tashkent was the site of the Second International Music Festival for countries of the Afro-Asian world,[51] and it was at Tashkent that an agreement was worked out between India and Pakistan after the war between these countries.

Uzbek political leaders also made an appearance on the international scene. In December 1955 Sharaf Rashidov—now Uzbek first party secretary and candidate member of the CPSU's Politburo—was a member of the USSR government delegation to India; and in May 1957 he accompanied Voroshilov on a tour of Asian countries. In 1957 Rashidov was a member of the Soviet delegation to the Asian-African Peoples Solidarity Conference in Cairo.

But while the window to the outside world has been partially reopened and Uzbekistan made an international showcase, and while Tashkent is the most important Soviet city in the East, control over foreign relations remains in the hands of Moscow. Access to and from the Uzbek SSR is the province not of Uzbeks but of Russians. The foreign role of the republic is determined many miles away in European Russia. Of course, Uzbeks benefit from the USSR's concern with the Afro-Asian world. This has probably resulted in investment of funds to restore monuments with the inten-

48 Kaushik, 1970: 254.
49 Abdushukurov, 1972: 306–354.

50 Kaushik, 1970: 256.
51 *Pravda Vostoka* (January 27), 1972: 3.

tion of impressing foreigners. Also, it has given Uzbeks an opportunity to exchange views with fellow Moslems from whom they

have been isolated for more than a generation. It is still too early to judge what will be the political consequences of all this.

Media

LANGUAGE DATA

Uzbek is a member of the Turkic family of languages.[52] Prior to the revolution various dialects were spoken in Turkestan; they were, however, branches of the same Turkic language tree. Students in Moslem schools also learned to read or at least to recite in Arabic, language of the Koran. Apparently, its role was to serve as *lingua franca* for religious purposes; it was not used for conversation. One objective of the dzhadidist (djadidist) reformers was to develop a common literary language, and thus they sought to reestablish Chaghatay, the court language and literary medium used in the time of Tamerlane.[53] This was the principal project of Fitrat, the dzhadidist writer and Bukharan political leader.

One major device employed by the Soviet leadership to integrate Uzbeks into a broader socialist community was a series of language reforms, conducted in order to forward "nationalizing" of language. First a Latin script was developed in the late 1920s for the various Central Asian peoples, among them the Uzbeks. This had political as well as modernizing implications: opponents of the Soviet regime argued that this language reform, as well as the 1925 national delimitation, was in essence a "fragmentation" policy aimed at undermining the pan-Islamic and pan-Turkic unity of the region.[54] Providing natives with a Latin alphabet tended to isolate them from Arabic culture and countries and, consequently, to further their assimilation into the Soviet community. In the late 1930s the Latin script was dropped in Uzbekistan, replaced by a Cyrillic alphabet adjusted to local speech patterns.[55] Thus, the process of

assimilation and integration into the Soviet Russian sphere was given an added thrust. In addition, it was felt that adoption of the Russian language by Uzbeks would be facilitated by this intermediary Cyrillic-Uzbek alphabet.

Clearly, the process of linguistic assimilation in Uzbekistan has not moved rapidly. Recent statistics indicate that Uzbeks are not inclined to renounce their native tongue for Russian. The findings of the 1959 and 1970 census show that, after a period of 20 to 30 years, Uzbeks much prefer their own language. (Relevant data are presented in Table 13.7) In both 1959 and 1970 only a small number of Uzbeks listed anything but Uzbek as mother tongue. In the 1970 census, respondents were asked to indicate their second language. It is striking that as late as 1970 only 13% cited Russian as second language. Statistics point to the importance of Russian for those Uzbeks living outside Uzbekistan. Of that group, 22% cited Russian as second language. Evidence indicates that bilingualism is highest among urban Uzbeks, and one would surmise that the more prominent the individual the more likely the tendency and the necessity. It is very rare for rural Uzbeks to adopt Russian as second language.

The language data indicate a very limited degree of assimilation into Soviet Russian culture, serving to document the vitality of the native tongue. There is also evidence of efforts to "de-Russify" the native language. As James Critchlow observes:

Russian vocabulary has been to some extent expunged from the national languages, reversing an earlier trend, and preferential treatment is now being given to the use of those languages for communications. . . .

De-Russification has become overt and official, implemented through such devices as conferences held in the Moslem republics to discuss "speech

---

52 Menges, 1967: 60–91.
53 Allworth, 1964: ch. 4.
54 Caroe, 1967: 143–149.
55 *Pravda Vostoka* (March 28, April 5), 1938. See also *Pravda Vostoka* (August 10, October 17), 1939.

Table 13.7

Native and Second Languages Spoken by Uzbeks

(in thousands)

| No. Uzbeks Residing | | | SPEAKING AS NATIVE LANGUAGE | | | | | | SPEAKING AS SECOND LANGUAGE[a] | |
| | | | Uzbek | | | Russian | | | Russian | Other Languages of Peoples of USSR |
	1959	1970	1959	1970	% Point Change 1959–1970	1959	1970	% Point Change 1959–1970	1970	1970[b]
in Uzbek SSR	5,038 (100%)	7,725 (100%)	4,970 (98.6%)	7,639 (98.9%)	+0.3	18 (0.4%)	26 (0.3%)	−0.1	1,005 (13%)	186 (2.4%)
in other Soviet republics	977 (100%)	1,461 (100%)	952 (97.4%)	1,417 (97%)	−0.4	13 (1.3%)	23 (1.6%)	+0.3	328 (22.4%)	118 (8%)
Total	6,015 (100%)	9,195 (100%)	5,921 (98.4%)	9,071 (98.6%)	+0.2	30 (0.5%)	49 (0.5%)	0	1,333 (14.5%)	303 (3.3%)

Sources: For 1970, *Nar khoz. 1972*: 32; *Itogi 1970*: IV: 20: 306. For 1959, *Itogi Uzbekistana, 1959*: tables 53, 54; *Itogi 1959*: table 53.

[a] No data are available for 1959, since no questions regarding command of a second language were asked in the 1959 census.

[b] Including Uzbek, if not native language.

culture." Commenting on one such conference organized in 1969 in Uzbekistan, an Uzbek writer revealed that its purpose was to rectify linguistic injustices of an earlier period, when numerous native words were purged from the Uzbek language in favor of Russian ones.[56]

LOCAL MEDIA

Given the backwardness of Turkestan and subsequently Uzbekistan, Soviet accomplishments in modernization cannot be gainsaid. At the minimum they are an impressive technical achievement, as attested by development of communications media (see Tables 13.8 and 13.9). There are 27 museums and 24 theaters in the Uzbek SSR; in 1971 almost 3.5 million attended these theaters. Uzbekistan can boast of 5,820 public libraries with holdings of over 32 million books and magazines, as well as a flourishing publications network. In 1971, 225 newspapers in all languages were published in the republic: 59 were in Russian and 139 in Uzbek.

Major republic newspapers are *Pravda Vostoka* [*Truth of the East*] in Russian and *Soviet Uzbekistani* in Uzbek, which are organs of the Uzbek Communist party appearing six times weekly in Tashkent. *Komsomolets Uzbekistana* in Russian and *Yosh Leninchi* [*Young Leninist*] in Uzbek, both Komsomol organs, are issued five times weekly.[57]

As Table 13.8 shows, 18 magazines were published in Russian in 1971 and the same number in Uzbek, although with a much higher per issue circulation. Among the most important periodicals published in the Uzbek language are: *Fan va Turmush* [*Science and Life*], journal of the Uzbek Academy of Sciences; *Gulistan* [*Prosperous Country*], journal of the Central Committee of the Communist party of Uzbekistan which offers fiction; *Gulkhan* [*Bonfire*], Komsomol monthly for ages 10 to 14; *Quncha* [*Small Bud*], another Komsomol magazine, for ages 5 to 10; *Mushtum* [*Fist*], satirical journal; *Saodat* [*Happiness*], a journal addressed to women; *Shark Yulduzi* [*Star of the East*], journal of the Uzbek Union of Writers, which offers fiction; and the pedagogical journal *Sovet Maktabi* [*Soviet School*]. *Partiya Turmushi* [*Party Life*] and *Uzbekistan Kommunisti*, organs of the Uzbek Central Committee of the Communist party, appear in both Uzbek and Russian. *Obshchestvennyye nauki v Uzbekistane* [*Social Sciences in Uzbekistan*] is a valuable journal published by the Social Science Section of the Uzbek Academy of Sciences.[58]

In 1971, 1,005 Russian books and brochures were published, amounting to a total volume of 6,957,000. Concomitantly, 833 titles were issued in Uzbek, amounting to 23,630,000 books and brochures in that language.[59] As another index of modern status, Table 13.9 shows the expansion of electronic media between 1960 and 1971. There were 13.6 wireless sets and 10.5 television sets per 100 population in the Uzbek SSR in 1971. While this is not a startling set of figures when compared with more developed countries, it places Uzbekistan in the forefront when comparison is with the more underdeveloped Afro-Asian countries. Given the large size of Uzbek families, many more people are being reached per unit of electronic network than in a situation where a more nearly nuclear family unit is the norm. Radio Tashkent broadcasts in Uzbek, Persian, Urdu, Uygur, and English.

A curious sidelight on the role of electronic media was furnished in 1967; the Tashkent newspaper *Pravda Vostoka* claimed that television was invented in Uzbekistan, when in 1928 an engineer named Gravossky "for the first time in the world cast a likeness of the human face on a screen."[60]

EDUCATIONAL, SCIENTIFIC, AND CULTURAL INSTITUTIONS

Accomplishments in the realm of education during the Soviet period have been impressive (see Table 13.10). In 1971 there

56 Critchlow, 1972: 21.
57 *Europa Yearbook*, 1972: 1,321.

58 *Ibid.*
59 See Table 13.8.
60 James Critchlow, "Broadcasting in the Uzbek SSR," *Central Asian Review* (1967): XV: 3: 261–262.

Table 13.8

Publications in Uzbek SSR

Language of Publication	Year	NEWSPAPERS[a]			MAGAZINES			BOOKS & BROCHURES		
		No.	Per Issue Circulation (1,000)	Copies/100 in Language Group[d]	No.	Per Issue Circulation (1,000)	Copies/100 in Language Group[d]	No. Titles	Total Volume (1,000)	Books & Brochures/100 in Language Group[d]
Russian	1959	58	373	28.4	N.A.	N.A.	N.A.	702	6,860	521.8
	1971	59	710	40.3	18	126	7.1	1,055	6,957	394.7
Uzbek[b]	1959	164	955	18.9	N.A.	N.A.	N.A.	887	14,046	278.5
	1971	139	2,753	35.7	18	2,903	37.6	833	23,630	306.4
Minority languages	1959	21	87	5.0	N.A.	N.A.	N.A.	185	768	43.9
	1971	26	247	6.9	2	18	0.5	135	687	19.2
Foreign languages (Polish)	1959	0	0	0	N.A.	N.A.	N.A.	(35)[c]	(154)	N.A.
	1971	N.A.	N.A.	N.A.	1	2	N.A.	(27)[c]	(652)	N.A.
All languages	1959	243	1,405	17.3	26	7,713	95.2	1,809[c]	21,828	269.3
	1971	225	3,715	31.5	39	3,048	25.8	2,050[c]	31,853	270.0

Sources: *Pechat' 1959:* 54, 128, 164; *Pechat' 1971:* 95, 158, 188.

[a] 1971 figures do not include *kolkhoz* newspapers.

[b] This figure may include publication in non-Soviet languages.

[c] Book totals as given in *Pechat'* sometimes differ from totals in language categories. The indication is that books are published in other languages, but no data is given. Figures in parentheses are the presumed production of books in other languages based on this discrepancy.

[d] Includes all native speakers of the language.

Table 13.9

Electronic Media and Films in Uzbek SSR

YEAR	RADIO					TELEVISION			MOVIES	
	No. Stations	No. Wired Sets (1,000)	Sets/100 Population	No. Wireless Sets (1,000)	Sets/100 Population	No. Stations	No. Sets (1,000)	Sets/100 Population	Seats (1,000)	Seats/100 Population
1960	N.A.	891[a]	10.1[d]	965[a]	10.9[c]	N.A.	118[a]	1.3[c]	231[b]	2.6[d]
1970	N.A.	1,303[a]	10.7[d]	1,627[a]	13.2[c]	N.A.	1,156[a]	9.4[c]	627[b]	5.1[d]
1971	N.A.	1,329[d]	10.6[d]	1,703[d]	13.6[c]	N.A.	1,315[c]	10.5[c]	N.A.	N.A.

[a] Source: Transport i svyaz' SSR, 1972: 296–298.
[b] Source: Nar. obraz. 1971: 325.
[c] Source: Nar. khoz. 1971: 572, 578.
[d] Computed from data cited above ([b] and [c]).

Table 13.10

Selected Data on Education in Uzbek SSR (1971)

Population: 12,526,000

		PER 1,000 POPULATION	% OF TOTAL
All Schools			
number of schools	9,234	.7	
number of students	3,407,000	272	
Newly opened elementary, incomplete secondary, and secondary schools			
number of schools	417		
number of student places	140,200	11.2	
Secondary special schools			
number of schools	168		
number of students	167,300	13.4	
Institutions of higher education			
number of institutions	38		
number of students	234,300	18.7	
Universities			
number of universities	2		
number of students			
total	27,199		
day students	12,205		44.8
evening students	6,319		23.2
correspondence students	8,675		31.8
newly admitted			
total	4,784		
day students	2,601		54.3
evening students	1,039		21.7
correspondence students	1,144		23.9
graduated			
total	4,369		
day students	2,263		51.7
evening students	674		15.4
correspondence students	1,432		32.7
Graduate students			
total number	3,230	.26	
in scientific research institutions	1,621		
in universities	1,609		
Number of persons with (in 1970) higher or secondary (complete and incomplete) education			
per 1,000 individuals, 10 years and older	458		
per 1,000 individuals employed in national economy	663		
Number of workers graduated from professional-technical schools	42,800	3.4	

Source: *Nar. khoz. 1972*: 438, 552, 554.

were 9,234 schools in the Uzbek SSR and a total student population of 3,407,000. There were 38 institutions of higher education with an enrollment of 234,300. The republic could also boast two universities with a student body of 27,199: 12,205 (44.8%) were full-time students and the rest were enrolled in evening school or correspondence courses.

There were 391,000 persons working in the areas of education and culture, as well as 64,000 in science and scientific services.

Repeatedly, Soviet writers draw attention to creation of a new Uzbek intelligentsia under the regime's auspices, taking pride in this accomplishment.[61] Table 13.11 presents the nationality composition of students in higher and middle-level specialist institutes as of 1960–1961 and 1970–1971. The tremendous expansion in number of students between these years is striking; equally if not more striking is the number of Uzbeks among this group. Total number of students in the higher teaching institutes doubled in the 10-year period; the Uzbek contingent tripled during the same time span. The Russian component kept pace among students in higher education; as the table shows, it almost doubled during this period. Specific focus on students in middle-range specialist institutes shows a 300% plus increase as a whole, a doubling plus in number of Russians, and a more than three-fold increase of Uzbeks.

One can also determine the number of Uzbeks in higher reaches of the educational scientific establishment. An examination of

the category "Scientific Workers," presented in Table 13.12, illustrates a rapid growth of the technical intelligentsia. Between 1960 and 1970 total number of scientific workers in the Uzbek SSR grew from 10,000 to over 25,000. Among this group Uzbeks increased from an initial 3,552 to over 11,000. In this same period, the number of Russians rose from 3,971 to 7,692.

A further consideration should be noted regarding higher education. While a student can choose between two parallel tracks, in which language of instruction is Uzbek in one program and Russian in the other, the separate "tracks" are really not considered equal. As one recent study of Uzbek education notes:

> An important qualification needs to be applied to the advanced training programs offered in Uzbekistan: differentiation has consistently been a factor in terms of two possible "tracks"—the "Russian program" and the "Uzbek program," denoting the language of instruction used in the majority of courses offered under the one or the other program. The Russian language program is reportedly the better of the two and sought after by aspiring young native students. This kind of differentiation reflects on the average native employee's ability to perform in the technical fields. It is also generally acknowledged, for example, that preference is usually given to a *Russian* or a Russian-trained person (from the so-called "Russian program").[62]

National Attitudes

REVIEW OF FACTORS FORMING
NATIONAL ATTITUDES

The history of Turkestan and the first phase of the Uzbek SSR offers an abundance of evidence of local opposition first to tsarist and later to Soviet rule. It would be inaccurate, however, to label all native resistance and political opposition as

"nationalist." Armed resistance to Russian expansion into Turkestan in the nineteenth century was led by traditional feudal elites. The Ferghana rebellion of 1898 as well as the native *dekkhan* revolt of 1916 lacked true nationalist direction, although both had an ethnic dimension.

In the period 1917–1924, it was not the Turkestani nationalists (i.e., dzhadidist [djadidist] intelligentsia) who posed the

---

61 For a volume devoted to this theme, see Valiev, 1966.

62 Medlin et al., 1971: 130.

major threat to Soviet rule in Turkestan. The nationalists were not numerous and lacked a mass base. For such a popular base one had to make an appeal on religious, not national, grounds. The main danger to Communist rule stemmed from the Basmachi bands, led for the most part by traditional elites and sustained by Moslem religious agitation against infidels as well as by anti-Russian feeling. Again, in the late

Table 13.11

National Composition of Student Body in Higher and Middle Specialist Institutes, Uzbek SSR

1960–1961, 1970–1971

	STUDENTS IN HIGHER INSTITUTES		STUDENTS IN MIDDLE-SPECIALIST INSTITUTES	
	1960–1961	1970–1971	1960–1961	1970–1971
Total	101,300	232,900	53,300	165,000
By nationality:				
Uzbeks	47,800	134,300	23,900	84,800
Russians	26,300	43,600	15,000	38,800
Tatars	6,000	11,500	4,200	12,200
Kazakhs	5,000	11,000	2,700	7,500
Ukrainians	2,500	4,000	1,300	3,000
Jews	2,900	4,700	1,100	2,000
Tadzhiks	1,800	4,800	800	3,400
Kara-Kalpaks	1,700	4,300	1,000	4,000
Turkmen	1,000	1,800	300	800
Kirgiz	700	1,500	300	1,100

Source: *Nar. khoz. Uzbekskoi 1970*: 269.

Table 13.12

National Composition of Scientific Workers in Uzbek SSR, 1960, 1970

	ALL SCIENTIFIC WORKERS		RANK			
			Doctor of Science		Candidate of Science	
	1960	1970	1960	1970	1960	1970
Total Scientific Workers	10,329	25,244	222	494	2,442	6,907
Uzbeks	3,552	11,258	78	258	821	3,636
Russians	3,971	7,692	80	121	915	1,624
Tatars	566	1,331	4	14	119	293
Kazakhs	138	506	3	11	26	119
Jews	857	1,644	32	50	275	524
Ukrainians	321	686	7	5	73	133
Tadzhiks	120	287	1	8	37	97
Kara-Kalpaks	134	362	N.A.	5	11	123
Armenians	207	424	8	11	54	104
Other Nationalities	403	1,054	9	11	111	254

Source: *Nar. khoz. Uzbekskoi 1970*: 270.

1920s, although Communist nationalists protested against collectivization in the Uzbek SSR, the reawakening of *Basmachestvo* posed the real threat to the Bolshevik regime.[63]

Still, Uzbek nationalists—more narrowly defined as the modernist, secular, native intelligentsia, conscious of a "nation" and intent on national independence in some form—did pose a problem for Moscow and its local representatives. The modern native intelligentsia's problem—and the major clue to its weakness—was that the traditional elite and peasant masses seemed as fully ill disposed toward it as they were toward the Russians. The Basmachi chiefs, after all, had killed dzhadidists, and in 1929 the radical poet Khamza was murdered in an Uzbek village for carrying out antireligious propaganda.[64] As Bennigsen writes, "Before 1917 among the Moslem public there was not, and there could not be, a consciousness of belonging to a modern, well-defined nation. Their consciousness was pre-modern, of a purely religious type." [65]

Unable to strike a responsive chord among their uneducated, deeply religious people, the dzhadidist (djadidist) intellectuals had been forced to collaborate with Russians, who seemed more attuned to their modernist and reformist aspirations. Within the Communist party during the 1920s, these nationalists carried on a struggle to enhance the scope of Uzbekistan's autonomy; simultaneously, they leaned on Russians for backing in the conflict with their own obscurantist co-religionists. Moscow was also able to use the more radically inclined Uzbek Communists, although they were few, to check those national politicians who wanted to enhance local autonomy and minimize dependence on Russians.

When industrialization and collectivization drew the Uzbek SSR into a tighter economic embrace with the rest of the USSR, the national Communists charged Moscow with making Uzbekistan a "cotton colony." [66] But a series of intraparty factional struggles and public trials had made it clear by the 1930s that the formula "national in form, socialist in content," in the Stalinist view, precluded realization of objectives usually associated with national independence from a colonial power.

Moscow's fear of nationalism led to destruction in the Great Purge of even those Uzbek Communists who seemed previously to have proved their loyalty to the center. In struggles of the 1920s and early 1930s these individuals had vigorously attacked the more nationalist-inclined natives. Now Stalin used the same charge of "bourgeois nationalism" against them.[67] A generation of Uzbek Communists was destroyed in 1937–1938. Stalin then raised to positions of power in the republic Uzbeks unconnected with the dzhadidist generation, completely dependent on Moscow, and beholden to him for their rapid upward mobility.[68]

Stalin and associates appeared to consider as "bourgeois nationalist" any attachment to the past and to local Moslem culture. After World War II, they embarked on periodic campaigns to eradicate "bourgeois nationalism," "localism," and "past remnants" in Uzbekistan and Central Asia.[69] When one scans the period from the Great Purge through the 1950s, one finds little evidence of any substantive nationalist expression in the Uzbek SSR posing any threat to Moscow. Nevertheless, the Uzbek party leadership continued to warn of the danger of bourgeois nationalism. At the First Congress of the Intelligentsia of Uzbekistan in 1956, N. A. Mukhitdinov, first party secretary, observed:

> With the liquidation of the exploiting classes in our country there was eliminated any soil for bourgeois nationalism. Socialist nations by their very nature are alien to chauvinism and nationalism. This does not mean that it is impossible to have sick localities and politically unhealthy attitudes, among them nationalism, with which it is necessary to carry on uninterrupted struggle.
>
> It is known that there are tenacious

---

63 Chugunov, 1972.
64 Khamza, 1970: 40.
65 Bennigsen, 1971: 176.
66 From the speech of Ikramoy, first secretary of the Uzbek CP, quoting "bourgeois nationalists." *Pravda Vostoka* (January 16), 1934: 1.

67 For a discussion of the Uzbek leaders Khodzhnaev and Ikramov, see *Kritika*: VIII: Nos. 2, 3.
68 Such was Usman Yusupov, who replaced Ikramov as Uzbek first secretary in September 1937. For his biography, see *Pravda Vostoka* (November 21), 1937: 1. Yusupov died on May 7, 1966; his obituary appeared in *Pravda Vostoka* (May 8), 1966: 3.
69 Caroe, 1967: ch. 14.

manifestations of bourgeois ideology, particularly nationalist remnants. And it is possible to root them out only with profound political-educational work. In connection with our discussion of the cult of the personality and the liquidation of its consequences in Uzbekistan, there began to be rumored that in Uzbekistan there was not in the past and that there is not now, nationalist remnants. This position at its roots is mistaken and dangerous.[70]

His successor as first party secretary, Sharaf Rashidov, sounded the same note in 1963:

> There is no ground—either social or political or economic—for nationalism in our land. But we cannot forget that vestiges of it are still tenacious among a certain segment of politically immature people . . . (and) always ready to break out to the surface.[71]

In a 1955 pioneering study, Richard Pipes published his findings on local attitudes, based on interviews with refugee Central Asian Moslems.[72] His conclusions have largely stood the test of time; most seem confirmed by reports of those who have recently visited Uzbekistan. Interviewed by Pipes were mainly middle-level intelligentsia. He reported the weakness of formal religious identification among the group, underlining the strong commitment to secularism and Westernization. They projected a deep respect for modern science and a complete rejection of traditional religion. As their own replies indicated, however, the old customs lived on and traditional mores remained alive in Uzbekistan. Pipes concluded:

> In clothes, as in other customs . . . the natives discard what is patently inconvenient and adopt from the Russians what is more practical, i.e. Western. They do not discard traditions for other than utility.[73]

They had not rejected the native language even when it was imperative to learn Russian but, rather, had become bilingual; they used Russian on the job, reverting to the native tongue in their private lives. As "de-nationalizing influence" of the Russians was not compelling in the area of language, this also proved true in the realm of intermarriage. Pipes reported:

> The informants unanimously agree that in Central Asia marriage between a Moslem girl and a Russian would be utterly unthinkable, since it would be prevented by the parents and male relatives of the girl. Several of the refugee informants stated the opinion that a girl who would evade parental disapproval and marry a Russian would be assassinated by her male relatives; one recalled the specific instance of an Uzbek opera star who was killed by her brother for having married a Russian. Intermarriage is considered an insult to the family and to the nation.[74]

Our data on language, based on censuses of 1959 and 1970, confirm Pipes' observations regarding vitality of the native tongue. So do statistics presented earlier in this chapter on rates of intermarriage.[75]

The findings regarding Russian-native tensions "vary considerably, depending upon the social status and level of education," leading Pipes to observe:

> On the whole, the interviews indicate that national friction is in an inverse ratio to social status and education: the higher the status, the less friction. Racial hostility appears strongest among the poorest rural inhabitants, among the plain soldiers, and the unskilled laborers; it seems least prevalent among the intelligentsia, the state and party officials, the well-to-do peasants and workers, and the army officers. By and large the refugees—despite their strong anti-Russian bias—agreed that the relations between Russians and Muslims are good, and they attached little significance to various incidents of national friction which, being prompted, they had been able to recall. There seems to be a deep-seated feeling that whatever the differences dividing them, both groups suffer from the same regime, that they are "in the same boat." [76]

Travelers do not usually find overt expressions of national antagonism between members of the Uzbek and Russian intelligentsia.

---

70 *I S"ezd*, 1957: 54–55.
71 *Pravda* (May 23), 1963, quoted in Pipes, 1964: 5.
72 Pipes, 1955: Parts I and II.
73 Pipes, 1955: Part I: 157.

74 Pipes, 1955: Part II: 300.
75 See section in this chapter on demography.
76 Pipes, 1955: Part I: 301.

Lower-class Uzbeks, however, do not seem as reconciled to Russian hegemony.[77]

"Nowhere in the Soviet Union is the influence of religion stronger than in Central Asia," a young Soviet scientist told a recent visitor to Tashkent.[78] "The Islamic influence is very powerful," he added. The same Western visitor also reported:

> When the director of Tashkent's large Pedagogical Institute died a couple of years ago, officials proposed to accord him the honor of burial in the Communist cemetery reserved for outstanding figures. His family refused, insisting on burial in the Uzbek cemetery with a Moslem mullah chanting prayers.
>
> At a restaurant in Bukhara the other evening a young man with a flair for modern fashion collapsed into a chair, impatiently ordered a beef dinner. . . . He explained that during the day his family was observing the month-long Moslem fast of Ramadan. Other educated Uzbeks said the same.
>
> Three teen-age boys on a park bench near the magnificent blue-domed Islamic monument of Samarkand, in telling a foreigner that they were Moslems evinced none of the common Soviet hesitancy to acknowledge religious affiliation.[79]

When the same Western reporter asked what was the most important local holiday, he expected the response to be that it was the approaching November anniversary of the Bolshevik revolution. Instead, he was informed that the most important date was November 8, celebration of the Islamic feast marking the end of Ramadan. A Soviet intellectual who had grown up in Uzbekistan told him:

There are two quite different groups of Uzbeks. The modern, educated, Europeanized Uzbeks, and the traditional ones, among whom Moslem influence is very strong. They observe national holidays in traditional ways, have Moslem weddings and funerals, and do not let their children intermarry with Russians.[80]

BASIC VIEWS OF SCHOLARS ON NATIONAL ATTITUDES

The official Soviet view of nationalities is that they are firmly integrated—that these various ethnic groups mesh together harmoniously today, and will perhaps melt together fully at some future point in time. Typical of the orthodox Soviet version of Uzbek history is the following:

> With the fraternal assistance of other Soviet republics, the Russian Republic in the first place, the peoples of Central Asia have overcome their economic and cultural backwardness, a legacy of feudalism and colonialism, within a very brief historical period, i.e. within the lifetime of one generation. They owe these magnificent successes to the advantages of the socialist system, to planned economic development and friendship and the mutual assistance of Soviet peoples.[81]

Or as the Uzbek historian, Kh. Inoyatov, stated it, success of Central Asian peoples in building socialism "in the fraternal family of Soviet peoples" was possible only as a result of the October socialist revolution. The victories were possible "only in the conditions of free development of the peoples, who had liberated themselves from oppression and exploitation, thanks to the implementation of the Leninist national policy and as a result of the disinterested aid of the great Russian people." [82] Sharaf

---

[77] In 1963 at a hotel in Samarkand, an Uzbek worker, in the presence of a Russian official, asked this writer, "Are workers in America always drunk?" and when I answered "No," the Uzbek responded: "All Uzbek workers are drunk because the Russians pay us only enough to get drunk." When the Russian suggested the Uzbek end the conversation, the Uzbek replied: "You [the Russian] are a political man, I am a man of the people; I speak when I want to."
Shortly after, I watched, unobserved, as this Uzbek was literally dragged out of the back of the hotel by four militiamen. He was then stuffed into the rear of what seemed to be a police wagon.
[78] Smith, 1972.
[79] Ibid.

[80] Ibid. An American student who studied at Tashkent noted social segregation even among urban youth: "In the student dormitory, social life was usually voluntarily separated along racial lines. The Europeans and the Turkic peoples kept with their respective groups." Quoted in Critchlow, 1972: 28.
[81] Kaushik, 1970: 250.
[82] Inoyatov, 1966: 150.

Rashidov was even more explicit regarding the key role of Russians and the Russian language:

> Turkestan, like other national outlands, was from the first days of Soviet rule an object of special concern for Vladimir Ilich Lenin and the Communist Party. Basing itself on the generosity and selflessness of the Great Russian nation, the Leninist Party rendered comprehensive aid to Turkestan. . . .
>
> For the Uzbek people the Russian language has become a second native language. . . . Everyone here considers it the highest honor to learn how to speak in the language of the great Lenin, in the language of the people who are elder brothers and closest friends.[83]

Not all Western students of the nationality question are as convinced that the "nationality problem" has been resolved in the USSR. In 1971 Zbigniew Brzezinski was quoted as observing: "It is not inconceivable that in the next several decades the nationality problem will become politically more important in the Soviet Union than the racial issue has become in the United States."[84] Many Western specialists who deal with Uzbekistan are somewhat more cautious in their projections, but most agree that difficulties for the Soviet regime are possible.

The attitude of Western scholars about the future of Uzbek nationalism depends to a large extent on the relative weight each places on Soviet modernization versus costs and political consequences of that process. The cost factor is largely calculated in terms of transcending, or perhaps eradicating, the native heritage and traditional society. The more negative the scholar's appraisal of the pre-Soviet period, and the greater the value he places on Soviet modernization successes, the less he seems inclined to credit national unrest and to anticipate an emergent national problem in the Uzbek SSR. One can reverse the process to account for the other major range of opinion: the greater the weight placed on the pre-Soviet heritage, and the greater the reservations regarding

accomplishments during the Soviet period, the more likely the scholar is to credit reports of present national differences and to anticipate more in the future.

In the first category one might place the study by A. Nove and J. A. Newth. These authors contend that the Communist accomplishment in modernization is placed in better perspective when compared to the stage of development in neighboring non-Communist countries of the Middle East.[85] On every major index of modernization, the Uzbek SSR and other Central Asian republics surpass these Middle Eastern peoples. Nor do the authors give much credit to the argument that the USSR operated solely, or mainly, as a colonial imperialist power in this region, draining off raw materials and returning little of worth to these dependencies.[86] Are they colonies? the authors ask. The answer they give is "yes and no"; for they observe that while the Central Asian republics are "to a great extent ruled from the outside," it is also true they "registered some notable economic and social gains and that the gains were partly paid for by the Russians."[87] They grant that

> . . . it may therefore be that Central Asian nationalism is still in a somewhat dormant state but that it will manifest itself in future years especially if the Russians are tactless or oppressive. . . .
>
> Already now, as is clear from travellers reports, *some* natives deeply resent the existing situation and are willing to say so. The problem . . . is how to assess public opinion in the absence of reliable information, and how to distinguish grumbles and grievances from real disloyalty. It is therefore right to end with a question mark.[88]

The classic statement stressing local unrest and disloyalty was presented by O. Caroe in the first edition (1953) of his study. He argued that "national delimitation," collectivization, suppression of traditional culture, and creation of artificial languages provided a rich store of discontent which fueled and provoked local unrest.

83 Quoted in Pipes, 1964.
84 *Newsweek* (January 12), 1970: 30.

85 Nove and Newth, 1967: ch. 8.
86 *Ibid.*: 113–115.
87 *Ibid.*: 120.
88 *Ibid.*: 121, 132.

In the introduction to the new edition of his book, Caroe seems less inclined to weigh lightly the positive impact of these changes during the Soviet period.[89] He also seems no longer as optimistic regarding the vitality of pan-Turanian unity in the region as a basis for an anti-Russian movement. Caroe implies that the international environment, especially the Sino-Soviet conflict, could stimulate rebirth of the demand for local independence.[90]

Geoffrey Wheeler is also impressed by the extent of westernization in Central Asia. While noting the limits of this process and the negative features of Soviet rule, he does not see any likelihood of a full-scale national independence movement emerging in the region.[91] The Sino-Soviet conflict and proliferation of new states in the Afro-Asian world may have an impact in the future. Wheeler notes the contradictory nature of the USSR's pressing for creation of these new states when the Western Powers are concerned, while displaying no inclination to surrender its tutelary role vis-à-vis its own Moslem people. And he observes:

> Whatever the correct definition of the present political status of the Central Asian peoples—colonial, dominion, autonomous, or sovereign—their destinies have lain in Russian hands for upwards of a hundred years and are likely to remain so. For them, therefore, the Western impact has meant primarily that their way of life and work and their culture have become progressively more and more Russian, and that the means of national expression have dwindled correspondingly and now seem destined to disappear altogether.[92]

Bennigsen and Lemercier-Quelquejay are also cautious in projections regarding the future of nationalism in Central Asia.[93] They provide an extensive analysis of the evidence showing the persistence of older cultural themes and norms that have remained viable in the face of Soviet modern-

ization. While not suggesting widespread national unrest, they draw our attention to the fact that the Soviet regime has provided Moslem peoples with all the essentials of a national identity, and perhaps with grounds for national antagonism toward the Russians. It is the growing new Moslem intelligentsia, created under Soviet auspices, they suggest, that could provide the focal point for a future national resurgence.[94]

In a study of emerging nationalism in the Uzbek SSR, Critchlow has gathered from recent Uzbek language writings evidence of restiveness among new native elites. These have taken such forms as an open campaign to expunge Russian words from Uzbek, pressures to replace Europeans with national cadres in key posts, glorification of the area's ancient pre-Russian and prerevolutionary past, implicit calls for strengthening of political and economic autonomy within the federal structure, and forging of links with other peoples of Moslem tradition in the USSR and abroad. Critchlow makes a strong case for an already emergent national restiveness in Uzbekistan.[95]

Indeed, the March 1973 speech of Sh. R. Rashidov, first secretary of the Communist party of Uzbekistan, reflected the difficulties implicit in the Soviet pattern of rule. While praising "the fraternal friendship" of the nationality groups as a "source of the Soviet State's insuperable strength," he stressed the need for improvement of "the people's ideological-political moral education." In particular, he pointed to lack of a well-directed atheistic education program, which he related to an "incorrect attitude toward women." His emphasis on religious survivals (i.e., illegal mullahs) throughout the rather lengthy speech is perhaps an indication of their current strength in Uzbekistan. Artists, writers, and musicians were also brought to task for their use of "[nationalistic] themes from the feudal past," "naked erotica," and "mysticism."[96] It is evident that the Soviet leadership must constantly be on guard to maintain its dominance over Uzbek cultural institutions.

89 Caroe, 1967: xv.
90 *Ibid.*: xxiii–xxxii.
91 Wheeler, 1964: Epilogue.
92 *Ibid.*: 233.
93 Bennigsen and Lemercier-Quelquejay, 1967: 224–230.

94 *Ibid.*: 222–223.
95 Critchlow, 1972: 18–27.
96 *JPRS 58565*, Translations on USSR Political and Sociological Affairs (March 26), 1973: CCCLIII: 1–28.

RECENT MANIFESTATIONS OF NATIONALISM

Nationalism in Historical Interpretation

If the term "Uzbek nationalists" is used to mean those who demand a fully independent state for an Uzbek or Turkic nation —complete sovereignty based on separation from the USSR—then Moscow has not had to confront Uzbek nationalists since the 1920s, certainly no later than the 1930s. Those directly connected with the dzhadidist (djadidist) generation were killed by 1938. If, however, we state the problem in narrower Marxist-Leninist—especially Stalinist—terms, the situation is somewhat different. "Cultural nationalism" or even "localism" (in the sense of giving priority to the local and republic context as opposed to the all-Union level) is a continuing and, it seems, growing area of difficulty. The Stalinist tendency to view all local patriotism, religious customs, and cultural patterns rooted in anything but the Soviet order as dangerous and consequently "bourgeois nationalist" is no longer the sole motif in Uzbekistan. Preoccupation with the local heritage need not be a danger to the integrity of the Soviet state, as Stalinists apparently believed. Nor is it necessarily in conflict with Soviet federalism. In a multinational state, this can be a social lubricant, sustaining and reinforcing integration of the larger unit as a whole.

Because of the extraordinary Soviet sensitivity to such national expressions, however, manifestations of Uzbek patriotism take on an unusual and indirect—one might even say subliminal—character. In general, native dress, music, and art are tolerated by the regime as long as these national manifestations are formal and symbolic, considered epiphenomena. A vital area where tension, if not conflict, emerges between local Uzbek and all-Union and Russian themes is in the region of historiography, where one can perceive below the surface a struggle among interpretations of the Uzbek and Turkic past. In essence, at issue is the question of the role of Russians and Communist system vis-à-vis the native people and culture. Four areas where the historical role of Russians versus natives will continue to emerge in future are the following:

1. *The tsarist conquest.* Since the 1930's, there has been a changing Russian position on this question[97] Growing native preoccupation with the pre-Russian period and cultural heritage is unlikely to lead to the simplified conclusion that before the Russian conquest their ancestors were totally lost in the Dark Ages. Whether the tsarist conquest was a "positive good," or even a "lesser evil," is arguable, as Soviet historians contend.

2. *The native revolt of 1916.* Soviet historians have sought to stress the class nature of this revolt and to play down or ignore its anti-Russian dimension. This is not likely to survive vigorous historical investigation. Already available is the study by T. Ryskulov (who has been rehabilitated) which does not neglect this aspect of the revolt.[98] Recent publications indicate Soviet historians have anticipated a reevaluation by native historians.[99] They have strongly restated the older interpretation, imposed as norm in the 1930s and minimizing the ethnic dimension.

3. *The Basmachi movement.* Portrayal of the Basmachi as bandits, nothing more than representatives of the exploiting classes,[100] is likely to be challenged by future native historians. Exploits of the Basmachi against vastly superior Russian forces and their historic persistence in the face of overwhelming odds are natural subjects for probing by Uzbeks in search of a true historical record.

4. *Uzbek national Communists.* While Moscow has refused to return dzhadidist (djadidist) nationalists to good favor, it has entered the risky area of

---

97 Rywkin, 1963: 92–95.
98 Ryskulov, 1925.
99 Pyaskovskii, 1960; Tursunov, 1962.
100 Shamagdiev, 1961; Chugunov, 1972.

rehabilitating Uzbek Communists killed by Stalin. Emergence of Akmal' Ikramov and Faizulla Khodzhaev as loyal Communists seems part of an effort to give Uzbeks safe national heroes who served the Communist system.[101] The difficulty with this step is in explaining why they were killed if they were loyal; this raises questions on the nature of the Communist system and on Russian motives in the Uzbek SSR. The solution to this dilemma now in vogue is to ignore the fact that in 1937–1938 these two leaders and many other Uzbeks were eliminated by Stalin. Recent biographies are silent about their disappearance from the scene and the story comes to an abrupt end in 1938.[102]

While these historical questions are largely, but not totally, on the future agenda, providing a kind of index of growing national tension, Critchlow has produced evidence of recent indications that local Uzbek patriotism is already on the scene.[103]

Overt Nationalism

But it is not just within the Uzbek governing system or through expression by Uzbek intellectuals that native-Russian antagonism has been manifested. In late April 1969 tension broke into the open: a riot erupted in Tashkent outside the Paskhator football stadium.[104] The Tashkent disturbance continued into early May 1969, and involved fighting between Uzbeks and Russians. One source reported as follows:

In mid-May there were large-scale national disturbances in a number of places in Uzbekistan. They took the form of spontaneous meetings and rallies, under the slogan "Russians, get out of Uzbekistan!" The disturbances assumed such a violent character that

troops were brought into Tashkent. About one hundred and fifty arrests were made in Tashkent and other towns. The majority were allowed to go free, but about thirty people were given fifteen days in prison for "petty hooliganism." According to unconfirmed rumours, one of those kept under arrest was Rashidova, daughter of the First Secretary of the Central Committee of the Communist Party of Uzbekistan, and another the son of one of the deputy chairmen of the Uzbek Council of Ministers.[105]

Vivid evidence of nationality difficulties in the Uzbek SSR has concerned the Crimean Tatars, deported to Central Asia after World War II. Many settled in Uzbekistan, and in 1968–1969 their efforts to obtain redress of grievances resulted in a trial at Tashkent in which some Tatars were sentenced.[106]

The Intelligentsia and Nationalism

One cannot help but be struck by the key role of non-Uzbeks in the republic's development. Even those impressed by modernization, and not inclined to stress national differences, grant the central role of "outsiders." Nove and Newth state:

The existence of political groups at the local level which were prepared to accept modernization as an ideal was a considerable asset to the Soviet authorities in this early phase; the conflict arose over the speed of modernization —the rate at which society was to be transformed, and the ideas and institutions which were to be jettisoned— rather than the direction in which society was to be moved.[107]

These conflicts, however, were not unimportant areas of divergence, but essential questions determining the nature of the modernization process and the character of its outcome. Today in the ranks of the party and intelligentsia in the Uzbek SSR, Russians continue to play a key role. A charac-

---

101 For an analysis of the rehabilitation of Khodzhaev and Ikramov, see *Kritika*: VIII: Nos. 2, 3.
102 Khasanov, 1970: 130; Khodzhaev, 1970: 66–68.
103 Critchlow, 1972: 23–26.
104 Reddaway, 1972: 402.

105 *Ibid.*: 402–403.
106 *Ibid.*: 259–261.
107 Nove and Newth, 1967: 119.

terization of this situation as "Russian imperialism" might seem not far off the mark; but one must agree with Nove and Newth that this is not a fully accurate description. It does not encompass the total power configuration, including the native component; nor does it provide sufficient insight into the likely future course of political dynamics. Russians do not rule alone and, although Moscow has a firm grip on key political posts, the local native intelligentsia has risen in the political and economic realm to occupy many important positions. As Bennigsen and Lemercier-Quelquejay note, a vital growing Moslem intelligentsia has been created by Moscow.[108] The key question concerns the local elite's attitudes, and the likelihood of the native intelligentsia rising to full control in its own republic.

This Soviet Uzbek intelligentsia, Pipes wrote, possesses "many of the characteristics which distinguish the Soviet intelligentsia as a whole," but also displays "certain traits engendered by special conditions prevailing in Central Asia." Regarding these special conditions, he added:

> By origin, language, culture and family ties, it is connected to the Moslem population; by training, work, and much of its world-outlook, it is identified with the Soviet regime. It thus belongs fully to neither of the two groups, constituting something of a third element which functions as a connecting link between the Russian-dominated regime and the native population.[109]

An analysis keyed to social class highlights the intelligentsia's integration within the broader framework of Soviet society; but this may be a deceptive guide to attitudes, perhaps leading to minimizing potential emergence of national and ethnic loyalties in a new guise. Critchlow has suggested as much.[110] The new elite's search for renewed native roots could take the form of "localism" and Uzbek patriotism. Having created a native Soviet intelligentsia to bypass nationalism and cement all-Union integration, Moscow may yet find that it has structured the basis for a series of new ethnic tensions.

The phenomenon may be linked to generational differences. As the second or third generation of the Soviet Uzbek intelligentsia emerges, one may find it less preoccupied with its debt to Moscow and more confident of its local status. One may find it contemplating the "colonial tie" as it seeks out its own cultural past. Perhaps there will also appear, as evidence already suggests, a search for symbols linking it with the masses and further differentiating it from other national branches of the Soviet intelligentsia. The new generation accepts the Soviet societal framework but takes Moscow's largesse for granted. Broad industrial trends tend of themselves to socialize the engineers and technicians to accept integration within a multinational Soviet system. But industrial society also breeds its own problems. To what degree, for instance, will ethnic tension unfold as Uzbeks emerge from the schools, armed with skills but confronted with Russians and Ukrainians occupying key positions, blocking the channels for mobility? Just as Western colonialism had its "white man's burden," so Moscow's modernization rationale revolved, implicitly if not explicitly, around a similar "Bolshevik burden." In the past dominance of Slavs in Central Asia could be justified to some degree on a technical nonpolitical basis, since natives lacked the wherewithal to create and manage a complex modern society. But skill and education are no longer the monopoly of Europeans, and a perception of colonialism might become the common currency explaining Russian dominance in elite positions in the Uzbek SSR. Moscow may yet be confronted with the dilemma of either granting full power to the native elite or running the risk of a growing native alienation. This would be stimulated by the very visible Russian presence there which could serve as a concrete focus for local unrest.

---

108 Bennigsen and Lemercier-Quelquejay, 1967.
109 Pipes, 1955: part II: 305.
110 Critchlow, 1972.

REFERENCES

Abdushukurov, 1972
R. Kh. Abdushukurov, *Torzhestvo leninskoi teorii perekhoda otstalykh stran k sotsializmu i kommunizmu minuya kapitalizm* (Tashkent: Izdatel'stvo Fan, Uzbekskoi SSR, 1972).

Aleskerov, 1967
Yu. N. Aleskerov, *Samarkand* (Tashkent: Izdatel'stvo Uzbekistan, 1967).

Allworth, 1964
Edward Allworth, *Uzbek Literary Politics* (The Hague: Mouton, 1964).

Allworth, 1967
Edward Allworth, ed., *Central Asia, A Century of Russian Rule* (New York and London: Columbia University Press, 1967).

Allworth, 1971
Edward Allworth, ed., *Soviet Nationality Problems* (New York: Columbia University Press, 1971).

Bennigsen, 1971
Alexandre Bennigsen, "Islamic or Local Consciousness Among Soviet Nationalities?," in Allworth, 1971.

Bennigsen and Lemercier-Quelquejay, 1967
Alexandre Bennigsen and Chantal Lemercier-Quelquejay, *Islam in the Soviet Union* (New York and London: Praeger and Pall Mall, 1967).

BSE, Yezhegodnik, 1972
Bol'shaya Sovetskaya entsiklopediya, Yezhegodnik (Moscow: Sovetskaya entsiklopediya, 1972).

Caroe, 1967
Olaf Caroe, *Soviet Empire* (New York: St. Martin's Press, 1967).

Carrère d'Encausse, 1971
Hélène Carrère d'Encausse, "Systematic Conquest, 1865 to 1884," in Allworth, 1971.

Chugunov, 1972
A. I. Chugunov, "Bor'ba a basmachestvom v Srednei Asii," *Istoriya SSSR*, 1972: 2.

Conolly, 1967
Violet Conolly, *Beyond the Urals, Economic Developments in Soviet Asia* (London: Oxford University Press, 1967).

Critchlow, 1972
James Critchlow, "Signs of Emerging Nationalism in the Moslem Soviet Republics," in Dodge, 1972.

Dodge, 1972
N. Dodge, ed., *Soviets in Asia* (Mechanicsville, Pa.: Cremona Foundation, 1972).

Ekonomicheskaya istorii, 1966
Ekonomicheskaya istorii sovetskogo Uzbekistana, 1917–1965 (Tashkent: Izdatel'stvo Fan, Uzbekskoi SSR, 1966).

Europa Yearbook, 1972
Europa Yearbook (London: Europa Publications, 1972).

Goldhagen, 1968
Erich Goldhagen, ed., *Ethnic Minorities in the Soviet Union* (New York: Praeger, 1968).

Gulyamova, 1962
M. Gulyamova, *Iz istorii formirovaniya Uzbekskoi sovetskoi intelligentsii (1933–1937)* (Tashkent: Izdatel'stvo Akademii Nauk Uzbeskoi SSR, 1962).

Inoyatov, 1966
Kh. Inoyatov, *Central Asia and Kazakhstan Before and After the October Revolution* (Moscow: Progress Publishers, 1966).

Iskhakov, 1960
Yu. I. Iskhakov, *Razvitie khlopkovodstva v Uzbekistane* (Tashkent: Gosudarstvennoe Izdatel'stvo Uzbekskoi SSR, 1960).

I S"ezd, 1957
I S"ezd Intelligentsii Uzbekistana, Stenografcheskii otchet (Tashkent: Gosudarstvennoe Izdatel'stvo Uzbekskoi SSR, 1957).

Istoriya Samarkand, 1970
Istoriya Samarkand v dvukh tomakh (Tashkent: Izdatel'stvo Fan, Uzbekskoi SSR, 1970).

Itogi 1959
Itogi vsesoyuznoi perepisi naseleniya 1959 goda SSSR (Moscow: Gosstatizdat, 1962).

Itogi 1970
Itogi vsesoyuznoi perepisi naseleniya 1970 goda (Moscow: Statistika, 1972–1973).

Itogi Uzbekistana 1959
Itogi vsesoyuznoi perepisi naseleniya 1959 goda: Uzbekskaya SSR (Moscow: Statistika, 1962).

Kary-Niyazov, 1955
T. N. Kary-Niyazov, *Ocherki istorii kul'tury sovetskogo Uzbekistana* (Moscow: Izdatel'stvo Akademii Nauk SSSR, 1955).

Kaushik, 1970
D. Kaushik, *Central Asia in Modern Times* (Moscow: Progress Publishers, 1970).

Khamza, 1970
Khamza Khakim-zade Niyazi, *Izbrannye Proizvedeniya* (Tashkent, 1970).

Khanazarov, 1963
Kh. K. Khanazarov, *Sbilzhenie natsii i natsional'nye yazyki v SSSR* (Tashkent: Izdatel'stvo Akademii Nauk, Uzbekskoi SSR, 1963).

Khasanov, 1970
Kh. Khasanov, *Tovarishch Akmal'* (Tashkent: Izdatel'stvo Uzbekistan, 1970).

Khodzhaev, 1970
Faizulla Khodzhaev, *Izbrannye Trudy, tom 1* (Tashkent: Izdatel'stvo Fan, 1970).

Kommunisticheskaya partiya Uzbekistana, 1968
Kommunisticheskaya partiya Uzbekistana v rezolyutsiyakh i postanovleniyakh s'ezdov (Tashkent: Izdatel'stvo Uzbekistan, 1968).

Kritika, 1971, 1972
D. Carlisle, "Faizulla Khodzhaev," *Kritika* (Cambridge, Mass.) (Fall 1971): VII: 1.
D. Carlisle, "Akmal' Ikramov," *Kritika* (Cambridge, Mass.) (Spring 1972): VIII: 3.

Medlin et al., 1971
William K. Medlin, William M. Cave, and Finley Carpenter, *Education and Development in Central Asia* (Leiden: E. J. Brill, 1971).

Menges, 1967
K. H. Menges, "People, Languages, and Migrations," in Allworth, 1967.

Nar. khoz. 1972
Narodnoye khozyaistvo SSSR (1922–1972). Yubileinyi statisticheskii yezhegodnik (Moscow: Statistika, 1972).

Nar. khoz. Uzbekskoi 1961
Narodnoe khozyaistvo Uzbekskoi SSR v 1961 (Tashkent: Izdatel'stvo Uzbekistan, 1962).

Nar. khoz. Uzbekskoi 1970
Narodnoe khozyaistvo Uzbekskoi SSR v 1970 (Tashkent: Izdatel'stvo Uzbekistan, 1971).

Nar. obraz., 1971
Narodnoye obrazovaniye, nauka i kul'tura v SSSR: Statisticheskii sbornik (Moscow: Statistika, 1971).

Narody, 1962
Narody srednei azii i Kazakhstana, tom I (Tashkent, 1962).

Nishanov, 1970
R. Nishanov, *Internatsionalizm—znamiya nashikh pobeda* (Tashkent, 1970).

Nove and Newth, 1967
A. Nove and J. A. Newth, *The Soviet Middle East: A Communist Model for Development* (New York: Praeger, 1967).

Park, 1957
Alexander G. Park, *Bolshevism in Turkestan 1917–1927* (New York: Columbia University Press, 1957).

Pechat' 1959
Pechat' SSSR v 1959 godu (Moscow: Kniga, 1960).

Pechat' 1971
Pechat' SSSR v 1971 godu (Moscow: Kniga, 1972).

Pierce, 1960
R. Pierce, *Russian Central Asia, 1867–1917* (Berkeley: University of California Press, 1960).

Pipes, 1955
R. Pipes, "Muslims of Soviet Central Asia: Trends and Prospects," *Middle East Journal* (1955): IX: 147–162, 295–308.

Pipes, 1964a
R. Pipes, "The Forces of Nationalism," *Problems of Communism*, January-February 1964.

Pipes, 1964b
R. Pipes, *The Formation of the Soviet Union: Communism and Nationalism 1917–1923*, rev. ed. (Cambridge: Harvard University Press, 1964).

Pyaskovskii, 1960
A. V. Pyaskovskii, ed., *Vosstaniye 1916 goda v Srednei Azii i Kazakhstane (sbornik dokumentov)* (Moscow: Izdatel'stvo Akademii Nauk SSSR, 1960).

Reddaway, 1972
Peter Reddaway, ed., *Uncensored Russia, Protest and Dissent in the Soviet Union* (New York: Cowles, 1972).

Ryskulov, 1925
T. Ryskulov, *Revolyutsiya i korennoye naseleniye Turkestana* (Tashkent, 1925).

Rywkin, 1963
M. Rywkin, *Russia in Central Asia* (New York: Collier Books, 1963).

Senyavskii and Tel'pukhovskii, 1971
S. L. Senyavskii and V. B. Tel'pukhovskii, *Rabochii class SSSR, 1938–1965* (Moscow: Mysl', 1971).

Shamagdiev, 1961
Sh. A. Shamagdiev, *Ocherki istorii grazhdanskoi voiny v Ferganskoi doline*, (Tashkent: Izdatel'stvo Akademii Nauk Uzbekskoi SSR, 1961).

Smith, 1972
Hedrick Smith, "Islam Retaining a Strong Grip on the Uzbeks," *New York Times*, November 22, 1972.

Sokol, 1954
E. D. Sokol, *The Revolt of 1916 in Russian Central Asia* (Baltimore: Johns Hopkins Press, 1954).

Sredneye obraz., 1962
Sredneye spetsial'noye obrazovaniye v SSR, statisticheskii sbornik (Moscow: Gosstatizdat, 1962).

Televideniye i radioveschaniye
Televideniye i radioveschaniye (Moscow, monthly).

Transport i svyaz', 1972
Transport i svyaz' SSR (Moscow: Statistika, 1972).
Tursunov, 1962
Kh. Tursunov, *Vosstaniye 1916 goda v Srednei Azii i Kazakhstane* (Tashkent: Gosudarstvennoye Izdatel'stvo Uzbekskoi SSR, 1962).
Uzbekistan, 1967
Sovietskii Soyuz: Uzbekistan (Moscow: Mysl', 1967).
Valiev, 1966
A. K. Valiev, *Formirovaniye i razvitiye*

sovetskoi natsional'noi intelligentsii v Srednei Azii (Tashkent: Fan, 1966).
Vitkovich, 1954
V. Vitkovich, *A Tour of Soviet Uzbekistan* (Moscow: Foreign Languages Publishing House, 1954).
Wheeler, 1964
G. Wheeler, *The Modern History of Soviet Central Asia* (New York: Praeger, 1964).
Zenkovsky, 1960
S. Zenkovsky, *Pan Turkism and Islam in Russia* (Cambridge: Harvard University Press, 1960).

14 | TADZHIKISTAN and THE TADZHIKS

Teresa Rakowska-Harmstone

General Information

TERRITORY[1]

The Tadzhik SSR, with an area of 54,900 square miles, is one of the smaller union republics, smallest in Soviet Central Asia. Situated in the southeastern corner of the Soviet Union, it is the southernmost Soviet republic except for Turkmenistan. Located between 36°40′ and 41°05′ north latitude, Tadzhikistan borders in the south on Afghanistan, with only the narrow "panhandle" separating it from Pakistan and India, and in the east on Chinese Sinkiang. The republic's internal boundaries are with Uzbekistan to the northwest, and with Kirgizia to the north.

Mountains cover 90% of the republic's surface. Its topography is dominated by three major mountain systems: the Tian-Shan chain in the north, the Hissar-Alay chain in the center and the Pamirs in the southeast. Tadzhikistan has the highest mountain ranges in the Soviet Union, comparable to the neighboring Himalayas. The Union's highest mountain, Peak Communism (24,733.5 feet) is in Tadzhikistan. This is also most earthquake-prone of the Soviet areas.

The climate varies with topography, temperatures ranging from subtropical highs in southwestern valleys (with extremes of up to 115° F.), to arctic lows in the eastern Pamirs (with extremes down to minus 58° F.). In addition to variability, climate is characterized by aridity, with average annual precipitation of less than eight inches. According to topography and climate, vegetation ranges from tropical crops in the southwest to Alpine meadow grasses in the mountains.

Human settlement clusters along river valleys. Tadzhikistan's rivers flow from the center southwestward (Kafirnigan and Vakhsh), westward (Zeravshan) to the Amu-Darya River, and to the northwest (Ferghana Valley of the Syr-Darya River).

Tadzhikistan lacks geographic and economic unity, as it divides into four distinct regions. In the north the Tadzhik part of the Ferghana Valley (the eastern part belongs to Kirgizia, the western to Uzbeki-

1 Based on Chumichev, 1968; Narzikulov and Riazantsev, 1956; *Sovetskii Soyuz* series; and Rakowska-Harmstone, 1970.

stan), connects with the rest of the republic by a narrow corridor between the two neighbor republics. Central Tadzhikistan surrounds the Zeravshan river valley, the lower reaches of which descend into Uzbekistan; southern Tadzhikistan, with the capital Dushanbe, centers on the southwestward-sloping valleys opening into Afghanistan. The Pamir region, including the whole of eastern Tadzhikistan, is a self-contained mountain area extending eastward and southward beyond the Soviet boundaries.

Mountains have traditionally favored isolation, with valleys as connecting links, crossroads, and, given the necessary irrigation, bases for fertile agricultural economy. Under Soviet rule much of this isolation has been overcome through mountain-to-valley resettlement, development of railroad and air transportation network, and increased exploitation of industrial resources and power potential of mountain rivers.

Tadzhikistan has many known natural resources, even though much of its area is still unexplored. The Ferghana Valley has polymetallic ores, cadmium, molybdenum, wolfram, copper, silver, and gold, as well as natural gas, petroleum, and coal. In the Hissar-Alay Mountains are such nonferrous metal ores as wolfram, antimony, mercury, and gluorspar. Reportedly, the region also boasts some of the largest coal deposits in Central Asia (in Fan-Iagnob). Little surveyed, the Pamir region has known deposits of rock crystal, gold, molybdenum, wolfram, asbestos, mica, lazurite, and coal. Natural gas and extensive rock salt deposits are found in the southwestern regions. In the republic as a whole is an extensive raw materials base for the construction materials industry and an impressive fuel and energy potential.

The territorial administrative division of the Tadzhik SSR includes two *oblasts,* one of which, Gorno-Badakhshan, is autonomous, coinciding with the Pamir geographic region; 40 rural *raions;* 17 cities (10 are directly under republic jurisdiction; only one, Dushanbe, has three urban *raions*); 40 urban-type settlements; and 274 rural Soviets.[2]

---

2 *Nar. khoz. TSSR 1970:* 52. Information is dated January 1, 1971.

ECONOMY

Upon incorporation into the Soviet Union, Tadzhikistan presented a classic case of economic backwardness. Its economy was based on primitive agriculture; crafts (such as silk weaving, pottery, and leather work) were highly developed, and there was a lively trade exchange of agricultural for craft products. With collectivization of agriculture and the new emphasis on cotton cultivation, development of the new socialist economy began in the 1930s. Industrialization started in the 1940s and progressed significantly in the 1960s. Nevertheless, Tadzhikistan's primary economic role in the Soviet economy has been that of producer and, lately, processor of cotton.

The economic growth index has been extremely high (see Table 14.1), but the image it projects tends to be misleading because of the relatively small absolute base. By the early 1970s Tadzhikistan was still at the lowest end of the Soviet development scale, with lowest per capita income of all union republics;[3] budget allocations,[4] share in long- and short-term bank loans,[5] and portion of all-Union investment funds[6] all fell below the proportionate share of its population in the Union total. This seemed to indicate that the gap between the republic and more developed parts of the USSR was widening.

As reflected in production of specific commodities, the country's weight in the USSR national economy is generally lower than the Tadzhik area or population share in the Union total (0.6% and 1.2%, respectively) (see Table 14.2). The few exceptions reflect Tadzhikistan's cotton specialization and continuation of traditional economic pursuits such as sericulture and sheep breeding. The republic is second in the USSR in production of raw cotton,

---

3 Hans Juergen Wagener, "Regional Output Levels in the Soviet Union," *Radio Liberty Research Paper,* 1971: 41.
4 1.0% in 1972; see *Pravda* (November 27), 1971.
5 In 1971 short-term, 0.9%; long-term, 0.4%. See "Data on the Development of the State Bank, USSR," *Dengi i Kredit,* 1971: 1.
6 For the 1960s, 0.6%; see Holubnychy, in Erich Goldhagen, *Ethnic Minorities in the Soviet Union* (New York: Praeger, 1968).

Table 14.1

Tadzhik SSR: Growth of Gross Industrial Production, 1913–1970

(in % of base year)

	1913	1940	1950	1960
1913	100			
1940	876	100		
1950	1,320	151	100	
1960	3,752	430	286	100
1969	7,905	907	602	211
1970	8,700	993	N.A.	231

Sources: *Nar. khoz. TSSR 1969*: 28; *Nar. khoz. 1970*: 138, 139, 140.

fourth in production of silk textiles, and sixth in production of cotton textiles. It carries or exceeds its economic weight in production of only a few other commodities such as hosiery, vegetable fats, refrigerators, canned goods, and wine. Light industry is more developed than heavy industry, but significant increases in absolute output figures in some branches of certain industries took place in the last decade: particularly in petroleum and natural gas extraction and production of mineral fertilizers. Neither fuel base nor hydroelectric potential is developed, however (see Table 14.3).

For transportation, roads and truck freight are far more important than railroads and rail freight; in 1971 length of the

Table 14.2

Tadzhik SSR: Weight in USSR National Economy, 1970

(% of total USSR)

Industrial Indicators		Agricultural Indicators	
Electrical energy	0.4	Number of collective farms	0.8
Petroleum	0.1	Number of state farms	0.6
Natural gas	0.2	Number of tractors	0.9
Coal	0.1	Sown area	0.4
Fertilizers	0.5	Gross grain crop	0.1
Metal-working lathes	0.7	Gross cotton crop	10.5
Agricultural machinery	0.4	Gross vegetable crop	1.0
Cement	0.9	Head of cattle	1.0
Bricks	0.8	Head of pig	0.1
Cotton yarn	11.0	Head of sheep and goats	1.8
Cotton textiles	1.3	Meat production	0.5
Silk textiles	3.5	Milk production	0.3
Knitted goods	1.9	Egg production	0.3
Leather shoes	0.9	Wool production	1.1
Home refrigerators	3.1		
Furniture	0.5	Sociocultural Indicators	
Animal fats	0.2	Manpower	0.6
Vegetable fats	2.5	Retail trade	0.8
Canned goods	1.6	Students in general schools of all kinds	1.6
Wine	1.3	Students in VUZ'y	1.0
		Scientific workers	0.5
Transport		Doctors (all kinds)	0.7
Railroad length	0.2	Movie facilities	0.7
Railroad freight	0.1	Books (total issue)	0.4
Road length (hard cover)	1.6	Newspapers (one issue)	0.6
Automobile freight	1.5		

Source: *Nar. khoz. 1970*: 70–74.

Table 14.3

Tadzhik SSR Industrial Production: Selected Commodities

	1940	1950	1960	1970	1971	1972 (Plan)
Electrical energy (bill. kWh.)	0.06	0.2	1.3	3.2[a]	3.3	3.6
Petroleum (1,000 ton)	30	20	17	181[b]	192	190
Natural gas (mill. m.^{3})	2	0.2	N.A.	388[c]	N.A.	N.A.
Mineral fertilizers (1,000 ton)	N.A.	N.A.	N.A.	252[d]	261	308
Cement (1,000 ton)	N.A.	17.2	134.2	871.7[e]	941	936
Bricks (mill. ton)	N.A.	N.A.	258	371[f]	N.A.	N.A.
Cotton textiles (mill. m.)	0.2	16.6	51.5	99.9[g]	97.9	121
Silk textiles	1,587	6,037	25,747	43,193[h]	44,500	44,900
Fiber cotton (1,000 ton)	60.9	71.1	137.4	235[i]	252	247
Raw silk (tons)	254	233	292	322[j]	355	370
Hosiery (mill. pairs)	0.2	1.1	5	25.5[k]	N.A.	N.A.
Leather shoes (mill. pairs)	0.5	0.8	3.1	6.1[l]	6.2	7.4
Meat (1,000 ton)	7	9.9	28.7	32.9[m]	N.A.	N.A.
Animal fats (1,000 ton)	0.1	1	2.3	2.1[n]	N.A.	N.A.
Vegetable fats (1,000 ton)	3.5	12.8	40.5	68.8[o]	76.5	81.9

Source: *Nar. khoz. 1970*: 180–259; *Nar. khoz. 1972*: 645.

[a] Lowest in USSR except for Turkmenia and Latvia.

[b] Lowest in USSR except for Georgia.

[c] Lowest in USSR except for Kirgizia

[d] Lowest in USSR except for Latvia, where none are produced. In TSSR production started in 1969.

[e] Fourth republic from bottom.

[f] Lowest in USSR.

[g] Sixth place in USSR after RSFSR, Ukraine, UzSSR, Estonia, Azerbaidzhan.

[h] Fourth place in USSR after RSFSR, Ukraine, UzSSR.

[i] Second place in USSR after Uzbekistan.

[j] Fourth place in USSR after Uzbekistan, Georgia, and Azerbaidzhan.

[k] Ninth place in USSR.

[l] Lowest in USSR except for Turkmenia.

[m] Lowest in USSR except for Turkmenia, Armenia, and Georgia.

[n] Lowest in USSR except for Turkmenia, Armenia, and Georgia.

[o] Fifth in USSR after RSFSR, Ukraine, Uzbekistan, and Moldavia.

rail network in the Tadzhik SSR was approximately 160 miles and length of hard-surface roads 5,270 miles, with rail freight of 4.1 million tons and truck freight of 151 million tons.[7]

Regional economic development has been very uneven. The northern Ferghana Valley constitutes the republic's economic heartland, and industry has been concentrated in two major cities: Dushanbe, the capital, and Leninabad. Agricultural production is centered in the valleys, with cotton cultivated in subtropical southern regions, particularly Vakhsh and Kafirnigan valleys, and grain in northern valleys and piedmont areas. In the post-1945 period the agricultural trend has been toward an increase in the area under cash crops (e.g., cotton) and in irrigated areas, with a proportional de-

crease in the area sown to grains. Area under fodder has also advanced substantially.

The acreage under cotton in 1970 was less than that for Uzbekistan and Turkmenistan, but Tadzhik cotton yield per acre was highest in the USSR.[8] Some of the cotton crop was of the fine long-fiber (Egyptian) variety.

Kolkhozy have been main units of agricultural production,[9] but *sovkhozy* and *sovkhoz* acreage are increasing.[10] In 1970 there were 282 *kolkhozy* and 89 *sovkhozy* in the Tadzhik SSR.[11] Since 1940 there has

---

7 *Nar. khoz. 1972*: 647.

8 *Nar. khoz. 1970*: 304, 319.

9 In 1969 total *kolkhoz* area was 18,294,542 acres (1,376,594 sown), total *sovkhoz* area, 4,629,665 acres (333,585 acres sown). *Nar. khoz. TSSR 1969*: 96, 99, 110.

10 From 21 in 1940 to 78 in 1969; *Nar. khoz. TSSR 1969*: 110.

11 *Nar. khoz. 1970*: 388, 396.

been a trend toward consolidation of *kolkhozy* into larger and more economically efficient entities.[12] The total of mechanized power in agriculture in 1970, in thousands of horsepower, was 2,858, with 1,771 in *kolkhozy*.[13] Mechanization of work in 1969 ranged from 74% in cotton, 50% in vegetable cultivation, to 22% in cotton picking. Livestock work (except for sheep shearing, 89% mechanized) was 90% nonmechanized.[14] Livestock figures have shown a steady increase since 1940, with 1970 total of 973,000 heads of cattle, 2.5 million heads of sheep and goats, 43,500 horses, and 61,600 pigs.[15] Still, these totals were below the combined numbers of sheep and goats, cattle and horses in 1928, prior to collectivization.[16]

The 1971 "Average annual number of total workers and employees" (including state farm workers and workers in agricultural enterprises, but not *kolkhozniki*) in Tadzhikistan constituted 20.6% of total population.[17] Average annual number of working *kolkhozniki* constituted 8.8% of the population. Women constituted 38% of the total for the workers and employees category, and 50% of working-age *kolkhozniki*. Share of women in the former category was lowest in the USSR; the Union average was 51%.[18]

The labor force constitutes a major problem area in Tadzhikistan as it does throughout Central Asia. The republic has lower

Table 14.4

Tadzhik SSR: Labor Force 1971

Average annual number of total workers and employees	620,000
Workers	422,000
Women in workers/employees category	238,000[a]
Average annual number of kolkhozniki	264,000[b]
Total workers and employees	620,000
Industry[c]	134,000
Agriculture	78,000
Transport	58,000
Communications	10,000
Construction	78,000
Trade	54,000
Communal economy	19,000
Health and social security	42,000
Education and culture	93,000
Science and services	18,000
Credit and social insurance	3,000
State and social organizations	17,000

Source: *Nar. khoz. 1972*: 649–650.

[a] 38% of total.

[b] 50% of kolkhozniki are women.

[c] Only Turkmenia had lower numbers of industrial production personnel. *Nar khoz. 1970*: 159.

labor participation rates, lower mobility, lower levels of urbanization, and a lower share in nonagricultural state sector employment than most other Soviet republics. Labor surpluses are building up among the republic's Asian population (see section on demography); most Asian labor remains in the countryside and few people emigrated outside the republic, because of lack of knowledge of the Russian language and lack of skills. The overall labor picture is further complicated by poor organization of work, high shares of manual labor, high labor turnover, low productivity, and influx of skilled Russian workers.[19] Speaking at a 1969 plenum of the Tadzhik party Central Committee, First Secretary Rasulov complained of labor surpluses in the countryside, while there were serious shortages of labor in industry and construction.[20]

Industrial labor productivity statistics for 1940–1970 reveal that Tadzhikistan

12 From 3,093 *kolkhozy* with average of 64 households, 612 acres sown area, and 348 heads of livestock (208 sheep and goats), per *kolkhoz* in 1940, to 302 *kolkhozy* with average of 771 households, 4,562 acres sown area, and 5,247 heads of livestock (3,897 sheep and goats) per *kolkhoz* in 1969 (*Nar. khoz. TSSR 1969*: 107–108). The USSR average of households per *kolkhoz* in the same year was 427 (i.e., almost half of the Tadzhik figure), but average acreage was almost double the Tadzhik figure (413 acres). *Nar. khoz. 1970*: 388, 396.
13 *Nar. khoz. 1970*: 373. Statistics in *Nar. khoz. TSSR 1969* reveal average figures. In 1969 there was an average of 47 tractors, 23 trucks, and 7 cotton combines per *kolkhoz* (pp. 107–108) and an average of 55 tractors, 26 trucks, and 3 grain combines per *sovkhoz* (p. 110).
14 *Nar. khoz. TSSR 1969*: 126.
15 *Ibid.*: 111. There were no pigs in Tadzhikistan prior to collectivization.
16 Rakowska-Harmstone, 1970: 58.
17 Calculated on basis of population of 3 million as per *Nar. khoz. 1972*: 644, as compared with 14% in 1956 (Rakowska-Harmstone, 1970: 59).
18 *Nar. khoz. 1970*: 516.

19 Feshbach and Rapawy, 1973.
20 *Pravda* (February 13), 1969.

Table 14.5

Selected Standard of Living Indicators for Tadzhik SSR, 1969

Social investment per inhabitant	172.8 rubles[a]
Average work week in industry	40.81 hours
Average monthly wage of workers and employees	112.9 rubles[b]
Money income per *kolkhoz* household per year	1,830 rubles[c]
Number of doctors	4,559[d]
Number of middle-level medical personnel	14,772
Number of hospitals	285
Number of hospital beds	27,675
Number of doctors per 10,000 people	15.7[e]
Number of middle-level medical personnel per 10,000 people	50.9[f]
Number of hospital beds per 10,000 people	95.4[g]

Source: *Nar. khoz. TSSR 1969*: 108, 186–188, 257–258.

[a] Compared with average of 248 rubles for USSR as a whole. *Nar. khoz. 1970*: 537

[b] Compared with 116.9 rubles, average in USSR national economy. *Nar. khoz. 1970*: 519.

[c] USSR average income was 1,870 rubles/household. *Nar. khoz. 1970*: 384.

[d] 60% were women.

[e] Lowest in USSR; next lowest (19) was in Uzbekistan and Moldavia. USSR average was 26/10,000. *Nar. khoz. 1970*: 690.

[f] Lowest in USSR. USSR average 84/10,000. *Nar. khoz. 1970*: 694.

[g] USSR average was 106.2/10,000; *ibid.*

had the lowest productivity increase of all Soviet republics during that period. Using 100 as the index for 1940, the republic's productivity was 257 in 1970, as compared to an average of 492 for the USSR as a whole. It remained the lowest with 1960 as base year, but moved up to third place from the bottom (ahead of Moldavia and Uzbekistan) with 1965 as base year.[21] No corresponding data are available for *kolkhoz* labor productivity, but its failure to improve was criticized at successive party congresses in 1966 and 1971.

While no national breakdown is available on urban-rural distribution of labor force, ample evidence exists that Asian labor was significantly underrepresented in urban and industrial employment. The CC CPSU resolution on work of the Tadzhik party in 1969 revealed that "there are notably few Tadzhiks among the industrial production personnel at enterprises in the chemical industry, machine building and metal processing," [22] Tadzhiks and Uzbeks together constituted only 30% of the labor force at construction of the Nurek Hydroelectric Station (Tadzhiks 25%) and 25%

of the labor force in Dushanbe Integrated Textile Mills (Tadzhiks 15%).[23] The central problem of the need to "form qualified labor cadres . . . among the indigenous population" was restated in almost identical words in the CC resolution, quoted above, the Tadzhik party plenum following it, and by First Secretary Rasulov at the 17th Congress of the party in 1971.[24]

HISTORY

The republic did not exist as a national unit prior to 1924 but the Tadzhiks, only Iranian group in Soviet Central Asia, share an ancient history with other people in an area that has been the crossroad of cultures for many centuries, with irrigation and trade hallmarks of its prosperity. Archaeology dates settlements there to 3,000 B.C., but Bactria and Sogd (sixth to fourth centuries B.C.) provide the first recorded history of Tadzhiks' Iranian ancestors. The Tadzhiks' history has been vitally

21 *Nar. khoz. 1970*: 163.
22 *Partiinaia zhizn* (January), 1969: 4.

23 Shorish, 1973: 3; Rosen, 1973: 4.
24 *Pravda* (February 13), 1969; *Kommunist Tadzhikistana* February 19), 1971.

affected by three milestones in pre-1917 Central Asian history: seventh-century Arab conquest; thirteenth-century Mongol invasion; and nineteenth-century Russian conquest.

The political power of Arab caliphates was ephemeral, but the Islam brought with them is today still the dominant unifying cultural and social force in the area. Under the impact of Islamic culture and Pax Arabia local dynasties flourished. Most important was the Samanid dynasty (903–999), ushering in a period of prosperity, power, and culture in medieval Central Asia. Bukhara, Samanid capital, became a great center of learning in the Arab world. In Soviet historiography the Samanid period is seen as the period when the Tadzhik nation and Tadzhik (Farsi) language were first formed, with the Empire being the one expression of Tadzhik political statehood prior to the Soviet period. The great medieval Persian literature developed in the ninth and tenth centuries (as represented by poets Rudaki and Firdousi) and the scientific discoveries of Avicenna are regarded as Tadzhik heritage; eastern Iranians (Tadzhiks) are regarded as generating influence in the subsequent development of Persian culture.

The thirteenth-century Mongol invasion destroyed the great Perso-Arabic civilization in Central Asia; for the next five centuries the area was cut off from Western influences. Iranians dispersed and mixed with successive waves of Turkic invaders from the East; Uzbeks, an offshoot of the Golden Horde, came into their present area in the fifteenth century. By the eighteenth century the settlement area of Central Asia was divided between independent and warring khanates of Bukhara, Khiva, Kokand, Hissar, and Badakhshan.

Russian eastward expansion reached Central Asia in the mid-nineteenth century, meeting British expansion from India and Afghanistan. As a result of conquest and treaty making, Russian Turkestan (under direct Russian military administration) was established in 1867; a Russian protectorate was established over Bukhara in 1868 and over Khiva in 1873; Kokand became the Ferghana Province of Turkestan in 1876; and the Turkmen were subdued in 1884. Demarcation of Russian and British spheres of influence left the Pamirs west of the Sarykol range and north of the river Panj to the Russians. Tadzhik historiography of the 1970s considers extension of Russia into Central Asia a progressive phenomenon, as it brought people there in contact with the historically superior capitalist system and eventually with the progressive influence of the Russian proletariat.

Under Russian rule, Turkestan began to develop economically, acquiring a dynamic, politically privileged minority of Russian settlers. Moslem masses, living within a traditional, largely ossified social system, had little contact with Russians and were little touched by the growing revolutionary fervor of the early twentieth century. The only Moslem reformers (known as dzhadidists [jadidists] or, in Bukhara, "Young Bukharans," were equally as unwelcome to Russians as to Moslem establishment. Outbreak of World War I in Turkestan was marked by sporadic Moslem resistance to labor conscription in 1916 (seen in Soviet historiography as a major uprising). When the revolution came in 1917, its various stages were fought out by the Russians among themselves, with the Tashkent soviet gaining ascendancy in October 1917. The Soviet was hostile to Moslem requests for autonomy, put forth first by a group of liberal Moslems and subsequently by a conservative-dominated Kokand government (which fell in 1918). The Soviets' "colonial" attitude toward Moslems and suppressive policies generated a conservative reaction and armed resistance, which became known as the Basmachi movement.[25] In Bukhara an abortive coup by Young Bukharans in 1918 was followed by an armed conquest from Tashkent in 1920; the emir fled to eastern Bukhara (present-day central Tadzhikistan), which became the center of Basmachi resistance for another year, until a Red Army pacification campaign came to a successful completion in 1921.

Following introduction of the New Economic Policy, Bolshevik policy in Turkestan became conciliatory toward the Moslems; much of the traditional way of life was resumed, including land tenure, operation of religious courts [Shariat], and free trade exchange. The influx of Russian cadres was accompanied by a genuine effort of the

25 The history of the Basmachi movement is summarized briefly in chapter on Kirgizistan.

party to educate indigenous cadres (so-called *korenizatsia*). Nevertheless, it took the following five years to overcome guerilla resistance in Tadzhikistan (there were two subsequent unsuccessful short-lived efforts in 1929 and 1931), and a further five years to overcome peasant resistance to the new social and economic policies. Pacification was carried out by the Red Army and Russian-dominated militia units; collectivization, largely by Russian officials, workers, and brigades, all leaving a legacy of lasting bitterness.

The Tadzhik ASSR was established in 1924 within Uzbekistan, as part of the process of national delimitation of Turkestan. At the same time the Basmachi movement revived in Tadzhikistan. It was finally subdued in 1926, as a result of strong punitive measures combined with economic concessions to peasants. First elections to the soviets took place in 1926, and formal governmental structure replaced a temporary network of revolutionary committees formed in 1925. Following 1926, the party's efforts were directed at fostering social change (through spread of mass education and liberation of women and the poor from their traditional bondage) and collectivization, including large-scale cultivation of cotton. Peasant resistance made it impossible, however, to implement land and water nationalization decrees until the early 1930s. In 1929 the Tadzhik ASSR was transformed into a union republic.

Changes at the all-Union level, consolidation of power by Stalin, and forced collectivization and industrialization caused an increase in resistance to these policies by local cadres in Central Asia. In Tadzhikistan the resistance culminated in a number of purges. There was a purge of the state apparatus in 1927–1928, and of the party apparatus in 1930–1931. The bitterly resisted collectivization campaign, completed in 1934, ended with a major purge of "bourgeois-nationalist elements" in the political apparatus. The 1934 purge affected 66% of total party membership, inclusive of the top leaders.[26] The leadership group purged in 1934 has never been rehabilitated; it is still referred to as "bourgeois-nationalist."

The post-1956 rehabilitation did, however, exonerate the successive leaders removed for "bourgeois-nationalism" during the second major wave of purges in 1937–1938, this time part of the all-Union purge of the "Right Opposition." By the end of the 1930s the Tadzhik political apparatus, virtually denuded of local cadres, was run outright by Russians sent out by central party and state authorities.

Economically, the period was dominated by efforts to develop large-scale cultivation of cotton, and to build a cotton-processing and light industry base in the republic. Direct control by Russian cadres continued throughout the war years, when the economy was redirected toward the war effort, with waves of deportees (including large contingents of Crimean Tatars and Volga Germans) resettled in the republic. New settlement policy also affected mountain people; many were resettled in cotton-growing valleys, a policy continuing through the post-1945 period.

The end of World War II marked a new period of economic progress (with greater relative emphasis on development of an industrial base) and cultural sovietization. Soviet-educated Tadzhik cadres were again promoted within the apparatus; they assumed formal directing positions, with Russian cadres relegated to behind-the-scenes control posts.[27] It is interesting to note the relative stability of tenure of Tadzhik party first secretaries since 1937; average length of tenure is nine years and the current first secretary, Dhabar Rasulov, has already been in office 12 years[28], as has the current chairman of the Council of Ministers. (The party's second secretary, however, was replaced in December 1970.) The Tadzhik political administration is frequently a target of all-Union criticism for economic shortcomings, as well as failures in implementation of social and cultural policies. A major scandal rocked Tadzhikistan in 1961, with the Tadzhik first secretary, the Russian second secretary, and a number of other leaders removed for alleged abuses of power in cadres policy, economic theft, falsification of economic

26 Party membership in January 1933 was 14,329; in January 1935, 4,791. Rakowska-Harmstone, 1970: 40, 100–101.

27 Rakowska-Harmstone, 1970: ch. 4.
28 Protopopov (Russian), 1937–1945; Gafurov (Tadzhik), 1945–1956; Ul'dahabaev (Tadzhik), 1956–1961; Rasulov (Tadzhik), 1961 to present (1973).

reports, and efforts at bypassing central controls.[29] The Tadzhik party was the one republican party singled out for special criticism following the 23d Congress of CPSU, in a December 1968 Central Committee CPSU resolution castigating Tadzhiks for economic shortcomings and poor educational policies.[30]

DEMOGRAPHY

Between the 1959 and 1970 censuses, total population increased from 1,980,547 to 2,899,602.[31] Tadzhikistan is still one of the least urbanized republics in the USSR, although percentage of urban population has grown considerably under Soviet rule. It is interesting to note that it increased only slightly between 1959 and 1970. Increase in percentage of urban population has been as follows:[32]

1913—	9%
1939—	17%
1959—	33%
1970—	37%
1971—	38%

The advance in urban population between 1959 and 1969 was due mainly to natural increase, reorganization of villages into urban-type settlements, and migration to the cities of "rural dwellers of the republic and other regions of the country." No distinction is made between migration from within the republic and from without.[33] Exact immigration statistics are not readily available from Soviet sources. Estimates compiled by Soviet and Western demographers, however, indicate that almost all urban immigration in Tadzhikistan in the 1959–1970 period came from outside the republic.

Soviet demographer V. V. Pokshishevskii estimated that between January 15, 1959, and January 1, 1968, net in-migration into the Tadzhik SSR was 161,000 people; a Western demographer's estimate for the 1959–1970 period came to 129,000.[34] Rural population in the Tadzhik SSR is predominantly Asian in ethnic composition (Tadzhik, Uzbek, and others) while urban population is dominated by European migrants into the republic.[35]

General urban population distribution is as follows:[36]

	1959	1970	1970 as % of 1959
Total urban population	646,178	1,076,700	166.6
City of Dushanbe	227,137	373,885	164.6
Raions under republic's jurisdiction	162,156	334,685	206.4
Leninabad Oblast	246,892	353,976	143.4
GBAO (Khorog city)	8,218	12,295	149.6

In Dushanbe Tadzhiks were only 24.2% of the population, compared with 42% for the Russians (1970).[37]

Leninabad Oblast (the Ferghana Valley part of the republic) and the city of Dushanbe have comprised the bulk of the republic's urban areas. It should be noted, however, that weight of these two units in total of urban population decreased from 73% to 67% in the last intercensal period. Largest increase in urban population was shown in the *raions* under republican juris-

diction. The trends indicate acceleration in industrialization and industrial construction in central Tadzhikistan. Still, distribution of urban population has remained extremely uneven. Average population density per square mile (in 1971) was 54.1, ranging, however, from 95.6 in Leninabad Oblast to 4.15 in the GBAO.[38]

Along with other Central Asian republics, the Tadzhik SSR has a much higher birth rate than the national average. In 1971 the

29 Rakowska-Harmstone, 1970: ch. 5.
30 "O rabote TsK Kompartii Tadzhikistana po vypolneniiu reshenii XXIII s"ezda KPSS," *Partiinaya zhizn'* (January), 1969: I: 3–8.
31 *Nar. khoz. TSSR 1970:* 286.
32 *Ibid.:* 285; *Nar. khoz. 1972:* 644.

33 *Nar. khoz. 1972:* 644.
34 For methods of calculation and more detail, see Leedy, 1973: 32–33.
35 *Itogi 1970:* IV: 295–300.
36 *Nar. khoz. TSSR 1970:* 286.
37 *Itogi 1970:* IV: 299.
38 *Nar. khoz. 1970:* 27–32.

republic had the highest crude birth rate in the Soviet Union, 36.8 per 1,000 population. Unlike birth rates for all other Soviet republics, the Tadzhik rate did not decline between 1960 and 1971. With the high birth rate and low steady death rate, the natural increase rate advanced from 28.4 per 1,000 in 1960 to 31.1 per 1,000 in 1971, highest of all the union republics.[39] The average annual rate of natural increase between 1959 and 1970 was 3.9% (compared with an average annual rate for the USSR as a whole of 1.3%).[40] Another Western source reported that in 1970 average number of children per woman in Tadzhikistan was 5.3.[41]

The extremely high birth rate was reflected in the republic's age structure; in 1970 more than one half of the population was below 20 years of age, and people below 45 constituted 84% of the population. The general picture was as follows (age groups as % of total):[42]

AGE GROUPS	1939	1959	1970
0–19 years of age	47.7%	46.7%	55.6%
20–44 years of age	37.0	34.6	28.5
45–69 years of age	13.3	15.8	12.8
Over 70 years of age	2.0	2.9	2.9

High birth rates, characteristic of the indigenous population, were felt predominantly in rural areas, creating huge labor surpluses, whose major impact will be felt in the next decade. Given the so-far-negligible rural-urban flow of the Asian population and concentration of non-Asian population in urban areas, Asian labor surplus and increasing numbers of younger indigenous population in the republic—not immediately absorbed into the socio-occupational structure—promise to become major problems.

This has already been reflected in occupational distribution of population, shown below for 1970 (as % of total population):[43]

	%
Employed (except those in private subsidiary agriculture)[44]	34.6[45]
Pensioners	7.8
Stipend holders	1.3
Dependents (including children, those in domestic work and families of *kolkhoz* members, workers and employees engaged in private subsidiary agriculture)	56.0
Other means of subsistence	0.3

Largest ethnic group in the republic in 1970 were Tadzhiks (56.2% of total), followed by Uzbeks and Russians. During 1959–1970 the high Tadzhik birth rate has been reflected in reversal of the trend of the preceding 30 years for Tadzhiks to decline as percentage of the republic's population. Correspondingly, the former steady increase in weight of the Russian group has been reversed. Fourth and fifth largest groups in the population (Tatars and Germans) were World War II deportees.

As a rule, no ethnic statistics are published for the party and government bodies, except occasionally for membership of the party as a whole and for general membership of the soviets. After 1945 general membership in the soviets tended to reflect ethnic composition of population; in the party Asian groups were underrepresented and European groups overrepresented. Ethnic breakdown of the Tadzhik party membership for 1962 was Tadzhiks, 45% of the total; Uzbeks, 16%; and Russians, 25%.[46]

The highest percentage of Russians in the total party membership in Tadzhikistan occurred during the final period of the Stalinist era; between 1948 and 1953 Russians constituted 29% to 30% of total membership (approximately triple their weight in total population), a higher percentage than in the period immediately following the two great purges of the 1930s. By 1954 the percentage had declined, and Russians constituted about a quarter of the membership from 1954 through 1962. In

---

39 Leedy, 1973: 25
40 *Ibid.*
41 Rosen, 1973: 63.
42 *Nar khoz. TSSR 1970*: 289. The third column does not add up to 100 in the source.
43 *Nar. khoz. TSSR 1970*: 294.

---

44 Those employed in a domestic capacity or in private subsidiary agriculture constituted 11% of the total.
45 This category included 78% of those of working age (86.8% if students were added).
46 Rakowska-Harmstone, 1970: 100.

Table 14.6
Ethnic Breakdown of Population of Tadzhikistan

(in thousands)

ETHNIC GROUP	1926[a]		1929		1939		1959		1970	
	Absolute No.	% of Total Republic	Absolute No.	% of Total Republic	Absolute No.	% of Total Republic	Absolute No.	% of Total Republic	Absolute No.	% of Total Republic
Tadzhiks	620.0	75.0	901.4	78.4	883.6	59.5	1051.2	53.1	1629.9	56.2
Uzbeks	N.A.	N.A.	206.3	17.9	353.6	23.8	455.0	23.0	665.7	23.0
Russians	5.6 }	0.7	N.A.	N.A.	153.0 }	10.3	262.6	13.3	344.1	11.9
Ukrainians			N.A.	N.A.			26.9	1.4	31.7	1.1
Tatars	N.A.	N.A.	N.A.	N.A.	N.A.	N.A.	56.9	2.9	70.8	2.4
Germans	N.A.	N.A.	N.A.	N.A.	N.A.	N.A.	32.6	1.6	37.7	1.3
Kirgiz	N.A.	N.A.	22.8 }	2.0	N.A.	N.A.	25.6	1.3	35.5	1.2
Kazakhs	N.A.	N.A.			N.A.	N.A.	12.6	0.6	8.3	0.3
Jews	N.A.	N.A.	N.A.	N.A.	N.A.	N.A.	12.4	0.6	14.6	0.5
Turkmen	N.A.	N.A.	16.4	1.4	N.A.	N.A.	7.1	0.4	11.0	0.4
Others	N.A.	N.A.	3.1	0.3	15.0	6.4	37.5	1.8	50.3	11.7

Sources: For 1926–1959, Rakowska-Harmstone, 1970: 42;
for 1970, *Nar. khoz. TSSR 1970*: 293.
[a] Within 1926 boundaries.

1966 total party membership was 73,283,[47] and in 1971, 86,732 (i.e., 3% of population), but no ethnic breakdown data were given.[48]

No direct information is available on ethnic composition of governing bodies of the party or state apparatus, but differences between European and Asian names allow for an approximate calculation of distribution of indigenous and European cadres. In the late Stalinist period a pattern of distribution was visible; weight of European cadres was considerably higher and that of local cadres considerably lower than their respective weight in the population. The Russian weight rose with importance of a given body. At the same time all representative positions (such as heads of party and government bodies) were staffed by indigenous Communists, control positions (e.g., second in command in both bodies, control of cadres distribution, security heads, and heads of certain key ministries) were in the hands of Europeans.[49] During 1948–1956 distribution of cadres in the Central Committee was Europeans, 28%; Asians, 72%. In the bureau of the Central Committee, average distribution was 50:50.[50] Following 1956 ratio of Europeans in the Central Committee declined somewhat, stabilizing at about one fourth of membership (24% of total in 1961 and 1963, increasing to 27% in 1971).[51] In the Central Committee bureau, European share in membership (including members and candidate members) fluctuated from 28% in 1958 to 35% in 1961, 25% in 1963 (58% under Khrushchev's bifurcation scheme),[52] and 38% in 1971.[53]

Since 1945 the Tadzhik party first secretary has always been a Tadzhik and the second secretary a Russian or Ukrainian. Similarly, the chairman of the republic's Presidium of the Supreme Soviet and the chairman of the Council of Ministers have always been Tadzhiks and their first deputies invariably Europeans. During 1948–

1956, most heads of ministries were of local origin, while most deputies were European. Though no similar information was available for 1971, it was reported that Slavs constituted 31.9% of ministries' staffs and committees attached to the Council of Ministers, including senior post in the Committee of State Security.[54]

Though no ethnic breakdowns for the Tadzhik CP are available, data have been published about Tadzhiks in the CPSU: 46,593 in 1967, 0.4% of total membership (up from 0.3% in 1961). Tadzhik representation in the CPSU was less than half their weight in the Soviet population (0.88%).[55]

CULTURE

Tadzhiks now claim a distinct ancient cultural heritage from the tenth-century Perso-Arabic Samanid Empire. Crystallization of the claim took place as a result of the development of Soviet nationality policy after 1929; the heritage, nevertheless, forms part of the general Central Asian heritage, which in recent times survived in the emirate of Bukhara.

Most authorities agree[56] that centuries of common historical and religious development resulted in growth of a Central Asian cultural heritage combining Persian, Arabic, and Turkic elements, and that there was no cultural differentiation between Tadzhiks and Uzbeks of the plains, except that Tadzhiks spoke Farsi and Uzbeks, Central Asian Turkic. Elite of the emirate spoke both languages and were also familiar with literary Arabic. This is not to say that differences did not exist between settlers of the populous valleys (Uzbeks and Tadzhiks) and Iranian groups in the mountains, such as the Galcha of central Tadzhikistan and western Pamir groups (Iagnob, Iazgulem, Rushan, Shugnan, Vakhan, and Vanch), who led an isolated existence and spoke Iranian dialects, some significantly different from Farsi of the plains. While most plains Tadzhiks con-

47 *Partiinaya zhizn'* (March), 1966: VI: 55.
48 First Secretary Rasulov gave these figures at the 17th Congress, Tadzhik party. *Kommunist Tadzhikistana* (February 19), 1971.
49 Rakowska-Harmstone, 1970: chs. 4, 5.
50 *Ibid.*
51 *Kommunist Tadzhikistana* (September 24), 1961, (December 27), 1963, and (February 20), 1971.
52 Rakowska-Harmstone, 1970: 105, fn. 8.
53 *Kommunist Tadzhikistana* (February 19), 1971.

54 Rosen, 1973: 66.
55 Mickiewicz, 1973: 164. *Nar. khoz. 1972*: 31.
56 See works by Alexandre Bennigsen and Lemercier-Quelquejay, Edward Allworth, Geoffrey Wheeler, and V. V. Bartol'd.

sidered themselves indistinguishable from Uzbeks, mountain Tadzhiks harbored a degree of antagonism against Uzbek overlords in principalities of western Bukhara. Mountain Tadzhik differences did not seem significant in development of emirate culture as they were marginal to the mainstream of cultural progress. Tadzhiks, like Uzbeks, are Sunni Moslem (unlike Iranians who are Shia Moslem); some Pamir Tadzhiks were Ismailites.

Contrary to official Soviet claims, a significant cultural revival took place in Central Asia in the second part of the nineteenth century (inclusive of the Bukhara emirate, despite the repressive attitude of emir and conservative clergy), producing an important intellectual elite, conversant with Persian, Arabic, and Turkic literary languages and the poetry, theology, philosophy, history, and geography of the Moslem world. This cultural elite was interested in modernization and emphasized the need to educate youth. The dzhadidist (jadidist) reform movement formed part of this elite. Some members, such as Sadriddin Aini (officially regarded as founder of the "Soviet Tadzhik literature"),[57] made a successful transition into the Soviet period. The present-day cultural elite of Tadzhikistan traces direct roots to this group.[58]

The 1924–1925 national delimitation of Soviet Central Asia following ethnic boundaries made it necessary to differentiate among particular national-cultural heritages of major ethnic groups. For Tadzhiks, this resulted in revival of the Samanid heritage and differentiation between their Persian roots and the Turkic heritage of the Uzbeks.[59]

The three sources of modern Tadzhik literature are classic literature, oral poetic tradition, and Russian and Soviet literature.

Classic literature included poetry of the first classical period (10th through 15th century), including works of famous Persian poets: Abulkhasan Rudaki (d. 941), Abu'l-Qasim Firdousi (934–1025) and his epic poem *Shakh Name* [*Book of Kings*], Omar Khayyam (1040–1123), Hafiz (d.

1389), and others. Present cultural policy permits only progressive elements of classical literature (atheism, antidespotism, humanism, praise of labor, struggle with oppressors, etc.) to be revived, while "reactionary" elements (feudalism, religious elements, erotica, etc.) are suppressed. Oral poetic tradition includes the Iranian version of the ancient Central Asian–Middle Eastern epos, *Gurguli*, and also folk songs, proverbs, and satirical plays, transmitted by itinerant professional singers called *hafiz*. These are promoted subject to the same constraints as promotion of classical literature. Russian models include both Russian literature (Gogol, Pushkin, Tolstoy, Chernyshevsky, etc.) and Soviet literature; in the latter, the two models which Tadzhik writers are particularly asked to imitate are Maxim Gorkii and Vladimir Maiakovskii.

Traditional Central Asian literature was synonymous with poetry. Modern Tadzhik literature places great stress on development of prose, especially dramaturgy, literary criticism, and children's literature.

Two major representatives of the new Tadzhik literature in the 1920s were Aini and a Persian revolutionary, Abul Qasim Lahuti (1887–1957). Numerous other writers, found too nationalistic by the party, were purged; development of the new Soviet literature began in the 1930s. In the current period literati represent a large group, including poets and prose writers; most prominent are Mirzo Tursun-zade (b. 1911), long-time chairman of the Union of Tadzhik Writers (since 1946), major spokesman on cultural matters as well as representative in contacts with other republics and foreign countries, and Mirsaid Mirshakar (b. 1912).

As reflected in the party press, major shortcomings of Soviet Tadzhik literature have been: idealization of and escapism into the past; failure to depict properly "Soviet reality" and to build themes of the new life; reluctance to develop new genres not employed in traditional literature; and promotion of cultural isolationism.

It appears that the Tadzhik and Uzbek masses, still confined largely to rural areas, have responded little to new cultural themes, and continue to live circumscribed by traditional customs. This is attested to by repeated criticisms in the press of the

---

[57] Sadridden Murad Khaja Zada Ayniy, 1878–1954.
[58] Allworth, "The Changing Intellectual and Literary Community," in Allworth, 1967.
[59] See section on history; Rakowska-Harmstone, 1970: ch. 7.

survival of old customs and attitudes, particularly in reference to religious observance and attitude toward women. The elite, which has been growing rapidly because of demographic factors as well as spread of educational opportunities, has reacted selectively, accepting modernization and accompanying opportunities, but emphasizing traditional heritage as means of new national legitimization. Even among elite, survival of the customary way of life is high, and a distinction is made between "public" life, which is modern, and "private" life, still conforming significantly to traditional norms. All available data indicate that Tadzhiks (and other Asians) tend to live as a totally separate community from, and have little contact with, Russians and other European elements in the republic.[60]

Post-World War II cultural policy in Tadzhikistan has centered on efforts to develop a new historiography, selectively to revive classical Persian literature, to build and modernize the Farsi language, and to promote national literature and arts. One aim of this policy is to endow Tadzhiks with new legitimacy as bearers of the ancient Samanid political and cultural role in the Persian-speaking world; another is to legitimize the Russian conquest as means through which Tadzhiks were able to progress directly from feudalism to socialism, assuming a modern national existence within the Soviet family of nations.

The Tadzhik reaction appears ambivalent: on the one hand, they have embraced the revival of the ancient heritage as means of constructing a separate national identity; on the other, they have resisted the Soviet and Russian elements which, under party policy, are an integral part of this revival.

EXTERNAL RELATIONS

Tadzhiks belong to the group of Soviet nationalities which can be characterized as "stay-at-homes," not only in terms of mov-

ing among the union republics (let alone abroad), but also in terms of moving among localities within the republic. This lack of geographical mobility is due to several factors: compactness of settlement; strong identification with traditional cultural patterns of life which make Tadzhiks feel uncomfortable in different cultural environments; and, by and large, lack of knowledge of Russian language and marketable skills. As a group, Tadzhiks tend to cluster in rural areas; while settlement in the cities has increased, even here it tends to cluster. Numerous data in local papers indicate that, when coming for employment into a modern environment, they feel uncomfortable and eventually return to their original localities. Language and education data (see sections on language and education of this chapter) confirm the lacks in skills and in Russian language facility.

Contacts with Other Ethnic Groups within USSR

The Tadzhik masses have little, if any, contact with other national groups, even within the republic, except with Uzbeks and other Asians such as Turkmen and Kirgiz (depending on locality). As far as can be determined, there is no movement of Tadzhik labor outside the republic's boundaries. There is ethnic intermixture within the republic at construction sites and industrial centers but, apparently, little cultural exchange.

The elite also tend to stay within the republic, with a few notable exceptions such as Bobodzhan Gafurovich Gafurov, ex–first secretary of the Tadzhik party, 1946–1956, historian and member of the AN SSSR, and the poet Mirzo Tursun-zade. The elite's lack of mobility is in part a result of the past nationality policy, which encouraged development of each nationality within its own area and culture (particularly in Central Asia after 1924 where the aim was to break the pan-Islamic unity of Turkestan), and in part preoccupation with building their own identity (a by-product of that policy). The elite, however, maintain numerous interethnic contacts—within the

---

60 Rakowska-Harmstone, 1970; Wheeler, 1964, 1966; Allworth, 1967, 1971.

republic, within Central Asia as a whole, and, to a lesser degree, with the other Soviet republics. In the 1950s and 1960s there has been official encouragement of "exchange of experiences" among elites of the various republics, but this takes the largely ritualized form of meetings between groups from the republics, such as cultural groups (exchanges of cultural delegations, fairs of one republic in another, etc.), in which Tadzhik delegates participate. The same applies to exchange of Komsomol delegations, not only among the republics, but among localities in each republic. In the case of Tadzhikistan, most exchanges take place with the Uzbek republic. Few Tadzhik party and government cadres serve outside the republic, although Uzbek and numerous European cadres are sometimes posted in Tadzhikistan.

Contacts with Foreign Countries

There was virtually no exchange with foreign countries prior to 1956 and inauguration of the policy of "peaceful coexistence." In line with Soviet policy of allowing the Tadzhik to pursue the ancient "leading role," however, cultural activists visited neighboring countries: for example, Mirzo Tursun-zade, standard-bearer of the new Tadzhik culture, visited British India in 1947 and Pakistan in the late 1940s.

Since 1956 there has been initiation of contacts with the Third World—particularly with Afghanistan, India, Pakistan, and Iran. These took shape primarily as exchanges of delegations—of all kinds, but mostly cultural. While not on a major foreign circuit like Tashkent, Dushanbe has been visited by numerous foreign delegations. Members of the Tadzhik political and cultural elite also go abroad; here again the two most prominent individuals are Gafurov and Mirzo Tursun-zade. Some Tadzhiks are also included in foreign aid missions to foreign countries; some are allowed to go on pilgrimages to holy places of Islam. In addition to delegation exchanges, Tadzhiks can listen to foreign broadcasts in Persian, and neighboring countries can receive Tadzhik broadcasts (if in Persian or Uzbek).

It is impossible to determine the existence and/or frequency of illegal border crossings, although some undoubtedly exist, especially in the mountainous areas. Early information indicates that gold for the Aga Khan has been collected in the Pamirs; some references were also made to crossing the Panj on inflated goat skins. Illegal contacts are made difficult by the party policy of systematic resettlement of mountain *kishlaks* into the valleys (started in the 1930s, this continued in the 1950s and 1960s) plus activities of the border guards. Numerous refugees from the old Bukhara live in Afghanistan, and some contacts are undoubtedly continued.

Relations with Third World countries— particularly those of the Middle East and southwest Asia—have been important in the light of Soviet foreign policy and also in view of the Sino-Soviet rivalry and the Chinese attitude as champion of Soviet Asian rights. It appears, however, that the frequency of contacts may have diminished in the early 1970s.

Media

LANGUAGE DATA

Tadzhik (Farsi) is unlike any other major language spoken in the Soviet Union; it is an Iranian language, very close to Persian. Basically, there are three official languages in Tadzhikistan: Tadzhik, titular language; Uzbek, language of the second major group; and Russian. For all practical purposes (as seen from statistics below), Russian is language of political, administrative, and economic activity, except at the local (i.e., rural) level. In places with concentrations of other *indigenous* minorities, such as Kirgiz and Turkmen, their languages are also used locally for official purposes. Tadzhik, originally in the Arabic alphabet, has been written in the Cyrillic alphabet since 1940 (as are all other languages used in the republic).

The multilingual character of the republic and its people is illustrated by language statistics provided by two population censuses (see Table 14.7). Each major Asian indigenous group (Tadzhik, Uzbek, Turkmen, and Kirgiz) showed extremely high adherence to national language as native language (above 98% of total), and correspondingly very low fluency in Russian (only 16% of Tadzhiks spoke Russian, and fewer of the other three groups). In each case, percentage of members of each group using their national language *increased* between 1959 and 1970. No information was available on change in percentage in each group speaking Russian, but it is unlikely that it has increased.

The other two Asian groups, not native to the area—Kazakhs and deported Tatars

—showed a higher degree of assimilation into the Russian language. With Kazakhs, assimilation was high only in comparison with indigenous groups. Tatars, on the other hand, showed the second highest degree of fluency in Russian among non-Russian ethnic groups (71% of total). For both groups, the percentage of those regarding national language as native language decreased between the two censuses; fluency in Russian was also likely to have increased during this period.

Virtually all Russians in the Tadzhik republic regarded Russian as native language, and there was no change in the intercensal period. Only 4% of the Russian population knew any other Soviet language fluently. Thus, Russian was the only language of communication for Russians in the republic. Therefore, they could not communicate with at least 85% of members of indigenous ethnic groups, including the titular nationality, except through interpreters. Given a concentration of Russians in the political, administrative, and eco-

Table 14.7

Languages Spoken by Major Ethnic Groups in Tadzhik SSR
1959 and 1970

(% of total)

	REGARD OWN NATIONAL LANGUAGE AS NATIVE LANGUAGE (%)		SPEAK OTHER SOVIET LANGUAGE FLUENTLY, 1970 (%)	
	1959	*1970*	*Russian*	*Other*
Total Population in Tadzhik SSR	96.7	97.2	16.9	7.5
Tadzhiks	99.3	99.4	16.6	6.0
Uzbeks	98.6	98.8	12.8	12.0
Russians	99.9	99.9	0.04	4.2
Tatars	89.6	86.5	71.3	7.5
Germans	88.7	81.4	72.7	0.9
Kirgiz	95.5	97.6	11.9	18.7
Ukrainians	44.3	52.6	46.2	9.8
Jews	23.2	19.9	50.5	10.3
Turkmen	96.3	97.9	10.7	13.8
Kazakhs	94.4	93.0	28.1	27.9

Source: *Nar. khoz. TSSR 1970:* 293.

nomic hierarchy and among professionals, specialists, and skilled labor, Tadzhiks, Uzbeks, and others who did not know Russian (a substantial majority) could not enter and/or ascend within the socio-economic and political structure of the republic. Language data also indicate that the modern Tadzhik political and cultural elite in the early 1970s could not have been larger than approximately 15% of their national group, as membership in the elite (even cultural) was predicated on knowledge of the Russian language.

Other European groups in the population showed a relatively high degree of assimilation into the Russian language, especially the Jews: only 20% regarded Yiddish language as their native language in 1970 (a decline of 3% from 1959); only 50% of the Jewish group were fluent in Russian, indicating assimilation into other languages. (It is puzzling that data show only 10% of the Jewish group fluent in other Soviet languages, leaving 20% unaccounted for in terms of fluency in any language.)

The Germans (war deportees) declined in percentage of those regarding German as native language, demonstrating the highest fluency in Russian among all groups. Only 50% of Ukrainians regarded Ukrainian as first language, but only 46% were listed as fluent in Russian, indicating an existence, side by side, of Russified and non-Russified Ukrainian groups. Ukrainians were the only non-Russian, nonindigenous group to show an increase in number of affiliations to the national language during the intercensal period.

The absence of a common language of communication in Tadzhikistan poses a major problem in economic-administrative work and political education work, for at least three languages (and frequently more) must be used to reach the mass of the people. This is particularly important to effectiveness of printed and electronic media. The need to boost the ratio of Russian speakers among non-Russian groups was stressed in the Central Committee CPSU special resolution of January 1969 censuring work of the Tadzhik Communist party.[61]

_____

61 *Partiinaya zhizn'*, 1969: I: 8.

Modernization of the Tadzhik, or Farsi, language under the Soviets included two alphabet reforms (Latinization in 1928–1930 and introduction of the Cyrillic alphabet in 1940), expurgation of "alien" elements (Arabisms and "archaisms"), and introduction of "internationalist" elements (Russian-derived modern scientific-technical and sociopolitical vocabulary) and modern grammatical constructions, also borrowed from Russian. A conference in Stalinabad (Dushanbe) in 1938 marked the victory of "internationalists" over "bourgeois-nationalists" in Tadzhik linguistic policy.

With destalinization, there has been some reversal in Russification of Tadzhik, with strong pressures exercised by the cultural elite to purify the language of unnecessary Russicisms (as at the Tashkent 1969 language conference). One major problem in formation of modern Tadzhik has been the significant difference between literary Farsi (base of modern Tadzhik) and the spoken language, and between Tadzhik and Iranian dialects spoken by numerous groups. Repeatedly, the press has reported on problems encountered by Tadzhik children in studying their native language.

Another aspect of linguistic policy, as in all other republics, has been promotion of study of Russian and its use as the common Soviet language. The problem has been scarcity of Russian teachers and quality of instruction: ignorance of Russian disqualifies substantial numbers of young Tadzhiks from progressing on the socioeconomic and political ladder, which requires mastery of the Russian language.

LOCAL MEDIA

Print Media

In Tadzhikistan in 1970, 52% of all books published and 36% of all periodicals (including periodically issued collections and bulletins) were published in the Tadzhik language; both percentages are below the weight of the titular nationality in total population. Eighty-four percent of all news-

Table 14.8

Native and Second Languages Spoken by Tadzhiks

(in thousands)

NO. TADZHIKS RESIDING			SPEAKING AS NATIVE LANGUAGE						SPEAKING AS SECOND LANGUAGE[a]	
			Tadzhik			Russian				Other Languages of Peoples of USSR 1970[b]
	1959	1970	1959	1970	% Point Change 1959–1970	1959	1970	% Point Change 1959–1970	Russian 1970	
in Tadzhik SSR	1,051 (100%)	1,630 (100%)	1,044 (99.3%)	1,620 (99.4%)	+0.1	4 (0.4%)	7 (0.4%)	0	270 (16.6%)	97 (6.0%)
in other Soviet republics	346 (100%)	506 (100%)	327 (94.6%)	484 (95.7%)	+1.1	3 (1.0%)	6 (1.2%)	+0.2	59 (11.7%)	159 (31.4%)
Total	1,397 (100%)	2,136 (100%)	1,371 (98.1%)	2,104 (98.5%)	+0.4	8 (0.6%)	13 (0.6%)	0	329 (15.4%)	256 (12.0%)

Sources: *Itogi SSSR 1959, Itogi TSSR 1959*: tables 53, 54; *Itogi 1970*: IV: 20, 295.

[a] No data are available for 1959, since no questions regarding command of a second language were asked in the 1959 census.

[b] Including Tadzhik, if not native language.

papers (including *kolkhoz* newspapers) were published in Tadzhik. Of all books published in national languages in the Soviet Union in 1970, 0.5% were in Tadzhik. Weight of the Tadzhik national group in the total Soviet population was 0.9%.[62]

The first Tadzhik language newspaper was published in 1925; the first Russian language newspaper in 1929. Numbers and circulation figures of newspapers and magazines tend to be misleading, as only a few have a general circulation. Many *raion* and city newspapers are issued irregularly with limited circulation. The circulation figures are not necessarily reflective of readership because of language and (in the villages) literacy problems, and also because of problems with distribution. No information is available for the 1960s but in the 1950s there were stoppages and delays in delivery, so that a paper arrived days, sometimes weeks, later.[63]

Major newspapers in the republic are two organs of the party, *Kommunist Tadzhikistana* in Russian and *Tochikistoni Sovieti* in Tadzhik, and two Komsomol papers, *Komsomolets Tadzhikistana* in Russian and *Komsomol Tochikistoni* in Tadzhik. All major periodicals appear to be in Tadzhik. They include *Khochgii kishloki Tochikiston* [*Agriculture of Tadzhikistan*], journal of the Ministry of Agriculture; *Khorpushtak* [*Hedgehog*], satirical journal published by the party; *Kommunisti Tochikiston,* party journal dealing with political theory; *Maktabi Soveti* [*Soviet School*], journal of pedagogical science; *Marshal* [*Torch*], Komsomol magazine for 10- to 15-year-olds; *Sadon Shark* [*Voice of the East*], journal of the Tadzhik SSR Union of Writers;[64] and *Zanoni Tochikiston* [*Women of Tadzhikistan*], popular magazine issued by the party.[65]

Many books published in Tadzhik are translations from the Russian, although there is a shortage of qualified translators. Marxist-Leninist classics were translated

and published only after 1945; most translations are economic and technical manuals and "how to" pamphlets. Translations of Russian literary works (prerevolutionary and Soviet) and masterpieces of Western literature are generally done by members of the Tadzhik elite. (In the 1950s this was for many an escape from prescribed themes for creative writing, allowing them to maintain their "productivity" quotas.) Russian and Western literature usually appears in multilingual editions.

Aesthetic quality of many books (especially of the classical Persian literature) has been high in decorations and setting, but paper and print are poor.

There has been a decline in share of books printed in Central Asian languages within the USSR total, from 3.7% in 1960 to 3.3% in 1970. In 1970 377 titles were published in Tadzhik (0.4% of total) as compared with 60,240 titles issued in Russian (76.3% of total). Total circulation in Tadzhik amounted to 4,118 (0.3% of Soviet total); Russian, 1,086,133 (79.7%).[66] In 1971, in the republic, 753 titles were published, with printing of 5,391,000.[67]

Classical literature is available in Tadzhik, Uzbek, and Russian translations, but in the Cyrillic alphabet and selective editions (passages considered "reactionary" are expurgated) for mass consumption. Access to mass editions of the original is precluded by lack of knowledge of the original alphabets and of Arabic, except among scholars. The state public library in Dushanbe has a collection of more than 20,000 ancient manuscripts in Eastern languages.[68]

"Uncritical" treatment of classical literature by the cultural elite was the subject of reiterated criticism in the 1950s. Since 1956, however, greater freedom to publish and read previously proscribed works has been evident. One example would be current availability of *The Adventures of the Four Dervishes*, attributed to Amir Hisrou Dehlevi. In 1951 issuance of this work by the Tadzhik state publishing house caused a major scandal.[69]

---

62 Percentage calculations based on *Nar. khoz. SSSR, 1972:* 673–679.

63 Rakowska-Harmstone, 1970: 214–218.

64 In the 1950s the fiction journal of the writers' union, listed under the title *Sharki Surkh* [*The Red East*], was criticized repeatedly for nationalistic leanings. Rakowska-Harmstone, 1970: 255, 262–267.

65 *Europa Yearbook,* 1972: 1,311.

66 *Nar. khoz. SSSR,* 1972: 673.

67 *Pechat'* 1971: 97.

68 *Kommunist Tadzhikistana* (January 25), 1946.

69 Rakowska-Harmstone, 1970: 264.

Table 14.9

Publications in Tadzhik SSR

Language of Publication	Year	NEWSPAPERS[a]			MAGAZINES			BOOKS & BROCHURES		
		No.	Per Issue Circulation (1,000)	Copies/100 in Language Group[e]	No.	Per Issue Circulation (1,000)	Copies/100 in Language Group[e]	No. Titles	Total Volume (1,000)	Books & Brochures/100 in Language Group[e]
Russian	1959	8	75	24.1	N.A.	N.A.	N.A.	166	881	283.5
	1971	5	185	45.6	4	14	3.5	339	1,452	357.8
Tadzhik[b]	1959	56	275	26.0	N.A.	N.A.	N.A.	441	2,707	256.7
	1971	50	663	40.6	7	363	22.2	397	3,853	236.0
Minority languages	1959	6[d]	51	8.3	N.A.	N.A.	N.A.	23	117	19.0
	1971	5	110	12.8	0	0	0	10	72	8.4
Foreign languages (Polish)	1959	0	0	0	N.A.	N.A.	N.A.	(2)[c]	(3)	N.A.
	1971	0	0	0	0	0	0	(7)[c]	(276)	N.A.
All languages	1959	70	401	20.3	14	117	5.9	632[c]	3,708	187.3
	1971	60	958	33.0	11	377	13.0	718[c]	5,653	195.0

Sources: *Pechat' 1959*: 58, 130, 165; *Pechat' 1971*: 97, 160, 189.

[a] 1970 figures do not include *kolkhoz* newspapers.

[b] Some come out in both Russian and Tadzhik languages; 14 came out in Tadzhik and Uzbek.

[c] Book totals as given in *Pechat'* sometimes differ from totals in language categories. The indication is that books are published in other languages, but no data is given. Figures in parentheses are the presumed production of books in other languages based on this discrepancy.

[d] This figure may include newspapers in non-Soviet languages.

[e] Includes all native speakers of the language.

Electronic Media and Films

There are three TV channels in Dushanbe: Dushanbe, Moscow, and Tashkent. Dushanbe and Tashkent programs were bilingual (Tadzhik and Russian and Uzbek and Russian, respectively), with language of a given program indicated in the listing. In both cases a substantial number of programs have no language designation. These include a major portion of musical offerings, but also spoken programs. In each case titles listed were in Russian, so it would be reasonable to assume that large sections of these programs are also in Russian; they can also be bilingual. Moscow programs are all in Russian.

A sample of weekly programs in June 1973 revealed that total number of TV broadcast hours in Dushanbe on all three channels was 222 hours and 35 minutes, longest number of hours on the Moscow program, shortest on the Tashkent program. Analysis of programs by language indicates that two thirds of programs seen in the city were in Russian; 20% had no language designation; 8% were in Tadzhik; and 5% in Uzbek. Dushanbe channel broadcasted 46% of its programs in Russian and only 22% in Tadzhik; for the Tashkent channel, 51% were in Russian and 18% in Uzbek.[70]

A rough analysis of program content on the Dushanbe channel shows that in one week items were distributed as follows: music programs, 21; literary programs, 18; educational programs, 13; 15-minute news broadcasts (half Russian, half Tadzhik), 11; movies, 14; agitation-propaganda programs, 8; special youth programs, 6; theater programs, 2; sports events, 3; repeat program called "Times," 3; and three separate editions of TV journal—for the family, newspaper journal, and health journal. Music programs included symphonic as well as local (Tadzhik and Uzbek) folk music and songs and a concert from Hindu movies; also, dance music and music to sleep by. Education programs (mostly in Tadzhik) included classroom science presentations and education for housewives in cleanliness and so on; the "agit-prop" items included two broadcasts on "friendship of the people," both in Tadzhik. Literary programs included storytelling and poetry, both Russian and Tadzhik; one story was from Estonia.

Many mountain localities and Pamir are outside the range of either TV station. The Ninth Five-Year Plan envisaged building relay lines Dushanbe-Pendzhikent-Aini (Zeravshan Valley westward), and Leninabad-Isfara. A planned satellite will make relay possible for Pamirs and other mountain regions.[71]

Dushanbe also has three radio programs. Only the "first" is listed in the paper; the other two are referred to as "musical and artistic" programs. In June 1973 Program One had a weekly total of 108 hours and 40 minutes broadcast time; 25% of broadcasts were in Russian, 29%, in Tadzhik, 3% in Uzbek, and 43% had no language designation. Program content distribution was similar to that on TV.

A spot sampling of three issues of *Kommunist Tadzhikistana*[72] revealed a substantial number of movie theaters in Dushanbe, many more playing in summer than in winter. All movie titles were listed in Russian and, except for recognizable Western films such as *The Snows of Kilimanjaro* and *Lady Hamilton,* most appeared to have been Russian movies. Only once was a movie listed with the special designation "in the Tadzhik language." Some titles were obviously on local themes, some (very few) appeared transliterated from local languages. Most appeared to have largely entertainment value, although many were on "approved" themes. The September 1972 issues listed four visits from abroad in the space of a month: Indian artistic group; orchestra from the German Democratic Republic; artistic group from Turkey; song-and-dance ensemble from Afghanistan.

Many rural areas seem to have few movie facilities and are not well serviced by mobile movie vans. Subject to repeated criticism in the 1940s and 1950s, the problem still continues. At the 16th Congress

---

70 *Kommunist Tadzhikistana* (June 1–3, 5–8), 1973.

71 *Televedeniye-radioveshcheniye*, 1972: X: 9.
72 September 22, 1972; January 3, 1973; June 1, 1973.

Table 14.10

Electronic Media and Films in Tadzhik SSR

YEAR	RADIO					TELEVISION			MOVIES	
	No. Stations	No. Wired Sets (1,000)	Sets/100 Population	No. Wireless Sets (1,000)	Sets/100 Population	No. Stations	No. sets (1,000)	Sets/100 Population	Seats (1,000)	Seats/100 Population
1960	N.A.	148[a]	6.9[d]	168[a]	7.9[c]	N.A.	8[a]	.4[c]	81[b]	3.8[d]
1970	N.A.	267[a]	8.9[d]	390[a]	13.1[c]	N.A.	216[a]	7.2[c]	183[b]	6.1[d]
1971	N.A.	277[d]	8.9[d]	415[d]	13.4[c]	N.A.	265[c]	8.6[c]	N.A.	N.A.

[a] Source: *Transport i svyaz' SSR*, 1972: 296–298.
[b] Source: *Nar. obraz.*, 1971: 325
[c] Source: *Nar. koz.*, 1972: 572, 578.
[d] Computed from data cited above ([b] and [c]).

Table 14.11

Literacy in Tadzhik SSR for Age Group 9–49

(% of total population)

	1959			1970		
	Total	Men	Women	Total	Men	Women
Total	96.2	98.0	94.6	99.6	99.8	99.4
Urban population	95.6	97.9	93.7	99.6	99.8	99.3
Rural population	95.5[a]	98.0	95.1[a]	99.6	99.7	99.5[a]

Source: *Nar. khoz. TSSR 1970*: 290.

[a] The ratio was higher in rural areas, mostly because more older women who are less literate live in the cities (as noted in source).

of the Tadzhik CP, First Secretary Rasulov complained that films are rarely if ever shown in faraway *kishlaks*.[73]

EDUCATIONAL INSTITUTIONS

Level of Education

The literacy rate in Tadzhikistan, as published in official statistics, compares favorably with any country in the world. During the Soviet era, it increased from 3.8% in 1926 (6.4% for men, 0.9% for women) to 99.6% (for age group from 9 to 49) in 1970 (see Table 14.11).

The data in Table 14.11 do not show a significant difference between rural and urban literacy; as the table footnote points out, however, they do not distinguish separately the older (and less literate) generation in either type of area. Also no distinction is made for literacy of different national groups. Numerous other indicators, discussed later in this section, reveal, however, that degree of literacy is lower among Asian groups than among Europeans. For Central Asia in general, Edward Allworth concludes that, despite real increases in literacy rate, large numbers of local people still receive little or no education.[74]

Data for education per 1,000 people, al-

though among the lowest in the USSR, also compare favorably with other countries, especially with neighboring Asian nations such as Afghanistan. (See Table 14.12.)

Language Policy in Education

Generally, the republic has a trilingual school system with Russian, Tadzhik, and Uzbek as languages of instruction. There are also some Kirgiz language schools in Kirgiz settlement areas and, possibly, some Turkmen language schools in Turkmen areas, although no hard information is available for the latter. The nonindigenous groups do not have their own language schools and, as far as is known, usually attend Russian language schools. In the 1950s (no information is available for the 1960s) there were also multilingual schools, where parallel classes were offered in major republican languages. Russian instruction is offered in local language schools but, by all accounts, it was and is very poor. Numerous complaints are voiced about the quality of Russian language instruction, particularly in the rural areas, and statistics on the Asian groups' knowledge of the Russian language bear this out. This is primarily because of a shortage of qualified teachers and textbooks. Since 1958 the Tadzhik SSR has basically adopted unchanged Thesis 19 of the 1958 Education Act, which provides that parents have an option to educate children in either

[73] *Partiinaya zhizn'*, 1966: 6.
[74] Allworth, 1973: 393.

Table 14.12

Selected Data on Education in Tadzhik SSR (1971)

Population: 3,096,000

		PER 1,000 POPULATION	% OF TOTAL
All Schools			
number of schools	3,084	1.0	
number of students	810,000	261.7	
Newly opened elementary, incomplete secondary, and secondary schools			
number of schools	113		
number of student places	31,800	10.3	
Secondary special schools			
number of schools	37		
number of students	36,000	11.6	
Institutions of higher education			
number of institutions	8		
number of students	45,900	14.8	
Universities			
number of universities	1		
number of students			
total	12,467		
day students	5,551		44
evening students	2,348		19
correspondence students	4,568		37
newly admitted			
total	2,448		
day students	1,247		51
evening students	460		19
correspondence students	741		30
graduated			
total	1,880		
day students	846		45
evening students	325		17
correspondence students	709		38
Graduate students			
total number	680	.22	
in scientific research institutions	348		
in universities	332		
Number of persons with (in 1970) higher or secondary (complete and incomplete) education			
per 1,000 individuals, 10 years and older	420		
per 1,000 individuals employed in national economy	602		

Table 14.12 cont.

	PER 1,000 POPULATION	% OF TOTAL
Number of workers graduated from professional-technical schools	12,900	4.2
Addendum (1969–1970 data):		
Schools of working and rural youth (including correspondence students) number of students	29,400	
Professional-technical schools and FZU number of students	16,500	
Students improving qualifications at work or special courses and in other ways (excluding political education network)	86,500	
Elementary, incomplete secondary, and secondary number of schools number of students	2,827 710,400	

Sources: *Nar. khoz. 1972*: 108, 439, 644, 651, 652, 654; for Addendum, *Nar. khoz. TSSR 1969*: 227, 228.

Table 14.13

Tadzhik SSR, Education per 1,000 People 10 Years of Age and Above

	1959			1970		
	Average ratio	*Men*	*Women*	*Average ratio*	*Men*	*Women*
People with higher and middle-level education, total	325	381	275	420	471	374
with completed higher	15	} 19	12	29	} 39	20
with incomplete higher	9			12		
with special middle	34			40		
with general middle	48	} 362	263	112	} 432	354
with incomplete middle	219			227		

Source: *Nar. khoz. TSSR 1970*: 291, 292.

Russian or local language schools, but, along with other Central Asian republics, it is pledged to improve study of the Russian language.

Instruction in most specialized technical and professional schools has generally been in the Russian language, largely because of a shortage of qualified teachers and because Russian is essential in occu-pations for which these schools prepare. Entry to these schools, until 1971, was predicated on an examination which included a test (oral or written, depending on the school) in the Russian language. In view of poor preparation in the language of most Tadzhik/Uzbek students who completed the eighth, tenth, or eleventh grades (different entry points are required by different schools), most were *de facto* barred from receiving professional-technical education. In turn, this contributed to the largely unskilled character of the Asian component of the Tadzhik labor force, affected ethnic composition of urban and industrial employment, and contributed to underemployment in rural areas. The language admissions policy began to change in 1971, presumably because of the Asian population explosion, increase in numbers of Asian secondary school graduates, and growing numbers of youth in the labor force, combined with linguistic facts of life.

A decree adopted in May 1971 provided that a qualified Tadzhik or Uzbek student may follow any area of specialization at a higher educational establishment in the republic without being fluent in, or even acquainted with, the Russian language.[75]

A selected sample of school admission ads in *Kommunist Tadzhikistana*, 1973, indicates the beginnings of change in accordance with the decree, although the Russian language is still prerequisite in some schools.

Admissions requirements for schools training for the Security Services (MVD schools) provide for an entry examination in Russian language and literature (written and oral), USSR history (oral), and a foreign language (oral), the latter only for the higher (4 years) school.[76]

Admissions to librarians' schools require examinations in both Russian and Tadzhik languages; to club managers' schools, in Tadzhik for Tadzhik language courses (both types of schools are run by the Ministry of Culture). Admissions to agricultural tekhnikum require an examination in all three languages (it is not specified whether only one language is required, depending on the language of instruction, or all three in each case). The finance-economic tekhnikum (in Dushanbe) offers instruction in different languages, depending on program to be pursued. A physical education tekhnikum admits graduates of 8-year schools on the basis of a Russian language dictation and an oral mathe-

matics exam plus graduates of 10-year schools on the basis of a written essay in Russian language and literature and an oral examination in Soviet history.[77]

General rules, published in *Kommunist Tadzhikistana* for 1973, provide that admission to middle medical schools for applicants with the 8-year base require a Russian language dictation and an oral mathematics examination; for applicants with the 10-year base, an essay in Russian language and literature and an oral chemistry examination. The rules also provide that an applicant who did not attend secondary schools in language of instruction of the tekhnikum where he is applying may, on request, take a written entry examination in Russian (after 8 years' education) or in Russian language and literature (after 10 years' education); such an applicant is also interviewed to ascertain his/her practical facility in the language of instruction. A curious wording of this provision seems to indicate either that Russian is still predominant language of instruction in tekhnikums or that tekhnikum students, regardless of language of instruction, are expected to have a degree of facility in Russian.

Another announcement of general rules of admission to specialized middle-level schools provides that, on entering schools with language of instruction other than Russian, an entry examination in the given language may be substituted for the entry examination in the Russian language.[78]

These announcements seem to indicate that in line with new policy an applicant may now enter technical-professional schools without a knowledge of Russian, but that it is far preferable and sometimes required (in medical schools and others) that he demonstrate an acquaintance with the language.

Nationality and Education

National breakdown of the student bodies in higher and specialized middle-level schools indicates that the three indigenous

75 Shorish, 1973: 98 from *Tochikistoni Soviet* (May 8), 1971.
76 *Kommunist Tadzhikistana* (June 1), 1973.

77 *Ibid.* (June 2), 1973.
78 *Ibid.* (May 23), 1973.

Table 14.14

Nationality of Students in Higher and Special Middle-Level Schools in Tadzhik SSR

ETHNIC GROUP	HIGHER SCHOOLS				SPECIAL MIDDLE SCHOOLS			% OF GROUP IN REPUBLIC POPULATION 1970
	1963–1964 S.I.[a]	Total[b]	1969–1970 % of Total	S.I.[a]	Total[b]	1969–1970 % of Total	S.I.[a]	
Tadzhik	84.4	21,051[b]	50	89.3	13,370[b]	39	79	56.2
Uzbek	82.6	7,835	19	82.6	5,370	15	65.2	23.0
Russian	178.0	8,901	20	166.6	9,793	29	241.7	11.9
Ukrainian	238.5	903	2	181.8	937	3	273.7	1.1
Kirgiz	38.4	117	0.4	33.8	166	1	83.3	1.2
Other	128.0	3,797	9	128.6	4,330	13	185.7	6.6
Total		42,604			33,966			

Sources: For 1963–1964 data, Shorish, 1973: 89, based on 1959 population; for 1969–1970 data, *Nar. khoz. TSSR 1969:* 241.

[a] S.I.: Selectivity Index. A ratio normally derived by dividing proportion of an age cohort of an ethnic group within the total number of students in an educational establishment, by its proportion in the population; in this case, by dividing proportion of students in higher (and secondary middle) education by proportion of their nationality in the population. This index was developed in Shorish, 1973: 89.

[b] In 1970–1971 school year, number of Tadzhik students in higher educational establishments in Tadzhikistan was 28,100; in special middle-level schools, 17,700. *Nar. khoz.* 1970: 651.

nationalities are still underrepresented, and that European groups are overrepresented. Curiously, the ratio of Tadzhiks and Uzbeks among students of higher educational institutions is higher than their ratio in specialized middle-level schools. This probably indicates that the bulk of Asian students in higher institutions attend faculties of humanities—with local language predominant—rather than the sciences or professional schools. It also points out the shortage of local people in the professional-technical strata (see Table 14.14).

The academic selectivity index of Tadzhiks (i.e., a comparative measure of the group's access to educational opportunities) (see note in Table 14.14) in the early 1930s was lowest among Central Asian nationalities, and lowest of the 18 major national groups in the Soviet Union: 7.1 in 1928 and 14.2 in 1931 and 1933. By 1959 it had increased substantially.[79] Still, in the 1960s Tadzhiks remained in the lowest place in Central Asia, even though in Tadzhikistan itself their index was higher than that of Uzbeks and Kirgiz. It was much lower, however, than the index for these latter two groups between 1963–1964 and 1969–1970, reflecting the decline in their proportion of the total population. The selectivity index for Asian groups is undoubtedly inflated, as it has been calculated on the basis of the total groups' proportion in the population, rather than proportion of the appropriate age group. Fertility rates of Tadzhiks and Uzbeks have been much higher than those of Russians and Ukrainians; thus, their proportion in the students' group is certainly larger than the weight of their groups in the population as a whole.

The academic selectivity index for Tadzhiks in higher educational establishments in the Soviet Union as a whole declined from 71% to 68% between 1959 and 1970. (Turkmen were the only other group to show a decline.) Considering the higher net growth rate in their group, the decline may have been caused by a decrease in number of Tadzhiks who study outside their republic.[80]

Women and Education

Asian women's attendance at specialized and higher schools has been notoriously low. In statistical data it has been reflected in a lower proportion of girls in school than in the USSR as a whole, although no information is available on national breakdown of girls in school. Most specialized and higher schools are located in urban areas, however, and attendance of non-Asian girls brings the statistics up.

The virtual absence of Tadzhik and Uzbek girls in secondary and higher educational institutions was subject of repeated criticism in the republican press during the 1940s and 1950s, as was the extremely high dropout rate of Asian girls between the fourth and tenth grades. In 1953 the Tadzhik minister of education revealed that, while Asian girls constituted 45% of the enrollment through the fourth grade of primary school, they accounted for only 19% of enrollment in grades 8 through 10, and very few graduated.[81] By the end of the 1960s a change was visible; girls (of all nationalities) accounted for 48% of enrollment in grades 9–11, and proportion of Asian girls must have been much higher than the previous 19% (see Table 14.16). Some of the dropout rate is reflected in student statistics in primary and secondary grades (see Table 14.15). Official statistics, however, do not reflect any differential in percentage of girls in grades 1 through 11 in 1969–1970 (see Table 14.16). The relatively low percentage of women in higher educational institutions (see Table 14.17), and overall low selectivity index of women in higher schools—70.4 in 1969–1970 as compared to men's index of 130.6 —is primarily the result of Asian women's poor participation. The low academic selectivity index of women has probably pulled down the index for the Tadzhik, Uzbek, and Kirgiz groups as a whole.

The proportion of women among teachers in the republic is also very low, especially among directors of primary and incomplete middle-level schools (see Table 14.18).

79 Shorish, 1973: 87–89.
80 *Ibid.*, 90–91.

81 *Kommunist Tadzhikistana* (August 26), 1953.

Table 14.15

Student Enrollment in Primary and Middle-Level Schools in Tadzhik SSR

GRADES	1950–1951	1969–1970
1–4	263,300	376,700
5–8	80,800	275,100
9–10	5,200	80,000
11	——	5,800

Source: *Nar. khoz. TSSR 1969:* 227.

Table 14.16

Enrollment of Girls in Primary and Middle Level Schools in Tadzhik SSR, 1969–1970

GRADES	% OF TOTAL
1–11	47.9
Of this:	
1–4	48
5–8	47.7
9–11	48.2

Source: *Nar. khoz. TSSR 1969:* 330.

Note: For data for 1940–1941 (but not for subsequent years), it was specified that the relatively high percentage of girls in the ninth to eleventh grades reflected the fact that there were more schools with higher grades in urban than in rural areas.

Table 14.17

Women Students in Higher Educational Establishments in Tadzhik SSR

YEAR	WOMEN IN % OF TOTAL	SELECTIVITY INDEX
1950–1951	35	70.4
1960–1961	29	58.0
1969–1970	35	70.4

Sources: Data for 1950 to 1951 and 1960–1961 from Shorish, 1973: 90; for 1960–1970, from *Nar. khoz. TSSR 1969:* 241.

Table 14.18

Women Teachers in Primary and Secondary Schools in Tadzhik SSR, 1969–1970

SCHOOLS AND FUNCTIONS	% OF TOTAL
All schools	33
Teachers in grades 1–4	38
Teachers in grades 5–10	37
Directors, primary schools	13
Directors, 8-year schools	8
Directors, middle schools	16

Source: *Nar. khoz. TSSR 1969:* 232.

CULTURAL AND SCIENTIFIC INSTITUTIONS

Despite a well-developed network of cultural and mass enlightenment institutions, complaints about failure to reach the masses have been voiced at every party congress (and in the press) during the 1950s and the 1960s, including the 17th Congress in 1971 and the 1969 CC CPSU resolution censuring work of the Tadzhik party. Part of this failure is usually ascribed to poor work of these institutions and to shortage and breakdown of technical facilities, including means of transportation (Tadzhik topography compounds the usual Soviet transportation problems). Another cause of the failure seems to involve a combination of linguistic problems, with the still largely traditional rural Asian population unresponsive to content of the message conveyed by the cultural enlightenment network. This includes artistic offerings which do not include at least some traditional content. Another aspect of the problem has been an absence of cultural facilities in many areas. The 1969 CC CPSU resolution stated that "a significant part of large *kishlaks* [villages] to this day do not have clubs, libraries and cinema facilities." [82]

---

[82] *Partiinaya zhizn'*, 1969: I: 5.

Table 14.19

Scientific Workers in Tadzhik SSR by Nationality, 1969

(end of year)

ETHNIC GROUP	NUMBER	% OF TOTAL	GROUP % in POPULATION	SELECTIVITY INDEX[a]
Total	4,725	100		
Tadzhiks	1,851	39	56.2	69.6
Uzbeks	380	8	23.0	34.8
Russians	1,648	35	11.9	291.7
Ukrainians	201	4	1.1	368.5
Other	645	14	7.8	175.0

Source: *Nar. khoz. TSSR, 1969*: 243.

[a] Calculated as described in Table 14.14, note a.

Table 14.20

Ethnic Tadzhik Scientific Elite in USSR Total, 1970

SCIENTIFIC WORKERS	ABSOLUTE NOS.	TADZHIK SPECIALISTS AS % OF ALL TADZHIKS IN USSR	% OF TADZHIKS IN USSR TOTAL FOR EACH CATEGORY OF SPECIALIST
1. Scientists	2,358	0.11	0.2
Doctors of Science	61		0.2
Candidates of Science	760		0.3
Aspirants	489		0.4
2. Specialists with unfinished higher education	29,600	1.38	0.4
3. Specialists with intermediate education	26,800	1.25	0.2
Total of 1, 2, and 3	58,758	2.75	

Source: *Nar. obraz. 1971*: 240, 270, 278.

Theaters in Tadzhikistan are located in urban centers, while numerous "folk art circles" reportedly serve the countryside. From time to time theater collectives go "on the road" to various localities (and outside the republic).

As far as is known, Dushanbe has four permanent theaters: the Aini Theater of the Opera and Ballet (only opera and ballet theater in the republic); Mayakovsky Russian Drama Theater; Lakhuti Tadzhik Drama Theater; and a recently (1971) established State Theater for Youth.[83] Drama collectives from other republics and from abroad visit the capital frequently.

In 1969 total number of scientific wor-

83 Allworth, 1973: 10.

kers in the republic was listed as 4,725, with 2,001 employed by scientific enterprises and 2,651 by higher educational institutions (see Table 14.14). Among them, 1,851 were Tadzhiks (39% of total). This compares with the figure of 2,206 for all Tadzhik scientific workers in the USSR in the same year (and 2,358 in 1970), indicating that 345 worked outside the republic.[84] Number of Tadzhik scientific workers increased substantially from 1950 (when total in the USSR was 168) and from 1960 (866).[85]

The combined share of Tadzhiks and Uzbeks among scientific workers was 47%, to 39% of Russians and Ukrainians, and 14% of others. The differential in the selectivity index of Asian and European groups was even greater than in the case of students in higher education and middle-level schools, indicating once more that the republic's scientific elite was dominated by immigrant groups (see Table 14.19).

Scientists and other specialists constituted only 2.75% of Tadzhiks in the USSR in 1970, with scientists accounting for only 0.11% of Tadzhiks.[86]

There were 1,755 women scientific workers in Tadzhikistan (no ethnic breakdown available): 6 were academicians and professors; 61, doctors; 49, senior scientific workers; and 369, junior scientific workers and assistants.[87]

In 1971 there were more than 119,000 certified specialists working in the national economy, and every third worker in the republic had a middle-level or higher education.[88]

Table 14.21

Selected Data on Scientific and Cultural Facilities and Personnel in Tadzhik SSR (1971)

Population: 3,096,000

Academy of Sciences	
number of members	39
number of scientific institutions affiliated with academy	18
total number of scientific workers	1,008
Museums	
number of museums	6
attendance	357,000
attendance per 1,000 population	115
Theaters	
number of theaters	11
attendance	1,201,000
attendance per 1,000 population	388
Number of persons working in education and culture	
total	93,000
number per 1,000 population	30
Number of persons working in science and scientific services	
total	18,000
number per 1,000 population	6
Number of public libraries	1,191
number of books and magazines in public libraries	7,712,000
Number of clubs	980

Source: *Nar. khoz. 1972*: 106, 451, 650.

National Attitudes

REVIEW OF FACTORS FORMING
NATIONAL ATTITUDES

Geographical position and difficult topography have exerted a significant influence on national attitudes in Tadzhikistan. Historically, location at the crossroads of nomadic and agricultural settlements has brought successive waves of culturally and ethnically different people. At the same time,

84 *Nar. khoz. 1970*: 658.
85 *Ibid.*
86 *Nar. obraz.*, 1971: 240, 270, 278.
87 *Nar. khoz. TSSR 1970*: 242.
88 First Secretary Rasulov at 17th Congress of Tadzhik CP. *Kommunist Tadzhikistana* (February 19), 1971.

remoteness and isolation of the area—and, internally, between mountains and valleys —has made for fragmentation and difficult communications. To this day three major parts of the republic are linked to other regions: the Tadzhik section of Ferghana Valley with other parts of that area; the Zeravshan Valley extending westward into Uzbekistan; the southern valleys southward. Pamir remains a self-contained isolated entity, northeastern territories shading into Kirgizia, inhabited by Kirgiz shepherds.

The modern elite's sense of unity is a new phenomenon for the republic as a whole even though its roots are in pre-1920 Bukhara. The sense of cultural unity among the people has its source in Islam and survival of traditional patterns of life, extending beyond the Tadzhik borders. It has gained cohesiveness in response to the alien cultural influence of the Russians. There is no agreement among scholars as to whether or not the new sense of Tadzhik identity transcends the Islamic bonds of the old Turkestan. There seems no doubt that the bonds are felt when dealing with the Russian element, the all-Union demands, and sovietization. There are also indications, however, that national priorities exist when dealing with other Central Asian republics, especially Uzbekistan, strongest and most important republic in the region, and that the cultural elite has evolved an identity based in the Persian heritage.[89]

The Tadzhik economy is still basically a one-crop (cotton) colonial-type economy, geared to all-Union requirements. Development of subsidiary industry and, in the 1960s, beginnings of heavy industry do not necessarily reflect the republic's needs. Material benefits are unevenly distributed and, despite significant increase in overall standard of living, that part of the countryside inhabited by Tadzhiks (and Uzbeks) lags far behind predominantly European urban areas. In addition, there is still a strong legacy of bitterness in the countryside left over from collectivization and there seems to be bitterness over forcible resettlement of mountain villages into cotton-growing valleys.

Lack of commitment to economic goals,

on the part of the elite as well as workers and peasants, can be gauged by persistence of shortcomings in fulfillment. Criticism of economic performance has been steady, with no apparent improvement—in 1961 when first and second Tadzhik party secretaries were removed along with many other members of the political elite; at the 16th Congress of the Tadzhik party in 1966; in a special resolution of the CC CPSU censuring work of the Tadzhik party in January 1969; at a subsequent February plenum of the Tadzhik CC; and at the 17th Congress of the Tadzhik party in February 1971.[90]

In agriculture, criticism centers on low labor productivity, failure to improve mechanization and develop specialization of *kolkhozes* and *sovkhozes*, to sow irrigated areas and fulfill irrigation plans. In cotton growing there are complaints about uneven yields. Similarly, livestock growing has not achieved planned goals. Livestock problems are frequently blamed on traditional attitudes. Sheep losses are connected with Moslem festivals; Moslems are still unwilling to raise pigs.

Attitudes of the Asian population (their unwillingness to move into urban industrial employment because of cultural alienation) contribute to a growing surplus of labor in the countryside and continuation in traditional roles of Asian youth educated in local language schools. On the other hand, poor instruction in the Russian language in rural schools has constituted an objective barrier to acquiring skills and moving into the industrial labor market. This cannot but influence attitude toward Russians, especially in view of the obvious preference shown immigrant skilled workers in industrial hiring.

The pre-Soviet historical period left Tadzhiks fragmented, with a sense of cultural identity within the broader Islamic unity of the area as a whole, but with a surviving, if largely inchoate, sense of a separate Iranian heritage. The sense of separate national identity, still within broader Islamic traditions but in a unique Tadzhik variant, has crystallized in the period of

89 Procyk, 1973: 123–133; Rosen, 1973: 71.

90 *Kommunist Tadzhikistana* (April 14), 1961 and (February 19) 1971; *Pravda* (February 13), 1969; *Partiinaya zhizn'* (March 6), 1966: 54–56, and (January 1) 1969: 3–8.

Soviet Tadzhik history, mainly as the result of two factors: resentment against Russian political ascendancy and rediscovery of Persian heritage promoted, paradoxically, by Soviet nationality policy. The reaction toward Russian hegemony has been successively reinforced in the period of Soviet history by the "colonial" attitude of Russian settlers after outbreak of the revolution, the civil war, and Red Army pacification campaign of 1921; forcible subversion of the traditional society in 1920–1921 and 1930–1931; the collectivization campaign and purges of the 1930s; the "Big Brother" syndrome of the 1940s and early 1950s; and continuation of Russian ascendancy in the sociopolitical and economic structure of the republic.

Resistance to Russian models and the search for (and return to) an indigenous heritage has been reflected in the field of cultural activity by the Soviet-educated Tadzhik elite. This is apparent in historiography—especially in evaluation of the Russian role in the history of Central Asia and that of national movements in resistance to Russian encroachments, and in insistence on treating national history as a unified whole rather than from the Leninist class viewpoint of division between "progressive" and "reactionary" streams. In linguistics this resistance is manifested in an effort to preserve Arabic and Persian roots and to resist "internationalization." In literature it is seen in resistance to Russian-Soviet models in form as well as content, and preservation of form and content of traditional models.

Conscious adherence to traditional heritage not only on the part of the new elite, but also of the rural masses, is illustrated by several cases of *kolkhozniki* responding favorably to quotes from Firdousi poems, not only exhibiting familiarity with poetry of the classical period, but quoting from it at length.[91] The search for ancient roots among the intelligentsia, on the other hand, has resulted in formation of a new conception of the motherland, a Tadzhik-Moslem *Vatan,* contrasted with the Soviet Union.[92] For both groups classical literature has become a source of inspiration, the mark of a separate national identity.

Cultural alienation of the community is reflected in the urban-rural dichotomy, *de facto* separation of urban (Russian) and rural (Tadzhik) communities, and differential in fertility rates.

The 1970 census data indicate an extremely high level of adherence to the national language and widespread ignorance of Russian. While this is in part a result of objective factors (poor facilities for teaching Russian), it is also a result of unwillingness of Tadzhiks and Uzbeks to learn Russian. As noted earlier, ignorance of Russian has also been a significant factor in underrepresentation of Tadzhik and other Asian groups in professional and higher education; recent changes in admissions policies of educational institutions, allowing access to Asians who do not know Russian, appear poorly implemented (see section on educational institutions). At the same time, the indigenous population's need to master the Russian language has been referred to as the pivotal question at all major party gatherings and in the CC CPSU censuring resolution.[93]

Crystallization of Tadzhik national identity within the traditional mold plus rejection of Soviet models and, by extension, of many aspects of modernization is best illustrated by the list of complaints heard in the party's discussion of shortcomings in its political education work among the masses, the elite, and youth. Through the 1960s, these have included general exhortation on: need to improve efforts to foster formation of a Marxist-Leninist world outlook among all strata of the population in the republic, including party membership; need to combat survivals of feudal ways of life and family relations, especially as expressed in attitudes toward women and in survivals of religious superstition; and need to combat bourgeois ideology. Need to work with youth came to the forefront in the late 1960s, not only in terms of fostering Marxist-Leninist outlook, but also to combat "hooliganism" and instill a "proper" attitude toward work. It has been revealed that weakening of atheistic propaganda has contributed to religious survivals,[94] that

91 Procyk, 1973: 128–129.
92 Rosen, 1973: 71.

93 Rasulov, 1972: 5.
94 At (February) 1969 CC CPT plenum.

nationalism and religion are connected,[95] that there has been a decline of women in the party membership. Traditional child marriages have continued, as has payment of bride price [kalym].[96] Serious problems in ideological work with young people have also been reported (16th Congress CPT and February 1969 plenum), not only in villages (many are never reached), but also in urban areas and within the Komsomol organization.[97]

The complaints also refer to "national survivals." Keynote is the exhortation to propagate "the Leninist ideas of friendship of the people and proletarian internationalism," which "should be in the center of attention of the Party, Soviet and Komsomol organs," and "strengthening of brotherly ties of the working people of the republic with all Soviet people" (February 1969 plenum CC CPT), frequently repeated phrases.[98]

Despite vociferous repetition of the list of complaints, no improvement has taken place, but rather a backsliding on the road of "survivals." It is significant that no penalties seem to have been meted out to the current Tadzhik party leadership, which has so far shown longevity of tenure as well as little more than lip service toward combating nationalist manifestations.

BASIC VIEWS OF SCHOLARS ON NATIONAL ATTITUDES

Western observers agree that the new generation in Tadzhikistan will effect far-reaching changes in national attitudes. Edward Allworth writes that these basic changes will be largely independent of politicians. The major catalyst will be the emerging elite, intellectuals who

. . . blend the typical young person's involvement in his immediate environ-

ment and disinterest in the recent, toilsome past, with an invulnerability among the educated to stereotypes provided by patriotic slogans about zealous internationalism, official "friendship" between ethnic groups, or insistent claims of older generations about the felicity of regional bilingualism, classless comradeship, and the unshatterable union of nationalities.[99]

According to Allworth, Central Asians (presumably including Tadzhiks) are downgrading the nationality conceptions coming from Moscow.

The new view deemphasizes administrative or political nationality by widening the distance in the USSR between the old (conservative, Russian?) and young (innovative, Central Asian) generations into the primary social and intellectual cleavage affecting the region, given local preeminence to personal identity once again.[100]

Robert Barrett emphasizes the new ties of Central Asians with Third World countries which support their resistance to Russification.

Those Central Asian writers and other intellectuals concerned for their future ethnic identity continue with the limited means available to them to ward off their complete absorption into the diluting stream of a colorless, conformist, multinational culture. They surely recognize that in such a potpourri the prevailing hue must come from the dominant ingredient, the Soviet Russian culture. Their desire to avoid this eventuality is enhanced daily by the developments in the former colonial areas outside the Soviet Union where nationalism is holding sway.[101]

Barrett's contention is that if Central Asians gain cultural hegemony the apparent balance in present nationality arrangements will be disrupted.

Barry Rosen claims that there is a tendency for Tadzhiks to diverge both from other Central Asians and Russians. He attributes this to:

95 Rasulov, 1972: 5.
96 From Resolution 69, Central Committee, Communist party, USSR, CC CP Tadzhikistan (February 1969) plenum, and Kommunist Tadzhikistana (January 15), 1970.
97 From 16th Congress, CPT, and February 1969 plenum.
98 Ibid.

99 Allworth, 1973: 17–18.
100 Ibid.
101 Barrett, 1973: 33–34.

1. the dichotomy created by separate urban Russian and rural Tadzhik societies
2. the Tadzhik political-administrative
   leadership which assumes a token representative role but does not negate
   traditional cultural patterns
3. the cultural policy of "national form
   and socialist content," which has
   helped to produce a Tadzhik identity.[102]

In an article entitled "An Awareness of
Traditional Tadzhik Identity in Central
Asia," Rosen writes:

> In terms of the nationality question
> Tadzhikistan represents a situation
> that is equally noticeable in much of
> Central Asia: the general deficit, so far
> as the indigenous ethnic groups are
> concerned, of rewards, representation,
> and recognition in the Soviet system.
> This situation encourages and insu-
> lates the local cultures, helps to main-
> tain the rural nature of the region's
> population, and to a certain extent
> puts demands on the dominant group,
> the Russians, to narrow the distinc-
> tions between themselves and these
> Central Asians.[103]

Soviet authorities are, as a result, left with
a dilemma: if they grant the responsibility
(i.e., autonomy) necessary to correct the
deficiencies, they will invite not only cultural but "political divergence based upon
distinctly ethnic grounds."
A further question which Rosen poses
relates to the predominantly rural character
of Tadzhikistan. It may be true that the
people, looking upon rural existence as an
ideal way of life, resist (Russian) industrialization of their country.

> At present, the Tadzhiks precisely fit
> the pattern of a society that rejects
> urbanization and thus opens the
> nationality question for reevaluation
> by frustrating the process of amalga-
> mation that draws people together
> from diverse ethnic groups. This pre-
> cludes mixing in the modern sense of
> the word.[104]

---

102 Rosen, 1973: 61–72.
103 *Ibid.*: 72.
104 *Ibid.*: 72.

RECENT MANIFESTATIONS OF NATIONALISM

A review of developments during the last
decade reveals a failure of attempts to integrate Tadzhiks into the Soviet body politic.
It offers evidence of their cultural alienation from Soviet (i.e., Russian) models,
nonassimilation to all-Union systemic
goals, and substitution of local goals
(couched frequently in traditional terms)
whenever possible. At the same time, a new
sense of separate national identity, com-
mencing with revival of classical Persian
heritage, is in process of transformation
into a modern nationalism.

Three factors seem crucial in these developments: formation of a new intellectual elite; persistence of traditional way of
life and attitudes and of Islam among the
rural-based masses; and presence of an
alien (Russian) community, which has
appropriated political power, acted as agent
of forcible change, and become a foil for
the emergent nationalism.

Growth of the new elite has resulted from
establishment of a broadly based educational system; this has made it possible for
Tadzhiks to study in their own language
and to become conscious of their heritage
within the parameters of Soviet nationality
policy. In competition with traditional
socializing agents the Soviet system has
failed. In search of legitimacy vis-à-vis the
Russian presence, the elite has turned to
traditional values providing a necessary
bond with the peasant rural community.
Their unequal political and economic position in their own republic has served to
reinforce that bond, fostering a negative
attitude toward the Russian model of
modernization, creating an urban-rural
dichotomy based on ethnic as well as social
distinctions.

Demographic trends, spread of education, and economic requirements of the
1960s have made preservation of this
dichotomy and existence of a separate (but
unequal) traditional Tadzhik community
increasingly untenable. The Tadzhik intellectual elite, still small in numbers, is
steadily growing; it is being exposed to
contacts not only with other Soviet national

elites but also with national elites of Third World countries. The rapidly growing numbers of rural youth are educated in local language schools, unable to make the transition into urban industrial employment because of the partially self-imposed culture gap. As a result, they are forced to continue in traditional roles, creating huge labor surpluses in the countryside, while European migration continues into urban and industrial areas short of skilled labor.

Combined with unequal distribution of material and cultural benefits between urban (largely Russian) and rural (Tadzhik) areas, with the Tadzhik subordinate status in the power structure, and with their new sense of national identity, the setting carries the seeds of a classically explosive political situation, comparable to that of French-speaking Quebec in the 1930s or preindependence India.

Given Tadzhik unwillingness to close the culture gap and to assimilate into the Soviet model and their increasingly stronger and self-assured pressure for a greater share of autonomy and benefits, the all-Union leadership finds itself in an uneasy dilemma. It can either give in and risk the danger of political demands following cultural and economic ones, or it can accelerate pressure for integration along the lines of the *sblizheniye-sliyaniye* [coming together and eventual fusion] formula, while at the same time attempting to alleviate economic problems.

There are signs of accommodations on the cultural front, largely to facilitate relief of economic pressure. There are also signs, however, of increased insistence on assimilation into the Soviet model, including, by the early 1970s, reinforcement of Russian element within the Tadzhik political hierarchy.

REFERENCES

Allworth, 1967
Edward Allworth, ed., *Central Asia, A Century of Russian Rule* (New York: Columbia University Press, 1967).

Allworth, 1971
Edward Allworth, ed., *Soviet Nationality Problems* (New York: Columbia University Press, 1971).

Allworth, 1973
Edward Allworth, ed., *The Nationality Question in Soviet Central Asia* (New York: Praeger, 1973).

Barrett, 1973
Robert J. Barrett, "Convergence and the Nationality Literature of Central Asia," in Allworth, 1973.

Bartol'd, 1956
V. V. Bartol'd, *A Short History of Turkestan: History of the Semirech'ye, Four Studies on the History of Central Asia,* translated from Russian by V. and P. Minorsky (Leiden: E. J. Brill, 1956).

Bennigsen and Lemercier-Quelquejay, 1967
Alexandre Bennigsen and Chantal Lemercier-Quelquejay, *Islam in the Soviet Union* (New York and London: Praeger and Pall Mall, 1967).

Chumichev, 1968
D. A. Chumichev, ed., *Tadzhikistan* (Moscow, 1968).

Europa Yearbook, 1972
Europa Yearbook (London: Europa Publications, 1972).

Feshbach and Rapawy, 1973
Murray Feshbach and Stephen Rapawy, "Labor Constraints in the Five Year Plan," *Soviet Economic Prospects for the Seventies: A Compendium of Papers Submitted to the Joint Economic Committee, Congress of the United States, June 27, 1973, 93rd Congress, First Session* (Washington, D.C.: Government Printing Office, 1973): 485–563.

Itogi 1970
Itogi vsesoyuznoi perepisi naseleniya 1970 goda (Moscow: Statistika, 1973): IV.

Itogi SSSR 1959
Itogi vsesoyuznoi perepisi naseleniya 1959 goda SSSR (Moscow: Gosstatizdat, 1962).

Itogi TSSR 1959
Itogi vsesoyuznoi perepisi naseleniya 1959 goda. Tadzhikskaya SSR (Moscow: Gosstatizdat, 1962).

Leedy, 1973
Frederick A. Leedy, "Demographic Trends in the USSR," *Soviet Economic Prospects for the Seventies: A Compendium of Papers Submitted to the Joint Economic Committee, Congress of the United States, June 27, 1973, 93rd Congress, First Session* (Washington, D.C.: Government Printing Office, 1973): 428–484.

Mickiewicz, 1973
Ellen Mickiewicz, ed., *Handbook of Soviet Social Science Data* (New York: Free Press, 1973).

Nar. khoz. 1970
Narodnoye khozyaistvo SSR v 1970 godu (Moscow: Statistika, 1971).

Nar. khoz. 1972
Narodnoye khozyaistvo SSR 1922–1972: Yubileinyi statisticheskii yezhegodnik (Moscow: Statistika, 1972).

Nar. khoz. SSSR 1972
Narodnoye khozyaistvo SSSR v 1972 godu (Moscow: Statistika, 1973).

Nar. khoz. TSSR 1969
Narodnoye khozyaistvo Tadzhikskoi SSR v 1969 godu: Statisticheskii yezhegodnik (Dushanbe, 1970).

Nar. khoz. TSSR 1970
Narodnoye khozyaistvo Tadzhikskoi SSR v 1970 goda: Statisticheskii yezhegodnik (Dushanbe, 1971).

Narzikulov and Riazantsev, 1956
I. K. Narzikulov and S. N. Riazantsev, eds., *Tadzhikskaya SSR: Ekonomiko-geograficheskaya kharakteristika* (Moscow, 1956).

Partiinaya zhizn'
Partiinaya zhizn' (Moscow, monthly).

Pechat' 1959
Pechat' SSSR v 1959 godu (Moscow: Kniga, 1960).

Pechat' 1971
Pechat' SSSR v 1971 godu (Moscow: Kniga, 1972).

Procyk, 1973
Anna Procyk, "The Search for a Heritage and the Nationality Question in Central Asia," in Allworth, 1973.

Rakowska-Harmstone, 1970
Teresa Rakowska-Harmstone, *Russia and Nationalism in Central Asia: The Case of Tadzhikistan* (Baltimore: Johns Hopkins University Press, 1970).

Rakowska-Harmstone, 1974
Teresa Rakowska-Harmstone, "The Dialectics of Nationalism in the USSR," *Problems of Communism* (May–June), 1974.

Rasulov, 1972
Dzhabar Rasulov, "Novaia Istoricheskaia Obshchnost' Ludei," *Zhurnalist* (1972): No. 11.

Rosen, 1973
Barry M. Rosen, "An Awareness of Traditional Tadzhik Identity in Central Asia," in Allworth, 1973.

Shorish, 1973
M. Mobin Shorish, "Who Shall Be Educated: Selection and Integration in Soviet Central Asia," in Allworth, 1973.

Sovetskii Soyuz
Sovetskii Soyuz: Tadzhikistan (Moscow: Mysl', 1969).

Televedeniye i radioveshchaniye
Televedeniye i radioveshchaniye, (Moscow, monthly).

Transport i svyaz'
Transport i svyaz' SSSR (Moscow: Statistikar, 1972).

Wheeler, 1964
Geoffrey Wheeler, *The Modern History of Soviet Central Asia* (New York: Praeger, 1964).

Wheeler, 1966
Geoffrey Wheeler, *The Peoples of Soviet Central Asia* (Chester Springs, Pa.: Dufour Editions, 1966).

Part V

OTHER NATIONALITIES

Inclusion in this part of three nationalities does not imply that they are alike. Rather, they are included here because they did not fit in the other groupings. Moldavians, though they have a union republic of their own, do not belong to any "group" in the USSR. Tatars and Jews were selected from among the many nonunion nationalities: Tatars because they are a well-known, rather important ethnic group in the heartland of the European RSFSR; Jews because of the significance and topicality of their case. Tatars have an autonomous republic but also a large dispersed population in the USSR. Officially, Jews have an autonomous province in Birobidzhan, but in reality they are a dispersed people; only a tiny minority live in this "Jewish province."

15 | THE JEWS in THE SOVIET UNION

Zev Katz

General Information

TERRITORY

The Jews of the USSR are a dispersed nationality without a home republic, but they are for the most part concentrated in certain historical areas of settlement.

In 1772 the first Russian imperial decree was issued establishing a Pale in the western and southwestern part of Russia within which Jews were allowed to settle. In 1804 the Caucasus was included in the Pale. A clear delimitation of the Pale was given by another decree in 1835: it consisted of Lithuania and most of Belorussia, the Ukraine, and "New Russia" (the southern RSFSR along the Black Sea). Jews already residing in the Baltic provinces were allowed to remain.[1] These traditional areas of settlement, together with major cities of the Soviet Union, are still main centers of Jewish population. According to the census,[2] Jews amount to about 20% of the popula-

tion in Chernovtsy, 13% in Odessa, and 9% in Kiev, while only 4% in Leningrad and about 4% in Moscow.[3] (See Table 15.2.)

During the 1920s and 1930s, Soviet authorities and the *Yevsektsiya* (see section on history) made attempts to settle the Jews on land in Jewish national districts (Kalinindorf in Kherson province, Novo-Zlatopol'ye and Stalindorf in the Ukraine, in the Crimea). A special government organization (KOMZET) was established for this purpose.[4] Most ambitious attempt was creation of the Jewish Autonomous Province in Birobidzhan, an area of 13,900 square miles close to the Chinese border. This province consists of plains along the Amur River, with extensive swamps and grassy steppes, as well as hilly areas rising toward the Bureya and Little Khingan ranges, covered by oak-conifer and dense taiga forests. As in other areas of the Far East, climate is monsoonic with very cold and dry winters (average 13°F.) and hot, moist summers (average

---

1 Greenberg, 1965: 10–11; Neustadt, 1970: 32. See also sections on history and demography.
2 Wherever no date is given, "census" refers to the 1970 census.

3 Decter, 1971: 18–20; Newth, 1969; Millman, 1971: 13–18.
4 Schwartz, 1951: 151–154.

Table 15.1

Comprehensive Data on Jews in USSR and by Union Republic, 1959–1970

RANKING BY 1959 CENSUS	REPUBLIC	ESTIMATED POPULATION (IN THOUSANDS)[b] 1970	POPULATION BY CENSUS (IN THOUSANDS) 1959	1970	% OF REPUBLIC POPULATION 1959	1970	% OF TOTAL JEWS IN USSR (1970 census)	NET INCREASE/ DECREASE IN % 1959–1970
	USSR total—Jews	3,000	2,268	2,151	1.1	0.9	100.0	− 5.2
	USSR total—population	—	208,827	241,720	100.0	100.0	—	+16.0
1	RSFSR[a]	1,100	875.0	808.0	0.7	0.6	37.6	− 7.6
2	Ukraine	1,000	840.0	777.0	2.0	1.6	36.2	− 7.5
3	Belorussia	250	150.0	148.0	1.9	1.6	6.9	− 1.3
4	Uzbekistan	130	95.0	103.0	1.2	0.9	4.8	+ 8.4
5	Moldavia	130	95.0	98.0	3.3	2.7	4.5	+ 3.2
6	Georgia	110	52.0	55.0	1.3	1.2	2.5	+ 5.8
8	Latvia	40	36.6	36.7	1.7	1.6	1.7	− 0.3
9	Kazakhstan	40	27.1	27.6	0.3	0.2	1.3	+ 1.8
10	Lithuania	35	25.0	24.0	0.9	0.8	1.1	− 4.0
11	Tadzhikistan	18	12.4	14.6	0.6	0.5	0.7	+17.7
12	Kirgizia	10	8.6	7.7	0.4	0.3	0.3	−10.5
13	Estonia	8	5.4	5.3	0.5	0.4	0.25	− 1.8
14	Turkmenia	5	4.1	} 46.1[c]	0.3	} 0.5[c]	} 2.1[c]	} + 0.4
7	Azerbaidzhan	100	40.2		1.1			
15	Armenia	N.A.	1.6		0.1			

[a] Including Dagestan ASSR. In both 1959 and 1970 there were approximately 22,000 Jews in Dagestan, comprising 2.0% (in 1959) and 1.6% (in 1970) of total population of ASSR.

[b] Estimates are from Decter, 1971: 18–21. See text for discussion of differences between estimates and census.

[c] In the 1970 census data are not given separately for the three republics of Turkmenia, Azerbaidzhan, and Armenia.

Table 15.2

Cities with Major Jewish Concentrations, 1959–1970

City	NO. JEWS		JEWS AS % OF TOTAL CITY POPULATION		ESTIMATED NOS.[b]
	1959	1970	1959	1970	1970
Moscow	250,000	251,500	4.1	3.6	500,000
Leningrad	168,641	162,587	5.1	4.1	300,000
Kiev	153,466	152,000	13.8	9.3	225,000
Odessa	over 100,000[a]	116,280	15.0	13.0	—
Kharkov	over 75,000[a]	76,211	8.0	6.2	—
Tashkent	50,445	56,000	5.4	4.0	—
Dnepropetrovsk	over 50,000[a]	68,776[c]	7.6	8.0	—
Kishinev	42,934	49,905	18.2	13.4	65,000
Chernovtsy	over 42,140[a]	37,221	28.2	19.9	50,000
Minsk	38,842	47,057	7.6	5.1	—
Riga	30,267	30,581	5.0	4.2	35,000
Baku	29,204	29,716	3.0	2.3	—
Lvov	over 20,000[a]	27,584[c]	4.9	5.0	—
Tbilisi	17,430	19,579	2.5	2.2	—
Vilnius	16,354	16,400	6.9	4.4	25,000
Samarkand	14,000	16,000	7.1	6.0	—
Alma-Ata	8,425	9,180	1.9	1.3	—
Tallinn	3,714	3,754	1.3	1.0	5,000

Sources: Millman, 1971: 13–18; *Census Data* (for Moscow and republics); Newth, 1969; *Itogi 1970*: IV: 98, 178, 187, 191, 200, 223, 258, 269, 279, 283, 320.

[a] Estimate by Newth, 1969, and Millman, 1971.

[b] Estimates from Decter, 1971: 18–20.

[c] Total urban population in province, almost all in main city.

68°F.). There are about 23 inches of rain per year. The attempt to settle substantial numbers of Jews in the area never succeeded, but it remains nominally an autonomous Jewish province.

During the Soviet period major migratory processes among the Jewish population have been largely in two directions:

1. From the previous Pale of Settlement area toward the East.
2. From the *Shtetl* (small, predominantly Jewish townships) in general to big cities and new industrial towns.

Traditionally, Jews were not allowed to own land or live in rural areas; as a result, they are highly urbanized. In 1887 their urban (town and hamlet) population amounted to 83%. In 1939 this figure was 87%; in 1959, 97%; in 1970, 97.8%.[5] Altogether, about two thirds of a million Jews are now living in four large cities. The exact number depends on definition of Jew used for the statistic; census estimates, relying primarily on self-identification, are lowest, while estimates that include those who are Jewish by passport or descent provide considerably higher figures. (See Table 15.2, e.g., 500,000 Jews in Moscow, 300,000 Jews in Leningrad, etc.)

ECONOMY

Before the revolution, Jews constituted about one third of total urban population of the Pale of Settlement. Most trade and

5 Baron, 1964; *Census Data*, 1959, 1970.

crafts in this area were in Jewish hands. Jewish businessmen, professionals, and merchants made significant contributions to development of a market economy and industrialization of Russia. Jewish enterprise played a key role in the sugar industry (33%) and in railways, building, banking, agricultural export companies, oil industry, and heavy industry. Some Jews became millionaires (e.g., Brodsky the sugar magnate) and successful merchants. Yet in 1897 about 50% were craftsmen, hired hands, and workers in small industries; about 40% were shopkeepers and commercial agents; 5% were professionals; and only 2.5% were farmers.[6]

World War I caused major dislocations in the Pale area. The Civil War brought large-scale pogroms and control of the whole economy by the Soviet government. By 1920 the Jewish role in traditional Russian economy had been largely destroyed. The New Economic Policy (1921–1927) allowed for a limited return to small-scale manufacture and trade, but many Jews were without work.

In the late 1920s and 1930s a major socio-occupational transformation took place among Soviet Jews. In 1926, 25% of the Jews in the Ukraine were artisans and 35% were hired workers. By 1939 fully 71% of Jews in the USSR were workers and employees working for state and public organizations; only 16% were artisans and 6% farmers. About 43% of the workers and employees were manual workers; the rest (30.5% of all Jews) were professionals and white-collar workers.

With beginning of the Five-Year Plans the country needed great numbers of literate and skilled bookkeepers, managers, traders, bureaucrats, propagandists, engineers, educators, and scientists. Jews adapted to these roles more quickly than many other nationalities; soon they became an integral part of the Soviet managerial-technological machine and of the political-cultural apparatus. In the 1930s, though Jews made up only about 2% of the population of the USSR, they accounted for 16% of all doctors and workers in cultural institutions, 14% of all students, and 13% of all scientists. This remains the socio-occupational profile of the majority of Jews in the USSR, apart from the Oriental communities, among whom there are still high percentages of artisans and of skilled and unskilled workers.[7] Since the 1930s Jewish participation in farming and manual labor has gone down while participation in white-collar work and the professions has increased.

Nonetheless, relative weight of Jews in the educated and creative manpower pool is constantly falling because of speedy growth of these strata. There is also well-documented discrimination in recruitment to some fields. In some categories even absolute numbers of Jews are going down, as indicated in Table 15.3.

Soviet Jews are the most educated and professionally advanced of USSR ethnic groups. If an estimate of 2,750,000 Jews by passport (as differentiated from "census Jews") is assumed, it appears that about one in four (including those not able-bodied as well) are in the educated labor pool (see Table 15.3)—a very high ratio by all counts. Jews in the USSR have 166 specialists (with higher or secondary specialized education) working in the economy per 1,000 Jewish population; Georgians are second with 45 per 1,000 and Moldavians are last with 12 per 1,000.[8] The discrepancy between Jews and other nationalities is similar, though less extreme, for scientists and students.[9]

HISTORY[10]

Through the Revolution

Jews first settled in Eastern Europe in the days of the Second Temple, several centuries B.C. Archaeological finds of the first century A.D. speak of organized Jewish communities in Greek city colonies along northern shores of the Black Sea. Like others in these cities, the Jews were craftsmen (potters, jewelers) as well as merchants in grain, fish, and slaves. They enjoyed certain rights of communal autonomy but not those of full citizenship. A stone inscription from Panthekapaion on the Kerch peninsula records a ceremony of manumission in the local syna-

6 Baron, 1964, *passim*; Ettinger, 1971: 4–5.

7 *Ibid.*
8 *Nar. obraz.*, 1971: 240.
9 *Ibid.* 196, 278; *Nar. khoz. 1972*: 105.
10 This section is based on the following sources: Sachar, 1972; Halpern, 1968; Dubnow, 1916–1920; Ettinger, 1970; Schwartz, 1951, 1966.

Table 15.3

Jewish Educated Manpower in USSR

	1963–1964	1967–1968	1970–1971	1972–1973
1. Students in higher education (including evening and external)	82,600	110,000	105,800	88,500
Jews as percentage of total	2.5	2.6	2.3	1.9
2. Students at specialized secondary schools	51,300	46,700	40,000	37,100
Jews as percentage of total	1.7	1.1	0.9	0.8
3. Working specialists with higher education	322,700	327,800	356,800	N.A.
Jews as percentage of total	7.1	6.3	5.2	N.A.
4. Working specialists with specialized secondary education	159,700	169,300	181,800	N.A.
Jews as percentage of total	2.4	2.2	1.8	N.A.
5. Scientific and academic workers	50,915	58,952	64,400	66,739[a]
Jews as percentage of total	8.3	7.7	6.9	6.7
6. Total Jewish specialists and students in USSR (1–4 above, including most of 5)	616,300	653,800	684,400	N.A.
Jews as percentage of total	3.5	3.0	2.0	N.A.

Sources: *Soviet Union—50 Years* (Moscow: Progress Publishers, 1968): 237–238; *Nar. khoz. 1967*: 803, 811. See also J. A. Newth, "Jews in the Soviet Intelligentsia," *Bulletin on Soviet Jewish Affairs*: No. 2 (July 1968): vii, 1–12; *Nar. khoz. 1970:* 651, 648. This table is adopted from Katz, 1970: 333.

[a] 1971 data.

gogue. Jewish colonies along the Black Sea were the first islands of monotheism in Eastern Europe.

In the seventh and eighth centuries A.D. nomadic Turkic tribes called Khazars settled between the Black and Caspian seas. They believed in a supreme God as well as in their magicians. Jews took advantage of their tolerance of other religions to settle in their commercial towns, such as Ethyl and Semander on the Caspian, lying along routes from the East into Byzantium. In the eighth or ninth century the royal house of Khazar and large portions of its nobility and population embraced the Jewish faith. The conversion to Judaism of such a major kingdom was a unique case in Jewish history, remaining something of a legend for many centuries.[11] Jews remained a distinct community in Khazaria until the end of the tenth century when the Khazar kingdom was defeated by Sviatoslav, grand duke of Kiev.

By the eleventh century, Kiev was center of a growing Slavic state and a commercial center on routes leading from Germany to Byzantium. There was a Jewish community in the town living in a quarter of its own; some were associated with the authorities and suffered during a revolt in 1113. The Jewish community in Kiev had a rabbi; a Jewish scholar in Kiev composed a commentary on the Bible in 1124. Rabbi Moses Raba of Kiev (twelfth century) corresponded with Jewish religious scholars in Germany and with heads of the great Yeshiva in Babylon. Also, holy books were sometimes transported from Babylon to Germany through the Kievan principality (Kiev Rus). There were small Jewish communities in other towns in Kiev Rus and in southern Poland, especially along the trade routes between Germany and Kiev. The Jewish community in Kiev disappeared with disintegration of the Kiev principality itself, but the Jewish presence in the Crimea continued through the centuries.

11 According to some sources, the royal house of Khazar came to its decision to accept Judaism only after prolonged disputes in which learned people of Islam and Christianity also presented their case. Israel Halpern points out, however, that there may have been political reasons for this decision by the Khazars, since acceptance of Judaism underscored their independence of neighboring Christian Byzantines to the west and Islamic Arabs to the south. Halpern, 1968: 86; Dubnow, 1916: 52.

Some Jews lived briefly in Moscow as foreign representatives, physicians, and merchants. But the authorities opposed permanent Jewish settlement, particularly after the so-called "Judaizers" sect appeared in the fifteenth century. This nominally Christian sect denied that Jesus was literally "a Son of God" as well as the principle of the Trinity, and opposed the official Russian Orthodox Church. Though some Jews may have exerted an influence on the movement, it was never part of the Jewish faith. It spread among considerable portions of the nobility and the Church, however, convincing Moscow that Jewish settlement within its domain was undesirable. This conviction remained largely unchanged until fall of the monarchy in 1917.

From the fourteenth century, Jews settled in large numbers in Poland, and from there they moved on to Lithuania and present lands of the Ukraine and Belorussia. This development was a result of persecution in Western Europe, accompanied by a high rate of natural increase. Only a few settlers in these lands came from areas previously inhabited by Jews in the south of Russia. The Polish kings and landlords encouraged settlement of foreigners, especially Germans and Jews, since their skills in crafts and commerce aided building of towns. Such urban settlements were a source of tax income as well as of economic and military strength and culture. The authorities granted them protection as well as certain privileges, including the right to practice their religion and autonomy in internal affairs. Jewish communities elected their own communal authorities [kahal]; they also developed a network of regional and interregional self-governing councils, capped by the so-called Council of Four Lands [Vaad Arba Haaratzot]. The council included elected representatives from Great Poland, Little Poland, Ruthenia, and Volynia (territories presently in the Ukraine and Belorussia). Later, representatives from Lithuania were added. At the end of the fifteenth century there had been only several tens of thousands of Jews in the combined territories of Poland and Lithuania; by middle of the seventeenth century they numbered hundreds of thousands.

This "golden age" of Polish Jewry came to an end with the Cossack uprising under Bohdan Khmelnitsky, 1648–1658. Forbidden to own land or engage in certain occupations, many Jews became linked to the economy of the Polish landlords, collecting taxes for them and owning country taverns. Jews were hated as foreigners and non-Christians. The Cossack-Tatar alliance against the Poles was victorious, conquering large areas and many towns with considerable Jewish populations. Cossacks tortured and massacred Jews and handed survivors over to Tatars as slaves. In 1654 Muscovite forces also swept into Polish-Lithuanian territories, killing many Jews, exiling others into the interior, forcibly converting some to Christianity, and selling some into slavery. What was for the Ukrainians a war of national liberation, for Moscow a historic victory, was, like the Spanish Inquisition or the later Nazi holocaust, a great calamity in the history of the Jewish people. Estimates of victims range from one hundred thousand to half a million; 700 Jewish communities were destroyed and many thousands turned into refugees.[12]

The number of Jews in Europe in the mid-eighteenth century has been estimated at 1.5 million. Largest community was in Lithuania-Poland. With three successive partitions of this state toward the end of that century, the majority of these Polish Jews found themselves under Russian rule. Though few Jews had been in their domain, the monarchs of Russia had already established a strong anti-Jewish tradition. Peter the Great, who labored at enticing foreigners to Russia, called Jews "rogues and cheats."[13] His successors expelled them from inner Russia and parts of the Ukraine. Catherine II, who ruled during the partitions of Poland, granted them religious rights and recognized the autonomy of the kahal (convenient for collecting taxes), but continued the restrictions placed on them during the period of Polish decline. In 1791 she created the Pale of Settlement. The legislation included stringent anti-Jewish rules outside the Pale.

During the nineteenth century the situation continued to seesaw. With the accession of new tsars or ministers, Jews often hoped for liberalization, but more often

---

12 Sachar, 1972: 240–241; Halpern, 1968: 212–265.
13 Sachar, 1972: 310.

reaction followed. Such was the case with Alexander I, who at first opened all schools to Jews and encouraged their settlement on land outside the Pale, but later ordered their exile from huge parts of the country-side and forbade them to lease land or keep taverns. Nicholas I's reign (1825–1855) has been described as "a relentless 30-year war against the Jews," whom he regarded as "leeches and parasites . . . an unassimil-able element." [14] Jewish youngsters (from 12 years of age) were liable to be inducted into 25 years of military service, which often meant forcible conversion to Chris-tianity and a "living death" of the individ-ual to his family and people. Compulsory education of Jewish children in government schools was decreed, recognition of au-tonomy of the *kahal* was withdrawn, and the Pale was narrowed, compelling 150,000 Jews to move.

Alexander II began as a liberal ruler. Talented, skilled, and wealthy Jews were allowed to settle outside the Pale, to study at universities, and even to enter govern-ment service. Forced military inductions were discontinued; a flowering of Jewish culture ensued. But toward the end of his reign reaction set in anew. After he was killed (in 1881) by revolutionaries and Alexander III became ruler, a new period of officially organized persecution began, lasting until 1917. Jews were expelled from Moscow (in 1891), civil service was closed to them, and settlement regulations were made more stringent. Possibilities for higher studies and work in the professions were severely limited. Many fell victim to the pogroms, while tsarist security forces stood by without interfering, so as "not to endanger the lives of the soldiers for the sake of a few Jews." [15] Even revolutionary *narodniks* regarded the pogroms as a pos-itive phenomenon; supposedly, they helped awaken the people from apathy.

Pogroms, official anti-Jewish legislation, and expulsions continued during the reign of Nicholas II, the last tsar. In 1903 the especially brutal Kishinev pogrom shook the Jewish world, bringing protests from many countries. The Black Hundred, an officially inspired reactionary organization,

instigated a huge wave of pogroms in autumn 1905 to divert the population from the evolving revolutionary movement.[16] In Odessa alone hundreds were wounded, with tens of thousands of shops and homes ran-sacked. Some Jews were active in the rev-olutionary movement and in self-defense organizations; many were hanged and thou-sands exiled to Siberia. In 1911 Mendel Beilis was put on trial in Kiev for murder-ing "a Christian child to use his blood for Passover matzo." The concocted trial evoked worldwide protests as well as active opposition by prominent Russian intellec-tuals. The jury's verdict was not guilty, and after two years in prison Beilis was re-leased.[17]

By the beginning of the twentieth cen-tury, nearly half of all Jews in the world were within the confines of the Russian Empire. On the eve of World War I their number was estimated at 6 million.[18] Con-fined to the Pale, persecuted, and poor, many Jews looked for a solution through emigration either to Palestine (Zionism) or to the liberal and richer countries in West-ern Europe and America. By 1914 hundreds of thousands had left.[19]

The first years of World War I and of the revolution (1914–1921) brought tragic events and momentous changes for Russian Jewry. At first, hundreds of thousands were exiled, killed, and wounded during the ad-vance and retreat of Russian forces (es-pecially by the Cossacks). Enthusiastically, Jews greeted fall of the monarchy in 1917 and establishment of the new democratic republic which repealed all discriminatory legislation against them. A short flowering of Jewish political and cultural activities ensued. For the first time, Jews held elec-tions to an all-Russian Jewish congress. They could move freely in the country, and people of Jewish origin were among leaders of the main political parties. Lenin's main opponent, prominent leader of the Men-sheviks, Julius Martov, was Jewish. So were

---

14 *Ibid.*: 313–315.
15 Ettinger, 1970: 124–131; Greenberg, 1965: 77–86.

16 Dubnow, 1920: 124–131; Greenberg, 1965: 77–86.
17 Greenberg, 1951: 88–91.
18 The 1897 census showed 5,215,800 Jews in Rus-sia, about 4.9 million in the Pale. For details see Schwartz, 1951: 10–14.
19 Soviet statisticians estimate that 600,000 Jews emigrated between 1897 and 1926. Schwartz, 1951: 14.

several top leaders of the Bolsheviks and of the young Soviet state: Leon Trotsky; Jacob Sverdlov, first "president" of the Russian soviet republic; Grigori Zinoviev, first chairman of the Third International; and many others. While parts of the Jewish population supported the Bolsheviks, many others opposed them and soon became their victims (rabbinical clergy, the rich, Zionists, and those active in non-Bolshevik political organizations). The Ukrainian nationalists, Cossacks, and Whites soon embarked on a policy of persecution and massacre of Jews reminiscent of the times of Khmelnitsky. During the revolution and civil war more than 100,000 Jews were killed; many more had property confiscated or trade forbidden. Jews in the western territories (Poland, Baltic areas, Moldavia) found themselves outside Soviet Russia.[20]

During the 1920s and 1930s Soviet Jewish life was revolutionized. All independent Jewish organizations, parties, publications and educational and religious institutions were liquidated. On the other hand, the Communist party organized Jewish institutions controlled by special Jewish sections of the party (Yevsektsiya). A Jewish culture was developed with Communist content (see section on culture). The Soviets made efforts to settle Jews on the land in several "Jewish national districts" in the south of Russia, and Ukraine, and the Crimea. Though some measure of anti-Jewish feeling was utilized by Stalinists against Trotsky, Zinoviev, and Kamenev (all Jews) there was no official anti-Semitism during the early period of Stalin's rule.[21] Jews occupied high positions: L. Kaganovich was one of Stalin's lieutenants; Maxim Litvinov was foreign minister; L. Mekhlis was a top security aide. In the early 1930s Jewish sections of the party were abolished, and swift decline in Jewish cultural institutions set in. Many died in purges of the 1930s, but not for being Jewish; in fact, the 1930s were a period of rapid assimilation, with many Jews shedding their identity in the belief that all other nationalities would do the same and become one Soviet nation. Losses among Jewish

writers and Yevsektsiya activists caused by the purges were a blow to Jewish culture, facilitating the trend toward assimilation.[22]

Birobidzhan

In March 1928 the Soviet government announced that the province of Birobidzhan in the Far East (see section on territory) would become a Jewish autonomous area, available for settlement. The motivations behind this were complex. Large numbers of Jews could not find work after destruction of the previous economic fabric in the Pale area. The urge to make Jews "productive" citizens was a Russian tradition from tsarist times.[23] Soviet leaders also hoped to utilize the "Zionist" urge to settle an empty swamp-and-forest area on the border with China. They also hoped to attract money, sympathy, and settlers from the Jewish diaspora. Inadvertently, they recognized in this manner the validity of the central tenet of Zionism: need for the Jewish people to settle in a land of their own where they could form a political unit. After thousands moved to Birobidzhan, the area was proclaimed a Jewish Autonomous Province in May 1934, but the grand plans for Jewish colonization of the area never materialized. By the mid–1930s Soviet industrialization was in full swing, providing employment opportunities at home for the skilled newly educated Jews. Collectivization and the purges in Birobidzhan made conditions there decreasingly attractive. Following negative reports from the USSR, support from the West dwindled. Birobidzhan was not the Holy Land and the Amur River was not the Jordan. During World War II further settlement was not allowed.

Ultimately, very few Jews settled in the area. Having been established as a Jewish Autonomous Province, however, the area remains designated as such, permitting the Soviets to assert that Soviet Jews have their own territorial entity within the USSR borders. Appropriately, there is a Jewish joke which more accurately assesses the situation:

20 Sachar, 1972: 381–383.
21 Popular anti-Semitism was especially strong during the 1920s; see Weinryb, 1970: 298–303; Schwartz, 1951.

22 Schwartz, 1951: 90–148; Gittelman, 1972: 2–5.
23 Abramsky, 1970: 62–67; Schwartz, 1951: 160–180.

Question: What is true about the Jewish Autonomous Province?
Answer: Well, it is not Jewish, nor autonomous—but it is a province—that's for sure.[24]

World War II and the Black Years

The Soviet-Nazi pact (August 1939) at the beginning of World War II marked a new stage in the history of Soviet Jewry. Litvinov was removed and other Jewish officials were quietly eliminated from conspicuous positions. About 2 million Jews were among the new Soviet citizens in incorporated areas of Poland, the Baltic states, and Moldavia. While many thousands of refugees from Nazi-occupied Poland were well received by Soviet authorities, others were forcibly driven back over the Nazi border and up to a quarter of a million were exiled by security police to camps in remote areas.[25] After the Nazi attack on the USSR (June 1941) a dual situation again developed. On the one hand, Jews fought bravely in the war, compiling one of the highest ratios of heroes of the Soviet Union among all nationality groups. A Jewish Antifascist Committee was created in Moscow, including the most prominent Soviet-Jewish personalities; it was the first "representative" Jewish body since 1917. Among other Soviet citizens, hundreds of thousands of Jews were evacuated to inner parts of the USSR, saved from extermination by the Nazis. But, on the other hand, during the same period anti-Semitism was revived in Soviet Russia—in the occupied territories, at the front, and in inner parts of the country, flooded by alien, often better educated, wealthier Jews. Nationalist and anti-Soviet local inhabitants, becoming allies of the Nazis, took a willing part in hunting down and killing approximately 2 million Jews in the occupied lands. Survivors, returning after liberation to their former areas, encountered anti-Semitism and official discrimination.[26]

With the beginning of the cold war, and with Stalin's ever deeper immersion in Russianism and hatred of the West, the situation for the Jews continued to be tenuous. According to his daughter Svetlana, the aging Stalin became more and more anti-Semitic. He did attempt to capitalize on Jewish nationalism to get the British out of Palestine, and the USSR supported partition and recognized the newly created State of Israel in May 1948. The appearance in Moscow of Golda Meir as the first Israeli envoy, however, eliciting manifestations of sympathy from Jews at the Moscow synagogue, was followed by a major anti-Jewish purge. The secret police had been preparing for this action; in February 1948 it had arranged the killing (through a traffic accident) of S. Mikhoels, the USSR's most famous Jewish actor, an outstanding former member of the Jewish Antifascist Committee. In the fall, a campaign against "rootless cosmopolitans" began. Thousands were imprisoned and died in the camps. The writers Leib Kvitko, Perets Markish, Itsik Fefer, Der-Nistor, David Bergelson, and others were imprisoned and later (August 1952) shot for supposed treason—serving foreign powers and attempting to make the Crimea Jewish and cut it off from the USSR.[27] In Soviet-controlled Hungary, Rumania, and Czechoslovakia purges and trials (such as the Slansky trial in 1952) with clear anti-Semitic features were organized under Soviet direction. In January 1953 the secret police "discovered" a "plot" by doctors who had allegedly poisoned Soviet leaders: among nine arrested, seven were Jewish. As anti-Jewish hysteria grew, Jews expected exile to Siberia; preparations for such a measure were under way. Then, on March 5, 1953, Stalin died suddenly. A few weeks later the Soviet government announced the "doctors' plot" was a police fabrication and the doctors were released (except for two who died in prison). At

---

24 Schwartz, 1951: 175–190; Schwartz, 1966: 192–197; Goldberg, 1961; Abramsky, 1970: 67–75. For a Soviet presentation on Birobidzhan today, see, e.g., *Soviet Life* (May), 1972: 17, an article written by Lev Shapiro, recently elected Jewish first party secretary there.
25 Redlich, 1971: 81–90. The estimate of 0.25 million Jewish deportees is by Zev Katz. Cf. Schwartz, 1966: 20–42.

---

26 Schwartz, 1966: 43–177. On the role of Jews in the Soviet armed forces during World War II, see Ainsztein, 1970: 269–287.
27 Sachar, 1972: 440. For extensive treatment of the period, see Gilboa, 1971, *passim*.

last, it was thought, the "Black Years" of Soviet Jewry were over.[28]

The death of Stalin, public renunciation of the "doctors' plot," and years of destalinization aroused great hopes among Soviet Jewry. Diplomatic relations with Israel, cut off during the "doctors' plot" (on February 11, 1953), were restored. A small rabbinical school was opened at the Moscow synagogue, a Yiddish literary journal began publication (in 1961), and concerts in Yiddish were allowed. Yet in all other respects official policy remained unchanged. Jews were still kept out of several fields of activity (diplomacy, foreign trade, party and security apparatus, responsible state positions). They were discriminated against in education, work, travel. During the campaign against economic crimes, for which the death penalty was reintroduced, Jews were hunted, accused, and sentenced with special zeal; more than half of those sentenced to death were Jewish. Following the destalinization campaign and loss of faith in the Communist ideology, many in the Soviet Union turned back to their national roots. Others turned to religion and to the democratic dissent movement, in which many Jews became active. Those who cherished their Jewishness came to realize that official policies would not change and that there was no possibility of a full dignified Jewish life for themselves and their children in the USSR.[29] The roots were laid for a rising demand for the right to emigrate.

DEMOGRAPHY

Introduction

There is a considerable divergence of opinion as to total number of Jews in the USSR. To some degree, the figure depends on one's definition of the term *Jew*. The following distinctions can be made:[30]

1. *"Census Jews."* Those declaring themselves Jewish or registered as such during an official census. Since many do not care to declare themselves Jewish in front of census takers and since there is no demand for documentary proof of "nationality," census estimates of Jews provide the lowest numbers.

2. *"Passport Jews."* Those registered as Jewish on the internal passport obligatory for every urban dweller in the USSR; 98% of Jews are urban dwellers. The registration as Jewish is entered in the passport for all offspring of two Jewish parents. Upon reaching the age of 16, the child of a marriage in which only one parent is Jewish may declare himself either Jewish or the nationality of the other parent. Once entered, the designation cannot be altered no matter what may be the individual's later feelings or religion.

3. *Jews by descent.* This category includes all persons with a Jewish parent or even grandparent, even if the person is registered as non-Jewish. It is in this sense that some attackers of Pavel Litvinov denigrated him as a "dirty Jew," since his grandfather was Jewish.[31]

4. *"Emigration Jews."* This category also includes non-Jews with Jewish family ties who, as such, may emigrate with their Jewish family. Among those emigrating to Israel are numerous Russians, Ukrainians, and others not ethnically Jewish but now Israelis for all practical purposes. This is potentially a large category.

Between 1959 and 1970 number of "census Jews" decreased by about 5% whereas total population of the USSR increased 16%. This decrease, however, was not evenly distributed among Jewish communities (see Table 15.1). Whereas in the RSFSR and the Ukraine there were declines of 8% and 7.5%, respectively, in Uzbekistan and Georgia there were increases of 8.4% and 6%. It appears that Oriental Jews added to their number, as did the Jews of Moldavia (+3.2%). Main losses were

---

28 Schwartz, 1966: 198–231; Weinryb, 1970: 307–311; Alliluyeva, 1967, *passim.*

29 Weinryb, 1970: 311–315. For events in recent years, see the section on manifestations of nationalism, and for a recent extensive treatment of anti-Semitism in the Soviet Union, see Korey, 1973, *passim.*

30 These categories are designated by the present author. But see Nove and Newth, 1970: 128–129.

31 K. Van Het Reve, *Dear Comrade: Pavel Litvinov and the Voices of Soviet Citizens' Dissent* (New York: Pitman, 1969).

among Jews in core areas of the Soviet Union. Jews registered minor losses in the Baltic area, part of which may have been a result of emigration to Israel.[32]

The number of "passport Jews" has not been published. Nove and Newth think that the Soviet authorities themselves do not know the exact figure because of lack of an accounting system for this purpose. At various times, however, Soviet sources have cited figures higher than those of the census (e.g., 2.5 million for 1965 and 3 million for the late 1960s, as compared with 2.268 million in the 1959 census).[33] Israeli and recent émigré sources often give number of Jews in the Soviet Union as 3–3.5 million.[34] These figures may refer to Jews by descent. As far as potential for emigration is concerned, number of Jews may be more than 3 million.

Although Soviet Jewry is usually regarded as one community, it consists of several distinct communities so different from each other that they are recognized as the same people only with great difficulty. These make up two broad categories: Ashkenazi and Orientals. Very few Soviet Jews are by origin Sephardic Jews, a group initially from Spain who form a third major category of world-wide Jewry. Most Ashkenazi are originally from the Polish territories to which they immigrated from Germany (see section on history). They spoke Yiddish (based on medieval German) and had a distinct religious and historical heritage. The Oriental communities do not understand Yiddish. They arrived in the Soviet Union from Asian countries and the Mediterranean, bringing distinctive religious and communal traditions. Over the centuries, they have adopted some customs of their neighbors, much as the Ashkenazi Jews have adopted from theirs. Subgroups within these two categories are described below.

A small subgroup of significance are Jews in the Jewish Autonomous Region of Birobidzhan, mostly Ashkenazi settlers from European parts of the USSR. In 1951 their

number was 14,269 or 8.8% of total population for the region. By 1970 their number had decreased to 11,452, 6.6% of the total. This appears to be the smallest percentage for a titular nationality within its own political unit. Also, the Jews of Birobidzhan amount to 0.5% of the total Jewish population of the USSR, an insignificant fraction by any criterion.[35]

Oriental Communities

1. *The Georgians.* Georgian Jews claim to stem from the ten tribes of Israel exiled by Babylon in the eighth century B.C. The Armenian historian Khorenatsi writes that an Armenian king received Jewish slaves from Nebuchadnezzar, and archaeological finds from the first centuries A.D. in Georgia bear evidence of Jewish settlement in the area at that time.[36] In 1804, when the tsar declared the Caucasus within the Pale of Settlement, many Ashkenazi Jews immigrated to the area, influencing the Oriental communities there.[37]

According to the 1959 census there were 51,580 Jews in Georgia; 37,720 declared Georgian as native language. Neustadt argues that number of Georgian Jews in Georgia in 1959 exceeded 85,000. Together with Georgian Jews living in Baku, Dagestan, and other parts of the USSR, their total is approximately 100,000.[38] Though some Georgian Jews were possibly not included in the census, it is difficult to see how more than half were missed. The 1970 census figure for all Jews in Georgia was 55,000; a more detailed breakdown is not yet available. An estimate of Altschuler of 45,000 Georgian Jews in 1959 and some 60,000 to 65,000 in 1970 seems more credible.[39]

Through all Soviet history, the Georgian Jews have kept their traditional way of life. They reside en masse in specific

---

32 See *Census data.* CDSP: XXIII: 16: 14–18; *Itogi 1970*: IV: 9–19.
33 *Atlas narodov mira*, 1964: 158; Rabinovich, 1967: 45.
34 Decter, 1971: 17. See also a letter of March 1967 written by Soviet-Jewish actors (Decter, 1971: 40) and Gittelman, 1972.

35 Abramsky, 1970: 73–74; Eliav, 1969: 179–180; *Itogi 1970*: IV: 76; Katz, 1968: 1–7.
36 Neustadt, 1970: 16–39; Decter, 1971: 21–23.
37 Eliav, 1969: 147–163.
38 Neustadt, 1970: 103–104.
39 M. Altschuler, "Kavim Lidmoto Hademografit Shel' Hakibutz Hayehudi Bevrit Hamoatzot," *Gesher*, (September) 1966: 9–30.

town areas, usually around a synagogue, adhering firmly to the large family in which the young are socialized in religious fashion. Even Soviet official ethnographers have recognized that under such conditions it is difficult to inject official ideology, and that Jews and Georgians live entirely separated lives.[40]

2. *Mountain (Tat) Jews.* Another Jewish community in the Caucasus (Daghestan) are the "mountain" or Tat Jews. They speak an Iranian language with Turkic additions, called Tat, and are variously referred to as descendants of the Khazars (see section on history) or as having arrived many centuries ago from Persian Azerbaidzhan (hence the language). Originally, they lived in mountain villages, but during the last few decades have moved to the cities, mostly along the Caspian Sea (Derbent, Makhachkala, and Baku). Though neighbors of the Georgian Jews for many centuries, they have little contact with them and possess a distinct culture of their own. Total number is estimated at a high of around 100,000,[41] and a low of around 45,000.[42]

3. *Bukharan Jews.* The Oriental Jews of Central Asia are usually referred to as Bukharan. They also speak a dialect of Persian (Tadzhik) and came into the area from Persia, settling along the famous "silk road" extending from the Far East to the Mediterranean. Under impact of contact with the Ashkenazi Jews of Russia, Jewish culture flourished in these areas during certain periods of the Middle Ages and again during the last decades of imperial Russia. Today main concentrations are in the Uzbek republic (Tashkent, Samarkand, Bukhara), but they also live in major towns of other republics (Ashkhabad, Dushanbe). Total number of Jews in Uzbekistan, including non-Bukharan, was 95,000 in 1959 and 103,000 in 1970. Some writers estimate the total of Bukharan Jews as around 100,000. A more realistic estimate for 1970 would stand at 60,000. Available data and estimates of the three major Oriental Jewish communities in the USSR are as shown in Table 15.4.

Ashkenazi Communities

1. *Western Jews.* The group commonly designated as "Western" Jews consists of communities of East European Jewry

---

40 *Ibid.*
41 Neustadt, 1970: 25–28; Eliav, 1969: 166–171; Decter, 1971: 18–21.
42 *Literaturnya entsiklopediya*: VII: 1, 203.

Table 15.4

Oriental Jews in USSR[a]

	1959	1970	ESTIMATES[b]
Georgian	52,000	55,000	60,000–100,000
Mountain (Tat)			45,000–100,000
Dagestan ASSR	21,500	22,149	
Neighboring ASSRs[c]	11,000	12,667	
Bukharan	95,000	103,000	60,000–100,000
Total	179,500	192,816	165,000–300,000

Sources: 1959 and 1970 censuses; Decter, 1971: 18; *Itogi 1970*: IV: 133, 135, 142, 147.

[a] These data include both local and nonlocal Jews.

[b] Eliav, 1969: 147; Neustadt, 1970: 25, 103–104, 145. According to high Western estimates, there are more than a quarter million Oriental Jews in the USSR. A more cautious estimate by this writer would put them at over 200,000. Decter (1971: 18, 20–24) estimates 225,000. And see M. Altschuler et al., *Yehudei Bukhara Vehayehudim Haharaiim* (Jerusalem: The Hebrew University, 1973).

[c] Chechen-Ingush, Kabardino-Balkar, North Osetia.

Table 15.5

"Western" Jews in USSR

	1959	1970	ESTIMATES 1970
Baltic			
Latvia	37,000	37,000	40,000
Lithuania	25,000	24,000	35,000
Estonia	5,400	5,300	8,000
Total	67,400	66,300	83,000
Former Polish Areas			
Western Ukraine	84,400	N.A.	100,000
Western Belorussia	10,000	N.A.	15,000
Total	94,400	N.A.	115,000
Former Rumanian Areas			
Moldavia	95,000	98,000	130,000
Bukovina (Chernovtsy province)	42,000	37,459	50,000
Total	137,000	135,459	180,000
Former Czechoslovak Areas			
Transcarpathia	12,000	10,862	15,000
Total in "new" Soviet areas	310,800	N.A.	393,000

Sources: *Census Data*; Eliav, 1969: 142–147; Decter, 1971: 18–21.

Note: These figures include *all* Jews in these areas, including non-Western Jews who settled there. Estimates are from the sources given above. To arrive at a *net* estimate of "Western" Jews in these territories, one third of the total should probably be subtracted. On the other hand, some of them moved to other areas. The net total of Western Jews is probably in the range of 300,000.

that were not Soviet until World War II. Most Western Jews were religious and Zionist, and many were Bundist and socialist. Their children received a traditional Jewish education in Yiddish and Hebrew. During the interwar period many emigrated to Palestine and the West, so that almost every family has relatives outside the USSR. Since the death of Stalin, such families kept contact with members abroad, and this exerted a powerful influence on their national attitudes. Most members of these communities experienced anti-Semitism before the war, Nazism, the anti-Jewish purge of the late 1940s, Khrushchev's economic purges, and anti-Israeli and anti-Jewish campaigns of the late 1960s. Many see no future for themselves except through emigration to Israel.

Western Jews include former Rumanian citizens (from Moldavia and Bukovina) and Jews in the Baltic countries (Estonia, Latvia, and Lithuania), plus former citizens of Poland, Czechoslovakia (from Transcarpathian Ruthenia), and Hungary who live in Soviet Russia. Total number may be cautiously estimated at 250,000; Decter and Eliav estimate it at 300,000 to 400,000.[43]

2. *Core Soviet Jews.* Core Jews are mainly of Ashkenazi origin, living in areas where the power of the Soviet system was established from the beginning. They have felt the full brunt of official atheist propaganda, Communist indoctrination, intense government education,

[43] Eliav, 1969: 141–147; Decter, 1971: 18–21.

and disruption of former social organizations and community structure.

Nove and Newth[44] subdivide these core Jews "into two streams . . . one an immigrant population (high frequency of mixed marriage), while the other group, remaining at home, were much more conservative." In broader terms, these categories can be identified with the Ukraine and Belorussia, on the one hand (territories largely within the former Pale of Settlement); on the other, the Russian SFSR, including major cities in European Russia as well as new industrial areas in the Urals, Siberia, and the Far East. Table 15.6 shows number of Jews in these categories.

Jews were traditionally active in revolutionary parties in tsarist Russia and became important participants in the Bolshevik party. Official figures put their percentage in 1922 at 5.2% of the party. Since then, the percentage has declined. It was 4.3% in 1927 and apparently remained the same in 1940; Western sources have estimated that Jews made up 2.8% of party membership in 1961 and about 1.6% in 1965.[45] Despite this decrease, they may still have the highest party membership relative to

population of any Soviet nationality, since even 1.6% is almost double their percentage in the total population.[46] In 1967 Jews constituted 0.8% of party membership in Turkmenia whereas in 1959 they were only 0.3% of total republic population.[47]

Jews were very prominent among the party leadership during the first years of Soviet power and all through Stalin's reign despite his late overt anti-Semitism. By now, however, there is not one Jewish member in the Politburo or party secretariat, or in other high government positions. Highest-ranking Jewish person is the deputy prime minister for supplies, V. Dymshits. Another is Alexsandr Chakovsky, editor of the *Literary Gazette*, leader of the conservative stream in the Writers Union, recently made a member of the party Central Committee. In 1972, for the first time in many years, a Jew, Lev Shapiro, was made first secretary of the party in the Jewish Autonomous Province of Birobidzhan.[48]

Age Structure

In the RSFSR only 15% of the Jewish population is in the 0–19 age bracket, whereas the Russians have 35% in this age

---

44 Nove and Newth, 1970: 144–145. See also Eliav, 1969: 140–143; on Jews in the Ukraine, see Newth, 1969: 16–19.
45 Rigby, 1968: 383–388.

46 Katz, 1970: 332–334; Newth and Katz, 1969: 37–38.
47 Artykov et al., 1967.
48 *Soviet Life* (May), 1972: 17.

Table 15.6

"Core" Soviet Jews

	1959	CENSUS 1970	ESTIMATES 1970
Old "Core" Communities			
Ukraine[a]	840,000	777,000	1,000,000
Belorussia[a]	150,000	148,000	250,000
Total	990,000	925,000	1,250,000
New Immigrant Communities			
Russian RSFSR[a]	878,000	808,000	1,100,000
Total	1,868,000	1,733,000	2,350,000

Sources: *Census Data*, 1971: 20; estimates by Decter, 1971: 18–20.
a These figures include a small number of Western and Oriental Jews who settled in these republics.

group; 43% of the Jewish population is over 50 years of age, whereas the comparable figure for Russians is 21.5%[49] The gap would be much wider were only Ashkenazi Jews considered, since the fertility rate is much higher among Soviet Oriental populations. Low weight in the 0–19 age group is a result of low fertility of non-Oriental Jews and high incidence of both intermarriage and assimilation. Altshuler found that in mixed marriages involving a Jewish spouse only 12% to 18% of offspring registered as Jewish.[50]

Data on language as related to age are given for the RSFSR only. Understandably, they show that among the older age groups a much higher percentage declare a Jewish language as native language. Among the middle-aged Jewish population, the percentage is much lower than average. For younger age groups (0 to 11 and 11 to 15 years), percentages are high (14.5% and 17.5%, respectively).[51] This may indicate the greater weight of Oriental children in the Jewish population.

Data on marriage indicate that Jewish men have a slightly higher ratio than that for Russians or Ukrainians. Jews (both men and women) generally marry later, however, which may contribute to their lower fertility.[52]

CULTURE

By the end of the eighteenth century Russian Jewry, encompassing Jews of Poland and Lithuania, had become a focus of world Jewish religion and culture. Just before the Polish areas became Russian, Rabbi Israel of Moldavia (the Baal Shem Tov) established the Hassidic movement, a tradition of serving God not only through scholarly study but through rejoicing in the Lord by song, prayer, and simple living. The Gaon of Vilna (Elijah) established a renowned Talmudic Academy, prototype for similar great religious schools proliferating in many towns of the Pale.[53]

In the nineteenth and early twentieth centuries, Russian Jewry was the source of many cultural and national trends which were to make up the content of modern Jewish life. This was especially so in the second half of the nineteenth century, during which there was a flowering of Yiddish and modern Hebrew literature (e.g., Mendele Mocher Sforim, Y. L. Perets, Sholem Aleichem, S. Chernichovsky).

Toward the end of the nineteenth century, a proto-Zionist movement in Russia, *Hovevei Tsion* [Lovers of Zion] emerged. In 1882, 13 years before Herzl's *Judenstaat*, Dr. Leon Pinsker published his Zionist tract *Autoemancipation*. In the early 1880s the first groups of young Russian Jews went as pioneers [*Bilu*] to settle in Palestine. Early in the twentieth century the *Bund*, part of the general social democratic movement in Russia, combined the philosophy of socialism with the demand for Jewish autonomy and Yiddish cultural development. Within Zionism several distinctive trends appeared, almost all led by Russian Jews: V. Jabotisnsky, founder of the nationalist Revisionist party: Ahad Ha'am, theoretician of "spiritual Zionism"; B. Borochov and N. Syrkin, ideologues of socialist Zionism; and rabbis L. Mohilover and H. Kalisher, founders of religious Zionism.

Religion was the mainstay of Jewish life in Russia. Before 1917 there were religious institutions in every little *shtetl*: synagogues and prayer houses, religious schools, Talmudic academies, rabbinical courts, and so on. Soon after the Bolshevik revolution and following the decree of January 23, 1918, Soviet authorities began a campaign aimed at closing synagogues and suppressing Jewish religious life. This gained momentum in 1921 when Yevsektsiya representatives closed many religious institutions by turning them into emergency homes of refuge for the starving population during the famine. A second major antireligious wave instigated by the authorities began in 1927–1928 and went on through most of the 1930s. The Nazi occupation liquidated whatever remained of Jewish prayer houses in all of the western USSR. After liberation by the Soviet army, restoration of synagogues was permitted only in very exceptional cases.[54]

---

49 *Itogi 1970*: 373. These data relate to the Russian republic only; there are no data for other republics.
50 Altshuler, 1970: 30–33.
51 *Itogi 1970*: 373.
52 *Itogi 1970*: 386. The data are only for several republics, including the Ukraine and Moldavia.
53 Sachar, 1972: 264–267.

54 Rothenberg, 1971: 39–66, and personal talks with Soviet émigrés by Z. Katz.

After the death of Stalin there was some relaxation of policy. In 1957 a small *yeshivah* was opened at the Moscow synagogue with 35 students, mostly from Georgia. A prayer book was printed in a limited edition. Several years later the *yeshivah* was crippled through denial of residence permits to students; only a few people employed in the Moscow synagogue were registered pro forma as "students." In the 1960s a new wave of synagogue closings was organized. There are numerous and conflicting figures for the present number of Jewish houses of worship in the USSR, varying mainly in whether they include only formally established synagogues (which are in separate houses and must have a responsible group of believers recognized by authorities) or also *minyan* type prayer groups (which meet in the dwelling of one of the believers and are often ad hoc informal groups active mainly during the holiday season). In 1959 Soviet reports to the UN gave number of existing synagogues as 450. By the early 1970s the number was reported at less than 100. (The lowest, most frequent figure given by Jewish organizations outside the USSR is 62.) The majority of these synagogues are in Oriental and "Western" Jewish communities (see section on geography); some may have been closed recently because of mass emigration to Israel.[55]

Despite all, the synagogue remains the only officially recognized Jewish institution in the USSR today; as such, it has acquired a new role. During Jewish religious holidays in the late 1960s and early 1970s many thousands of nonreligious Jewish people, especially youth, gathered around the synagogues to sing, dance, talk, and generally demonstrate their Jewish identity. In 1972–1973 police tried to prevent such demonstrations and bar access to synagogues. In several places a number of young people were arrested. The synagogues continue to be meeting places for Jewish and non-Jewish visitors from abroad with Soviet Jews. The rabbi of the Moscow synagogue is often presented as spokesman on matters of Soviet Jewish affairs. From talks with émigrés it appears that "return to the synagogue" is a manifestation of Jewish national revival (Zionism) and a return to Jewish tradition rather than to Jewish religion.

EXTERNAL RELATIONS

The Jews of Russia, like Jewish communities elsewhere, have historically maintained close relations with co-religionists abroad. They have been strongly influenced by Jewish spiritual trends in Central Europe (*Haskalah*, political Zionism, religious reform). Until 1917 Russian Jews were part of international Jewish organizations, traveling abroad often for business, study, or pleasure. Many migrated to Western countries, creating bonds of family, friendship, community, and politics across the borders of Russia. Also, world Jewry and world public opinion took to heart the grave plight of Russian Jewry, especially during the pogroms—and to a degree were able to influence tsarist policy.

These relations ended after 1917, though fragmentary connections persisted until the late 1920s. A small number of Jews were still allowed to emigrate. An American Jewish charity organization, the Joint Distribution Committee, was allowed to provide aid during the famine of the early 1920s and to help finance Jewish settlement of the land in the late 1920s.[56] Even in the 1930s, Soviet authorities worked actively to get foreign (especially American) Jewish support for the Birobidzhan venture. During the war the Jewish Antifascist Committee was created to mobilize Jewish support in the West for the war in general and the USSR in particular. Representatives of the committee traveled to the United States and Britain to address Jewish gatherings. When the cold war came, they were first to pay, becoming victims of the "purge of the cosmopolitans" (see section on history).

The first and second waves of pioneer immigrants to Palestine between 1880 and 1914 were predominantly Jews from Russia. They established the first Jewish agricultural colonies, created the first *kibbutz* settlements, and founded the Histadrut

---

55 Rothenberg, 1971: 39–66, and personal talks with Soviet émigrés by Z. Katz. See also A. Yodfat, "Jewish Religious Communities in the USSR," *Soviet-Jewish Affairs*, 1971: II: 61–67.

---

56 See Abramsky, 1970: 66–67.

(Jewish Federation of Labor) and the main political parties which remain dominant forces of Israeli politics today. Though the Zionist movement was suppressed along with all other non-Bolshevik groups, some radically left Zionist groups were quasi-legally active until late in the 1920s.[57] But after 1939 Soviet Jewry again experienced the influence of non-Soviet Jews from Poland and the newly annexed territories. Many were religious, Zionist, and highly knowledgeable about Jewish history and culture. There was a high incidence of intermarriage between Russian and refugee Jews during the war; afterwards, a number of Russians along with foreign spouses were able to return to Poland, and from there emigrate to Israel and the West.

Presence of Israeli diplomatic representatives in the Soviet Union after the USSR's recognition of Israel in 1948 added a new dimension to the world of Soviet Jewry. Meetings with these diplomats, who toured the country as extensively as possible, had a profound impact on both sides, as witnessed by the later struggle of Oriental Jewish communities for emigration to Israel. From such contacts came the first extensive reports on conditions of Jews in the USSR.[58] In the mid–1950s tourism from the West and later from Israel was again allowed; since the 1960s many thousands of Soviet Jews have been allowed to emigrate to Israel. Several thousand have arrived in Europe and the United States. Jews in the West have become active in campaigning for the rights of Soviet Jews. These developments have created a strong bond between Soviet Jews, Israel, and the West.[59]

Media

LANGUAGE DATA

In the census of 1897, 96.9% of all Jews in Russia (including Polish Jews) regarded Yiddish as mother tongue (in some areas of the Pale it was up to 99.3%). In 1926 the percentage was 70.4%, with 90.7% in Belorussia and 23.5% in the Caucasian republics (where the mother tongue of Oriental Jews was not Yiddish).[60]

By 1959 only 17.9% gave Yiddish as mother tongue (75% in Lithuania, 50% in Moldavia, 32% in Kiev province, and 26% in Mogilev and Gomel). Together with Oriental Jews who gave their own Jewish language as mother tongues, almost half a million Jews (21.5% of all Soviet Jews) regarded Yiddish or another Jewish language as their own language.[61]

According to the 1959 census, distribution of Jewish languages as mother tongue was as follows:[62]

Georgian-Jewish	35,673
Tadzhik-Jewish	20,763
Tat-Jewish	25,225
Crimean Tatar–Jewish	189
Total Oriental Jewish	81,850
Yiddish	405,936
Soviet total	487,786

In 1970, 17.7% of Jews declared Yiddish or another Jewish language as mother tongue, a decrease of 3.8% since 1959. Russian was the mother tongue for 78.2%, an increase of 2.7% since 1959; 16.3% were also fluent in Russian as second language. Thus, fully 94.5% of Soviet Jews knew Russian well.[63] In addition to 381,000 who gave Jewish languages as native tongue, 166,500 knew a Jewish language as second language, for a total of 547,500. In addition, 28.8% of the Jewish population knew languages of other Soviet nationalities, one of the highest percentages for any ethnic group.[64]

57 Goldman, 1960, *passim.*
58 Eliav, 1969.
59 See section on manifestations of nationalism.
60 Schwartz, 1951: 18–21.
61 Ettinger, 1970: 38–40.
62 *Itogi 1959*: 184, 188. The 1970 census does not include these data.

63 *Itogi 1959*: 184, 188; *Nar. khoz. 1972*: 32.
64 *Itogi 1959*: 184, 188; *Nar. khoz. 1972*: 32; *Itogi 1970*: IV: 20.

Table 15.7

Jewish Population in USSR: Identification with Jewish Languages by Republic, 1959–1970

RANKING BY JEWISH NATIVE LANGUAGE 1970	REPUBLIC	JEWISH LANGUAGE		
		As Native Language		As Native or Second Language[a]
		1959 %	1970 %	1970 %
14	RSFSR	13.4	11.8	21.3
13	Ukraine	16.9	13.1	20.2
12	Belorussia	N.A.	17.8	28.3
4	Moldavia	50.0	44.7	52.1
2	Lithuania	69.0	61.9	63.0
3	Latvia	47.9	46.2	49.4
10	Estonia	24.8	21.5	24.8
6	Uzbekistan	49.6	37.5	42.3
1	Georgia	72.3	80.9	—
9	Kazakhstan	22.7	22.8	27.6
8	Kirgizia	30.3	26.7	33.5
11	Tadzhikistan	23.2	19.9	21.9
7	Turkmenia	N.A.	30.2	36.7
5	Azerbaidzhan	35.2	41.3	46.6
—	Armenia	N.A.	N.A.	N.A.

Sources: *Itogi 1970*: 96, 102–103, 202, 223, 253, 263, 273, 280, 284, 295, 306, 317; *Kommunist Tadjikistana* (May 6), 1971; *Zarya vostoka* (May 8), 1971; *Turkmenskaya iskra* (May 22), 1971; *Bakinskii rabochii* (May 21, 22), 1971.

[a] No such question was asked during the 1959 census.

Like Jews in other countries, Jews in the Soviet Union possess considerable linguistic ability. Many know English and German; Lithuanian Jews often know some Polish; Moldavians understand Rumanian; Bukharan and mountain Jews understand some Persian, and many in all communities can follow Hebrew as well.[65]

Under Soviet conditions it is reasonable to accept data on native languages as indicator of national consciousness. Census data on Jews reveals a highly differentiated situation. Highest rate of knowledge of native language is predictably registered among Jews outside the core area: Lithuania (62%), Latvia (46%); and among Orientals: Azerbaidzhan (41%), Uzbekis-

tan (37.5%), and Turkmenia (30%). If autonomous republics are also included, Dagestan is highest of all with 87%, followed by the Kabardino-Balkar republic with 79%. Lowest is the RSFSR (Russian Federation) with less than 12%, followed by the Ukraine with slightly more than 13%, mainly because several areas are included in which knowledge of Yiddish (and national consciousness) is high—Bukovina, Transcarpathia, western Ukraine. Ratio between Lithuania and the RSFSR for Jews speaking native languages is 5.3: 1. Figures for those declaring a Jewish language as second language are especially high in areas where Jewish as mother tongue is low.

Greatest ratio of acculturation can be seen in large Slav cities, especially those outside the traditional Pale areas: Kharkov (4.8%), Leningrad (5.2%), Novosibirsk

---

65 English is popular among the educated of the younger generation, and German among those who know some Yiddish.

(7.0%), and Moscow (7.6%). Even in the traditional centers of Jewish culture in Slav areas percentages are low: Odessa (9.0%), Minsk (11.2%), and so on. At the other end are cities in peripheral areas such as Chernovtsy, Riga, and Kishinev, where almost half of the Jews declared Yiddish as native tongue. Cities with large numbers of Oriental Jews also show a high ratio for a Jewish native tongue: Tbilisi (40.5%), Tashkent (32.5%), and Baku (26.9%).[66]

LOCAL MEDIA

In the second half of the nineteenth century a Jewish book publishing and periodical press appeared. On the eve of World War I, 13 Yiddish and 2 Hebrew dailies were published in Russia, with total circulation of several hundred thousand. Though suppressed during the war, the Jewish press flourished after the February revolution; in 1917–1918, 170 periodicals were issued. Shortly thereafter, Communist publications multiplied and non-Communist ones were closed down. By 1935 there were Jewish dailies in Moscow, Kharkov, Minsk, and Birobidzhan. Ten Jewish periodicals appeared in the Ukraine alone, including one for children and one for artisans, as well as nondaily papers in Kiev, Berdichev, Odessa, Kremenchug, and in the Jewish national districts. In the late 1930s, however, a decline set in. By 1939 even the great Moscow newspaper Emes [Truth] was closed and in the whole of the RSFSR only the Birobidzhan paper remained. In the same year only seven periodicals were left in the whole country, with a circulation of 38,700 for a population of 3 million. During World War II a Yiddish newspaper (Ainikeit) was again published in Moscow, and a limited revival of Jewish cultural activity set in; it was extinguished in 1948.[67]

In all of the USSR today there were only two publications in Yiddish. One is the monthly Sovetish Heimland [Soviet Father-land], published in Moscow since 1961 (at first as a bimonthly) with a stated circulation of 25,000, a considerable number sold abroad. It is edited by Aron Vergelis (formerly a minor poet in Birobidzhan) who has assumed the role as spokesman for Soviet Jewry. Although it deals mostly with Soviet themes, sometimes it has items of Jewish interest, including a sheet for self-study of Yiddish, news on Jewish concerts, meeting of Yiddish writers organized by the monthly, and Jewish cultural news from abroad.[68]

Other publication is the thrice-weekly Birobidzhaner Shtern [Birobidzhan Star], mostly a two-page translation into Yiddish of the province newspaper in Russian. Soviet official statistics for 1970 give the circulation of Birobidzhaner Shtern as 12,000, making for 4.28 copies per 100 in the Yiddish language group. Since total number of Jews in Birobidzhan was about 14,000 in 1959, it seems that a large part of the printing is sent outside of the region.

During certain periods it was possible to subscribe to the Folksshtime [People's Voice], published in Poland, which often contained rather different information than that in the Soviet press. After the paper published articles with implied criticism of Soviet policy regarding Jewish culture, its entry into the USSR terminated. It has been possible to read Hebrew publications of the Israeli Communist party in some Soviet public libraries.

The fate of Jewish book publishing has been similar. There was a period of marked expansion of Yiddish publishing and of Soviet Jewish literature in the 1920s and early 1930s, followed by a decline and finally total annihilation in the late 1940s. At the peak of this activity, in 1932, 653 titles of Yiddish books were printed, with a circulation of more than 2.5 million.[69] Since 1959 about two dozen books in Yiddish have been published in the USSR; in 1970 four such books were issued, amounting to 3.56 copies per 100 in the language group, a ratio of 1:135 compared with the Lithuanians. The year 1970 was a very good

---

66 Itogi 1970: 20, 98, 103, 107, 133–147, 170–191, 253–283, 317–320.
67 Brumberg, 1968; Abramsky, 1970; Friedberg, 1970: 94.

68 See, e.g., Sovetish Heimland, 1972: 1, 2; Pechat' 1970: 10, 68 gives circulation of this journal as 12,000 only. See Table 15.8.
69 Schwarz, 1951: 139–141.

Table 15.8

Native and Second Languages Spoken by Jews

NO. JEWS RESIDING		SPEAKING AS NATIVE LANGUAGE						SPEAKING AS SECOND LANGUAGE[a]	
		Jewish Languages[b]		% Point Change	Russian		% Point Change	Russian	Other Languages of Peoples of USSR[c]
1959	1970	1959	1970	1959–1970	1959	1970	1959–1970	1970	1970
in Birobidzhan Autonomous Province									
14,269 (100%)	11,452 (100%)	N.A.	1,970 (17.2%)	N.A.	N.A.	9,479 (82.8%)	N.A.	1,804 (15.7%)	1,783 (15.6%)
in all Soviet republics									
2,268,000 (100%)	2,151,000 (100%)	488,000 (21.5%)	381,000 (17.7%)	−3.8	1,733,000 (76.5%)	1,682,000 (78.2%)	+2.7%	351,000 (16.3%)	619,000 (28.8%)

Sources: *Itogi 1959*: 184, 188; *Census Data, 1970*: 16; *Nar. khoz. 1972*: 32; *Itogi 1970*: 76.

[a] No data are available for 1959, since no questions regarding command of a second language were asked in the 1959 census.

[b] Including Yiddish, Georgian, Tadzhik, Tat, and Crimean Tatar Jewish.

[c] Including Jewish, if not the native language.

Table 15.9

Jewish Publications

Language of Publication	Year	NEWSPAPERS[a]			MAGAZINES			BOOKS & BROCHURES		
		No.	Per Issue Circulation (1,000)	Copies/100 in Language Group	No.	Per Issue Circulation (1,000)	Copies/100 in Language Group	No. Titles	Total Volume (1,000)	Books & Brochures/100 in Language Group
Russian	1959	N.A.	N.A.	N.A.	N.A.	N.A.	N.A.	N.A.	N.A.	N.A.
	1971	N.A.	N.A.	N.A.	N.A.	N.A.	N.A.	N.A.	N.A.	N.A.
Jewish	1959									
	1970	1[b]	12[c]	4.28[d]	1	12	4.28	4	10	3.56
	1971									
Minority languages	1959	N.A.	N.A.	N.A.	N.A.	N.A.	N.A.	N.A.	N.A.	N.A.
	1971	N.A.	N.A.	N.A.	N.A.	N.A.	N.A.	N.A.	N.A.	N.A.
Foreign languages	1959	N.A.	N.A.	N.A.	N.A.	N.A.	N.A.	N.A.	N.A.	N.A.
	1971	N.A.	N.A.	N.A.	N.A.	N.A.	N.A.	N.A.	N.A.	N.A.
All languages	1959	N.A.	N.A.	N.A.	N.A.	N.A.	N.A.	N.A.	N.A.	N.A.
	1971	N.A.	N.A.	N.A.	N.A.	N.A.	N.A.	N.A.	N.A.	N.A.

Source: *Pechat' 1970*: 10, 68.
Note: Figures given here are the only ones available for Jewish publications.
[a] 1970 figures do not include *kolkhoz* newspapers.
[b] Three times per week.
[c] Total population of Jews in Birobidzhan is about 11,500.
[d] Based on an estimated 280,000 who declared Yiddish as their mother tongue.

year; there were years in which only one or no Yiddish books appeared.[70]

Apart from a brief news bulletin in Yiddish on Birobidzhan Radio, there are no radio or television programs in Yiddish or in Russian on Jewish themes anywhere in the USSR. Due to their great interest in current events and in the world outside, Soviet Jews are avid listeners to foreign radio (Voice of Israel programs as well as Western stations). Oriental Jews who understand Farsi listen to broadcasts in Persian by various stations.[71]

EDUCATIONAL INSTITUTIONS

The tsarist regime did not generally allow secular schools to teach in the language of the nationalities. Nevertheless, the Jews of Russia had a widely ramified network of their own religious schools. Jewish schools in the Russian language were also permitted. The Ministry of Education reported that 773 Jewish secular schools and 7,743 hadorim [primary religious schools] were active in 1912, as well as 147 Talmud Torah [religious high schools]. Altogether, some 400,000 Jewish children were enrolled in these schools.[72]

Secular schools taught mostly in Russian and religious schools in Yiddish, with some Hebrew. During the last years of the Russian Empire, Yiddish and Hebrew were quietly introduced into secular schools.[73] During World War I and the civil war the movement for Jewish schools was vastly strengthened, with certain contending political forces proclaiming support.[74]

During the early years of Bolshevism, Lenin and Stalin fought against "Jewish cultural autonomy" as opposed to Marxism. But, soon after the Bolshevik revolution, the Soviet government began an energetic campaign encouraging Jewish-Yiddish schools to teach in the Bolshevik spirit. The first Soviet decree on Jewish schools was published in August 1918. The 1920s were a period of expansion of Soviet-Jewish culture. By 1931 there were 1,100 Jewish schools with 130,000 pupils, from four-year primary schools to teachers' colleges and technical high schools. There was also a Jewish Department at the Communist University of the Toilers of the West in Moscow.[75]

The Jewish schools were organized and run under the supervision of Yevsektsia (see section on history), suddenly abolished in March 1930. Many of its leaders and activists fell victim to subsequent purges of the 1930s, and during this decade Jewish schools declined swiftly until few remained. World War II spelled an end to these schools. Several attempts to reestablish them after the war were nipped in the bud by Soviet authorities. Under Stalin's rule the party no longer needed special Jewish sections or schools.[76]

No Jewish schools have been allowed in the USSR since, and not a single Jewish education institution is in existence today. For other dispersed nationalities, some without even an autonomous province of their own, there are government arrangements for teaching in their languages (e.g., Germans, Poles, and Crimean Tatars). There are also schools for minority groups outside their republic in Central Asia. Not so for the Jews.

Recently, Jewish people awaiting departure for Israel have created unofficial Hebrew seminars and small private schools on Jewish topics. These are known to exist in Moscow as well as elsewhere in the USSR. Jewish education is transmitted mostly within the family, from generation to generation, especially among Oriental Jews.[77] Jews, however, are prominent as teachers, university professors, and students in USSR educational institutions, especially in cities with large Jewish communities.[78]

It is generally known that Soviet Jews, like Jews in other countries, have taken advantage of educational opportunities available in a modern society. The 1970 census data corroborate that, despite official and

---

70 Pechat' 1970: 10, 68.
71 Chronicle (London): No. 1; also conversations with émigrés by Zev Katz. Moscow's Radio Peace and Progress" broadcasts in Hebrew to Israel.
72 Vestnik Ope (February), 1914; Schulman, 1971: 2–15.
73 Schulman, 1971: 18–25.
74 Ibid.: 35–45.

75 Kantor, 1934: 172ff.; Schulman, 1971: 56–95.
76 Schulman, 1971: 146–165.
77 Personal information from talks with émigrés held by Z. Katz. See also Jews in Eastern Europe (November), 1971: 107–135.
78 See section on the economy.

unofficial discrimination, they have achieved a high standard of education, remaining the most educated ethnic group in the Soviet Union.

Of every 1,000 Jews in the RSFSR, 10 years old and above, 344 have a higher education, compared with 43 for Russians, a ratio of 8:1. Corresponding ratios for other republics are 8.5:1 in Moldavia; 7:1 in Belorussia; 6.5:1 in the Ukraine; and 5.5:1 in Latvia. In relation to less educated (non-Christian) nationalities, ratios are even greater: Jews to Tatars, 15.5:1; to Chechens, 49:1; and to Nentsy (a formerly pagan northern people), 115:1. All these figures are for Jews within a given republic and for the dominant nationality within the same republic; there are no data for all Jews which can be compared with all members of an entire nationality in the USSR.[79]

A similar pattern is evident in data on educated manpower in the USSR: 81% of employed Jews in Moldavia have a higher or secondary education (including incomplete secondary) whereas the figure for Moldavians is 43.5%; in the Ukraine the figures are 91.5% and 63.7%, respectively. The census documents the socio-occupational structure of Jews in the Soviet Union: in the RSFSR more than two thirds of Jews (68.2%) are specialists with higher or secondary special education; in the Ukraine, Latvia, and Belorussia, about half; in Moldavia, about 40%. The respective ratios for local nationalities move from 7% for Moldavians to 19% for Russians and 20% for Latvians. Percentage of Jewish specialists among their working population is 7 times higher than that of Moldavians and about 3.5 times higher than that of Russians.[80]

The above data may serve to explain the situation of Soviet Jewry today. As an urban population with a tradition for learning, Jews have been "too successful" in the area of education. The official and unofficial efforts to stem their advance in education succeed in making it more difficult, but cannot radically change the situation. Ultimately, such efforts simply make Jewish citizens more conscious of their problem. Relative exclusion from the sensitive polit-ical and security areas is additionally frustrating to this highly educated, active population.[81] Some react by hiding their Jewishness (assimilation); others look for a solution outside the USSR.

CULTURAL AND SCIENTIFIC INSTITUTIONS

In the 1920s and 1930s the Ukrainian Academy of Sciences included an Institute of Jewish Proletarian Culture and the Belorussian Academy included a Jewish Sector. These were described as "a laboratory of scientific thought in the field of Jewish culture." In particular, these two institutions concentrated on history of the revolutionary movement within the Jewish population and on its socioeconomic status.[82]

In 1919 a Jewish state theater was established in Moscow. The Soviet state took special interest in it, and Jewish theatrical art flourished with such institutions as Jewish Theatrical College in Minsk, Jewish departments at Kiev Institute for Drama and Minsk Jewish State Theater. By 1934 there were 18 permanent Jewish theaters in the USSR; but by the end of the 1930s their number had diminished considerably, further decreasing as a result of World War II. In 1948, after the murder of Mikhoels by the secret police, Jewish State Theater in Moscow was closed. Since then, there has been no permanent Jewish theatrical establishment in the USSR.[83]

Several temporary groups of professional actors and concert artists have made appearances in Yiddish, well attended by Jews. Amateur theater groups exist in Vilnius, Birobidzhan, and Riga. In March 1967 seven prominent Soviet-Jewish actors addressed a letter to the CPSU leadership asking permission to establish a state Jewish theater in Kiev. Permission was not granted. In the meantime, a number of prominent Jewish artists (e.g., Nehama Lifshits, M. Goldblatt) left for Israel.[84]

---

79 *Itogi 1970*: IV: 405, 449, 475–476, 480, 483, 513, 516, 518.
80 *Ibid.*: 577, 579, 588, 590, 614, 618, 632–633.

81 Personal information from talks with émigrés by Zev Katz.
82 Schwartz, 1951: 138–139.
83 *Ibid.*: 140–142.
84 Decter, 1971: 39–40; *Soviet Life* (May), 1972: 17.

Though without scientific or cultural institutions of their own, Jews have made significant contributions to development of Soviet science and culture. The famous Soviet MiG planes were built by Mikoyan (an Armenian) and Gurevich (a Jew). Abram Yoffe was father of the Soviet school of atomic physics and teacher of Kurchatov, father of the Soviet atomic bomb. The physicist Lev Landau was regarded as "the Soviet Einstein." The economist Evsei Liberman is recognized as a leader of the Soviet economic reform of the middle 1960s. Gersh Budker and Vladimir Veksler are among prominent Soviet scientists in the science cities of Dubno near Moscow and Akademgorodok near Novosibirsk. L. Gurevich is designer of the Soviet flax combine harvester. Soviet-Jewish musicians—such as D. Oistrakh, E. Gillels, and L. Kogan—are known all over the world much as the "Russian" masters of chess, Tal and Botvinik.[85]

Jewish contribution to Soviet literature has been great, from Isaac Babel and Osip Mandelshtam to Ilya Ehrenburg, Boris Pasternak, and Samuil Marshak to Yuli Daniel, Aleksandr Galich, and Mikhail Vysotsky. Among Jews active in Soviet creative arts are Sergei Eisenstein in films, Maya Plisetskaya in ballet, Arkady Raikin in popular comedy, and Elena Bystritskaya in theater (Russian woman hero in film version of Sholokov's *Quiet Is the Don*).

In present-day Soviet sociology Igor Kon, Yuri Levada, and Ovsei Shkaratan have made significant contributions. Igor Kon is the only Soviet social scientist who has addressed himself to the roots of modern ethnic prejudice. Levada and Shkaratan have been objects of party criticism for ideological "mistakes."[86]

National Attitudes

REVIEW OF FACTORS FORMING NATIONAL ATTITUDES

For the last several decades formal indicators point to steady assimilation of Jews into Soviet culture. They are without a potent national area of their own. National increase is below replacement levels; the 1970 census indicated that their numbers had decreased 5% since 1959. They have no viable cultural institutions (apart from a monthly journal and a few concerts). Jewish religion is practiced by small groups, mostly over 50 years of age. In spite of these factors, a major national revival movement has emerged among Jews in the USSR. Its clearest manifestation is the desire for mass emigration to Israel.

Parallel to the movement for emigration is considerable evidence of large-scale assimilation. The situation is complex: on the one extreme, there are outright assimilationists who easily deny their Jewishness; on the other, there are traditional Oriental Jews and extremist Zionists. The following factors influence Jewish attitudes in the USSR; none are mutually exclusive, and their impact on major Jewish subgroups varies:

1. anti-Semitism
2. official Soviet doctrine and policies
3. revival of nationalism among Soviet ethnic groups
4. Israel
5. Jewish diaspora
6. Judaic religion
7. previous personal and group experience
8. dissent movement

During the first two decades after the revolution, the Bolsheviks actively discouraged anti-Semitism. Nevertheless, as an identifiable group, Jews found themselves hated for supporting the Soviet government or for becoming successful and prosperous

85 Rabinovich, 1967, *passim*; *Zionism*, 1970; J. Turkevich, *Soviet Men of Science* (Princeton, N.J.: Van Nostrand, 1963): 69,409.
86 Igor Kon, "Psikhologiya predrassudka," *Novy Mir*, 1966: 9.

in its service. At the same time they were often resented as private traders and blamed for speculation. During World War II, anti-Semitism intensified in all parts of the USSR.[87] Since the war it has acquired a new form: political anti-Semitism, basically motivated by ideological and political concerns. Jews are excluded first and foremost from the general political sphere (consisting of party and state leadership and security and diplomatic services). Jewish culture has been practically extinguished and ethnic identity suppressed in the interests of political expediency as understood by the Soviets. (Political expediency was also the basis of the Soviet leadership's attitude toward other nationalities—Crimean Tatars, Meskhi Turks, and Germans in the USSR.)[88] Political anti-Semitism is different from its racial or national variety: it does not exclude all Jews. Those prepared to accept the option of total assimilation are accepted into the fold, though not quite equal to Russians and other Soviet nationalities. This inherent contradiction in Soviet official policy—assimilation accompanied by discrimination—has a decisive impact on attitudes of both assimilated and nationally conscious Jews.

To this present-day picture must be added the long history of Jewish persecution from early tsarist and Soviet periods to the "Black Years" under Stalin. The tragedy of World War II which resulted in deaths of an estimated 1 to 2 million Soviet Jews compounds the picture. Except for Oriental communities, no Jewish family in the USSR is not affected by the holocaust.[89]

Revival of nationalism in the USSR has been a powerful factor in shaping Jewish attitudes. The original idea of everyone giving up previous ethnic identification to become Soviet was recognized to be unrealistic in the early 1930s as Stalin identified more and more with Russianism. The most recent wave of Russian nationalist literature (both of the legal and *samizdat* variety) must have had a devastating effect on Jews, especially those who had assimilated into Russian culture. Among glaring examples of anti-Semitic literature are the novels by Ivan Shevtsov, *In the Name of the Father and*

Son and Love and Hate. The central character in the latter is a Jew depicted as a mother-killer, swindler, pervert, and drug pusher; 200,000 copies of this book were published.[90]

Among *samizdat* materials, the journal *Veche* has reprinted anti-Semitic materials from writings of Slavophiles of the last century, arguing for a return to Orthodox Russianism. *Slovo natsii* takes a flagrantly racist position, blaming white Americans for despoiling the race by too lax a policy toward blacks. Not unnaturally, such assimilated Jews as Chakovsky and Pomerants fight this phenomenon as best they can. The former publishes attacks on it in *Literaturnaya Gazeta*, of which he is an editor; the latter writes powerful *samizdat* essays from the position of a dissident democratic Russian-Jewish writer and critic.[91]

Nationalism is also growing among other minority nationalities. Jews are often caught in the middle: local nationalists regard them as alien Russianizers and sovietizers and Russians regard them as Jews (i.e., non-Russians). Some Jews have made great contributions to development of the national culture and economy of many republics. But when they identify with the local population, they are again apt to arouse the ire of Russianizers, official and unofficial. It has been reported by recent émigrés that certain minority groups (Armenians, Georgians, Latvians) have adopted a sympathetic attitude toward the Jewish movement for emigration and toward Israel in general. Ukrainian activists have appealed for condemnation of anti-Semitism and a new relationship between Jews and Ukrainians.[92]

At the same time, forces for integration of Jews into Soviet society exert a powerful influence. Generations in the Russian environment have had their effect. Many Jews have immersed themselves in Russia and its culture, accepting Soviet ideology so deeply that they hold to it even after destalinization and the disenchantments of recent years. The Soviet Union is a huge country with much potential and, despite

---

87 See section on history.
88 *Chronicle*, 1968–1972; Reddaway, 1972, *passim*.
89 Decter, 1971: 25; Schwartz, 1965; Ettinger, 1971.

90 W. Bergman, *Soviet Jewish Affairs*, 1971: I: 119–125.
91 Pomerants: 123–127; *Samizdat Documents*: 103, 590, 1,020.
92 Dzyuba, 1970; Katz, 1973; Reddaway, 1972.

numerous obstacles, many Jewish citizens find careers and professional satisfaction.

Another strong assimilative force—especially for the young in newly opened areas—is intermarriage. There are no fully representative data on amount of intermarriage between Jews and non-Jews, but several partial surveys on intermarriage have been conducted in a number of Soviet cities and in several republics of the USSR. Following are findings by Western writers based on these surveys.

Nove and Newth, extrapolating from 1959 census data, show that intermarriage within the Pale was lower than without. In an attempt to discern a general pattern, Altshuler found that Jewish intermarriage in an old district of Tashkent inhabited mainly by Bukharan Jews was 7.7% of all marriages involving a Jewish partner (in 1962); whereas, in a modern central district inhabited by Ashkenazi Jews, the figure stood at 33.7% (up from 19.2% in 1926). A Vilnius study showed that rate of intermarriage was higher for Jewish men than for Jewish women.

Gittelman estimates that present rate of Jewish intermarriage in the USSR is between 20% and 35%. Though high, this is somewhat lower than in the 1930s and not unprecedented in other Jewish communities (e.g., Jews in Germany in the 1920s and in some North American communities in the 1950s). Since dispersal of the Jewish population is much higher than that of other ethnic groups, Armstrong sees the fact that most Jewish marriages are still endogamous as an indication of strong national cohesiveness.[93]

As to consequences of Jewish intermarriage, a detailed Soviet report indicates that the children of mixed couples "usually choose that nationality, the language and culture of which are most familiar." [94] This would mean that the great majority of children from mixed marriages with Jews choose Russian nationality.

Evidence suggests, however, that several factors mitigate the acculturative effects of intermarriage. When the father has a pro-

nouncedly Jewish family name or the Jewish side of the family is dominant or Jewish consciousness is high or the Jewish spouse is well known as Jewish, it is difficult for children to register as non-Jews. Edward Kuznetsov, who received a death sentence (later commuted to life imprisonment) in the Leningrad "highjackers" trial, is the son of a mixed marriage and was registered as Russian in his passport; yet he is regarded, and regards himself, as Jewish. Several leaders of the Jewish movement for emigration to Israel have non-Jewish spouses.[95]

BASIC VIEWS OF SCHOLARS ON NATIONAL ATTITUDES

The Soviet View

Soviet leaders, from Lenin to Khrushchev, have been rather outspoken in their views about Jews as a people and as individuals. Soviet theory differentiates between *natsiya* [nation], *national'nost'* [nationality in the sense of ethnic group], *narod* [a people, in the sense of ethnic community], and *narodnost'* [small ethnic group, not fully constituted as a nationality]. Lenin, and Stalin writing under Lenin's guidance,[96] consistently stated that Jews were not a *nation* since they lacked such essential characteristics as a common territory, language, and common economy. But they did recognize that Jews "had a common religion, origin, and certain relics of national character" (Stalin) and "a common descent and nationality" (Lenin).[97]

After 1917 Soviet Bolsheviks granted Jews the rights of a nationality and even some degree of cultural and organizational separateness (e.g., Yevsektsiya, Jewish schools). At the same time, the Soviets deny that the Jews in the Soviet Union belong to

93 Altshuler, 1970: 30–32; Gittelman, 1972: 20–30; Nove and Newth, 1970: 143–145; Armstrong, 1971: 62–67. These findings are similar to those reached from conversations with recent émigrés.
94 *Lit. gaz.* (January 24), 1973: 13.

95 Talks with émigrés by Zev Katz.
96 See Stalin's book *Marksizm i natsional'no-kolonial'nyi vopros* which appeared in 1913; an English translation, *Marxism and the National and Colonial Question*, was published in London by Martin Lawrence, undated. See also *Filosofskii slovar* (Moscow: Izd. Polit. Lit., 1963): 298–301.
97 Lenin, 1937: 293; Stalin, 1936: 6–8; Korey, 1970: 76–77. See also detailed discussion in Schwartz, 1951: 24–58; for a recent discussion in USSR on "nation," see Miller, 1970: 48–51.

the same group as Jews outside—that they are *one* people.[98]

Among Soviet leaders, M. Kalinin was most outspoken in arguing for preservation of Jewish nationality. In 1934 he spoke about the need of Jews "to have a state of their own." A 1936 Soviet decree stated that "for the first time in the history of the Jewish people its ardent desire to create a homeland of its own, to achieve national statehood, is being realized"—in Birobidzhan.[99]

The Soviet view that Jews need a state of their own reappeared in statements in 1947–1948 when the USSR supported partition of Palestine and was among the first to recognize Israel. It would appear that in accord with Soviet official theory the Jews—or at least the Israeli Jews—should be recognized as a nation, since they display the necessary features: territory, language, culture, and common economy.

Stalin's personal views are relatively well documented. When still a young delegate to the London party conference (in 1903), he reported that someone remarked "jokingly" that since most opposition to the Bolsheviks was Jewish and the great majority of Bolsheviks were non-Jewish "a little pogrom could take care of things." There is some evidence that during his struggles against Trotsky, Zinoviev, and Kamenev (all Jews) his followers utilized anti-Jewish feelings to gain support. In 1931 Stalin answered a question from the Jewish Telegraphic Agency, condemning anti-Semitism as "a phenomenon profoundly hostile to the Soviet system." The statement was later (in 1936) made public by Molotov, appearing in *Pravda*.[100] Evidence of Stalin's strong anti-Semitism in the latter years of his rule comes from his daughter Svetlana and from Khrushchev. According to them, he regarded Jews as treacherous and dishonest.[101]

In several talks with foreigners, Khrushchev admitted that "anti-Semitic sentiments still existed" in the USSR, explaining that the "indigenous inhabitants in the republics

. . . have created new cadres and they would take it amiss should the Jews want to occupy the foremost positions in them." He argued that Jews "surround themselves with Jewish collaborators," and that they always argue about everything and do not agree among themselves in the end.[102] He also explained that there were no Jewish schools and no Jewish theater in the Soviet Union because there was no demand for them, since the Jews preferred to send their children to Russian schools. As to attitudes of present leaders, it was reported that Kosygin attacked F. Kriegel, leader of the Czechoslovak Spring, calling him "this Galician Jew." [103]

Western Views

John Armstrong has developed the notion of "mobilized diasporas," using Soviet Jews, "an ethnic minority that performs a special function in the modernization process," as model. Members of such groups are, he claims, more urban oriented, higher educated, and possess a greater degree of managerial and language skills than the local population. Also, their women are more involved in the labor force. Because of these scarce qualities, "mobilized diasporas" obtain a disproportionate share of key positions in a modernizing society. When the local nationality develops an educated stratum of its own, however, "this apparently favored position of the minority group arouses jealousy. The diaspora group becomes subject to discrimination and usually ceases its specialized functions." [104]

Leonard Schapiro sees the fate of Soviet Jewry as intricately bound up with the fate of the Soviet political system: "The Jew suffers more than the other Soviet citizen from the circumstance that he lives in a totalitarian state, in which the principles of tolerance and equality before an independent law are not observed." He points out that much of what Jews suffer is directed not against Jews alone but, rather, against

98 *BSE*, 1952: 15.
99 *Pravda* (November 26), 1926; Goldberg, 1961: 171–174; Schwartz, 1951: 174, 181.
100 *Pravda* (November 30), 1936; Lestchinsky, 1930: 263; Weinryb, 1970: 302–303.
101 Alliluyeva, 1967: 197–198, 206, 217; Khrushchev, 1971, *passim*.

102 Korey, 1970: 89–92. See also Khrushchev, 1971.
103 Levenberg, 1970: 39–40. Other reports relate this incident to the then first secretary of the Ukraine, P. Shelest.
104 Armstrong, 1967: 131–135.

any nationality (especially of the diaspora kind) and any religion in the USSR. But "the national consciousness of the Jew, where it exists, revolves around . . . religion and Zionism. . . . Propaganda against priests does not . . . arouse hostile feelings against Armenians or Georgians or Russians. In contrast, lurid stories about the immorality of a rabbi . . . suitably caricatured with a hooked nose and other distinctive Jewish features stimulate hostility against Jews as such." Moreover, this "creates a sense among non-Jews that the Soviet authorities treat the Jews as second-class citizens, and that the Jews are, therefore, 'fair game.' The same line of reasoning applies to anti-Zionism." [105]

Rothenberg points out that "the anti-Judaic propaganda impugning the ethics and historical past of the Jewish people charts a distorted and maligned picture of the Jew. The negative assumption applies to every Jew and the onus of disproving the assumption lies on each Jewish individual." [106] While not disputing the effect of anti-Zionist propaganda campaigns, J. Frankel comes to the conclusion that this propaganda "was not part of a general policy directed against Jews per se. Rather, it represents ad hoc responses to new moves in the campaign for the freedom of Jews to emigrate to Israel—moves from inside and outside Russia." There is deep division between "would-be Leninist attitudes and neo-Stalinist attitudes" among people in the Soviet Union. The latter attitude finds expression in extremely harsh trials and crude intimidation; the former, in attempts at persuasion and greatly stepped-up emigration. [107]

Alex Inkeles sees attitudes toward Jews as a function of stress which develops when there is a "shift from class interest to ethnic interest: a class-based party becomes a ruler of an ethnic nation-state and comes to identify the class interest with the ethnic interests." Also, under Soviet conditions there has been a very high rate of social mobility into the elite; its new members bring with them many folk prejudices including anti-Jewish feelings. Moreover, the Soviet system has not done away with the socioeconomic reasons for anti-Semitism: good positions are scarce, and success of Jews in competition for these positions breeds ill feeling. Of two possible responses to the situation, "to deny one's identity more and more . . . [or] to build a heightened identity," Inkeles believes that the second is taking place in the Soviet Union. Anti-Semitism also plays a role for relieving tensions between the USSR and countries of Eastern Europe which are in a difficult period of transition (e.g., when Jews are used as scapegoats during a crisis). [108]

Zvi Gittelman attempts to discern the specific and complex processes going on among Soviet Jewry, to point out their simultaneous occurrence and contradictory effects. Jews undergo a rapid (and mostly willing) process of linguistic assimilation into Russian and of general Russian acculturation. But, as mentioned, this leads to total assimilation for some Jews, while others become more nationally conscious. "Jews in the USSR are culturally Russian but legally and socially Jews. This split personality creates an internal dissonance the resolution of which can be achieved by becoming wholly Jewish or wholly Russian." Soviet authorities create this contradictory situation: on the one hand, they press the Jew into assimilation while at the same time they make it impossible. [109]

Views of Soviet Writers and Dissenters

The problems of anti-Semitism and emigration to Israel have become significant themes for more liberal Soviet writers and dissenters in the post-Stalin period. A main character in Ehrenburg's *Thaw* was a Jewish doctor suffering during the doctors' plot period. *Babi Yar* was the name of the well-known poem by Yevtushenko as well as a book by A. Kuznetsov. The largely unknown letter by writer Boris Polevoi to the party Central Committee asking for revival of Jewish culture in the USSR was one of many similar activities among members of

105 Schapiro, 1970: 6–9.
106 Rothenberg, 1971: 217–218.
107 Frankel, 1972: 53–54. See also Ben-Shlomo, 1970, *passim*.

108 Inkeles, 1971: 76–85.
109 Gittelman, 1972: 1–5, 33–48.

the Soviet intelligentsia. Jewish personages are prominent in Solzhenitsyn's *First Circle*.[110]

Among dissenters, Yuli Daniel and A. Sinyansky have included passages on anti-Semitism in their stories. A. Marchenko described anti-Jewish prejudice in Soviet prison camps and A. Amalrik among Soviet students. At first, the dissent movement did not take an active stand on the Jewish issue but Jewish national revival became stronger and, as authorities intensified their struggle against it, prominent dissenters became more involved. Sakharov, the brothers Medvedev, Chalidze, and others have published appeals in support of the right of Soviet Jews to emigrate to Israel and condemning anti-Jewish discrimination in the USSR. Roi Medvedev devoted a special paper to the Middle East and the Jewish problem in the Soviet Union. In his book *On Socialist Democracy*, he argues that Jews have been living for hundreds of years in Russia and therefore should be regarded as a rooted [*korenoye*] population, much like any other. He stated also that development of the previously backward nationalities had reached a level at which there was no longer need to give them preference in appointments, which should be made without reference to nationality.[111]

RECENT MANIFESTATIONS OF NATIONALISM

Recent manifestations of Jewish nationalism are inextricably linked with recent events in the USSR, especially in the post-Khrushchev period. Immediately after the removal of Khrushchev there was an improvement in the situation of Soviet Jews. The economic trials were discontinued. An editorial in *Pravda* explicitly condemned manifestations of anti-Semitism in the country.[112] A virulent anti-Jewish booklet (*Judaism Without Embellishments*), published under the auspices of the Ukrainian Academy of Sciences by Trofim Kichko, aroused world-wide protests—even among Communist parties in the West. Officially criticized by the Ideological Committee, CPSU, it was reportedly withdrawn.

From 1964 to 1967 (until June) there was also improvement in relations between the USSR and Israel. Cultural and tourist exchanges widened (including a visit by the Soviet writer K. Simonov to Israel and a tour by Israeli singer Geula Gill in the Soviet Union). Also, for the first time, several thousand Soviet Jews (mostly older citizens) were allowed to emigrate to Israel. Simultaneously, however, the Soviets were becoming ever more involved in support of the Arab position in the Middle East.[113]

The Six-Day War in June 1967 led to far-reaching changes in the Soviet position. Diplomatic relations with Israel were severed; the minuscule but significant emigration was halted. Soviet media undertook a vicious and vituperative campaign against Israel, Zionism, and Judaism—with direct and indirect anti-Semitic features.[114] The previously rebuked Kichko reappeared with a new book published in Kiev (*Judaism and Zionism*), in which Judaism was presented primarily as "a creed teaching poisonous hatred for all other peoples," one advocating "thievery, betrayal and perfidy." All during this period, the Soviet Union became more and more involved on the side of the Arab countries against Israel. On the other hand, the Jewish writer Ehrenburg freely expressed satisfaction with the Israeli victory in the Six-Day War and criticized Soviet policies.[115]

In 1968 the pattern of blaming an "international Zionist alliance which was playing the role of a secret channel between reactionary forces in the Imperialist states [primarily the United States, German Fed-

110 Ehrenburg, *The Thaw* (London: Mayflower-Dell, 1955); A. Solzhenitsyn, *The First Circle* (New York: Bantam Books, 1968); *Politicheskii dnevnik* (Amsterdam: Herzen Foundation, 1972): 102–105.

111 *On Trial* (New York: Harper & Row, 1966); A. Amalrik, *Involuntary Journey to Siberia* (New York: Harcourt, Brace, Jovannovich, 1970); A. Marchenko, *My Testimony* (London: Pall Mall, 1969); A. Sakharov, *Progress, Coexistence and Intellectual Freedom* (New York: Norton, 1968); Roi Medvedev, *Kniga o sotsialisticheskoi demokratii* (Amsterdam: Herzen Foundation, 1972).

112 *Pravda* (September 5), 1965.

113 Weinryb, 1970: 315–316; Decter, 1971: 29–30; Lawrence, 1970: 33–44; Cang, 1969: 147–167.

114 For an extensive review see Korey, 1973, *passim*.

115 Korey, 1970: 45–46; Katz, 1968: 27; Frankel, 1972, *passim*; A. Werth, *Russia: Hopes and Fears* (London: Cresset Press, 1969): 242.

eral Republic, and Britain] and Israeli militarists" for anti-Soviet developments, spilled over into Eastern Europe. In March 1968 during student riots in Warsaw, the Polish first secretary of the party, V. Gomulka, with active support of the Soviets, blamed the "Zionists" as instigators and initiated a major expulsion of Jews from Poland. During the Soviet-Czechoslovak crisis, Soviet leaders consciously used anti-Semitism to weaken and split the Czechoslovak Spring movement, demanding elimination of the Jewish leaders E. Goldstuecker, F. Kriegel, and O. Šik. In the USSR similar procedures were used to weaken the growing dissent movement, in which Jews were playing a significant role.[116]

In the fall of 1968 Soviet authorities again began to issue exit visas for Israel for some while denying them to others. Pressure mounted from those not allowed to leave. Learning from tactics of the dissent movement, they arranged sit-ins, circulated appeals inside the USSR, and sent protest documents to prominent personalities outside the Soviet Union. In this way the foreign press was constantly kept informed. Soviet security police conducted a constant campaign of harassment, suppression, and arrests in an attempt to limit the extent of the movement for emigration.

In November 1968 a Kiev engineer, Boris Kochubievsky, who had criticized Soviet policies toward Jews and Israel, was arrested and later sentenced to three years' imprisonment. Similar cases were later reported from Odessa, Kharkov, Sverdlovsk, Moscow, Riga, and other places. When in March 1970 the Soviet Foreign Ministry arranged a press conference in which prominent Soviet Jewish personalities condemned Zionism and supported the official policies, a group of Jewish activists made a statement denying the right of these people to speak in the name of Soviet Jewry and demanding permission to emigrate to Israel.[117]

In June 1970 arrests of the so-called "hijackers" began. Thirty-four Jews were arrested: first in Leningrad, then in Riga, Kishinev, and Tbilisi. In December two were

sentenced to death in Leningrad (Eduard Kuznetsov and Mark Dymshits) and nine were condemned to various terms of imprisonment. Several other trials followed. An attempt to hijack a plane to escape from the Soviet Union to Israel was regarded by the court as an act of treason. The harsh sentences and prospective executions aroused a global response, and the USSR supreme court commuted the death sentences to life imprisonment. Instead of weakening the movement for emigration, however, the trials strengthened it, providing worldwide support and recognition. In Spring 1971 a world conference of Jewish communities convened in Brussels to deliberate on the position of Soviet Jewry. In Moscow, Jewish national activists from all over the USSR staged several demonstrations, including a sit-in in the building of the Central Committee, CPSU. A *samizdat* Jewish chronicle entitled *Exodus* appeared. Following these developments Soviet authorities allowed a relatively large-scale emigration to Israel, continuing at the time of this writing.[118]

The exact numbers in the Jewish emigration from the USSR are unavailable since neither Israel nor the USSR publishes official figures, and unofficial figures often vary. Table 15.10 shows estimates based on several sources.

By the end of June 1974 more than 100,000 Jews had left the Soviet Union— about 8,500 before the Six-Day War and some 93,000 since. In June 1973 the *New York Times* reported that Brezhnev had assured the United States that Jewish emigration would continue "at the rate of 36,000 to 40,000 a year," and in June 1974 a figure of 50,000 a year was mentioned.[119]

Data on composition of the emigration are even more scarce. Estimates of composition are given in Table 15.11.

According to these estimates, Georgian Jews may complete an almost total exodus to Israel within several years; almost half have emigrated already. About one in every three Baltic Jews has left, and within several years the overwhelming majority will have done so. Altogether, Western and Oriental Jews comprising only 20% to 25%

116 Korey, 1970: 43–52; Lendvai, 1971, *passim*; *Soviet Jewish Affairs*, 1971: 1; 1972: 3; and other issues.
117 *Jews in Eastern Europe*, 1969, 1971 (various issues); Katz, 1970: 328–329; *Redemption*, 1970, *passim*.

118 *Jews in Eastern Europe*, 1971: IV: 6–7; *Soviet Jewish Affairs*, 1970–1972 (various issues).
119 *New York Times* (June 2), 1973, (June 24), 1974.

Table 15.10

Jewish Emigration from USSR to Israel

up to 1964[a]		4,667
1965		750
1966		1,613
1967		1,412
	Total up to 1967	8,442
1968		231
1969		3,033
1970[b]		1,000
1971		12,923
1972		32,200
1973[c]		33,000
1974[d]	(first 6 months)	10,000
	Total since 1967	92,387
	Grand total	100,829

Sources: Gittelman, 1972: 9–10; Schroeter, 1972: 3–4; personal information of Zev Katz; *Klitat Aliyah* (Jerusalem: Ministry of Absorption, March 1974).

[a] The figure was given by Prime Minister Kosygin during a visit to Ottawa in October 1971.

[b] Figures up to 1971 were released by the Jewish Agency.

[c] Official figures of the Israeli Ministry of Absorption.

[d] Estimated by Zev Katz. Cf. *Jews in the USSR* (June 6), 1974.

of the total make up 70% of émigrés. So far only about 1% of Core Jews have left (altogether; 20,000). In the émigré total they amount to some 20%, though they are about 70% of total Jews in the USSR.

The reasons for this differentiated behavior lie partly in history and background of the different Jewish communities (see sections on demography and history), but it also results from planning of central authorities and different attitudes of local and national leadership. Core Jews live in the large cities, centers of Soviet power, culture, science, and education. Many are educated or "important," and the authorities place all kinds of obstacles in the way of emigration. In the list of Soviet Jews reportedly submitted to the Soviets by U.S. representatives (asking for their release), there are few Oriental Jews but many Core Jews. Knowledgeable observers think that the Soviets regard the Oriental Jews as expendable and the Western Jews as nationalist (Zionist) and therefore undesirable (or dangerous). Certainly, the latter designation applies also to Jewish activists from among Core Jews; they are suppressed, harassed, imprisoned, or allowed to leave. Basic policy seems to allow departure of Jews least assimilable into contemporary Slavic Soviet society (especially Oriental Jews, whose childhood was spent in non-Soviet areas)

Table 15.11

Jewish Emigration from USSR by Community

(up to June 1974)

	TOTAL NO. IN USSR (1,000)	TOTAL EMIGRATED (1,000)	% OF ALL ÉMIGRÉS	% OF GROUP EMIGRATED	POTENTIAL TOTAL EMIGRATION (1,000)
Georgians	60	27.4	27	47.0	45.0 (75%)
Central Asian (Bukharan)	100	7.1	7	4.0	55.0 (55%)
Baltics	80	25.4	25	32.5	60.0 (75%)
Ukraine (including Bukovina)	1,000	15.3	15	1.5	250.0 (25%)
Moldavia	130	10.1	10	8.0	97.5 (75%)
RSFSR	1,000	10.1	10	1.0	200.0 (20%)
Other (Belorussian, mountain Jews)	385	6.1	6	1.5	115.5 (30%)
Total	2,755	101.5	100		823.0

Source: Estimates by Zev Katz.

but to retain Soviet-educated, professionally competent Jews of the core areas. As for re-emigration, some 1,300 Soviet emigrants left Israel up to April 1974; of these 138 gathered in Vienna waiting for permits to return to the USSR; 40 were allowed to do so and 28 returned to Israel. In 1973–1974 several thousand of those allowed to leave for Israel went from Vienna to other countries.[120]

The estimates of potential emigration given in Table 15.11 are based on information about past behavior and motivation. Should these variables change, so will the potential for emigration. If the estimates are correct, total emigration potential in the near future is three quarters of a million. Of these some 150,000 have already received affidavits from Israel.[121]

---

[120] Israeli Public Council for Soviet Jewry, Scientists Committee, *Newsbulletin*, No. 38.

[121] *Jews in the USSR*, (June 14) 1974.

REFERENCES

Abramsky, 1970
    C. Abramsky, "The Biro-Bidzhan Project, 1927–1959," in Kochan, 1970: 62–75.
Ainsztein, 1970
    R. Ainsztein, "Soviet Jewry in the Second World War," in Kochan, 1970: 269–287.
Alliluyeva, 1967
    Svetlana Alliluyeva, *Twenty Letters to a Friend* (New York: Harper & Row 1967).
Alliluyeva, 1969
    Svetlana Alliluyeva, *Only One Year* (New York: Harper & Row, 1969).
Altshuler, 1970
    Mordekhai Altshuler, "Mixed Marriages amongst Soviet Jews," *Soviet Jewish Affairs* (December 1970): VI: 30–33.
Armstrong, 1967
    John A. Armstrong, *Ideology, Politics and Government in the Soviet Union*, rev. ed. (New York: Praeger, 1967).
Armstrong, 1968
    John A. Armstrong, "The Ethnic Scene in the Soviet Union: The View of the Dictatorship," in Goldhagen, 1968: 3–49.
Armstrong, 1971
    John A. Armstrong, "Soviet Foreign Policy and Anti-Semitism," *Soviet Jewry* (1971): 62–75.
Artykov et al., 1967
    A. Artykov et al., *Kommunisticheskaya partiya Turkmenistana v tsifrakh (1925–1966)*, (Ashkhabad: Turkmenistan, 1967).
Atlas narodov mira, 1964
    Atlas narodov mira (Moscow: BSE, 1964).
Baron, 1964
    Salo Baron, *The Russian Jew under Tsars and Soviets* (New York: Macmillan, 1964).

Ben-Shlomo, 1970
    Zeev Ben-Shlomo, "The Current Anti-Zionist Campaign in the USSR," *Soviet Jewish Affairs*, May 1970.
Brumberg, 1968
    Joseph (and Abraham) Brumberg, "Sovyetish Heymland," *The Unredeemed*, 1968: 83–96.
BSE, 1952
    Bol'shaya Sovetskaya Entsiklopediya (Moscow: Bol'shaya Sovetskaya entsiklopediya, 1952).
Cang, 1969
    Joel Cang, *The Silent Millions* (London: Rapp & Whiting, 1969).
Census Data, 1959, 1970
    See *Itogi 1959, Itogi 1970*. Also:
    "Census Data: Age, Education, Nationality," CDSP, XXIII: 16: 14–18.
    Vechernaya Moskva (June 7, 1971): 2.
    Sovetskaya Kirgiziya (May 5, 1971): 3–4.
    Kommunist Tadzhikistana (May 6, 1971): 1–3.
    Sovetskaya Latviya (June 23, 1971): 2.
    Pravda vostoka (April 28, 1971): 2.
    Kazakhstanskaya pravda (June 9, 1971): 1, 3.
    Sovetskaya Litva (May 11, 1971): 1–2.
    Turkmenskaya iskra (July 11, 1971): 1–2.
Chronicle
    Chronicle of Current Events (London: Amnesty International Publications, 1970–1971); in Russian, *Khronika tekushchikh sobytii*, Samizdat Documents series of Radio Liberty.
Chronicle (London)
    Khronika zashchity prav v SSR (London and New York: Khronika Press).
Davies, 1969
    Eduard Davies, "In the Theater of Soviet

Central Asia," *Soviet Jewish Affairs* (January 1969): III: 32–33.

Decter, 1971
Moshe Decter, "Jewish National Consciousness in the Soviet Union" and "Epilogue," *Soviet Jewry* (1971): 1–41, 17–104.

Dubnow, 1916, 1918, 1920
S. M. Dubnow, *History of the Jews in Russia and Poland* (Philadelphia: Jewish Publication Society of America, 1916: I; 1918: II; 1920: III.

Dzyuba, 1970
Ivan Dzyuba, *Internationalism or Russification? A Study in the Soviet Nationalities Problem* (London: Weidenfeld & Nicholson, 1970).

Eliav, 1969
Arie L. Eliav (Ben-Ami), *Between Hammer and Sickle* (New York: Signet Books, 1969).

Ettinger, 1970
S. Ettinger, "The Jews in Russia at the Outbreak of the Revolution," in Kochan, 1970: 14–28.

Ettinger, 1971
S. Ettinger. *Shorasheha shel 'Hasheelah Hayehudit' Bevrit Hamoatsot* [*Roots of Jewish Problem in USSR*], paper for Brussels Conference on Soviet Jewry, 1971 (unpublished).

Frankel, 1972
Jonathan Frankel, "The Anti-Zionist Press Campaigns in the USSR 1969–1971: Political Implications" (Jerusalem: Hebrew University, Soviet and East European Research Center, Research Paper No. 2, 1972).

Friedberg, 1969
Maurice Friedberg, "Jewish Contributions to Soviet Literature," *Soviet Jewish Affairs* (January 1969): 3.

Friedberg, 1970
Maurice Friedberg, "Jewish Contributions to Soviet Literature," in Kochan, 1970: 208–217.

Gilboa, 1971
Yehoshua Gilboa, *The Black Years of Soviet Jewry* (Boston: Little, Brown, 1971).

Gittelman, 1972
Zvi Gittelman, *Assimilation, Acculturation, and National Consciousness Among Soviet Jews* (Ann Arbor: University of Michigan [mimeo], December 1972).

Goldberg, 1961
B. Z. Goldberg, *The Jewish Problem in the Soviet Union* (New York: Crown, 1961).

Goldhagen, 1968
Erich Goldhagen, ed., *Ethnic Minorities in the Soviet Union* (New York: Praeger, 1968).

Goldman, 1960
Guido Goldman, *Zionism Under Soviet Rule, 1917–1928* (New York: Herzl Press, 1960).

Greenberg, 1965
Louis Greenberg, *The Jews in Russia* (New Haven: Yale University Press, 1965): I, II.

Halpern (Heilpern), 1968
Israel Halpern (Heilpern), *Yehudim Ve-Yahadut Be-Mizrach Eiropa* [*Eastern European Jewry*] (Jerusalem: Magness Press, Hebrew University, 1968).

Inkeles, 1971
Alex Inkeles, "Anti-Semitism as an Instrument of Soviet Policy," in *Soviet Jewry*, 1971: 76–85.

Itogi 1959
Itogi vsesoyuznoi perepisi naseleniya 1959 goda SSSR (Moscow: Gosstatizdat, 1962).

Itogi 1970
Itogi vsesoyuznoi perepisi naseleniya 1970 goda (Moscow: Statistika, 1973): IV.

Jews in Eastern Europe
Jews in Eastern Europe, E. Litvinoff, ed. Periodical newsletter published in London.

Kantor, 1934
Yakov Kantor, *Natsional'noye stroitel'stvo sredi yevreyev SSSR* [*National Construction among USSR Jews*], Z. Ostrovsky, ed. (Moscow: Vlast' Sovetov, 1934).

Katz, 1968
Zev Katz, "The Anomaly of the Jewish Autonomous Region in Birobidzhan," *Soviet Jewish Affairs* (July 1968): 2.

Katz, 1970
Zev Katz, "After the Six-Day War," in Kochan, 1970: 321–336.

Katz, 1973
Zev Katz "The New Nationalism in the USSR," *Midstream* (February 1973): 3–13.

Kochan, 1970
Lionel Kochan, ed., *The Jews in Soviet Russia since 1917* (London: Oxford University Press, 1970).

Korey, 1970
William Korey, "The Legal Position of Soviet Jewry: A Historical Enquiry," in Kochan, 1970: 76–98.

Korey, 1971
William Korey, "Myths, Fantasies, and Show Trials: Echoes of the Past," in *Soviet Jewry*, 1971: 42–61.

Korey, 1973
William Korey, *The Soviet Cage: Antisemitism in Russia* (New York: Viking, 1973).

Khrushchev, 1971
Nikita Khrushchev, *Khrushchev Remembers* (Boston: Little, Brown, 1971).

Lawrence, 1970
Gunther Lawrence, *Three Million More* (Garden City, N.Y.: Doubleday, 1970).

Lendvai, 1971
Paul Lendvai, *Anti-Semitism Without Jews* (Garden City, N.Y.: Doubleday, 1971).

Lenin, 1937
V. I. Lenin, *Sochineniya* [*Collected Writings*], 3rd ed. (Moscow, 1937): XVII, cited by Korey, 1970.

Lestschinsky, 1930
J. Lestschinsky, *Tswishn Lebn un Toit* (Wilno: n.p., 1930).

Levenberg, 1970
S. Levenberg, "Soviet Jewry: Some Problems and Perspectives," in Kochan, 1970: 29–43.

Miller, 1970
J. Miller, "Soviet Theory on the Jews," in Kochan, 1970: 44–61.

Millman, 1971
Ivor Millman, "Jewish Population in the USSR," *Soviet Jewish Affairs* (June), 1971: I: 13–19.

Nar. khoz. 1966
Narodnoye khozyaistvo SSSR v 1966 godu. (Moscow: Statistika, 1971).

Nar. khoz. 1970
Narodnoye khozyaistvo SSSR v 1970 godu. (Moscow: Statistika, 1971).

Nar. khoz. 1972
Narodnoye khozyaistvo SSSR 1922–1972, Yubileinyi yezhegodnik (Baku: Azerbaidzhan Gosizdat, 1972).

Nar. obraz., 1971
Narodnoye obrazovaniye, nauka i kul'tura v SSSR: statisticheskii sbornik (Moscow: Statistika, 1971).

Neustadt, 1970
Mordekhai Neustadt, *Yehudei Gruzia* [*Jews of Georgia*] (Tel Aviv: Am Oved, 1970).

Newth, 1969
J. A. Newth, "Statistics on Ukrainian Jewry," *Soviet Jewish Affairs* (January), 1969: 3.

Newth and Katz, 1969
J. A. Newth and Z. Katz, "Proportion of Jews in the Communist Party of the Soviet Union," *Soviet Jewish Affairs,* 1969: IV: 37–38.

Nove and Newth, 1970
A. Nove and J. A. Newth, "The Jewish Population: Demographic Trends and Occupational Patterns," in Kochan, 1970: 125–158.

Politicheskii dnevnik, 1972
Politicheskii dnevnik [*Political Diary*] *1964–1970* (Amsterdam: Herzen Foundation, 1972).

Pomerants
G. Pomerants, *Neopublikovannoye* (printed underground in USSR and published anonymously in West, no date).

Rabinovich, 1967
Solomon Rabinovich, *Jews in the Soviet Union* (Moscow: Novosti, 1967).

Redemption, 1970
Redemption, Jewish Freedom Letters from Russia (New York: American Jewish Conference on Soviet Jewry, 1970).

Reddaway, 1972
Peter Reddaway, ed., *Uncensored Russia* (New York: Cowles, 1972).

Redlich, 1971
S. Redlich, "The Jews in Soviet Annexed Territories 1939–41," *Soviet Jewish Affairs* (June), 1971: I: 81–90.

Rigby, 1968
T. H. Rigby, *Communist Party Membership in the USSR, 1917–1967* (Princeton, N.J.: Princeton University Press, 1968).

Rothenberg, 1971
Joshua Rothenberg, *The Jewish Religion in the Soviet Union* (New York: Ktav and Brandeis University, 1971).

Sachar, 1972
Abram Leon Sachar, *A History of the Jews,* rev. ed. (New York: Knopf, 1972).

Schapiro, 1970
L. Schapiro, "Introduction," in Kochan, 1970: 1–14.

Schroeter, 1972
Leonard Schroeter, "How They Left: Varieties of Soviet Jewish Experience," *Soviet Jewish Affairs,* 1972: II: 2.

Schulman, 1971
Elias Schulman, *A History of Jewish Education in the Soviet Union* (New York: Ktav and Brandeis University, 1971).

Schwartz, 1951
Solomon M. Schwartz (Schwarz), *The Jews in the Soviet Union* (Syracuse: Syracuse University Press, 1951).

Schwartz, 1966
Solomon M. Schwartz (Schwarz), *Yevrei v Sovetskom Soyuze (1939–1965)* [*Jews in the Soviet Union: 1939–1965*] (New York: American Jewish Committee, 1966).

Soviet Jewish Affairs
Also published as *Bulletin on Soviet and East European Affairs* (London: Institute of Jewish Affairs).

Soviet Jewry, 1971
Perspectives on Soviet Jewry (New York: Academic Committee on Soviet Jewry and

Anti-Defamation League of B'nai Brith, 1971).

Stalin, 1936
Joseph Stalin, *Marxism and the National and Colonial Question* (London: Lawrence & Wishart, 1936).

The Unredeemed, 1968
The Unredeemed, Anti-Semitism in the Soviet Union, R. I. Rubin, ed. (Chicago: Quadrangle, 1968).

Weinryb, 1970
B. D. Weinryb, "Antisemitism in Soviet Russia," in Kochan, 1970: 288–320.

Zionism, 1970
Zionism: Instrument of Imperialist Reaction (Moscow: Novosti, 1970).

16 THE TATARS and THE TATAR ASSR

Gustav Burbiel

In the USSR "Tatar" is today applied to two distinct ethnic groups: Kazan Tatars, who have an autonomous republic on the Volga and Kama rivers to the east of Moscow, and Crimean Tatars, exiled by Stalin during World War II from the Crimean peninsula on the Black Sea to Central Asia.[1] Throughout much of their history these groups have shared a common culture. Eventually, Russian conquest and settlement led to their geographical separation and partial dispersion.

Some 2.5 million Kazan Tatars live in the Tatar and Bashkir ASSRs, and another 1.5 million in adjoining territories. (Other Tatars live in Siberia and in other areas and large cities of the RSFSR, as well as in the five Central Asian republics. Number of Tatars in the remaining union republics is negligible.) Soviet statistics do not distinguish between Kazan and Crimean Tatars,[2] but the latter are estimated to number about 300,000.[3]

This chapter deals with Kazan Tatars and the Tatar ASSR. Occasionally, however, we refer to Tatar-Bashkirs as one group. Bashkirs are a neighboring Turkic people with close historical, cultural, and demographic links to Tatars. They live primarily in the Bashkir ASSR in which, however, there are more Tatars than Bashkirs.[4] About one third of the Bashkirs regard Tatar as their mother tongue. Thus, the line of distinction between the two groups is unclear and topic for dispute, but differences do exist. Indeed, a rise in a distinct Bashkir national consciousness has been observed.

General Information

TERRITORY

The historical homeland of the Tatar-Bashkirs stretches from the Oka-Don lowlands and the Volga uplands in the west to the Siberian slopes of the Ural Mountains in the east. In the north it extends to the Vyatka-Uval uplands near Kirov. In the

---

1 Cf., e.g., *Malaya Sovetskaya entsiklopediya* (Moscow: Sovetskaya entsiklopediya, 1960): IX: 131.

2 *Itogi 1970*: IV: 9, 12–17, 329.

3 Petition by Crimean Tatars to Supreme Soviet of the USSR, July 1972, Reuters dispatch from Moscow of August 17, 1972.

4 See footnote 26.

south its boundaries run along the southern section of the Volga upland, on the right bank of the Volga, to the Caspian lowland and the city of Astrakhan.

This territory, boundaries of which approximate those of the Khanate of Kazan (early 1400s–1552), is now administratively divided into the Tatar ASSR (in the center); the Bashkir, Mari, Udmurt, Chuvash, and Mordvinian ASSRs; and parts of 10 *oblasty* of the RSFSR.[5] Present-day Tatar and Bashkir ASSRs comprise about a quarter of this historic homeland.

The Tatar ASSR (26,250 square miles) lies at the confluence of the Volga and Kama rivers, extending from the lower Belaya (Aghidel) River in the east to the Sviyaga, a right affluent of the Volga, in the west. The Volga and Kama rivers divide the republic into three distinct natural regions: (1) right bank of the Volga, with moderate continental climate, black earth, and deciduous (mainly oak) woodlands; (2) right bank of the Kama, in the northern coniferous forest zone with more extreme climate and podzolic soils; and (3) left bank of the Kama, with moderate dry climate and black-earth wooded steppe.

ECONOMY

Tatars took an active part in industrial development of Russia as early as the eighteenth century. Between 1750 and 1800 Tatar entrepreneurs built textile factories near Kazan. By 1814 these factories accounted for 75% of all textile manufacturing in Russia. A Tatar leather factory was established in Kazan in 1781; in 1812 there were 18 such factories, 13 owned by Tatars. In 1854, 10 of 13 soap factories in Kazan were owned by Tatars; in addition, Tatar enterprises produced candles, paper, paint, and metal goods.[6]

By 1913 there were 388 industrial plants in the area inhabited by Tatars: output for that year totaled 99 million rubles.[7] Nevertheless, because of a manpower surplus many Tatars emigrated to seek work in other industrial centers such as the Donbas, Baku, Astrakhan, the Urals, and Siberia. From 1906 to 1910 alone, 219,000 Tatars left the province of Kazan to search for work elsewhere.[8]

Good transport facilities, large labor force, and secure location in the interior led the Soviets to speed up industrialization of the area. Postwar discovery of oil turned the Tatar ASSR into one of the Soviet Union's most important economic areas. Today the ASSR has highly developed oil, chemical, and engineering industries. In 1971 oil output was 102.6 million tons, highest by far in the USSR.[9] Tatar oil is piped to Moscow, Yaroslav, Ryazan, Odessa, Novorossiisk, Orsk, Ishimbay, Saratov, Kuibyshev, and other industrial centers.[10] The Tatar ASSR is first in manufacture of fur goods, photographic film,[11] film gelatine, and liquid gas.[12] Heavy machinery, optical instruments, medicines, and high-heat-resistant glass instruments are among other items manufactured in Tataristan.[13] The production of timber, building materials, and textiles is expanding. Clothing and food are important industries. Among major industrial centers in the republic are Chistopol, Elabug, Bugulma, Almat, and Leninogorsk.

---

5 Projected borders of the Tatar state of Idel-Ural, proclaimed in November 1917 (see section on history), did not stretch as far west and north as those of the Khanate of Kazan. However, its eastern and southern borders were shifted more toward east and south. In the west the border ran along the western edge of today's Chuvash ASSR, through the Ulyanovsk oblast, hitting the Volga west of Togliatti, then followed the river to Volgograd. Thus all of Gorkiy oblast, Mordvinian ASSR, and Penza oblast and half of Ulyanovsk and Saratov oblast were outside Idel-Ural. In the north the border followed the northern edge of present Mari ASSR and ran through southern Kirov oblast, middle Udmurt ASSR, lower Perm oblast and, passing north of Sverdlovsk, to Tyumen. At Tyumen the border followed the Tobol river to the present boundary of Kazakh SSR. In the southwest it went to Astrakhan and then east along the Caspian Sea to the Emba river.

6 Devletchin, 1958: 72, quoting Bertold Spuler, *Der Islam* (Berlin, 1949), XXIX: 2: 170.
7 *Ibid.*, quoting *Revolyutsionnyi vostok* [*Revolutionary East*] (Moscow, 1935): I: 21: 156.
8 *Ibid.*, quoting *Revolyutsionnyi vostok* (1934): V: 27: 162.
9 Total oil output in the USSR for 1971: 371.8 million tons. *Nar. khoz.* 1972: 137, 736.
10 *Qazan Utlary*, 1972: XI: 142.
11 The Tatar ASSR supplies half of all film used in the USSR. *Qazan Utlary*, 1972: V: 4–7.
12 *Qazan Utlary*, 1972: XI: 141.
13 *Ibid.*, 1972: 5.

The capital city, Kazan (population 904,000),[14] has shipyards, railroad yards, and auto repair works. Typewriters, calculating machines, agricultural implements, and aircraft are manufactured there, and about half of all fur processing in the USSR is done in the city. It also has clothing, shoe and felt-boot industries, and large food processing plants.

The Tatar ASSR supplies the Chuvash, Bashkir, and Mari ASSRs and the Gorky and Kuibyshev *oblasty* with electric energy.[15] Total output in 1971 was 16.7 billion kwh.[16]

Largest automobile works in the Soviet Union (13.4 million square feet) were under construction on the Kama River in the early 1970s.[17] About 2,000 industrial products manufactured in the Tatar ASSR are exported to 60 countries in Europe, Asia, Africa, and America.[18]

Industrial production in 1969 in the Tatar ASSR was 337 times as large as in 1913 (compared with 119 for the RSFSR and 121 for the entire USSR).[19] Despite this enormous industrial expansion, however, large numbers of Tatars still seek work outside their native homeland. In fact, the republic's population has grown only 8.4% since it was created in 1920.[20]

Since 1970, when construction began on the new automobile works on the Kama, an unspecified number of Tatars seem to have returned to their native republic with the intention of staying on after completion of the huge project. But there has also been an influx of non-Tatars of 40 nationalities.[21]

Another important factor in the republic's economy is agriculture. Wheat and rye are grown throughout its territory, but wheat predominates in the northwest. Oats are grown south of the Kama River and millet and hemp north of it. Hemp is also grown in the area southwest of the Volga. Other agricultural products include leguminous plants and fodder crops. Dairy cattle are raised extensively along the Kama River,

and poultry along the Volga River.[22] In 1970 there were 588 collective and 167 state farms.

HISTORY

Today's Kazan (or Volga) Tatars are descendants of the Volga-Kama Bolgars, the Qypchaq Turks from Central Asia who came to the Volga-Ural region in the thirteenth century, and Turkicized Finnish tribes. The Turkic-speaking Bolgars appeared in the region in the seventh century. By the ninth century they had formed a state which expanded gradually to include those Bashkirs living west of the Urals. They accepted Islam in 922 A.D. The Bolgar state eroded during the early 1200s when Mongol-Tatars under Batu invaded the area and established the Golden Horde. The Mongols, a small minority in the conquering force, were quickly assimilated by the Turkic majority, and the Bolgars and Qypchaq Turks became ethnically dominant elements in the Golden Horde. During the second half of the fourteenth and into the fifteenth centuries the Bolgars moved further north and west; merging with the Turks and Finns, they became known as "New Bolgars" and, finally, "Kazan Tatars."

During the first half of the fifteenth century the Golden Horde broke up into the khanates of Kazan, Astrakhan, Crimea, and Siberia and the Noghay Horde. The Khanate of Kazan also included the Turkic-speaking Chuvash, western Bashkirs, and most Finnish-speaking Mordvinians, Maris, and Udmurts, all formerly part of the Bolgar state. The Khanate of Kazan remained a formidable opponent of Muscovy for more than a century. Finally, it succumbed to superior Russian power in 1552, opening the way for Russian expansion toward the East.

During the two centuries following the fall of Kazan, Moslem Tatars were subjected to political persecution and severe economic and religious pressures[23] which forced large numbers to leave their homes and move eastward to Bashkiristan, the Urals, and

14 As of January 1, 1971. *Nar. khoz. 1972*: 22.
15 *Qazan Utlary*, 1972: XI: 142.
16 *Nar. khoz. 1972*: 736.
17 *Qazan Utlary*, 1972: 5.
18 *Ibid.*: XI: 142.
19 *Ibid.*: 141.
20 Total population of the Tatar ASSR in 1920 was 2,919,300: one half (1,459,600) were Tatars. Devletchin, 1958: 70.
21 *Qazan Utlary*, 1972: XII: 22.

22 Shabad, 1951.
23 In 1744–1755, in the area of Kazan alone, 418 of 536 mosques with schools were destroyed. *Tarikh'*, 1959: 230.

beyond. Others moved to the lower Volga region in the south. Their situation began to improve after the Pugachev uprising of 1774. Although Pugachev and his armies—consisting mainly of Tatars, Bashkirs, and Chuvash—were eventually defeated, the uprising brought Tatars important religious and economic concessions. A decree in 1788 established the muftiat of Orenburg, giving Islam official status in Russia, and in 1792 Tatars were granted extensive rights in Russia's trade with Turkestan, Iran, and China. Since they spoke a similar language and shared the same religion as their Turkic trading partners, Tatars soon controlled most of Russia's trade with the Moslem East. This period of Tatar-Russian cooperation lasted for more than half a century until the 1860s, when Tatars were subjected to new organized attempts at Christianization and Russification. Tatars responded with local uprisings and manifestations of a still more fanatic adherence to Islam. Some emigrated to Turkey.

At the same time, Russian conquest of Turkestan in the second half of the nineteenth century created a new situation to which Tatars were compelled to adjust. Combined with a growing realization that European education was necessary to win equality with Russians, and with awareness of Turkey's turn toward Europe, this change resulted in an increasing orientation toward Europe and an awakening of Tatar national consciousness. Three Kazan Tatars, Shihabeddin Mardjani (1818–1889), Husseyin Fayeshani (1821–1866), and Qayyum Nasiri (1825–1902) were responsible for early reforms in religion and education. The Paris-educated Crimean Tatar Ismail Bay Gaspiraly (1851–1914), under the motto "Unity of Language, Thought and Action," promoted unity of all Turkic peoples in the Russian Empire and introduction of European methods of education. With the Kazan Tatar Yussuf Aqchura and the Azerbaidzhani Topchybashev, he was instrumental in formation of the "Union of Moslems of Russia" in 1906.

Under the more liberal conditions of early twentieth-century Russia, Tatar political and cultural life progressed rapidly. The Tatar press was by far the most important Turkic press in the empire. Tatar newspapers and journals of various political views—appearing in such national centers as Kazan, Ufa, Orenburg, Astrakhan, Troitsk, and Uralsk—were distributed throughout the empire. In the Moslem struggle for greater personal and political freedom and for social and economic changes, Tatars assumed leadership. Fall of the Russian monarchy in 1917 forced them to reexamine their position within the Russian state and to reassess their political, national, and cultural relations with Petrograd.

In May 1917 a congress of all Moslems of Russia was held in Moscow under the motto of national unity. The congress elected a "free" Mufti (the liberal and progressive Tatar scholar Ghalimdjan Barudi), declared political equality of the sexes, prohibited polygamy, decided to form Moslem national military units, and demanded abolition of private landed property and introduction of the eight-hour working day. The delegates, however, were split on the question of whether Moslem autonomy should be territorial within a federal republic or cultural in a unified but democratic Russian republic. To coordinate joint political action, the congress established the Moslem National Council [*Milli Shura*].

In July 1917 a united Moslem congress convened in Kazan, proclaiming cultural autonomy of the "Moslem Turko-Tatars of Inner Russia and Siberia." It named a national administration headed by the Sorbonne-educated Kazan Tatar Sadri Maqsudi (formerly leader of the Moslem faction in the Russian parliament [*Duma*]). In November this administration convened in Ufa, organizing free multiparty elections to a national parliament of 120 members. On November 29 it declared territorial autonomy of the state of Idel-Ural,[24] which existed until the middle of April 1918 when its National Council and National Assembly were officially dissolved by Bolsheviks. A few days earlier, on March 23, 1918, Bolsheviks issued a decree calling for forma-

---

24 Bashkirs participating in the Moscow congress subsequently held their own congress in Orenburg and, under the leadership of Zeki Velidi Togan, established on August 1, 1917, a "Bashkir Central Council," whose principal task was solution of the land question. On November 29, 1917, Bashkirs proclaimed national autonomy within a "Little Bashkiria," which lasted until February 4, 1918.

tion of a Soviet socialist Tatar-Bashkir republic (Soviet version of the state of Idel-Ural).[25] The decree had considerable political impact, gaining the support of many Tatar-Bashkir intellectuals for the Bolsheviks, but it evoked opposition from practically all Russian Communists in the Volga-Ural region. Its implementation was delayed by outbreak of the civil war, and eventually the decree was rescinded. Idel-Ural was broken up into smaller components. The Bashkir ASSR was established March 23, 1919 (enlarged July 14, 1922); the Tatar ASSR, on June 25, 1920. Formation of two small separate Tatar and Bashkir autonomous republics instead of the promised Soviet socialist Tatar-Bashkir republic undermined the strength of Moslem unity, leaving three quarters of the Tatar population outside the boundaries of the Tatar republic and more Tatars than Bashkirs living in Bashkiristan.[26] Moreover, it relegated the USSR's fifth largest ethnic group to a political-administrative status inferior to that of smaller groups granted union republics.

As a result, Tatar-Bashkir intellectuals who had joined the Bolsheviks in 1917 became disillusioned. Dissatisfaction also spread among leading Tatar-Bashkir Communists. Mirsayit Sultanghaliev[27] began to work, in part with exiled Moslem nationalists, toward establishment of a genuinely autonomous Tatar-Bashkir state. Expelled from the Communist party in 1923, he set

up a clandestine political network aimed at formation of an independent "Federated Peoples Socialist Republic of Turan," which was to comprise Tatars, Bashkirs, the five Central Asian republics (Kazakh, Kirgiz, Uzbek, Turkmen, and Tadjik), and possibly Chuvashia and Azerbaidzhan.[28] Sultanghaliev was eliminated, and during the 1930s purges Tatar-Bashkirs lost virtually their entire intelligentsia.

Tatar-Bashkir national life revived somewhat in the more liberal atmosphere after Stalin's death and particularly after the 20th Party Congress. Publication of many Tatar classical cultural works was allowed, a fact of great importance not only for Tatar literature but for national education and cultural life in general. Percentage of Tatars in key posts and other positions in the administrative apparatus of their republic is approaching their percentage of the population. Tatars also hold important positions in industry and economy. Because they have an autonomous and not a union republic, however, Tatars as a group are more restricted, with fewer rights than those nationality groups possessing union republics. For example, on account of their ASSR status, the 6 million Tatars have only 11 deputies in the Soviet of Nationalities, whereas the 1 million Estonians and 1 million Kirgiz have 32 deputies each.

This paradox has not gone unnoticed by Soviet authorities. A 1966 study in the Tatar ASSR by the Institute for State and Law of the Academy of Sciences[29] called for extension of rights of the Tatar ASSR to correspond with the republic's high cultural and economic level. Some steps have been taken in that direction: for example, the Supreme Soviet of the Tatar ASSR and its executive organs have received a stronger role in management of enterprises and organizations ultimately controlled by higher organs of the RSFSR. State organs of the Tatar ASSR have been granted more rights and privileges in apartment building, culture, consumer goods production, water pollution, and other areas.[30]

---

25 The decree was signed by Stalin and by Mullanur Vakhitov, chairman of the Central Moslem Commissariat, Ghalimdjan Ibrahim and Sherif Manatov, both members of the same commissariat, and Dimanshtein, secretary of People's Commissariat for the Nationalities (see *Tatarstan*, 1925–1926: 239).

26 According to the 1970 census there were 898,092 Bashkirs and 947,986 Tatars in the Bashkir ASSR.

27 Mirsayit Sultanghaliev was highest-placed Moslem in the Communist hierarchy, chairman of the Moslem Commissariat in Kazan, chairman of the Central Moslem Military Soviet and later (in 1920) one of Stalin's primary assistants in the People's Commissariat for Nationalities (NARKOMNATS). He was first Communist leader in history to organize a national Communist movement in his own country and ranks with M. N. Roy in his emphasis on revolutionary primacy of the underdeveloped world. Seton-Watson, 1960: 87. See also section of this chapter on recent manifestations of nationalism.

---

28 The state would have had a population of over 30 million, 75% Turkic Moslems. The attempt ended with his arrest and trial in 1929.

29 *Sovetskoye gosudarstvo i pravo*, 1967: 4.

30 *Tatarstan Kommunisty*, 1972: XI: 16.

Table 16.1

Distribution of Tatars in USSR 1959–1970

TERRITORY	1959		1970		
	Tatar Population (in thousands)	% of All Tatars	Tatar Population (in thousands)	% of All Tatars	% Increase 1959–1970
RSFSR, total	4,075	82.0	4,758	80.2	16.8
Tatar ASSR	1,345	27.1	1,536	25.9	14.2
Bashkir ASSR	769	15.5	945	15.9	22.9
Central Asia	588	11.8	750	12.7	27.6
Kazakh SSR	192	3.9	288	4.9	50.0
Other Republics	113	2.3	135	2.2	19.5
Total	4,968	100.0	5,931	100.0	19.4

Source: *Itogi 1970*: IV: 9, 12–17, 329.

DEMOGRAPHY

According to the 1970 census there were 5,931,000 Tatars in the USSR in that year,[31] an increase of 19.4% over 1959. Their distribution in the USSR and rates of growth since 1959 are summarized in Table 16.1. Total population of the Tatar ASSR in 1970 was 3,131,000, an increase of about 9.9% over the 1959 total. The Tatar population increased considerably faster (14.2%) and its share of the republic's total population increased from 47% to 49%.

The balance between the two principal ethnic groups in the Tatar ASSR (Tatars and Russians) has remained quite stable ever since the republic was established, as Table 16.2 shows.

Fifty-three percent of the population of the Tatar ASSR lived in urban areas in 1970, but only 38.6% of Tatars in the republic did so. They constituted 36% of total urban population, a slight increase over 1959. According to the Bureau of Statistics of the Tatar ASSR, the percentage of Tatars in such major cities as Kazan (33.2%),[32] Almat (43.6%), and Minzele (35.9%)[33]

Table 16.2

Tatars and Russians in Tatar ASSR

(% of Total Population)

YEAR	% TATAR	% RUSSIAN
1920	50.0	N.A.
1924	51.1	40.9
1926	45.0	43.0
1939	50.4	41.8
1956	49.0	43.0
1959	47.0	43.9
1970	49.0	42.4

Source: *Dergi*, 1958: XIV: 70.

remained virtually unchanged from 1959 to 1968.[34]

In 1970 proportion of Tatars in the Bashkir ASSR was 24.7% or 947,986, up from 23.3% or 768,566 in 1959.[35] Together, Tatar-Bashkirs made up 48.1% of the republic's total population, up from 45% in 1959.[36] In 1970, 25.9% of Tatars and 72%

---

31 Neither 1959 nor 1970 census distinguishes between Kazan and Crimean Tatars.

32 Up from 19.4% in 1924. *Bish yil echende Tatarstan*, 1925–1926: 233–234.

33 In comparison, Uzbeks make up 33.8% in Tashkent, Kirgiz are 9.4% in Frunze, and Turkmen 29.8% in Ashkhabad. *Sovetskaya etnografiya*, 1967: 5.

34 *Sovetskaya etnografiya*, 1970: III: 6.

35 *Ibid.*, 1972: VI: 40.

36 In 1970 Russians made up 40.5% (down 1.9% from 1959) of total population of the Bashkir ASSR. The remaining 11.3% consisted of Chuvash (126,638), Mari (109,638), Ukrainians (76,005), Mordvinians (40,745), Udmurts (27,918), Belorussians (17,985), and others. *Itogi 1970*: IV: 131.

of Bashkirs lived in their respective republics.[37] Approximately 70% of Tatar-Bashkirs
lived within the borders of Idel-Ural as proclaimed in 1917. Outside their historical
borders, but within the RSFSR, Tatars live in
large numbers in and around Moscow
(158,500 in 1970) and Leningrad (38,250
in 1970).[38] In Siberia there were approximately 350,000 to 400,000 Tatars in 1970.[39]

Of Tatars in Central Asia, 574,000, or
more than half (up 29% since 1959), live
in Uzbekistan, where they are concentrated
mainly in and around Tashkent, Samarkand, Andijan, and Ferghana. In 1959, 65%
of Tatars in Uzbekistan lived in urban areas.
In Kazakhstan, Tatars numbered 284,000 in
1970 (up 50% since 1959), mostly in the
"virgin lands" region and in the south. Two
thirds of Tatars in Kazakhstan live in the
cities. In the Kirgiz SSR most of the 69,000
Tatars live in and around Osh. The number
of Tatars in Turkmenistan is small: 36,000
(up 20% since 1959), 87% living in and
around the cities. In Tadzhikistan, in 1970,
Tatars numbered 71,000 (up 24.5% since
1959); 75% live in urban areas.[40]

As of November 16, 1970, 109,200 Tatars
with higher education and 173,500 with
specialized secondary education were employed in the national economy. At the end
of 1970 there were 11,617 Tatars listed as
scientific workers.[41]

Data available for pre-war years indicate
that Tatar party representation tended to
be noticeably lower than the Tatar share of
population. After World War II, however,
Tatar party membership rose more rapidly
and on January 1, 1974, was only 5.6%
short of their percentage of the republic's
total population, as the following figures
show:

	TATARS IN POPULATION	TATARS IN PARTY	
	%	%[43]	Number[44]
1922		19.8	
1926	48.3[42]		
1927		32.4	
1930		36.3	
1946		37.2	20,309
1959		40.0	40,000
1970	49.0		
1974		43.4	82,230

Chairman of the Presidium of the Supreme Soviet, Tatar ASSR (Salikh Batyev),
chairman and vice chairman of the Soviet of
Ministers, Tatar ASSR (Ghabdulkhaq
Abdrazyaqov and Khasanov), and first
secretary of Tataristan Oblast Committee,
Communist party, USSR (Fikret Tabeyev),
are Tatars. In the Bashkir ASSR positions of
chairman of the Presidium, Supreme Soviet
(Fayezrahman Zaghafuranov), and vice
chairman, Soviet of Ministers (Ghabbas
Shafiqov), are held by Bashkirs. Of 61
delegates[45] from the Tatar ASSR participating in the 23rd Party Congress in 1966, 29
were Tatars; of 60 delegates from the Bashkir ASSR 34 were Tatar-Bashkirs.[46] The
report on the 24th Party Congress (1971)
does not indicate delegates' home territories.

In 1959 labor unions in Tataristan had a
total of 672,000 members; by 1966 membership had grown to 915,000.[47]

CULTURE

Tatars have a rich written heritage in the
Tatar language, which has roots in the ancient common Turkic literature and was
molded and developed under the all-per-
vading influence of Islam until well into the
nineteenth century. Despite the enormous
importance of religion, however, Tatar poets
were also greatly attracted by legends and

37 *Sovetskaya etnografiya*, 1972: VI: 40.
38 Practically all Bashkirs live within the historical
borders of Idel-Ural.
39 Excluding those west Siberian territories falling
within the borders of Idel-Ural.
40 *Itogi 1970*: IV: 202, 223, 284, 295, 306.
41 *Nar. obraz.*, 1971: 240, 270.
42 Data from Rigby, 1968: 369.
43 Data for 1922, 1927, 1930 from Rigby, 1968: 369;
for 1946 and 1974 from *Tatarstan Kommunisty*,
1974: II: 38; for 1959 from *Tatarstan ASSR Tarikhy*,
1970: 620.
44 Data for 1946 and 1974 from *Tatarstan Kommunisty*, 1974: II: 38; for 1959 from *Tatarstan
ASSR Tarikhy*, 1970: 620.
45 According to *Tatarstan ASSR Tarikhy*, the Tatar
ASSR sent 64 delegates (see p. 654), but the "Stenographic Report of the 23rd Congress of the Communist Party of the USSR" (Moscow, 1966:
389–623) lists names of only 61 delegates.
46 "Stenographic Report of the 23rd Party Congress": 389–623.
47 *Tatarstan ASSR Tarikhy*, 1970. No ethnic breakdown given.

themes of romantic love. Furthermore, early Tatar literature mirrored historical and social events, national customs, and traditions. By the nineteenth century traditional Islamic forms were subjected to the modernizing influence of Turkish reform movements and Russian and Western European writing with which Tatar intellectuals were familiar. This introduced new types of Tatar prose—novels, novellas, dramas, and comedies.

In the later nineteenth century, literature became important in the struggle for cultural and social reforms and for spreading new ideas. Educational reforms, oppression of Moslems in Russia, emancipation of Tatar women, and the fight against religious fanaticism were among topics treated in the literature of that period.

After the revolution of 1905 a group of liberal democratic writers[48] emerged. Working under the comparative freedom prevailing until 1917–1918, they lifted Tatar literature to new heights which—except perhaps for the first 10 to 15 years after the Bolshevik revolution—have not since been equaled. This period is generally referred to as the "golden age" of classical Tatar literature. Major issues raised in works of this period were: hard life of workers, peasants, and rural poor; education of the young generation; national aspirations of the Tatar people; love for Tatar homeland and language; anti-Tatar discrimination among Russians; and role of youth in the revolution. When the Bolshevik revolution came, Tatar literature had firmly established itself as an effective vehicle for realization of social, political, and national-cultural aspirations.

Up to creation of the two separate Tatar and Bashkir republics, Tatar was the common literature for Tatars and Bashkirs. No distinction was made between Tatar and Bashkir writers, both using the Tatar literary language, but the Bolsheviks set about creating a separate Bashkir literature based on the Bashkir dialect. Until the late 1920s

Tatar literature had been comparatively unrestricted, and the ranks of prerevolutionary writers were swelled by many new writers of the younger generation.[49] Important topics included prerevolutionary times, the revolution and civil war, conflict between old and new, birth of a new life and a new man, formation of a new moral order.

Stalin's more repressive nationality policy initiated a tragic chapter in Tatar life and literature. In the process Tatars lost almost all political leaders, and only a handful of writers survived the disaster.[50] After Stalin's death Tatar literature began to revive, especially after the 20th Congress of the CPSU. Practically all of the previously arrested and "convicted" Tatar writers were rehabilitated (most posthumously) and many of their works republished. Literature received further stimulus in 1963–1964 and has since managed to produce some impressive works, reflecting concern for human problems and issues as well as love for the homeland, mother tongue, culture, and history. They are often remarkably candid in presentation and criticism of existing social and national conditions. Tatar literature showed remarkable resilience, recovering much of its old vigor and aggressiveness.[51]

Tatar dramas first appeared in the late 1800s. Due to conservatism of the Moslem clergy and Tatar society, however, performances were held in private homes. The first public theater performance, also marking official establishment of the Tatar theater, took place in Kazan in 1906. Tatar theaters opened in Ufa, Orenburg, Astrakhan, Uralsk, and other cities soon thereafter. Repertory companies began to travel all over the country, performing even in Siberia and Central Asia. Until the Bolshevik revolution, repertoire consisted mainly of comedies and dramas written by such renowned Tatar playwrights as Ghaliasghar Kamal (1879–1933), regarded as the father of Tatar theater, Karim Tinchurin

---

48 These included Ghabdulla Tuqay, Madjit Ghafuri, Ghaliasghar Kamal, Sharif Kamal, Fatih Amirhan, Ghalimdjan Ibrahim, Fathi Burnash, F. Sayfi Qazanly, Karim Tinchurin, Ghayaz Ishaqi, Mirkhaydar Fayzi, Saghit Soncheley, Derdemend, Saghit Remi, Shaykhzade Babich, and others.

49 For example: Shamil Usman, Naqi Isanbat, Qavi Nadjmi, Hassan Tufan, Tadji Ghizzat, Ghomar Bashir, Hadi Taqtash, Shaykhi Manur, Ghumir Tolymbay, Ghadel Qutuy, Ghabdrahman Minski, Riza Ishmorat, Mirsay Amir, Amirhan Yeniki, Fatih Husni, and others.
50 Bashir, 1965: II: 363.
51 Burbiel, 1969: 40–46.

(1887–1947), Fatih Amirhan (1866–1926), Ghayaz Ishaqi (1878–1954), and Mirhaydar Fayzi (1891–1928). Tatar translations of Russian and West European plays were also included. The first Tatar musical was shown in 1916–1917 and the first opera in 1925. During the 1920s theaters also presented numerous satirical plays mocking both old-fashioned bourgeoisie and Bolsheviks.

During the 1930s purges Tatars lost practically all prerevolutionary writers, and the theater declined sharply. Until the 1956 20th Party Congress its repertoire consisted, with certain exceptions, of poorly written and rather primitive propaganda plays. Subsequent rehabilitation and return to the people of a large part of their literary heritage, as well as relaxation in party control over literature and art, gave new life to the Tatar theater. Today, theater repertoires comprise both modern plays and prerevolutionary classics, as well as Russian and foreign dramas, comedies, and operas in Tatar translation.[52]

As direct heirs to the culture of the Bolgar state (9th–12th centuries) bequeathed by Moslem ancestors, Bolgars, and other Qypchaq tribes, Tatars have traditionally been part of the Islamic world. For centuries Islam has played a tremendous role in social, economic, political, cultural, and spiritual development. Continued deep adherence to the principles and spiritual values of Islam enabled Tatars to resist attempts at Christianization by Russian neighbors and this tradition limits the success of Russification today.

Awakening of Tatar national consciousness in the second half of the nineteenth century and steady growth of Turko-Tatar nationalism (Turkism) after the revolution of 1905 led to reform and modernization in Islam without, however, diminishing its importance in Tatar life. Until after the Bolshevik revolution, Islam formed the roof under which Moslems of Russia rallied in efforts to unite and coordinate their political and cultural actions.

Today Moslems of the Volga-Ural area and Siberia (mostly Tatar-Bashkirs) are under jurisdiction of the Spiritual Director-ate for the Sunni Moslems of European Russia and Siberia, with headquarters in Ufa, Bashkir ASSR.[53] Data showing exact strength of Islam in territories administered by this directorate are unavailable. Two studies published in 1970 and 1971, however, show that adherence to Islam or Islamic practices among Tatars living in rural areas of the Tatar ASSR is strong. According to the 1971 study,[54] one fifth of Tatar men and more than a third of Tatar women (average for both sexes 30.4%) questioned believe in Islam, while approximately another fifth were undecided. Furthermore, more than half (50.9%) favored circumcision and about two fifths (39.9%) said they celebrated Moslem holidays. Also, the study showed how the Moslem clergy, by presenting religious rites as part of the national heritage, wins the undecided over to Islam.

The other study, published in 1970,[55] showed an even higher percentage of Tatars celebrating such Moslem holidays as *Qurban Bayram* and *Ramadan* and favoring circumcision, particularly when questioned by Tatar interviewers. The following data are from the 1970 study:

	NATIONALITY OF INTERVIEWER	
	Tatar	*Russian*
Celebrate Moslem holidays	44%	34%
Don't celebrate	24	41
Indifferent	28	—
Difficult to answer	4	25
Favor circumcision	59	45
Against circumcision	11	18
Difficult to answer	20	5
No answer	10	32

EXTERNAL RELATIONS

Tatars and Bashkirs are part of the large family of Turkic peoples inhabiting a broad belt of territories stretching from Chinese Turkestan (Sinkiang) and Mongolia in the

---

52 Nurullin, 1966; see also publications of Ghaliasghar Kamal Tatar State Academy Theater, Kazan, 1970.

53 There are three more directorates: one for Central Asia and Kazakhstan, one for the north Caucasus, and a third for Transcaucasia.
54 *Sovetskaya etnografiya*, 1971: 1.
55 *Ibid.*, 1970: 2.

east, across Central Asia and portions of Siberia, to the middle Volga basin, the eastern Caucasus, and the eastern Mediterranean in the west. These people number about 75 million, approximately 33 million living in the Soviet Union. Occupying the northwestern corner of this huge area, the Tatar-Bashkirs have since early times had contact with Finno-Ugric and Slavic peoples dwelling among them or in territories adjoining their western borders.

After loss of independence to the Russians, Tatar-Bashkir relations with the latter remained generally strained, though there were periods of cooperation. An enterprising people, Tatars developed a fairly strong merchant class which established close trade relations with other Turkic peoples in Central Asia. Cultural ties between the Tatar-Bashkirs and other Turkic peoples had, of course, existed for centuries and, with the Tatar national and cultural renaissance in the second half of the nineteenth century, and especially after the revolution of 1905, Kazan became the most dynamic enlightened Turko-Tatar center in Russia. With pan-Turkism as political ideal, Tatars sought to unite all Turkic peoples of Russia into one nation. Kazan reformers maintained strong cultural relations with liberal circles in Ottoman Turkey. Turkish, they thought, should become common language of the united Turkic peoples of Russia. Turkey was viewed as the home of all Turks, and many Tatars went there to study or take up permanent residence.[56] During World War I most Tatar-Bashkirs sympathized with Turkey and hoped for a victory for Russia's enemies. After the Bolshevik takeover, many prominent Tatar-Bashkirs and other Turkic intellectuals found a haven in Turkey. However, the pan-Turkic idea was also pursued by Tatar Communists who, under the leadership of Sultanghaliev, tried to establish a Socialist People's Republic of Turan. According to Soviet historians, Sultanghaliev's underground organization maintained close relations with Basmachis in Turkestan and émigré circles in Turkey and Germany.[57]

As part of a general policy of discouraging integration of Turkic peoples into one nation, Bolsheviks for more than 30 years kept them isolated from each other and from the outside world. This isolation ended for Central Asian Moslems when, after rapprochement of the Soviet Union with the Asian and African world, their usefulness for foreign policy became apparent to Moscow. Tatars were kept isolated for a much longer time. (Kazan was opened to foreign tourists only in the late 1960s.) With relaxation of this policy, Tatar-Bashkirs and other Turkic peoples of the USSR began to reestablish mutual relations.[58]

Turkish cultural festivals were organized and the study of Turkic culture intensified. In Central Asia, Moscow, Leningrad, and other surrounding regions, Tatars again became active in matters concerning their original homeland (Idel-Ural). The desire was expressed to establish stronger cultural ties with both Tatar and Bashkir republics.

Tatar writers and officials are now permitted to travel abroad, and several have published travelogues in the journal *Qazan Utlary*. The minister of education of the Tatar ASSR, Mirza Makhmutov, traveled to Chile in 1971 to acquaint himself with the school system in that country.[59] The literary critic Rafael Mostafin made a trip to Syria, North Korea, and Singapore in 1970 and to East Germany in 1971.[60] The well-known writer Ayaz Ghiladjev traveled in Turkey as member of a Tataristan tourist delegation.[61] Other countries visited by Tatars within the last six years were Egypt, Iraq, India, Nepal, Turkey, Greece, Italy, France, England, Denmark, Sweden, and the United States.

Tatar emigration is directed mainly toward Turkey, the United States, and Finland. In Turkey there are several thousand Kazan Tatars. The Kazan Tatar Culture and Relief Society publishes a 64-page cultural and literary magazine called *Kazan*, appearing in Istanbul once every 3 months. The journal is in Turkish, but examples of Tatar literature are usually given in Tatar with Turkish translation.

In the United States there are about

---

56 Traditionally, Turkish policy has permitted any Turkish immigrant to become a citizen of Turkey immediately on the basis of ethnic and linguistic kinship.

57 Bennigsen and Lemercier-Quelquejay, 1967: 184.

58 See *Qazan Utlary*, 1966, and the Bashkir literary magazine *Aghidel* of the same year.

59 *Qazan Utlary*, 1972: 2.

60 *Ibid.*, 1971: 2, 3, 4; 1972: 4.

61 *Ibid.*, 1970: 8.

1,500 to 2,000 Tatars, most living in New York and San Francisco. They have no community organ.

In Finland Tatars are settled mainly in Helsinki and Tampere. Community organ is *Mahalle Heberlere* [*Community News*], published in Tatar with the Arabic alphabet.

Unlike Tatars in Turkey or the United States, the Tatar community in Finland maintains cultural relations with Tataristan, and artists and scholars from the Tatar ASSR have given concerts and lectures in Tatar communities in Helsinki and Tampere.[62]

Media

LANGUAGE DATA

Both Tatar and Bashkir belong to the northwestern, or Qypchaq, group of Turkic languages. The difference between Tatar and Bashkir is basically phonetic; vocabulary and grammar are similar. Kazakh and Kirgiz also belong in the Qypchaq group. While these latter two languages are closely related to one another, however, they differ from Tatar and Bashkir languages in phonetics, grammar, and vocabulary. A Tatar-speaking person cannot readily understand Kazakh without special study. Although it does not belong to the Qypchaq group, Uzbek is closer to Tatar than is Kazakh.

Until the late 1920s both Tatars and Bashkirs used the Arabic alphabet which their ancestors, the Volga Bolgars, had used since the ninth century.[63] In 1927 the Arabic alphabet was officially (against strong opposition) replaced by the Latin alphabet.[64] Twelve years later, in 1939–1940, in line with Soviet nationality policy toward Russification, the Latin alphabet was in turn replaced by a modified Cyrillic alphabet.[65] This last alphabet change gave the Soviets a convenient opportunity to reprint, in the new Cyrillic alphabet, only those works they considered acceptable, relegating all others to oblivion.

In 1970,[66] 89.2% (down almost 2% since

1959[67]) of Soviet Tatars considered Tatar their mother tongue. The rest indicated Russian, Bashkir, Kazakh, Uzbek and, to a lesser extent, other languages. Percentage of Tatars claiming Tatar as first language varies from more than 98% in the Tatar ASSR to 71% in Leningrad, and it is still lower among smaller groups of Tatars living in the Soviet Far East.[68] Almost two thirds (62.5%) of Tatars in the USSR are fluent in Russian. As would be expected, this percentage is lower in the Tatar ASSR, especially in rural areas, and higher in areas where Tatars live in a more or less totally Russian environment.

In 1969 the percentage of Tatars in rural areas of the Tatar ASSR who had a command of the Russian language (degree not indicated) was as follows:[69]

AGE	COMMAND OF RUSSIAN
16–17	25.0%
18–22	27.9
23–27	31.6
28–34	23.8
35–49	16.5
50–59	11.8
60 and over	5.6

---

62 *Ibid.*, 1969: IX: 192.
63 Qurbatov, 1960: 25.
64 *Ibid.*: 77.
65 *Ibid.*: 105.
66 *Itogi 1970*: IV: 20.

67 *Sovetskaya etnografiya*, 1972: VI: 44, quoting the same census, gives 93.6% for 1959 and 90.5% for 1970.
68 *Itogi 1970*: IV: 70, 74, 77. See also section of this chapter on factors forming national attitudes.
69 *Voprosy filosofii*, 1969: 12. Cf. *Itogi 1970*: IV: 144, 370. Data are given there separately for urban and rural Tatars in the Tatar ASSR, and separately for all Tatars by age. No data are available for urban Tatars by age.

Table 16.3

Native and Second Languages Spoken by Tatars
(in thousands)

NO. TATARS RESIDING			SPEAKING AS NATIVE LANGUAGE						SPEAKING AS SECOND LANGUAGE[a]	
			Tatar			Russian			Russian	Other Languages of Peoples of USSR
	1959	1970	1959	1970	% Point Change 1959–1970	1959	1970	% Point Change 1959–1970	1970	1970
in Tatar ASSR	1,345 (100%)	1,536 (100%)	1,330 (98.9%)	1,513 (98.5%)	−0.4	15 (1.1%)	23 (1.5%)	+0.4	841 (54.8%)	2 (0.1%)
elsewhere in USSR	3,623 (100%)	4,395 (100%)	3,243 (89.5%)	3,776 (85.9%)	−3.6	334 (9.2%)	585 (13.3%)	+4.1	2,868 (65.3%)	92 (2.1%)
Total	4,968 (100%)	5,931 (100%)	4,573 (92.0%)	5,289 (89.2%)	−2.8	349 (7.0%)	608 (10.3%)	+3.3	3,709 (62.5%)	94 (1.6%)

Sources: *Itogi 1959* and *Itogi RSFSR 1959*: tables 53, 54; *Itogi 1970*: IV: 20, 144

[a] No data are available for 1959, since no questions regarding command of a second language were asked in the 1959 census.

Tatar is also the mother tongue of approximately one third of the Bashkir population.[70]

LOCAL MEDIA

According to the Tatar journal *Azat Khatyn* [*Free Woman*], a total of 121 newspapers and 11 journals were published in the Tatar ASSR in 1970.[71] These figures include local and *kolkhoz* publications. *Qazan Utlary* lists five republican and 71 district newspapers and eight journals for 1966.[72] But the *Letopis' Periodicheskikh Izdanii SSSR 1961–1965* [*Chronicle of Periodical Publications of USSR 1961–1965*] lists 90 newspapers, 6 republican, 22 city, and the rest district papers.[73] Seventy-eight newspaper editions in all languages (excluding local and *kolkhoz* papers) with combined circulation of 860,000 (up from 801,000 in 1970) and 11 journals with total circulation (usually monthly) of 948,000 appeared in the Tatar ASSR in 1971.[74] According to the same source, total number of Tatar language newspapers appearing inside and outside the Tatar ASSR in 1971 was 81 with total circulation of 731,000 (up from 77 newspapers with total circulation 703,000 in 1970).[75]

Of Tatar language newspapers appearing inside the Tatar ASSR, the following are republican:

Soviet Tatarstany [*Soviet Tataristan*], with circulation of 131,000 in 1970,[76] organ of Tatar *Oblast'* Committee, CPSU, since April 13, 1917.

Sotsialistik Tatarstan [*Socialist Tataristan*], also organ of the Tatar *Oblast'* Committee, CPSU, with circulation of 150,000 in 1972.[77]

Tatarstan Jashlere [*Tatar Youth*], Komsomol organ, present circulation unknown.

Jash Lenenche [*Young Leninist*], organ of the Pioneers.

All newspapers with a republic-wide circulation are published in the capital city of Kazan. Tatar language newspapers also appear in the cities of Almat, Bogelma, Buinsk, Jelabuga, Zelenogorsk, Leninogorsk, Tetyush, and Chistay; these, however, are not distributed widely and have primarily local readerships.[78]

Most important Tatar newspaper outside the Tatar ASSR is *Qyzyl Tang* [*Red Dawn*]. This paper, published in Ufa, is also a party organ with a circulation approximately that of *Sotsialistik Tatarstan*.

By far the most significant Tatar journal is *Quzan Utlary* [*Lights of Kazan*][79] It is a monthly literary and sociopolitical journal, organ of the Tataristan Union of Writers. Since the mid–1950s the journal has followed a consistent liberal line and its monthly circulation has grown from 6,000 in 1957 to nearly 90,000 in 1972. It enjoys great popularity among Tatar readers inside and outside the Tatar ASSR as well as among Tatar-Bashkir intelligentsia, peasants, workers, and members of the armed services.

Other important journals include:

Azat Khatyn [*Free Woman*], illustrated sociopolitical and literary journal for women. It has appeared since 1926; in November 1972 circulation was 303,500.

---

70 The 1970 census is not clear on this point. Indicating that 66.2% of Bashkirs in the USSR considered Bashkir as their mother tongue, the census gives no complete information on mother language of the remaining 33.8% of Bashkirs. For the Bashkir ASSR the census gives these figures: of 892,248 Bashkirs in the BASSR, 563,702 or 63.2% indicated Bashkir, 13,422 or 1.5% Russian, 315,124 or 35.4% "other languages" as their mother tongue. According to the 1959 census, 344,556, or 36.1% of the then 953,801 Bashkirs in the USSR indicated Tatar as mother tongue. *Itogi 1970*: 9, 131; *Itogi 1959*: 300, 302.

71 *Azat Khatyn*, 1970: 7. Divergencies between figures in the text and the media tables in this section reflect differences in inclusion (e.g., with or without *kolkhoz* papers), sources, and dates.

72 *Qazan Utlary*, 1966: XI: 93.

73 *Letopis' periodicheskikh izdanii SSSR 1961–1965* (Moscow, 1967): II: 313–326.

74 *Pechat' 1971*: 184, 154. These figures do not include local or kolkhoz newspapers.

75 *Ibid.*, 69. These figures include local newspapers and exclude only kolkhoz newspapers.

76 *Sovet Mektebe* [*Soviet School*], 1970: XII: 30.

77 *Tatar Calendar*, 1972.

78 *Sovet Mektebe*, 1972: XI: 62.

79 From 1932–1965 it appeared under the name *Soviet Adabiaty* [*Soviet Literature*].

Sovet Mektebe [*Soviet School*], organ of Ministry of Education of the Tatar ASSR. In November 1972 circulation was 21,646.

Yalqyn [*Flame*], monthly organ of the Tataristan Pioneers, with circulation of 71,346 in 1970.

Tatarstan Kommunisty [*Communist of Tataristan*], organ of the Tatar *Oblast'* Committee, CPSU. In Tatar it had a circulation of 17,246 in November 1972, while in Russian its circulation was roughly comparable (17,854 in November 1972).

Chayan [*Scorpion*], official satirical journal, appearing twice monthly. In June 1972 circulation was 240,500 (up from 40,000 in November 1966).

Idel [*Volga*], almanac for young writers and readers. Its publication began in connection with the fiftieth anniversary of the Tatar ASSR in 1970.[80]

Export abroad of Tatar and Bashkir newspapers is prohibited, but most journals can be obtained through subscription.

In 1971, 583 books and booklets were published in the Tatar ASSR, with total circulation of 7,472,000.[81] In the USSR, 302, with total circulation of 4,538,000, were in Tatar (up from 195 books and booklets with an edition of 2,891,000 in 1970).[82]

A considerable portion of the Tatar-Bashkir literary heritage remains "taboo" (it is not republished). Also taboo are all works of Tatar-Bashkirs who have emigrated abroad. Those classics whose republication is permitted are chronically out of print. Often reprints appear in intervals of 10 years or more. Contemporary novels are also hard to get because their editions are usually small.[83] The reason for this is Moscow's publishing policy, highly discriminatory in that it is guided not by a nation's size, cultural, and educational level or needs but solely by its political-administrative status—as a union or autonomous republic, for example. Consequently, 6 million Tatars and approximately 400,000 Bashkirs who consider Tatar their mother tongue, although they constitute the fifth largest ethnic group in the USSR, are allotted lower publishing quotas than the smaller nationalities in union republics. Thus, by contrast, in 1971, 817 books and booklets with total circulation of 9,922,000 copies were published in Azeri for 4,380,000 Azerbaidzhanis, and 657 titles with 13,189,000 copies in Kazakh for 5.3 million Kazakhs.[84]

In 1970 there were 900,000 radio sets and wired loudspeakers (no breakdown available) in the Tatar ASSR.[85] Broadcasts are in Tatar and Russian (no breakdown available). Number of television sets in that year totaled 300,000.[86] There are two daily programs in Russian and Tatar (again, no breakdown available).[87] The republic has a motion picture studio and (in 1972) 2,500 movie theaters (see section on cultural institutions).

Foreign press organs (mostly Communist ones) are quoted in the Tatar press, but news items are usually classified by capitals of countries from which the news has been received. Only foreign radio station broadcasting in Tatar is Radio Liberty; its Tatar program totals 4 hours per day at present.

Foreign films are shown in the Tatar ASSR. In fact, in 1966 almost a quarter of all films shown in the republic were from countries of the "socialist camp," and 66% were Soviet (Russian and films from other union republics).[88] Presumably, the rest (9.2%) were from nonsocialist countries.

A study conducted by the Institute of Ethnography, Academy of Sciences, USSR, on the subject of social-ethnic aspects of rural culture in the Tatar ASSR reveals that among the rural population radio is most widespread means of mass communication.[89] Tatars listen to the Tatar language radio programs from Kazan because they understand them. The local radio not only

---

80 For a time it seemed as though the first issue would also be the last, but two years later the second issue appeared.

81 *Pechat'* 1971: 80.

82 *Ibid.*: 11. Of 302 Tatar books and booklets, 132 were belles-lettres and 106 titles were translations into Tatar (total edition 2,058,000; up from 84 translated titles with an edition of 1,287,000 in 1970).

83 The three-volume *Selected Works* by Fatih Husni, for years the most popular Tatar novelist, appeared in 1966–68 with an edition of 14,000 copies for each of the first two volumes, 12,000 for the third.

84 *Pechat'* 1971: 10.

85 *Azat Khatyn*, 1970: VI: 7.

86 *Ibid.*

87 *Sovet Mektebe*, 1970: XII: 29.

88 *Qazan Utlary*, 1966: XI: 93.

89 *Sovetskaya etnografiya*, 1971: I: 3–13.

Table 16.4

Publications in Tatar ASSR and in Tatar Language in USSR

Language of Publication	Year	NEWSPAPERS			MAGAZINES			BOOKS & BROCHURES		
		No.	Per Issue Circulation (1,000)	Copies/100 in Language Group[c]	No.	Per Issue Circulation (1,000)	Copies/100 in Language Group[c]	No. Titles	Total Volume (1,000)	Books & Brochures/100 in Language Group[c]
Russian	1959	N.A.	N.A.	N.A.	N.A.	N.A.	N.A.	N.A.	N.A.	N.A.
	1970	N.A.	N.A.	N.A.	N.A.	N.A.	N.A.	N.A.	N.A.	N.A.
Tatar[a]	1959	87	263	6.9	8	97	2.5	353	4,149	108.72
	1970	77	703	13.3	6	533	10.1	195	2,891	54.7
	1971	81	731	N.A.	10	742	N.A.	302	4,538	N.A.
Minority languages	1959	N.A.	N.A.	N.A.	N.A.	N.A.	N.A.	N.A.	N.A.	N.A.
	1970	N.A.	N.A.	N.A.	N.A.	N.A.	N.A.	N.A.	N.A.	N.A.
Foreign languages	1959	N.A.	N.A.	N.A.	N.A.	N.A.	N.A.	N.A.	N.A.	N.A.
	1970	N.A.	N.A.	N.A.	N.A.	N.A.	N.A.	N.A.	N.A.	N.A.
All languages[b]	1959	105	366	12.8	N.A.	N.A.	N.A.	609	6,158	216.1
	1970	78	801	25.6	11	653	20.9	441	4,619	147.5
	1971	78	860	N.A.	11	948	N.A.	583	7,472	N.A.

Sources: *Pechat' 1959:* 37, 61, 133, 160, 163; *Pechat' 1970:* 11, 60, 69, 80, 154, 184; *Pechat' 1971:* 11, 60, 69, 80, 184. Data for Tatars are scarce since they are not included in the tables of union republic nationalities See text for data from other sources.   [a] Figures for Tatar language include all Tatar language books, journals, and newspapers published in the USSR;   [b] Tatar ASSR only.   [c] Includes all native speakers of the language. separate data on Tatar ASSR not available.

Table 16.5

Electronic Media and Films in Tatar ASSR

YEAR	RADIO					TELEVISION			MOVIES	
	No. Stations	No. Wired Sets (1,000)	Sets/100 Population	No. Wireless Sets (1,000)	Sets/100 Population	No. Stations	No. sets (1,000)	Sets/100 Population	Theaters[d]	Attendance/100 Population
1960	N.A.	371.4[a]	13.0[e]	N.A.	N.A.	N.A.	N.A.	N.A.	1,329	1,408
1965	N.A.	381.4[a]	12.4[f]	N.A.	N.A.	N.A.	N.A.	N.A.	2,075	1,686
1969	N.A.	397.8[a]	12.7	(500)[b]	16.0	N.A.	300[c]	9.6	2,348	1,778

[a] *TsSU RSFSR, 50 let Tatarskoi ASSR*, 1970: 109.
[b] Estimate. See text.
[c] 1970. See text.
[d] Theaters and mobile screening units.
[e] Population figures for 1959.
[f] Population figures for 1966.

satisfies interest in local news but also meets the need for national music. Almost all requests for musical radio programs made by Tatars living in villages are for Tatar national music. This interest is especially noticeable among the rural intelligentsia, whose letters always contain such requests. Besides the interest in traditional folk music, there is also a great interest in contemporary music.

According to the same study, 58% of Tatars and 48% of Russians in the Tatar ASSR read newspapers regularly. Records of subscriptions to periodicals as of January 1, 1969, show that 790 persons per 1,000 subscribed in Tatar districts while in Russian districts the ratio was 610/1,000. Tatars are especially interested in the republican press, that is, in Tatar language publications.

The same source indicated that while Russians read only books published in their own language, 63.9% of Tatar readers read books solely in Tatar. About one quarter of readers in the Tatar ASSR read both Tatar and Russian, and 11.1% Russian only. Workers read mostly books in the Tatar language only; the intelligentsia generally reads both Tatar and Russian. Tatars appear to go to the movies somewhat more frequently than do Russians. If films deal with Tatar national themes, the audience is usually only Tatar.

More than 10% of Tatars and 17.7% of Russians watch television. Languages of television broadcasts were not indicated in the source.[90]

EDUCATIONAL INSTITUTIONS

Until 1918 the Tatar educational system was closely tied to religious institutions. It included both primary schools [mekteps] and schools of higher learning [medreses], both under the administration of Moslem clergy. Tsarist colonial policy froze any prospect for development of this system and was also responsible for destruction of a considerable number of mosques along with their schools. With the Tatar cultural renaissance of the late 1800s, school modernization became a central issue of national life. After the 1905 revolution, school reform and building of new schools progressed rapidly. In 1911 there were 1,822 mekteps and medreses (with 132,000 pupils) in the school district of Kazan. In the district of Ufa there were 1,500 mekteps and medreses with 53,000 pupils.[91]

Large medreses existed in Kazan, Ufa, Orenburg, Troitsk, and several major villages in 1911. The Muhammediye medrese, built in Kazan in 1901 by Ghalimdjan Barudi, a progressive religious leader and later mufti of Orenburg, became well known among Moslems of Russia. Its curriculum comprised Koran science, Hadith [prophetic tradition relating to acts and utterances of Mohammed and associates], Islamic history, Arabic language and literature, Turkish language and literature, Russian, natural science, artihmetic, and geography. The medreses in Kazan attracted students from all over Moslem Russia.[92] By the time of the Bolshevik revolution most young Tatar men and women were literate.[93] Achievements in the field of education are especially impressive since the Russian state did not allocate financial support for Moslem schools. Tatar schools were usually established by progressive clergy, rich merchants and industrialists, and voluntary contributions.

Reorganization of the educational system began in 1918. In the course of the Tatarization [korenizatsiya] decreed in 1921, the Tatar language was given official status in Tataristan and a number of institutions of higher learning (among them the Society for Tatar Studies) were established. In 1930–1931, more than 96% of all Tatar children were receiving their entire education in their mother tongue.[94]

In 1927 Arabic script was replaced by the Latin alphabet, and Kazan appeared on its way to establishing itself firmly as the foremost cultural center of Moslems of the USSR.[95] Then a more repressive Soviet

---

90 *Ibid.* The study reflects the situation in the late sixties. Since then the television audience may have expanded considerably. See also Bennigsen and Lemercier-Quelquejay, 1960: 225.

91 *Tatary,* 1967.
92 *Dergi,* 1958: XIII: 16.
93 *Qazan Utlary,* 1968: XI: 144.
94 *Dergi,* 1960: XX: 55, quoting *Revolyutsiya i natsionalnosti* (Moscow, 1933): XII: 63.
95 Samoylovich, 1925: 1–2.

Table 16.6

Selected Data on Education in Tatar ASSR (1969–1970)

Population: 3,131,600 (1970)

		PER 1,000 POPULATION
All Schools		
number of schools	3,446	1.1
number of students	827,100	264.1
Secondary special schools		
number of schools	52	
number of students	45,900	14.7
	(Tatars 18,100)	
Institutions of higher education		
number of institutions	11	
	+ 3 branches	
	of other	
	institutions	
number of students	61,000	19.5
	(Tatars 22,600)	
Universities		
number of universities	1	
number of students		
total	9,007	
day students	5,340	
evening students	1,561	
correspondence students	2,106	
newly admitted		
total	1,726	
day students	1,125	
evening students	302	
correspondence students	299	
graduated		
total	1,659	
day students	915	
evening students	322	
correspondence students	422	
Graduate students (1969)		
total number	1,052	0.3
in scientific research institutions	132	0.04
in Vuzy	920	0.3
Number of persons with (in 1970) higher or secondary (complete and incomplete) education		
per 1,000 individuals, 10 years and older	468	
per 1,000 individuals employed in national economy	664	
Number of workers graduated from professional-technical schools, 1969	23,100	7.4

Source: *Nar. obraz.*, 1971: VIII: 8–11, 160; *TsSU RSFSR,
50 let Tatarskoi ASSR*, 1970: 136, 153, 157, 164.

nationality policy toward Tatars, emphasizing Russification, began in 1929–1930, and put a halt to the burgeoning Tatar cultural life. In Fall 1929 the Society for Tatar Studies, denounced as a "center of nationalism," was closed. In the following three years extensive purges were carried out in Pedagogical Institute of the East and Tatar schools for preparation of national cadres. In 1939–1940, in a further move toward Russification, the Latin alphabet was replaced by the Cyrillic in a somewhat modified form.

Since then general level of education in the Tatar ASSR has risen considerably. In 1970 total number of schools was 3,236:[96] 1,480 were Tatar and Tatar-Russian (mixed), 130 Chuvash and Chuvash-Russian, 36 Udmurt, 20 Mari, and 2 Mordvinian.[97] In addition, in 1958 there were approximately 2,000 Tatar schools outside the border of the Tatar ASSR;[98] 1,225 in the Bashkir ASSR and the rest in other ASSRs and provinces of the RSFSR. No Tatar schools are permitted in other union republics.[99] At present, only primary and secondary education is offered in Tatar; higher education is normally in Russian. Exceptions to this rule can be found in National Pedagogical Institute and Tatar Philological Faculty of Kazan University.[100] In 1970 the Faculty had 250 students, many planning to become teachers.[101]

Soviet conditions have resulted in increased Tatar attendance at Russian schools. While in 1948 less than half of all children in the Tatar ASSR attended Russian schools, by 1966 their percentage had increased to almost two thirds. Approximately one quarter of all Tatar children attended Russian schools in 1969.[102] During the same period, percentage of Russian schools in the Tatar ASSR rose from 42.8% to 44.9%. By 1968, however, there was a slight drop to 44.2%.[103] Nevertheless, number of Tatar children attending Tatar schools also rose steadily. In 1971, 211,000 Tatar children in the Tatar ASSR received their education in Tatar,[104] up from 170,000 in 1965.[105] The number completing secondary education in Tatar schools rose from 41,000 in the 1950s to 68,000 in the 1960s.[106]

According to the 1970 census, average level of education in the Tatar ASSR was slightly over the average for the RSFSR. In the Tatar ASSR, 664 of every 1,000 employed persons (up from 456 in 1959) had had a higher or secondary education (including 8-year secondary). (Average for the RSFSR was 656 per 1,000, up from 440 per 1,000 in 1959.)[107] In 1970, 87,000 Tatars were studying in institutes of higher learning and 98,000 in specialized secondary schools. There were 11,617 Tatar scientific workers. Of Tatars employed in the national economy, 109,200 had had a higher education, with 173,500 receiving specialized secondary education.

In republics with large Tatar populations, average level of education of Tatars was somewhat below that of Russians but considerably above that of other Turkic groups.[108]

In Tatar language schools, study of Russian is compulsory beginning in the first grade. In fact, as shown below in a tabulation for the 1972–1973 school year, total hours per week dedicated to Russian language and literature exceed total of hours reserved for Tatar language and literature.[109]

---

96 Nar. obraz., 1971: 34.
97 Tatarstan Kommunisty, 1971: XII: 13.
98 Devletchin, 1960, quoting Natsionalnyye shkoly RSFSR za 40 let (Moscow, 1958).
99 This may be interpreted as discriminatory Soviet educational policy. For example, there are Armenian schools in Georgia, Kazakh and Tadzhik schools in Uzbekistan, and Uzbek schools in Kirgizistan and Tadzhikistan. However, Belorussians and Ukrainians are denied the right to an education in their native languages outside the borders of their own republics. Tatars are denied this right except in the RSFSR. There are no restrictions on Russian schools; they may be established anywhere in the Soviet Union. Crimean Tatars did receive permission to conduct classes in the Crimean Tatar language in their areas of deportation after partial rehabilitation in 1967.
100 Dergi, 1960: XX: 55.
101 UNESCO Features, 1970: II: 571.

102 Voprosy filosofii, 1969: XII: 134.
103 Ibid.
104 Tatarstan Kommunisty, 1971: XII: 13.
105 Qazan Utlary, 1966: XI: 89.
106 Tatarstan Kommunisty, 1971: XII: 13.
107 Izvestia (April 17), 1971.
108 See Itogi 1959, volumes for individual republics, tables 57 and 57a, and Itogi 1970: IV: 623, 625, 637, 639, 643.
109 Data from Soviet Mektebe, 1972: 7.

WEEKLY HOURS BY GRADE LEVEL

Subject	I	II	III	IV	V	VI	VII	VIII	IX	X	Total
Tatar language and literature	8	7	7	5	5	4.5	4	3	2	2	47.5
Russian language and literature	6	8	7	7	9	6.5	6	5	6	5	65.5
Foreign languages	0	0	0	0	2	2	2	2	2	2	12

Russian schools in the Tatar ASSR are required to provide 2 hours of Tatar per week in grades 2 to 8, but this rule is not always observed.[110]

In 1970 there were 723,000 pupils in 3,236 schools in the Tatar ASSR: 420,000 were in schools with grades 5 to 10; 52,000 were in general secondary schools (8–10 grades only); and 47,700 were in 39 specialized secondary schools [*tekhnikum*].[111] Of Tatar schools, 60% were elementary, 27% were 8-year, and 30% secondary.[112] The 11 higher educational establishments had 60,300 students. The University of Kazan, founded in 1804, had 8 faculties, 60 chairs, and 9,007 students. It provides specialist training in radiophysics, electronics, biochemistry, astronomy, geodesy, and so on, and for 150 years has also been an important center for Oriental studies. In 1970 there were 1,770 libraries in the Tatar ASSR.[113]

CULTURAL AND SCIENTIFIC INSTITUTIONS

A branch of the Academy of Sciences of the USSR is located in Kazan, with 39 scientific research institutions. The director of its Ghalimdjan Ibrahim Institute of Language, Literature, and History is M. Mokharramov, a Tatar.

The work of the Kazan Film Studio is limited mostly to production of documentaries and local language sound tracks for full-length films. In 1971 the studio produced 4 documentaries and 36 newsreels in Russian, Tatar, and Chuvash.[114] Newsreels dealt with the four autonomous republics on the Volga served by the Kazan Film

Table 16.7

Selected Data on Scientific and Cultural Facilities and Personnel in Tatar ASSR (1969)

Population: 3,131,600 (1970)

Museums
number of museums	10
attendance	1,113,000
attendance per 1,000 population	355

Theaters
number of theaters	9
attendance	1,722,500
attendance per 1,000 population	550

Number of public libraries	1,763
number of books and magazines in public libraries	17,263,000

Number of clubs	2,553

Source: *TsSU RSFSR, 50 let Tatarskoi ASSR*, 1970: 8, 166–168. Because data on Tatars and Tatar ASSR do not appear in sources for union republics, this table is less complete than comparable tables in other chapters.

Studio. Furthermore, the studio produced Bashkir, Tatar, Chuvash, Mari, and Udmurt synchronized sound tracks for 70 full-length films, producing one artistic film about the famous Tatar composer Salikh Saydashev.

In 1972 there were 2,500 movie theaters in the Tatar ASSR.[115] In 1966 the average urban resident of the republic went to the movies 15 to 22 times per year; the figure was 7.9 to 13.6 times per year for those in the countryside.[116] Nine state theaters and 48 "people's" theaters and music ensembles operated in Tataristan in 1972; among

---

110 *Qazan Utlary*, 1973: IV: 164.
111 *Nar. obraz.*, 1971: 34.
112 *Sovetskaya etnografiya*, 1972: VI: 47.
113 *Nar. obraz.*, 1971: 35 .
114 *Qazan Utlary*, 1972: XI: 155, 156.

---

115 *Sovet Mektebe*, 1972: XI: 62.
116 *Qazan Utlary*, 1966: XI: 90–93.

them were Tatar State Academy Theater
and Tatar State Opera and Ballet Theater,
both in Kazan, and Tataristan Song and

Dance Ensemble. There are also eight
museums, a conservatory, and Tatar State
Philharmonic Society.[117]

National Attitudes

REVIEW OF FACTORS FORMING
NATIONAL ATTITUDES

Tatars are the most Westernized of
Turkic peoples of the USSR. They were the
first Turks to develop a middle class, and
on the eve of World War I possessed a
rather large proletariat. Since most Tatar
workers lived outside of Tataristan (in the
Donets Basin and industrial regions of the
Urals and Siberia), however, they did not
exert much political influence in their
homeland. The first Tatar socialists emerged from the more radical section of the
young bourgeois intelligentsia, and early
Tatar communism was dominated by non-
proletarian elements.[118]

Since then a new generation has grown
up, with a new intelligentsia. As evidenced
by Tatar and Bashkir publications (particularly the Tatar literary monthly *Qazan
Utlary* and the Bashkir literary magazine
Aghidel), this new generation is just as
firmly attached to its national values and
culture as was the old generation. The
Tatar-Bashkir intelligentsia has become
very outspoken in demands for improvements, especially in the cultural and
national sectors. This attitude is also shared
by the Tatar diaspora in Central Asia and
other parts of the Soviet Union.

On the other hand, there have been instances of Tatars, especially youth in the
cities, displaying relative indifference toward their own culture and language,
provoking open criticism from such well-
known Tatar intellectuals as writer and
former chairman of the Tatar Writers'
Union, Ghomar Bashir, who decried "Euro-

peanization" and advocated youth working
among their own people.[119]

Tatar men of letters have been among the
most ardent, articulate defenders and pro-
moters of the Tatar language and culture.
Through their literary writings, critical
articles, and speeches at conferences and
congresses, they have contributed (and continue to contribute) to strengthening Tatar
national consciousness, particularly among
the young. Throughout the post-Stalinist
period they have worked untiringly to popu-
larize the language and culture and to alert
or sharpen public awareness toward current national problems. The Tatar Writers'
Union headquarters in Kazan has become
a veritable mecca to Tatars from all over
the Soviet Union. In addition, Tatar writers
frequently travel throughout the Tatar
ASSR to meet readers and discuss their own
works, as well as literature in general.

In spite of the fact that Tatars hold only
a small majority over the Russians in the
Tatar ASSR, Russification does not seem
to have made significant headway. Tatars
have lived with Russians for centuries and,
as we have seen, balance between Tatar
and Russian population in their republic
has, with slight fluctuations, existed ever
since its establishment. According to
Ghomar Usmanov, premier of the Tatar
ASSR, and Murkhazid Valiyev, party secretary for ideology, this balance is not expected to change in the near future.[120]

As the 1959 census has shown, Tatars
residing in the Tatar ASSR and in *oblasts*
and other autonomous republics lying within their historical borders have preserved
their language to a very high degree. More

---

117 *Sovet Mektebe*, 1972: XI: 62.
118 Bennigsen and Lemercier-Quelquejay, 1967:
50–51.

119 *Sovet Adabiaty* [*Soviet Literature*], 1957: 11.
Note: *Sovet Adabiaty* is the old name for the journal
Qazan Utlary.
120 *New York Times* (March 25), 1970.

than 98% of Tatars in the Tatar ASSR gave Tatar as their mother tongue. In the Bashkir ASSR the percentage was 97.6% and in the Mordvinian ASSR, 98.5%; elsewhere in the Volga-Viatka region the percentage ranged from 92% to 98%. For Tatars in Central Asia the figure was 90% (with the remaining 10% divided between Russian and local Turkic languages); in the Siberian *oblast* of Omsk, 94%. Even in large Russian cities, such as Moscow and Leningrad, the great majority of Tatars, 78% and 71%, respectively, considered Tatar their mother tongue.[121] Moreover, a considerable number of those who gave Russian as their mother tongue undoubtedly retained a command of Tatar. For example, of Tatars in Kazan who indicate Russian as their mother tongue, 19.2% continue to speak Tatar at home.[122]

Alexandre Bennigsen of the Sorbonne considers the Soviet army the principal instrument of Russification. To this the educational system should be added. Unavailability of higher education in the republic and the obvious advantage of knowing Russian induces many parents to send their children to Russian schools at a very early age. This disrupts Tatar socialization processes, contributing to the process of Russification.

BASIC VIEWS OF SCHOLARS ON NATIONAL ATTITUDES

Geoffrey E. Wheeler, retired director of the Central Asian Research Centre in London, and Alexandre Bennigsen and Chantal Lemercier-Quelquejay, both of l'Ecole Pratique des Hautes Etudes, Sorbonne, seem rather optimistic about the future of Moslems in the USSR. They have expressed the opinion that Islam and the USSR Moslems

may prove more than a match for the Russians and that the latter have up to now failed in attempts to assimilate them.

Wheeler writes that even convinced Communists may be Moslems at heart.[123] In his opinion, Soviet Moslems are technically, mentally, and spiritually far better fit to undertake government of their people than many former colonial Moslem countries whose independence the Soviet government has so eagerly advocated. Silent but persistent struggle is sensed, if not thoroughly comprehended, by Soviet authorities. Though less spectacular than the triumphant progress of the Arab and Ottoman armies during their earlier empires, it demonstrates just as strikingly the inherent vitality and integrity of Islam as a social force, and in the long run may prove just as effective.

Bennigsen and Lemercier-Quelquejay argue that the new generation's attitude toward fundamental problems facing the Moslem peoples is reminiscent of that of Sultanghaliyev. "Like him and perhaps even more than him, they are firmly attached to this national culture, not only in its form but also in its content." [124] That Moslem Tatars wish to preserve their religion and traditional heritage—even if that heritage is scarcely compatible with proletarian culture—is obvious, according to Bennigsen and Lemercier-Quelquejay. Their idealization of the Moslem past brings them into conflict with the Russians. Finally—and here one can detect most clearly the influence of Sultanghaliyev—they seem to want to relate their own notion of communism to antecedents other than those of the Russian Bolsheviks, implying that "Oriental communism" is an original concept.

Bennigsen and Lemercier-Quelquejay go on to state that, more than his predecessors of the 1920s and 1930s, the Moslem intellectual of today is emerging as a real representative of his people. His national consciousness is at once more keenly felt, more rational, and, in the final analysis, more firmly hostile to Russian influence

---

121 Among other non-Slavic groups residing in and around Leningrad, the percentage of those indicating the language of their nationality as their mother tongue was the following: Estonians (14,067), 26.1%; Armenians (9,437), 32.7%; Latvians (8,752), 31.5%; Lithuanians (5,017), 41.5%. *Itogi RSFSR, 1959:* 312.

122 *Sovetskaya etnografiya,* 1972: II: 33.

123 Bennigsen and Lemercier-Quelquejay, 1967: Foreword.

124 *Ibid.*

than that of any other sector of the Moslem population.[125]

It should be noted here that Tatars and Bashkirs have traditionally belonged to the most devout group of Soviet Moslems and that long before the Bolshevik revolution they had developed a rather strong national consciousness.

A study of ethnosocial structure of the urban population (mostly Kazan) of the Tatar ASSR published the following results:[126]

Tatars residing in Kazan had, on the average, 47.8% Tatar friends and 42.4% Russian friends. For the Russians the figures were 58.3% Russian and 31.9% Tatar friends.

In Kazan 87.4% of the Tatars had spouses of their own nationality, 10.7% were married to Russians. Of the Russians in Kazan, 91.6% were married to persons of their own nationality; more than 5% were married to Tatars. The percentage of intermarriage was higher among intellectuals, lower among unskilled workers.

More than half (51.4%) of the children born of Russian mothers and Tatar fathers chose Tatar as their nationality.

RECENT MANIFESTATIONS OF NATIONALISM

In contrast to Crimean Tatars, whose struggle for return to their homeland has attracted worldwide attention, no evidence has up to now been received that Kazan Tatars and Bashkirs have produced any *samizdat*. Nevertheless, substantial evidence vouches for existence of Tatar-Bashkir nationalism.

For Tatars and Bashkirs, preservation of national integrity, culture, and language against the current Russification drive of the Soviet government is an important issue. Tatars and Bashkirs in the party and government apparatus of their respective republics, as well as the Tatar-Bashkir intelligentsia, use every opportunity (sessions of Supreme Soviet of USSR and RSFSR,

writers' congresses, conferences of scientists and professional groups, publications, etc.) to speak up on behalf of their people and promote the interests of their republics.

It is in literature, however, that Tatar nationalism becomes most conspicuous. Besides a few prominent scientists. Soviet poets, playwrights, novelists, and journalists constitute practically the only group in the population which has succeeded in establishing a forum for raising, within certain limits, important issues confronting the people. By skillfully using literary characters, Tatar writers have conveyed thoughts and ideas which could never be expressed directly through other communications media. Since literature is extremely popular among Tatars and Bashkirs, it is an excellent means of reaching large segments of the population.[127]

Anti-Russian feeling is reflected, for example, in the Tatar novel *Yamashev* by Atilla Rasih.[128] In the story, set in prerevolutionary years at the turn of the century, a "negative" character, the Tatar Jaghfer, confronts the "positive" social democrat Yamashev. He is told by the latter that after socialism all nations will prosper, and this is the major theme of the work. During the ongoing argument between the two, however, Jaghfer as a Tatar suffers certain indignities and disillusionment; it is not difficult for Tatar readers to identify mainly with the "negative" Jaghfer.

Another example is found in a poem by Ildar Yuziev entitled "What Things Does the Smith Make?" [129] The author enumerates all kinds of things, such as fish hooks, nails for caskets, wolf traps, and so on. Among them:

> Locks which lock up the writer in jail
> Hoops to lay around the necks of the
>   freedom loving.

Besides furnishing youth with a solid foundation by acquainting it with the national heritage, Tatar literature tackles such topics as Russification, discrimination

125 *Ibid.*: 225.
126 *Sovetskaya etnografiya*, 1970: 3.

127 See Burbiel, 1969: 40–46.
128 Published in *Qazan Utlary* (1967: 9–12), its author is one of the more important modern Tatar writers. Husseyn Yamashev was a leading Tatar social democrat (1882–1912).
129 *Qazan Utlary*, 1972: V: 80. Ildar Yuziev is a prominent contemporary Tatar poet.

against Tatars, intermarriage, forced assignment of Tatars to work outside their republic, distortion and vilification of their image, promotion of education in schools, exposure of existing class differences in Soviet society, corruption among party and government officials, and exploitation of workers by the existing Soviet labor system. This is done with the aim of stimulating the reader's national feelings, fostering a devotion to the welfare of his people and native homeland, showing him the injustices and shortcomings of Soviet society.

Nationalism and anti-Russian feelings among Tatars and Bashkirs have also been reported by recent émigrés from the Soviet Union. In 1969 Ukrainian Information Service Smoloskyp (Baltimore, Md.) reported a document in which a pro-Russian Ukrainian living in Ufa, Bashkir ASSR, warned against nationalism in Ufa, Kazan, and other republics. The document consisted of a letter written to a CPSU Central Committee member in Moscow by a Ukrainian "renegade" who had married a Christian Tatar woman and was teaching in an institute of higher learning in Ufa.

The author of the letter cited a number of examples of contempt toward everything Russian among Tatars in Bashkiria and in the Georgian, Baltic, Kirgiz, Moldavian, and Ukrainian republics. Most examples are of events happening in Ufa during the author's residence in that city. He claimed that cadres were selected by nationality (i.e., from among the native people) even if they were "blockheads." In the same manner professors' chairs were filled, and the same applied to universities and medical institutions.

According to this author, the secretary of the Ufa party committee had said that it was not necessary to invite specialists and scholars from the outside, that they already had their own, and that, in general, the Bashkir ASSR was ready to become an independent state.

The letter also reported on a banquet given in May 1966 by local authorities to celebrate the day of victory. Seating was according to nationality. Tatars sat and talked together in their own language, and Russians sat as though they were guests or poor relatives.

In institutions of higher education, nationalism is (not surprisingly) implanted by members of social science departments. Incidents at the Institute of Agriculture were related in the Ukrainian's letter. A teacher began his seminar in Tatar. Russians asked him to speak so that they too could understand. He obliged. Teachers gathered in their departments and talked in their own language; when Russians were among them, they behaved as if they weren't there. At a party committee meeting of the institute, Tatars (rector, vice rector and heads of social science departments) switched to their language as though the Russians were not there at all.

The letter also alleged that 90% of inmates of a privileged local sanatorium were Tatars and Bashkirs, although Russians made up half the population of the Bashkir ASSR.

Finally, the author writes, "The great Russian people, who have led Tatars, Bashkirs . . . out of the darkness of slavery, injustice . . . are little by little encroached upon here, but this process will go on more rapidly if measures to stop it are not taken on a state-wide level." [130]

---

[130] *Ukrains'kiy visnyk*, 1971: I–II: 111–118.

REFERENCES

Azat Khatyn
  Azat Khatyn (Free Woman) (Kazan, monthly).
Bashir, 1965
  Ghomar Bashir, *Selected Works* (Kazan, 1965).

Battal-Taymas, 1966
  Abdullah Battal-Taymas, *Kazan Türkleri* [*Kazan Turks*] (Ankara, 1966).
Bennigsen and Lemercier-Quelquejay, 1960
  Alexandre Bennigsen and Chantal Lemercier-Quelquejay, *Les mouvements*

nationaux chez les Musulmans de Russie —le "Sultangalievisme" au Tatarstan (Paris and La Haye: Mouton, 1960).

Bennigsen and Lemercier-Quelquejay, 1967
Alexandre Bennigsen and Chantal Lemercier-Quelquejay, *Islam in the Soviet Union* (New York and London: Praeger and Pall Mall, 1967).

Burbiel, 1969
Gustav Burbiel, "Like the Proverbial Phoenix, the Rich and Resilient Tatar Writing Re-emerges as a National Tool," *Mid East: A Middle East North African Review* (Washington), October 1969.

Dergi
Dergi. Turkish language journal, Institute for Study of USSR (Munich).

Devletchin, 1958
T. Devletchin, "Tataristanin bugünkü ekonomikasi" [Economy of Tataristan Today], *Dergi*, 1958: 14.

Devletchin, 1960
T. Devletchin, "Education among the Kazan Tatars in the Soviet Period," *Dergi* (Munich), 1960: 20.

Itogi 1959
Itogi vsesoyuznoi perepisi naseleniya 1959 goda (Moscow: Gosstatizdat, 1962).

Itogi 1970
Itogi vsesoyuznoi perepisi naseleniya 1970 goda (Moscow: Statistika, 1973).

Itogi RSFSR 1959
Itogi vsesoyuznoi perepisi naseleniya 1959 goda, RSFSR (Moscow: Statistika, 1963).

Letopis, 1966
Letopis periodicheskikh izdanii SSSR 1961–1965 (Moscow: Kniga, 1966).

Mende, 1936
Gerhard von Mende, *Der nationale Kampf der Russlandtürken* (Berlin, 1936).

Nar. khoz. 1970
Narodnoye khozyaistvo SSSR v 1970 godu (Moscow: Statistika, 1971).

Nar. khoz. 1972
Narodnoye khozyaistvo SSSR 1922–1972: Yubileinyi statisticheskii yezhegodnik (Moscow: Statistika, 1972).

Nar. obraz., 1971
Narodnoye obrazovaniye, nauka i kul'tura v SSSR: statisticheskii sbornik (Moscow: Statistika, 1971).

Nurullin, 1966
Ibrahim Nurullin, *XX joz bashy tatar adabiaty* [*Tatar Literature at Beginning of 20th Century*] (Kazan, 1966).

Pechat' 1959
Pechat' SSSR v 1959 godu (Moscow: Kniga, 1960).

Pechat' 1970
Pechat' SSSR v 1970 godu (Moscow: Kniga, 1971).

Pechat' 1971
Pechat' SSSR v 1971 godu (Moscow: Kniga, 1972).

Qazan Utlary
Qazan Utlary [*Lights of Kazan*] (Kazan, monthly).

Qurbatov, 1960
Kh. Qurbatov, *Tatar telenen alfavit hem orfografie tarikhy* (Kazan, 1960).

Rigby, 1968
T. H. Rigby, *Communist Party Membership in the USSR 1917–1967* (Princeton, N.J.: Princeton University Press, 1968).

Samoylovich, 1925
A. Samoylovich, "Twenty Days in Kazan," *Vestnik nauchnogo obshchestva Tatarovedeniya* (January–April 1925): 1–2.

Seton-Watson, 1960
Hugh Seton-Watson, *From Lenin to Khrushchev* (New York: Praeger, 1960).

Shabad, 1951
Theodore Shabad, *Geography of the USSR: A Regional Study* (New York: Columbia University Press, 1951).

Sovet Mektebe
Sovet Mektebe [*Soviet School*] (Kazan).

Sovetskaya etnografiya
Sovetskaya etnografiya (Moscow, quarterly).

Tatar Calendar, 1972
Tatar Calendar (Kazan: Tatar Kitap Neshriaty, 1972).

Tatarstan, 1925–1926
Bish jyl echende Tatarstan [*Tataristan in First Five Years*] (Kazan, 1925–1926).

Tatarstan ASSR Tarikhy, 1970
Tatarstan ASSR Tarikhy (Kazan: Tatar Kitap Neshriaty, 1970).

Tatarstan Kommunisty
Tatarstan Kommunisty (Kazan, monthly).

Tatary, 1967
Tatary srednego povolzh'ya i priural'ya (Moscow, 1967).

Togan, 1969
Zeki Velidi Togan, *Hatiralar* [*Memoires*] (Istanbul, 1969).

TsSU RSFSR, 50 let Tatarskoi ASSR, 1970
TsSU RSFSR, 50 let Tatarskoi ASSR (Kazan: Statistika, 1970).

Ukrains'kiy visnyk, 1971
Ukrains'kiy visnyk [*Ukrainian Herald*] (Paris and Baltimore: PIUF and Smoloskyp, 1971).

Voprosy Filosofii
Voprosy Filosofii (Moscow, monthly).

17 | MOLDAVIA and THE MOLDAVIANS

Stephen Fischer-Galati

Since various national designations used in this chapter may confuse the reader, the following definitions could prove helpful: *Rumanian Moldavia* is a portion of northeastern Rumania. *Bessarabia*, formerly part of Rumania Moldavia, was annexed by Russia in 1812, restored to Rumania in 1918, annexed by the USSR in 1940. *Moldavian Autonomous SSR*, the original Soviet "Moldavian" republic, was established in 1924 as part of the Ukrainian SSR, consisting of a portion of the USSR whose boundaries included a significant Rumanian resident population. *Moldavian SSR* is the present union republic consisting of the Moldavian Autonomous SSR plus Bessarabia. *Moldavians* are members of the officially designated titular nationality of Moldavia; basically, ethnic Rumanians.

General Information

TERRITORY

The Moldavian Soviet Socialist Republic was formed on August 2, 1940, through incorporation of the central section of Bessarabia into the Moldavian Autonomous SSR. Smallest of the constituent republics of the USSR, it covers an area of 13,012 square miles.[1] The Moldavian SSR lies to the extreme southwest of the USSR, bordering on Rumania, by the river Prut, to the southwest and on the Ukrainian SSR to the north, northeast, and southeast. The Moldavian SSR has 32 districts, 20 towns, and 33 urban settlements.[2] Its capital is Kishinev.

Central portion of the republic is a plateau known as the Bessarabian-Moldavian upland, which rises to 1,410 feet and extends westward beyond the Prut. The

---

1 Shabad, 1951: 464.

2 *BSE, Yezhegodnik.*, 1971: 151.

upland is composed of young sedimentary rock, mainly limestone, covered with a layer of loess. Its higher wooded portions, known as the Kodry, have podsolic soils supporting deciduous forests of oak, ash, and maple. North of the plateau lies the level treeless Bel'tsy steppe, and to the south the dry Budzhak steppe. Both are covered with rich black-earth soils. In the south, tree vegetation is found only in the flood plains of the lower Dnestr and Prut rivers.[3]

The republic is one of the warmest regions of the European USSR, with a mean annual temperature of 50°F. In January average temperatures range from 27°F. in the south to 23°F. in the north. In July the respective temperatures are 68°F. and 73°F.[4] Yearly precipitation varies between 22 inches in the north and 12–16 inches in the south. Most rains occur in June and July.[5] The prevalent winds are northeasterly.

Construction materials constitute the chief mineral resources. Vast gypsum deposits lie in the vicinity of Lipkany, in the extreme north. Granite, chalk, and cement rock are found in the Dnestr Valley.[6]

ECONOMY

Agriculture, including livestock raising, is chief economic activity of the Moldavian SSR. Moldavia includes about one third of the vineyard acreage of the USSR. Grain crops, of which corn is most widely cultivated, occupy 75% of total cultivated area, representing 83% of total area of the republic. Aside from corn, winter wheat, barley, and winter rye are main grain crops. Chief industrial crops are tobacco, sugar beets, soybeans, sunflowers, flax, and hemp. Main processing industries are fruit and vegetable canning, wine making, distilling, flour milling, vegetable oil extraction, tobacco processing, and sugar refining. Of lesser importance are tanning, knitting, woodworking, and quarrying industries.[7]

Animal husbandry, while well developed

in terms of needs of the republic, is significant in terms of total USSR figures only with respect to pig raising—3.8% of the total. The actual number of pigs in the Moldavian SSR reached 1,573,000 in 1970, in contrast to 1,187,000 in 1965. By contrast, the number of beef and dairy cattle was lower in 1970 (903,000) than in 1965 (914,000). Number of sheep and goats also declined: the figures for 1970 and 1965 were 1,417,000 and 1,676,000 respectively.[8] Livestock and animal products accounted for 30% of gross value of Moldavian agricultural output in 1970.[9]

Moldavia ranks first among union republics in production of wine and related products. In 1970 the winemaking industry produced 64.7 million gallons of grape wine as against 42.2 million gallons in 1965. Wine production in 1970 was approximately 18% of the total for the USSR.[10] In 1970 the canning industry produced 945.8 million tins of canned food (about 5% of the USSR total) as against 684.8 million in 1965.[11] In the same year the vegetable oil industry produced 159,000 tons of vegetable oil as against 132,700 tons in 1965. The increase in production figures of other branches of the food industry since 1965 has been much less spectacular.[12] However, the ruble value of Moldavia's food industry output in 1970 reached 2.3 billion as against 1.5 billion in 1965. The average annual volume of the gross output of agriculture increased by 26.7% since 1965, and general growth in gross industrial production ranks among the highest for union republics.[13]

Light industry, primarily tanning, footwear, and knitwear, has also developed rapidly since 1965, as have the machine-building and metal-working industries. Even so, the food processing industry represents approximately 60% of total industrial structure as against 25% for light industry and 15% for heavy industry.[14] In terms of total industrial development, Moldavia still has lowest productivity, lowest

---

3 *Moldaviya*, 1970: 17–27; Shabad, 1951: 464.
4 *Moldaviya*, 1970: 28–33.
5 *Ibid.*: 33.
6 Shabad, 1951: 464.
7 *Moldaviya*, 1970: 101–134.

---

8 *BSE, Yezhegodnik*, 1971: 153.
9 *Nar. khoz.* 1972: 222.
10 *BSE, Yezhegodnik*, 1971: 152; Shabad, 1951: 466–467.
11 *BSE, Yezhegodnik*, 1971: 152.
12 *Ibid.*
13 *Pravda* (April 4), 1971: 2–3.
14 *BSE, Yezhegodnik*, 1971: 152.

capital investment, and lowest rate of industrial employment of all union republics.[15]

Statistics indicative of standard of living uniformly rank Moldavia well below other European republics of the USSR. They suggest that in these aspects of development Moldavia is more closely comparable to Central Asia than to the rest of the European USSR. In 1970 savings per capita averaged 93.70 rubles, less than half the USSR average. Trade turnover per capita was 488 rubles, compared to 639 for the USSR as a whole and 956 for Estonia, most favored republic in this respect. In 1971 number of doctors per 10,000 inhabitants (21.5) was well below the USSR average (28.3), but equally far above Rumania's 14.1 doctors per 10,000 in 1968. In number of television sets per 100 population, Moldavia also compared favorably with Rumania (11.5 versus 6.4), although not with the average for the USSR (14.5).[16]

HISTORY

On October 12, 1924, an Autonomous Moldavian Soviet Socialist Republic was established as part of the Ukrainian Soviet Socialist Republic to formalize the Kremlin's opposition to incorporation of Bessarabia into Rumania at the end of World War I and to provide a political nucleus for eventual reunification of all "Moldavians." [17] From its inception the Moldavian republic was an instrument of Soviet political action against Rumania.

The boundaries were drawn so as to include a substantial segment of the Rumanian population east of the Dnestr, but by no means all Rumanian-speaking inhabitants of Transdnistria and the Ukraine; only 30% of the republic's population was Rumanian. It has been suggested this was done to "prove" relative proportion of Moldavians in the area stretching from Rumanian Moldavia to Odessa was similar, thus invalidating

Rumania's claim that its seizure of Bessarabia was justified by the overwhelmingly Rumanian character of that province.[18] These demographic arguments were supplemented by "historic proofs" stressing Russia's historic rights to Bessarabia, based on possession of the province at the time of the Bolshevik revolution and the allegedly illegal dismemberment and subsequent transfer to Rumania in 1918 of the Democratic Moldavian Republic, first established in December 1917.[19]

Soviet claims to Bessarabia can be challenged on both demographic and historic grounds. Historically, Bessarabia was part of the Rumanian principality of Moldavia; its incorporation into Russia in 1812 was prompted by strategic and political considerations related exclusively to Russo-Turkish relations and Great Power interests. Return to the principality of Moldavia of parts of Bessarabia at the Congress of Paris of 1856 was again a decision of the powers, as was restitution of those same sections to Russia at the 1878 Congress of Berlin. And, despite determined efforts by the tsarist regime to Russify Bessarabia between 1812 and 1917 (largely through settlement of Ukrainians, Russians, and Jews), over two thirds of the inhabitants of Bessarabia were Rumanians at the time of the Bolshevik revolution. The Democratic Moldavian Republic, established in 1917 by the dominant Rumanian political forces in Bessarabia, was expressly anti-Bolshevik in character, intended as an instrument to allow incorporation of the province into Rumania should its autonomy be threatened by the Bolsheviks. In fact, therefore, union of the Moldavian republic with Rumania in April 1918 was voluntary.[20]

The Autonomous Moldavian Soviet Socialist Republic, theoretical reincarnation of the Democratic Moldavian Republic of 1917, was assigned by Moscow the task of working toward reincorporation of Bessarabia through propaganda as well as through revolutionary action within Bessarabia proper. Promotion of Moldavian culture in the autonomous republic by the

15 Cole and German, 1970: 127, 133, 160, 163–164, 166, 171, 177.
16 *Nar. khoz. 1970*: 564, 579; *Nar. khoz. 1972*: 515ff., 610, 616. *Statistical Abstract of the U.S.*, 1971: 800, 822.
17 Clark, 1927: 239ff.

18 Babel, 1926: 198–233.
19 The most eloquent and most thoroughly documented statement of the Soviet position is by J. Okhotnikov and N. Batchinsky, *La Bessarabie et la paix europeenne* (Paris, 1927).
20 Clark, 1927: 151–157.

Ukraine, development of a national "Moldavian" language and literature, and sporadic revolutionary activity exported to Bessarabia by members of the Communist party were, however, ineffectual.[21] Reincorporation of Bessarabia into the USSR was made possible only by Soviet military action early in June 1940, when the USSR, on the basis of secret provisions of the Molotov-Ribbentrop pact of August 1939, was permitted by Hitler to march into and annex Bessarabia and northern Bukovina. It was then that the Moldavian Soviet Socialist Republic was established as a union republic, with boundaries changed to improve its "Moldavian" image by transferring 1,900 of 3,200 square miles of the former autonomous republic to the Ukraine and incorporating most of Bessarabia into the Moldavian SSR.

After the 1941 German attack on the USSR, the Moldavian republic and the area previously comprising the autonomous republic were overrun by Rumania allied with Berlin, largely to recover Bessarabia.[22] Only in 1944 was legitimacy of the Moldavian SSR formally guaranteed when the Soviet-Rumanian Armistice Convention recognized the legality of the Soviet annexation of Bessarabia and northern Bukovina. Reaffirmation of this agreement by the Rumanian peace treaty of 1947 closed de jure if not de facto the Bessarabian and "Moldavian" questions.[23] But the history of the Moldavian SSR must be understood precisely in the context of the "illegal" reopening of these questions by "forces inimical" to the USSR.

The history of the Moldavian SSR since 1947, and particularly since development of the Rumanian "independent" (or anti-Soviet) course in the early 1960s, has been characterized by consistent Russian attempts to strengthen bases of Soviet power in Moldavia and to isolate the republic from Rumania and Rumanian influences.[24] The former aim has been implemented by securing control of the party and state apparatus by non-Moldavians, by systematic

Communist indoctrination of the Moldavian population, and by development of the republic's economy. The latter aim is pursued by cultural propaganda designed to prove the historic validity and legitimacy of the Moldavian republic, by constant attacks against pro-Rumanian nationalist manifestations on the part of the Moldavians, and by virtual elimination of all personal contacts between Soviet Moldavians and Rumanian Moldavians. These policies, carried out by several first secretaries of the Moldavian Communist party—by Leonid Brezhnev himself in the fifties—have proven satisfactory to the Kremlin, and possibilities for change from the present status of the Moldavian SSR appear inconceivable at this time.

DEMOGRAPHY

The Moldavian SSR was inhabited by 3,568,873 people in 1970, a 24% increase over the 2,884,477 inhabitants recorded in the census of 1959.[25] It recorded the highest birth rate (20.7 per 1,000) and the lowest death rate (6.8 per 1,000) of all European union republics;[26] 2,304,000 ethnic Moldavians, or 85.4% of total 2,698,000 Moldavians in the USSR, lived in the republic, constituting 64.6% of the population; percentage of Moldavians had declined from 65.4% recorded in 1959. Similarly, the percentage of Ukrainian inhabitants of the republic decreased from 14.6% in 1959 to 14.2% in 1970 while that of the third largest nationality, Russians, increased from 10.2% to 11.6%. Of remaining nationalities, Turkish-speaking Gagauzy represent 3.5% of the population, Jews 2.7%, and Bulgarians 2.1%.[27] Population density of 274 inhabitants per square mile is highest in the USSR.

The 1970 census records a substantial increase in size of urban population since the previous census was taken in 1959. Total urban population rose from 642,300 (or 22.3% of total population of the Moldavian SSR) in 1959 to 1,130,000 (or

21 Ibid., 261–276: Okhotnikov and Batchinsky, 1927: 149–153.
22 Cioranesco et al., 1967: 165ff.
23 Ionescu, 1964: 91, 129–131.
24 Cioranesco et al., 1967: 196ff.; Fischer-Galati, 1967: 55ff., 78ff.

25 Sovetskaya Moldaviya (May 5), 1971: 1.
26 Cole and German, 1970: 105.
27 Sovetskaya Moldaviya (May 5), 1971: 1; Itogi 1970: 14.

31.4% of the total) in 1970.[28] Population of the capital, Kishinev, increased from 216,000 in 1959 to 374,000 in 1970 and, among other major towns, that of Tiraspol from 63,000 to 106,000, Beltsy from 61,000 to 102,000, and Bendery from 38,000 to 43,000. Nevertheless, level of urbanization of the Moldavian SSR is lowest of all union republics.

Little specific information is available with respect to social structure of the population of the Moldavian SSR. Some relevant data from the 1970 census have been released, including evidence of an increase in number of workers and employees, accounting for a major share of the large increase in the republic's urban population. In 1959, there were 113,000 white-collar employees and 294,000 workers, representing, respectively, 3.9% and 10.2% of total population.[29] In 1970 corresponding figures were 269,000 (7.4% of total population) and 675,000 (18.7%).[30] Number of full-time students (at all levels) in 1970 is given as 891,000 or 25% of population, but no breakdown between urban and rural students is available;[31] 46.6% of total 1,604,000 employed inhabitants of the republic are engaged in agriculture, including 570,000 *kolkhozniki*.[32]

In 1959, 90% of Moldavians lived in rural areas while 67% of Russians in the republic were urban dwellers. The pattern was similar in 1970: 82% of Moldavians were still in rural areas, while the urbanized Russian population had grown to 77%.[33] According to other sources, of 113,000 employees, only 35,000 (31%) were Moldavians, and of total number of specialists with higher education employed in the Moldavian SSR in 1959 one third each were Moldavians and Russians, 17% Ukrainians, and the rest members of other nationalities.[34] No such detail has been published for 1970, but calculations based on the available data indicate that 31% of

persons with higher education in Moldavia are Moldavian.[35] The insignificance of the number of Moldavians classified as "scientific workers" is striking. In 1955, of 223,893 recorded for the USSR as a whole, only 305 (.015%) were listed as Moldavians.[36] By 1971 there were 2,624 Moldavian "scientific workers," 8.5 times as many; but they still amounted to only 0.26% of the USSR total, much less than their weight in the overall Soviet population (1.1%). Thus, Moldavians are grossly underrepresented in leading social strata, even in their own republic.

Information is also limited with respect to membership in political and professional organizations. In 1970 the Supreme Soviet of the Moldavian SSR consisted of 315 deputies, including 113 women.[37] Membership of the Communist party as of January 1, 1971, was 110,131, exclusive of 5,033 candidate members. The Party's Central Committee consisted of 210 members and candidate members, 163 workers and members of collective farms.[38] The Leninist Union of Communist Youth had a membership of 338,139 at the beginning of 1971.[39] At that time membership in professional unions reached 1,041,926.[40]

Data on actual or relative representation of different nationalities in political organizations are scarce. On the basis of studies on composition of the republic's party organization and Central Committee made available during the 1960s, it has been established that in 1963 party membership was 34.6% Moldavian, as compared to 36.9% Russian and 23.5% Ukrainian.[41] Only 1.3% of the Moldavian population belonged to the party in contrast with 7.3% of the Russian and 3.8% of the Ukrainian.[42] For the CPSU as a whole, Moldavians are most underrepresented of republic nationalities, constituting 0.4% of CPSU membership in January 1972, versus 1.1% of total Soviet population in the 1970 census.[43]

28 *Sovetskaya Moldaviya* (May 5), 1971: 1.
29 *Manchester Guardian* (April 29), 1966. The Russian word *sluzhashchiye*, translated as "employees," implies white-collar occupation.
30 *Nar. khoz. 1972*: 612.
31 *Moldaviya*, 1970: 234.
32 *Ibid.*: 612–613.
33 *Manchester Guardian* (April 29), 1966; *Itogi 1970*: IV: 276–278.
34 *Pravda* (October 27), 1961: 3–4.

35 *Itogi 1970*: III: 18; IV: 380, 513.
36 Tsameryan and Ronin, 1962: 99.
37 *BSE, Yezhegodnik*, 1971: 151.
38 *Ibid.*: 152.
39 *Ibid.*
40 *Ibid.*
41 Rigby, 1968: 381.
42 *Ibid.*
43 *Kommunist vooruzhennykh sil* (December), 1972: XXIV: 12.

No comparable statistics are available for determining configuration of the CPM Central Committee on the basis of nationality; however, the supreme body of the party, the bureau of the Central Committee, elected at the 13th Congress of the Moldavian party in February 1971, consisted of nine members—five Russian, three Ukrainian, and one Moldavian.[44] An analysis of incomplete data on composition of Supreme Soviet and Council of Ministers by nationality suggests that nearly two thirds of the leading cadres are Russians and the rest about equally divided between Moldavians and Ukrainians.

CULTURE

The Moldavian SSR, both within the framework of the Soviet Union and as Bessarabia in the context of Rumanian civilization, has always been on the periphery of Rumanian and Russian culture. The population of Bessarabia and of the Moldavian republic has produced no writers, artists, musicians, or other intellectuals who have made a mark in the history of Moldavian civilization. Primary reason for this has been the isolation of Rumanian inhabitants of these areas from the mainstream of cultural life of pre-World War II Rumania and tsarist or Soviet Russia. Writers—including such well-known figures as Grigore Urechie, Miron Costin, Gheorghe Asachi, and Bogdan Petriceicu Hajdeu— practiced their craft outside Bessarabia, usually in the cultural center of Iasi, capital of historic Moldavia, identifying with Moldavian intelligentsia rather than with Bessarabian peasant masses or non-Rumanian urban dwellers.[45] Writers and artists making contributions to Moldavian culture within the borders of Soviet Moldavia have attained little distinction. This is due primarily to a preponderance of Russian and Ukrainian authors and artists in the Moldavian SSR, and also to customary restrictions imposed upon all authors and artists by the Soviet regime. The literary works of

such better known Moldavian writers as L. S. Delianu or A. P. Lupan are limited to socialist-realist themes and as such have cultural value mainly in terms of Soviet plans for cultural development of the Moldavian SSR.[46]

The aspects of culture encouraged by the Kremlin are limited to those involving raising educational level of the population, disseminating propaganda through printed word, theater, and other media of communication, and preserving and developing folk culture, particularly in the spheres of music and dancing. In these terms much has been achieved.

Illiteracy, among the highest of all Rumanian provinces prior to incorporation of Bessarabia into the Moldavian republic, has been eliminated. The educational system, extremely backward before World War II, consisted in 1970 of 2,617 regular primary and secondary schools, 46 secondary special educational institutions, and 8 institutions of higher learning with total number of students 795,000, 51,700, and 44,800, respectively.[47] The Academy of Sciences of the Moldavian SSR, established in August 1961, by 1971 had as many as 17 academicians.[48] In 1970 there were 7 theaters, including the opera theater, 1,925 choirs and 420 orchestral ensembles, exclusive of 247 ensembles specializing in folk music. Also in 1970 there were 1,897 public libraries with holdings of 17.1 million books and newspapers, 22 museums, and 1,749 film projectors; 1,710 books were published in 11,778,000 copies in 1970. In the same year 201 newspapers and periodical publications appeared in the Moldavian SSR.[49] (See also sections on media and on educational and cultural institutions.)

Impressive as these statistics may be, they require qualification: the republic's cultural activities, except for folklore, are dominated by non-Moldavians. This is also true of higher educational institutions.[50] Content of cultural activities is also non-Moldavian, if

44 BSE, Yezhegodnik, 1971: 151.
45 Constantinescu et al., 1969: 425–443; 532–542.

46 Ocherk, 1963: 93–223.
47 Moldaviya, 1970: 93–94, 234; Pennar, 1971: 311–323.
48 BSE, Yezhegodnik, 1971: 153–154.
49 Ibid. 154–155.
50 Moldaviya, 1970: 81–100.

not anti-Moldavian in the historic sense, because it denies the Rumanianism of the Moldavians' national origin and cultural
heritage even in relation to contemporary
Communist Rumania. This is true even of
folkloristic cultural manifestations in music
and the dance which were historically
linked to, if not the same as, those of
Rumanian Moldavia, now stylized to blur
and minimize that organic relationship.
Customs of Moldavians, based on the
Rumanian rural patriarchal society and
steeped in a profound and fundamentalist
Rumanian Orthodox tradition, have also
been subject to attack in the predominantly
rural territories.[51] Collectivization of agriculture, which affected the peasant only
after the incorporation of Bessarabia into
the Moldavian republic, was a major cultural as well as economic blow, since Bessarabia was one of the oldest strongholds of
private ownership of rural property in
Rumania.[52]

The extent to which urbanization, sovietization, and education have affected cultural
values and traditions of the rural masses is
difficult to assess. Probably, essential elements of the Rumanian peasant culture
have not been obliterated. However, almost
no data other than that related to "nationalist manifestations" is available with respect
to youth, educated, urban, or nonresident
(the latter approximately 15% of total
population) Moldavians which would permit intelligent assessment of cultural transformation and current values of these
important segments of the Rumanian population of the Moldavian SSR.

EXTERNAL RELATIONS

External relations of the Moldavian SSR
are determined primarily by the republic's
underdeveloped economy and its geographic
location with respect to the Socialist Republic of Rumania.

Relations with other component republics
of the USSR appear limited to normal inter-
republic affairs. Special political and economic ties linking Moldavia to the Ukraine
(as autonomous republic within the Ukrainian SSR) before annexation of Bessarabia
and in the years immediately following
World War II have been eliminated in recent years. Due to the proximity of Rumania, with its historic national ties with
Moldavia, relations with that country have
always been restricted, all but ceasing since
1964 when legitimacy of the annexation of
Bessarabia was *de facto* questioned by
Bucharest.[53]

The only external relations, exclusive of
foreign trade arrangements, mentioned in
the press and by official speakers of the
Moldavian SSR are those with Bulgaria and
Hungary, restricted to exchanges of information in the field of agricultural production and processing.[54] Still, contracts for
reciprocal trade, concluded by the Ministry
of Trade of the Moldavian SSR and its
counterparts in socialist countries, are in
force between Moldavia and Hungary and
Czechoslovakia, and bilateral foreign trade
arrangements concluded by trading delegations are in effect with all European socialist
countries.[55]

Media

LANGUAGE DATA

What in official post–1945 terminology is
called the "Moldavian" language is one of
the regional dialects of Rumanian. Therefore, Moldavians and other Rumanians
understand each other readily, and we refer
to the "Moldavian" language in quotations.
The Soviet regime has imposed the use of

---

51 *Ibid.*, 81–93.
52 Cioranesco et al., 1967: 254–256.

53 Fischer-Galati, 1967: 99ff.; *New York Times* (November 6), 1971.
54 *Pravda* (April 4), 1971: 3.
55 *Sovetskaya torgovlya* (January 24), 1967.

Table 17.1

Native and Second Languages Spoken by Moldavians

(in thousands)

NO. MOLDAVIANS RESIDING			SPEAKING AS NATIVE LANGUAGE						SPEAKING AS SECOND LANGUAGE[a]	
			"Moldavian"		*% Point Change*	Russian		*% Point Change*	Russian	*Other Languages of Peoples of USSR*[b]
	1959	1970	1959	1970	*1959–1970*	1959	1970	*1959–1970*	1970	1970
in Moldavian SSR	1,887 (100%)	2,304 (100%)	1,853 (98.2%)	2,251 (97.7%)	−0.5	25 (1.3%)	46 (2.0%)	+0.7	781 (33.9%)	37 (1.6%)
in other Soviet republics	328 (100%)	394 (100%)	255 (77.7%)	312 (79.2%)	+1.5	55 (16.8%)	67 (17.0%)	+0.2	193 (49.0%)	60 (15.2%)
Total	2,214 (100%)	2,698 (100%)	2,108 (95.2%)	2,563 (95.0%)	−0.2	79 (3.6%)	113 (4.2%)	+0.6	974 (36.1%)	97 (3.6%)

Sources: *Itogi SSSR 1959* and *Itogi Moldavii 1959*: tables 53, 54; *Itogi 1970*: IV: 20, 276.

[a] No data are available for 1959, since no questions regarding command of a second language were asked in the 1959 census.

[b] Including "Moldavian," if not native language.

Cyrillic script in the republic. Thus, written "Moldavian" appears different from Rumanian.

According to data provided by the 1970 census, 95.0% of all Moldavians in the USSR (2,563,000 of 2,698,000) regard "Moldavian" as native language, a slight decrease from 1959 when 95.2% did so (see Table 17.1).

In the Moldavian SSR where 85.4% of the USSR's Moldavians live, 97.7% claimed that their native language was "Moldavian." In addition, 33.9% gave Russian as a second language of fluency, as did nearly half of the 394,000 Moldavians living in other parts of the Soviet Union.[56]

Of 1,264,957 non-Moldavian inhabitants of the republic, only 13,790 consider "Moldavian" their native tongue and only 173,612 speak it as a second language. Only 40.3% of total urban population of the republic, and 42.7% of the population of Kishinev, speak "Moldavian" as either first or second language.[57]

LOCAL MEDIA

In 1971, 192 newspapers and periodicals of all types, with total per issue circulation of approximately 3,280,000 copies, were published in the Moldavian SSR.[58] About 45% of these publications were in "Moldavian" and 55% in Russian, although circulation of the "Moldavian" language publications was nearly twice as large as that of the Russian language publications.[59] The principal newspaper, official publication of the republic party organization and government, is *Sovetskaya Moldaviya*, in Russian; an identical version in "Moldavian," *Moldova Socialista*, is printed for use of Moldavian inhabitants. Both papers, dailies, are typical of republican newspapers in that they carry relatively little news of strictly republican character. No recent circulation figures are available for these newspapers but it is known that total circulation of "Moldavian" language newspapers in 1971 was 1,364,000 as against 651,000 for Russian language newspapers (see Table 17.2).[60] The seven republic-level newspapers included four in "Moldavian," two in Russian, and one with both "Moldavian" and Russian editions. Of four city newspapers, those of Kishinev and Tiraspol have both "Moldavian" and Russian editions, while those of Bel'tsy and Bendery appear in Russian only.[61]

Most important periodical is the party journal *Kommunist Moldavii*, published in Russian; its theoretical articles show no regional characteristics.

As far as can be ascertained by reading several publications in "Moldavian," the Moldavian press is the Russian press in translation. The "Moldavian" language used is staid and artificial in comparison with that currently used in the Rumanian press, and to a Rumanian reader would appear written by foreigners. It is unknown whether the Rumanian press is available in Moldavia but, on the basis of statements by party spokesmen, it would appear that Rumanian language newspapers published outside the Moldavian SSR are not circulated in the republic.[62]

Little information is available on listening and viewing habits of the Moldavian population.[63] Official programming, as far as known, is more regionally oriented in radio than in television transmission. About 12–15 hours a day are devoted to broadcasting of local materials by local radio stations.[64] Dissemination of news, foreign and domestic, adheres strictly to patterns established by Moscow. Extent of reception of foreign broadcasts is unknown. No information is available with respect to reception or popularity in Moldavia of broadcasts emanating from BBC, Radio Free Europe, Radio Liberty, or other Western stations. It is known, however, that broadcasts and television transmissions originat-

56 *Sovetskaya Moldaviya* (May 5), 1971; *Pravda* (April 17), 1971.
57 *Itogi 1970*: IV: 276–279.
58 *Pechat' 1971*: 159, 189. "Periodicals" include bulletins, scientific notes, and other serial publications not included in the category *zhurnaly* (magazines).
59 *Moldaviya*, 1970: 236.

60 Hopkins, 1970: 198.
61 *Gazentyi mir*, 1971: 52–53.
62 *Sovetskaya Moldaviya* (February 16), 1967. See also *New York Times* (November 6), 1971.
63 Available data on electronic media are provided in Table 17.3.
64 Hopkins, 1970: 259.

Table 17.2

Publications in Moldavian SSR

Language of Publication	Year	NEWSPAPERS[a]			MAGAZINES			BOOKS & BROCHURES		
		No.	Per Issue Circulation (1,000)	Copies/100 in Language Group[d]	No.	Per Issue Circulation (1,000)	Copies/100 in Language Group[d]	No. Titles	Total Volume (1,000)	Books & Brochures/100 in Language Group[d]
Russian	1959	45	231	54.1	N.A.	N.A.	N.A.	415	3,142	735.5
	1971	62	651	102.2	9	48	7.5	1,192	5,161	810.1
"Moldavian"	1959	49	384	20.6	N.A.	N.A.	N.A.	411	3,244	173.6
	1971	49	1,364	60.2	11	492	21.7	613	6,960	307.2
Minority languages	1959	2[b]	4	6.7	N.A.	N.A.	N.A.	7	37	6.2
	1971	0	0	0	0	0	0	5	93	14.0
Foreign languages	1959	0	0	0	N.A.	N.A.	N.A.	(14)[c]	(140)	N.A.
	1971	0	0	0	0	0	0	(23)[c]	(232)	N.A.
All languages	1959	96	619	21.5	10	90	3.1	847[c]	6,563	227.5
	1971	111	2,015	56.5	20	540	15.0	1,833	12,446	348.7

Sources: *Pechat' 1959*: 56, 129, 165; *Pechat' 1971*: 96, 159, 189.

a 1971 figures do not include Kolkhoz newspapers.

b This figure may include publications in non-Soviet languages.

c Book totals as given in *Pechat'* sometimes differ from totals in language categories. The indication is that books are published in other languages, but no data is given. Figures in parentheses are the presumed production of books in other languages based on this discrepancy.

d Includes all native speakers of the language.

Table 17.3

Electronic Media and Films in Moldavian SSR

YEAR	RADIO					TELEVISION				MOVIES	
	No. Stations	No. Wired Sets (1,000)	Sets/100 Population	No. Wireless Sets (1,000)	Sets/100 Population	No. Stations	No. sets (1,000)	Sets/100 Population		Seats (1,000)	Seats/100 Population
1960	N.A.	397[a]	13.1[d]	236[a]	7.8[c]	N.A.	21[a]	.7[c]		123[b]	4.1[d]
1970	N.A.	617[a]	17.0[d]	577[a]	15.9[c]	N.A.	417[a]	11.5[c]		315[b]	8.7[d]
1971	N.A.	649[d]	17.7[d]	642[d]	17.5[c]	N.A.	465[c]	12.7[c]		N.A.	N.A.

[a] *Transport i svyaz' SSR*, 1972: 296–298.
[b] *Nar. obraz.*, 1971: 325.
[c] *Nar. khoz. 1972*: 610, 616.
[d] Computed.

ing in Rumania are received and viewed in the Moldavian SSR.[65] The party has repeatedly attacked the nature of these transmissions because of their anti-Russian orientation, warning Moldavians against listening to foreign propaganda.[66] All this indicates that massive Soviet efforts at indoctrination and isolation through vast use of network media originating in the USSR have not been altogether successful.

EDUCATIONAL INSTITUTIONS

In 1971 Moldavia had 2,165 primary and secondary schools with 804,000 students, 45 secondary specialized educational institutions with 52,400 students, and 8 institutions of higher education with 43,800 students (see Table 17.4). The increase in number of students at each level since 1961 was impressive since in that year respective enrollment figures were 545,000, 19,200, and 17,200.[67] Nevertheless, the Moldavian SSR ranks next to last among all union republics in percentage of inhabitants who had either attended or completed a course of instruction in a secondary or higher educational institution. In 1970 only 39.7% of inhabitants of Moldavia had a complete or incomplete secondary or higher education, and only 50.8% of the employed population had similar qualifications in contrast to all-Union percentages of 48.3% and 65.3%, respectively.[68]

In the school year 1970–1971, 199,000 of a total of 734,000 students enrolled in primary and secondary schools were attending urban schools.[69] The proportion of urban versus rural school attendance (27.1% vs. 72.9%) was somewhat higher than that recorded during the school year 1962–1963 (23.7% vs. 76.3%).[70] Still, the growth did not keep pace with size of urban population of the Moldavian SSR (from 22% in 1959 to 32% in 1970), indicating a sustained higher birth rate in the countryside.

A significant decline in instruction in the

"Moldavian" language has occurred since the end of World War II. In 1955–1956, 27% of schools, embracing 33% of the student body, used Russian as medium of instruction.[71] This figure exceeded percentage of Russians living in Moldavia more than threefold.[72] That trend was accelerated in the 1960s when the doctrine of supremacy of the Russian language as "the language of the common struggle of the peoples of our country for Communism" was officially advanced in the Moldavian SSR.[73]

The unfavorable situation in education and with respect to language is most evident in the area of higher education. As late as the academic year 1966–1967 the percentage of Moldavian students in Soviet institutions of higher education was 0.6% whereas the Moldavian population in the USSR amounted to 1.1% of the total.[74] Specific data compiled for the academic year 1960–1961 on the basis of students per 10,000 of each ethnic group gives an even better picture of the development of higher education among different national groups living in the republic. There were 51 Moldavian, 70 Ukrainian, 150 Russian, and 129 Jewish students in *vuzy* (institutions of higher education) per 10,000 of their respective nationalities in the 1960–1961 school year; the USSR average was 111 per 10,000 inhabitants. In 1970–1971 there were 114 Moldavian students per 10,000 of their population, a significant increase but again the lowest ratio of all union republic nationalities.[75]

Official explanations for the small proportion of Moldavian students in higher education center on inadequacy of preparation in rural schools, particularly in the Russian language.[76] This appears accurate but does not take into account the corollary reason: stringency of the Russian language requirements of *vuzy*, given that Russian is not the republic's predominant language. The small proportion of Moldavians is also related to Russification of the elementary and secondary schools. This is because the majority of students attending institutions of higher learning, whether Moldavian or

65 *Sovetskaya Moldaviya* (February 16), 1967.
66 *Ibid.*
67 *Moldaviya*, 1970: 234; *Sovetskaya Moldaviya* (May 5), 1971.
68 *Pravda* (April 17), 1971.
69 *Nar. obraz.*, 1971: 64–65.
70 Pennar et al., 1971: 314–315.

71 *Ibid.*: 315.
72 *Ibid.*
73 *Sovetskaya Moldaviya* (December 19), 1965.
74 Pennar et al., 1971: 319.
75 *Ibid.* See also *Nar. obraz.*, 1971: 196.
76 *Uchitelskaya gazeta* (July 13), 1967.

Table 17.4

Selected Data on Education in Moldavian SSR (1971)

Population: 3,670,000

		PER 1,000 POPULATION	% OF TOTAL
All Schools			
number of schools	2,165	.6	
number of students	804,000	219.1	
Newly opened elementary, incomplete secondary, and secondary schools			
number of schools	65		
number of student places	37,300	10.2	
Secondary special schools			
number of schools	45		
number of students	52,400	14.3	
Institutions of higher education			
number of institutions	8		
number of students	43,800	11.9	
Universities			
number of universities	1		
number of students			
total	7,635		
day students	4,035		53
evening students	0		
correspondence students	3,600		47
newly admitted			
total	1,346		
day students	940		70
evening students	0		
correspondence students	406		30
graduated			
total	1,412		
day students	855		61
evening students	0		
correspondence students	557		39
Graduate students			
total number	756	.2	
in scientific research institutions	460		
in universities	296		
Number of persons with (in 1970) higher or secondary (complete and incomplete) education			
per 1,000 individuals, 10 years and older	397		
per 1,000 individuals employed in national economy	508		
Number of workers graduated from professional-technical schools	21,300	5.8	

Source: *Nar. khoz. 1972*: 108, 438, 607, 614, 615, 617.

of other nationality, specialize in education (68% in 1960–1961, in contrast to 20.6% in agricultural studies and 9.5% in public health)[77] and therefore must be prepared to teach in Russian.

No breakdown by nationality is given for instructional staffs of any educational institution in the Moldavian SSR. It is safe to infer that Moldavian teachers are still predominant in rural school system and that Russian teachers are dominant in urban and higher education systems.

CULTURAL AND SCIENTIFIC INSTITUTIONS

The Moldavian SSR has standard Soviet cultural institutions including, at the beginning of 1971, 8 theaters, 1,925 choruses, 420 orchestras, 247 orchestras of Moldavian folk music, 1,775 houses of culture, 22 museums, and 1,897 public libraries.[78] The data provide no specific information as to urban-rural distribution of national representation or composition.

Only rudimentary information is available from Soviet and Moldavian sources with respect to scientific institutions, except for the Moldavian Academy of Sciences, established in 1961.[79] In 1970 the academy had 17 academicians and 20 corresponding members. From fragmentary data it would appear that a majority of the academicians and section heads are Russian and that the principal spheres of scientific investigation are mathematics, geology, and history.[80] The academy's scientific contributions appear generally undistinguished (for additional data, see Table 17.5). Among its works are monographs on the Moldavian working class in 1940–1965 and history of the Moldavian intelligentsia, as well as collections of research papers in philosophy and sociology.[81]

Table 17.5

Selected Data on Scientific and Cultural Facilities and Personnel in Moldavian SSR (1971)

Population: 3,670,000

Academy of Sciences	
number of members	36
number of scientific institutions	
affiliated with academy	20
total number of scientific workers	721
Museums	
number of museums	21
attendance	1,956,000
attendance per 1,000 population	532
Theaters	
number of theaters	8
attendance	1,197,000
attendance per 1,000 population	326
Number of persons working in education and culture	
total	120,000
number per 1,000 population	33
Number of persons working in science and scientific services	
total	23,000
number per 1,000 population	6
Number of public libraries	1,865
number of books and magazines in public libraries	17,926,000
Number of clubs	1,787

Source: *Nar. khoz. 1972*: 106, 451, 617.

---

77 Pennar et al., 1971: 318.
78 *BSE, Yezhegodnik*, 1971: 154–155. Later 1971 figures: libraries down to 1,865; museums to 21. *Nar. khoz. 1972*: 106, 451.
79 *BSE, Yezhegodnik*, 1971: 153–154.
80 *Ibid.*
81 V. K. Vizer et al., *Razvitiye rabochego klassa Moldavskoi SSR (1940–1965)* (Kishinev: Moldavian Academy of Sciences, 1970); A. I. Babii, *Formiro-* *vaniye Moldavskoi intelligentsii* (Kishinev: Shtinitsa, 1971); V. N. Yermuratsky et al., *Filosofskiye i sotsiologicheskiye issledovaniya v Moldavii* (Kishinev: Moldavian Academy of Sciences, 1970).

National Attitudes

REVIEW OF FACTORS FORMING
NATIONAL ATTITUDES

The nationalism of Moldavians, according to party critics, is rooted in continuing adherence to pre–World War II traditions, both social and national.[82] This criticism implies nonreconciliation, if not opposition, to social and cultural change and the de-Rumanization to which Moldavians have been subjected under Soviet rule.

Historically, nationalism of the Rumanian population of Bessarabia was characterized by anti-Russianism and anti-Semitism.[83] Opposition to Russia, based primarily on tsarist Russification of Bessarabia, was if anything exacerbated by the Bolshevik revolution and Communist activities in Bessarabia in the interwar years. As beneficiaries of drastic land reforms prior to union with Rumania in 1918, the Rumanian peasants of Bessarabia were at all times fearful of Bolshevik agrarian policies. Rumanian intellectuals always regarded Russians as foreign oppressors.[84] A corollary factor influencing anti-Russian and anti-Bolshevik sentiments of Rumanians was anti-Semitism. The urban centers of Bessarabia, particularly Kishinev, were essentially Jewish towns and Russians were held responsible for planting normally non-Rumanian-speaking Jews in cities as well as in certain rural areas of Bessarabia in the nineteenth and early twentieth centuries. Moldavian anti-Semitism was intensified by Bolshevik policies, which not only temporarily emancipated the Jews but sought to rely on parts of the Jewish population of Bessarabia for execution of their plans and programs, both before and after incorporation of Bessarabia into Rumania and again after reincorporation of Bessarabia into the Soviet Union during World War II. It is noteworthy that the Rumanians from Bessarabia were among the most virulent exponents of anti-Russian and anti-Semitic programs of such extremist right-wing Rumanian organizations as the Iron Guard and the League of National Christian Defense during the interwar years, and that the only pogroms by Rumanians recorded in World War II occurred in Bessarabia following reoccupation of that province by Rumanian armies during World War II.[85]

This right-wing Rumanian nationalism, so prevalent among the young, intellectuals, and even peasant masses, at least until definitive return of Bessarabia to the USSR in 1944, has evidently not been eradicated; rather, it has been converted into a more explicitly Moldavian nationalism. Collectivization of agriculture did not lessen Moldavian anti-Russianism. Restrictions imposed upon Moldavian youth with respect to higher educational and professional opportunities appear to contribute toward maintenance of anti-Soviet attitudes. Imposition of Soviet cultural policies, offensive to the deeply religious orientation and prejudices of the Moldavian masses, appear also to increase nationalism.[86]

Moldavian nationalism has also flourished in recent years because of revival of historic nationalism in Rumania proper and the Soviet Union's negative reaction to this.[87] Appeals emanating from Rumania for reunification through Rumanianism of all natives throughout the world have most directly affected those most proximate to Rumania itself.[88] The Moldavian response to Communist Rumania's neonationalism appears limited to identification with a Rumanian historical rather than Communist tradition. Rulers of the Soviet Union, however, have cut off contacts between Moldavians and Rumanians while attempting

---

82 *Pravda* (April 4), 1971: 2–3.
83 Fischer-Galati, 1969: 373–395; 1971: 112–121; Weber, 1966: 500–573.
84 Boldur, 1943: 1ff.

85 Cioranesco et al., 1967: 165ff.; Weber, 1966: 517ff.
86 Fischer-Galati, 1970: 15–37; *Scinteia* (May 7), 1966; *Sovetskaya Moldaviya* (March 2), 1966.
87 Swearingen, 1971: 355–364; *Pravda* (April 4), 1971: 2–3.
88 *Tribuna Romaniei*, 1972: 1–3; 1973: 4–6.

to perfect and legitimize a "Moldavian" historic tradition and nationality separate from the Rumanian. This process does not entail abandonment of discriminatory socioeconomic and cultural policies toward Moldavian inhabitants of the republic. For all these reasons Moldavian nationalism has continued to manifest itself.[89] The "Moldavianization" of Rumanian "bourgeois," Christian, anti-Russian, anti-Communist, and anti-Semitic nationalism may have changed, albeit superficially, the historic character of Bessarabian nationalism, but it would seem to have transplanted it, not rooted it out.

BASIC VIEWS OF SCHOLARS ON NATIONAL ATTITUDES

There are no studies by leading Western scholars on attitudinal factors affecting Moldavians or, for that matter, even Rumanian inhabitants of historic Bessarabia. Several Western scholars such as Henry L. Roberts,[90] Eugen Weber,[91] and Stephen Fischer-Galati,[92] concerned with Rumanian national attitudes in historic Moldavia, are in agreement on the essentially anti-Russian and anti-Semitic character of Moldavian nationalism. The anti-Russian and particularly the anti-Communist bases of Moldavian nationalism are stressed by G. Cioranesco et al. in a recent study on Russo-Rumanian relations.[93] Contemporary Rumanian scholars, for obvious political reasons, have failed to mention Bessarabia by name during the past three decades, paying no attention to problems of Rumanian inhabitants of the Moldavian SSR.

Soviet scholars have also shied away from study of attitudinal factors affecting Moldavians: the few venturing into this field have stressed, routinely and dogmatically, the historically pro-Russian and more recently pro-Communist sentiments of Moldavians. Among the more conspicuous exponents of the view that Moldavians are

Russophiles by tradition and Communists by conviction are S. Afteniuk[94] and V. A. Surilov.[95] Their contentions on the eternal brotherhood of Moldavians and Russians and on the slanderous propaganda emanating from falsifiers of history with respect to alleged Moldavian anti-Communist and anti-Russian sentiments cannot be taken seriously. Similar theses, in a strictly historical context, have been propounded in the collection *Istoriya Moldavii*, edited by A. D. Udal'tsov and L. V. Cherepnin,[96] and in *Istoriya Moldavskoi SSR*, edited by L. V. Cherepnin and other Moldavian scholars.[97] Even more distorted theses, stressing the "eternal friendship" among Moldavians, Russians, and Ukrainians, were presented at several Moldavian-Ukrainian-Russian "friendship conferences"; the "scholarly findings" of the most notorious, held in Kishinev in November 1958, were published by the Moldavian academy in 1961.[98] Their contentions cannot be considered scholarly contributions; in fact, the politically delicate problems connected with Moldavians and their attitudes account either for absence or falsification of data related to attitudinal factors. Essentially, Soviet sources argue that "the Moldavian language, much like the Rumanian, belongs to the East-Roman group of languages," and that the Moldavians are a separate nationality, quite apart from the Rumanians.[99] Western views of Moldavia, including those of this writer, can be summarized as follows.

The Moldavian SSR is among the most artificial of union republics: its very name and national composition are based on obfuscation of historical reality. The majority of the republic's inhabitants are Rumanians separated by artificial means from Rumanian inhabitants of historic Moldavia. Historic arguments provided by Soviet historians, politicians, and propagandists with

89 *Pravda* (April 4), 1971: 2–3; *Sovetskaya Moldaviya* (August 3), 1971.
90 Roberts, 1951: 1ff.
91 Weber, 1966: 501–574.
92 Fischer-Galati, 1969: 373–395; Fischer-Galati, 1971: 112–121.
93 Cioranesco et al., 1967: 1ff.

94 Afteniuk, 1957: 1ff.
95 Surilov, 1967: 1ff.
96 Udal'tsov and Cherepnin, 1951: I.
97 Cherepnin et al., 1968: I, II.
98 *Vekovaya Druzhba*, 1961: 1ff.
99 *BSE*, 1954: XXVIII: 105. Moldavia has been selected by Soviet ethnographers as the first union republic to be studied in connection with a survey of national attitudes based on a pilot study conducted in the Tatar ASSR. The extent to which the results of this study are published will be interesting to observe. *Sovetskaya Etnografiya*, 1972: III: 3–20.

respect to Moldavian national characteristics, language, and historic evolution and aspirations are baseless, serving only as a screen for obscuring historic reality. Leaders of the USSR and the Moldavian SSR—aware of the true history of the republic, reasons for its formation, and dangers of proximity of Soviet Moldavia to Rumanian Moldavia —are pursuing a conscious policy of isolating the predominantly rural population from the political and urban technological order, dominated by Russians and to a lesser extent Ukrainians. The Soviet regime has encouraged development of traditional agricultural pursuits with resultant economic prosperity for the peasantry. It has also encouraged maintenance of traditional Moldavian folk culture. In both sovietization of traditional forms of rural life through collectivization of agriculture and de-Rumanization of the essence of Moldavian folklore and way of life, however, securing allegiance of the population to the Soviet order and to aims of leaders of the Kremlin and of the Moldavian SSR has been at best tenuous.

Historic and national ties linking Moldavians of the republic with Rumanian inhabitants of Moldavia "across the river" have apparently not been severed by the Soviet regime despite the "iron curtain" erected on the eastern bank of the Prut. Yet the virtual isolation of Soviet Moldavians from Rumanian Moldavians is indicative of the delicacy of the Moldavian question in the USSR. Alone of all union republics, the Moldavian SSR has an equivalent, in the greater Soviet empire in Eastern Europe, in adjoining socialist Rumania. Leaders of the Socialist Republic of Rumania have legally relinquished all rights to reincorporation into Rumania of most territory now comprising the Moldavian SSR. Still, they are constantly trying to remind the republic's Moldavian inhabitants of their Rumanianism and of their national ties with brethren in Rumanian Moldavia.

RECENT MANIFESTATIONS OF NATIONALISM

According to the first secretary of the Moldavian Communist party, I. I. Bodyul, "harmful phenomena" (euphemism for bourgeois-nationalist manifestations) occurred in Moldavia as late as the 24th Congress of the CPSU in April 1971. Illustrations and details were not provided by Bodyul then or, for that matter, by any critic of Moldavian nationalism in recent years, but identification of the phenomena does provide a clue as to the nature of the nationalist manifestations:

> We still encounter instances of the penetration into literature and the arts of works that represent a distorted view of socialist reality. . . . We cannot regard as normal the obsession of certain creative workers with the archaic past and the glorification and poeticization in their works of long-outworn customs and traditions and their contraposition to our own times. . . . Playing upon the people's respectful attitude toward the past, upon feelings of national distinctiveness, the authors of such works essentially preach the idea of the classless, uncritical acceptance of the past, and therefore create conditions for the activization of harmful survivals, especially among young people, and prepare the soil for the penetration of alien views and sentiments into the people's minds.[100]

Attacks of this kind, together with countermeasures designed to invalidate "unhealthy" nationalist attitudes, have been frequent since publication in Rumania, in December 1964 within the context of rising Soviet-Rumanian tension, of *Notes on the Rumanians*.[101] That book, consisting of notes written by Marx himself on the "rape of Bessarabia" by tsarist Russia in 1812, was not circulated in the Moldavian SSR but its contents became known there. First major public denunciation of the volume, of the implicit Rumanian claims to Bessarabia, and of acceptance by Moldavians of the validity of this propaganda emanating from "certain bourgeois quill drivers," was by Bodyul on the occasion of the 12th Congress of the Moldavian Communist party in March 1966. While reiterating the validity of historic Russian claims to Bessarabia, he went so far as to declare that the Moldavian people had enthusiastically welcomed incorporation of Bessarabia into the "Motherland" in 1940 and that those questioning

---

100 *Pravda* (April 4), 1971: 3.
101 Marx, 1964: 1ff.

this view should be set straight by party activists.[102]

Despite these admonitions, nationalist manifestations and sentiments survived long enough to evoke even more extreme official statements. In February 1967 the same Bodyul followed the customary castigation of nationalism with the statement that "our children and future generations must know that their fathers did not conceive of a life for themselves outside of Russia" and with the demand that a concerted campaign for "elucidation in depth of the real history of the Moldavian people" be initiated at once.[103]

Repetition of such statements and admonitions—combined with continuing efforts to indoctrinate believers and skeptics alike with official Soviet theories regarding Moldavians' past and present aspirations —may be partly preventive in character. It may also represent a case of overreaction by rulers of the USSR and the Moldavian republic. Nevertheless, constant repetition of this party line by historians, the press, and other media of communication is indicative of a survival of nationalism, providing substantiating evidence for the validity of Bodyul's criticisms of 1971.[104]

102 *Sovetskaya Moldaviya* (March 2), 1966.
103 *Ibid.* (February 16), 1967.

104 *Moldaviya*, 1970: 63–100.

REFERENCES

Afteniuk, 1957
    Semen Yakovlevich Afteniuk, V *bratskoi sem'e narodov SSSR* (Kishinev: Kartia Moldoveniaske, 1957).
BSE, 1954
    Bol'shaya Sovetskaya entsiklopediya 2nd ed. (Moscow: Bol'shaya Sovetskaya entsiklopediya, 1954).
BSE, *Yezhegodnik*, 1971
    Bol'shaya Sovetskaya entsiklopediya, Yezhegodnik (Moscow: Sovetskaya entsiklopediya, 1971).
Babel, 1926
    Antony Babel, *La Bessarabie: Etude historique, ethnographique et economique* (Paris, 1926).
Boldur, 1943
    Alexandru V. Boldur, *Basarabia romaneasca* (Bucuresti, 1943).
Cherepnin et al., 1968
    L. V. Cherepnin et al., *Istoriya moldavskoi SSR* (Kishinev: Kartia Moldoveniaske, 1965, 1968): I–II.
Cioranesco et al., 1967
    C. Cioranesco et al., *Aspects des relations russo-roumaines* (Paris, 1967).
Clark, 1927
    Charles Upson Clark, *Bessarabia* (New York, 1927).
Cole and German, 1970
    J. P. Cole and F. C. German, *A Geography of the U.S.S.R.*, 2nd ed. (London: Butterworth, 1970).

Constantinescu et al., 1969
    Miron Constantinescu et al., *Istoria Romaniei* (Bucuresti: Editura Didactica, 1969).
Fischer-Galati, 1967
    Stephen Fischer-Galati, *The New Rumania: From People's Democracy to Socialist Republic* (Cambridge: M.I.T. Press, 1967).
Fischer-Galati, 1969
    Stephen Fischer-Galati, "Rumanian Nationalism," in Peter F. Sugar and Ivo J. Lederer, eds., *Nationalism in Eastern Europe* (Seattle: University of Washington Press, 1969): 373–395.
Fischer-Galati, 1970
    Stephen Fischer-Galati, "The Socialist Republic of Rumania," in Peter A. Toma, ed., *The Changing Face of Communism in Eastern Europe* (Tucson: University of Arizona Press, 1970): 15–37.
Fischer-Galati, 1971
    Stephen Fischer-Galati, "Fascism in Rumania," in Peter F. Sugar, ed., *Native Fascism in the Successor States, 1918–1945* (Santa Barbara: Clio Press, 1971): 112–121.
Gazetnyi mir, 1971
    Gazetnyi mir (Moscow: Izdatel'stvo politicheskoi literatury, 1971).
Hopkins, 1970
    Mark W. Hopkins, *Mass Media in the Soviet Union* (New York: Pegasus, 1970).

Ionescu, 1964
Ghita Ionescu, *Communism in Rumania, 1944–1962* (London: Oxford University Press, 1964).

Itogi 1970
Itogi vsesoyuznoi perepisi naseleniya 1970 goda (Moscow: Statistika, 1972–1973).

Itogi Moldavii 1959
Itogi vsesoyuznoi perepisi naseleniya 1959 goda Moldavskaya SSR (Moscow: Gosstatizdat, 1962).

Itogi SSSR, 1959
Itogi vsesoyuznoi perepisi naseleniya 1959 goda SSSR (Moscow: Gosstatizdat, 1962), summary volume and volumes on 15 republics.

Marx, 1964
Karl Marx, *Insemnari despre romani* (Bucuresti, 1964).

Moldaviya, 1970
Moldaviya (Moscow: Mysl', 1970).

Nar. khoz. 1970
Narodnoye khozyaistvo SSSR v 1970 godu (Moscow: Statistika, 1971).

Nar. khoz. 1972
Narodnoye khozyaistvo SSSR 1922–1972, Yubileinyi statisticheskii yezhegodnik (Moscow: Statistika, 1972).

Nar. obraz., 1971
Narodnoye obrazovaniye, nauka i kul'tura v SSSR: statisticheskii sbornik (Moscow: Statistika, 1971).

Ocherk, 1963
Ocherk istorii moldavskoi sovetskoi literatury (Moscow, 1963).

Okhotnikov and Batchinsky, 1927
J. Okhotnikov and N. Batchinsky, *La Bessarabie et la paix européenne* (Paris, 1927).

Pechat' 1959
Pechat' SSSR v 1959 godu (Moscow: Kniga, 1960).

Pechat' 1970
Pechat' SSSR v 1970 godu (Moscow: Kniga, 1971).

Pennar et al., 1971
Jaan Pennar et al., *Modernization and Diversity in Soviet Education with Special Reference to Nationality Groups* (New York: Praeger, 1971).

Rigby, 1968
T. H. Rigby, *Communist Party Membership in the USSR* (Princeton, N.J.: Princeton University Press, 1968).

Roberts, 1951
Henry L. Roberts, *Rumania: Political Problems of an Agrarian State* (New Haven: Yale University Press, 1951).

Shabad, 1951
Theodore Shabad, *Geography of the USSR: A Regional Survey* (New York: Columbia University Press, 1951).

Surilov, 1967
V. A. Surilov, *O natsional'no gosudartsvenom samôpredelenii moldavskogo naroda* (Kishinev, 1967).

Swearingen, 1971
Rodger Swearingen, ed., *Leaders of the Communist World* (New York: Free Press, 1971).

Televideniye i radioveshchaniye
Televideniye i radioveshchaniye (Moscow, monthly).

Transport i svyaz' SSSR, 1972
Transport i svyaz' SSSR (Moscow: Statistika, 1972).

Tsameryan and Ronin, 1962
I. P. Tsameryan and S. L. Ronin, *Equality of Rights between Races and Nationalities in the USSR* (Paris: UNESCO, 1962).

Udal'tsov and Cherepnin, 1951
A. D. Udal'tsov and L. V. Cherepnin, eds., *Istoriya Moldavii* (Kishinev, 1951): I.

Vekovaya druzhba, 1961
Vekovaya druzhba. Materialy nauchnoi sessii instituta istorii moldavskogo filiala A.N. SSSR (Kishinev, 1961).

Weber, 1966
Eugen Weber, "Romania," in Hans Rogger and Eugen Weber, eds., *The European Right: A Historical Profile* (Berkeley: University of California Press, 1966): 501–574.

APPENDIX:
Comparative Tables for the
Major Soviet Nationalities

Zev Katz and Frederic T. Harned

The first 23 tables in this Appendix bring together the basic demographic, political, economic, educational and cultural data developed in this volume. These data are aggregated in two ways: (1) by nationality, and (2) by union republic. In the first case, data are provided for members of the 17 nationalities analyzed in this volume—i.e. the titular nationalities of the 15 union republics (whether resident in the specific SSR or not) plus Tatars and Jews. In the second case the unit for which data are provided is the union republic; where data are available, the Tatar ASSR (part of the RSFSR) is also included in these tables and set in italics to distinguish it from the union republics. The exception to these statements is Table A.1 which presents data by union republic and also, where available, for Tatars and Jews (both of the latter set in italics).

The remaining tables, A.24–A.29, attempt to arrive at more complex indications of national development and vitality. The ranking in these tables were derived as follows:

Table A.24 presents a ranking for *national political vitality*, arrived at by combining the rankings for population growth (Table A.2), titular nationality as percent of republic population (Table A.6), concentration of nationality in republic population (Table A.7), percentage for whom the national language is native (Table A.8), and weight of nationality in CPSU (Table A.11).

In Table A.25, a ranking for *economic development* was developed by combining rankings for produced income per capita (Table A.15), savings per capita (Table A.16), and trade turnover per capita (Table A.17).

Table A.26 gives a ranking for *sociocultural development*, reached by combining rankings for urbanization (Table A.9), educational standards (Table A.18), students in higher education (Table A.19), scientists (Table A.20), doctors (Table A.21), and books (Table A.23) per population.

In Table A.27, a combined ranking for *sociocultural and economic development* is given by combining indicators in Tables A.25 and A.26.

Table A.28 presents a ranking for *overall national development*, reached by combining indicators in tables A.24 and A.27.

In Table A.29, nationalities are grouped into broad ethnic-geographic categories and a ranking developed for *overall development by ethnic-geographic category*, using indicators from tables A.24, A.25, and A.26.

The above approach—obtaining cumulative rankings by adding individual rankings —has the virtue of simplicity; however, the results cannot be taken as definitive statements of the relative political vitality and economic and sociocultural development of Soviet nationalities. Use of different criteria or more refined and complex calculations for Tables A.24–A.29 would probably have produced somewhat different conclusions. Nevertheless, it is unlikely that the differences would be extreme—that is, that a nationality's rank in any table would switch from high to low or vice versa if a different approach were used.

Some rankings would also change if all data used in tables A.1–A.23 were uniformly available by nationality. In some instances, data on a particular indicator were not available for a particular *nationality*, and data on that indicator for the *national republic* were used instead. Validity of the rankings thus obtained depends on weight of the nationality in its republic. Most important instance of error introduced by this approach is the relative ranking of Kazakhs and Uzbeks in tables A.24–A.28. Most evidence suggests that Uzbeks are generally more developed than Kazakhs; Kazakhs rank higher in the tables because most Kazakh data available were for the Kazakh SSR, in which the more highly developed Slavs are a majority of the population.

Thus, the assessments in tables A.24–A.29 are very rough, subject to correction and refinement. Still, they are useful in providing an overall picture whose outlines would be difficult to discern directly from the mass of separate data on which they are based.

Table A.1

Basic Data on Union Republics, Tatar, ASSR, and Jews

	AREA (SQ. MI.)	POPULA-TION (1970 CENSUS)	DEVELOPMENT RANK OF TITULAR NATION-ALITY[a]	LANGUAGE GROUP OF TITULAR NATIONALITY	ALPHABET	RELIGION	MODE OF ACCESSION TO USSR
RSFSR	6,592,818	130,079,000	1	Slavic	Cyrillic	Christian/predominantly Russian Orthodox, also other Christian sects, Islamic, Buddhist	Proclaimed November 7, 1917, as Federative Soviet Socialist Republic; became union republic with establishment of USSR in December 1922; presently includes 12 autonomous national republics, 5 autonomous provinces.
Ukrainian SSR	233,089	47,126,000	7	Slavic	Cyrillic	Christian/Russian Orthodox, Uniate	After brief independence (1918–1919), constituted as Soviet republic allied with RSFSR; since December 1922 union republic within USSR.
Belorussian SSR	80,134	9,002,000	11	Slavic	Cyrillic	Christian/Russian Orthodox, Catholic	Established as Belorussian Soviet Republic, allied with RSFSR, after brief struggle between national independence movement and pro-Bolshevik forces; in December 1922 became union republic within USSR.
Estonian SSR	17,413	1,356,000	3	Finno-Ugric	Latin	Christian/predominantly Lutheran	Independent republics, 1918–1940; taken over by Soviet forces in 1940, incorporated as union republics in USSR.
Latvian SSR	24,595	2,364,000	6	Indo-European/ Baltic	Latin	Christian/Lutheran, Catholic	
Lithuanian SSR	25,173	3,128,000	4,5	Indo-European/ Baltic	Latin	Christian/predominantly Catholic	

438

Republic				Language	Script	Religion	History
Armenian SSR	11,175	2,492,000	4,5	Indo-European/Caucasian	Armenian	Christian/Armenian (Gregorian) Church	Brief independence (1918–1920) terminated with victory of Red Army. Transcaucasian Soviet Federation of Socialist Republics created in 1921; became union republic with creation of USSR in December 1922. Separate national units were autonomous republics until December 1936 when units became full union republics of USSR.
Georgian SSR	26,757	4,686,000	2	Ibero-Caucasian	Georgian	Christian/Georgian Orthodox Church	
Azerbaidzhan SSR	33,425	5,117,000	8	Turkic	Cyrillic	Islamic/Shia	
Kazakh SSR	1,048,305	13,009,000	10	Turkic	Cyrillic	Islamic and Christian	Turkestan Soviet Republic within RSFSR proclaimed in spring 1918. After period of war with local independence movements, Red Army established rule in 1920. Kazakh (called at first Kirgiz) Autonomous SSR within RSFSR established in August 1920. Soviet authorities also recognized autonomy of People's Republics of Khiva (Khorezm) and Bukhara. In 1924–1925 these autonomous units and Turkestan republic were abolished and Turkmen, Uzbek, and Kirgiz SSRs were created. Tadzhiks had at first autonomous republic within Uzbek SSR (1924); in 1929 transformed into union republic. Kazakh ASSR became union republic in December 1936.
Kirgiz SSR	76,100	2,933,000	12	Turkic	Cyrillic	Islamic	
Turkmen SSR	187,200	2,159,000	9	Turkic	Cyrillic	Islamic	
Uzbek SSR	172,741	11,780,000	13	Turkic	Cyrillic	Islamic	
Tadzhik SSR	54,900	2,900,000	15	Iranian	Cyrillic	Islamic	

Table A.1 (continued)

	AREA (SQ. MI.)	POPULATION (1970 CENSUS)	DEVELOPMENT RANK OF TITULAR NATIONALITY[a]	LANGUAGE GROUP OF TITULAR NATIONALITY	ALPHABET	RELIGION	MODE OF ACCESSION TO USSR
Moldavian SSR	13,012	3,569,000	14	Romance	Cyrillic	Christian/East Orthodox	Autonomous Moldavian Republic within Ukrainian SSR created in October 1924. In June 1940 Soviet forces entered Bessarabia (previously under rule of Rumania) and in August 1940 union republic of Moldavia comprising both territories proclaimed.
Tatar ASSR	26,250	2,850,000[c]	N.A.	Turkic	Cyrillic	Islamic, about 2% Christian	*Established in May 1920 as autonomous republic within RSFSR.*
Jews[b]	(Birobidzhan 13,900)	(total population of nationality in USSR 2,151,000)	N.A.	Yiddish	Hebrew	Judaism	*Jewish Autonomous Province within RSFSR, decreed in March 1928.*

[a] See Table A.28 for derivation of this ranking.

[b] Not a national republic; only a small minority live in the "Jewish Autonomous Oblast" of Birobidzhan. Data are given for Jewish nationality where applicable.

[c] Includes Tatars in ASSR and elsewhere in the USSR.

Table A.2

Major Soviet Nationalities: Size, Growth, and Weight

Ranked by Weight in Total USSR Population, 1970

RANK	NATIONALITY	POPULATION (IN THOUSANDS)			GROWTH (%)		RANK BY 1959–1970 GROWTH	% OF TOTAL USSR POPULATION	
		1926	1959	1970	1926–1970	1959–1970		1959	1970
	USSR Total	147,082	208,827	241,720	64.3	15.8		100.0	100.0
1	Russians	77,791	114,114	129,015	65.8	13.1	13	54.65	53.37
2	Ukrainians	31,195[a]	37,253	40,753	[a]	9.4	14	17.84	16.86
3	Uzbeks	3,989	6,015	9,195	130.1	52.9	2	2.88	3.80
4	Belorussians	4,739[a]	7,913	9,052	[a]	14.4	12	3.79	3.74
5	Tatars	3,311	4,968	5,931	80.0	19.4	10	2.38	2.45
6	Kazakhs	3,968	3,622	5,299	33.5	46.3	6	1.73	2.19
7	Azerbaidzhani	1,713	2,940	4,380	155.7	49.0	5	1.41	1.81
8	Armenians	1,568	2,787	3,559	127.0	27.7	7	1.33	1.47
9	Georgians	1,821	2,692	3,245	78.2	20.5	9	1.29	1.34
10	Moldavians	279[a]	2,214	2,698	[a]	21.9	8	1.06	1.12
11	Lithuanians	41[a]	2,326	2,665	[a]	14.6	11	1.11	1.10
12	Jews	2,672	2,268	2,151	−19.5	−05.2	17	1.09	0.89
13	Tadzhiks	981	1,397	2,136	117.7	52.9	1	0.67	0.88
14	Turkmen	764	1,002	1,525	99.6	52.2	3	0.48	0.63
15	Kirgiz	763	969	1,452	90.3	49.8	4	0.46	0.60
16	Latvians	151[a]	1,400	1,430	[a]	2.1	15	0.67	0.59
17	Estonians	155[a]	989	1,007	[a]	1.8	16	0.47	0.42
	All Other	11,181	13,958	16,227	45.1	16.3		6.68	6.71

Sources: *Nar. khoz.* 1972: 31; *Itogi 1959*: 84.

[a] Does not include population in territories subsequently incorporated into USSR; 1926–1970 growth rates not computed for these nationalities.

441

Table A.3

Size, Growth, and Weight of Major Nationalities by Geographic-Ethnic Group

NATIONALITY GROUP	POPULATION (IN THOUSANDS)			GROWTH (%)		WEIGHT IN TOTAL USSR POPULATION (%)	
				1926–	1959–		
	1926	1959	1970	1970	1970	1959	1970
Slavs[a]	113,725	159,280	178,820	57.2	12.3	76.3	74.0
Other Europeans[b]	3,298	9,197	9,951	201.7[d]	8.2	4.4	4.1
Islamic[c]	15,489	20,913	29,918	93.2	43.1	10.0	12.4
Armenian-Georgian	3,389	5,479	6,804	100.8	24.2	2.6	2.8

Source: Calculated from data in Table A.2.

NOTE: The Islamic group has the highest rate of growth and the "other Europeans" the lowest (ratio 5.25:1). The Slav ratio is second lowest (ratio 3.5:1). Since the Slavs together amount to about three quarters of the population, they will remain the predominant group for a long time even if they continue losing in relative weight to the Islamic group.

[a] Russians, Ukrainians, Belorussians.

[b] Estonians, Latvians, Lithuanians, Moldavians, Jews.

[c] Uzbeks, Tatars, Kazakhs, Aberbaidzhani, Tadzhiks, Turkmen, and Kirgiz.

[d] Reflects incorporation of territories inhabited by these peoples in 1939–1945.

Table A.4

Republic Populations, 1959–1970

Ranked by Growth Rate

RANK	REPUBLICS	POPULATION (IN THOUSANDS)		% GROWTH	% OF USSR POPULATION	
		1959	1970	1959–1970	1959	1970
	USSR total	208,827	241,720	16	100.0	100.0
1	Tadzhik SSR	1,981	2,900	46	0.95	1.20
2	Uzbek SSR	8,261	11,960	45	3.96	4.95
3	Turkmen SSR	1,516	2,159	42	0.73	0.89
4	Kirgiz SSR	2,066	2,933	42	0.99	1.21
5	Armenian SSR	1,763	2,492	41	0.84	1.03
6	Kazakh SSR	9,153	12,849	40	4.38	5.32
7	Azerbaidzhan SSR	3,698	5,117	38	1.77	2.12
8	Moldavian SSR	2,885	3,569	24	1.38	1.48
9	Georgian SSR	4,044	4,686	16	1.94	1.94
10	Lithuanian SSR	2,711	3,128	15	1.30	1.29
11	Estonian SSR	1,197	1,356	13	0.57	0.56
12	Latvian SSR	2,093	2,364	13	1.00	0.98
13	Ukraine SSR	41,869	47,126	13	20.05	19.50
14	Belorussian SSR	8,056	9,002	12	3.86	3.72
15	RSFSR	117,534	130,079	11	56.28	53.81
16	Tatar ASSR	2,850	3,131	10	1.36	1.29

Sources: *Izvestia* (April 17), 1971; *CDSP*, 1971: XXIII: 16: 16–18; *Itogi 1970*: I: 12.

Table A.5

Adult Population (Over 20) of Republics, 1959–1970

Ranked by Growth Rate of Total Population, as in Table A. 4

RANK	REPUBLICS	ADULT POPULATION (IN THOUSANDS)		% OF TOTAL POPULATION OF REPUBLIC		% OF USSR ADULT POPULATION	
		1959	1970	1959	1970	1959	1970
	USSR Total	130,656	149,747	62.57	61.95	100.0	100.0
1	Tadzhik SSR	1,057	1,287	53.36	44.38	0.8	0.9
2	Uzbek SSR	4,405	5,401	53.32	45.16	3.4	3.6
3	Turkmen SSR	819	987	54.02	45.72	0.6	0.7
4	Kirgiz SSR	1,144	1,433	55.37	48.86	0.9	1.0
5	Armenian SSR	976	1,266	55.36	50.80	0.7	0.8
6	Kazakh SSR	5,217	6,870	57.00	53.47	4.0	4.6
7	Azerbaidzhan SSR	2,032	2,397	54.95	46.84	1.6	1.6
8	Moldavian SSR	1,677	2,079	58.13	58.25	1.3	1.4
9	Georgian SSR	2,524	2,855	62.41	60.93	1.9	1.9
10	Lithuanian SSR	1,746	2,048	64.40	65.47	1.3	1.4
11	Estonian SSR	839	957	70.09	70.58	0.6	0.6
12	Latvian SSR	1,466	1,687	70.04	71.36	1.1	1.1
13	Ukraine SSR	27,489	31,538	65.65	66.92	21.0	21.1
14	Belorussian SSR	4,976	5,624	61.77	62.48	3.8	3.8
15	RSFSR	74,290	83,316	63.21	63.87	56.9	55.6
16	Tatar ASSR	1,707	1,853	59.89	59.18	1.3	1.2

Source: *Itogi 1970*: II: 12–75, 157.

NOTE: Moslem republics have most youthful populations; Estonia and Latvia, the oldest.

Table A.6

Titular Nationality as Percent of Republic Population, 1959–1970

Ranked by % of Population, 1970

RANK	REPUBLIC	MEMBERS OF TITULAR NATIONALITY RESIDING IN REPUBLIC (IN THOUSANDS)		TITULAR NATIONALITY AS % OF TOTAL REPUBLIC POPULATION		% POINT CHANGE
		1959	*1970*	*1959*	*1970*	*1959–1970*
1	Armenian SSR	1,552	2,208	88.0	88.6	+0.6
2	RSFSR	97,864	107,748	83.3	82.8	−0.5
3	Belorussian SSR	6,532	7,290	81.1	81.0	−0.1
4	Lithuanian SSR	2,151	2,507	79.3	80.1	+0.8
5	Ukraine SSR	32,158	35,284	76.8	74.9	−1.9
6	Azerbaidzhan SSR	2,494	3,777	67.5	73.8	+6.3
7	Estonian SSR	893	925	74.6	68.2	−6.4
8	Georgian SSR	2,601	3,131	64.3	66.8	+2.5
9	Turkmen SSR	924	1,417	60.9	65.6	+4.7
10	Uzbek SSR	5,044	7,734	61.1	64.7	+3.6
11	Moldavian SSR	1,887	2,304	65.4	64.6	−0.8
12	Latvian SSR	1,298	1,342	62.0	56.8	−5.2
13	Tadzhik SSR	1,051	1,630	53.1	56.2	+3.1
14	*Tatar ASSR*	*1,345*	*1,536*	*47.2*	*49.1*	*+1.9*
15	Kirgiz SSR	837	1,285	40.5	43.8	+3.3
16	Kazakh SSR	2,723	4,161	30.0	32.6	+2.6

Sources: *Izvestia* (April 17), 1971; *CDSP*, 1971: XXIII: 16: 16–18; *Itogi 1959*: 203; *Itogi 1970*: IV: 144.

NOTE: Nations *increasing* as percentage of their republic's population, 1959–1970: all non-Europeans plus Lithuanians. Nations *decreasing* as percentage of their republic's population, 1959–1970: all Europeans except for Lithuanians.

Table A.7

Concentration of Titular Nationality in Republic, 1959–1970

Ranked by % of Total Population of Nationality in USSR

Who Live in Own Republic

	1959			1970		
RANK	NATIONALITY	% LIVING IN RESPECTIVE REPUBLICS	RANK	NATIONALITY	% LIVING IN RESPECTIVE REPUBLICS	NET CHANGE IN % POINTS 1959–1970[a]
1	Georgians	96.6	1	Georgians	96.5	−0.1
2	Latvians	92.7	2	Lithuanians	94.1	+1.8
3	Lithuanians	92.3	3	Latvians	93.8	+1.1
4	Turkmen	92.2	4	Turkmen	92.9	+0.7
5	Estonians	90.3	5	Estonians	91.9	+1.6
6	Kirgiz	86.4	6	Kirgiz	88.5	+2.1
7	Ukrainians	86.3	7	Ukrainians	86.6	+0.3
8	Russians	85.8	8	Azerbaidzhani	86.2	+1.4
9	Moldavians	85.2	9	Moldavians	85.4	+0.2
10	Azerbaidzhani	84.8	10	Uzbeks	84.1	+0.3
11	Uzbeks	83.8	11	Russians	83.5	−2.3
12	Belorussians	82.5	12	Belorussians	80.5	−2.0
13	Tadzhiks	75.2	13	Kazakhs	78.5	+3.3
14	Kazakhs	75.2	14	Tadzhiks	76.3	+1.1
15	Armenians	55.0	15	Armenians	62.0	+7.0
16	*Tatars*	*27.0*	16	*Tatars*	*25.9*	*−1.1*
	Mean Concentration:	84.33			85.39	+1.06

Source: Computed from census returns cited in tables
A.4 and A.6.

NOTE: Except for marginal decrease in percent of Georgians in Georgia, Russians, Belorussians, and Tatars were the only nationalities to become less concentrated in their own republics. Highest gains in concentration are among Armenians, Kazakhs, Kirgiz, and Lithuanians.

[a] Sequence of nationalities as in 1970 column.

Table A.8

Speakers of Languages of Major Nationalities of USSR, 1970

Ranked by % Identifying Language as Mother Tongue

RANK	LANGUAGE	NATIVE SPEAKERS	FLUENT AS SECOND LANGUAGE	TOTAL SPEAKERS	% NATIONALITY IDENTIFYING LANGUAGE AS MOTHER TONGUE
1	Russian	141,830,564	41,937,995	183,798,559	c
2	Turkmen	1,514,980	50,996	1,565,976	98.9
3	Kirgiz	1,445,213	41,493	1,486,706	98.8
4	Uzbek	9,154,904	543,023	9,697,727	98.6
5	Tadzhik	2,202,671	261,248	2,463,919	98.5
6	Georgian	3,310,917	190,115	3,501,032	98.4
7	Azerbaidzhani	4,347,089	263,160	4,610,249	98.2
8	Kazakh	5,213,694	146,057	5,359,751	98.0
9	Lithuanian	2,625,608	152,523	2,778,131	97.9
10	Estonian	974,649	69,520	1,044,169	95.5
11	Latvian	1,390,162	215,376	1,605,538	95.2
12	"Moldavian"	2,607,367	283,426	2,890,793	95.0
13	Armenian	3,261,053	147,727	3,408,780	91.4
14	Tatar[a]	5,493,316	344,414	5,837,730	89.2
15	Ukrainian	35,400,944	5,618,837	41,019,781	85.7
16	Belorussian	7,630,007	903,024	8,533,031	80.2
17	Jewish[b]	381,571	166,571	547,649	17.7

Source: *Itogi 1970*: IV: 20, 76, 331–332, 333–359.

[a] Complete data available only for RSFSR, Kazakhstan, Georgia, and Central Asia.

[b] Includes Yiddish and other languages of Jews in USSR. Data not available on non-Jewish speakers of the language except in Jewish national region (Birobidzhan); however, number of such speakers is estimated to be negligible.

[c] Precise statistic not available; all other evidence indicates that virtually all who identify themselves as of Russian nationality speak Russian as their native language.

Table A.9

Urban-Rural Distribution, 1959–1970, by Nationality

Ranked by Urban Percentage

RANK	NATIONALITY	1959		RANK	NATIONALITY	1970	
		% Urban	% Rural			% Urban	% Rural
1	Jews	95.3	4.7	1	Jews	97.9	2.1
2	Russians	57.7	42.3	2	Russians	68.0	32.0
3	Armenians	56.5	43.5	3	Armenians	64.8	35.2
4	Latvians	47.5	52.5	4	Estonians	55.1	44.9
5	Tatars	47.2	52.8	5	Tatars	55.0	45.0
6	Estonians	47.0	53,0	6	Latvians	52.7	47.3
7	Ukrainians	39.2	60.8	7	Ukrainians	48.5	51.5
8	Georgians	36.1	63.9	8	Lithuanians	46.7	53.3
9	Lithuanians	35.1	64.9	9	Georgians	44.0	56.0
10	Azerbaidzhani	34.8	65.2	10	Belorussians	43.7	56.3
11	Belorussians	32.4	67.6	11	Azerbaidzhani	39.7	60.3
12	Turkmen	25.4	74.6	12	Turkmen	31.0	69.0
13	Kazakhs	24.1	75.9	13	Kazakhs	26.7	73.3
14	Uzbeks	21.8	78.2	14	Tadzhiks	26.0	74.0
15	Tadzhiks	20.6	79.4	15	Uzbeks	24.9	75.1
16	Moldavians	12.9	87.1	16	Moldavians	20.4	79.6
17	Kirgiz	10.8	89.2	17	Kirgiz	14.6	85.4
	USSR average	47.9	52.1		USSR average	56.0	44.0

Sources: *Itogi 1959*: 190–196; *Itogi 1970*: IV: 20, 27, 28.

NOTE: Highest urbanization: Jews, Russians, Armenians, Latvians, Tatars (highest Islamic group), Estonians. Lowest urbanization: Central Asians plus Moldavians. Only three nationalities—Jews, Russians, and Armenians —are above USSR mean level of urbanization. They and Tatars are only peoples exceeding urbanization levels of their respective republics. Tatars are far more urbanized than other Moslem peoples, who, with Moldavians, are grouped at bottom of urbanization ranking. In 1970 urbanization ratio between lowest group (Moldavians) and highest (Jews) was 1:6.7 and second highest (Russians), 1:4.7. The gap closed somewhat in comparison with 1959.

448 APPENDIX

Table A.10

Urban-Rural Distribution, 1959–1970, by Republic

Ranked by Urban Percentage

RANK	REPUBLIC	1959		RANK	REPUBLIC	1970		% INCREASE IN URBAN POPULATION
		% Urban	% Rural			% Urban	% Rural	1959–1970
1	Estonian SSR	56	44	1	Estonian SSR	66	34	36.1
2	Latvian SSR	56	44	2	RSFSR	64	36	37.0
3	RSFSR	52	48	3	Latvian SSR	64	36	30.3
4	Armenian SSR	50	50	4	Armenian SSR	61	39	80.2
5	Azerbaidzhan SSR	48	52	5	Ukraine SSR	56	44	41.0
6	Turkmen SSR	46	54	6	Tatar ASSR	54	46	45.4
7	Ukraine SSR	46	54	7	Lithuanian SSR	53	47	61.2
8	Kazakh SSR	44	56	8	Kazakh SSR	52	48	70.7
9	Georgian SSR	42	58	9	Azerbaidzhan SSR	51	49	52.3
10	Tatar ASSR	42	58	10	Georgian SSR	48	52	35.6
11	Lithuanian SSR	39	61	11	Turkmen SSR	48	52	57.1
12	Kirgiz SSR	34	66	12	Belorussian SSR	46	54	69.6
13	Uzbek SSR	34	66	13	Tadzhik SSR	38	62	80.3
14	Tadzhik SSR	33	67	14	Kirgiz SSR	38	62	67.2
15	Belorussian SSR	31	69	15	Uzbek SSR	37	63	68.5
16	Moldavian SSR	22	78	16	Moldavian SSR	33	67	90.7
	USSR total	48	52		USSR total	56	44	36.0

Sources: *Nar. khoz. 1972*: 499–725; *Itogi 1959*: 20–29.

NOTE: With some exceptions, republics with a low urban percentage had a very high growth of the urban population in 1959–1970, and those with a high urban percentage had a lower growth. The ratio between highest (Estonia) and lowest (Moldavia) closed somewhat (from 2.5 in 1959 to 2.0 in 1970).

Table A.11

National Composition of CPSU, January 1, 1972

Union Republic Nationalities Only

Ranked by Weight Index

RANK	NATIONALITY	NO.	%	WEIGHT INDEX[a]
1	Georgians	242,253	1.66	1.24
2	Russians	8,927,400	61.02	1.14
3	Armenians	223,372	1.52	1.04
4	Ukrainians	2,333,750	15.95	0.95
5	Belorussians	511,981	3.50	0.94
6	Azerbaidzhani	206,184	1.41	0.78
7	Kazakhs	246,393	1.68	0.77
8	Estonians	45,454	0.31	0.74
9	Latvians	60,843	0.42	0.71
10	Lithuanians	93,271	0.64	0.58
11	Kirgiz	45,205	0.31	0.52
12	Uzbeks	282,918	1.93	0.51
13	Turkmen	43,111	0.29	0.46
14	Tadzhiks	57,271	0.39	0.44
15	Moldavians	58,062	0.40	0.36
	Other Nationalities	1,253,821	8.57	1.28
	Total	14,631,289	100.00	1.00

Source: *Kommunist vooruzhennykh sil*, 1972: XXIV: 12.

[a] Weight Index: Nationality's % of party divided by % of 1970 population.

Table A.12

National Composition of CPSU by

Geographic-Ethnic Group,

January 1, 1972

GROUP[a]	% OF PARTY	WEIGHT INDEX[b]
All Slavs	80.47	1.09
Russians	61.02	1.14
Other Slavs	19.45	0.94
Other Europeans	1.77	0.43
Islamic	6.01	0.48
Armenian-Georgian	3.19	1.14

Source: Calculated from data in Table A.11.

[a] See note in Table A.3.

[b] See note in Table A.11.

Table A.13

Republic Communist Party Organizations by Population

Ranked by Size Relative to Population, 1971

RANK	REPUBLIC	JAN 1, 1959 SIZE	% OF 1959 POPULA- TION	INDEX[a]	JAN 1, 1971 SIZE	% OF 1970 POPULA- TION	INDEX[a]
	USSR	8,708,000	4.16	1.00	14,455,000[c]	5.98	1.00
1	RSFSR	5,799,540[b]	4.93	1.19	9,252,822[b]	7.11	1.19
2	Georgian SSR	208,584	5.16	1.24	296,375	6.32	1.06
3	Latvian SSR	65,947	3.15	0.75	127,753	5.40	0.90
4	Estonian SSR	33,382	2.78	0.66	73,168	5.40	0.90
5	Armenian SSR	80,350	4.56	1.10	130,353	5.23	0.87
6	Azerbaidzhan SSR	143,730	3.89	0.93	258,549	5.05	0.84
7	Ukraine SSR	1,388,488	3.32	0.80	2,378,789	5.05	0.84
8	Belorussian SSR	203,477	2.52	0.61	434,527[d]	4.83	0.81
9	Kazakh SSR	318,000	3.42	0.82	575,439	4.42	0.74
10	Lithuanian SSR	54,324	2.00	0.48	122,469	3.92	0.66
11	Uzbek SSR	202,865	2.50	0.60	428,507	3.63	0.61
12	Kirgiz SSR	61,646	2.98	0.72	104,632	3.57	0.60
13	Turkmen SSR	45,225	2.98	0.72	69.862	3.24	0.54
14	Moldavian SSR	54,324	1.88	0.45	115,164	3.23	0.54
15	Tadzhik SSR	48,225	2.43	0.58	86,407	2.98	0.50

Sources: *BSE, Yezhegodnik*, 1960, 1971; *Nar. khoz. 1972:* 10.

NOTE: Party members in the Soviet army units stationed in a republic are counted as members of that republic's party.

$$\text{Index} = \frac{\text{\% of republic population in republic CP}}{\text{\% of USSR population in CPSU}}$$

[a]

[b] Computed by subtracting total of other republic parties from CPSU total.

[c] Membership as of March 1971.

[d] Membership as of January 1, 1970.

Table A.14

Weight of Republic Communist Party Organizations in Adult Population[a]

Ranked by Size Relative to Adult Population, 1971

RANK	REPUBLIC	JANUARY 1959 PARTY MEMBERS AS % OF ADULT POPULATION	INDEX[b]	JANUARY 1970 PARTY MEMBERS AS % OF ADULT POPULATION	INDEX[b]
	USSR	6.66	1.00	9.65	1.00
1	RSFSR	7.81	1.17	11.11	1.15
2	Aberbaidzhan	7.07	1.06	10.78	1.12
3	Georgia	8.27	1.24	10.38	1.08
4	Armenia	8.24	1.24	10.30	1.07
5	Kazakhstan	6.10	0.92	8.38	0.87
6	Uzbekistan	4.61	0.69	7.93	0.82
7	Belorussia	4.09	0.61	7.73	0.80
8	Estonia	3.98	0.60	7.65	0.79
9	Latvia	4.50	0.67	7.57	0.78
10	Ukraine	5.05	0.76	7.54	0.78
11	Kirgizia	5.39	0.81	7.30	0.76
12	Turkmenistan	5.52	0.83	7.08	0.73
13	Tadzhikistan	4.56	0.68	6.71	0.70
14	Lithuania	3.11	0.47	5.98	0.62
15	Moldavia	3.24	0.49	5.54	0.57

Sources: As for Table A.13, plus *Itogi 1970*: I, table 3

NOTE: Because more of populations are adult, Baltic states fall in ranking compared to Table A.13.

[a] Adult population = 20 years and over.

$$^{b} \text{Index} = \frac{\% \text{ of republic adult population in republic CP}}{\% \text{ of USSR adult population in CPSU}}$$

Table A.15

Produced National Income by Republic, 1960–1970

Ranked by Rubles Per Capita

	1960[a]			1970[b]	
1	Estonia	872	1	Estonia	1,587
2	Latvia	855	2	Latvia	1,574
3	RSFSR	732	3	Lithuania	1,336
4	Turkmenia	708	4	RSFSR	1,332
5	Ukraine	658	5	Ukraine	1,158
6	Lithuania	636	6	Belorussia	1,092
7	Kazakhstan	601	7	Kazakhstan	979
8	Azerbaidzhan	590	8	Moldavia	969
9	Belorussia	552	9	Armenia	923
10	Armenia	530	10	Turkmenistan	878
11	Moldavia	521	11	Georgia	871
12	Uzbekistan	506	12	Kirgizia	797
13	Georgia	501	13	Azerbaidzhan	737
14	Kirgizia	492	14	Uzbekistan	728
15	Tadzhikistan	443	15	Tadzhikistan	673
	USSR average	678		USSR average	1,194

Source: *Narodnoye khozyaistvo Latviiskoi SSR 1972*
(Riga: Statistika, 1972): 56.

NOTE: Produced National Income is a Soviet unit for measuring performance of the economy; it is not identical to any Western measure. See Campbell et al., 1973: 122–146. Measured by this unit the Baltic republics rank highest, the Slavs second; except for Kazakhstan, Moslem republics are lowest. The numbers for Armenia and Georgia are low because they do not include the product of the unofficial private sector, especially large in these republics.

[a] Computed from 1960–1970 growth rates, in "comparative prices."

[b] In "actual prices."

Table A.16

Money in Savings Accounts by Republic, 1960–1970

Ranked by Rubles Per Capita

	1960			1970	
1	RSFSR	61.81	1	Estonia	297.20
2	Estonia	59.90	2	Armenia	252.09
3	Georgia	53.09	3	Georgia	248.08
4	Latvia	51.98	4	Latvia	240.02
5	Ukraine	46.92	5	Lithuania	237.15
6	Armenia	45.89	6	RSFSR	216.15
7	Kazakhstan	35.26	7	Ukraine	194.17
8	Azerbaidzhan	32.18	8	Belorussia	161.89
9	Lithuania	32.13	9	Kazakhstan	139.58
10	Kirgizistan	31.85	10	Kirgizistan	103.34
11	Belorussia	31.69	11	Azerbaidzhan	102.40
12	Turkmenistan	28.96	12	Turkmenistan	97.27
13	Tadzhikistan	24.43	13	Moldavia	93.70
14	Uzbekistan	24.11	14	Tadzhikistan	87.03
15	Moldavia	21.66	15	Uzbekistan	79.72
	USSR average	52.24		USSR average	192.78

Source: Computed from *Nar. khoz. 1970*: 563–564.

NOTE: In 1970 the Balts and Armenia-Georgia were at the top, the Slavs in the middle, and the Moslem republics and Moldavia at the bottom.

Table A.17

Trade Turnover by Republic, 1960–1970

Ranked by Rubles Per Capita

1960			1970		% INCREASE 1960–1970
	Republic	Rubles/Capita		Republic	Rubles/Capita	
USSR mean		376	USSR mean		639	70
1	Estonia	530	1	Estonia	956	80
2	Latvia	518	2	Latvia	944	82
3	RSFSR	414	3	Lithuania	702	115
4	Kazakhstan	374	4	RSFSR	700	69
5	Lithuania	327	5	Ukraine	582	82
6	Turkmenistan	324	6	Belorussia	579	112
7	Ukraine	319	7	Kazakhstan	557	50
8	Georgia	307	8	Armenia	507	72
9	Armenia	295	9	Georgia	492	60
10	Kirgizistan	286	10	Moldavia	488	108
11	Uzbekistan	284	11	Turkmenistan	466	44
12	Belorussia	273	12	Kirgizistan	466	63
13	Azerbaidzhan	267	13	Uzbekistan	417	47
14	Tadzhikistan	253	14	Azerbaidzhan	397	49
15	Moldavia	235	15	Tadzhikistan	396	57

Sources: 1960: *Ekonomika Litvy, 1970*: 457, computed on
basis of 1959 population; 1970: *Nar. khoz. 1970*: 579
(1970 population figures).

NOTE: Baltic republics at top followed by Slavs. Armenia-Georgia are relatively low because these data do not
reflect the unofficial private market. Moslem republics
and Moldavia are at bottom.

Table A.18

People with Higher and Secondary (Complete and Incomplete) Education per 1,000 People Aged 10 Years and Older, by Republic

Ranked by 1970 level

RANK	REPUBLIC	1939	1959	1970
	USSR	108	361	483
1	Georgian SSR	165	448	554
2	Latvian SSR[a]	176	431	517
3	Armenian SSR	128	445	516
4	Estonian SSR[a]	161	386	506
5	Ukraine SSR	120	373	494
6	RSFSR	109	361	489
7	Turkmen SSR	65	387	475
8	Azerbaidzhan SSR	113	400	471
9	Kazakh SSR	83	348	470
10	Tatar ASSR	89	359	468
11	Uzbek SSR	55	352	456
12	Kirghiz SSR	46	342	452
13	Belorussian SSR	92	304	440
14	Tadzhik SSR	40	325	420
15	Moldavian SSR	57	264	397
16	Lithuanian SSR	81	232	382

Sources: *Nar. obraz.* (August), 1971; *JPRS*, Translations on Political and Social Affairs: No. 180: 29–34.

[a] Significantly exceeded USSR averages in 1939, before incorporation in the USSR.

Table A.19

Students in Higher Educational Institutions by Nationality, 1970–1971

Ranked by Student-Population Ratio (Relative Weight)

RANK	NATIONALITY	NO. STUDENTS[a]	PER 1,000 POPULATION OF NATIONALITY	% OF TOTAL STUDENTS IN USSR	RELATIVE WEIGHT[b]
	USSR	4,580,600	18.95	100.00	1.00
1	Jews	105,800	49.19	2.31	2.60
2	Georgians	87,800	27.06	1.92	1.43
3	Armenians	81,500	22.90	1.78	1.34
4	Russians	2,729,000	21.15	59.58	1.12
5	Azerbaidzhani	86,000	19.35	1.88	1.04
6	Kazakhs	100,300	18.93	2.19	1.00
7	Lithuanians	49,800	18.69	1.09	0.99
8	Kirgiz	26.400	18.18	0.58	0.97
9	Estonians	17,900	17.78	0.39	0.93
10	Uzbeks	150,700	16.39	3.29	0.87
11	Ukrainians	621,200	15.25	13.56	0.80
12	Latvians	21,800	15.24	0.48	0.81
13	Tatars	87,000	14.67	1.90	0.78
14	Turkmen	22,500	14.75	0.49	0.78
15	Belorussians	130,200	14.38	2.84	0.76
16	Tadzhiks	28,100	13.16	0.61	0.69
17	Moldavians	30,800	11.42	0.67	0.60

Source: *Nar. obraz.*, 1971: 196.

NOTE: The ratio between lowest (Moldavians) and highest (Jews)—1:4.33; second highest (Russians)—1:2.38.

[a] Includes students in evening and correspondence studies.

[b] Relative Weight $= \dfrac{\text{\% of All Students (USSR)}}{\text{\% of All Population (USSR)}}$

Table A.20

Scientific Workers by Nationality

Ranked by Relative Weight Index, 1971

RANK	NATIONALITY	1960			1971			POINT CHANGE IN WEIGHT INDEX 1960–1971
		No.	% of Total	Index[a]	No.	% of Total	Index[a]	
	USSR	354,158	100.0	1.00	1,002,930	100.0	1.00	
1	Jews	33,529	9.47	8.69	66,793	6.66	7.48	−1.21
2	Armenians	8,001	2.26	1.70	22,056	2.20	1.50	−0.20
3	Georgians	8,306	2.35	1.82	19,411	1.94	1.45	−0.37
4	Russians	229,547	64.81	1.19	666,059	66.41	1.24	+0.05
5	Estonians	2,048	0.58	1.23	4,959	0.49	1.17	−0.06
6	Latvians	2,662	0.75	1.12	6,262	0.62	1.05	−0.07
7	Lithuanians	2,959	0.84	0.76	8,751	0.87	0.79	+0.03
8	Azerbaidzhani	4,972	1.40	0.99	13,998	1.40	0.77	−0.22
9	Ukrainians	35,426	10.00	0.56	107,475	10.72	0.64	+0.08
10	Belorussians	6,358	1.80	0.47	20,538	2.05	0.55	+0.08
11	Tatars	3,691	1.04	0.44	12,619	1.26	0.51	+0.11
12	Turkmen	707	0.20	0.42	1,946	0.19	0.40	−0.02
13	Kazakhs	2,290	0.65	0.38	8,629	0.86	0.39	+0.01
14	Kirgiz	586	0.17	0.37	2,100	0.21	0.35	−0.02
15	Uzbeks	3,748	1.06	0.37	12,928	1.29	0.34	−0.03
16	Tadzhiks	866	0.24	0.36	2,550	0.25	0.28	−0.08
17	Moldavians	590	0.17	0.16	2,624	0.26	0.23	+0.07

Source: *Nar. khoz. 1972*: 105.

NOTE: Jews, Armenians, and Georgians, with a very high weight ratio, have gone down considerably. Russians have gone up, though considerably "over-represented."

$$^a \text{Index} = \frac{\% \text{ of USSR scientific workers}}{\text{Weight (\%) of total USSR Population}}$$

Table A.21

Doctors per 10,000 Inhabitants by Republic: 1960, 1966, 1971

Ranked by Number

1960	DOCTORS PER 10,000 POPULATION	1966	DOCTORS PER 10,000 POPULATION	CHANGE IN RANK	1971	DOCTORS PER 10,000 POPULATION	CHANGE IN RANK
USSR average	20.0	USSR average	24.6		USSR average	28.3	
Georgia	33.0	Georgia	35.5	0	Georgia	36.8	0
Latvia	26.4	Latvia	32.6	0	Latvia	36.2	0
Armenia	24.0	Estonia	30.7	+1	Estonia	33.8	0
Estonia	23.9	Armenia	28.4	−1	RSFSR	30.1	+1
Azerbaidzhan	23.7	RSFSR	25.8	+1	Armenia	29.4	−1
RSFSR	20.8	Ukraine	24.8	+1	Lithuania	28.6	+2
Ukraine	19.9	Azerbaidzhan	24.1	−2	Ukraine	28.3	−1
Turkmenia	18.7	Lithuania	23.1	+2	Belorussia	26.7	+1
Tatar ASSR	N.A.	Belorussia	22.6	+2	Azerbaidzhan	25.1	−2
Lithuania	17.4	Turkmenia	21.4	−2	Tatar ASSR	23.5	+1
Belorussia	16.4	Tatar ASSR	19.7[a]	−2	Kazakhstan	22.9	+2
Kirgizia	15.4	Kirgizia	19.4	0	Turkmenia	21.9	−2
Moldavia	14.3	Kazakhstan	18.9	+1	Moldavia	21.5	+1
Kazakhstan	14.1	Moldavia	18.5	−1	Kirgizia	21.4	−2
Uzbekistan	13.8	Uzbekistan	17.9	0	Uzbekistan	21.0	0
Tadzhikistan	12.7	Tadzhikistan	15.4	0	Tadzhikistan	16.5	0

Sources: 1966: *Soviet Union 50 Years*, 1969: 261; 1971: *Nar. khoz.* 1972: 101–118. See Ellen Mickiewicz, *Handbook of Soviet Social Science Data* (New York: Free Press, 1973): 101–118.

NOTE: All European republics rise in rank or stay the same; two out of three Transcaucasus republics fall in rank; Moslem republics cluster at the bottom, led by Tatar ASSR and Kazakhstan. High-low ratio in 1966 was 2.3:1 and in 1971 2.2:1.

[a] 1965 data.

Table A.22

Books Published in Languages of Major Soviet Nationalities, by Language, 1970

Ranked by Copies/100 Speakers of Language[a]

RANK	LANGUAGE	NO. BOOKS	TOTAL VOLUME (1,000)	SPEAKERS OF LANGUAGE (1,000)	COPIES/100 SPEAKERS OF LANGUAGE
1	Estonian	1,346	9,290	1,044	889.7
2	Latvian	1,165	11,870	1,606	739.3
3	Russian	60,216	1,033,333	183,799	562.2
4	Lithuanian	1,415	12,019	2,778	432.6
5	Georgian	1,613	12,963	3,501	370.3
6	Turkmen	308	3,796	1,566	242.4
7	Uzbek	925	23,203	9,698	239.3
8	Kazakh	634	12,807	5,360	238.9
9	Ukrainian	3,112	92,800	41,020	226.2
10	Kirgiz	410	3,322	1,487	223.4
11	Armenian	822	7,224	3,409	211.9
12	Moldavian	550	6,102	2,891	211.1
13	Azerbaidzhani	850	8,857	4,610	192.1
14	Tadzhik	377	4,118	2,464	167.1
15	Belorussian	430	9,371	8,533	109.8
16	Tatar[b]	195	2,891	5,838	49.5
17	Jewish	4	10	548	1.8

Sources: *Pechat' 1970*: 10–11; *Itogi 1970*: IV: 20, 76, 331–332, 333–359.

NOTE: Balts and Russians are high. Some Moslem nationalities are relatively high. Belorussians and Tatars are at the bottom and Jews very low. By copies/100 speakers, Russian is third after Estonian and Latvian. Cf. Table A.8 which shows predominance of Russian in other ways.

[a] Native speakers and all fluent in the language as a second language, with exceptions noted in Table A.8

[b] Discrimination against Tatars in the field of book publishing was especially obvious in 1970. Comparative figures for 1959 and 1971 are:

1959:	353	4,149	—
1971:	302	4,538	77.7

Table A.23

Books, Periodicals, and Newspapers Published in Titular Languages,
by Union Republic, 1970

% of Total Titles Published

REPUBLIC	BOOKS	PERIODICALS[a]	NEWSPAPERS[b]	NATIONAL GROUP % IN POPULATION OF EACH REPUBLIC
RSFSR	93	95	93	82.2
Ukraine	37	35	80	74.9
Belorussia	21	26	75	81.1
Uzbekistan	44	27	57	64.7
Kazakhstan	31	16	37	32.4
Georgia	73	73	86	66.8
Azerbaidzhan	64	64	80	73.8
Lithuania	64	70	81	80.1
Moldavia	31	22	47	64.6
Latvia	52	52	64	56.8
Kirgizia	47	40	55	43.8
Tadzhikistan	52	36	84	56.2
Armenia	75	73	88	88.6
Turkmenia	65	43	70	65.6
Estonia	74	74	72	68.2

Source: *Nar. obraz.*, 1971: 359–363, 369–370, 378–379.

[a] Including periodically issued collections and bulletins.

[b] Including *kolkhoz* newspapers.

Table A.24

Index of National Political Vitality

RANK	NATIONALITY	GROWTH	NAT % REP	CONC REP	NAT LANG	NAT CPSU	CUM IND	MEAN IND
1	Georgians	9	8	1	6	1	25	5.0
2	Russians	13	2	11	1	2	29	5.8
3	Turkmen	3	9	4	2	13	31	6.2
4	Azerbaidzhani	5	6	8	7	6	32	6.4
5	Lithuanians	11	4	2	9	10	36	7.2
6	Uzbeks	2	10	10	4	12	38	7.6
7,8	Kirgiz	4	15	6	3	11	39	7.8
7,8	Armenians	7	1	15	13	3	39	7.8
9	Ukrainians	14	5	7	15	4	45	7.0
10	Estonians	16	7	5	10	8	46	9.2
11	Tadzhiks	1	13	14	5	14	47	9.4
12	Belorussians	12	3	12	16	5	48	9.6
13,14	Latvians	15	12	3	11	9	50	10.0
13,14	Kazakhs	6	16	13	8	7	50	10.0
15	Moldavians	8	11	9	12	15	55	11.0
	Tatars	10	14	16	14		high:low = 2.2:1	
	Jews	17			17			

Growth   —Population growth (Table A.2).

Nat % Rep —Nationality as percentage of republic population (Table A.6.).

Conc Rep —Concentration of nationality in its republic (Table A.7.).

Nat Lang   —Percentage who declared the national language as native (Table A.8).

Nat CPSU —Weight of nationality in CPSU (Table A.11).

Cum Ind   —Cumulative index (sum of all indicators).

Mean Ind —Mean index $\left(\dfrac{\text{cumulative index}}{\text{number of indicators}} \right)$.

Table A.25

Index of Economic Development

RANK	NATIONALITY	PI CAP	SAV CAP	TR CAP	CUM IND	MEAN IND
1	Estonians	1	1	1	3	1
2	Latvians	2	4	2	8	2.22
3	Lithuanians	3	5	3	11	3.67
4	Russians	4	6	4	14	4.67
5	Ukrainians	5	7	5	17	5.67
6	Armenians	9	2	8	19	6.33
7	Belorussians	6	8	6	20	6,67
8,9	Georgians	11	3	9	23	7.67
8,9	Kazakhs	7	9	7	23	7.67
10	Moldavians	8	13	10	31	10.33
11	Turkmen	10	12	11	33	11.00
12	Kirgiz	12	10	12	34	11.33
13	Azerbaidzhani	13	11	14	38	12.67
14	Uzbeks	14	15	13	42	14.00
15	Tadzhiks	15	14	15	44	14.67
					high:low = 14.7:1	

Pi Cap   —Produced income per capita (Table A.15).

Sav Cap   —Savings per capita (Table A.16).

TR Cap   —Trade turnover per capita (Table A.17).

Cum Ind   —Cumulative index (sum of indicators).

Mean Ind   —Mean index $\left(\dfrac{\text{cumulative index}}{\text{number of indicators}} \right)$.

Table A.26

Index of Socio-cultural Development

RANK	NATIONALITY	U/R	STU	EDU	BOK	SCI	DOC	CUM IND	MEAN IND
1	Georgians	9	2	1	5	3	1	21	3.50
2	Russians	2	4	6	3	4	4	23	3.83
3	Estonians	4	9	4	1	5	3	26	4.33
4	Armenians	3	3	3	11	2	5	27	4.50
5,6	Latvians	6	12	2	2	6	2	30	5.00
5,6	Jews	1	1		17	1		20	5.00
7,8	Lithuanians	8	7	16	4	7	6	48	8.00
7,8	Ukrainians	7	11	5	9	9	7	48	8.00
9	Azerbaidzhani	11	5	8	13	8	9	54	9.00
10	Kazakhs	13	6	9	8	13	11	60	10.00
11	Turkmen	12	14	7	7	12	12	64	10.67
12	Tatars	5	13	10	16	11	10	65	10.83
13	Belorussians	10	15	13	15	10	8	71	11.83
14	Uzbeks	15	10	11	6	15	15	72	12.00
15	Kirgiz	17	8	12	10	14	14	75	12.50
16,17	Tadzhiks	14	16	14	14	16	16	90	15.00
16,17	Moldavians	16	17	15	12	17	13	90	15.00

high:low = 4.3:1

U/R —Urban-rural division (Table A.9).

Stu —Students per population (Table A.19).

Edu —Educational standards of population (Table A.18).

Bok —Books per capita (Table A.23).

Sci —Scientists per capita (Table A.20).

Doc —Doctors per capita (Table A.21).

Cum Ind —Cumulative index (sum of all indicators).

Mean Ind —Mean index $\left(\dfrac{\text{cumulative index}}{\text{number of indicators}} \right)$.

Table A.27

Index of Sociocultural and Economic
Development

RANK	NATIONALITY	CUM IND	MEAN IND
1	Estonians	29	3.22
2	Russians	37	4.11
3	Latvians	38	4.22
4	Georgians	44	4.88
5	Armenians	48	5.33
6	Lithuanians	51	5.67
7	Ukrainians	65	7.22
8	Kazakhs	83	9.22
9	Belorussians	91	10.11
10	Azerbaidzhani	92	10.22
11	Turkmen	97	10.78
12	Moldavians	100	11.11
13	Kirgiz	109	12.11
14	Uzbeks	114	12.67
15	Tadzhiks	134	14.89

Cum Ind = Cumulative Index: Sum of all indicators in
    Tables A.25 and A.26.

$$\text{Mean Ind} = \text{Mean Index: } \frac{\text{Cum Ind}}{\text{number of indicators}}.$$

Table A.28

Composite Index: Overall Development of Soviet Nationalities

RANK	NATIONALITY	SOC, CULT, & ECON	NAT POL VITAL	CUM IND	COMP IND
1	Russians	37	29	66	4.71
2	Georgians	44	25	69	4.93
3	Estonians	29	46	75	5.42
4,5	Lithuanians	51	36	87	6.21
4,5	Armenians	48	39	87	6.21
6	Latvians	38	50	88	6.28
7	Ukrainians	65	45	100	7.14
8	Azerbaidzhani	92	32	124	8.86
9	Turkmen	97	31	128	9.14
10	Kazakhs	83	50	133	9.50
11	Belorussians	91	48	139	9.93
12	Kirgiz	109	39	148	10.57
13	Uzbeks	114	38	152	10.86
14	Moldavians	100	55	155	11.07
15	Tadzhiks	134	47	181	12.92
				high:low = 2.74.:1	

Soc, Cult, & Econ—Index of sociocultural and economic development (Table A.27).

Nat Pol Vital   —Index of national-political vitality (Table A.24).

Cum Ind   —Cumulative index (sum of all indicators).

Comp Ind   —Composite index $\left(\dfrac{\text{cumulative index}}{\text{number of indicators.}} \right)$.

Table A.29

Composite Index: Development of Soviet Nationalities by Geographic-Ethnic Group[a]

Ranked by Composite Index (column 4)

Mean Index for Group

RANK	NATIONALITY	NAT POL VITAL	ECON DEVEL	SOC & CULT DEVEL	COMP IND
1	Armenian-Georgian	6.4	7.00	4.00	5.57
2	Balts	8.8	2.30	5.77	5.97
3	Slavs	7.5	5.67	7.88	7.26
4	Islamic	7.9	9.58	11.53	10.31

Source: Tables A.24, A.25, A.26, A.28.

Nat Pol Vital = National political vitality; see Table A.24.
Econ Devel = Economic development; see Table A.25.
Soc & Cult Devel = Social and cultural development; see Table A.26.

Comp. Ind. = Composite index, from Table A.28.
[a] Excluding Moldavians, Tatars, Jews.

Summary

Despite decades of far-reaching modernization, and official Soviet declarations notwithstanding, there are still immense differences among the major Soviet nationalities. In the tables based on indicators of level of economic and sociocultural development, these differences are fairly consistent; that is, the nationalities appear in about the same order, with Balts, Russians, and the Georgian-Armenian group at the top, Islamic nationalities at the bottom, and non-Russian Slavs in between. This is also the order of tables A.28 and A.29.

In Table A.24, however, the order is entirely different, because the table reflects demographic data, such as natural growth and national concentration in the republic, which are high for nationalities at a low level of development. As a result, Islamic nationalities like Turkmen and Azerbaidzhani occupy a high position, while Latvians and Estonians rank low.

Certain individual nationalities score consistently a similar position: Moldavians are low and Russians are high on almost all indicators. While some Soviet nationalities are urbanized, wealthy, well educated, and industrialized, others are still mainly rural-agricultural, poor, and with low standards of education. Though differences are narrowing in some respects, they are widening in others. It is questionable whether major gaps among the Soviet nationalities can be closed in the foreseeable future.

REFERENCES

BSE, Yezhegodnik, 1960
  Bol'shaya Sovetskaya entsiklopediya, Yezhegodnik (Moscow: Bol'shaya Sovetskaya entsiklopediya, 1961).
BSE, Yezhegodnik, 1971
  Bol'shaya Sovetskaya entsiklopediya, Yezhegodnik (Moscow: Bol'shaya Sovetskaya entsiklopediya, 1972).
CDSP
  Current Digest of the Soviet Press, published by Joint Committee on Slavic Studies.
Ekonomika Litvy 1970
  Ekonomika i kul'tura Litovskoi SSR v 1970 godu. Statisticheskii yezhegodnik (Vilnius: Statistika, 1971).
Itogi 1959
  Itogi vsesoyuznoi perepisi naseleniya 1959 goda SSSR (Moscow: Gosstatizdat, 1962).
Itogi 1970
  Itogi vsesoyuznoi perepisi naseleniya 1970 goda (Moscow: Statistika, 1972–1973).

Kommunist vooruzhennykh sil
  Kommunist vooruzhennykh sil (Moscow, monthly).
Nar. khoz. 1970
  Narodnoye khozyaistvo SSSR v 1970 godu. (Moscow: Statistika, 1971).
Nar. khoz. 1972
  Narodnoye khozyaistvo SSSR 1922–1972. Yubileinyi statisticheskii yezhegodnik (Moscow: Statistika, 1972).
Nar. obraz., 1971
  Narodnoye obrazovaniye, nauka i kul'tura v SSSR: statisticheskii sbornik (Moscow: Statistika, 1971).
Pechat' 1970
  Pechat' SSSR 1970 godu (Moscow: Kniga, 1971).
Soviet Union, 1969
  Soviet Union—50 Years: Statistical Returns (Moscow: Progress Publishers, 1969).

INDEX